SOCIOLOGY
THE CORE

To my sons,
Nels and Brad

SOCIOLOGY
THE CORE

FOURTH EDITION

James W. Vander Zanden
The Ohio State University

McGraw-Hill, Inc.
New York   St. Louis   San Francisco   Auckland   Bogotá   Caracas
Lisbon   London   Madrid   Mexico City   Milan   Montreal   New Delhi
San Juan   Singapore   Sydney   Tokyo   Toronto

SOCIOLOGY
The Core

Credits and Acknowledgments appear on page 471, and on this page by reference.

This book is printed on acid-free paper.

1 2 3 4 5 6 7 8 9 0   DOC   DOC   9 0 9 8 7 6 5

ISBN 0-07-067021-8

ISBN 0_07_114834_5

9 780071 148344

This book was set in Minion by The Clarinda Company.
The editors were Jill S. Gordon and Sheila H. Gillams;
the production supervisor was Paula Keller.
The cover was designed by John Hite.
The photo editor was Barbara Salz.
R. R. Donnelley & Sons Company was printer and binder.

Cover photo: © 94 Bilderberg, The Stock Market

Library of Congress Cataloging-in-Publication Data

Vander Zanden, James Wilfrid.
        Sociology: the core / James W. Vander Zanden. — 4th ed.
        p.   cm.
        Includes bibliographical references (p.   –   ) and indexes.
        ISBN 0-07-067021-8
        1. Sociology.   I. Title.
HM51.V354   1996   95-16831
301—dc20

Contents in Brief

Contents

Preface

We are about to enter the twenty-first century—a rather awesome thought. Perhaps even more daunting, students currently taking a first course in sociology will live out the greater part of their lives in the new century. The education that students receive should allow them to live fuller, richer, and more fruitful lives. Indeed, such a goal is ultimately the bedrock upon which we build and justify our careers as educators and sociologists.

The introductory course in sociology affords students the opportunity to grasp the power of the sociological imagination in understanding and mastering their social world. As a science of social organization and interaction, sociology provides a new vision of social life. It encourages us to scrutinize aspects of our social environment that we might otherwise ignore, neglect, or take for granted. Sociology equips us with a special form of consciousness, suspending the belief that things are simply as they seem. In sum, sociology is a liberating science.

☐ Providing the Core

A course in sociology should broaden the horizons of students, sharpen their observational skills, and strengthen their analytical capabilities. But as the store of sociological knowledge has grown, many instructors have felt it necessary to transmit more and more material to their students. This trend is reflected in many mainline introductory sociology textbooks that are little more than information catalogs. Unhappily, students are finding themselves overwhelmed with concepts, principles, and data, and the first course in sociology is rapidly becoming unmanageable. Under these circumstances, sociology loses its vitality as a "way of seeing" and becomes simply a body of information that students must mechanically memorize and regurgitate on examinations.

This text aims to make the introductory course manageable for instructors and students alike. It provides the core of sociology—the basic foundations of the discipline. It strips away many peripheral concerns and presents the essentials of sociology. In so doing, it aims to supply a solid foundation in sociological concepts and principles without compromising the integrity of the discipline. The coverage of many key topics—theory, culture, socialization, groups, formal organization, deviance, social stratification, race, gender, power, the family, religion, and social change—is equal to, and in many cases exceeds, that found in most other introductory textbooks.

A core text serves as a home base for students while allowing greater latitude to instructors. It is an aid to pedagogy, a coherent presentation of sociological materials. Instructors can supplement the text with papers, readers, or monographs that meet their unique teaching needs. It would be presumptuous for any sociologist to program another sociologist's course. So I have attempted to provide a solid resource—a common intellectual platform—with the hope that each instructor will find it a sound foundation and go on his or her own way from there. Simultaneously, students can use the core text as a "second voice," available 24 hours a day, 365 days a year, and move at their own pace, irrespective of their educational backgrounds.

☐ Bringing Students In

The text seeks to make sociology come alive as a vital and exciting field, to relate principles to real-world circumstances, and to attune students to the dynamic processes of our rapidly changing contemporary society. In this way the study of a science comes to captivate student interest and excite student imagination. In my classes at Ohio State University, I have attempted to foster and encourage a sociological consciousness through student projects and journals. I have asked the students to observe particular events and then interpret them with sociological concepts and principles. Through this process I have hoped to encourage students to begin thinking like sociologists. The insights supplied by the students are often quite interesting. A sampling of this material is provided in boxes labeled "Doing Sociology." The boxes allow students to teach other students by bringing the full drama, color, and richness of the human experience to the learning process. In this edition, I have included eight new "Doing Sociology" boxes, seven of which summarize the classroom experiences of sociology instructors and their students as told in *Teaching Sociology*.

□ Pedagogical Aids

In selecting pedagogical aids for the text, I decided to use those that provide the most guidance with the least clutter. Each chapter opens with an outline of its major headings, which allows students to review at a glance the material to be covered. Each chapter concludes with a numbered summary that recapitulates the central points and allows students to review what they have read in a systematic manner, and with a list of key terms and definitions that provides students with a convenient means of reviewing key concepts. The terms most essential to the core of sociology are set in **boldface** type and are defined as they are presented in the text.

□ Ancillary Materials

Accompanying *Sociology: The Core* is a complete package of learning and teaching aids. The student Study Guide, prepared by Meg Wilkes Karraker, offers major learning objectives for each chapter; matching and multiple-choice items that review key concepts; questions for review; and selected readings.

The Instructor's Manual, prepared by John Henderson, Scottsdale Community College, includes chapter-by-chapter techniques for reinforcing the textual material, classroom ideas, student projects, and annotated lists of films and additional readings.

The Print Test Bank, prepared by John Henderson, contains fifty to sixty multiple-choice items and five to ten essay questions per chapter. This test bank is also available in floppy disk for use on IBM-compatible and Macintosh computers.

An extensive set of 80 four-color high-quality acetate overhead transparencies for introductory sociology are available from McGraw-Hill along with a new videodisc, *Points of Departure* (also available on videotape), based on NBC news footage as well as a diverse video library.

□ Acknowledgments

I would like to thank the following reviewers for their many helpful comments and suggestions: Sarah A. Coleman, Mohawk Valley Community College; Timothy E. Evans, Community College of Allegheny County; Lee Frank, Community College of Allegheny County; Ellsworta F. Fuhrman, Virginia Polytechnic Institute and State University; Meg Wilkes Karraker, University of St. Thomas; Beverly Quist, Mohawk Valley Community College; James W. Robinson, Louisiana State University–Eunice; Charles Rogers, Mohawk Valley Community College; and Ellen Rosengarten, Sinclair Community College.

JAMES W. VANDER ZANDEN

SOCIOLOGY
THE CORE

Chapter 1

DEVELOPING
A SOCIOLOGICAL
CONSCIOUSNESS

"No man [or woman] is an island, entire of itself," wrote the English poet John Donne some four centuries ago. He was drawing our attention to the fact that every person may be many things, but above all each of us is a social being. As infants we are born into a social environment; we become genuinely human only in this environment; and we take our places within the human enterprise in such an environment. Indeed, we cannot be human all by ourselves. What we think, how we feel, and what we say and do are shaped by our interaction with other people in group settings. It is the web of meanings, expectations, behavior, and structural arrangements that result when people interact with one another in society that is the stuff of the science we term sociology. Thus we may define **sociology** as the scientific study of social interaction and organization.

Judged by ancient folklore, myths, and archeological remains, human beings have had a long interest in understanding themselves and their social arrangements. They have pondered why people of other societies order their lives in ways that differ from theirs. They have reflected on the reasons that members of their society violate social rules. They have wondered why some people become wealthy while others experience abject poverty. They have been bewildered by episodes of mass hysteria, revolution, and war. Yet it has been only in the past 150 years or so that human beings have sought answers to these and related questions through science. This science—sociology—pursues the study of social interaction and group behavior through research governed by the rigorous and disciplined collection and analysis of facts.

But many of us are not simply interested in understanding society and human behavior. We would also like to improve the human condition so that we and others might lead fuller, richer, and more fruitful lives. To do this, we need knowledge about the basic structures and processes involved in the social enterprise. Sociology, through its emphasis on observation and measurement, allows us to bring rigorous and systematic scientific thinking and information to bear on difficult questions associated with social policies and choices, including such themes as poverty, health, immigration, crime, and education. Many people interested in these issues do not realize that more is needed than a "loving heart." Put another way, knowledge must inform action.

Sociological writings often find application in practical matters (Barber, 1988). For instance, the U.S. Supreme Court placed heavy reliance on social science findings regarding the effects of segregation on children in reaching its historic 1954 decision declaring mandatory school segregation unconstitutional (Klineberg, 1986; Jackson, 1990). Similarly, research on the nursery school experiences of children was influential in leading government officials to establish the Head Start program in 1965 and later to provide rigorous follow-up programs so that the effects of Head Start do not "wash out" over time (Zigler Styfco, 1993). The purpose of Head Start is to provide preschool educational opportunities for economically disadvantaged youngsters so that they may become financially independent. Social science research has also dramatically changed our ideas about crime, poverty, aging, mental illness, alcoholism, foreigners, foreign cultures, and behavioral differences in men and women. As the result of this and other research, Americans today have a quite different view of human behavior and social institutions than their parents did only a generation ago (Sterba, 1982; Ferriss, 1988).

Increasingly, people are coming to recognize the centrality of the social and behavioral sciences to the nation's health and science agenda. For instance, a 1993 study released by the American Medical Association shows that at least $1 out of every $4 Americans spend on health care each year goes to treat conditions that result from alcohol abuse, drug use, smoking, street and domestic violence, and other behaviors that are potentially changeable through social interventions (*New York Times*, February 23, 1993,

B/7). Indeed, sociologists may deliberately design studies to evaluate public policies or to inform us about social conditions, such as those that assess the effects of various criminal justice programs (Sampson and Laub, 1990; Langan, 1991), the social consequences of mass unemployment (Buss and Redburn, 1983), and the social impact that highways and high-technology actions have on people's lives and the physical environment (Freudenburg, 1986). Further, the collection of census and other national statistical data, which is the foundation of many federal and state policies on health, education, housing, and welfare, is based on sample survey and statistical techniques developed by sociologists and other social scientists. Sociology, then, is a powerful scientific tool both for acquiring knowledge about ourselves and for intervening in social affairs to realize various goals.

□ The Sociological Perspective

The sociological perspective invites us to look beyond the often neglected and taken-for-granted aspects of our social environment and examine them in fresh and creative ways (Berger, 1963). We find that there are many layers of meaning in the human experience and that things are not always what they seem. Networks of invisible rules and institutional arrangements guide our behavior. And we continually evolve, negotiate, and rework tacit bargains with family members, friends, lovers, and work associates as we steer our lives along the paths of everyday activity. Many of these understandings are below the usual threshold of our awareness (Collins and Makowsky, 1984), and so as we look behind the outer edifice of the world and scrutinize the hidden fabric, we encounter new levels of reality (see "Doing Sociology," which examines how we navigate across crowded campus sidewalks). This approach to reality—a special form of consciousness—is the core of the sociological perspective.

Doing Sociology: Navigating across Campus

Consider what happens as you navigate crowded campus sidewalks and intersections. If you and your classmates were to move like two sets of robots, each set maintaining its line of march, you would constantly knock one another down. Yet somehow you manage to minimize collisions. What crash avoidance devices do you employ in routing your movement across campus? Students in introductory sociology classes at Ohio State University have examined this matter and have identified a number of social mechanisms.

(Left) Notice the step-and-slide maneuver the man is making to effect a "clean pass." *(Right)* Notice how the woman communicates through eye contact with the man her intention of crossing in front of him. Both parties must take account of each other in devising their movements if they are to avoid a collision. (Don McCarthy)

☐ Cultural rules assist us by providing guidelines for navigating walkways. They dictate that we use the right side of the walk. They define for us the "first come, first through" principle at crowded intersections. And they provide that men should defer to women, the young to the elderly, and the able-bodied to the handicapped. We need not invent a new solution for each sidewalk encounter. Instead, we employ common understandings or ready-made answers that were devised by earlier generations of Americans. Accordingly, we do not cross the campus in a haphazard or random fashion,

NEW LEVELS OF REALITY

We can gain an appreciation for the sociological perspective by considering a classic study carried out by social scientist Elliot Liebow (1967) in a downtown Washington, D.C., African-American neighborhood. Thirty-seven years old and white, he began "hanging out" on a corner in front of the New Deal Carry-out Shop. Liebow won the trust of twenty or so African-American men, listened carefully, and faithfully told their stories in the study he titled *Tally's Corner.*

The shop is located a short distance from the White House in a blighted section of the city. It is open seven days a week, serving a diverse clientele coffee, hamburgers, french fries, hot dogs, and submarine sandwiches. The men come to the corner to eat, to enjoy easy talk, to banter with women who pass by, to "horse around," to see "what's happening," and in general to pass the time. Some of the men are close friends, some do not like others, and some think of others as enemies.

but we move in accordance with established cultural formulas or recipes.

☐ Even if we were to program robots to remain on the right side of the walk, they would collide at intersections. So in crossing the campus, we need to communicate our intentions. For the most part, we accomplish this task on the nonverbal level. At about 15 or 20 feet, we ordinarily size up the situation by glancing at pedestrians we are likely to encounter at an intersection and occasionally establish fleeting eye contact with them. We then shut down eye contact until we are about 3 to 5 feet apart. At this distance we establish brief eye contact, signaling to others that we recognize their presence. However, we usually do not hold the visual contact unless we wish to take an assertive or aggressive stance. Simultaneously, we mentally calculate our own and the other person's pace and make appropriate adjustments to avoid a collision. In doing so, we may "negotiate" with the other individuals—we slow our pace to signal to them that we would like them to increase their pace, or we quicken our pace to ask them to slow their pace. Additionally, we mutually inform one another of our anticipated route through body language. We may incline our heads, shoulders, or bodies and dart our eyes in the direction we are headed.

☐ Numbers make a difference. The lone individual is at a disadvantage, and groups at an advantage. A lone individual is likely to give way or detour around a group of people (even stepping off the sidewalk), whereas a group is likely to ignore a lone individual and continue on course in an assertive fashion.

☐ Pedestrians "compress" themselves in crowded settings. For instance, individuals cooperate to effect a "clean pass." When they are about 5 to 6 feet apart, each person slightly angles his or her body, turns the shoulders, and takes a slight step to the side; hands are pulled inward or away to avoid hand-to-hand contact; bodies are twisted backward to maximize face-to-face distance. Likewise, students often pull their backpack or books toward a more central and less exposed position.

☐ In the course of navigating campus sidewalks, people are constantly sizing one another up, especially in terms of their basic roles and physical attractiveness. Men tend to hold their gaze longer when looking at women than when looking at men. Likewise, men seem to be permitted greater leeway in "looking over" women than women are permitted in "looking over" men. If individuals are interested in one another, after a few paces they follow up with a backward glance.

The following scene is typical of a weekday morning in this Washington neighborhood (Liebow, 1967:29):

A pickup truck drives slowly down the street. The truck stops as it comes abreast of a man sitting on a cast-iron porch and the white driver calls out, asking if the man wants a day's work. The man shakes his head and the truck moves on up the block, stopping again whenever idling men come within calling distance of the driver. At the Carry-out corner, five men debate the question briefly and shake their heads no to the truck. The truck turns the corner and repeats the same performance up the next street. In the distance, one can see one man, then another climb into the back of the truck and sit down. In starts and stops, the truck finally disappears.

The white truckdriver views the African-American streetcorner men as lazy and irresponsible, unwilling "to take a job even if it were handed to them on a platter." But Liebow discovered quite a different picture. Indeed, most of the men on the corner that morning had jobs. Boley had a weekday off because he worked Saturdays as a member of a trash collection crew. Sweets worked nights mopping floors and cleaning up trash in an office building. Tally had come back from his job after his employer had concluded that the weather was not suitable for pouring concrete. And Clarence had to attend a funeral at eleven o'clock.

Also on the corner that morning were a few men who had been laid off and who were drawing unemployment compensation. They had nothing to gain by accepting work that paid little more, and frequently less, than they received in unemployment benefits. And there were a small number like Arthur, able-bodied men who had no visible means of support but who did not want a job. The truckdriver had assumed that the Arthurs were representative of all the streetcorner men. Finally, not to be forgotten, the man on the porch turned out to be severely crippled by arthritis.

The truckdriver thought that able-bodied men like Arthur do not work because they are lazy and undependable. Like many middle-class Americans, he believed that inner-city African-American men live only for the moment, indulging their whims and satisfying their current appetites with little thought for long-term consequences. Rather than providing for a wife and children, saving their money, and investing in a future, the men appear to squander their limited resources in a lifestyle consumed by gambling, alcohol, drugs, and "high living."

But Liebow found these stereotyped images to be wrong. He discovered that streetcorner men and middle-class men differ not so much in their attitudes toward the future as in the different futures they see ahead of them. Middle-class men command sufficient financial resources to justify the long-term commitment of resources to money market funds, savings accounts, mutual funds, stocks, and bonds. They hold jobs that offer the promise of upward mobility in corporate or professional careers. And they can reasonably expect their children to pursue a higher educa-

tion. But it is otherwise for streetcorner men, who are obliged to expend all their resources maintaining themselves in the present. Thus when streetcorner men squander a week's pay in two days, it is not because, like animals or children, they are unconcerned with the future. They do so precisely because they are aware of the future and the hopelessness of their prospects.

Like many privileged Americans, the white truckdriver had located the job problems of inner-city men in the men themselves—or, more precisely, in their lack of willingness to work. Given this interpretation, social policy might best be directed toward changing the motivations of streetcorner men and encouraging them to develop those values and goals that lead to occupational achievement. But Liebow's research revealed a quite different state of affairs. The streetcorner men and other American men did *not* differ in their fundamental values or goals. The men on the corner also wanted stable jobs and marriages. However, they had continually discovered that jobs are only intermittently available, almost always menial, often hard, and invariably low-paying. Jobs as dishwashers, janitors, store clerks, and unskilled laborers lie outside those tracks that typically lead to advancement in the United States, and thus the jobs offer no more in the future than they do in the present. Moreover, armed with models of other men in their community who have failed, streetcorner men are uncertain of their ability to carry out their responsibilities as husbands and fathers.

In seeking an explanation for their behavior, Liebow looked beyond the individual men to the *social fabric* in which the men were enmeshed. He turned his investigative eye upon the social arrangements that are external to individuals but that nonetheless *structure* their experiences and place constraints on their behavior. In like fashion sociologist William Julius Wilson (1987, 1991) has shown that African-American poverty and disadvantage persist in our nation's central cities because hundreds of thousands of low-skill jobs—primarily involving physical labor—have disappeared over the last three decades. Blue-collar jobs in manufacturing had been a main avenue of job security and mobility for the disadvantaged. Indeed, many problems of the inner city—high rates of welfare dependency, teenage pregnancy, drug abuse, and crime—are also in part outgrowths of this fundamental problem of male joblessness (Anderson, 1990; Huff-Corzine, Corzine, and Moore, 1991; Wilkie, 1991). Wilson contends that the primary forces making for the plight of inner-city African Americans are not discrimination, pathological values, or welfare dependency, but the changing structure of the nation's economy and the widening class division among African Americans. In sum, society—and more particularly its groups and institutions—provides the framework for sociology, not the individual. The sociological perspective allows us to bring previously inaccessible aspects of human life to social awareness and gain a window on the social landscape that we often overlook or misunderstand.

THE SOCIOLOGICAL IMAGINATION

We have stressed that a basic premise underlying sociology is the notion that only by understanding the society in which we live can we gain a fuller insight into ourselves. C. Wright Mills (1959) termed this quality of the discipline ("The Promise" of sociology) the **sociological imagination**—the ability to see our private experiences and personal difficulties as entwined with the structural arrangements of society and the historical times in which we live. We usually go about our daily activities bounded by our own narrow orbit. Our viewpoint is limited to our school, job, family, and neighborhood. The sociological imagination allows us to break out of this contracted vision and discern the relationship between our personal experiences and broader social and historical events.

Mills, an influential but controversial sociologist, pointed out that our personal troubles and public issues "overlap and interpenetrate to form the larger structure of social and historical life."

Take, for instance, the job difficulties experienced by many Americans in the early 1990s. The restructuring and downsizing of corporate America (see Chapter 8) compounded the effects of economic recession. The economic malaise had a devastating effect on the employment ranks of the nation's youth: Nearly 2 million fewer young people were employed in 1993 than in 1989 (Bernstein, 1993). Teens and young adults are always hit harder in bad times and take longer to experience the upturns. At the same time, the level of skill required for many jobs is climbing rapidly, leaving unskilled young workers out in the cold. Significantly, of the nation's jobless workers, some three-quarters received no unemployment benefits. Mills (1959:9) contended that we cannot look to the "personal character" of individuals to explain their employment problems under these sorts of circumstances:

The very structure of opportunities has collapsed. Both the correct statement of the problem and the range of possible solutions require us to consider the economic and political institutions of the society, and not merely the personal situation and character of a scatter of individuals.

Social and historical forces will also provide the external constraints governing the career opportunities of many students currently enrolled in the nation's colleges and universities. Labor Department economists calculate that while skill levels in the workplace rose during the past decade, the supply of college graduates rose even faster. The outlook for the next 12 years seems even more problematic. Although the percentage of new jobs requiring a college degree will continue to rise, the economists calculate that the supply of new workers with a college degree will continue to exceed demand. Should current job and educational trends continue, some 30 percent of college graduates entering the work force from 1990 to 2005 will work in jobs that do not require a college degree—a trend that could boost the percentage of "underemployed" college graduates to one in four (Koretz, 1992). Thus the developing

THE WALL STREET JOURNAL

PERSONNEL DIRECTOR

"That salary's less than my tuition last year!"

From *The Wall Street Journal*—Permission, Cartoon Features Syndicate.

private job frustrations of many younger Americans must be understood within the context of the structural factors operating in the larger society and the workplace (see Chapter 12).

We see the operation of the sociological imagination in other spheres of life as well. Mills (1959:9) was especially concerned with issues of war and peace:

The personal problems of war, when it occurs, may be how to survive it or how to die in it with honor; how to make money out of it; how to climb into the higher safety of the military apparatus; or how to contribute to the war's termination. . . . But the structural issues of war have to do with its causes; with what types of men it throws up into command; with its effects upon economic and political, family and religious institutions, with the unorganized irresponsibility of a world of nation-states.

In sum, the sociological imagination allows us to penetrate our social world and identify the links between our personal biographies and the larger social forces of life—to see that what is happening to us immediately is a minute point at which our personal lives and society intersect.

MICROSOCIOLOGY AND MACROSOCIOLOGY

Mills emphasized that our personal troubles and public issues overlap and interpenetrate to form the larger structure of social life. Sociologists seek to extend this insight by distinguishing between the micro, or small-scale, aspects of the social enterprise and the macro, or large-scale, structural components. When we focus upon the former elements, we examine behavior close-up and observe what happens as people interact on a face-to-face basis. Sociologists term this level **microsociology**—*micro*- meaning "small," as in the word "microscope." Microsociology entails the detailed study of what people say, do, and think moment by moment as they go about their daily lives. Liebow's study of the African-American men on the Washington streetcorner provides an illustration of microsociology. Liebow wanted to find out how the men saw themselves, how they dealt with one another in face-to-face encounters, and how they balanced their hopes and aspirations with their real-world experiences. Microsociology, then, deals with everyday life—a woman and a man initiating a conversation on a bus, several youngsters playing basketball on an inner-city playground, guests at a bridal party or baby shower, a police officer directing traffic at a busy intersection, a barbershop quartet performing before an audience, a routine encounter between pupils and teacher in a specific classroom, or a meeting of a school board.

Alternatively, sociologists turn their investigative eye upon the "big picture" and study social groups and societies. When they view life at this level, each person is analogous to one dot among the many dots that compose a larger picture, much in the manner of dots on a television screen. This approach is termed **macrosociology**—*macro*- meaning "large." Macrosociology focuses upon large-scale and long-term social processes, including the state, social class, the family, the economy, culture, and society. At this level sociologists direct their attention to the changes in the structure of a religion sect, the impact of population dynamics and computer technologies on the work force, shifts in the racial and ethnic composition of a city, the transition of a nation from socialism to capitalism, or the dynamics of intergroup rivalries. When we examine the lives of Liebow's streetcorner men from a macrosociological perspective, we gain a picture of the institutional constraints that minority and economically disadvantaged men face and that limit their job opportunities.

The microsociological and macrosociological levels are not independent of one another (Mehan, 1992). The circumstances of the streetcorner men testify to this fact. The American economy is structured so that millions of Americans are locked in dead-end jobs. We can most appropriately think of the distinction between "micro" and "macro" as one of degree rather than as one of "either-or" entities (Lawler, Ridgeway, and Markovsky, 1993). Larger structures are composed of the repetitive patterns of interaction on the micro level. Simultaneously, macro structures frame the purposeful encounters through which people relate to one another on the micro level. Indeed, within these encounters, microstructures emerge and organize future encounters. At the same time, microstructures forge links among encounters and macrostructures and afford the mechanisms by which macrostructures evolve and change. In sum, complex interconnections and feedback loops between the micro and macro levels contribute to an emergent and diverse social order (Mouzelis, 1992).

□ The Development of Sociology

Just as we must seek an understanding of our private experiences and personal difficulties in the structural arrangements and the historical times in which we live, so we must locate the origins of

"Nobody has all of the answers, gentlemen. . . . What bothers me is we have all of the questions."

From *The Columbus Dispatch* © 1994 Tribune Media Services, Inc. Reprinted by permission: Tribune Media Services.

sociology in the social milieu of the period in which it developed. The political revolutions ushered in by the French Revolution in Europe in 1789 and continuing through the nineteenth century provided a major impetus to sociological work. Many individuals were troubled by the chaos and disorder that characterized Europe, and they longed for the more peaceful and relatively orderly days of the Middle Ages. But more sophisticated thinkers recognized that the clock could not be turned back and that they would have to seek new foundations of order in society (Ritzer, 1983; Lepenies, 1988).

Simultaneously, an additional force was at work. The Industrial Revolution that swept many Western nations resulted in large numbers of people leaving a predominantly agricultural setting for work in factories. New social and economic arrangements arose to provide the many services required by emergent capitalism. The excesses of the industrial system led some thinkers like Karl Marx to scrutinize the operation of social and economic institutions and to propose alternatives to them. Let us turn, then, to a brief consideration of the contributions of six particularly influential sociologists and to the emergence of sociology in the United States.

AUGUSTE COMTE AND HARRIET MARTINEAU

Auguste Comte (1798–1857) is commonly credited with being the founder of sociology and as having coined the name "sociology" for the new science. He emphasized that the study of society must be scientific, and he urged sociologists to use systematic observation, experimentation, and comparative historical analysis as their methods. Indeed, he went so far as to construct a "hierarchy of the sciences," with sociology as the "queen" science. Although this hierarchy allowed Comte to assert the importance of his new science and to separate it from social philosophy, his grandiose image of sociology is not shared by contemporary sociologists (Turner, 1982; Ritzer, 1983).

Comte divided the study of society into social statics and social dynamics. **Social statics** involves those aspects of social life that have to do with order and stability and that allow societies to hold together and endure. **Social dynamics** refers to those aspects of social life that have to do with social change and that pattern institutional development. Although the specifics of his work no longer direct contemporary sociology, Comte exerted enormous influence on the thinking of other sociologists, particularly Herbert Spencer, Harriet Martineau, and Emile Durkheim.

While Comte was laying the theoretical foundations for sociology, the English sociologist Harriet Martineau (1802–1876) was paving the way for the new discipline through her observations of social behavior in the United States and England. Like Comte, she insisted that the study of society represents a separate scientific field. Among her contributions was the first book on the methodology of social research, *How to Observe Manners and Morals,* published in 1838. She also undertook the comparative study of the stratification systems of Europe and the United States. Martineau showed how the basic moral values of the young American nation shaped its key institutional arrangements. Throughout her career Martineau was an ardent defender of women's rights. In masterly fashion she showed the similarities between the position of women in the Western world and that of American slaves and called for freedom and justice in an age in which they were granted only to white males (Rossi, 1973; Dergan, 1991).

HERBERT SPENCER

Herbert Spencer (1820–1903), an English sociologist, shared Comte's concern with social statics and social dynamics. He viewed society as having important similarities to a biological organism and depicted it as a *system,* a whole made up of interrelated parts. Just as the human body is made up of organs like the kidneys, lungs, and heart, so society is made up of institutions like the family, religion, education, the state, and the economy. Like biologists who portray an organism in terms of its structures and the functional contributions these structures make to its survival, Spencer described society in similar terms. This image of society is in line with what sociologists now call structural-functional theory, a perspective about which we will have more to say in Chapter 2.

Spencer handled social statics by means of the organic analogy. But he had an even greater interest in social dynamics. He proposed an evolutionary theory of historical development, one that depicted the world as growing progressively better. Intrigued by the Darwinian view of natural selection, Spencer applied the concept of survival of the fittest to the social world, an approach termed **Social Darwinism.** He sought to demonstrate that government should not interfere with the natural processes going on in a society. Only in this manner would people who were "fit" survive and those who were "unfit" die out. If this principle were allowed to operate freely, human beings and their institutions, like plants and animals, would progressively adapt themselves to their environment and reach higher and higher levels of historical development (Richards, 1988).

Spencer's Social Darwinist outlook shows that the ideas we hold about ourselves and the universe are shaped by the social age in which we live.

Spencer did much of his serious writing at the height of laissez-faire capitalism, and so it is hardly surprising that he embraced the doctrine that rugged individualism, unbridled competition, and noninterference by government achieve the greatest positive good. Spencer's Social Darwinist ideas were used extensively within England and the United States to justify unrestrained capitalism. John D. Rockefeller, the American oil tycoon, would echo Spencer and observe: "The growth of a large business is merely a survival of the fittest. . . . This is not an evil tendency in business. It is merely the working out of a law of nature" (quoted by Lewontin, Rose, and Kamin, 1984:26).

KARL MARX

Although Karl Marx (1818–1883) considered himself a political activist and not a sociologist, in truth he was both—and a philosopher, historian, economist, and political scientist as well. He viewed science not only as a vehicle for understanding society but also as a tool for transforming it. Marx was especially anxious to change the structure of capitalist institutions and to establish new institutions in the service of humanity. Although born in Germany, Marx was compelled to spend much of his adult life as a political exile in London.

Marx has influenced sociological thinking both by his penetrating insights and by the fact that some sociologists have constructed their work specifically *against* his theory (Gurney, 1981). Prior to the 1960s, most American theorists dismissed Marx as an ideologue whose partisan sympathies barred him from producing serious scientific work. But as young American sociologists were drawn into the civil rights and antiwar movements of the 1960s and early 1970s, they began to give serious attention to Marx's ideas. In the intervening three decades, American sociologists have come to accord Marx his rightful place among the giants of sociological thought (Ritzer, 1983).

Marx tried to discover the basic principles of history. He focused his search on the economic environments in which societies develop, particularly the current state of their technology and their method of organizing production (such as hunting and gathering, agriculture, or industry). At each stage of history, these factors dictate the group that will dominate society and the groups that will be subjugated. He believed that society is divided into those who own the means of producing wealth and those who do not, which gives rise to **class conflict** (see Chapters 6 and 8). All history, he said, is composed of struggles between classes. In ancient Rome, it was a conflict between patricians and plebeians and between masters and slaves. In the Middle Ages, it was a struggle between guildmasters and journeymen and between lords and serfs. And in contemporary Western societies that sprouted from the ruins of the feudal order, class antagonisms revolve about the struggle between the oppressing capitalist class or bourgeoisie and the oppressed working class or proletariat. The former derive their income through their ownership of the means of production, primarily factories, which allows them to exploit the labor of workers. The latter own nothing except their labor power and, because they are dependent for a living on the jobs provided by capitalists, must sell their labor power in order to exist.

Marx's perspective is called **dialectical materialism,** the notion that development depends on the clash of contradictions and the creation of new, more advanced structures out of these clashes. The approach depicts the world as made up not of static structures but of dynamic processes—a world of *becoming* rather than *being.* In the Marxian view of history, every economic order grows to a state of maximum efficiency; at the same time, it develops internal contradictions or weaknesses that contribute to its decay. The roots of an opposing order already begin to take hold in an old order. In time, the new order displaces the old order, while simultaneously absorbing its most useful features. In this manner society is propelled from one historical stage to another as each new order triumphs over the old. Marx depicted slavery as being displaced by feudalism, feudalism by capitalism, capitalism by socialism, and ultimately socialism by communism (the highest stage of society).

Marx portrayed political ideologies, religion, family organization, education, and government as making up the **superstructure** of society. The economic base of society—its mode of producing goods and its class structure—influences the forms that other institutions take. When one class controls the critical means whereby people derive their livelihood, its members gain the leverage necessary to fashion other aspects of institutional life—the superstructure—in ways that favor their class interests. However, the economic structure does not shape the superstructure in only a one-way direction (see Chapters 8, 10, and 12). Aspects of the superstructure act upon the economic base and modify it in a reciprocal relationship. For this reason, as we shall see in Chapters 6 and 8, Marx thought that when the working class became armed with a revolutionary ideology that fostered its class consciousness, it would overturn the existing social order and establish one that would pursue humane goals (Boswell and Dixon, 1993).

Within a century of his death, governments claiming to be run on Marxist principles had been installed in nations with more than a third of the world's population. But by the 1990s communist governments in Eastern Europe and the Soviet Union had been toppled, and many one-time socialists had come to embrace free-market concepts. We should emphasize, however, that Marxism is not synonymous with communist movements or states. Although Marx thought that the collapse of capitalism would usher in a more humane society, he had very little to say about socialism or communism (of Marx's entire opus of writings, less than 1 percent is about socialism). Indeed, Marx does not mention central planning in his writings; he was a utopian who seemingly assumed that once socialism had supplanted capitalism, many of the world's problems would sim-

ply evaporate. Rather, Marx centered his attention on capitalism and its internal dynamics (the capitalism of today is far different from that of Marx's time). Ironically, his concepts and analysis also afford insights on the disintegration of contemporary communist states. (The Soviet Union depended for its existence on total, centralized economic and political control by the Communist party, but the authoritarian control produced a nation that was too backward to compete with other Western nations and too weak politically to maintain dominance over its Eastern European and non-Russian empire.) More significantly, much in the manner of Plato's contribution to philosophy and Sigmund Freud's contribution to psychology, Marx advanced a mode of inquiry designed to reach a reality lying buried beneath the surface of history and our everyday social experiences. While many of his specific predictions proved wrong, ideas traceable to Marx's work echo throughout much of today's political debate in the United States. He sought to redress the gap between the rich and the poor (consider the controversies currently swirling about tax legislation) while championing limits on the working day, rules for factory safety, and elements of many contemporary taken-for-granted social welfare programs.

We will have a good deal more to say about Marx in the chapters that follow, particularly in our consideration of social stratification in Chapter 6 and power in Chapter 8. For our purposes here, suffice it to note that Marx is now recognized by most sociologists as a major figure in sociological theory. Today he is better known and understood, and more widely studied, than at any time since he began his career in the 1840s. Much of what is valuable in his work has now been incorporated in mainstream sociology, particularly as it finds expression in the conflict perspective we will consider in Chapter 2. In sum, for most sociologists, much as for most historians and economists, Marx's work is too outdated to follow in its particulars, yet too important to ignore (Boswell and Dixon, 1993).

EMILE DURKHEIM

Whereas Marx saw society as a stage upon which classes with conflicting interests contested with one another, the French sociologist Emile Durkheim (1858–1916) focused his sociological eye on the question of how societies hold together and endure. The principal objection Durkheim had to Marx's work was that Marx attributed too much importance to economic factors and class struggle and not enough to social solidarity (Bottomore, 1981; Turner, 1990). Central to Durkheim's (1897/1951) sociology is the notion that social integration is necessary for the maintenance of the social order and for the happiness of individuals. In particular, he suggested that happiness depends on individuals' finding a sense of meaning outside themselves that occurs within the context of group involvement. Durkheim sought to demonstrate that the destruction of social bonds has negative consequences and under some circumstances can lead individuals to commit suicide. Other sociologists have picked up on this central idea and have shown how the breakdown of group bonds can contribute to deviant behavior (Merton, 1968) and participation in social movements (Kornhauser, 1959).

In *The Division of Labor in Society* (1893/1964), Durkheim examined social solidarity. He distinguished between the types of solidarity found in early and modern societies. In early societies the social structure was relatively simple, with little division of labor. People were knitted together by the fact that they engaged in essentially similar tasks as jacks-of-all-trades. They derived a sense of oneness because they were so much alike, what Durkheim termed **mechanical solidarity.** Modern societies, in contrast, are characterized by complex social structures and a sophisticated division of labor. People perform specialized tasks in factories, offices, and schools. Since each person performs a relatively narrow range of tasks, no one person can be self-sufficient, and all must depend upon others in order to survive. Under these circumstances, soci-

ety is held together by the interdependence fostered by the differences among people, what Durkheim labeled **organic solidarity.**

In examining social solidarity and other sociological questions, Durkheim ascribed ultimate social reality to the group, not to the individual. He contended that the distinctive subject matter of sociology should be the study of social facts. **Social facts** are aspects of social life that cannot be explained in terms of the biological or mental characteristics of the individual. People experience the social fact as external to themselves in the sense that it has an independent reality and forms a part of their objective environment. As such, the social fact serves to *constrain* their behavior. Illustrations include social rules, maxims of public morality, patterns of family living, and religious observances.

Viewed in this manner, the social fact takes on the qualities of a "thing," a reality in its own right that is independent of its manifestation in particular individuals. Since the social fact is real and external, like the physical and biological aspects of the human environment, it has implications for individuals and their behavior. The hallmark of this independent reality is the resistance it poses to our inclinations and the counterpressure it places on our actions. For instance, individuals cannot flout moral and legal rules without tangible evidence of social disapproval (Benoit-Smullyan, 1948). Durkheim insisted that the explanation of social life must be sought in society itself. Society, he said, is more than the sum of its parts; it is a system formed by the association of individuals that comes to constitute a reality with its own distinctive characteristics.

Durkheim convincingly demonstrated the critical part social facts play in human behavior in his book *Suicide* (1897/1951), a landmark study in the history of sociology. Whereas earlier sociologists were given to armchair speculation, Durkheim undertook the painstaking collection and analysis of data in order to test his theory. Moreover, he used statistical techniques for studying human populations. In doing so, he was the first major sociologist to face up to the complex problems associated with the disciplined and rigorous study of social life.

In his study of suicide, Durkheim used population data gained from government records statistically to refute theories that explained suicide in terms of climatic, geographic, biological, or psychological factors. As an alternative, he proposed that suicide is a social fact—a product of the meanings, expectations, and structural arrangements that evolve as people interact with one another. As such, suicide is explainable by social factors. Durkheim investigated suicide rates among various groups of Europeans and found that some groups had higher rates than others. Protestants had higher rates than Catholics; the unmarried, higher rates than the married; and soldiers, higher rates than civilians. Moreover, suicide rates were higher in times of peace than in times of war and revolution, and higher in times of economic prosperity and recession than in times of economic stability. On the basis of these findings, he concluded that different suicide rates (as distinct from the individual case, which is a matter for psychology) are the consequence of variations in social solidarity. Individuals who are enmeshed in a web of social bonds are less inclined to suicide than individuals who are weakly integrated into group life.

MAX WEBER

No sociologist other than Marx has had a greater impact on sociology than the German sociologist Max Weber (1864–1920). Significantly, as we will see in later chapters, a good deal of Weber's work represented a debate with the ghost of Marx. Although finding much of value in Marx's writings, Weber disagreed with Marx on a number of important matters. Over the course of his career, Weber left a legacy of rich insights for a variety of disciplines, including economics, political science, and history. Among sociologists, he is known not only for his theoretical contributions but for a number of specific ideas that in their own right

have generated considerable interest and research. His sociological work covered a wide range of topics, including politics, bureaucracies, social stratification, law, religion, capitalism, music, the city, and cross-cultural comparison.

Weber believed that sociologists can derive an *understanding* of their subject matter in a manner that is unavailable to chemists and physicists. In investigating human behavior, sociologists are not limited to such objective criteria as weight and temperature; they can examine the "meanings" individuals bring to their interactions with one another. Consequently, Weber contended that a critical aspect of the sociological enterprise is the study of the intentions, values, beliefs, and attitudes that underlie people's behavior. Weber employed the German word **Verstehen**—meaning "understanding" or "insight"—in describing this approach for learning about the subjective meanings people attach to their actions. In using this method, sociologists mentally attempt to place themselves in the shoes of other people and identify what they think and how they feel. Whereas Durkheim argued that sociologists should direct their investigations primarily to social facts that lie beyond the individual, Weber thought it also essential that sociologists examine the definitions people use in shaping their behavior.

Another notable sociological contribution made by Weber is his concept of the ideal type. An **ideal type** is a concept constructed by a sociologist to portray the principal characteristics of a phenomenon. The term has nothing to do with evaluations of any sort. Rather, it is a tool that allows sociologists to generalize and simplify data by ignoring minor differences in order to accentuate major similarities. In Chapter 4 we will see how Weber employed the notion of the ideal type to devise his model of bureaucracy, and in Chapter 10 how he used it to examine the connection between Calvinism (the Protestant ethic) and capitalism. Weber contended that if sociologists are to establish cause-and-effect relationships, they must have concepts that are defined in a precise and unambiguous manner. The ideal type affords such a standard, especially in the study of concrete historical events and situations. It serves as a measuring rod against which sociologists can evaluate actual cases.

In his writings, Weber stressed the importance of a **value-free sociology.** He insisted that sociologists must not allow their personal biases to affect the conduct of their scientific research. Weber recognized that sociologists, like everyone else, have individual biases and moral convictions regarding behavior. But he insisted that sociologists must cultivate a disciplined approach to the phenomena they study so that they may see facts as they are, and not as they might wish them to be. By the same token, Weber recognized that objectivity is not neutrality. *Neutrality* implies that a person does not take sides on an issue; *objectivity* has to do with the pursuit of scientifically verifiable knowledge. Weber saw a role for values in certain specific aspects of the research process—namely, in selecting a topic for study and in determining the uses to which the knowledge is put. Clearly, data do not speak for themselves; they must be interpreted by scientists. For his part, Weber was led to study bureaucracy because it was an important part of the Germany in which he lived. Moreover, Weber was not afraid to express a value judgment or to tackle important issues of the day (Ritzer, 1983).

AMERICAN SOCIOLOGY

The sociologists we have considered thus far have been of European origin. Were sociologists to establish a sociological Hall of Fame, Comte, Martineau, Spencer, Marx, Durkheim, and Weber would unquestionably be among its first inductees. Yet as sociology entered the twentieth century, Americans assumed a critical role in its development. In the period preceding World War I, an array of factors provided a favorable climate for sociology in the United States (Hinkle, 1980). As in Europe, the Industrial Revolution and urbanization gave a major impetus to sociological study. An added factor was the massive immigra-

tion of foreigners to the United States and the problems their absorption and assimilation posed for American life. Further, both sociology and the modern university system arose together. In Europe, by contrast, sociology had a more difficult time becoming established because it had to break into an established system of academic disciplines.

A number of individuals like Lester F. Ward (1841–1913) played an important part in the development of sociology in the United States. Ward was influenced by Spencer's ideas, but unlike Spencer he was an advocate of social reform. He thought that sociologists should identify the basic laws that underlie social life and then use this knowledge to improve human society. William Graham Sumner (1840–1910), who as a professor at Yale taught the first sociology course in the United States, was also influenced by Spencer. And like Spencer, he adopted a survival-of-the-fittest approach. Sumner provided sociology with the distinction between folkways and mores (see Chapter 2) and in-groups and out-groups (see Chapter 4). W. E. B. DuBois (1868–1963), a leading African-American intellectual and one of the founders of the National Association for the Advancement of Colored People, took sociology out of the ivy tower and provided impetus to investigative field work. While at the University of Pennsylvania, DuBois gathered material on the African-American community of Philadelphia, which appeared as *The Philadelphia Negro* in 1900. Between 1896 and 1914, DuBois led the annual Atlanta University Conferences on Negro Problems that produced the first reliable sociological research on the South.

Contributions of considerable significance to sociology were also made by sociologists at the University of Chicago, where the first department of sociology in the United States was established in 1893. Here sociologists like William I. Thomas (see Chapter 3 for discussion of the Thomas theorem), Robert E. Park and Ernest W. Burgess (see Chapter 11 for a discussion of the concentric circle model), and George Herbert Mead (see Chapter 3 for a discussion of the self) carried out their work, a good deal of which centered on Chicago itself. Chicago was viewed as a "social laboratory," and it was subjected to intense and systematic study. Included in this research were investigations of juvenile gangs, immigrant ghettos, wealthy Gold Coast and slum life, taxi-dance halls, prostitution, and mental disorders.

During this period, Chicago sociologists trained an estimated half of the sociologists in the world at the time. Significantly, a number of the world's most capable female social scientists were among the university's graduates. But its department of sociology was largely a male world, one that afforded a hostile environment to the political activism espoused by many of the women. The women's world of sociology was centered at Hull House, a Chicago settlement house cofounded in 1889 by Jane Addams and Ellen Gates Starr. Hull House served as a model for the social reform activities and the civic, recreational, and educational programs that came to be identified with settlement houses throughout the nation. The juvenile court system and workers' compensation were products of the two women's efforts. Addams and Starr also pioneered campaigns for women's suffrage, better housing, improvements in public welfare, stricter child-labor laws, and the protection of working women. The women of Hull House are credited with inventing the research procedures of community case studies and of demographic mapping that would later become hallmarks of Chicago sociology (Deegan, 1988; Fitzpatrick, 1990).

During the 1940s and until the mid-1960s, sociologists at Columbia, Harvard, and the University of California at Berkeley took the lead and established the major directions for sociological research and theory. Paul L. Lazarsfeld and his colleagues crafted techniques for surveying public attitudes, while Talcott Parsons, Robert K. Merton, and Kingsley Davis refined models that portrayed society as a system made up of parts with interrelated functions. The leaders of American sociology insisted that the discipline should remain outside social problems and concern itself strictly with the enlargement of sociological knowledge.

The social turmoil of the 1960s and early 1970s brought to sociology many students who were student power, civil rights, and peace activists. These "new breed" sociologists contended that the doctrine of sociological neutrality was a cloak concealing moral insensitivity—a crass disregard for such things as the sufferings of the poor and minorities, the destructiveness of war, and the high social costs of crime. These sociologists looked to the writings of C. Wright Mills and other proponents of the sociological imagination for their inspiration. They also broke with established sociological theory and sought new directions in theory and research, including the dramaturgical approach discussed in Chapter 3 and the ethnomethodological perspective examined in Chapter 4 (also see Agger, 1991, and Maynard and Clayman, 1991).

The evolution of sociology continues, making for a much more diverse, and many would say richer, discipline than it was a few decades ago. Simultaneously, new questions and issues have surfaced. A number of sociologists have embraced ideas deriving from Jacques Derrida and Michel Foucault's deconstructionism. Such approaches—variously termed "poststructuralism" and "postpositivism"—contend that truth is relative, that all perceptions are mediated by an individual's cultural, racial, socioeconomic, and gender identities, and that science is only one of many ways of knowing the world. At the same time, foreign social theorists, including Anthony Giddens in England, Jürgen Habermas in Germany, and Pierre Bourdieu in France, have afforded major new avenues of intellectual stimulation. Sociologist Neil J. Smelser summarizes current matters by noting that a "peaceful pluralism" seems to be arising within sociology from the diversity: "It's not a vigorous or vicious period of polemics, but of a generally accepted idea that there is a variety of legitimate approaches and subjects—a kind of catholicism" (quoted by Coughlin, 1992:A8).

□ Conducting Research

The sociologists we have considered have provided us with important theoretical insights regarding the nature and workings of social life. However, theory that is not confirmed by facts is merely speculation that has little solid value. We require both theoretical understanding and facts, and for this reason both theory and research are essential components of the sociological enterprise (see Chapter 2). Theory inspires research that can verify or disprove it. Research provides findings that permit us to accept, reject, or modify our theoretical formulations, while simultaneously challenging us to craft new and better theories. Although some people dismiss theory and research as esoteric undertakings, there is good practical reason for them. For instance, the nation's former surgeon general, C. Everett Koop, has documented that behavior patterns account for at least half of the fatalities in seven of the ten largest categories of causes of death in the United States (yet the proportion of the budget that the National Institutes of Health allot to research on human behavior hovers at the 4 percent level) (Raymond, 1990a).

Sociologist William B. Sanders (1974) points out that sociological research resembles detective work. Both entail initial perplexity and conjecture, the search for evidence, perceptive reasoning, false leads, and, ideally, a final sense of triumph. For example, consider how the great fictional detective Sherlock Holmes went about sizing up situations. Here is Holmes's account of how he figured out that Dr. Watson had recently returned from Afghanistan (Doyle, 1927:24):

Here is a gentleman of medical type, but with the air of a military man. Clearly an army doctor, then. He has just come from the tropics, for his face is dark, and that is not the natural tint of skin, for his wrists are fair. He has undergone hardship and sickness, as his haggard face says clearly. His left arm has been injured. He holds it in a stiff and unnatural manner. Where in the tropics could an English army doctor have seen such hardship and got his arm wounded? Clearly in Afghanistan.

Underlying both sociology and detective work is the notion of *causality,* an idea that merits closer examination.

THE LOGIC OF SCIENCE

As we go about our daily lives, we typically assume that when one event occurs, another event, one that ordinarily follows the first, will do so again. Science makes a similar assumption—namely, that every event or action results from an antecedent cause. Indeed, a primary objective of science is to decide what causes what. Sociologists assume that crime, racism, social inequality, and marriages do not simply "happen," but that they have causes. Moreover, they assume that under identical conditions, the same cause will always produce the same effect. So sociologists, like other scientists, proceed on the assumption that cause-and-effect relationships prevail in the universe. Otherwise social life would be unintelligible because events would occur in a random or haphazard manner and be utterly unpredictable.

Scientists have typically assumed that truth is not a matter of belief but of objective reality that can be *empirically* tested—in other words, data can be gathered and analyzed by means of careful observation and meticulous measurement. According to this view, the reality established by science is believed to be the same for all people regardless of what they think about it. Consequently, the facts discovered by one scientist can be verified by other scientists. Even so, in practice science is not a collection of facts; science is a *process,* a form of social behavior (Kuhn, 1962; Cole, 1992). Science is what scientists do. And what scientists do is carried on in the context of other people and groups of people. It is this element that injects subjectivity into the scientific enterprise. For instance, all of us have values—notions of what is desirable, correct, and good. Even at our best, values subtly invade our work. Additionally, our culture provides a lens through which we view and define reality.

Although science is a human activity and as such is affected by social life, the key to science is

Drawing by D. Fradon; © 1992 The New Yorker Magazine, Inc.

found in its approach to data—the rigorous, disciplined attempt to look as objectively as is humanly possible at the phenomena studied. Sociologists are enjoined to avoid such emotional involvement in their work that they cannot adopt a new approach or reject an old answer when their findings indicate that this is required. At the heart of the scientific enterprise is a skepticism that dictates that ideas be checked against observable evidence. This scientific approach is centered in the way scientists go about testing for linkages among variables. A **variable** is the term scientists apply to something that they think influences (or is influenced by) something else. It usually occurs in different amounts, degrees, or forms. For example, heat is one variable that causes water to boil; atmospheric pressure is another. The variables sociologists typically study have to do with social conditions, attitudes, and behaviors. In studying political behavior, for example, sociologists commonly examine such variables as differences in race, gender, age, religion, and socioeconomic standing. They also frequently appraise the social climate of the times as it finds expression in such variables as the state of international tensions and the rates of unemployment, interest, and inflation.

In investigating cause-and-effect relationships, scientists distinguish between the independent and the dependent variable. The **independent variable** is the variable that causes an effect. The **dependent variable** is the variable that is affected. The causal variable (the independent variable) precedes in time the phenomenon it causes (the dependent variable). For example, as the temperature gets warmer, air can hold more water. The temperature—a measure of heat—is the independent variable and the amount of water suspended in the air is the dependent variable. Similarly, as the socioeconomic level of women (independent variable) increases, the mortality rate of their infants decreases (the dependent variable). In their research, scientists typically attempt to hypothesize the relationship they expect to find between the independent and dependent variables. Such a statement—or **hypothesis**—is a proposition that can then be tested to determine its validity.

Doing Sociology: Does the Super Bowl Winner Portend the Stock Market?

Between 1967 and 1993 the winner of the Super Bowl has foreshadowed the performance of the stock market in 24 of the 27 years. See the table below. If a National Football Conference (NFC) team wins the Super Bowl, the stock market (measured by the Dow Jones Industrial Average) typically posts a gain for the year. If an American Football Conference (AFC) team wins, it tends to be a down year. If the winner is an AFC team whose roots are in the old National Football League (NFL)—the Cleveland Browns, the Pittsburgh Steelers, and the Indianapolis (formerly Baltimore) Colts—it is counted as an up year. Additionally, the exceptions have typically involved narrow margins. The years the Super Bowl indicator did not work are in bold type. Would you find it prudent to invest your money on the basis of this relationship? Explain. What are the dangers associated with equating correlation with causation? Can you identify factors that may bias the Super Bowl indicator? For instance, are there as many AFL as old NFL teams (eleven versus seventeen teams). In how many years did the market rise?

Year	Winner	Dow Change	Year	Winner	Dow Change
1967	Green Bay (NFL)	15.2	1981	Oakland (AFC)	−9.2%
1968	Green Bay (NFL)	4.3	1982	San Francisco (NFC)	19.6
1969	N.Y. Jets (AFL)	−15.2	1983	Washington (NFC)	20.3
1970	**Kansas City (AFL)**	**4.8**	1984	L.A. Raiders (AFC)	−3.7
1971	Baltimore (AFC)*	6.1	1985	San Francisco (NFC)	27.7
1972	Dallas (NFC)	14.6	1986	Chicago (NFC)	22.6
1973	Miami (AFC)	−16.6	1987	New York (NFC)	2.3
1974	Miami (AFC)	−27.5	1988	Washington (NFC)	11.9
1975	Pittsburgh (AFC)*	38.3	1989	San Francisco (NFC)	27.0
1976	Pittsburgh (AFC)*	17.9	**1990**	**San Francisco (NFC)**	**−4.3**
1977	Oakland (AFC)	−17.3	1991	New York (NFC)	20.3
1978	**Dallas (NFC)**	**−3.2**	1992	Washington (NFC)	4.2
1979	Pittsburgh (AFC)*	4.2	1993	Dallas (NFC)	13.7
1980	Pittsburgh (AFC)*	14.9			

*Formerly NFL.

SOURCE: *USA Today,* January 24, 1994, p. B1. Copywright 1994, *USA Today.* Reprinted with permission.

Scientists spend a good deal of their time attempting to figure out how one thing relates to another. They seek to determine the degree of association that exists between an independent and a dependent variable. If the variables are causally related, then they must be correlated with one another. A **correlation** exists if a change in one variable is associated with a change in the other variable. Since the mortality rate of infants decreases as the socioeconomic level of women increases, the two variables are said to be correlated.

Correlation, however, does not establish causation (Cole, 1972). See the box. For instance, the death rate is considerably higher among hospitalized individuals than among nonhospitalized individuals. Yet we would be wrong to conclude on the basis of this correlation that hospitals cause death. Likewise, the amount of damage resulting from a fire is closely associated with the number of fire engines that are on the scene. Again, we would be wrong to conclude that fire engines cause greater fire damage. In these latter cases the correlation is *spurious*—the apparent relationship between the two variables is produced by a third variable that influences the original variables (severe sickness is associated both with admission to hospitals and with death; similarly, a large, uncontrolled fire is associated both with extensive damage and the mobilization of multiple firefighting units). In order to combat the likelihood that their research will be contaminated by third variables, scientists employ controls, a matter we will consider at greater length a little later in the chapter when we deal with experimentation.

STEPS IN THE SCIENTIFIC METHOD

The scientific method is a way of finding out about the world that relies on the rigorous and disciplined collection of facts and a logical explanation of them. It finds expression in a systematic series of steps that seek to ensure maximum objectivity in investigating a problem. Ideally sociological research follows this step-by-step procedure, although in practice it is not always possible. Even so, the following steps provide useful guidelines for conducting research (see Figure 1.1).

1. *Selecting a researchable problem.* The range of topics available for social research is as broad as the range of human behavior. Thus we need to find a problem that merits study and that can be investigated by the methods of science. For instance, two social scientists, Donald G.

Dutton and Arthur P. Aron (1974), were intrigued by the seeming connection between states of high anxiety and sexual attraction, a link first noted by the first-century Roman poet Ovid. Ovid had advised men that an excellent time to arouse romantic passion in women was while watching gladiators disembowel one another in the arena. Presumably the emotions of fear and repulsion excited by the grisly scene somehow translated themselves into romantic interests.

2. *Reviewing the literature.* Rather than plunging hastily into a research venture, Dutton and Aron surveyed the literature dealing with sexual attraction and states of strong emotion. This review told them about other research that had been undertaken, suggested a variety of leads, and saved them from duplicating work others had already done. For instance, ethologist Niko Tinbergen (1954) had found a connection between "aggression" and courting behaviors in some animal species, and a number of psychologists had experimentally documented the existence of similar linkages in human behavior (Clark, 1952; Barclay and Haber, 1965).

3. *Formulating a hypothesis.* After reviewing the literature, researchers commonly arrive at a tentative guess regarding the relationship they believe exists between two variables. They state this relationship in the form of a hypothesis. For instance, Dutton and Aron sought to test the hypothesis that a state of high anxiety (the independent variable) heightens sexual attraction (the dependent variable). But before undertaking their research, they had to develop operational definitions of their variables. In developing an **operational definition,** scientists take abstract concepts and put them in a form that permits their measurement. Dutton and Aron (1974:511) operationalized their hypothesis as follows: "An attractive female is seen as more attractive by males who encounter her while they experience a strong

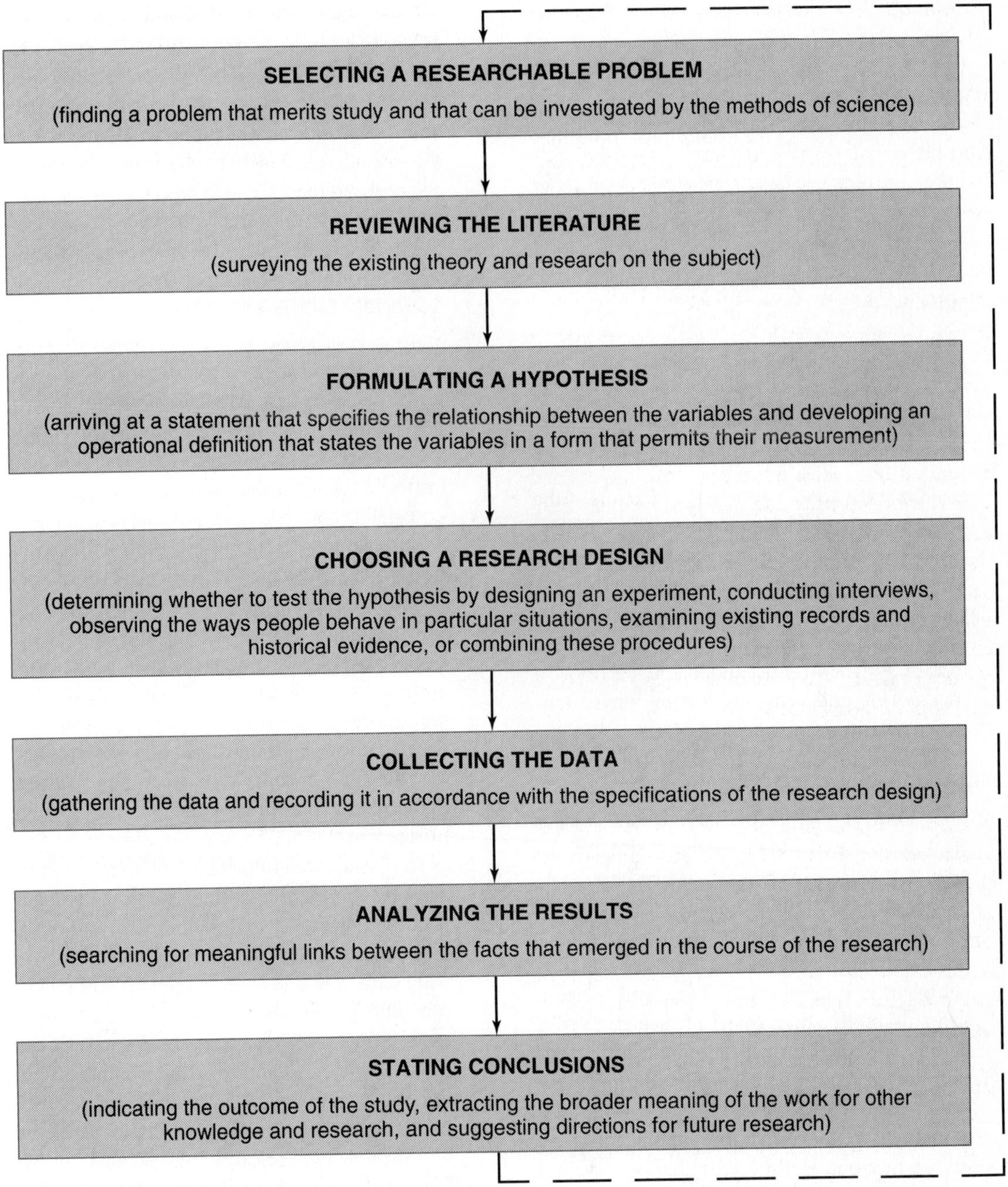

SELECTING A RESEARCHABLE PROBLEM

(finding a problem that merits study and that can be investigated by the methods of science)

REVIEWING THE LITERATURE

(surveying the existing theory and research on the subject)

FORMULATING A HYPOTHESIS

(arriving at a statement that specifies the relationship between the variables and developing an operational definition that states the variables in a form that permits their measurement)

CHOOSING A RESEARCH DESIGN

(determining whether to test the hypothesis by designing an experiment, conducting interviews, observing the ways people behave in particular situations, examining existing records and historical evidence, or combining these procedures)

COLLECTING THE DATA

(gathering the data and recording it in accordance with the specifications of the research design)

ANALYZING THE RESULTS

(searching for meaningful links between the facts that emerged in the course of the research)

STATING CONCLUSIONS

(indicating the outcome of the study, extracting the broader meaning of the work for other knowledge and research, and suggesting directions for future research)

Figure 1.1   THE STEPS IN THE SCIENTIFIC METHOD
The chart shows the steps researchers commonly follow in investigating a problem.

emotion (fear) than by males not experiencing a strong emotion."

4. *Choosing a research design.* Once researchers have formulated and operationalized their hypothesis, they have to determine how they will collect the data that will provide a test of it. Depending on the nature of their hypothesis, they might design an experiment, conduct interviews, observe the way people behave in particular situations, examine existing records and historical evidence, or combine these procedures. Dutton and Aron undertook a field experiment in which they used the real world as their laboratory. The researchers introduced the independent variable into a natural setting to determine its impact on behavior.

5. *Collecting the data.* The actual collection of the data plays a critical part in the research enterprise. Dutton and Aron collected their data near two footbridges hikers use to cross the Capilano River in North Vancouver, Canada. The first or "experimental" bridge is a 450-foot-long structure suspended 230 feet above a rock canyon and a rushing stream; it has a tendency to tilt, sway, and wobble, creating the impression that one could easily fall over the side. The second or "control" bridge is a wide, solid wood bridge farther upriver that is only 10 feet above a small, shallow stream. An attractive female interviewer approached male hikers who had crossed either of the bridges and explained that she was doing a project for her psychology class. The men were asked to complete a brief questionnaire and write a short dramatic story based on a picture of a young woman from the Thematic Apperception Test (TAT). When the men (termed *subjects*) completed their questionnaires, the woman gave each man her name and telephone number in the event that he "desired more information about the study."

6. *Analyzing the results.* Once researchers have their data, they must analyze them to find answers to the questions posed by their research project. Analysis involves a search for meaningful links between the facts that have emerged in the course of the research. As revealed by the content of the stories, Dutton and Aron found that the men who had crossed the wobbly suspension bridge were more sexually aroused than the men who had crossed the solid bridge. Additionally, half of the men on the high-fear bridge called the young woman, whereas only 13 percent of those on the low-fear bridge called her.

7. *Stating conclusions.* After completing their analysis of the data, researchers are ready to state their conclusions. They typically accept, reject, or modify their hypothesis. Additionally, researchers usually seek to extract broader meaning from their work by linking it to other knowledge and theory. In this case, Dutton and Aron accepted the hypothesis that strong emotion increases sexual arousal. And they suggested that their findings offer support in favor of the labeling theory of emotions, a perspective that parallels the symbolic interactionist approach we will discuss in Chapter 2. The two researchers concluded that love is a combination of physiological arousal and the application of the appropriate label to the feelings. Presumably, the men on the high, wobbly bridge had defined their inner stirrings of fear as romantic attraction. This labeling is encouraged by the popular stereotype that depicts a pounding heart, shortness of breath, and trembling hands (also the physical symptoms of fear) with falling in love. In another study Dutton and Aron also found that men who expected to receive electric shocks were much more attracted to an attractive female confederate (a person in league with the experimenters) than were men who did not expect to be shocked. Such research suggests that love, or at least infatuation, arises when we define our inner feelings of arousal as love. So in their daily lives people find it easy to pick up on the romantic cues that abound in their environment and decide that they are "in love." Such

findings lend support to the symbolic interactionist perspective (discussed in Chapter 2) that seeks to explain how we go about interpreting and giving meaning to our experiences.

RESEARCH METHODS

We have emphasized that the scientific method allows researchers to pursue answers to their questions by gathering evidence in a systematic manner. Although no single method can eliminate uncertainty, the steps embodied in the scientific method maximize the chances for deriving information that is relevant, unbiased, and economical. Four major techniques of data collection are available to sociologists: experiments, surveys, observation, and archival research. Let us examine each of these research designs in turn.

Experiments. The ideal design for scientific research is one that allows researchers either to accept or to reject a hypothesis. In order to do so, scientists attempt to control all the relevant variables to eliminate other explanations for their findings. The **experiment** best meets this requirement. In the experiment, researchers work with two groups that are identical in all relevant respects. They introduce a change in one group— the **experimental group**—but not in the other group—the **control group.** The two groups are identical except for the variable that the researchers introduce in the experimental group. The control group affords a neutral standard against which the changes in the experimental group can then be measured. This procedure allows sociologists to test the effects of an independent variable on a dependent variable.

We commonly think of experiments as being performed in a laboratory setting, and this is the case for much medical research and for a good deal of the research done by psychologists and social psychologists. However, sociologists are much more likely to perform field experiments of the sort conducted by Dutton and Aron than they

are to undertake laboratory experiments. Sociologists usually wish to maximize the natural quality of the setting in which people interact. They want to observe various forms of social behavior under the conditions where they normally occur. Further, sociologists can use more representative subject populations than college students. And finally, in contrast to laboratory settings, where some subjects inhibit their behavior because they are afraid to appear incompetent or unattractive, the subjects of field experiments are unlikely to be "on guard" or seek the experimenter's goodwill by doing what is "expected" of them.

Although the field experiment seems to provide an ideal combination of the strict rules of experimentation with the realism of natural settings, it does have disadvantages (Deaux and Wrightsman, 1984). For one thing, it is difficult to control the independent variable and to get a good "fix" on the dependent variable. And, in contrast to laboratory scientists, researchers in the field have no control over unexpected intrusions that may reduce or destroy the effectiveness of the changes they make in the independent variable. Then too, there is an ethical question. Is it reasonable for sociologists to involve people in an experiment without their knowledge or consent? Most social scientists believe that such research is permissible so long as it does not disrupt a person's daily life, the setting is a public one, and the independent variable does not harm them. We will return to the matter of ethics later in the chapter.

Surveys. Methods that rely on observation attempt to describe and portray behavior as it occurs. But some aspects of behavior are not directly accessible to observation, particularly those having to do with people's values, beliefs, attitudes, perceptions, motivations, and feelings. Further, individuals may be willing to report but not permit researchers to observe some of their private behaviors, particularly their sexual activity, religious practices, and drug use. And since the spontaneous occurrence of some events is unpredictable, trained observers cannot always be on the scene. Under these circumstances, the **survey** is a valuable tool in the researcher's arsenal. Survey data are typically gathered in one of two ways. In the first, the researcher interviews people by reading them questions from a prepared questionnaire. In the second, people receive a questionnaire in the mail, fill it out, and return it by mail.

In both interview and questionnaire surveys, researchers have to pay close attention to their sampling procedures. Should they wish information about a large population, they do not need to contact every member of that population. Instead, they can draw on a small sample to derive broad generalizations. Public opinion pollsters like the Gallup, Harris, and CBS News organizations employ a small sample of approximately 1,500 individuals to tap the opinion of more than 250 million Americans. However, there is a troubling development: Deluged by a growing number of telephone and mail solicitations and demands on their time, more and more Americans are refusing to participate in survey research (Goyder, 1987; Rothenberg, 1990; Dillman, 1991).

The rationale underlying sampling procedures is easy to grasp. By way of illustration, consider a jar filled with 80,000 blue, green, red, purple, and white marbles. You would not have to count all the marbles to determine their proportions. All you would need do is randomly select 1,000 marbles, sort them into appropriate piles by color, and count them. You could then estimate the proportions of the various marbles with great confidence and with only a small margin of error, so long of course as each marble in the jar has an equal chance of being represented in the count. Physicians proceed on a similar assumption when they test your blood by taking only a few drops of it.

When it comes to social behavior, however, the matter is more complicated than it is with marbles and blood. Sociologists typically employ either a random sample or a stratified random sample in their research. In the **random sample** researchers select subjects on the basis of chance so that every individual in the population has the

"I quit ringing doorbells—I just read their bumper stickers."

From *The Wall Street Journal*—Permission, Cartoon Features Syndicate.

same opportunity to be chosen. Should sociologists prefer greater precision, they can use a **stratified random sample.** They then divide the population into relevant categories, such as age, gender, socioeconomic level, and race, and draw a random sample from each of the categories. Thus if African Americans constitute 12 percent of the population and Hispanics 9 percent, African Americans will comprise 12 percent of the sample and Hispanics 9 percent.

Designing good questionnaires is not easy. The wording of the questions, their number, and the format in which they appear are all critical matters. For instance, the wording of a question may systematically bias the answers. A New York Times/CBS News survey found that only 29 percent of respondents said they favored a constitutional amendment "prohibiting abortions." But in response to a later question in the same survey, 50 percent said they favored an amendment "protecting the life of an unborn child"—which amounts to the same thing (Dionne, 1980). At times politicians seek to use this tactic to their advantage (Deaux and Wrightsman, 1984; Ladd, 1987; Bradburn and Sudman, 1988). For example, a question that begins "I agree that Candidate X" is more likely to produce a positive response than a question that begins "Does Candidate X." A good deal of pretesting is required to ensure that questions are understandable, unbiased, and specific enough to elicit the desired information.

Probably the major difficulty with self-report information has to do with the issue of its accuracy (Schuman and Scott, 1987; Cose, 1990). Because individuals are involved in the data they are reporting, they may intentionally or unwittingly supply biased reports. For example, they may withhold or distort information because, if they were to tell the truth, they would feel threatened or face a loss in self-esteem. Further, many people lack the self-insight required to provide certain kinds of information. At least 10 percent of the population lacks the literacy necessary to comprehend even the simplest question. Then too, from 20 to 70 percent of the people who receive a questionnaire in the mail fail to complete or return it, distorting the sample's representativeness.

Observation. As baseball's Yogi Berra once observed, "You can observe a lot just by watching." Indeed, observation is one of the most pervasive activities in which we engage as we go about our everyday lives. It is also a primary tool of sociological inquiry. Observation becomes a scientific technique when it (1) serves a clear research objective, (2) is undertaken in a systematic rather than haphazard manner, (3) is carefully recorded, (4) is related to a broader body of sociological knowledge and theory, and (5) is subjected to the same checks and controls applied to all types of scientific evidence (Selltiz, Wrightsman, and Cook, 1976).

Anthropologists have long employed observation as a primary tool for studying non-Western peoples. And as early as the 1920s, sociologists trained at the University of Chicago employed the technique as the cornerstone of their studies of hobo life (Anderson, 1923), prostitution (Thomas, 1923), and gang behavior (Thrasher, 1927). Sociologists typically observe people in one of two ways. They may observe the activities of people without intruding or participating in the activities, a procedure termed **unobtrusive observation.** Or sociologists may engage in activities with the people that they are studying, a technique called **participant observation.**

Elliot Liebow's (1967) study of the African-American streetcorner men, which we discussed earlier in the chapter, involved participant observation. Liebow, a white, began his study by hanging out on the corner in front of the New Deal Carry-out Shop. Here he initiated a conversation with a 31-year-old African-American man, Tally Jackson. Over the course of the next four hours the two men struck up a friendship as they drank coffee, watched people pass by, and chatted. Over the next several weeks, Liebow often ate breakfast and lunch at the Carry-out and began occasionally putting a dime in the jukebox. The streetcorner men were at first suspicious of Liebow, but Tally allayed their distrust by sponsoring Liebow as his friend.

Within a number of months, Liebow was well enough known and accepted by the streetcorner men that he was free to go to their rooms or apartments, needing neither an excuse nor an explanation for doing so. Yet even so, the fact that he was white, college-educated, and "doing research" made him an "outsider." Liebow (1967:253) observes:

> [B]ut I also was a participant in a full sense of the word. The people I was observing knew that I was observing them, yet they allowed me to participate in their activities and take part in their lives to a degree that continues to surprise me. Some "exploited" me, not as an outsider but rather as one who, as a rule, had more resources than they did. When one of them came up with the resources—money or a car, for example—he too was "exploited" in the same way. I usually tried to limit money or other favors to what I thought each would have gotten from another friend had he the same resources as I. I tried to meet requests as best I could without becoming conspicuous. I was not always on the giving end and learned somewhat too slowly to accept food or let myself be treated to drinks even though I knew this would work a hardship on the giver.

In many situations observation is the only way to gather data. At times people are unable or unwilling to tell about their behavior: They may lack sufficient self-insight to report on it, or because their behavior is illicit, taboo, or deviant, they may be reluctant to do so. For instance, we may wish answers to such questions as, Why and how are people drawn to crack and heroin? How is the drug market structured? How does drug use affect the social and economic life of the community? What is its role in crime and violence? Some of the most informative answers we possess on these questions have come from researchers who have undertaken streetwise unobtrusive observation while living and working in drug-ridden communities (Holden, 1989; Anderson, 1990). But observation also has many of the same limitations as the field experiment. Additionally, there is the practical problem of applying observational procedures to phenomena that occur over a long period, such as a certain historical era. For these types of investigation, archival data are particularly useful.

Comparative and Historical Research. We may learn a good deal about deviance, work, sexual behavior, family life, leisure, and other matters within the United States and other Western societies. But do these insights hold for non-Western peoples? And do they hold for earlier historical periods? To answer these sorts of questions, sociologists need to look to other societies and other historical periods to test their ideas. Comparative and historical research is well suited to the task (Wallerstein, 1974; Tilly, 1984; Ragin, 1987; McMichael, 1990; Kiser and Hechter, 1991). One approach involves archival research. **Archival research** refers to the use of existing records that have been produced or maintained by persons or organizations other than the researcher. Sources include census data, government statistics, newspaper reports, books, magazines, personal letters, speeches, folklore, court records, works of art, and the research data of other social scientists. A new

utilization of data already collected for some other purpose may have considerable value and merit.

Comparative and historical materials have provided us with valuable insights on issues relating to the nation-state. A good illustration is sociologist Theda Skocpol's landmark study, *States and Social Revolution* (1979). Skocpol had a number of concerns, including testing Marx's theory of revolution. In her study, Skocpol looked for similarities in the societal conditions that existed at the time of the French (1787–1800), Russian (1917–1921), and Chinese (1911–1949) revolutions. She then studied data from nations where revolutions failed or did not take place: Germany in 1848 and Russia in 1905 (revolutions that failed), England in the seventeenth century (a political revolution), and Prussia in the early 1800s and Japan in the late 1860s (where basic structural change was initiated by a ruling elite). Although Skocpol found much of value in Marx's theory of revolution, she was also critical of it. Whereas Marx saw the state as the coercive instrument of the ruling class, Skocpol (1979:27) depicts it as "a structure with a logic and interests of its own not necessarily equivalent to, or fused with, the interests of the dominant class in society" (see Chapter 8).

Skocpol also traces the roots of the French, Russian, and Chinese revolutions to the political crises that developed in the nations' "old-regime states." The crises developed when the countries became enmeshed in long-term international conflicts that resulted in military defeat. Simultaneously, domestic class tensions, particularly those between the landed aristocracy and the peasantry, made the agrarian masses receptive to revolutionary activity. On the basis of her comparative historical analysis, Skocpol has concluded that successful social revolutions pass through three stages: An old regime's state apparatus collapses; the peasantry mobilizes in class-based uprisings; and a new elite consolidates political power.

Significantly, knowledge is not static. Using historical materials and comparisons in novel and imaginative ways, sociologist Jack Goldstone (1991) has brought additional sophistication to the state-centered theory of revolutions. Goldstone does not change the core of Skocpol's approach: Revolutions arise because of the breakdown of the state from above rather than insurgence from below. However, he implicates somewhat different social forces in the breakdown. Whereas Skocpol locates the state's crisis in military strain resulting from geopolitical conditions, Goldstone looks to mechanisms associated with population growth:

1. Rapid population growth pressures food and commodity prices, placing fiscal strain on state budgets (for instance, the cost of maintaining a standing army)
2. Price hikes undermine old elites, give birth to new elites, and intensify competition and conflicts among elites
3. Population pressures contribute to food shortages, flooded labor markets, falling wages, mounting poverty, and youthful unrest, and these in turn feed popular revolts

Goldstone demonstrates that population change often functions as an imperceptible process of which individuals are seldom fully aware but which nonetheless has vast social repercussions. However, because both Skocpol and Goldstone stress state breakdown, they are basically variants on the same model (Collins, 1993; Foran, 1993b).

Archival research has the advantage of allowing researchers to test hypotheses over a wider range of time and societies than would otherwise be possible. We gain greater confidence in the validity of a hypothesis when we can test it in a number of cultures and historical periods rather than restrict ourselves to a single group in the present time and place. However, the technique also has its disadvantages. The major problem is that missing or inaccurate records often prevent an adequate test. And when material is available, it is frequently difficult to categorize in a way that gives an answer to a research question (Deaux and Wrightsman, 1984).

Conclusion. Differences among sociologists with respect to their preferences in research methodology occasionally lead to rancor. Even so, most sociologists agree that nothing is to be gained from intellectual antagonism and the distancing of one group from the others. Such differences typically derive from the considerable diversity found among sociologists in research interests and styles of inquiry. This is as it should be. Indeed, as Leonard I. Pearlin (1992:9) observes, ". . . differences permit each to give something to the other." So even if sociologists are planted firmly in one or another camp, most of them are at least prepared to dip into one or more of the other camps for new insights and modes of inquiry. This approach increases the opportunities and potential for synergistic exchanges (the notion that joint action, when taken together, increases the effectiveness of each approach).

RESEARCH ETHICS

We are reminded of the dangers inherent in science gone awry by the American government's sponsoring of radiation experiments on human subjects—including more than 200 babies—during the cold war. Because sociological knowledge can have positive and negative consequences for individuals and institutions, ethical considerations must govern sociological research. Yet in conducting research, sociologists confront a dilemma. On the one hand, they must not distort or manipulate their findings to serve untruthful, personal, or institutional ends. On the other hand, they are obligated to consider people as ends and not means. Because of the possible conflicts between these various responsibilities, the American Sociological Association (1989) has provided a code of ethics to govern the behavior of its members. Among these principles are the following:

Sociologists should not misuse their positions as professional social scientists for fraudulent purposes or as a pretext for gathering intelligence for any organization or government. Sociologists should not mislead respondents involved in a research project as to the purpose for which that research is being conducted.

The process of conducting sociological research must not expose respondents to substantial risk of personal harm. Informed consent must be obtained when the risks of research are greater than the risks of everyday life. Where modest risk or harm is anticipated, informed consent must be obtained.

Sociologists must not coerce or deceive students into serving as research subjects.

No sociologists should discriminate in hiring, firing, promotions, salary, treatment, or any other conditions of employment or career development on the basis of sex, sexual preference, age, race, religion, national origin, handicap, or political orientation.

In sum, because sociological knowledge can be a form of economic and political power, sociologists must exercise care to protect their discipline, the people they study and teach, and society from abuses that may stem from their professional work.

Summary

1. The sociological perspective encourages us to look beyond the often neglected and taken-for-granted aspects of our social environment and examine them in fresh and creative ways. As we look behind the outside of our social world and scrutinize the hidden fabric, we encounter new levels of reality.

2. The ability to see our private experiences and personal difficulties as entwined with the structural arrangements of our society and the historical times in which we live is the essence of the sociological imagination. The sociological imagination allows us to break out from the narrow vision that usually characterizes our daily activities.

3. The sociologist Auguste Comte is commonly credited with being the founder of sociology. He emphasized that the study of society must be scientific, and he urged sociologists to employ systematic observation, experimentation, and comparative historical analysis as their methods. Additionally, he divided the study of society into social statics and social dynamics.

4. Herbert Spencer depicted society as a system, a whole made up of interrelated parts, an image he based upon the organic analogy. He also set forth an evolutionary theory of historical development, one that depicted the world as growing progressively better.

5. Karl Marx has influenced sociological thinking both by his penetrating insights and by the fact that some sociologists have fashioned their work specifically against his theory. He focused his search for the basic principles of history on the economic environments in which societies develop. At each stage of history, the current state of a society's technology and its method of organizing production dictate the group that will dominate the society and the groups that will be dominated. Thus he believed that society is divided into

those who own the means of producing wealth and those who do not, giving rise to class conflict.

6. Emile Durkheim was especially concerned with social solidarity, distinguishing between mechanical and organic solidarity. He contended that the distinctive subject matter of sociology should be the study of social facts—those aspects of social life that cannot be explained in terms of the biological or mental characteristics of the individual. People experience the social fact as external to themselves in the sense that it has an independent reality and forms a part of their objective environment.

7. Max Weber left a legacy of rich insights for a variety of disciplines, including sociology. He said that a critical aspect of the sociological enterprise is the study of the intentions, values, beliefs, and attitudes that underlie people's behavior. Weber employed the German word *Verstehen* in describing his approach for learning about the subjective meanings people attach to their actions. Other ideas that Weber contributed to sociology were his notions of the ideal type and a value-free science.

8. Science assumes that every event or action results from an antecedent cause—that is, cause-and-effect relationships prevail in the universe. Scientists spend a good deal of their time attempting to figure out how one thing relates to another. In so doing, they find the steps associated with the scientific method a helpful procedure. These steps entail selecting a researchable problem, reviewing the literature, formulating a hypothesis, choosing a research design, collecting the data, analyzing the results, and stating conclusions.

9. Four major techniques of data collection are available to sociologists: experiments, surveys, observation, and archival research. In the experiment, researchers work with two groups that are identical in all relevant respects. They introduce a change in one group—the experimental group—but not in the other group—the control group. The procedure allows sociologists to test the effects of an independent variable on a dependent variable. Surveys allow sociologists to investigate people's values, beliefs, attitudes, perceptions, motivations, and feelings. Interviewing and questionnaires constitute the primary techniques for gathering survey data. Observation is a valuable tool when people lack sufficient self-insight to report on their behavior or when they are reluctant to do so. Archival research allows sociologists to test hypotheses over a wider range of time and societies than would otherwise be possible.

10. It is important that sociologists observe the ethics of their discipline in carrying out research. They have an obligation not to expose their subjects to substantial risk or personal harm in the research process and to protect the rights and dignity of their subjects.

Glossary

archival research The use of existing records that have been produced or maintained by persons or organizations other than the researcher.

class conflict The view of Karl Marx that society is divided into those who own the means of producing wealth and those who do not, giving rise to struggles between classes.

control group The group that affords a neutral standard against which the changes in an experimental group can be measured.

correlation   A change in one variable associated with a change in another variable.

dependent variable   The variable that is affected in an experimental setting.

dialectical materialism   The notion in Marxist theory that development depends on the clash of contradictions and the creation of new, more advanced structures out of these clashes.

experiment   A technique in which researchers work with two groups that are identical in all relevant respects. They introduce a change in one group, but not in the other group. The procedure permits researchers to test the effects of an independent variable on a dependent variable.

experimental group   The group in which researchers introduce a change in an experimental setting.

hypothesis   A proposition that can be tested to determine its validity.

ideal type   A concept constructed by a sociologist to portray the principal characteristics of a phenomenon.

independent variable   The variable that causes an effect in an experimental setting.

macrosociology   The study of large-scale and long-term social processes.

mechanical solidarity   A form of social integration that characterized early societies in which a sense of oneness was derived from the fact that all the members of the society engaged in essentially similar tasks.

microsociology   The detailed study of what individuals say, do, and think moment by moment as they go about their daily lives.

operational definition   A definition developed by taking abstract concepts and putting them in a form that permits their measurement.

organic solidarity   A form of social integration that characterizes modern societies. A society is held together by the interdependence fostered by the differences among people.

participant observation   A technique in which researchers engage in activities with the people that they are observing.

random sample   A sampling procedure in which researchers select subjects on the basis of chance so that every individual in the population has the same opportunity to be chosen.

Social Darwinism   The application of evolutionary notions and the concept of survival of the fittest to the social world.

social dynamics   Those aspects of social life that have to do with social change and that pattern institutional development.

social facts   Those aspects of social life that cannot be explained in terms of the biological or mental characteristics of the individual. People experience the social fact as external to themselves in the sense that it has an independent reality and forms a part of their objective environment.

social statics   Those aspects of social life that have to do with order and stability and that allow societies to hold together and endure.

sociological imagination   The ability to see our private experiences and personal difficulties as entwined with the structural arrangements of our society and the historical times in which we live.

sociology   The scientific study of social interaction and organization.

stratified random sample   A sampling procedure in which researchers divide a population into relevant categories and draw a random sample from each of the categories.

superstructure   The notion of Karl Marx that political ideologies, religion, family organization, education, and government constitute a level of social life that is primarily shaped by the economic institution.

survey   A method for gathering data on people's beliefs, values, attitudes, perceptions, motivations, and feelings. The data can be derived from interviews or questionnaires.

unobtrusive observation   A technique in which researchers observe the activities of people without intruding or participating in the activities.

value-free sociology   The view of Max Weber that sociologists must not allow their personal biases to affect the conduct of their scientific research.

variable   The term scientists apply to something they think influences (or is influenced by) something else.

Verstehen   An approach to the study of social life developed by Max Weber in which sociologists mentally attempt to place themselves in the shoes of other people and identify what they think and how they feel.

Chapter 2

CULTURE
AND SOCIAL
STRUCTURE

The story of the mutiny on the *Bounty* and of the subsequent settlement on Pitcairn Island is a perennial favorite. Many of us harbor a secret dream that we might escape to a modern-day Garden of Eden, especially when it is situated on a lovely Pacific islet. And the chords of the imagination vibrate readily to the romance and drama of the mutiny and to the tale of crime and murder that accompanied the first days on Pitcairn. But our interest in Pitcairn derives primarily from another fact—it offers a unique social experiment in the founding of a society and the fashioning of a new culture.

As most of us know, in 1789 mutineers led by Fletcher Christian seized the *Bounty* shortly after the ship had departed from Tahiti. They put Lieutenant William Bligh, the ship's captain, and eighteen of his men adrift in a small cutter. The mutineers then returned to Tahiti. Sixteen of the men decided to remain on the island, while another nine, including Christian, elected to seek another island where they might escape British retribution. They induced six Tahitian men and twelve Tahitian women to sail with them to Pitcairn Island.

Imagine the problems that confronted the English and Tahitian colonists when they arrived on Pitcairn, an uninhabited South Pacific island that is less than 2 square miles in area. How would they find food? How would they protect themselves from the elements? How would they maintain order? How would they manage their sexual relationships, a matter of no small concern since there were fifteen men and twelve women? How would they provide for the children born of these unions?

In finding solutions to their problems, the English and Tahitian colonists could not fall back on genetically programmed answers such as those that permit ants, bees, termites, and other social insects to live a group existence. They lacked built-in responses and highly specialized appendages that would prepare them for a particular environmental niche. Instead, *Homo sapiens* are organisms for which the environment had become primarily a thing to shape and not a thing by which to be shaped. The Pitcairn Islanders were not prisoners of their genes. For similar reasons, human beings find it possible to live in Arctic regions the way the Inuit (Eskimo) peoples do, in deserts as the Arab nomads of the Sahara do, and in space in special craft as astronauts do. The foundations of this adaptation are to be found in culture and society, the topics of this chapter.

Culture refers to the social heritage of a people—those learned patterns for thinking, feeling, and acting that are transmitted from one generation to the next, including the embodiment of these patterns in material items. It includes both **nonmaterial culture**—abstract creations like values, beliefs, symbols, norms, customs, and institutional arrangements—and **material culture**—physical artifacts or objects like stone axes, computers, loincloths, tuxedos, automobiles, paintings, hammocks, and domed stadiums. **Society** refers to a group of people who live within the same territory and share a common culture. Very simply, culture has to do with the customs of a people, and society with the people who are practicing the customs. Culture provides the fabric that enables human beings to interpret their experiences and guide their actions, whereas society represents the networks of social relations that arise among a people.

In fashioning a new society, the Pitcairn Islanders had the combined heritage of two cultures to draw on. Their ancestors in England and Tahiti had been confronted with similar problems of social living. Not surprisingly, the cultural patterns they evolved were a blend of their different backgrounds. Take subsistence. Since Pitcairn ecologically resembles Tahiti more than England, their food patterns consisted principally of Tahitian items, including yams, taros, sweet potatoes, pumpkins, peas, bananas, breadfruit, and coconuts. However, their tools—metal hoes, spades, and mattocks—were of English origin. Since the women took responsibility for the preparation and cooking of food, the nonmaterial aspects of Tahitian culture came to dominate in household arrangements (for instance, as in Tahiti, the Pitcairn Islanders ate their meals in the late morning and in the early evening). And Pitcairnese language evolved as a stew of eighteenth-century English, Polynesian, and seafaring terms.

Eighteen years passed before the colonists were visited by outsiders, but even then guests came only rarely and stayed but a short time. In 1833 a Captain Freemantle found the residents to be "a well-disposed, well-behaved, kind, hospitable people." They had evolved deep attachments to their island and strong bonds of social unity. Yet the early years on Pitcairn were difficult. Things went rather peaceably and prosperously for about 2 years, at which time the English and Tahitian men had a falling out over the women. Two of the Tahitian men were murdered, leading to eight years of intermittent strife and bloodshed. Even so, an underlying cooperation and division of labor sustained life on the island as the colonists built homes, cultivated gardens, fished, caught birds, and constructed pits for trapping wild hogs. Had the hand of every human being been turned against that of every other person, Pitcairn society would have disintegrated.

At its height, Pitcairn Island was home to more than 250 people. Today there are only 9 families, numbering some 38 residents. Recently Dea Birkett (1991:74) visited the descendants of the mutineers and Tahitians. Birkett found a social order where "the good of one is subservient to the good of all. If what is best for an individual is not best for the island, then that individual had better forget it and just fit in." Pitcairner Tony Washington says, "This island fosters the sense of belonging to a group, the sense of belonging to Pitcairn" (Birkett, 1991:78). Islanders are distrustful of allegiances that threaten loyalty to the island. Consequently, romantic love is discouraged. Indeed, in 1991, one unpopular young couple were removed from Pitcairn on the technicality that they were walking about holding hands. It seems that social life on Pitcairn is powerfully framed by two unrelenting and unalterable facts: The island is tiny and utterly remote. Birkett (1991:68) observes,

"Disappointments, feuds and tensions inevitably fester. And there is nowhere to go when the pressures . . . prove too much."

☐ Components of Culture

As our account of the Pitcairn Islanders testifies, culture provides individuals with a set of common understandings that they employ in fashioning their actions. In doing so, it binds the separated lives of individuals into a larger whole, making society possible by providing a common framework of meaning. Only by sharing similar perspectives with one another—designs and ways of life—can we weave integrated webs of ongoing interaction. Culture allows us to "know" in rather broad terms what we can expect of others and what they can expect of us. Simultaneously, culture affords a kind of map or a set of guideposts for finding our way about life. It provides a configuration of dos and don'ts, a complex of patterned mental stop-and-go signs that tell us about the social landscape: "Notice this," "Ignore that," "Avoid this action," and "Do that" (Kluckhohn, 1960:21). If we know a people's culture—their design for living—we can understand and predict a good deal of their behavior. Let us examine more carefully a number of key components of culture.

NORMS

If we are going to live our lives in group settings, we must have understandings that tell us which actions are permissible and which are not. Only in this way do our daily lives take on an ordered and patterned existence. And only in this way can we determine which behaviors we can legitimately insist others perform and which they can legitimately insist we perform. For instance, when we enter a clothing store, begin a college course, get married, or start a new job, we already have some idea regarding the expectations that will hold for

us and others in these settings. Such expectations are norms. **Norms** are social rules that specify appropriate and inappropriate behavior in given situations. They tell us what we "should," "ought," and "must" do, as well as what we "should not," "ought not," and "must not" do. In all cultures, the great body of rules deals with such matters as sex, property, and safety.

Norms afford a *means* by which we orient ourselves to other people. They provide social definitions that allow us to shape our actions so that we can align them with those of other people. But norms are also *ends*. We and others attribute to them an independent quality, making them "things" in their own right (Stokes and Hewitt, 1976; Reno, Cialdini, and Kallgren, 1993). They become standards by which individuals appraise one another's actions and reward and punish various behaviors. People attach a good deal of importance to some norms, called **mores** (singular **mos**), and they mete out harsh punishment to violators. Other norms, called **folkways,** they deem to be of less importance, and they exact less stringent conformity to them (Sumner, 1906).

Folkways.   Folkways have to do with the customary ways and ordinary conventions by which we carry out our daily activities. We bathe, brush our teeth, groom our hair, wear shoes or sandals, wave greetings to friends, mow our lawns, and sleep in beds. We view people who violate folkways, especially those who violate a good number of them, as somehow "different" and even "strange." However, ordinarily we do not attach moral significance to folkways. For example, we may regard people who wear soiled clothing as crude but not as sinful, and people who are late for appointments as thoughtless but not evil. Gossip and ridicule are important mechanisms for enforcing folkways.

Mores.   People take a less benign approach to violators of mores. Murder, theft, rape, treason, and child molestation bring strong disapproval and severe punishment in the United States.

Mores are seen as vital to a society's well-being and survival. People usually attach moral significance to mores, and they define people who violate them as sinful, evil, and wicked. Consequently, the punishment for violators of a society's mores is severe; they may be put to death, imprisoned, cast out, mutilated, or tortured.

Folkways and mores are distinguished by the fact that they are usually enforced by people acting in a spontaneous and often collective manner. Consider contemporary Pitcairn Island. Says Pastor Rick Ferret, one of two outsiders employed on the island, "The islanders are frightened of retribution. They're scared that if they say or do something against someone, that person will get back at them at some later date. You can't walk away from it here" (Birkett, 1991:76). For example, when one Pitcairner cut down another's banana tree, he was greeted the next morning with 3-inch nails planted in the mud path outside his house. Additionally, social censure is achieved through the ancient but formidable weapon of gossip: "Rumors reach the culprit within hours. Once accused in absentia, even if only a few hundred yards away, you are as good as guilty" (Birkett, 1991:76).

Laws. A society's mores are an important source of laws. **Laws** are rules that are enforced by a special political organization composed of individuals who enjoy the right to use force. As anthropologist E. A. Hoebel (1958: 470–471) observes: "The essentials of legal coercion are general acceptance of the application of physical power, in threat or in fact, by a privileged party, for a legitimate cause, in a legitimate way, and at a legitimate time." The people who administer laws may make use of physical force with a low probability of retaliation by a third party (Collins, 1975). Laws tend to be the result of conscious thought, deliberate planning, and formal declaration. They can be changed more readily than can folkways and mores.

Since you are a member of numerous groups, other people—your family members, friends, neighbors, and coworkers—may also benefit or suffer from your conduct. So if you are arrested or fired, others may experience spillover effects. Indeed, group members are often held accountable for one another's actions. Some American corporations link their employees through group incentive plans, and military boot camps punish everyone in the barracks for one recruit's misconduct. Such spillover effects give group members a stake in regulating one another's behavior. However, in the case of some groups, for instance, criminal and revolutionary organizations, a person's peers often have a stake in helping the violator avoid detection and punishment (Heckathorn, 1988, 1990).

VALUES

Whereas norms are rules for behavior, **values** are broad ideas regarding what is desirable, correct, and good that most members of a society share. Values are so general and abstract that they do not explicitly specify which behaviors are acceptable and which are not. Instead, values provide us with criteria and conceptions by which we evaluate people, objects, and events as to their relative worth, merit, beauty, or morality. The major value configurations within the dominant American culture include the assignment of high importance to achievement and success, work and activity, efficiency and practicality, material comfort, individuality, progress, rationality, patriotism, and democracy (Williams, 1970). People tend to appeal to values as the ultimate rationales for the choices they make in life.

At times different norms are based on the same values. For instance, two Americans may both place a premium on the same value—social equality. However, one may express this sentiment by supporting affirmative action programs and the other by opposing such legislation as "reverse discrimination," favoring instead "color-blind" civil rights laws.

Likewise, for much of this century the value of freedom was embodied in quite different norms in the United States and pre-1991 Russia (the Soviet Union). Americans express the value in terms of legal rights associated with free speech, freedom of religion, and other Bill of Rights guarantees. Pre-1991 Russians defined freedom in terms of such guarantees as the right to a job, an education, and medical care. As Russians have discovered in recent years, it may be quite disruptive to shift from one system of norms to another. Indeed the nineteenth-century French social critic Alexis de Tocqueville drew an important connection between the values of a people and its experience with democracy. In his classic *Democracy in America* (the product of traveling widely in the United States in the 1830s), de Tocqueville depicted the "habits of heart" that animated the new nation's experiment in democracy and persuasively argued that democracy cannot be mechanically transplanted from one culture to another. Today it would be well to remind ourselves of de Tocqueville's insights. The guiding premise of American policy makers seems to be that Western cultural values in general, and American values in particular, are unequivocally good and should be exported to Slavic nations. Yet as contemporary sociologist Stjepan G. Meštrović (1991) demonstrates, such premises are unrealistic because not all habits of the heart in Eastern Europe are benign. They include such troublesome forces as racism, anti-Semitism, revanchistic nationalism, and authoritarianism. Western democratic institutions cannot be simply transplanted onto Slavic soil without first establishing how Slavic values affect the way the peoples of Eastern Europe and Russian will experiment with democracy. Rather than democracy, the next step could well be charismatic leaders who offer to restore order and produce ultranationalist, fascist regimes.

Values are not etched in granite for all time (Rokeach and Ball-Rokeach, 1989). The advice columns of Ann Landers mirror many of the changes that have taken place in American attitudes over the past 30 years (Hays, 1984). In 1955, Landers was a bit Victorian. Although many of the letters came from wretchedly unhappy wives, Landers emphasized that the bond of marriage was virtually indissoluble. And in contrast to the "child-free" couple of the later "me decade," she portrayed the "childless" couple of 1955 as "a tragedy." Even in the early 1960s, we gain from the columns an image of a society guided by traditional values. But by 1970 many barriers had come down, and the columns dealt casually with homosexuality, runaway children, and marijuana. A decade later, Landers was even less likely to reply in a conservative tone. One letter of the 1980s thanked Ann for her "nonjudgmental" advice on what to do should a married lover suffer a heart attack in a hotel room. And in one of her spicier columns, Landers printed a piece by a physician who advocated masturbation as a means for dealing with sexual frustrations. The somewhat Victorian Ann had grown to accept new ideas regarding what constitutes proper behavior, as had Americans in general.

SYMBOLS AND LANGUAGE

Norms and values are nontangible aspects of social life, what sociologists term "nonmaterial culture." But if they lack a physical existence, how can we get a handle on them? How in the course of our daily lives can we talk to one another about rules and standards, mull over them in our minds, and appraise people's behavior in terms of them? The answer has to do with symbols. **Symbols** are acts or objects that have come to be socially accepted as standing for something else. They come to represent other things through the shared understandings people have. Consider the word "computer," a symbol that when spoken or written stands for a physical object. It becomes a vehicle of communication because a community of users (Americans) agree that the symbol and the object are linked. Hence symbols are a powerful code or shorthand for representing and dealing with aspects of the world about us (Hewitt, 1979).

Symbols assume many different forms. Take gestures—body postures or movements with social significance (Hiller, 1933). Whereas Americans shake their heads to show a negative reaction, the inhabitants of the Admiralty Islands make a quick stroke of the nose with a finger of the right hand. Turks display negation by throwing their heads back and then making a clucking noise with the tongue. By virtue of their culture, Americans will misinterpret the meanings of these gestures. Objects such as flags, paintings, religious icons, badges, and uniforms also function as social symbols. But probably the most important symbols of all are found in **language**— a socially structured system of sound patterns (words and sentences) with specific and arbitrary meanings. Language is the cornerstone of every culture. It is the chief vehicle by which people communicate ideas, information, attitudes, and emotions to one another. And it is the principal means by which human beings create culture and transmit it from generation to generation.

The Significance of Symbols.   We can gain an appreciation for the part that symbols, particularly words, play in our daily lives by recalling the experiences of Helen Keller. As most of us know, Helen Keller was stricken with a severe illness at the age of 21 months that left her deaf and blind. In her autobiography, *The Story of My Life* (1904), she recounts that in her early years she remained imprisoned in her body, having only nebulous and uncertain links to the outside world. Later, through the skilled and patient teaching given her by Anne Mansfield Sullivan, she learned the American Sign Language for the deaf.

In the following passage from her autobiography, Helen Keller (1904:21–24) tells of her early experiences:

Have you ever been at sea in a dense fog, when it seemed as if a tangible white darkness shut you in, and the great ship, tense and anxious, groped her way toward the shore with plummet and sounding-line, and you waited with beating heart for something to happen? I was like that ship before my education began, only I was without compass or sounding-line, and had no way of knowing how near the harbour was.

. . . The morning after my teacher came she led me into her room and gave me a doll. When I had played with it a little while, Miss Sullivan slowly spelled into my hand the word "d-o-l-l." I was at once interested in this finger play and tried to imitate it. When I finally succeeded in making the letters correctly I was flushed with childish pleasure. Running downstairs to my mother I held up my hand and made the letters for doll. I did not know that I was spelling a word or even that words existed; I was simply making my fingers go in monkey-like imitation. In the days that followed I learned to spell in this uncomprehensible way a great many words, among them pin, hat, cup and a few verbs like sit, stand, and walk. But my teacher had been with me several weeks before I understood that everything has a name.

One day, while I was playing with my new doll, Miss Sullivan put my big rag doll into my lap also, spelled "d-o-l-l" and tried to make me understand that "d-o-l-l" applied to both. Earlier in the day we had had a tussle over the words "m-u-g" and "w-a-t-e-r." Miss Sullivan had tried to impress it upon me that "m-u-g" is mug and that "w-a-t-e-r" is water but I persisted in confounding the two. In despair she had dropped the subject for the time, only to renew it at the first opportunity. . . .

We walked down the path to the well-house, attracted by the fragrance of the honeysuckle with which it was covered. Some one was drawing water and my teacher placed my hand under the spout. As the cool stream gushed over one hand she spelled into the other the word water, first slowly, then rapidly. I stood still, my whole attention fixed upon the motions of her fingers. Suddenly I felt a misty consciousness as of something forgotten—a thrill of returning thought; and somehow the mystery of language was revealed to me. I knew then that "w-a-t-e-r" meant the wonderful cool something that was flowing over my hand. That living word awakened my soul, gave it light, hope, joy, set it free! . . . I left the well-house eager to learn. Everything had a name, and each name gave birth to a new thought. (Copyright 1902, 1903, 1905 by Helen Keller. Reprinted by permission of Doubleday & Co., Inc.)

Only as Helen Keller grasped the significance of symbols, particularly words, did she acquire an intelligent understanding of her environment. Indeed, the change it brought revolutionized her personality. The association between a word and an experience allowed her to use the symbol in the absence of the experience. She could now conceive of water apart from its actual presence. By virtue of symbolic expression, "reality" becomes internally coded in a condensed and more easily manipulated mental form. Thus Helen Keller was reluctant to apply the term "idea" or "thought" to her mental processes before she learned how to employ words. Of equal significance, she could share her experiences with other people and they could share their experiences with her. The ability to use symbols, especially language, was the ticket that admitted Helen Keller to social life and hence to full humanness.

Human beings live their lives primarily within symbolic environments. Other organisms may communicate by means of gestures, sounds, touch, and chemical odors, but the meanings of these signals are genetically programmed within them (Colgan, 1983). Psychologists have trained chimpanzees and gorillas to use American Sign Language, but human intervention was first necessary. Presumably some of the apes have understood that meanings are attached to the symbols. For instance, upon seeing a watermelon for the first time, the chimp Washoe invented the phrase "drink fruit" to refer to it and likewise labeled a swan a "water bird." Similarly, the gorilla Koko learned to devise novel names for new objects, such as "finger bracelet" for a ring, "white tiger" for a zebra, and "eye hat" for a mask. But even though various apes have displayed notable achievements, nobody is likely to mistake their capacities for those of a normal 3-year-old human child (Limber, 1977; Gould, 1983; Pinker, 1994). The skills exhibited by the chimps are related to human skills, but they are clearly not equivalent to human skills (Terrace, 1979; de Luce and Wilder, 1983; Maugh, 1990).

The Linguistic Relativity Hypothesis. The languages found among the world's people are quite diverse. Arabs have some 6,000 words that are connected in some way with the camel, involving colors, breeds (different lineages), classes (such as milk camels, riding camels, marriage camels, and slaughter camels), states of pregnancy (some 50 words), and their current activities (such as grazing, conveying a caravan, and participating in a war expedition). Inuits (Eskimos) make minute distinctions among different kinds of snow and snowfall. And Americans have a vast number of words pertaining to automobiles, involving make, year, model, body type, and accessories.

Do these linguistic differences mean that if people speak a certain language, they experience a different social reality than do people who speak another language? In other words, does our language shape the way we perceive and interpret the world? Edward Sapir (1949) and his student Benjamin L. Whorf (1956) answer these questions affirmatively. In what has been termed the **linguistic relativity hypothesis,** Sapir and Whorf contend that languages "slice up" and conceptualize the world of experience differently, creating different realities for us. Hence no two languages shape the thought of people in quite the same fashion. Conceived in these terms, the hypothesis means that we selectively screen sensory input in the way we are programmed by our language, admitting some things while filtering out others. Consequently, experience as it is perceived through one set of linguistically patterned sensory screens is quite different from experience perceived through another set (Hall, 1966).

Few sociologists challenge the basic premise of the linguistic relativity hypothesis that the words people use reflect their chief cultural concerns—camels, snow, automobiles, or whatever. But most contend that regardless of their culture, people can make the same distinctions made by Arabs with regard to camels, Inuits with regard to snow, and Americans with regard to automobiles. They may lack a word to name each distinction, but they are still capable of recognizing it. Rather than determining thought, language is viewed as simply helping or hindering certain kinds of thinking. Viewed in this manner, language reflects the distinctions that are of practical importance in the life of a community. In like fashion, the idioms and vernacular of sociologists, lawyers, prostitutes, baseball players, college students, drug dealers, and stamp collectors all reflect their special interests and concerns.

□ Cultural Unity and Diversity

The great merit of culture is that it permits human beings to circumvent the slowness of genetic evolution. Behavior patterns that are wired into organisms by their genes do not allow rapid adaptation to changing conditions. In contrast, cultural change can be rapid. Indeed, some social scientists contend that cultural evolution has swamped biological evolution as the chief source of behavior change for human beings. The functioning of the human brain is no longer rigidly prescribed by genetic programs. Instead, genes have allowed the construction of a liberated brain, one that permits a flexible repertoire of responses. The more culture human beings have acquired, the more biological capacity for culture has then evolved, leading to more culture, and so on (Lewontin, Rose, and Kamin, 1984; Wilson, 1988). The fact that culture has increasingly usurped nature as the primary moving force in human development has implications for cultural unity and diversity, a matter to which we now turn our attention.

CULTURAL UNIVERSALS

Although culture provides guideposts for daily living—a blueprint or map for life's activities—these guideposts often differ from one society to another. The "oughts" and "musts" of some societies are the "ought nots" and "must nots" of other societies; the "good" and "desirable" among this people are the "bad" and "undesirable" among that people. And so it goes. Should this fact of cultural variation lead to the conclusion that cultures are different in all respects and hence not compa-

rable? Or to put the question another way, can we realistically speak of **cultural universals**—patterned and recurrent aspects of life that appear in all known societies?

There are indeed such common denominators or cultural constants. The reason is not hard to come by. All people confront many of the same problems (Schwartz and Bilsky, 1987; Wilson, 1988; B. D. Smith, 1989). They must secure a livelihood, socialize children, handle grief, deal with deviants, provide for sex, and so on. Culture represents an accumulation of solutions to the problems posed by human biology and the generalities of the human situation.

George Peter Murdock and his associates at Yale University (1950b) have developed a classification of cultural components that has universal application. They list some eighty-eight general categories of behavior that are found among all cultures, including "food quest," "clothing," "settlements," "property," "travel and transport," "fine arts," "social stratification," "kinship," "political behavior," "death," "religious practices," and "infancy and childhood." The eighty-eight categories are subdivided into additional topics. For example, "funeral rites" always include expressions of grief, means for disposing of the corpse, and rituals to define the relations of the dead with the living. It should be emphasized, however, that universal components at no point include the specific details of actual behavior. The universals relate to broad, overall categories and not to the *content of culture* (Snarey, 1987). Consider marriage. Although marriage is found in all cultures, some societies favor monogamy (one spouse), others polyandry (plural husbands), and still others polygyny (plural wives) (see Chapter 9).

CULTURAL INTEGRATION

The items that form a culture tend to constitute a consistent and integrated whole. In the words of William Graham Sumner (1906: 5–6), the parts are "subject to a strain of consistency with each other." However, perfect integration is never achieved for the obvious reason that historical events constantly exert a disturbing influence. Nor is it sufficient merely to know the traits of a people. Two cultures could have identical inventories of items and yet be substantially different (Kluckhohn, 1960). We need to know how the various ingredients are interrelated. An analogy may prove helpful. Take a musical sequence of three pitches, C, E, and G. Knowing this information does not allow us to predict the type of sensation that the playing of these pitches is likely to produce. We need to know the relationship between the pitches. In what order will they be played? What will be the duration each will receive? How will the emphasis be distributed? And will the instrument on which they are played be a horn, a piano, or a violin?

Many early anthropologists made the error of viewing culture as so loosely knit together that the main task of cultural analysis consisted of disentangling the various elements and showing from which people they came. They portrayed culture as just so many patches and shreds that somehow coexisted. But increasingly social scientists have come to recognize that the parts of a culture comprise a closely interwoven fabric, so that a change in one part has consequences for other parts and for the whole. For this reason, an element undergoes modification in the process of being diffused from one society to another. Occasionally, the modification of a cultural trait may take the form of *syncretism*—the blending or fusing of the trait with a like element in another culture. Our contemporary Christmas and Easter holidays are examples. In pre-Christian times, many European peoples carried out midwinter and spring ceremonies. The midwinter festival often included games, dancing, exchange of gifts, and general merrymaking. These elements have entered into the celebration of Christmas and are summed up in the traditional greeting, "Merry Christmas!" Early Christians simply found it advantageous to locate Christmas and Easter at times of already existing festivals.

ETHNOCENTRISM

Once we acquire the cultural ways peculiar to our own society, they become so deeply engrained that they seem second nature to us. Additionally, we have difficulty conceiving of alternative ways of life. Anthropologist Ralph Linton (1945:125) notes:

It has been said that the last thing which a dweller in the deep sea would be likely to discover would be water. He would become conscious of its existence only if some accident brought him to the surface and introduced him to air. Man, throughout most of his history, has been only vaguely conscious of the existence of culture and has owed even this consciousness to contrasts between the customs of his own society and those of some other with which he happened to be brought into contact.

Given these tendencies, it is hardly surprising that we should judge the behavior of other groups by the standards of our own culture, a phenomenon sociologists call **ethnocentrism.** Sumner (1906: 13) described this point of view as one "in which one's own group is the center of everything, and all others are scaled and rated with reference to it."

It was ethnocentrism that led China's Emperor Chien Lung to dispatch the following message to Great Britain's George III in reply to the latter's request that the two nations establish trade ties:

Our Celestial Empire possesses all things in prolific abundance and lacks no produce within its own borders. There is, therefore, no need to import the manufactures of outside barbarians in exchange for our own produce. But as the tea, silk, and porcelain, which the Celestial Empire produces, are absolute necessities to European nations and to yourselves, we have permitted, as a signal mark of favor, that foreign business houses [at Canton] be supplied, and your country thus participate in our beneficence. . . . As your Ambassador can see for himself, we possess all things. I set no value on objects strange or ingenious, and I have no use for your country's manufacturers. . . . I do not forget the lonely remoteness of your island, cut off from the world by intervening wastes of sea, and I overlook your excusable ignorance of the usages of our Celestial Empire. I have consequently commanded my Minister to enlighten your Ambassador on the subject. (Gargan, 1986:5)

Ethnocentrism is found among families, tribes, nations, cliques, colleges, fraternities, businesses, churches, and political parties. The notion that one belongs to the "best people" provides a kind of social glue cementing people together. Feelings of group pride, belonging, and collective self-awareness promote solidarity and stability. But at the same time these feelings generate intergroup conflict. Ethnocentrism, then, is a double-edged feeling. It fosters a sense of oneness, overriding divisions within a group and binding together people who otherwise are divided by economic conflicts and social gradations. And it sets people apart by promoting a longing not to belong to any other group. See the box on the Nacirema.

CULTURAL RELATIVISM

Ethnocentrism gets in the way of the scientific study of culture. We cannot grasp the behavior of other peoples if we interpret it in the context of *our* values, beliefs, and motives. Rather, we must examine their behavior in the light of *their* values, beliefs, and motives. This approach, termed **cultural relativism,** views the behavior of a people from the perspective of their own culture. In sharp contrast to ethnocentrism, cultural relativism employs the kind of value-free or neutral approach advocated by Max Weber (see Chapter 1).

Anthropologist Elman Service (1973:10) came to appreciate the importance of cultural relativism in the course of his fieldwork among the Havasupai Indians of the Southwest. In interviewing an old man about the tribe's culture, the anthropologist periodically asked why the people behave as they do. The man would answer: "That's the way we do." Service observes: "I was looking for a key to Havasupai culture, afraid of not finding it, and right there I patently overlooked the truth: There is no key to understanding culture except on its own terms."

A perspective characterized by cultural relativism does not ask whether or not a particular trait is moral or immoral, but what part it plays in the life of a people. For instance, among some Inuit peoples, the elderly infirm are left behind to perish in the cold. Rather than condemning the practice, social scientists examine the behavior in the context of Inuit culture, where it is defined as a humane measure (Murdock, 1934). The Inuits believe that individuals experience in the next world a standard of health similar to that which they enjoyed in the period preceding death. Consequently, the Inuits see the practice as minimizing the disabilities and infirmities their loved ones will encounter in the hereafter. By the same token, social scientists point out that the practice is adaptive for a people whose subsistence is precarious and who must strictly limit their dependent population. For Americans who are appalled at the Inuit custom, it is worth noting that many Japanese find quite abhorrent our practice of placing our elderly infirm in nursing homes rather than caring for them at home.

SUBCULTURES AND COUNTERCULTURES

Cultural diversity may also be found within a society. In many modern nations, the members of some groups participate in the main culture of the society while simultaneously sharing with one another a number of unique values, norms, traditions, and lifestyles. These distinctive cultural patterns are termed a **subculture.** Subcultures abound in American life and find expression in various religious, racial, ethnic, occupational, and age groups.

The Old Order Amish are a case in point. The Amish are a religious sect that originated in Germany and Switzerland during the Reformation conflicts of the sixteenth century. Because of religious persecution, many Amish migrated to Pennsylvania in the early 1700s. Most Amish families live on farms, although a minority work in skilled crafts like carpentry, furniture making, and blacksmithing. They believe in a literal interpretation of the Bible and turn their backs on modern standards of dress, "progressive" morality,

Doing Sociology: The Nacirema

Peoples throughout the world differ in a great many ways, and so anthropologists are not too surprised when they come across a society whose customs seem strange and exotic. Some 45 years ago anthropologist Horace Miner (1956) encountered such a people—the Nacirema—who have developed elaborate rituals about the care of their bodies. It seems that the Nacirema are so preoccupied with their bodies that they begin indoctrinating their children in their special ritual practices as soon as possible. Indeed, the Nacirema are quick to punish youngsters and shun adults who violate the rituals.

Although the Nacirema obsessively seek to project an appearance of being in robust health, they view the human body as naturally ugly and vulnerable to debilitation and disease. So the Nacirema constantly find themselves in a predicament. They attempt to deal with the dilemma by indulging in magical practices and rituals that they believe will avert the ravages of illness and old age. Each dwelling has at least one shrine devoted to the care of the body. Although many families have more than one household shrine, the rituals that they undertake there are private and secret. Nacirema parents typically discuss the ceremonies only with their youngsters, and then merely to initiate them into their mysteries.

Over time Miner established rapport with several natives, who described the rituals to him and allowed him him to examine a number of shrines. It seems that the focal point of each shrine is a chest built into the inside of a household wall. In this chest the Nacirema maintain an array of charms and magical potions that they secure from herbalists who provide the preparations in return for gifts. The curative potions are contrived by influential and powerful medicine men and women who write down the ingredients in a secret, ancient language.

Other priestlike practitioners also seek to involve themselves in the ritual practices. Miner (1956: 505) describes them as follows:

In the hierarchy of magical practitioners, and below the medicine men in prestige, are specialists whose designation is best translated "holy-mouth-men." The Nacirema have an almost pathological horror of and fascination with the mouth, the condition of which is believed to have a supernatural influence on all social relationships. Were it not for the rituals of the mouth, they believe that their teeth would fall out, their gums bleed, their jaws shrink, their friends desert them, and their lovers reject them.

As Miner's anthropological work demonstrates, the Nacirema are a magic-ridden people. He confesses, despite his professional credentials, that he finds it difficult to understand

"worldly" amusement, automobiles, and higher education. Above all, the Amish value hard physical work and believe that those who do not find joy in work are somehow abnormal. Far from being ashamed of their nonconformity to "worldly standards," the Amish pride themselves on being a "peculiar people" who separate themselves from the world (Hostetler, 1980; Batutis, 1987; Raymond, 1990b).

Youth culture is another example of a subculture. Western nations have postponed the entrance of their adolescents into adulthood for economic and educational reasons and have segregated them in schools and colleges. In doing so, they have spawned conditions favorable to the development of unique cultural patterns among their youth. These cultural patterns find expression in fads having to do with recordings, enter-

how they have managed to endure as a people because they are so weighed down by demanding body rituals. Like Miner, many of us—given our advanced civilization—find it easy to discern the crudity and irrelevance of the Nacirema's magical practices.

Have you recognized the Nacirema? Miner wrote about the Nacirema—"American" spelled backwards—as a spoof on anthropologists. But as his commentary suggests, it is helpful to stand back from our culture and see it in a more "objective light."

Kim D. Schopmeyer (Henry Ford Community College) and Bradley J. Fisher (Southwest Missouri State University) (1993) have their students in introductory sociology classes read Miner's paper on the Nacirema. They then ask students to write a brief paragraph in answer to a question like this one: How would you feel if you learned you would be spending the next year living among the Nacirema? In somewhat similar fashion

Richard C. Monk and Joel Henderson (1986) asked their students to respond to the question: Would you like your sister to marry a Nacireman?

Schopmeyer and Fisher (1993:150) then read a number of student reactions in class. Here are some examples:

In comparison to my own culture, it is hard for me to believe that there could be a culture like that of the Nacirema.

They believe in things that, to me, are totally off the wall. Maybe it's because of the way I was brought up, but I don't think I could relate to their way of living. Their standards are totally different from ours.

This article both shocked and intrigued me. Why would people live with pain and sadistic behavior? And what makes them feel so obligated to take it? It made me pity them and wonder about what I'd do for my own society.

I was surprised to know that people like this still exist. Their culture is so different from ours. People in our culture would resist if they were told to do some of the things these people did. I am glad I live in the culture that I live in, and not with the Nacirema.

As you might infer, Schopmeyer and Fisher designed these exercises to help students confront the biases associated with being "insiders" to their own society and "outsiders" to others. Ethnocentrism entails the dual judgment that the ways of one's own society are "normal" and "natural" while those of other societies—because they are different—are "abnormal" and so "inferior." In sum, ethnocentrism leads to an uncritical acceptance of one's own society and its practices (the bias associated with the insider) and a revulsion or intolerance toward other societies (the bias associated with the outsider).

---

tainment idols, and dance steps, personal adornment and hairstyles, and distinctive jargons. Standards revolving about masculinity and femininity also have high priority. For boys, the critical signs of manhood are physical mastery, athletic skill, sexual prowess, risk taking, courage in the face of aggression, and a willingness to defend one's honor at all costs. For girls, the most admired qualities are physical attractiveness, personal vivaciousness, the ability to manipulate delicately various sorts of interpersonal relationships, and skill in exercising control over sexual encounters.

Large corporations like American Telephone & Telegraph (AT&T) also have distinctive subcultures (Langley, 1984). For over 100 years, AT&T cultivated an incredibly strong service ethic, captured by a picture of an early Bell System lineman fighting to keep telephone lines open during a

Table 2.1 SUBCULTURAL BEHAVIOR: A SAMPLER OF SLANG IN LEISURE ACTIVITIES

CLIMBING/MOUNTAINEERING

To crater: When a climber falls a long way and ultimately hits ground.

A screamer: A long fall of twenty or more feet during which the climber has ample time to scream before the rope catches him.

Sew up a route: To put so much protection in place that falling is almost impossible; generally implies being intimidated by a route.

Deadpoint: A lunge where a climber grabs the handhold at the precise moment of weightlessness, just before gravity begins to pull him down.

SNOWBOARDING

Sick ripper: Really good rider.

Fakie: Backward.

Corduroy: Perfectly groomed snow.

Bone: To take maneuver to its most radical extent. Same as tweak, such as: "He tweaked that air."

Toasted edges: Dull edges.

SKIING

To biff: Fall or wipe out.

Auger: To drill into deep powder and become buried.

Loud powder: Icy snow.

Mambo: Describes skiers noodling their turns, swinging their hips.

MOUNTAIN BIKING

Face plant: When a rider goes over handlebars and lands on head, face.

Getting down into granny: Using the smallest gear for hill climbing.

Big cookie: Opposite of granny or pixie gear.

Thrashed: Feeling terrible, completely exhausted, same as bonked.

HIKING/BACKPACKING

Toxic socks: A thru-hiker's socks after weeks on the trail.

Yellow blazing: When a hiker takes to road instead of walking trail.

Green Tunnel: Appalachian Trail, much under a canopy of trees.

AEROBIC EXERCISE

Patting the head: Take from top.

Four by fours: Doing each sequence or combination four times.

Turn it up: Go harder and faster.

Like you mean it: Emphasize move.

Cross the top: Travel length of step.

RAFTING/KAYAKING

Super duck: High-performance one-person inflatable raft.

Cranking: A river with fresh infusion of rain or snow.

Crash and burn: Flipping a raft, usually at the top of a rapid.

Squirt: To dive back end of boat down so front is up in the air.

Enders: To dive nose of boat down into a hydraulic, or hole, and stand it up on end.

Mystery move: To intentionally sink a squirt boat while keeping one's head above water.

SURFING

Chillin' like a megavillain: Relaxing.

Hangin' lom: Hanging out.

O-ring: Kook, idiot.

Tea bag: Bodyboard with a leash.

Creetch: To wander, usually aimlessly.

Cringe: To pursue, to want.

Wettie: Wet suit.

Shuck: Forget that (reduced from shuckle, which was reduced from shuckle bail).

Left-hander, right-hander: Indicates which direction the wave is breaking while facing shore.

Session: A period of time spent surfing.

Filthy: Great, unreal, terrific.

Crip: Good, as in "That was a crip wave."

FISHING

Stick-up: Fallen trees or other structures poking above the surface of the water.

Professional overrun: A polite term. Pro fishermen don't often have backlashes but occasionally do find bird's nests in their reels.

Riprap: A built-up area in water, usually rock, that is artificial.

SOURCE: *USA Today,* April 23, 1992, p. 11C. Copyright 1992, *USA Today.* Reprinted with permission.

This famous illustration, showing an intrepid AT&T lineman working to keep the telephone lines open during a blizzard, demonstrates the commitment to service that has long been a component of AT&T's corporate subculture. (Courtesy of AT&T)

blizzard. This mission shaped the company's organizational structure, the kind of people it hired, and their shared value system. The breaking up of the Bell System in 1984 had a profound impact on its corporate culture. With AT&T free to enter competitive high-technology markets, the company had to abandon many of its earlier values and standards. And because it no longer operates in a regulated environment, the company has had to face fierce challenges from competitors. In its struggles to fight off aggressive competitors and adjust to the new telephone era, AT&T has undertaken wave after wave of layoffs and transfers, eliminating more than 100,000 jobs, or a fourth of its payroll. Streamlining, downsizing, and cost cutting has led some AT&T clients to complain that their service has been hurt. In its determination to become efficient and flexible, At&T may well be jeopardizing its reputation for reliability which long has been one of its central assets (Keller, 1992). Recent restructuring at International Business Machines (IBM) involving corporate cutbacks has strained the firm's ethos of "respect for the individual" that ruled out pay cuts, layoffs, and forced transfers (Kneale, 1987; Carroll, 1991).

When subcultures do not fit, corporate mergers and acquisitions frequently fail. Combinations appeal to business leaders because they assume that the marriages will provide more market power, greater profits, and more organizational synergy. Yet the leaders are often disappointed. A variety of studies, both in the United States and abroad, reveal that most companies would have profited more by banking their money rather than buying another company. It seems that prospects for a good corporate marriage are particularly slim if the acquiring firm has an authoritarian culture, whereas the target company values freedom, teamwork, and flexibility (Cartwright and Cooper, 1993).

At times the norms, values, and lifestyles of a subculture are substantially at odds with those of the larger society and constitute a **counterculture.**

A counterculture rejects many of the behavioral standards and guideposts that hold in the dominant culture. The "hang-loose" orientation found among some youth in the early 1970s had a good many countercultural overtones. The young people questioned the legitimacy of the Establishment, rejected the hard-work ethic of their elders, turned to drugs in a search for new experiences, and "dropped out" of middle-class life. Controversy surrounding youthful involvement in the hang-loose counterculture resurfaced in the late 1980s when Judge Douglas H. Ginsburg was compelled to withdraw as a Supreme Court nominee after it was disclosed that he had used marijuana as a youth; the debate widened when Democratic presidential contenders Senator Albert Gore, Jr., and Bruce Babbitt admitted that they too had used marijuana in the 1960s (Dionne, 1987). Delinquent gangs, Satanic cults, and the survivalist right are other illustrations of counterculture groups.

□ Social Structure

Earlier in the chapter we noted that culture has to do with the customs of a people, and society with the people who are practicing the customs. Culture supplies the framework that allows people to interpret events and guide their actions; society consists of the actual web of relationships that people enter into as they go about their daily activities. For the most part, people do not interact in a haphazard or random manner. Rather, their relationships are characterized by social ordering. Sociologists apply the term **social structure** to this social ordering—the interweaving of people's interactions and relationships in more-or-less recurrent and stable patterns. It finds expression in a matrix of social positions and the distribution of people in them.

Social structure provides an organized and focused quality to our group experiences, and it allows us to achieve our collective purposes. By virtue of social structure, we link certain of our experiences, terming them, for example, "the family," "the church," "the neighborhood," and "General Motors." In somewhat similar fashion, we perceive physical aspects of our experience as structures—parts organized into wholes—and not as isolated elements. For example, when we look at a building we do not simply see lumber, shingles, bricks, glass, and other components, but a house; when we look at a tailless amphibian, we do not merely see bulging eyes, smooth spotted skin, and long hind legs, but a frog. In so doing, we relate an experience to other experiences in terms of some larger, more inclusive context.

Social structure gives us the feeling that life is characterized by organization and stability. For example, consider the social structure of your college. Each semester you enter new classes, yet you have little difficulty attuning yourself to unfamiliar classmates and professors. Courses in sociology, calculus, American history, English composition, and physical education are offered year after year. A new class enters college each fall, and another class graduates each spring. Football games are scheduled for Saturday afternoons in the autumn, and basketball games for evenings during the winter months. Deans prepare budgets, allocate funds, and manage their academic domains. At the same time new students, professors, coaches, players, and deans pass through the system and in due course make their exits. Yet even though the actual people that comprise a college change over time, the college endures. Likewise, a clique, a family, a rock band, an army, a business organization, a religious group, and a nation are social structures. Social structure, then, consists of the recurrent and orderly relationships that prevail among the members of a group or society.

Sociologists view social structure as a *social fact* of the sort described by Emile Durkheim (see Chapter 1). We experience a social fact as external to ourselves—as an independent reality that forms a part of our objective environment. Consequently, social structures constrain our behavior and channel our actions in certain directions. When you entered college for the first time, you felt somewhat awkward because as yet you did not fit into your college's way of doing things. The college's way is social structure, the shape or form that a particular organization has taken through the years as students, professors, and administrators have interacted on a regular basis.

Although we use motionless structural terms as a convenient means for describing and analyzing social life, we should not allow this practice to blind us to the dynamic and changing qualities of social structure. As sociologist William H. Sewell, Jr. (1992:27), observes: "Structure is dynamic, not static; it is the continually evolving outcome and matrix of a process of social interaction." Thus a college is not a fixed entity that, once created, continues to operate perpetually in the same manner. All social ordering must be continually created and re-created through the interweaving and stabilizing of social relationships. For this reason, organized social life is always undergoing modification and change (Coleman, 1993) (see Chapter 12). Let us take a closer look at social structure by examining its major components.

STATUSES

In our daily conversations, we use the word "status" to refer to a person's ranking as determined by wealth, influence, and prestige. However, sociologists employ **status** somewhat differently to mean a position within a group or society. It is by means of statuses that we locate one another in various social structures. Mother, mayor, priest, friend, supervisor, male, captain, child, Cuban-American, customer, professor, and convict are all statuses.

A status has been likened to a ready-made suit of clothes (Newcomb, 1950). Within certain limits, the prospective buyer can choose regarding matters of style and fabric. But an American is not free to choose the costume of a Chinese peasant or that of a Hindu prince. We must choose from among the suits presented by our society. Furthermore, our choice is limited to a size that will fit, as well as by our pocketbooks. Having made our choice within these limits, we can have certain alterations made. But apart from minor modifications, we tend to be limited to what retailers already have on their racks. Statuses too come ready-made, and the range of choice among them is limited. Societies commonly limit competition for statuses with reference to gender, age, and social affiliations. For instance, realistically, not every American can be elected president. Women, African Americans, and members of the lower class suffer severe handicaps from the outset. This observation brings us to a consideration of ascribed and achieved statuses.

Ascribed and Achieved Statuses. We have greater control over some of our statuses than others. Some statuses are assigned to us by our group or society and termed **ascribed statuses.** Age and gender are common reference points for the ascription of statuses. For instance, one cannot legally drive a car (age 16 or 17), vote (age 18), become president (age 35), or receive Social Security retirement benefits (age 62) without being the requisite age. Race, religion, family background, and socioeconomic status are also common bases for assigning statuses to individuals.

Other statuses we secure on the basis of individual choice and competition. We call these **achieved statuses.** No society ignores the fact that individuals differ from one another, and all societies recognize individual accomplishment and failure. This fact is reflected in the allocation of some statuses on the basis of individual achievement. Quarterback, choir director, physician, actor, college student, church deacon, county sheriff, pickpocket, president of Exxon, coal miner, and scuba diver are illustrations of achieved statuses.

Master Statuses. Some of our statuses overshadow other of our statuses both in our own minds and in those of other people as well. A

"O.K., you be the doctor, and I'll be the Secretary of Health and Human Services."

Drawing by Bernard Schoenbaum; © 1993 The New Yorker Magazine, Inc.

master status is a key or core status that carries primary weight in a person's interactions and relationships with others. For children, age is a master status; similarly, gender is a master status in most societies. Additionally, race and occupation are particularly critical statuses in American life. Master statuses tend to lay the framework within which our goals are formulated and our training is carried out (Adler and Adler, 1989).

ROLES

A status carries with it a set of culturally defined rights and duties, what sociologists term a **role.** These expectations define the behavior people view as appropriate and inappropriate for the occupant of a status. Quite simply, the difference between a status and a role is that we *occupy* a status and *play* a role (Linton, 1936).

Sociologists have taken the notion of role from the theater, an analogy suggested by William Shakespeare in *As You Like It* (Act II, Scene 7):

All the world's a stage,
And all the men and women merely players.
They have their exits and their entrances;
And one man in his time plays many parts.

Actors perform their roles in accordance with a script (analogous to culture), what the other actors say and do, and the reactions of the audience. But the theater analogy also has its weaknesses. Whereas the theater is a world of make-believe, in life our parts are real. And as we go about our daily activities, we are seldom conscious of "acting" according to a script. Moreover, in life we must do a good deal of improvising, continually testing and changing our actions in accordance with the behavior of other people.

Roles allow us to formulate our behavior mentally so that we can shape our actions in appropriate ways. In doing so, we collect the particulars of an unfolding situation and identify *who does what, when, and where.* Roles permit us to assume that in some respects we can ignore personal differences and say that for practical matters people are interchangeable. For example, every American "knows" that a physician is "a person who treats sick people" and a carpenter is "a person who uses lumber to build houses." In sum, roles enable us to collapse or telescope a range of behaviors into manageable bundles.

Role Performance.   A role is the *expected* behavior we associate with a status. **Role performance** is the *actual* behavior of the person who occupies a status. In real life a gap often exists between what people should do and what they actually do. And people vary in how they implement the rights and duties associated with their roles. You frequently take such differences into account when you select one professor over another for a given course. One professor may have a reputation for coming late to class, lecturing in a relaxed, informal manner, and assigning difficult term papers. Another professor may be a distinguished authority in the field, monitor class attendance, and assign take-home examinations. Regardless of which professor you select, you will still occupy the status of student and play its associated role. However, you will have to modify your behavior somewhat depending upon your selection.

Role Set.   A single status may have multiple roles attached to it, constituting a **role set.** Consider your status as a student. The status of student involves one role as a pupil, one role as a peer of other students, one role as a loyal supporter of your school's teams, one role as a user of the library, and one role as a "good citizen" of the college community. In fact, a role does not exist in isolation. Instead, it is a bundle of activities that are meshed with the activities of other people. For this reason, there can be no professors without

students, no wives without husbands, no blacks without whites, and no patients without physicians.

Roles impinge on us as sets of norms that define our **duties**—the actions others can legitimately insist that we perform—and our **rights**—the actions we can legitimately insist that others perform (Goffman, 1961a). Every role has at least one reciprocal role attached to it. Hence, the rights of one role are the duties of the other role. For instance, your rights as a student—to receive authoritative material in lectures, to be administered fair exams, and to be graded objectively—are the duties of your professor. And your duties—to read assigned materials, take exams, and attend classes—are your professor's rights.

One way individuals are linked together in groups is through networks of reciprocal roles. Role relationships tie us to one another because the rights of one end of the relationship are the expectations of the other. Groups consist of intricate complexes of interlocking roles, which their members sustain in the course of interacting with one another. People experience these stable relationships as social structure—a school, a hospital, a family, a gang, an army, and so on.

Role Conflict.   **Role conflict** results when individuals are confronted with conflicting expectations stemming from their simultaneous occupancy of two or more statuses. A football coach whose son is a member of the team may experience role conflict when deciding whether to make his own son or another more talented player the starting quarterback. African-American police officers at times are placed in a somewhat similar dilemma when their supervisors expect them to be loyal to the police department and African-Americans expect them to be loyal to the African-American community. Some college students report that they experience role conflict when their parents pay them a campus visit. They feel they are "on stage" before two audiences holding somewhat contradictory expectations of them. One way to handle role conflict is to subdivide or compartmentalize one's life and assume only one of the incompatible roles at a time. For instance, college students may attempt to segregate their school and home experiences so they do not have to appear before their parents and peers simultaneously.

Role Strain. **Role strain** occurs when individuals find the expectations of a single role incompatible, so that they have difficulty performing the role. Consider the relationship physicians have with their patients (Klass, 1987). Doctors are expected to be gentle healers, humanitarians, and self-sacrificing saviors of the sick. Simultaneously, they are expected to be small-business retailers of knowledge that they have obtained at considerable cost and sacrifice. While aggressive bill collecting is consistent with the small-business-retailer aspects of the role, it is inconsistent with that of the gentle healer. Supervisors often confront similar difficulties. They wonder: "Should I be a good Joe and mix with my staff, or should I maintain my distance from them?" They are asked to be both commanding parent figures and reassuring, comforting big brothers or sisters. For the most part there are few well-defined or accepted answers to the dilemmas posed by these contradictory expectations.

GROUPS

Statuses and roles are building blocks for more comprehensive social structures, including groups. Sociologists view a **group** as two or more people who share a feeling of unity and who are bound together in relatively stable patterns of social interaction. As previously pointed out, roles link us within social relationships. When these relationships are sustained across time, we frequently assign group properties to them. Four things usually happen as a result of these attributions. First, we come to think of the relationships as encompassed by boundaries, so that people are either "inside" or "outside" a group. Second, we attribute an "objective" existence to groups and treat them as if they are real and exact things. Third, we view a group as having a distinct subculture or counterculture—a set of unique norms and values. And fourth, we develop a sense of allegiance to a group that leads us to feel we are a unit with a distinct identity. We will examine these features at some length in Chapter 4.

A group is more than a collection of people. Sociologists distinguish it from an **aggregate,** which is simply a collection of anonymous individuals who are in one place at the same time. Shoppers in a mall, individuals waiting in line for football tickets, an audience at a concert, and a crowd watching a hockey game are examples of aggregates. Individuals shift in and out of an aggregate rather easily and frequently. Since the people interact with one another only transiently and temporarily, patterns of social ordering are short-lived. However, this quality should not lead us to dismiss aggregates as inconsequential. As we will see in Chapter 12, they provide the foundation for many forms of collective behavior.

A group also differs from a **category,** a collection of people who share a characteristic that is deemed to be of social significance. Common categories include age, race, gender, occupation, and educational attainment. Often categories are little more than statistical groupings. However, information regarding such categories can have important uses. For instance, if we know the age distribution of a population, we can make projections that anticipate the demand for various social services, including Social Security and Medicare benefits (see Chapter 11). Further, people who are aware that they share certain traits may be motivated to interact. They may even establish organizations to advance their common interests. For example, some women have banded together in the League of Women Voters and the National Organization for Women (NOW) by virtue of an awareness that they are a social category that shares certain problems.

INSTITUTIONS

Groups assume a particularly important part in institutional life. Sociologists view **institutions** as the principal instruments whereby the essential tasks of living are organized, directed, and executed. Each institution is built about a standardized solution to a set of problems. The family institution has as its chief focus the reproduction, socialization, and maintenance of children; the economic institution, the production and distribution of goods and services; the political institution, the protection of citizens from one another and from foreign enemies; the religious institution, the enhancement of social solidarity and consensus; and the educational institution, the transmission of the cultural heritage from one generation to the next. Admittedly this classification oversimplifies matters. An institution may perform more than one function, and several institutions may contribute to the performance of the same function.

As sociologists typically define an institution, it encompasses both the notion of cultural patterns and social structure. Thus institutions constitute (1) the more or less standardized solutions (cultural patterns) that serve to direct people in meeting the problems of social living, and (2) the relatively stable relationships that characterize people in actually implementing these solutions. Conceived in this way, a cluster of cultural patterns (a set of norms, values, and symbols) establishes the behavior that is expected of us as a certain kind of person (for instance, a student) in relation to certain other kinds of people (for example, a professor, dean, teaching assistant, departmental secretary, registrar, or bursar). This set of cultural patterns locates us within a network of relationships. The concept of institution, then, implies that we are bound within networks of relationships (groups) in which we interact with one another (play our roles) in terms of certain shared understandings (cultural patterns) that define the behavior expected of us as given kinds of people (statuses). In the chapters that follow we will have

considerably more to say on these . ticular, Chapters 8, 9, and 10 ex. institutions.

SOCIETIES

Societies represent the most comprehensive and complex type of social structure in today's world. As we noted earlier in the chapter, *society* refers to a group of people who live within the same territory and share a common culture. By virtue of this common culture, the members of a society typically possess similar values and norms and a common language. Its members perpetuate themselves primarily through reproduction and comprise a more-or-less self-sufficient social unit. A society can be as small as a tribal community of several dozen people or as large as modern nations with hundreds of millions of people.

Although we often use the term "nation-state" interchangeably with "society," the two are not necessarily the same. As we will see in Chapter 8, a state is a political entity centering on a government. Among many peoples of the world, the state binds together nationality and tribal groups that in their own right constitute societies. Consider Europe. A large number of European nation-states contain multiple nationality groups, including Great Britain (Scottish, Welsh, and English), Belgium (Flemings and Walloons), and Switzerland (Germans, Italians, and French). In 1993 Czechoslovakia split into two nations—the Czech Republic and Slovakia—according to nationality (Czechs and Slovaks). Similarly, many African nation-states contain multiple tribal groups: 250 in Nigeria, 200 in Zaire, and 130 in Tanzania. Political self-determination for one nationality is often incompatible with political self-determination for another.

Sociologists have classified societies in a good many ways. One popular approach is based on the principal way in which the members of a society derive their livelihood (Lenski and Lenski, 1982). Clearly, survival confronts all peoples with the problem of how they will provide for such vital needs as food, clothing, and shelter. And the manner in which they solve the problem has vast consequences for other aspects of their lives.

Hunting and gathering societies represent the earliest form of organized social life. Individuals survive by hunting animals and gathering edible foods. Because their food-gathering techniques rather quickly reduce the supply of animals and plants in a locality, the people are constantly on the move. Moreover, their society is typically small, consisting of about fifty or so members. Large and complex forms of social organization are virtually impossible at this level of development. Kinship—ties by blood and marriage—is the foundation for most relationships. Specialized and enduring work groups, governments, and standing armies are unknown.

Some 10,000 or so years ago, human beings learned how to cultivate a number of plants on which they depended for food. They became less dependent on the whims of nature than their hunting and gathering ancestors had been. The digging stick, and later the hoe, provided the basis for *horticultural societies*. Horticulturalists clear the land by means of "slash and burn" technology, raise crops for 2 to 3 years, and then move on to new plots as the soil becomes exhausted. Their more efficient economies allow for the production of a social surplus—goods and services over and above those necessary for human survival. This surplus becomes the foundation for social stratification; the specialization of some economic, political, and religious roles; a growth in the importance of warfare; and more complex forms of culture and social structure (Lenski, 1966; Haas, 1993). Even so, the upper limit for most horticultural communities is about 3,000 persons.

Five to six thousand years ago, in fertile river valleys such as those of the Middle East, the plow heralded an agricultural revolution and the emergence of *agrarian societies* (Childe, 1941). Plowing stirs up the fertile elements in the soil that in semiarid regions sink beneath the reach of plant

THE WALL STREET JOURNAL

"Like you I was an anthropologist, then I discovered it takes the natives four hours a day, hunting and fishing, to earn a living for their families."

From *The Wall Street Journal*—Permission, Cartoon Features Syndicate.

roots. Additionally, the harnessing of animal power (such as oxen) and the discovery of the basic principles of metallurgy greatly enhanced the value of the plow. These innovations meant larger crops, more food, expanding populations, and even more complex forms of social organization. In time sophisticated political institutions emerged, with power concentrated in the hands of hereditary monarchs. Continuing advances in both productive and military technologies contributed to a substantial growth in the power of the state, the size of the territory it controlled, and the emergence of large capital cities. The massive pyramids of Egypt, the great cathedrals of medieval Europe, the roads and aqueducts of Rome, and the far-flung irrigation systems of the Middle East and China are products of agrarian societies.

About 250 years ago, the Industrial Revolution gave birth to *industrial societies* whose productive and economic systems are based on machine technologies. The energy needed for work activities came increasingly from hydroelectric plants, petroleum, and natural gas rather than from people and animals. Economic self-sufficiency and local market systems were displaced by complex divisions of labor, exchange relationships, and national and international market systems. The ability to read and write, limited to a small minority in agrarian societies, became essential in advanced industrial societies and led to the growth of educational institutions. Many activities that were once the responsibility of families were relinquished to other institutions. Populations grew and people increasingly congregated in cities. Large-scale bureaucracies and formal organizations came to predominate in both the private and public spheres, finding expression in big business, big unions, big universities, big hospitals, and big government.

Some social analysts contend that the United States is currently moving in the direction of a *postindustrial society* (Bell, 1973). Other metaphors have been applied to the new and revolutionary patterns, including the *third wave* (Toffler, 1980), *megatrends* (Naisbitt, 1982), and the *postcapitalist* world (Drucker, 1993). In the postindustrial society, increasing numbers of workers find employment in tertiary industry centering on the provision of services rather than the extraction of raw materials and the manufacture of goods. Simultaneously, new techniques permit the automation of many processes in the workplace with the introduction of computers and complex feedback regulation devices. All these changes are being accompanied by the knowledge explosion based on the creating, processing, and distribution of information (Block, 1990; Hage and Powers, 1992). We will have considerably more to say on these matters in Chapter 12.

☐ Perspectives in Sociology

Thus far in the chapter we have considered the units that comprise culture and social structure. More particularly, we have looked at a number of the crucial building blocks—norms, values, symbols, and language—that provide the foundations of culture. In a similar manner, we have examined the components of social structure—statuses, roles, groups, institutions, and society. The discussion has been largely descriptive. But how are we to bind together such a great mass of material—facts and concepts—so that we can grasp and comprehend them all at once? How are we to see relationships among the concepts and uncover implications that are not evident in isolated pieces of data? How are we to organize our search for knowledge regarding the many different, and often puzzling, aspects of human behavior? Clearly we need some sort of tool. A theoretical perspective provides such a tool. A **theoretical perspective** is a general approach to phenomena that affords a set of assumptions and interrelated concepts for depicting the world.

Through the years, sociology has come to be characterized by a number of theoretical perspectives. The adherents of each perspective ask somewhat different questions about society and provide different views of social life. We do not need to accept only one model and reject all the others; rather, theoretical perspectives are tools—mental constructs—that allow us to visualize something. Any model necessarily limits our experience and presents a tunnel image. But a good model also increases the horizon of what we can see, serving like a pair of binoculars. It provides rules of inference through which new relationships can be discovered and suggestions about how the scope of a theory can be expanded. Within contemporary sociology there are three major perspectives: the functionalist, the conflict, and the symbolic interactionist. We will be returning to them throughout the book. For now, let us briefly examine each in turn.

THE FUNCTIONALIST PERSPECTIVE

The structural-functional—or, more simply, functionalist—perspective draws substantially upon the ideas of Auguste Comte, Herbert Spencer, and Emile Durkheim (see Chapter 1). Its theorists take a broad view of society and focus on the macro aspects of social life. In the 1950s and early 1960s, the functionalist theories of Talcott

Parsons (1949, 1951) and his students occupied center stage in American sociology. Indeed, some proponents such as Kingsley Davis (1959) argued that the approach was, for all intents and purposes, synonymous with sociology.

Society as a Social System. Functionalists take as their starting point the notion that society is a system. A **system** is a set of elements or components that are related to each other in a more-or-less stable fashion through a period of time. Hence functionalists focus on the parts of society, particularly its major institutions, such as the family, religion, the economy, the state, and education. They identify the structural characteristics of the institutions much as biologists describe the principal features of the body's organs. They then appraise the functions of the institutions. For instance, as we noted earlier in the chapter, the family is said to have as its chief focus the reproduction, socialization, and maintenance of children.

One of the features of a system stressed by functionalists is its tendency toward *equilibrium,* or balance, among its parts and among the forces operating on it. Hence change in one institution has implications for other institutions and for the community or society as a whole. For instance, as women have been drawn into the wage economy, they have tended to postpone marriage and have fewer children. In turn, the schools have seen enrollments fall and authorities have often had to close school buildings. Some institutions may also change more rapidly than others, contributing to social dislocations. As increasing numbers of mothers with preschool children enter the paid labor force, new arrangements are required to take care of the children during the day. Yet licensed day-care facilities are currently available for fewer than one out of six of the children with working mothers. So many children, especially those from low-income homes, are currently receiving inadequate care.

Functions and Dysfunctions. Within system analysis, functionalists pay particular attention to the functions performed by a system's parts, especially its institutions, roles, cultural patterns, social norms, and groups. **Functions** are the observed consequences that permit the adaptation or adjustment of a system (Merton, 1968). Functionalists say that if a system is to survive, certain essential tasks must be performed; should these tasks go unperformed, the system fails to maintain itself—it perishes. If society is to exist, let alone flourish, its members must make provision for certain functional requirements. Institutions are the principal structures whereby these critical tasks for social living are organized, directed, and executed. Each institution is built around a standardized solution to a set of problems.

Robert K. Merton (1968) points out that just as institutions and the other parts of society can contribute to the maintenance of the social system, they can also have negative consequences. Those observed consequences that lessen the adaptation or adjustment of a system he terms **dysfunctions.** Take poverty. As shown by sociologist Herbert J. Gans (1972), poverty has both functional and dysfunctional properties. In conducting his analysis, Gans was serving neither as an apologist nor as a critic of poverty. Rather, he sought to identify the part poverty plays within American life. In terms of its functions, the existence of poverty ensures that the nation's "dirty work" is done—those jobs that are physically dirty, dangerous, temporary, dead-end, poorly paid, and menial. Poverty also creates jobs for those who serve the poor or who "shield" the rest of the population from them—police, social workers, numbers runners, Pentecostal ministers, loan sharks, and drug pushers. Of course, large numbers of poor people may be simultaneously dysfunctional for society. Poverty intensifies a variety of social problems, including those associated with health, education, crime, and drug addiction. And the victims of poverty often experience a sense of alienation from society and as a consequence withhold their loyalty from the system.

Manifest and Latent Functions.   Merton (1968) also distinguishes between manifest functions and latent functions. **Manifest functions** are those consequences that are intended and recognized by the participants in a system; **latent functions** are those consequences that are neither intended nor recognized. This distinction draws our attention to the fact that people's *conscious* motivations for engaging in a behavior are not necessarily identical with the behavior's *objective* consequences. This distinction helps to clarify what otherwise may seem to be irrational social patterns. Consider the ceremonials of the Hopi Indians of the Southwest that are designed to produce rain. Science informs us that the manifest function of the rituals is not achieved; the ceremonials do not control meteorological events. But the concept of latent functions allows us to examine the consequences of the rituals not for the rain gods but for the Hopi themselves. The rituals provide occasions on which the scattered members of the society assemble to engage in a common activity imbued with intense emotional fervor. In so doing, the ceremonials afford a means of collective expression by which the Hopi people achieve a sense of social solidarity. In sum, what outsiders may see as irrational behavior is actually functional for the group itself.

Social Consensus.   Functionalists also assume that most members of a society agree on what is desirable, worthwhile, and moral, and what is undesirable, worthless, and evil. In other words, they share a *consensus* regarding their core values and beliefs. Most Americans accept the values and beliefs that inhere in the democratic creed, the doctrine of equal opportunity, and the notion of personal achievement. And until recent years, most Russians accepted the desirability of a society fashioned in accordance with the communist creed. (Consequently, it is hardly surprising that a good many of them now find it exceedingly difficult to embrace and implement many of the subtleties of a market economy.) Functionalists say that a high degree of consensus provides the foundation for social integration and stability. By virtue of a long socialization process, people come to accept the rules of their society, and so for the most part they live by them.

Evaluation of the Functionalist Perspective. The functionalist perspective is a useful tool for describing society and identifying its structural parts and the functions of these parts. It provides a "big picture" of the whole of social life, particularly as it finds expression in patterned, recurrent behavior and institutions. For some purposes, it is clearly helpful to "shut down" social processes and describe behavior at a given point in time. An anatomist does much the same thing when examining a cell under a microscope or a cadaver in a laboratory. Thus from the functionalist perspective we derive primarily a static picture—a sort of snapshot—of social life at a particular time in history.

However, such an approach does not provide us with the entire story of social life. The functionalist approach has difficulty dealing with history and processes of social change. It fails to grasp the never-ending flow of action that occurs among people. Yet the real world consists of transition and flux. Moreover, the functionalist perspective tends to exaggerate consensus, integration, and stability while disregarding conflict, dissensus, and instability. The problems that structural-functional theory has in dealing with change, history, and conflict have led critics to charge that it has a conservative bias and that it tends to support existing social arrangements. Such is not the case with the conflict perspective: It paints quite a different picture of social life.

THE CONFLICT PERSPECTIVE

Conflict theorists, like functionalists, focus their attention on society as a whole, studying its institutions and structural arrangements. Yet the two perspectives are at odds on a good many matters (Dahrendorf, 1959; Lenski, 1966). Where functionalists depict society in relatively static terms,

Doing Sociology: Applying the Sociological Perspectives

Fraternities and sororities have long been a fixture on many American college and university campuses. As part of a class project to apply the major sociological perspectives to an aspect of college life, introductory students at Ohio State University examined fraternities and sororities. Viewed from the functionalist perspective, the Greeks were seen as parts of a larger whole or system that constitutes the educational enterprise. More partic-

ularly, the Greek houses seem to function as social arrangements that assist college youth in weakening their emotional bonds with their parents and moving into the larger world, including the academic community. They allow youth to establish meaningful ties with peers, to exercise independence from adult controls, and to realize identities and acquire statuses in which their own activities and concerns are paramount. And the group living that characterizes Greek life enables young people to cultivate relationships and skills characterized by sociability, self-assertion, competition, cooperation, and mutual understanding among equals. By the same token, Greek involvement in

campus charity drives and support for intercollegiate athletic programs foster the esprit de corps so essential for college and university allegiances. However, fraternities and sororities may also have dysfunctional properties because social and status distinctions may provide the focus for campus dissension and obligations to the Greek community may take precedence over educational concerns.

Viewed from the conflict perspective, fraternities and sororities were seen within the context of a larger social and economic order characterized by class, racial, and gender conflicts and inequalities. The Greeks appear to mirror and reproduce these social arrangements. Within

conflict theorists emphasize the processes of change that continually transform social life. Where functionalists stress the order and stability to be found in society, conflict theorists emphasize disorder and instability. Where functionalists see the common interests shared by the members of a society, conflict theorists focus upon the interests that divide. Where functionalists view consensus as the basis of social unity, conflict theorists insist that social unity is an illusion resting on coercion. And where functionalists often view existing social arrangements as necessary and justified by the requirements of group life, conflict theorists see many of the arrangements as neither necessary nor justified.

Diversity of Approaches. Although conflict theory derives much of its inspiration from the work

of Karl Marx, the conflict framework is not necessarily Marxian (see Chapter 1). Indeed, it draws on many diverse currents, including the work of such sociologists as Georg Simmel (1908/1955, 1950), Lewis Coser (1956), and Randall Collins (1975; Kemper and Collins, 1990). Moreover, because Marx's theory is so encyclopedic, a great many theorists have claimed to be working within the guidelines set down by his work, even though irreconcilable differences set them apart in warring camps. Further, although class conflict is the core of Marxian theory, many contemporary sociologists view conflict as occurring among many groups and interests—religion versus religion, race versus race, consumers versus producers, taxpayers versus welfare recipients, sunbelt versus snowbelt states, central city residents versus suburbanites, the young versus the elderly, and so on.

their fraternity and sorority houses, privileged youth are prepared for their future lives in corporate and other large-scale organizational structures. Young people must subordinate and relegate their individual needs and aspirations to the dictates and requirements of the Greek organization in much the same manner they later will be required to in large law and accounting firms, business establishments, government bureaus, hospitals, and universities. Additionally, the hierarchical structure of authority and the division of labor in the Greek houses equip youth for similar types of relationships in the bureaucratic structures of the larger world. And the social life provided by the Greeks reflects the "country-club" type of etiquette and interpersonal social skills that will be required of corporate officials and professionals. Thus, from the conflict perspective the Greek system seems to be an aspect of elitist arrangements by which the established order is perpetuated from one generation to the next.

The sociology students saw symbolic interactionists as taking a somewhat different view of fraternities and sororities. Here the emphasis falls on the ways that members of the Greek community fashion shared meanings that provide the foundations for social relationships. Greek emblems and rituals facilitate a consciousness of oneness, symbolizing the reality of the group and the relation of members to it. Simultaneously, these same mechanisms identify and highlight the boundaries of the group. An important characteristic of such boundaries is that they face in two directions. Not only do the boundaries limit Greek members from moving out to other interaction possibilities, but they prevent non-Greek members from entering the Greek sphere. Members become aware of the contours of the group; they know what kinds of experiences "belong" within its precincts and what kinds do not. In the course of their social interaction, the youth construct the reality we know as the fraternity and sorority system.

Sources of Conflict. While the conflict perspective encompasses a variety of approaches, most of them assume that human societies operate under conditions of perpetual scarcity for many of the resources people require. Wealth, prestige, and power are always in limited supply, and so gains for one individual or group are often associated with losses for others. The question then becomes: Which party will win and which party will lose? **Power**—the ability to control the behavior of others, even against their will—provides the answer. As we will see in Chapter 8, power determines the outcome of the *distributive question* of who will get what, when, and how (Lasswell, 1936). And power also answers the question of which group will be able to translate its preferences for behavior (its values) into the operating rules for others—for instance, who will define whom as deviant and make their definitions of deviance stick (see Chapter 5). Conflict theorists ask how some groups acquire power, dominate other groups, and effect their will in human affairs. In so doing, they look at who benefits and who loses from the way society is organized.

How Society Is Possible. If social life is fractured and fragmented by confrontations between individuals or groups, how is a society possible? We pointed out how functionalists say that society is held together primarily by a consensus among its members regarding core values and norms. Conflict theorists reject this view; they maintain that society is often held together in the face of conflicting interests in one of two ways. Under one arrangement, one group enjoys sufficient power to make and enforce rules and shape institutional life so that its interests are served. Many conflict theorists regard the state—government and the rules it promulgates—as an instrument of oppression employed by ruling elites for their own benefit (functionalists tend to view the state as an organ of the total society, functioning to promote social control and stability). Under another arrangement, there are so many overlapping and divided interest groups that people can win or lose jointly, depending on their willingness to cooperate and compromise. Thus rewards can often be maximized and losses minimized by entering into alliances against outsiders (Sprey, 1979).

Evaluation of the Conflict Perspective. The conflict perspective provides a welcome balance to functionalist theory. Indeed, since the strengths of the one perspective tend to be the weaknesses of the other, the two approaches complement one another in many ways. Where the functionalist approach has difficulty dealing with history and social change, the conflict approach makes these matters its strength. And where the conflict approach has difficulty dealing with some aspects of consensus, integration, and stability, the functionalist approach affords penetrating insights.

Admittedly, some proponents of the functionalist and conflict schools find their differences so great that they see no basis for reconciliation. Even so, any number of sociologists have taken on the task. For instance, Ralf Dahrendorf (1959) and Gerhard E. Lenski (1966) view society as basically "Janus-headed" and contend that the functionalists and conflict theorists are simply studying two aspects of the same reality. They note that both consensus and conflict are central features of social life. Additionally, both approaches have traditionally taken a holistic view of social life, portraying societies as systems of interrelated parts (van den Berghe, 1963).

Other sociologists such as Lewis Coser (1956) and Joseph Himes (1973), drawing upon the seminal work done by Georg Simmel (1908/1955),

"*Of course undergraduates aren't going to read Habermas and Foucault. But if I don't assign them, people will think I haven't read them.*"

Cartoon © 1993 by Vivian Scott Hixson. Reprinted by permission.

suggest that under some circumstances conflict is *functional* for society. It quickens group allegiances and loyalties and thus is a social glue that binds people together. For example, the Black Power movement of the 1960s and early 1970s provided African Americans with a sense of dignity, belonging, self-worth, and pride. And conflict may also prevent social systems from ossifying by exerting pressure for change and innovation. The civil rights movement, although challenging established interests and racist patterns, may have contributed to the long-term stability of American institutions by bringing African Americans into the "system." However, it is clear that conflict can be dysfunctional for an existing system, a fact highlighted by contemporary news headlines. Russia's empire, for some 70 years bound as the Soviet Union, has broken up; Yugoslavia's Croats want to shake loose of the Serbs; Slovaks seek to separate from the Czechs; and Quebec's French-speaking separatists wish to secede from Canada.

THE INTERACTIONIST PERSPECTIVE

The functionalist and conflict perspectives take a big-picture approach to sociology, focusing on the macro or large-scale structures of society. In contrast, the interactionist perspective has traditionally been more concerned with the micro or small-scale aspects of social life. Sociologists like Charles Horton Cooley (1902/1964), George Herbert Mead (1934/1962), Manford Kuhn (1964), and Herbert Blumer (1969) have turned their attention to the individuals who make up society and have asked how they go about fitting their actions together. As with the functionalist and conflict perspectives, a number of themes recur in the various formulations of interactionist thought.

Symbols.   Interactionists emphasize that we are social beings who live a group existence. However, in contrast to ants, bees, termites, and other social insects, we possess few, if any, innate behaviors for relating ourselves to one another. If we are largely lacking in such inborn mechanisms, how is society possible? Interactionists find the answer in the ability of human beings to communicate by means of symbols. Because they stress the importance of social interaction and the symbols people use to attune themselves to one another, these sociologists are called *symbolic interactionists.*

Meaning: Constructing Reality.   Following in the tradition of George Herbert Mead (1863–1931), symbolic interactionists contend that we act toward people, objects, and events on the basis of the *meanings* we impart to them. Meaning is not something that inheres in things; it is a property that derives from, or arises out of, the interaction that takes place among people in the course of their daily lives (Blumer, 1969). Put another way, reality does not exist "out there" in the world but is *manufactured* by people as they intervene in the world and interpret what is occurring there. As social philosopher Alfred Schutz (1971) points

out, there are strictly speaking no such things as facts, pure and simple. We select facts from a universal context through the activities of our mind, and for this reason all "facts" are human creations. Accordingly, symbolic interactionists say that we experience the world as **constructed reality.**

An illustration may help in grasping this point. Some cloudless night, look up into the northern heavens and find the seven stars that form the Big Dipper. Then attempt to discern in this combination of stars the image first of a bear, then of a wagon, and finally of a bushel basket. Most Americans have great difficulty identifying the latter objects. They conclude: "It just looks like a dipper and that's all there is to it." Other people have known this same set of stars by different names. The ancient Syrians saw the configuration as the Wild Boar; the Hindus, as the Seven Sages; the Greeks, as the Great Bear; the Poles, as the Heavenly Wagon; and the Chinese, as the Northern Bushel.

The interesting thing about all this is the influence the assignment of such names—symbolic word handles—has had on how people view this celestial configuration. From their writings, it is clear that the ancient Greeks did not just call these stars the Great Bear; when they looked into the northern sky, they *saw* the figure of a bear. Nor does it matter to most of us that some 200 other stars are visible in the same constellation—Ursa Major—and that these stars offer an infinite number of combinations and configurations. In the case of the dipper, we single out seven specific stars, label them a "dipper," and in turn we see a "dipper." For their part, the ancient Greeks saw a bear; the Syrians, a wild boar; and so on.

In a somewhat similar manner, symbolic interactionists view society as a continually *generated* and *regenerated* reality that we "create" moment by moment as we interact with one another (as we undertake "joint actions" that give birth to a "constructed collective" or "constituted order"). As each of us "encounters" society, it is something independent of us. We give "it" a name—"the

United States," "Canada," or "India," and we come to treat the United States, Canada, and India as *objects*. For example, we act *as if* the United States is real, and in so doing *make* it real. We recite the Pledge of Allegiance, talk about "America's" relations with Russia, debate with others about "what is wrong with this country," pay taxes to the "United States," extol "the American way of life" in Fourth of July speeches, commemorate "American history" at such battlefield shrines as Valley Forge and Gettysburg, and honor "America's soldier heroes" on Memorial and Veterans Days. What holds for society as a whole also holds for smaller groups, organizations, and communities. In sum, by treating society and its parts as "things," we give them existence and continuity (Hewitt, 1979). All this leads symbolic interactionists to say that if sociologists are to understand social life, they must understand what people actually say and do from the viewpoint of the people themselves. Put another way, sociologists must get "inside people's heads" and view the "world" as it is seen, interpreted, acted upon, and shaped by the people themselves. This orientation is strongly influenced by Max Weber's concept of *Verstehen* (see Chapter 1).

Fashioning Behavior. Symbolic interactionists portray us as creatively constructing our actions in accordance with the meanings we attribute to a situation. In fashioning our behavior, we use symbols to define our perceptual inputs, mentally outline possible responses, imagine the consequences of alternative courses of action, eliminate unlikely possibilities, and finally select the optimal mode of action (Stryker, 1980). We mentally rehearse our actions before we actually act and, upon acting, serve as audiences to our own actions (see Chapter 3). This implies that a certain amount of indeterminacy or unpredictability—even chance—inheres in human behavior because we must continually fashion meanings and devise ways to fit our actions together (Manis and Meltzer, 1994). Consequently, much of our behavior has a tentative and developing quality to it: We

map, test, devise, suspend, and revise our overt actions in response to the actions of others. So we are at least as likely to shape "social structure" as to be shaped by it.

Evaluation of the Interactionist Perspective. The interactionist perspective has the advantage of bringing "people" into the panorama of sociological investigation. It directs our attention to the activities of individuals as they go about their everyday lives. We see people not as robots mechanically enacting behavior prescribed by social rules and institutional arrangements, but as social beings endowed with the capacity for thought. Through interaction they acquire the symbols and the meanings that allow them to interpret situations, assess the advantages and disadvantages of given actions, and then select one of them. Thus from interactionists we gain an image of human beings as individuals who actively fashion their behavior, as opposed to an image of individuals who simply respond in a passive manner to the external dictates of structural constraints.

However, the interactionist perspective has its limitations. In their everyday lives people do not enjoy total flexibility in shaping their actions. Although interactionists acknowledge that many of our actions are guided by systems of preestablished meanings, including culture and social order, some like Herbert Blumer (1969) downgrade the part social structure plays in our lives. Critics contend that symbolic interactionism can lead to a marked overemphasis on the immediate situation and an "obsessive concern with the transient, episodic, and fleeting" (Meltzer, Petras, and Reynolds, 1975:85). The perspective tends to overlook the connectedness that outcomes have to one another, particularly the links that exist among episodes of interaction (Weinstein and Tanur, 1976).

In contrast with traditional formulations of the interactionist perspective, functionalists remind us that society has a patterned, recurrent quality to it that limits the latitude people have in forging their actions. And conflict theorists alert us to the fact that social arrangements are not neutral, but allocate the burdens and benefits of society unequally among different groups. To rectify some of these difficulties, a number of sociologists such as Sheldon Stryker (1980, 1987; Stryker and Statham, 1985) and Guy E. Swanson (1992) have recently undertaken to introduce structural and large-scale components into interactionist thought. Stryker attempts to bridge social structure and the individual with such concepts as "position" and "role." We took a somewhat similar approach earlier in the chapter when we undertook to link the small-scale or micro aspects of social life with its large-scale or macro aspects. We saw that the intertwined patterns of action and interaction form the foundation for groups and societies.

USING THE THREE PERSPECTIVES

The details of the three sociological perspectives will become clearer as we encounter them in the chapters to come. As we noted, each theoretical approach has its advantages and its disadvantages. (Table 2.2 is a summary of the major theoretical

Table 2.2 MAJOR THEORETICAL PERSPECTIVES IN SOCIOLOGY

	Functionalist	*Conflict*	*Interactionist*
Primary level of analysis	The large-scale or macro aspects of the social enterprise	The large-scale or macro aspects of the social enterprise	The small-scale or micro aspects of the social enterprise
Nature of society	A social system made up of interdependent parts	A social order characterized by competing interest groups, each of which pursues its own interests	A social reality that people create and re-create anew as they interact with one another
Foundations of social interaction	Social consensus among the members of society that derives from shared beliefs and values	Individuals and groups engaged in conflict and the exercise of power and coercion	People who attribute meaning to one another and to objects and events with symbols
Focus of study	Social order and the maintenance of the social system through the performance of essential functions	The interests that divide the members of society and foster social change	The development of the self and the dynamic interplay between the individual and society
Advantages	Depicts the big picture of social life, especially as it finds expression in patterned recurrent behavior and institutions	Is capable of dealing with historical processes and providing insight on institutional and societal change	Portrays people as active social beings who have the ability to think and fashion meaningful social arrangements
Disadvantages	Has difficulty dealing with historical processes and the mechanisms of social change	Has difficulty dealing with social consensus, the integration of society, and institutional stability	Has difficulty dealing with the large-scale organizational components of society and with relations among organizations and societies

perspectives.) Each portrays a different aspect of reality and directs our attention to some dimension of social life that the other neglects or overlooks. Functionalism highlights the functions and dysfunctions of poverty in terms of the operation of the larger society. Conflict theorists portray the inequalities that flow from the way society is organized, and they show who gains and who loses from these arrangements. Interactionists suggest that people define certain circumstances as deviating from what they perceive to be an ideal standard of living, assign an unfavorable meaning to these conditions, and apply the label "poverty" to them. Hence, each approach offers a somewhat different insight.

Further, each perspective affords a more effective approach, a better "fit," to some kinds of data—some aspects of social life—than other perspectives do. Each approach may have some merit and need not necessarily preclude the accuracy of another perspective in explaining given data or predicting particular outcomes. Indeed, each approach is useful precisely because it provides us with some piece of information regarding the exceedingly complex puzzle of social life. Just as carpenters find that a chisel, a plane, and a saw are useful tools that complement one another as they go about building a house, so we will find that all three perspectives are useful sociological tools for describing and analyzing human behavior. Moreover, in recent years any number of currents have fed a diffuse movement toward a theoretical integration of the three perspectives. These trends toward synthesizing sociological thinking have done more than breathe new life into older orthodoxies. They have also inspired the breaking of new ground (Giddens, 1984, 1990; Alexander, 1988; Ritzer, 1990; Colomy, 1991).

Summary

1. Culture provides individuals with a set of common understandings that they employ in fashioning their actions. In so doing, it binds the separated lives of individuals into a larger whole, making society possible by providing a common framework of meaning. Only by sharing similar perspectives with one another can we weave integrated webs of ongoing interaction.

2. Norms are social rules that specify appropriate and inappropriate behavior in given situations. They afford a means by which we orient ourselves to other people. And they are also ends; we and others attribute to them an independent quality, making them "things" in their own right. Folkways, mores, and laws are types of norms. Whereas norms are rules for behavior, values are broad ideas regarding what is desirable, correct, and good that most members of a society share. Values are so general and abstract that they do not explicitly specify which behaviors are acceptable and which are not.

3. Symbols are acts or objects that have come to be socially accepted as standing for something else. Symbols assume many different forms, but language is the most important of these. Language is the cornerstone of every culture. It is the chief vehicle by which people communicate ideas, information, attitudes, and emotions. And it is the principal means by which human beings create culture and transmit it from generation to generation.

4. Cultural universals are patterned and recurrent aspects of life that appear in all known societies. The reason for such common

denominators or cultural constants is not hard to come by. All people confront many of the same problems. Culture represents an accumulation of solutions to the problems posed by human biology and the human situation. The items that form a culture tend to constitute a consistent and integrated whole.

5. Once we acquire the cultural ways peculiar to our own society, they become so deeply ingrained that they seem second nature to us. Additionally, we have difficulty conceiving of alternative ways of life. Given these facts, it is hardly surprising that we should judge the behavior of other groups by the standards of our own culture, a phenomenon sociologists term "ethnocentrism." Ethnocentrism gets in the way of the scientific study of other cultures. We must examine their behavior in the light of their values, beliefs, and motives, an approach termed "cultural relativism."

6. Cultural diversity does not occur only between societies. It may also be found within a society in the form of subcultures. Subcultures abound in American life, finding expression in various religious, racial, ethnic, occupational, and age groups. At times the norms, values, and lifestyles of a subculture are at odds with those of the larger society, making it a counterculture.

7. For the most part people do not interact with one another in a haphazard or random manner. Instead, their relationships are characterized by social ordering. Sociologists apply the term "social structure" to this social ordering—the interweaving of people's interactions and relationships in recurrent and stable patterns. Social structure is a social fact of the sort described by Emile Durkheim.

8. Status represents a position within a group or society. It is by means of statuses that we locate one another in various social structures. We have greater control over some of our statuses than others. Some are assigned to us—ascribed statuses; others we secure on the

basis of individual choice and competition— achieved statuses. A status carries with it a set of culturally defined rights and duties, what sociologists term a role. A role is the expected behavior we associate with a status. Role performance is the actual behavior of the person who occupies a status. A single status may have multiple roles attached to it, constituting a role set.

9. Statuses and roles are building blocks for more comprehensive social structures, including groups. Roles link us within social relationships. When these relationships are sustained across time, we frequently attribute group properties to them. Sociologists distinguish groups from aggregates and categories.

10. Institutions are the principal instruments whereby the essential tasks of social living are organized, directed, and executed. Each institution is built around a standardized solution to a set of problems. As sociologists typically define an institution, it encompasses the notions of both cultural patterns and social structure.

11. Societies represent the most comprehensive and complex type of social structure in today's world. By virtue of their common culture, the members of a society typically possess similar values and norms and a common language. One particular approach for classifying societies is based on the way people derive their livelihood: hunting and gathering societies, horticultural societies, agrarian societies, industrial societies, and postindustrial societies. Another approach rests on the distinction between traditional and modern types.

12. The structural-functional—or, more simply, functionalist—perspective draws substantially upon the ideas of Comte, Spencer, and Durkheim. Its proponents take as their starting point the notion that society is a system. They identify the structural characteristics and functions of institutions. Functionalists

also typically assume that most members of a society share a consensus regarding their core beliefs and values.

13. Although the conflict approach draws much of its inspiration from the work of Karl Marx, its framework is not necessarily Marxian. While class conflict constitutes the central core of Marxian theory, many contemporary sociologists view conflict as occurring among many groups and interests. The conflict perspective provides a welcome balance to functionalist theory.

14. Symbolic interactionists contend that society is possible because human beings have the ability to communicate with one another by means of symbols. They say that we act toward people, objects, and events on the basis of the meanings we impart to them. Consequently, we experience the world as constructed reality.

Glossary

achieved status   A status that individuals secure on the basis of choice and competition.

aggregate   A collection of anonymous individuals who are in one place at the same time.

ascribed status   A status assigned to an individual by a group or society.

category   A collection of people who share a characteristic that is deemed to be of social significance.

constructed reality   Our experience of the world. Meaning is not something that inheres in things; it is a property that derives from, or arises out of, the interaction that takes place among people in the course of their daily lives.

counterculture   A subculture—norms, values, and lifestyle—that is at odds with the ways of the larger society.

cultural relativism   A value-free or neutral approach that views the behavior of a people from the perspective of their own culture.

cultural universals   Patterned and recurrent aspects of life that appear in all known societies.

culture   The social heritage of a people; those learned patterns for thinking, feeling, and acting that are transmitted from one generation to the next, including the embodiment of these patterns in material items.

duties   Actions that others can legitimately insist we perform.

dysfunctions   Observed consequences that lessen the adaptation or adjustment of a system.

ethnocentrism   The tendency to judge the behavior of other groups by the standards of one's own culture.

folkways   Norms people do not deem to be of great importance and to which they exact less stringent conformity.

functions   Observed consequences that permit the adaptation or adjustment of a system.

group   Two or more people who share a feeling of unity and who are bound together in relatively stable patterns of social interaction.

institutions   The principal instruments whereby the essential tasks of living are organized, directed, and executed.

language   A socially structured system of sound patterns (words and sentences) with specific and arbitrary meanings.

latent functions   Consequences that are neither intended nor recognized by the participants in a system.

laws   Rules that are enforced by a special political organization composed of individuals who enjoy the right to use force.

linguistic relativity hypothesis   The view that different languages slice up and conceptualize the world of experience differently.

manifest functions   Consequences that are intended and recognized by the participants in a system.

master status A key or core status that carries primary weight in a person's interactions and relationships with others.

material culture Physical artifacts or objects created by the members of a society.

mores Norms to which people attach a good deal of importance and exact strict conformity.

nonmaterial culture Abstract creations like values, beliefs, symbols, norms, customs, and institutional arrangements created by the members of a society.

norm A social rule that specifies appropriate and inappropriate behavior in given situations.

power The ability to control the behavior of others, even against their will.

rights Actions that we can legitimately insist that others perform.

role A set of expectations (rights and duties) that define the behavior people view as appropriate and inappropriate for the occupant of a status.

role conflict The situation in which individuals are confronted with conflicting expectations stemming from their simultaneous occupancy of two or more statuses.

role performance The actual behavior of the person who occupies a status.

role set The multiple roles associated with a single status.

role strain The situation in which individuals find the expectations of a single role incompatible, so that they have difficulty performing the role.

social structure The interweaving of people's interactions and relationships in more-or-less recurrent and stable patterns.

society A group of people who live within the same territory and share a common culture.

status A position within a group or society; a location in a social structure.

subculture A group whose members participate in the main culture of a society while simultaneously sharing a number of unique values, norms, traditions, and lifestyles.

symbol An act or object that has come to be socially accepted as standing for something else.

system A set of elements or components related to each other in a more-or-less stable fashion through a period of time.

theoretical perspective A general approach to phenomena that affords a set of assumptions and interrelated concepts for depicting the world.

values Broad ideas regarding what is desirable, correct, and good that most members of a society share.

Chapter 3

SOCIALIZATION

In comparison with other species, we enter the world as amazingly "unfinished" beings. We are not born human, but become human only in the course of interaction with other people. Our humanness is a social product that arises in the course of **socialization**—a process of social interaction by which people acquire the knowledge, attitudes, values, and behaviors essential for effective participation in society. By virtue of socialization, a mere biological organism becomes transformed into a person—a genuine social being.

Were it not for socialization, the renewal of culture could not occur from one generation to the next. Human beings are uniquely dependent upon a social heritage—the rich store of adaptations and innovations that countless generations of ancestors have developed over thousands of years. Through culture, each new generation can move on from the achievements of the preceding one. Without socialization, society could not perpetuate itself beyond a single generation. Individuals would lack those common understandings necessary to align their actions and to bind their separated lives into a larger whole. Both the individual and society are mutually dependent on socialization. It blends the sentiments and ideas of culture to the capacities and needs of the organism (Davis, 1949:195).

We gain an appreciation of the importance of socialization when we examine the cases of children reared under conditions of extreme isolation. Sociologist Kingsley Davis (1949) reports on two cases from the 1940s. Anna and Isabelle were illegitimate children whose mothers had kept them hidden in secluded rooms over a period of years. They received enough care to be kept alive. When local authorities discovered them, they were about 6 years of age. They were extremely retarded and displayed few human capabilities or responses.

Anna was placed in a county home and later in a school for retarded children. She was able to learn to talk in phrases, walk, wash her hands, brush her teeth, follow simple instructions, play with a doll, and engage in other human activities.

Just how fully she might have developed is not known since she died of hemorrhagic jaundice at age 10. In contrast, Isabelle received special training from the members of the faculty of Ohio State University. Within a week after training was begun, she attempted her first vocalization. Isabelle progressed rapidly through the stages of learning and development typical of American children. She finished the sixth grade at age 14 and was judged by her teachers to be a competent, cheerful, well-adjusted student. Isabelle is reported to have completed high school, married, and had her own normal family. The cases of Anna and Isabelle testify that much of the behavior we regard as somehow given in the human species does not occur unless it is put there through communicative and social contact with others.

More recently, attention has been drawn to the case of Genie, who was discovered at the age of 13 after having experienced a childhood of severe and unusual deprivation (Curtiss, 1977; Rymer, 1993). From the age of 20 months she had been locked in a small room and harnessed to an infant's potty seat. Her father beat her frequently, especially when she made sounds. Under these circumstances, she never developed language. At age 13 Genie came to the attention of authorities and was admitted to a hospital. She was malformed, incontinent, and malnourished. On attainment and maturity tests she scored in the range of a 1-year-old. She could understand no more than twenty words, including "mother," "red," "blue," "bunny," and "jewelry box." She could also spit out a number of self-protective phrases like "Stopit!" and "Nomore!" Specialists at nearby University of California at Los Angeles (UCLA) designed a program to rehabilitate and educate her.

In the course of her training, Genie managed to pick up a vocabulary and acquired the ability to string words together in phrases ("one black kitty," "little bad boy," "bad orange fish—no eat—bad fish"). But she never attained the rudiments of grammar: Her speech remained slow and

resembled a somewhat garbled telegram. Additionally, her behavior was not "normal." When encountering a stranger who caught her fancy, she would ignore social norms, physically grasp the person, and refuse to let go. She would approach strangers, stand directly in front of them, and without observing an acceptable distance, peer directly into their faces. Additionally, she masturbated as often as possible, anywhere and everywhere. Over the years Genie become the focus of custody suits, countersuits, and scathing accusations of malfeasance, neglect, and exploitation among academics. Nor did Genie end up living happily ever after; tragically, she was consigned to a state institution. One hypothesis psychologists have advanced to explain Genie's language deficiencies is that there are critical periods in the development of language capabilities and that gaps occurring in these periods cannot be successfully bridged once children enter puberty.

☐ Foundations for Socialization

Human socialization presupposes that an adequate genetic endowment and an adequate environment are available. As we noted in Chapter 2, psychologists have taught chimpanzees and gorillas a great many things, including the use of symbols. Yet the methods by which the animals must be trained are quite different from the relatively spontaneous way in which children acquire language and many other skills. Nothing has happened in the evolution of chimps and gorillas that allows them to produce their own symbols, although they evidently have the mental capabilities to make use of those fashioned by people. Thus chimps and gorillas lack the unique capacity for language and thought that characterizes normal human beings. Clearly, if human socialization is to occur, an appropriate genetic endowment is necessary. By the same token, the cases of Anna, Isabelle, and Genie testify to the inadequacy of our biological equipment for producing a normal

"Now I'm going to show you something that's in bad taste, so you'll know what bad taste is."

Drawing by W. Miller; © 1992 The New Yorker Magazine, Inc.

human personality in the absence of social interaction. Humanness, then, is a product of both hereditary and environmental factors. The "desocialization" experiments described in the box provide evidence of the tremendous hold socialization processes have upon us.

NATURE AND NURTURE

Every February, as spring arrives, many children on the Mediterranean island of Sardinia suddenly become listless. Over the following 3 months their schoolwork suffers; they fall asleep at their desks; and they complain of feeling dizzy and nauseous. In the United States, the behavior would be ascribed to spring fever, boredom, or a collective effort to disrupt the schooling process. But Sardinian teachers know that children and adults can die of the affliction, particularly after urinating

quantities of blood. An estimated 35 percent of Sardinians suffer from the disorder (Harsanyi and Hutton, 1979).

Scientists investigated the disease and found that it is a hereditary condition associated with the lack of a single enzyme called glucose-6-phosphate dehydrogenase (or G-6-PD). However, the Sardinians display the symptoms only during the spring, suggesting that a victim's lack of G-6-PD is not the only factor activating the disease. Researchers reasoned that something in the environment had to be taking advantage of the enzyme deficiency. In other words, although the genetic defect may have been the gun, an environmental factor had to be pulling the trigger. They found that the Italian fava bean is the culprit and that susceptible Sardinians can remain free of attacks by not eating the plant and its products. Indeed, under the circumstances of a bean-free diet, the disorder can be viewed as entirely environmental in origin because it shows up in the presence of the fava bean but not in its absence.

In recent years, research of the sort undertaken among the Sardinians has shown the complex relationships that exist between heredity and environment. And the old nature-nurture controversy, debated for centuries, had been found to be a nonissue. Even the classical Greek philosophers argued over whether ideas are innate to the human mind or are acquired through experience. At first scientists asked *which* factor, heredity or environment, is more important in fashioning a particular trait, such as a mental disorder or an individual's intelligence. Later they attempted to determine *how much* of the differences they found among people could be attributed to differences in heredity and *how much* to differences in environment. More recently, many of them have phrased the question in terms of *how* specific hereditary and environmental factors *interact* to produce particular characteristics and behaviors.

The early phrasing of the question caused untold difficulties. Carried to its logical conclusion, the either-or dichotomy defines biologically inborn behavior as that which appears in the absence of environment, and learned behavior as that which does not require an organism. The "how much" question also poses difficulties. It assumes that nature and nurture are related in such a way that the contribution of one is *added* to the contribution of the other. Yet in real life, the two factors *work together* to produce a given outcome, as in the case of the Sardinian disorder. Genes determine the range of potential possibilities, but the environment selects among them.

Organisms are not passive objects programmed by internal genetic forces, nor are they passive objects shaped by the external environment. Hereditary and environmental factors interpenetrate and mutually determine each other. By way of analogy, consider the baking of a cake: The taste of the completed product is the result of a complex interaction among the components—butter, sugar, flour, salt, and so on—exposed for a certain period to oven temperature. The outcome is not dissociable into some percentage of flour, butter, and the like, although each component makes its contribution (Lewontin, Rose, and Kamin, 1984; Rossi, 1984).

The human situation is even more complex than that found among other organisms. As children develop, their behavior becomes less and less dependent on *maturation*—changes in an organism that unfold more or less automatically in a set, irreversible sequence due to physical and chemical processes. Instead, learning comes increasingly to the forefront. Significantly, in learning, the human organism modifies itself by responding: The mind is not *revealed* as children mature; it is *constructed*. For this reason, human beings are not locked into an unchangeable physical body or social system.

So in a world in which complex developmental interactions are always occurring, process and history assume paramount importance. Individuals become active agents shaping both themselves and their environments. As they act on and modify the world in which they live, they *in turn* are shaped and transformed by their own actions. *Human beings literally change themselves through*

acting. This dynamic interplay between an individual and the environment is the foundation of human intelligence, knowledge, and culture. In sum, behavior influences the functions of the brain, and in turn function influences the brain's architecture, so that experience produces lasting changes in the structure and function of the brain (Locke, 1993).

SOCIAL COMMUNICATION

If they are to adapt to their environment, human beings must be able to communicate with one another. Indeed, all social interaction involves communication. **Communication** refers to the process by which people transmit information, ideas, attitudes, and mental states to one another. It includes all those verbal and nonverbal processes by which we send and receive messages. Without the ability to communicate, each human being would be locked within a private world such as that experienced by Helen Keller before she acquired language. Communication allows us to establish "commonness" with one another so that senders and receivers can come together through a given message. Communication is an indispensable mechanism by which human beings attain social goals. It permits them to coordinate complex group activities, and as such it is the foundation for institutional life.

Verbal Communication. Language has enabled human beings alone of all animals to transcend biological evolution. Whereas biological evolution works only through genes, cultural evolution takes place through the linguistic transmission of information. For example, evolutionary processes took millions of years to fashion amphibians—creatures that can live on land or in water. In contrast, second amphibians—astronauts who can live in the earth's atmosphere or in the space outside it—have "evolved" in a comparatively short period of time. Human anatomy did not alter so that people could live in space. Rather, human beings increased their knowledge to the point

Doing Sociology: Just Standing There and Doing Nothing

Sociologist Bernard McGrane (1993a) asks his students at California's Chapman University to undertake a "field experiment" in which they remain unoccupied and unemployed—doing nothing for 10 minutes—to "see" what they can see. He finds that this setting fosters a "beginner's mind" as contrasted to an "expert's mind" (a mind-set consumed by cultural knowledge, judgments, theories, and the like). Whereas the expert's mind is constrained by a limited number of preconceived possibilities, the beginner's mind is ready for anything and open to everything. In brief, the beginner's mind does not know in advance what it will experience; it is open, flexible, and receptive to moment-by-moment happenings.

McGrane prefers that the students undertake the experiment in a "busy place," standing still and doing nothing for 10 minutes. They are instructed not to pretend that they are waiting for someone because that would be "doing waiting." Nor are the students to project an image of "sightseeing," "people-watching," or "doing relaxation" time (activities defined by norms) Moreover, they are not to occupy their minds by "daydreaming" or "planning their future." In sum, the students are told literally to stand (not sit or lie down) and *do nothing.*

As you can imagine, the students typically find this task to be arduous and perplexing. They have difficulty moving beyond their everyday commonsense notions and explanations. Sociologist Emile Durkheim noted this phenomenon a century ago in his *Rules of Sociological Methods* (1895/1938:xxxvii):

The impulses of common sense are so deeply ingrained in us that it is difficult to eradicate them from sociological discussion. When we consciously free our thoughts of them, they still mold our unconscious judgments. . . . The reader must bear in mind that the ways of thinking to

---

where they could employ it to complement and supplement their anatomy. They were able to make themselves spaceworthy.

What is the source of this amazing human facility? For years many social scientists asserted that infants come into the world essentially unprogrammed for language use. But then linguists began noticing similarities in languages throughout the world. It seems that all languages have nouns and verbs and allow individuals to ask questions, give commands, and deny statements. Moreover, children acquire language with little difficulty, despite the fact that they must master an incredibly complex, abstract set of rules for transforming strings of sounds into meanings. Even deaf children have a strong bias to communicate in languagelike ways (Goldin-Meadow, 1983; Goldin-Meadow and Mylander, 1984). And speakers can understand and produce an infinite set of sentences, even sentences they have never before heard or uttered.

In 1957, the eminent linguist Noam Chomsky put these observations together to suggest that human beings possess an inborn language-generating mechanism, what he terms the **language acquisition device.** As viewed by Chomsky (1957, 1975, 1980), the basic structure of language is biologically channeled, forming a sort of prefabricated filing system to order the words and phrases that make up human languages. All a child needs to do is learn the peculiarities of his or her society's language.

Chomsky's hypothesis has attracted interest as well as controversy. Social scientists have pointed out that simply because a biological predisposition for the development of language may be

which he is most inclined are adverse, rather than favorable, to the scientific study of social phenomena; and he must consequently be on guard against his first impressions.

McGrane asks his students to write up their observations for class. Students have a wide range of experiences. One student indicates that she became "rather disturbed" and describes a sense of being at sea in the world. Another student reports that she had difficulty doing nothing because our society's norms of "being constantly busy" had become so ingrained. Still another student recounted that he initially set about to figure out and plan how to do the experiment before concluding that McGrane's ground rules made the "law of doing" nonapplicable. And then there was Aimee who was accosted by a security guard, told she was "loitering," and instructed to leave the premises. The guard activated her internal sense of being a "nobody" to which her prior socialization had accustomed her to respond by affording an appropriate explanation for her behavior (she was a student doing a sociology assignment). But Aimee resisted her programming in accordance with this desocialization experiment.

In sum, McGrane's students experienced an extremely strong undertow in the course of the experiment that seemingly pulled them back out into "the societal sea"—an undertow that not only derived from external societal constraints but from internalized social guidelines *inside* them. Moreover, a number of the students recognized that their sense of identity—their self-image and definitions of who and what they were—is situated in a social environment and sustained by that environment. The students began to engage in sociological questioning, thinking about the ordinary, taken-for-granted aspects of social life. In being unoccupied—completely and genuinely unoccupied—the students attained a sense of becoming desocialized, even unglued. Shutting down "the great social machine," then, is hardly an easy task.

anchored in the human brain does not mean that environmental factors play no part in the acquisition of language. For instance, children do not seem to learn language simply by hearing it spoken. Two cases highlight the point. A boy with normal hearing but with deaf parents who communicated by American Sign Language was exposed daily to television, with the expectation that he would learn English. Because he suffered from asthma, he was confined to his home, where his interactions were limited to people who communicated in sign language. By the time he was 3, he was fluent in sign language, but he neither understood nor spoke English (Moskowitz, 1978).

Similarly, a child born with a nonfunctioning immune system was kept in a germ-free bubble environment for the first 4 years of his life, when a bone marrow transplant provided him with a normal immune response and allowed him to return home. During his years of isolation, he communicated with the outside world by means of gestures. When released from the hospital environment, he had considerable difficulty using language and rarely initiated a conversation. Although the child had been encouraged to speak while hospitalized, his life in isolation had not provided a context in which to use language (Holland, 1983). These cases suggest that to learn a language, children must be able to *interact* with people in that language.

In sum, the acquiring of language cannot be understood by examining genetic factors and learning processes in isolation from one another. Instead, complex and dynamic interactions occur among biochemical processes, maturational factors, learning strategies, and the social environment. No aspect by itself can produce a language-using human being. Although infants possess a genetically guided ground plan that leads them toward language, that ability can be acquired only in a social context.

Nonverbal Communication. Verbal symbols are only the tip of the communication iceberg. Nonverbal messages abound, and we "read" a good deal into them without necessarily being aware of doing so. On the basis of his experiments, psychologist Albert Mehrabian (1968) concludes that the total impact of a message is 7 percent verbal, 38 percent vocal, and 55 percent facial. Another specialist, Raymond L. Birdwhistell (1970:197), suggests that "no more than 30 to 35 percent of the social meaning of a conversation or an interaction is carried by its words."

One situation in which you are very likely aware of nonverbal communication is the pickup scene of a singles bar or a party. A rather standardized form of eye contact precedes the verbal contact. If, while gazing about a room, a man and woman spot each other and become interested, they signal with eye contact. For example, the man will hold the woman's gaze, look away, and then look back quickly once or twice. If the woman responds in kind, they may maneuver within speaking distance and strike up a conversation. A woman may also send a "flirt" sign—a sudden smile and a quick turning of the head downward or to the side. On the other hand, if you establish and hold eye contact with a stranger on an elevator, it is perceived to be a threatening communication. Similarly, in American culture you generally do not stare at another person unless you are talking (Mazur et al., 1980; Mazur, 1985).

Affirmative action programs have brought diversity to the workplace, creating the need for greater sensitivity among managers and employees regarding people's cultural backgrounds. For instance, white Americans define eye contact in the course of a conversation as showing respect.

THE WALL STREET JOURNAL

"*What do you mean we don't communicate? Just yesterday I faxed you a reply to the recorded message you left me on your answering machine.*"

From *The Wall Street Journal*—Permission, Cartoon Features Syndicate.

But many Latinos do not, and many Americans of Asian ancestry deem eye contact with a boss to be an exceedingly disrespectful behavior. Potential conflicts may arise when white bosses consider Hispanic or Asian employees furtive or rude for casting their eyes about the room. Multicultural training programs seek to teach employers and employees to look beyond their culture-bound notions about what constitutes "proper" and "improper" behavior (Fost, 1992).

There are a good many nonverbal communication systems, including the following:

Body language: Physical motions and gestures provide signals. The "preening behavior" that accompanies courtship is a good illustration. Women frequently stroke their hair, check their makeup, rearrange their clothes, or push the hair away from the face. Men may adjust their hair, tug at their tie, straighten their clothes, or pull up their socks. These are signals that say, "I'm interested in you. Notice me. I'm an attractive person."

Paralanguage: Nonverbal vocal cues surrounding speech—voice pitch, volume, pacing of speech, silent pauses, and sighs—provide a rich source of information. Paralanguage has to do with *how* something is said rather than with *what* is said. One of the least obvious types of paralanguage is silence. Silence can communicate scorn, hostility, defiance, and sternness, as well as respect, kindness, and acceptance.

Proxemics: The way we employ social and personal space also contains messages. For instance, students who sit in the front rows of a classroom tend to be the most interested, those in the rear are more prone to mischievous activities, and students on the aisles are primarily concerned with quick departures (Sommer, 1969).

Touch: Through physical contact such as touching, stroking, hitting, holding, and greeting (handshakes), we convey our feelings to one another. However, touch can also constitute an invasion of privacy, and it can become a symbol of power when people want to make power differences visible. For example, a high-status person might take the liberty of patting a low-status person on the back or shoulder, something that is deemed inappropriate for the subordinate.

Artifacts: We commonly employ objects, including certain types of clothing, makeup, hairpieces, eyeglasses, beauty aids, perfume, and jewelry, that tell other people our gender, rank, status, and attitude. For instance, at a singles bar, clothing and hairstyle tell potential mates what we are and are not and say "See me" or "Skip me."

Some aspects of nonverbal communication, such as many gestures, are especially susceptible to cultural influence (Ekman, Friesen, and Bear, 1984). The American "A-Okay" gesture made by joining the thumb and forefinger in a circle has quite different meanings, depending on the culture. An American tourist will find that what is taken to be a friendly sign in the United States has an insulting connotation in France and Belgium: "You're worth zero!" In southern Italy it means "You're a jerk," and in Greece and Turkey it conveys an insulting or vulgar sexual invitation (see Figure 3.1).

However, some facial expressions seem to have universal meanings. For example, in situations of threat and intimidation, people often use glares that very closely resemble the stare-down behavior observed in monkeys and apes. To investigate these matters, Paul Ekman and his associates (1980, 1987, 1988) selected a group of photographs they thought depicted surprise, disgust, fear, anger, sadness, and happiness. They showed the photos to people from five different cultures and asked them to say what the person in each photo was feeling. The overwhelming majority of the subjects identified the emotions in the same way. Even the Fore, a people in a remote part of New Guinea who had had little contact with outsiders and virtually no exposure to mass media, labeled the pictures in the same basic way. It appears, then, that the ways of displaying and interpreting certain feelings may be universal, which suggests a strong biological component. Even so, each culture provides its own "display rules," which regulate how and when given emotions may be exhibited and with what consequences.

DEFINITION OF THE SITUATION

From our discussion it is clear that human beings live in both a symbolic and a physical environment. People do not respond directly to stimuli from their sense organs but assign *meanings* to the stimuli and formulate their actions on the basis of these meanings. For example, a "pen" is not merely a collection of visual, aural, and tactile stimuli. We give meaning to it as an object with

Kiss on the cheek: *How many are appropriate? Zero to one in Britain, two on most of the Continent, three in Belgium and French-speaking Switzerland—and in Paris, four.*

The V sign: *What Churchill meant was "victory"—but the same signal with the knuckles turned out is England's and Australia's equivalent of the American middle finger.*

Tapping the nose: *In England, Scotland, and, strangely, Sardinia, this means, "You and I are in on the secret." But if a Welshperson does it, he means, "You're really nosy."*

Twisting the nose: *The French gesture of putting one's fist around the top of the nose and twisting it signifies that a person is drunk, but it is not a gesture used in other cultures.*

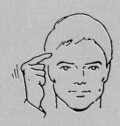

Tapping the temple: *Do this almost anywhere in Europe if you want to say someone or something is crazy—except in Holland, where the gesture means, "How clever!"*

Thumbs up: *This gesture was employed by Roman emperors to spare the lives of gladiators in the Colosseum. It is now favored by American and Western European airline pilots, truck drivers, and others to mean "All right." But in Sardinia and northern Greece, it is an insulting gesture paralleling the middle-finger gesture of American society.*

Thumb-and-index circle: *America's "OK" sign means just that in much of Europe—though not in Germany, where it is an obscene anatomical reference.*

The chin rub: *That's what people in France, French-speaking Switzerland and Belgium do when they're bored. Don't try it elsewhere: no one will get it.*

The wave: *Careful with this friendly greeting while in Greece. It could be misinterpreted as "Go to hell." When Greeks wave goodbye, they show the backs of their hands.*

Figure 3.1 SYMBOLIC GESTURES: BARRIERS TO CROSS-CULTURAL COMMUNICATION

(SOURCE: Text from "In Athens, It's Palms In," which appeared in *Newsweek*, November 12, 1990. Copyright © 1990, Newsweek Inc. All rights reserved. Reprinted by permission.)

which we can write. We may also infer from the quality of the pen something about the social rank of the user. And we may attribute magical powers to the pen as a "good luck" piece for taking unusually difficult examinations.

What we have been saying adds up to this: As we go about our everyday lives, we interpret the world about us. Our symbolic environment mediates the physical environment so that we do not simply experience stimuli, but rather a definition of the situation. A **definition of the situation** is the interpretation or meaning we give to our immediate circumstances. It is "reality" as perceived by people, the intersection of time and space within which they carry out their actions. Consequently, facts do not have an inherent or uniform existence apart from the persons who observe and assign meaning to them. "Real" facts are the ways in which people define various situations.

Because of differing definitions, people vary in their perceptions of and reactions to different situations. Take a gun. To a soldier it means one thing, to an armed robber another, to a holdup victim still another, to a hunter another, and to a gun control advocate quite another. A man mowing the lawn may be seen as beautifying his yard, avoiding his wife, getting exercise, supporting neighborhood property values, annoying a neighbor who is attempting to sleep, or earning a living by mowing lawns.

Although our definitions of the situation may differ, it is only as we arrive at common understandings that we are able to fit our action to the actions of other people. Whatever we do—play football, chat with a friend on the telephone, rob a store, make love, give a lecture, cross a busy intersection, or purchase a book—we must attribute a similar meaning to the situation if we are to achieve joint action with others. Moreover, a definition of the situation arrived at on one occasion may not hold for future occasions. Viewed in this manner, culture may be thought of as the agreed-upon meanings—the shared definitions of situations—that individuals acquire as members of a society. Socialization is the process by which

these shared definitions are transmitted from one generation to the next.

Sociologists point out that our definitions influence our construction of reality. William I. Thomas and Dorothy S. Thomas (1928:572) captured this insight in what has become known as the **Thomas theorem:** "If [people] define situations as real, they are real in their consequences." The Thomas theorem draws our attention to the fact that people respond not only to the objective features of a situation but also to the meaning the situation has for them. Once the meaning has been assigned, it serves to shape not only what people do or fail to do but also some of the consequences of their behavior. For example, for a good many generations whites defined blacks as racially inferior. Since whites controlled the centers of institutional power, they allocated to blacks a lesser share of the privileges and opportunities of society. By acting upon their racial definitions, whites fashioned social structures—institutional arrangements—in which blacks have enjoyed fewer advantages than whites. Blacks are less well educated, hold more menial jobs, live in poorer housing, and have poorer health than whites. So whites have created a social order characterized by institutional discrimination.

□ The Self

We not only arrive at definitions of the situation; we also arrive at self-definitions as we supply answers to the question: Who am I? These answers constitute what sociologists call the **self**—the set of concepts we use in defining who we are. The formation of the self is a central part of the socialization process. It is not a biological given but emerges in the course of interaction with other people. Sociologist J. Milton Yinger (1965:149) observes:

[T]he self is formed out of the actions of others, which become part of the individual as a result of his having *identified with these others and responded to himself in their terms. Retrospectively, one can ask "Who am I?" But in practice, the answer has come before the question. The answer has come from all the definitions of one's roles, values, and goals that others begin to furnish at the moment of birth. "You are a boy; you are my son; you are French"; "You are a good boy and fully a part of this group" (with rewards confirming the words); or "You are a bad boy" (with significant others driving the point home by the sanctions they administer).*

The self represents the ideas we have regarding our attributes, capacities, and behavior. In everyday speech, we note the existence of the self in such phrases as "proud of oneself," "talking to oneself," "losing control of oneself," "ashamed of oneself," "testing oneself," "hating oneself," and "loving oneself." These conceptions represent the heart of our humanness, our awareness that each of us is a unique being apart from other beings and is the same person across time. The image that each of us has that we are a distinct, bounded, coherent being gives us a feeling of psychic wholeness. Individuals who are the victims of some forms of severe mental illness, particularly schizophrenia, lack a stable self-conception and clear self-boundaries—a distinct indication of where they begin and end. Many of them therefore feel at sea in a flood of stimuli (Elliott, Rosenberg, and Wagner, 1984).

The self contributes to an **egocentric bias** in which we typically place ourselves at the center of events (Zuckerman et al., 1983; Kulik, Sledge, and Mahler, 1986; Dunning et al., 1990; Schlenker, Weigold, and Hallam, 1990). By virtue of the egocentric bias, we overperceive ourselves as the victim or target of an action or event that in reality is not directed at us. For instance, when a professor singles out a particularly good or poor exam for a few preliminary remarks before returning the papers to the class, we commonly overestimate the likelihood that one of the papers belongs to us (Fenigstein, 1984). In similar fashion, we tend to overestimate the likelihood that we, rather than another member of a group, will be chosen to participate in an experimental demonstration. And if

we are lottery players, we sense that our ticket has a far greater probability of being selected a winner than it in fact has (Goleman, 1984; Greenwald and Pratkanis, 1984). Thus the egocentric bias results in each of us experiencing life through a self-centered filter. This skewed view of reality shapes our perception of events and later our recall of the events from memory.

We typically think of the self in static terms as an "entity" or "thing." But as the concept is employed by symbolic interactionists, it also has dynamic properties. Symbolic interactionists point out that we can be objects of our own action. We mentally take a place on the outside and, from this vantage point, become an audience to our own actions. Viewed in this manner, the self is a process by which we devise our actions in order to fit them to the ongoing actions of other people. Sociologists such as Charles Horton Cooley, George Herbert Mead, and Erving Goffman have contributed a good deal to our understanding of these matters. Let us turn, then, to a consideration of their insights.

CHARLES HORTON COOLEY: THE LOOKING-GLASS SELF

At the beginning of this century, the notion was prevalent in both scientific and lay circles that human nature is biologically determined. Charles Horton Cooley (1864–1929) vigorously challenged this assertion. He maintained that people transform themselves and their worlds as they engage in social interaction. In particular, Cooley (1902/1964) contended that our consciousness arises in a social context. This notion is best exemplified by his concept of the **looking-glass self**—a process by which we imaginatively assume the stance of other people and view ourselves as we believe they see us. Our ability to take the perspective of another person is a basic requirement of all social behavior. Indeed, recent research suggests that the looking-glass self functions as a "magnifying glass" during self-perception, so that what people see in themselves while others are present has an extra-powerful impact on their behaviors and self-images (Tice, 1992).

Self-Awareness. Cooley suggests that the looking-glass self is an ongoing mental process characterized by three phases. First, we imagine how we appear to others. For example, we may think of ourselves as putting on weight and becoming "fat." Second, we imagine how others judge our appearance. We are aware, for instance, that people typically think of obese people as unattractive. Third, we develop some sort of self-feeling such as pride or mortification on the basis of what we perceive others' judgments to be. In this case, we are likely to experience anxiety or embarrassment regarding our "obese" state. The looking-glass self entails a subjective process and need not accord with objective reality. For example, victims of anorexia nervosa willfully starve themselves, denying that they are actually thin or ill, in the belief that they are too fat.

The notion of the looking-glass self does not imply that our self-conception changes radically every time we encounter a new person or a new situation. Accordingly, it is useful to distinguish between self-images and self-conceptions (Turner, 1968; Swann and Hill, 1982; Marsh, 1986). A **self-image** is a mental conception or picture that we have of ourselves which is relatively temporary; it changes as we move from one context to another. Our **self-conception** is a more overriding view of ourselves, a sense of self through time—"the real me," or "I myself as I really am." Layers of self-images typically build up over time and contribute to a relatively stable self-conception. For the most part, this succession of self-images *edits* rather than supplants our more crystallized self-conception or identity.

Shyness. Since human beings are capable of self-awareness, they often experience shyness. *Shyness* is a general tendency to be tense, inhibited, and awkward in social situations. Surveys show that as many as 40 percent of adult Americans consider themselves shy. Even such celebrities as Barbara Walters, England's Prince Charles, Terry Bradshaw, Fred Lynn, Catherine Deneuve, Carol Burnett, and Warren Beatty define themselves as shy (Zimbardo, 1978). The Japanese tend to have a very high prevalence of shyness—about 60 percent. One reason seems to be that the Japanese have what is described as a "shame culture," in which individuals experience considerable pressure not to let their families down (Cheek, 1983).

Shyness takes a heavy human toll because it creates a barrier for people in achieving happiness and fulfilling their potential. Shy people are commonly big losers—in school, in business, in love, in any arena of life where people meet their needs in the course of social interaction with others. They seem too self-aware, too preoccupied with their own adequacy and the adequacy of their behavior. Consequently, their spontaneity is impaired—they are unable to "let themselves go"—and they hold back from immersing themselves in ongoing social interaction (Asendorpf, 1987, 1989; Bruch et al., 1989).

Choking. *Choking* is behavior in which we fail to perform up to our level of skills and abilities by virtue of experiencing social pressure (Baumeister, 1984). Like shyness, it arises when the selfhood process goes awry. For example, we often become self-conscious when we are expected to provide an excellent performance. Thus in athletic competition we may attempt to ensure the correctness of our execution—the coordination and precision of our muscle movements—by monitoring our performance. But such self-monitoring disrupts the automatic or overlearned nature of execution. Consequently, we become susceptible to mistakes. In the final and decisive game of a championship series, such as baseball's World Series, the home team tends to choke and accordingly is at a decided disadvantage. A home crowd usually claps, shouts, and moans in response to the breaks and exploits of the home team, whereas the visitor's exploits are met either with silence or expressions of frustration. During the regular season and in early games of the World

Series, such behavior may be a source of inspiration to the home team. But when a championship is imminent, fear of failing to win it before a support audience compounds the pressures and intensifies the players' self-consciousness. As a result, they become "uptight" and error-prone (Baumeister and Steinhilber, 1984).

GEORGE HERBERT MEAD: THE GENERALIZED OTHER

George Herbert Mead (1863–1931) elaborated on Cooley's ideas and contributed many insights of his own. Mead (1934/1962) contended that we gain a sense of selfhood by acting toward ourselves in much the same fashion that we act toward others. In so doing, we "take the role of the other toward ourselves." We mentally assume a dual perspective: We are simultaneously the *subject* doing the viewing and the *object* being viewed. In our imagination, we take the position of another person and look back on ourselves from this standpoint.

Mead designates the subject aspect of the self-process the "I" and the object aspect the "me." Consider what sometimes happens when you contemplate whether or not to ask your professor a question. You think, "If I ask a question, he'll consider me stupid. I'd better keep quiet." In this example, you imagine the attitude of the professor toward students. In so doing, you mentally take the role of the professor and view yourself as an object or "me." It is you as the subject or "I" who decides that it would be unwise to ask the question. The use of personal pronouns in the statement illustrates the object-subject dimensions.

According to Mead, the key to children's development of the self resides in their acquisition of language. By virtue of language, we arouse the same tendencies in ourselves that we do in others. We mentally say to ourselves, "If I want to get this person to respond this way, what will it take to do so? What would it take to get me to act in this fashion?" Mead uses the example of an instructor who asks a student to bring a chair to the class-

room. The student probably would fulfill the request, but if not, the instructor would most likely get the chair herself. To ask the student to secure the chair, the instructor first must conjure up the act within her own mind. Language allows us to carry on an internal conversation. We talk and reply to ourselves in much the same manner that we carry on a conversation with others. In this fashion, we judge how other people will respond to us.

Sociologist Ralph Turner (1968) has clarified and extended Mead's ideas on the self. Turner points out that when speaking and acting, we typically adopt a state of *preparedness* for certain types of responses from the other person. If we wave to a professor, ask a police officer a question, or embrace a friend, we expect that the other person will respond with some action that will appropriately fit our own. As the other person responds, we enter a phase of *testing* and *revision.* We mentally appraise the other's behavior, determining whether or not it accords with our expectations. In doing so, we assign meaning to that behavior. We then plan our next course of action. For instance, if the person has responded in an unanticipated manner, we might terminate the interaction, attempt to "go back" and reassert our original intention, disregard the other's response, or abandon our initial course of action and follow the other person's lead. Consequently, symbolic interactionists say that the process of self-communication is essential to social interaction.

According to Mead, children typically pass through three stages in developing a full sense of selfhood: the "play" stage, the "game" stage, and the "generalized other" stage. In play, children take the role of only one other person at a time and "try on" the person's behavior. The model, usually an important person in the life of the child, such as a parent, is called a **significant other.** For example, a 2-year-old child may examine a doll's pants, pretend to find them wet, reprimand the doll, and take it to the bathroom. Presumably the child views the situation from the viewpoint of the parent and acts as the parent would act (Andersen and Cole, 1990).

Whereas in the play stage children take the role of only one other person at a time, in the game stage they assume many roles. As in the case of an organized game such as baseball, individuals must take into account the roles of a good many people. For example, if the batter bunts the ball down the third-base line, the person playing first base must know what the pitcher, third baseman, shortstop, and catcher will do. Each player must see his or her role as meshed with those of the other players. Likewise in life. Children must become familiar with the expectations that hold for a variety of roles if they are to play their own roles successfully.

In Mead's third stage, children recognize that they are immersed within a larger community of people and that this community has very definite attitudes regarding what constitutes appropriate and inappropriate behavior. The social unit that gives individuals their unity of self is called the **generalized other.** The attitude of the generalized other is the attitude of the larger community. Although we gain our conceptions of given rules from particular people (our mother, a teacher, or a peer), these notions are generalized or extended to embrace all people within similar situations. To think about our behavior, then, is to interact mentally with ourselves from the perspective of an abstract community of people. According to Mead, the generalized other is the vehicle by which we are linked to society. By means of the generalized other, we incorporate, or internalize, the organized attitudes of our community within our own personalities so that social control becomes self-control.

ERVING GOFFMAN: IMPRESSION MANAGEMENT

Erving Goffman (1922–1982) has provided an additional dimension to our understanding of the self. Cooley and Mead examined how our self-conceptions arise in the course of social interaction and how we fashion our actions based on the feedback we derive about ourselves and our behavior from other people. Goffman (1959) directs our attention to another matter. He points out that only by influencing other people's ideas of us can we hope to predict or control what happens to us. We have a stake in presenting ourselves to others in ways that will lead them to view us in a favorable light, a process Goffman calls **impression management.** In doing so, we use both concealment and strategic revelation. For example, a taxi driver may attempt to disguise from a passenger the fact that they have mistakenly been traveling in the wrong direction, and a young professor fresh out of graduate school may spend several hours preparing and rehearsing a lecture in hopes of appearing "knowledgeable" to her students. You are probably aware of engaging in impression management when deciding what to wear for a particular occasion, such as a party, a physician's appointment, a job interview, or a date (Leary and Kowalski, 1990).

Goffman sees the performances staged in a theater as an analytical analogy and tool for depicting and understanding social life, a perspective he calls the **dramaturgical approach.** He depicts social life as a stage on which people interact; all human beings are both actors and members of the audience, and the parts are the roles people play in the course of their daily activities. Goffman illustrates his approach by describing the changes that occur in waiters' behavior as they move from the kitchen to the dining room. As the nature of the audience changes, so does their behavior. "Frontstage" in the dining room, the waiters display a servile demeanor to the guests. "Backstage" in the kitchen, they openly flaunt and otherwise ridicule the servility they must portray frontstage. Further, they seal off the dirty work of food preparation—the gristle, grease, and foul smells of spoiled food—from the appetizing and enticing frontstage atmosphere. Hence, as people move from situation to situation, they drastically alter their self-expression. They undertake to define the situation for others by generating cues that will lead others to act in ways they wish.

Although Goffman is commonly classed by sociologists with interactionists, his work departs in significant ways from classical symbolic interactionist formulations (Gonos, 1977; Drew and Wootton, 1988; Hare and Blumberg, 1988; Deegan, 1989). Symbolic interactionists see each situation as somewhat unique, as freshly built up piece by piece out of the peculiar combinations of activities and meanings that operate in a particular setting. Goffman (1974) depicts social life as "frames"—structures—that have an invisible but real existence behind the visible social transactions of everyday life. These basic frameworks of understandings provide stable rules that people use in fashioning their behavior. Thus Goffman sees action as guided more by a mechanical adherence to rules than by an active, ongoing process of interpersonal negotiation.

□ Socialization across the Life Course

Socialization is a continuing, lifelong process. The world about us changes and requires that we also change. The self is not carved in granite, somehow finalized for all time during childhood. Life is adaptation—a process of constant renewing and remaking. Three-year-olds are socialized within the patterns of a nursery school, engineering students within their chosen profession, new employees within an office or plant, a husband and wife within a new family, religious converts within a sect, and elderly patients within a nursing home.

In one way or another, all societies have to deal with the **life course** that begins with conception and continues through old age and ultimately death. The concept makes reference to the interweave of age-graded trajectories with the vicissitudes of changing social conditions and future options. Sociological interest in the life course has gained considerable momentum in recent years. Many sociologists find the life course framework a

"The problem is to get rid of the perception *that we receive perks but not get rid of the perks."*

Drawing by Handelsman; © 1991 The New Yorker Magazine, Inc.

more compelling tool than the traditional socialization framework for dealing with questions that concern life span continuity and change (Elder, 1994). For instance, our early adult career choices have vast implications for our later retirement and old-age experiences by influencing the adequacy of our adaptive skills and economic resources (Clausen, 1993).

Upon the rich tapestry supplied by the organic age grid, societies weave varying social arrangements (Riley, 1987, 1988a, b). A 14-year-old girl may be expected to be a middle school student in one culture and a mother of two in another; a 45-year-old man may be at the peak of a business career, still moving up in a political career, retired from a career as a professional football player, or dead and worshipped as an ancestor in some other society (Datan, 1977). All cultures divide biological time into socially relevant units. While birth, puberty, maturity, aging, and death are biological facts of life, it is society that gives each its distinctive meaning.

Some peoples extend their stages of life to include the unborn and the deceased. Australian aborigines think of the unborn as the spirits of departed ancestors. These spirits are believed to enter the womb of a passing woman and gain rebirth as a child (Murdock, 1934). Likewise, Hindus regard the unborn as the spirits of persons or animals who lived in former incarnations (Davis, 1949). The dead may also be seen as continuing members of the community. Anthropologist Ralph Linton (1936:121–122) found that when a Tanala of Madagascar died, the individual was defined as merely surrendering one set of rights and duties for another:

Thus a Tanala clan has two sections which are equally real to its members, the living and the dead. In spite of rather half-hearted attempts by the living to explain to the dead that they are dead and to discourage their return, they remain an integral part of the clan. They must be informed of all important events, invited to all clan ceremonies, and remembered at every meal. In return they allow themselves to be consulted, take an active and helpful interest in the affairs of the community, and act as highly efficient guardians of the group's mores.

Hence each society shapes the processes of development in its own image, defining the stages it recognizes as significant.

Modern societies are ordered in ways that formally structure people's preparation for new roles. Schools and colleges are designed to transmit various skills, mental hospitals to teach healthier patterns of adjustment, prisons to "resocialize" convicts through rehabilitation programs, and conferences and seminars to familiarize a firm's staff with its operating procedures. Role socialization commonly involves three phases (Mortimer and Simmons, 1978). First, people think about, experiment with, and try on the behaviors associated with a new role, what sociologists term **anticipatory socialization.** Children informally acquaint themselves with such adult roles as spouse and parent by "playing house."

Apprenticeship, intern, probationary, and rehabilitation programs are more institutionalized arrangements for acquiring new roles. Second, once individuals assume a new status, they find that they must continually alter, adapt, and remake their roles to fit changing circumstances. For instance, as a couple enters marriage, they must evolve new interpersonal skills because much of the marital role was hidden from them as children. Third, as individuals move through the life course, they not only enters roles but must disengage or exit from many of them. Such rituals as graduation exercises, marriage, retirement banquets, funerals, and other rites of passage are socially established mechanisms for easing some role transitions. Let us take a closer look at some of the transitions that center on life course roles.

CHILDHOOD

In the Middle Ages, the concept of childhood as we know it was unheard of. Children were regarded as small adults (Ariès, 1962). The arts and documents of the medieval world portray adults and children mingling together, wearing the same clothes, and engaging in many of the same activities. The world we think proper for children—fairytales, games, toys, and books—is of comparatively recent origin. Until the seventeenth century, Western words for young males— "boy," *garçon* (French), and *Knabe* (German)— were used to denote a man of 30 or so years of age who enjoyed an independent position. No special word existed for a young male between the ages of 7 and 16. The word "child" expressed kinship, not an age period (Plumb, 1972). Only around the year 1600 did a new concept of childhood begin to emerge.

The notion that children should be attending school rather than working in factories, mines, and fields is of relatively recent origin. Significantly, the first industrial workers in the United States were nine children hired in 1791 as employees of a Rhode Island textile mill. In the 1820s, half of the cotton mill workers in New Eng-

Doing Sociology: The Selfhood Process

According to symbolic interactionists, we mesh our actions with those of other individuals through the selfhood process. In our imagination, we step out of ourselves into the role of another person and attempt to view ourselves from his or her perspective. We use symbols, particularly language, to arouse the same tendencies and dispositions in ourselves as we do in others. Thus we talk and reply to ourselves in much the same manner that we carry on a conversation with

other people. We become objects to ourselves, mentally monitoring and assigning meaning to our behavior and to other people's responses. For instance, when we provide a vocal utterance, a flirtatious glance, a wave of the hand, a shrug of the shoulder, or a clenched fist, we hope to signal something to another person. As the other person responds to us, we enter a phase of testing and revision. We interpret the other's behavior, noting whether or not it falls within the range of behaviors we anticipated. As we appraise the other's behavior and assign meaning to it, we plan our subsequent course of action. Thus, social interaction involves us in a process of

self-communication. In the two episodes presented below, students in an introductory sociology course analyze their behavior in terms of the selfhood process:

Early in the quarter I went to the dining hall with my new neighbor, Hank. All I knew about Hank was his name. I did not know what he was like or what his interests were. Accordingly, I was uncertain how I should act toward him. After we had gotten our food and were sitting down at the dining table, I put a napkin on my lap and said, "Would you please pass me the salt?" As Hank did so, I said to myself, "Gee, what am I going

---

land were children who worked 12- to 15-hour days. Even as late as 1924, the National Child Labor Committee estimated that 2 million American children under 15 were at work, the majority as farm laborers.

Whatever definitions they hold of children, societies begin socializing them as soon as possible. Most infants are fairly malleable in the sense that within broad limits they are capable of becoming adults of quite different sorts. The magnitude of their accomplishments over a relatively short period of time is truly astonishing. For example, by their fourth birthday most American children have mastered the complicated and abstract structure of the English language. And they can carry on complex social interactions in accordance with American cultural patterns.

The "social capital" contained within a family's environment is of vital consequence in channeling and shaping children's futures. A family's

social capital consists of (1) financial capital—the financial resources available to the household, (2) human capital—the cognitive skills and educational attainment of the parents, and (3) social capital—the dynamic relationships and resources that provide the interlock between a family and the community (Coleman, 1988, 1990). Many contemporary American children find their futures severely compromised by the inadequacy of their family's social capital. A wide-ranging, 3-year study of young American children under the auspices of the Carnegie Corporation of New York paints a bleak picture of disintegrating families, persistent poverty, high levels of child abuse, insufficient medical care, and poor-quality child care that threatens the youngsters' growth into healthy and responsible adults (Chira, 1994b) (see Chapters 6 and 9).

Children display people-oriented responses at very early ages. Even before their first birthdays,

to talk to this guy about?" I responded, "Perhaps I had better ask him what his major is?" I did. Hank answered in a dull monotone, "Electrical engineering." I thought to myself, "This guy is a cement block to talk to. Maybe I am too serious with him. My voice sounds serious and I seem uptight. I had better open things up somewhat." I said to myself, "If he were 'me,' what would 'I' want to hear that wasn't so serious?" In so doing I took a dual perspective, the "me" being the object aspect and the "I" the subject aspect. I responded to myself, "I like partying." So I asked, "Do you party?" Bingo!

His eyes came alive and he pulled himself into an upright posture. I found a topic of mutual interest and we then hit it off quite well.

I drove home late Friday evening. I take a back highway that has little traffic on it. I had my headlights on high when a car approached also with glaring beams. I said to myself, "I want that motorist to turn down his headlights. What would it take to signal me to cut my lights?" I responded, "I would lower my beams if someone flicked his lights." So I flicked my lights from high to low a number of times, but the motorist did not respond. I thought to myself,

"That motorist either doesn't think we are close enough to reduce his beams, or he has forgotten that he set them on high." As we got nearer, I said to myself, "I'll just leave my beams on high. I don't envy the guy a bit. I've replaced my headlamps with more powerful ones that throw more light than standard beams. Heck, if this joker wants to play 'Blind the other driver,' I'll go along with it. He'll get it a lot worse than I will." When we were about an eighth of a mile apart, he turned his beams down to regular strength. I mentally said to myself, "Okay, fair play. I'll cut mine as well." And I proceeded to do so.

children are already contributors to social life (Rheingold, Hay, and West, 1976; Leung and Rheingold, 1981; Lewis et al., 1989). For instance, they will point at objects—a window display, an airplane, an automobile, or a picture of a cereal box—to call other people's attention to them. In doing so, children demonstrate not only that they know other people can see what they see but also that others will look at what interests them. By 2 years of age, children can make a doll do something as if it were acting on its own. In so doing, they reveal an elementary ability for representing other people as independent agents. Most 3-year-olds can make a doll carry out several role-related activities, revealing knowledge of a social role (for instance, pretend to be a doctor and examine a doll). Four-year-olds can typically act out a role, meshing the behavior with that of a reciprocal role (for example, pretend that a patient doll is sick and a doctor doll examines it, in the course of

which both dolls make appropriate responses). During the late preschool years, children become capable of combining roles in more complicated ways (for instance, being a doctor and a father simultaneously). Most 6-year-olds can pretend to carry out several roles at the same time.

During the preschool years, children view the self and the mind as simply parts of the body (Damon and Hart, 1982; R. Johnson, 1990). However, between 6 and 8 years of age, they begin to distinguish that people are unique not only because they look different but because they have different feelings and thoughts. They come to define the self in internal rather than external terms and recognize the difference between psychological and physical attributes (Selman, 1980). The number of dimensions along which children conceptualize other people increases throughout childhood. The greatest development occurs between 7 and 8 years of age; then the rate of change in conceptualization slows. Indeed, the differences between children who are 7 years old and those who are 8 are frequently greater than the differences between 8-year-olds and 15-year-olds (Livesley and Bromley, 1973; Barenboim, 1981).

ADOLESCENCE

In much of the world, adolescence is not a socially distinct period in the human life course (Burbank, 1988). Although young people everywhere undergo the physiological changes associated with puberty, children frequently assume adult responsibilities by age 13 and even younger. In the United States, adolescence appears to be an "invention" of the past 100 years (Kett, 1977; Troen, 1985; Raphael, 1988). As the nation changed from a rural to an urban society, the role of children altered. They no longer had a significant economic function in the family once the workplace became separated from the home. In time, mandatory school attendance, child labor laws, and special legal procedures for "juveniles" established adolescence as a well-defined social reality.

During adolescence, individuals undergo changes in growth and development that are revolutionary. After years of inferiority, they suddenly catch up with adults in physical size and strength. Accompanying these changes is the rapid development of the reproductive organs that signals sexual maturity.

In the view of neo-Freudians like Erik Erikson (1963, 1968), the main task of adolescence is to build and confirm a reasonably stable identity. As they go about their everyday lives, people interact with one another on the basis not so much of what they actually are, as of what conceptions they have of themselves and others. Erikson (1968:165) suggests that an optimal feeling of identity is experienced as a sense of well-being. "Its most obvious concomitants are a feeling of being at home in one's body, a sense of 'knowing where one is going,' and an inner assuredness of anticipated recognition from those who count."

For adolescents, Erikson says, the search for identity becomes particularly acute. Like trapeze artists, adolescents must release their hold on childhood and reach in midair for a firm grasp on adulthood. In the process, many young people confront role confusion and a blurred self-image. Their uncertain identities lead them to search for a stable anchorage by overcommitting themselves to cliques, loves, and social causes.

Erikson's view of adolescence is in keeping with a long psychological tradition that has portrayed adolescence as a period of "storm and stress." Social scientists have suggested that Western nations make the transition from childhood to adulthood a particularly difficult one (Raphael, 1988; Hamburg and Takanishi, 1989). At adolescence, boys and girls are expected to stop being children, yet they are not expected to be men and women. The definitions given them by society are inconsistent. Many non-Western societies make the shift in status more definitive by providing **puberty rites**—initiation ceremonies that symbolize the transition from childhood to adulthood. Adolescents may be subjected to thoroughly distasteful, painful, and humiliating experiences during such rituals, but they are then pronounced grown up. Boys are often terrorized, ceremonially painted, and circumcised; girls are frequently secluded at menarche. But the tasks and tests are clear-cut, and young people know that if they accomplish the goals set for them, they will acquire adult status (Herdt, 1982; Gilmore, 1990). Mild versions of puberty rites in Western societies include the Jewish bar mitzvah and bat mitzvah, the Catholic confirmation, securing a driver's license, and graduation from high school and college.

In recent years, however, a growing body of research has led social scientists to challenge the view that adolescence among American youth is inherently a turbulent period (Savin-Williams and Demo, 1984; Rosenberg, 1986, 1989; Nottelmann, 1987). Although the self-images and self-conceptions of young people change, the changes are not invariably "stormy." Rather than experiencing dramatic change and disruption, adolescents gradually fashion their identities based on their sexual circumstances and their evolving competencies and skills. Indeed, for most youth, overall self-esteem increases with age across the adolescent years. But there are exceptions. Changes in the social environment, such as the transition to middle or junior high school, can in some cases have a disturbing effect, especially for girls (Nottelmann, 1987; Simmons and Blyth, 1987; Clausen, 1991).

Although the media make a good deal out of generational differences between adolescents and their parents, the notion of a "generation gap" vastly oversimplifies matters. Research suggests that both the family and the peer group are important anchors in the lives of most teenagers. However, the relative influence of the two groups varies with the issue involved. The peer group has the greater influence when the issues have to do with musical tastes, personal adornment, and entertainment idols, and in some cases with marijuana use and drinking. But the family has the greater influence when the issues have to do with future life goals, fundamental behavior codes, and core values (Steinberg, Elmen, and Mounts, 1989; Gecas and Seff, 1990). In many cases, a substantial proportion of young people see no reason to distinguish between the value system of their parents and that of their friends. In part this is because many teenagers select as friends individuals who share attitudes that are compatible with those of their families (Cohen, 1983).

Adolescence may also be experienced somewhat differently by men and women. According to a survey of 3,000 youngsters commissioned by the American Association of University Women, young women emerge from adolescence with a poorer self-image, relatively lower expectations for life, and substantially less self-confident attitudes than young men (Gilligan, Rogers, and Tolman, 1991). Eleven-year-old girls typically maintain the self-confidence they exhibit during the elementary school years. But by age 15 or 16, they increasingly say, "I don't know. I don't know. I don't know." During adolescence they come to fear rejection and anger, and so they mute their voices and repress their autonomy. Young women apparently internalize Western cultural norms that call upon them to be "nice" girls who avoid being "mean and bossy."

YOUNG ADULTHOOD

Recent developments in the Western world—the growth of service industries, the prolongation of education, and the enormously high educational demands of postindustrial society—have lengthened the transition to adulthood (Buchmann, 1989). In some respects our society appears to be evolving a new status between adolescence and adulthood: youth—men and women of college and graduate school age (Keniston, 1970; Neugarten and Neugarten, 1987a, b). In leaving home, youth in their late teens or early twenties may choose a transitional institution, such as the military or college, to start them on their way. Or young people may work (provided they can find a job) while continuing to live at home. During this time, a roughly equal balance exists between being in the family and moving out. Individuals become less financially dependent, enter new roles and living arrangements, and achieve greater autonomy and responsibility. With the passage of time, the center of gravity in young people's lives gradually shifts away from the family of origin.

The developmental tasks confronting individuals from 18 to 30 years of age typically center on the two core tasks Sigmund Freud (1938) called *love* and *work*. Through adult friendships, sexual relationships, and work experiences, they arrive at initial definitions of themselves as adults. Ideally, they develop the capacity to experience a trusting, supportive, and tender relationship with another person (Erikson, 1963). They may cohabit with a sexual partner or marry and begin a family. And they may lay the groundwork for a career or develop one career and then discard it. They may also drift aimlessly, which often precipitates a crisis at about age 30.

In making their way through the early years of adulthood, and for that matter the middle and later years as well, individuals are strongly influenced by **age norms**—rules that define what is appropriate for people to be and to do at various ages. A cultural timetable—a sort of societal "Big Ben"—defines the "best age" for a man or woman to finish school, settle on a career, marry, become a parent, hold a top job, become a grandparent, and retire (Kimmel, 1980; Heckhausen, Dixon, and Baltes, 1989). Individuals tend to set their personal "watches" by this **social clock,** and most people readily report whether they themselves are "early," "late," or "on time" with regard to major life events (Neugarten and Neugarten, 1987a, b).

However, variations do occur in the setting of one's social clock, so that the higher the social class, the later the pacing of age-linked events tends to be. Early adulthood typically lasts longer for a person in the middle class than for a member of the working class. Further, the life cycle in our society appears to be becoming more fluid; many traditional norms and expectations are changing, and age is losing many of its customary meanings. As a result, we may be witnessing what sociologist Bernice L. Neugarten (1979) has called an "age-irrelevant society" in which there is no single appropriate age for taking on given roles. She notes that it is no longer unusual to encounter the 28-year-old mayor, the 30-year-old college president, the 35-year-old grandmother, the 50-year-old retiree, the 65-year-old new father, and the 70-year-old student.

Some psychologists, like Erik Erikson (1963), have undertaken the search for what they view as the regular, sequential periods and transitions in the life cycle. They depict life as a succession of stages that resemble a stairway made up of a series of steplike levels. Erikson's chief concern is with psychological development, which he divides into the eight major stages of development described in Table 3.1. Each stage poses a unique task that revolves about a crisis—a turning point of increased vulnerability and heightened potential.

According to Erikson, the crises posed by each stage must be successfully resolved if healthy development is to take place. Consequently, the interaction that occurs between an individual and society at each stage can change the course of personality in a positive or a negative direction. Gail Sheehy took a somewhat similar approach in her best-selling book *Passages* (1976). She too contends that each stage in life poses a unique set of problems that must be resolved before a person can successfully advance to the next stage. By passing from one stage to the next—*passages*—each individual acquires new strengths and evolves an *authentic identity.*

Daniel J. Levinson (1986; Levinson et al., 1978) has also approached adulthood from a stage perspective. He and his associates at Yale University studied forty men in their midthirties to midforties. They designate six periods ranging from the late teens or early twenties to the late forties (see Figure 3.2). In Levinson's view, the overriding task confronting individuals throughout adulthood is the creation of a structure for life. But the structure does not become established once and for all time; it must be continually modified and reappraised. Transition periods tend to loom within 2 or 3 years of, and on either side of, the symbolically significant birthdays—20, 30, 40, 50, and 60. By interacting with the environment, each person formulates goals, works out means to achieve them, and modifies assumptions.

Some social scientists believe that unexpected events in our lives shape our development far more than the predictable transitions, such as marriage, parenthood, and retirement (Peterson, 1984; Rosenfeld and Stark, 1987). They contend that stage theories overlook the vast differences that characterize the human experience. Adult life is not the same thing for men and women and for rich and poor. Moreover, these social scientists contend that people are prepared for the major transitions of life by age norms and social clocks. Consequently, people have a tendency to take the transitions in their stride and do not perceive them as crises or unusually stressful events.

Table 3.1 ERIKSON'S EIGHT STAGES OF DEVELOPMENT

Development Stage	Psychosocial Crisis	Predominant Social Setting	Favorable Outcome
1. Infancy	Basic trust vs. mistrust	Family	The child develops trust in itself, its parents, and the world.
2. Early childhood	Autonomy vs. shame, doubt	Family	The child develops a sense of self-control without loss of self-esteem.
3. Fourth to fifth year	Initiative vs. guilt	Family	The child learns to acquire direction and purpose in activities.
4. Sixth year to onset of puberty	Industry vs. inferiority	Neighborhood; school	The child acquires a sense of mastery and competence.
5. Adolescence	Identity vs. role confusion	Peer groups and out-groups	The individual develops an *ego identity*—a coherent sense of self.
6. Young adulthood	Intimacy vs. isolation	Partners in friendship and sex	The individual develops the capacity to work toward a specific career and to involve himself or herself in an extended intimate relationship.
7. Adulthood	Generativity vs. stagnation	New family; work	The individual becomes concerned with others beyond the immediate family, with future generations, and with society.
8. Old age	Integrity vs. despair	Retirement and impending death	The individual acquires a sense of satisfaction in looking back upon his or her life.

SOURCE: Adapted from *Childhood and Society,* Second Edition, by Erik H. Erikson, by permission of W. W. Norton & Company, Inc. Copyright 1950, © 1963 by W. W. Norton & Company, Inc. Copyright renewed 1978, 1991 by Erik H. Erikson.

People locate themselves during the life course not only in terms of social timetables but also in terms of **life events**—turning points at which people change some direction in the course of their lives. Some of these events are related to social clocks. But many are not, such as suffering severe injury in an accident, being raped, winning a lottery, or undergoing a born-again conversion. Some life events are associated with internal growth or aging factors like puberty or old age. Others are the consequences of group life, including wars, national economic crises, and revolutions. Still oth-

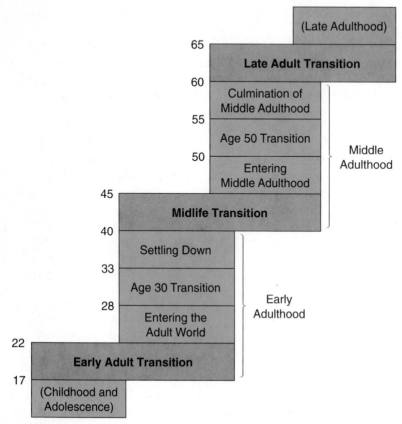

Figure 3.2 LEVINSON'S PERIODS OF MALE DEVELOPMENT
Daniel J. Levinson conceives of male development as characterized by a succession of stages.
Each stage requires the restructuring of critical aspects of a man's assumptions regarding
himself and the world. (SOURCE: From *The Seasons of a Man's Life* by Daniel Levinson et al. Copyright
© 1978 by Daniel J. Levinson. Reprinted by permission of Alfred A. Knopf, Inc.)

ers derive from happenings in the physical world, including fires, hurricanes, floods, earthquakes, or avalanches. And some have a strong inner or psychological component, such as a profound religious experience, the decision to leave one's spouse, or the death of a parent. Not surprisingly, gender impacts a person's experience of life events. For instance, men are more likely than women to report being distressed by work and financial events; women are more strongly influenced by exposure to negative events within the family (Conger et al., 1993). (Also see Chapter 7.)

Even coming of age at a certain point in time and experiencing certain decisive economic, social, political, or military events can have a profound impact on a person's life. For instance, Glen H. Elder, Jr. (1974, 1985, 1986) finds that the Great Depression of the 1930s and World War II had quite different consequences depending on the age and sex of those experiencing these events. While boys born between 1920 and 1921 typically derived positive benefits from their experiences during the Great Depression, it was otherwise for boys born between 1928 and 1929. The older boys, who were adolescents during much of the 1930s, assisted their families and themselves during the economically difficult times, but the younger boys had little opportunity to do so. Additionally, during World War II, most of the older boys entered military service, gaining a wide range of experience and educational and vocational benefits that opened new avenues for upward social mobility. By contrast, the boys born between 1928 and 1929 experienced the war on the home front and remained dependent on their families during the stressful years.

MIDDLE ADULTHOOD

Middle adulthood lacks the concreteness of infancy, childhood, and adolescence. It is a catchall category that is rather nebulous. Sometimes "middle adulthood" is used to refer to people over 30, a time in life when men and women presumably have "settled down" with families and careers. But it is also employed to denote "middle-aged" individuals—those roughly between 45 and 64 years of age. Whichever meaning is attached to "middle adulthood," the core tasks remain much the same as they were for men and women in young adulthood and revolve about love and work. We will defer our discussion of the love dimension since much of what we will have to say in Chapter 9 deals with intimacy issues and lifestyle options.

The central portion of the adult life span of both men and women is spent in work. As we will see in Chapter 8, people work for a great many reasons. Although economic considerations predominate, work also structures time, provides a context in which to relate to others, affords an escape from boredom, and sustains a sense of self-worth. The fact that someone will pay us for our work is an indication that what we do is needed by others and that we are a necessary part of the social fabric. Increasingly, for women as well as men, a paid job is defined as a badge of membership in the larger society. Overall, job satisfaction tends to be associated with the opportunity to exercise discretion, accept challenges, and make decisions.

Levinson (1986; Levinson et al., 1978) finds that in their early thirties men tend to establish their niche in the world, dig in, build a nest, and make and pursue long-range plans and goals. They usually have some dream or vision of the future that lies ahead of them. In their midthirties to late thirties, men seek to break out from under the authority of others and assert their independence. They often believe that their superiors control too much, delegate too little, and are insufficiently imaginative and aggressive. In their early forties men begin assessing where they stand in relation to the goals they earlier set for themselves. They may sense a gap between "what I've got now" and "what it is I really want," leading to an interval of soul-searching. Around 45, some men experience a "midlife crisis." Stereotypes depict men of this age as "flipping out"—leaving their wives for women young enough to be their daughters, quitting their jobs to become beachcombers, or drinking to excess. Yet most individuals are able to resolve the midlife transition through a continuous process of self-evaluation that may entail a modification of some aspirations and a reassessment of priorities. Most men gradually bring their aspirations in line with their attainments without severe upset and turmoil (Mortimer and Simmons, 1978; Goleman, 1989).

Although there is a growing interest in adult development, studies dealing with phases in adult female development have lagged behind those of men. Even so, evidence suggests that women progress through the same developmental periods as did the men in Levinson's study and at roughly the same ages. But although the timing of the periods and the nature of the developmental tasks are similar, the ways women approach these tasks and the outcomes they achieve are different. To a considerable extent, these differences derive from the greater complexity of women's visions for their future and the difficulties they encounter in living them out. Unlike men, most women do not report dreams in which careers stand out as the primary component; women are more likely to view a career as insurance against not marrying or a bad marriage and difficult economic circumstances. Instead, the dreams of most women contain an image in which they are immersed in a world centered in relationships with others, particularly husbands, children, and colleagues (Roberts and Newton, 1987). These findings parallel the work of psychologist Carol Gilligan (1982; Gilligan, Ward, and Taylor, 1989; Winkler, 1990), who finds that men see autonomy and competition as central to life, whereas women view life as a means for integrating themselves within the larger human enterprise. Gilligan believes that the development of women is not a steady progression but rather the recovery in adulthood of confidence, assertiveness, and a positive sense of self that Western society compels them to compromise during adolescence. We will have more to say on these matters in Chapter 7 when we examine gender roles in American life.

LATER ADULTHOOD

Like other periods of the life course, the time at which later adulthood begins is a matter of social definition. In preindustrial societies, life expectancy is typically short and the onset of old age is early. For instance, one observer reported that among the Arawak of Guyana (South America), individuals seldom lived more than 50 years and between the thirtieth and fortieth years in the case of men, and even earlier in the case of women, "the body, except the stomach, shrinks, and fat disappears [and] the skin hangs in hideous folds" (Im Thurn, 1883). Literary evidence also reveals that during the European Renaissance, men were considered "old" in their forties (Gilbert, 1967). Currently, a new division is emerging in many Western nations between the "young-old" and the "old-old" (Neugarten and Neugarten, 1987a, b). The young-old are early retirees who enjoy physical vigor, new leisure time, and new opportunities for community ser-

vice and self-fulfillment. The old-old include those who are of advanced age and suffer various infirmities.

Societies differ in the prestige and dignity they accord the aged. In many rural societies, including imperial China, elders enjoyed a prominent, esteemed, and honored position (Lang, 1946). Among the agricultural Palaung of North Burma, long life was deemed a privilege reserved for those who had lived virtuously in a previous incarnation. People showed their respect to older people by being careful not to step on their shadows. Young women cultivated an older appearance because women acquired honor and privilege in proportion to their years (Milne, 1924). In contrast to these cultural patterns, youth is the favored age in the United States. We have restricted the roles open to the elderly and accord them little prestige. Indeed, the older the elderly become, the more likely Americans are to stereotype them unfavorably. They are depicted as troublesome, cranky, touchy, and sickly beings. In some respects, the very old have become the nation's lepers.

Despite the unfavorable stereotypes that persist regarding the elderly, the actual picture is substantially different. Only 12 persons out of 1,000 in the 65 to 74 age group live in nursing homes. The figure rises to 59 for those 75 to 84, and to 237 for those over 85. Overall, only 1 American in 5 who is over 65 will ever be relegated to a nursing home. Additionally, about 3 percent of the elderly who live at home are bedridden, 5 percent are seriously incapacitated, and another 11 to 16 percent are restricted in mobility. On the other hand, from one-half to three-fifths of the elderly function without any limitation (and 37 percent of those 85 and over report no incapacitating limitation on their activity). Additionally, there is a huge variation from person to person in mental decline. A high level of verbal ability, a successful career or some other active involvement throughout life, and continuing keen mental interests are predictors for good mental function in old age (Goleman, 1994).

Old age entails exiting from some social roles. One of the most important of these exits is retirement from a job. On the whole, Americans are now retiring at earlier ages than in previous generations. The proportion of men aged 65 and over who were gainfully employed dropped from 68 percent in 1890, to 48 percent in 1947, to only 16 percent today. About 8 percent of women over 65 hold jobs or are seeking work, down from 9.5 percent in 1971. Of equal social significance, employed men aged 55 to 64 declined from 89 percent in 1947 to 69 percent currently, a drop of 20 percentage points. In government, nearly two out of three civil servants retire before age 62. The Bureau of Labor Statistics estimates that by the year 2000 only one in four men 60 years of age and over will be working (Lewin, 1990).

Traditionally, retirement has been portrayed as having negative consequences for the elderly because occupational status is a master status—an anchoring point for adult identity. Much of postretirement life is seen as aimless, and giving structure to the long, shapeless day is believed to be the retired person's most urgent challenge. Further, sociologist Irving Rosow (1974) contends that in the United States people are not effectively socialized to old age. The social norms that define the expectations for old age are few, weak, and nebulous. Complicating matters, the elderly have little motivation to conform to a "roleless role"—a socially devalued status. Even if there were definitive norms for guiding people's behavior in old age, Rosow says that few people would want to conform to role expectations that exclude them from equal opportunities for social participation and rewards.

In recent years the negative view of retirement has been challenged (Parnes, 1981; Palmore et al., 1985; Parnes et al., 1985; Bosse et al., 1991). For one thing, attitudes toward work and retirement seem to be changing. Moreover, research reveals that money is what is most missed in retirement, and that when people are assured an adequate income, they will retire early (Beck, 1982; Horn and Meer, 1987). One long-term survey of 5,000 men found that most men who retire for reasons

"What's this I hear about you adults mortgaging my future?"

From *The Wall Street Journal*—Permission, Cartoon Features Syndicate.

other than health are "very happy" in retirement and would, if they had to do it over again, retire at the same age. Only about 13 percent said they would choose to retire later if they could choose again (Parnes, 1981). Overall, when people are healthy and their incomes are adequate, they express satisfaction with retirement (Herzog, House, and Morgan, 1991).

Many elderly individuals also experience another role loss, that of being married. Although three out of four American men 65 and over are married and living with their wives, the same holds true for only one out of three women. This results from the fact that women typically outlive men by 7 to 8 years and from the tradition that women marry men older than themselves. Research by Helena Znaniecki Lopata (1973, 1981) reveals that the higher a woman's education and socioeconomic class, the more disorganized her self-identity and life become after her husband's death. However, once their "grief work" is accomplished, these women have more resources to form a new lifestyle. Overall, negative long-term consequences of widowhood appear to derive more from socioeconomic deprivation than from widowhood itself (Balkwell, 1981; Bound et al., 1991). Of interest, Lopata found that about half of the widows in her study lived alone, and most of them said they much preferred to do so. Only 10 percent moved in with their married children. Those who lived alone cited their desire to remain independent as their chief reason.

DEATH

A diagnosis of impending death requires that an individual adjust to a new definition of self. To be defined as dying implies more than the presence of a series of biochemical processes (De Vries, 1981). It entails the assumption of a social status, one in which social structuring not only attends but shapes the dying experience. Consider, for instance, the different social definitions we typically attribute to a 20-year-old who has been given a 5-year life expectancy and those we attribute to a healthy 80-year-old. Likewise, hospital personnel give different care to patients based on their perceived social worth. In a study of a hospital emergency room, sociologist David Sudnow (1967) found that different social evaluations led the staff to work frantically to revive a young child but to acquiesce in the death of an elderly woman. Finally, although death is a biological event, it is made a social reality through such culturally fashioned events as wakes and funerals.

Changes in medical technology and social conditions have made death a different experience than in earlier times. Dying in the modern world is often drawn out and enmeshed in formal bureaucratic processes (Nuland, 1994). Only a few

generations ago, most people died at home and the family assumed responsibility for laying out the deceased and preparing for the funeral. In recent times, death has been surrounded by taboos that in large measure have kept the subject out of sight and out of mind. Today the nursing home or hospital cares for the terminally ill and manages the dying experience. A mortuary—euphemistically called a "home"—prepares the body and makes the funeral arrangements or arranges for the cremation of the remains. As a result, the average American's exposure to death is minimized. The dying and the dead are segregated from others and placed with specialists for whom contact with death has become a routine and impersonal matter (Strauss and Glaser, 1970; Ariès, 1981; Kamerman, 1988).

Institutional control of dying has reduced individual autonomy. Personal needs and desires are often subordinated to organization needs. Indeed, much criticism has been leveled at the way modern organizations and technology structure the care of the terminally ill. Public opinion surveys reveal that eight out of ten Americans believe patients should be allowed to die under some circumstances, and about half say some incurably ill people have the moral right to commit suicide. Only 15 percent say that doctors and nurses should always do everything possible to save a patient's life. Fifty-nine percent would want their doctors to stop administering life-sustaining treatment if they had a terminal illness and were experiencing a great deal of physical pain. Significantly, a third of adult Americans can imagine themselves taking the life of a loved one who was suffering terribly from a terminal illness (Times Mirror Center for the People and the Press, 1990). In sum, Americans tend to favor a quick transition between life and death. But the belief "the less dying, the better" has come up against an altered biomedical technology in which individuals are increasingly approaching death through a "lingering trajectory." Many people have a profound fear of being held captive in a state between life and death—as "vegetables" sustained entirely by life-support equipment. Consequently, growing numbers of Americans are coming to the view that too much is done for too long a period at too high a cost, all at the expense of basic human considerations and sensitivities.

Recent developments, including the considerable sales of a do-it-yourself suicide manual (Derek Humphry's 1991 book *Final Exit*), widespread fascination with the assisted-suicide crusade of Dr. Jack Kevorkian, and various ballot initiatives authorizing physician-assisted suicide, suggest that a growing number of Americans want greater control of their lives when they confront long-term suffering and impending death. So Americans are increasingly grappling with the issue of **euthanasia**—painlessly putting to death an individual who suffers from an incurable and painful disease. For some people euthanasia is the first step in a nightmare scenario reminiscent of Nazi Germany. They fear that with time euthanasia would become more and more involuntary, with poor people, the elderly, and the infirm increasingly induced to accept a fatal drug dosage. For others it is an emergent civil rights issue: whether one has the right to determine or control the circumstances of one's own death. Individuals on both sides believe that the nation is embarking on a struggle as emotional, protracted, and ethically difficult as the battle over abortion.

Over the past two decades another approach has emerged—the hospice movement that seeks a more humane approach for the care of the terminally ill. A **hospice** is a program or mode of care that attempts to make the dying experience less painful and emotionally traumatic for patients and their families. Advocates of the hospice approach say that it is difficult for physicians and nurses in hospital settings to accept the inevitability of death. Hospitals are geared to curing illness and prolonging life, and consequently incurable illness and death are sources of embarrassment to them. Thus proponents of hospice care insist that other institutional arrangements are required.

Whenever possible, hospice treatment is administered in the patient's home. Visiting physicians, nurses, social workers, and volunteers provide emotional and spiritual help in addition to medical care. A number of hospitals and nursing homes have also established hospice units. The emphasis of hospice approaches falls on comfort and care rather than on attempts to prolong life. Patients receive painkilling medication on an as-needed basis, and they are also provided with antidepressive and antianxiety drugs should they be required. Most hospice programs also offer follow-up bereavement care for family members.

In recent years, Elisabeth Kübler-Ross (1969, 1981) has contributed a good deal to the movement to restore dignity and humanity to death. She contends that when medical personnel and the family know that a patient is dying and attempt to hide the fact, they construct a barrier that prevents all the parties from preparing for death. Moreover, the dying person typically sees through the make-believe. Kübler-Ross has found that it is better if everyone is allowed to express his or her genuine emotions and if these feelings are respected. Surveys show that four out of five persons would want to be told if they had an incurable illness.

Although there are different styles for dying—just as there are different styles for living—Kübler-Ross (1969) finds that dying people typically pass through five stages in accommodating themselves to impending death: *denial* that they will die, *anger* that their life will shortly end, *bargaining* with God or fate to arrange a temporary truce, *depression* or "preparatory grief," and *acceptance.* Not everyone passes through all the stages, and individuals slip back and forth between stages. And a great many other factors also influence the dying experience, including differences in gender, ethnic membership, personality, the death environment, and the nature of the disease itself. Death cannot be understood except in the total context of a person's previous life and current circumstances. In sum, over the past decade or so, public and professional awareness of the dying person's experience has increased dramatically and has given impetus to a more humane approach to death.

Summary

1. Socialization is the process of social interaction by which people acquire those behaviors essential for effective participation in society. Were it not for socialization, the renewal of culture could not occur from one generation to the next. And in the absence of socialization, society could not perpetuate itself beyond a single generation. Both the individual and society are mutually dependent on socialization.

2. Human socialization presupposes that an adequate genetic endowment and an adequate environment are available. Organisms are not passive objects programmed by internal genetic forces, nor are they passive objects shaped by the external environment. Hereditary and environmental factors interpenetrate and mutually determine each other. The dynamic interplay between an individual and the environment is the foundation of human intelligence, knowledge, and culture.

3. If they are to adapt to their environment, human beings must be able to communicate. Communication refers to the process by which people transmit information, ideas, attitudes, and mental states to one another. It includes all those verbal and nonverbal processes by which we send and receive messages.

4. People do not respond directly to stimuli from their sense organs, but assign meanings to the stimuli and formulate their actions on the basis of these meanings. Our symbolic environment mediates the physical environment so that we do not simply experience stimuli, but rather a definition of the situation. A definition of the situation is the interpretation or meaning we give to our immediate circumstances. Our definitions influence our construction of reality, an insight captured by the Thomas theorem: "If [people] define situations as real, they are real in their consequences."

5. We not only arrive at definitions of the situation; we also arrive at self-definitions as we supply answers to the question, Who am I? Charles Horton Cooley contended that our consciousness arises in a social context. This notion is exemplified by his concept of the looking-glass self—a process by which we imaginatively assume the stance of other people and view ourselves as we believe they see us. It consists of three phases. First, we imagine how we appear to others. Second, we imagine how others judge our appearance. And third, we develop some sort of self-feeling such as pride or mortification on the basis of what we perceive others' judgments of us to be.

6. George Herbert Mead elaborated upon Cooley's ideas and contributed many insights of his own. He contended that we gain a sense of selfhood by acting toward ourselves in much the same fashion that we act toward others. In so doing, we "take the role of the other toward ourselves." We mentally assume a dual perspective: Simultaneously we are the subject doing the viewing and the object being viewed. According to Mead, children typically pass through three stages in developing a full sense of selfhood: the play stage, the game stage, and the generalized other stage.

7. Erving Goffman has provided an additional dimension to our understanding of the self. He points out that only by influencing other people's ideas of us can we hope to predict or control what happens to us. Consequently, we have a stake in presenting ourselves to others in ways that will lead them to view us in a favorable light, a process Goffman calls impression management. In so doing, we use

the arts of both concealment and strategic revelation.

8. Socialization is a continuing, lifelong process. All societies have to deal with the life cycle that begins with conception and continues through old age and ultimately death. Upon this organic age grid, societies weave varying social arrangements. Some of these arrangements have to do with childhood. Though societies differ in their definitions of childhood, they all begin the socialization process as soon as possible. The magnitude of children's accomplishments over a relatively short period of time is truly astonishing. For instance, they display people-oriented responses at very early ages.

9. In much of the world, adolescence is not a socially distinct period in the human life span. Although people everywhere undergo the physiological changes associated with puberty, they frequently assume adult responsibilities by age 13 and even younger. In the view of Erik Erikson, the main task of adolescence is to build and confirm a stable identity. But adolescence is not necessarily a turbulent period. Nor does a sharp generation gap separate American adolescents from their parents.

10. The developmental tasks confronting young adults revolve about the core tasks of work and love. Ideally they develop the capacity to experience a trusting, supportive, and tender relationship with another person. And they lay the groundwork for a career. In making their way through the early years of adulthood, individuals are strongly influenced by age norms and tend to set their personal "watches" by a cultural Big Ben, the social clock. Some social scientists have looked for stages through which young adults typically pass. Others believe that unexpected events play a more important role in development.

11. Middle adulthood is a somewhat nebulous period. The core tasks remain much the same as they were in young adulthood. Increasingly, work is coming to be defined for both men and women as a badge of membership in the larger society. Although economic considerations predominate, people also work as a means to structure their time, interact with other people, escape from boredom, and sustain a positive self-image. As they pass through the middle years, adults confront a variety of changing circumstances and challenges to which they must fashion adaptations.

12. Like other periods of the life span, the time at which later adulthood begins is a matter of social definition. Further, societies differ in the prestige and dignity they accord the aged. Old age often entails exiting from some social roles. One of the most important of these exits is retirement from a job. Some sociologists have portrayed retirement in negative terms, but this view has recently been challenged. Overall, when people are healthy and their incomes are adequate, they typically express satisfaction with retirement. Many elderly adults also experience another role loss, that of being married. Women are more likely to be widowed than are men.

13. A diagnosis of impending death requires that an individual adjust to a new definition of self. It entails the assumption of a social status, one in which social structuring not only attends but shapes the course of the dying experience. Changes in medical technology and social conditions have made death a different experience from that of earlier times. Dying in the modern world is often drawn out and enmeshed in formal bureaucratic processes. The hospice movement has arisen to provide a more humane approach to the dying experience.

Glossary

age norms Rules that define what is appropriate for people to be and to do at various ages.

anticipatory socialization The process in which people think about, experiment with, and try on the behaviors associated with a new role.

artifacts Objects, such as certain types of clothing, makeup, or jewelry, we employ to tell other people our gender, race, status, and attitude.

body language Physical motions and gestures that provide social signals.

communication The process by which people transmit information, ideas, attitudes, and mental states to one another.

definition of the situation The interpretation or meaning we give to our immediate circumstances.

dramaturgical approach The sociological perspective associated with Erving Goffman that views the performances staged in a theater as an analytical analogy and tool for depicting social life.

egocentric bias The tendency to place ourselves at the center of events so that we overperceive ourselves as the victim or target of an action or event that in reality is not directed at us.

euthanasia Painlessly putting to death an individual who suffers from an incurable and painful disease.

generalized other The term George Herbert Mead applied to the social unit that gives individuals their unity of self. The attitude of the generalized other is the attitude of the larger community.

hospice A program or mode of care that attempts to make the dying experience less painful and emotionally traumatic for patients and their families.

impression management The term Erving Goffman applied to the process whereby we present ourselves to others in ways that will lead them to view us in a favorable light.

language acquisition device The view associated with Noam Chomsky that human beings possess an inborn language-generating mechanism. The basic structure of language is seen as biologically channeled, forming a sort of prefabricated filing system to order the words and phrases that make up human languages.

life course The interweave of age-graded trajectories with the vicissitudes of changing social conditions and future options that characterizes the life span from conception through old age and death.

life events Turning points at which people change some direction in the course of their lives.

looking-glass self The term that Charles Horton Cooley applied to the process by which we imaginatively assume the stance of other people and view ourselves as we believe they see us.

paralanguage Nonverbal cues surrounding speech—voice, pitch, volume, pacing of speech, silent pauses, and sighs—that provide a rich source of communicative information.

proxemics The way we employ social and personal space to transmit messages.

puberty rites Initiation ceremonies that symbolize the transition from childhood to adulthood.

self The set of concepts we use in defining who we are.

self-conception An overriding view of ourselves; a sense of self through time.

self-image A mental conception or picture we have of ourselves that is relatively temporary; it changes as we move from one context to another.

significant other The term George Herbert Mead applied to a social model, usually an important person in an individual's life.

social clock The personal "watch" individuals use to pace the major events of their lives, which is based on cultural age norms.

socialization A process of social interaction by which people acquire the knowledge, attitudes, values, and behaviors essential for effective participation in society.

Thomas theorem The notion that our definitions influence our construction of reality. It was stated by William I. Thomas and Dorothy S. Thomas: "If [people] define situations as real, they are real in their consequences."

Chapter 4

SOCIAL GROUPS
AND FORMAL
ORGANIZATIONS

We often do not appreciate the part groups play in our lives until we are separated from them. When we leave home to attend college, get married, or take a job, many of us experience "homesickness"—nostalgia for a group from which our immediate ties suddenly have been severed. Groups provide the structure by which we involve ourselves in the daily affairs of life. It is is hardly surprising, therefore, that living alone may be hazardous to your health. Heart attack patients living alone are nearly twice as likely to suffer another heart attack—and more likely to die of an attack—within 6 months. Additionally, accidents, suicides, psychiatric disorders, alcoholism, and even tuberculosis are more common among socially isolated individuals. When we confront difficulties, the social support and feedback of others can be of immense help. For instance, cancer patients who enjoy the strong emotional support of family, friends, or spouses typically survive substantially longer than those who lack such support. Cancer specialists at Stanford University find that support groups add an average of 18 months to the lives of women in advanced stages of cancer, appreciably longer than any of the chemotherapy medications they might take (Goleman, 1991a). Even your success or failure at college may depend upon your involvement in groups. After 5 years of study, researchers at Harvard concluded that the most effective strategy that undergraduates can pursue is to make alliances with fellow students, faculty members, and advisers and not try to brave the educational experience alone (DePalma, 1991).

Prisoners who are maintained in solitary confinement reveal some of the appalling consequences of social isolation. Their orientation to the world about them is often profoundly altered (Grassian, 1983:1452–1453). One prisoner held in solitary confinement at the Massachusetts Correctional Institution at Walpole observes: "Everything gets exaggerated. After a while, you can't stand it. Meals—I used to eat everything they served. Now I can't stand the smells—the meat—the only thing I can stand to eat is the bread."

Another says, "What really freaks me out is when a bee gets into the cell—such a small thing." Many inmates report difficulties with thinking, concentration, and memory. One prisoner reports: "I can't read. . . . Your mind's narcotized . . . sometimes I can't grasp words in my mind that I know." In some cases, inmates in solitary confinement impulsively mutilate themselves. "I cut my wrists—cut myself many times when in isolation. Now, it seems crazy. But every time I did it, I wasn't thinking—lost control—cut myself without knowing what I was doing." Given the critical importance of groups, it is hardly surprising that rebellious convicts at the South Ohio Correctional Facility gradually fashioned a highly disciplined community in the prison wing they controlled for 11 days in 1993. The makeshift rebel community included a health clinic to treat injured prisoners, a corps of lookouts, and security squads (Ruth and Brooks, 1993).

As we pointed out in Chapter 2, a **group** consists of two or more people who share a feeling of unity and who are bound together in relatively stable patterns of social interaction. Groups are not tangible things; rather, they are products of social definitions—sets of shared ideas. As such they constitute constructed realities. In other words, we make groups real by treating them *as if* they are real, a clear application of the Thomas theorem (see Chapter 3). We fabricate groups in the course of our social interaction as we cluster people together in social units: families, teams, cliques, nationalities, races, labor unions, fraternities, clubs, corporations, and the like. In turn we *act* on the basis of these shared mental fabrications, creating an existence *beyond* the individuals who are involved. As we pointed out in Chapter 2, groups are social structures that have an existence apart from the particular relationships individual people have with one another. For this reason, many groups like colleges, sports teams, religious orders, ethnic groups, political parties, and business organizations have an existence that extends beyond the life spans of specific people.

What we have been saying adds up to this: The whole is greater than the sum of its parts. Groups have distinctive properties in their own right apart from the particular individuals who belong to them. In this sense, they are *social facts* (see Chapter 1). Groups resemble chemical compounds more than they do mixtures. For example, although hydrogen and oxygen are both gases at room temperature, they form a chemical compound— water—whose properties are different in kind from either hydrogen or oxygen. It is the joining of molecules—and the bonding of people— that produces qualitatively new entities. Accordingly, we can speak of families, cliques, clubs, and organizations without having to break them down into the separate interactions that compose them.

□ Group Relationships

Life places us in a complex web of relationships with other people. As we noted in Chapter 3, our humanness arises out of these relationships in the course of social interaction. Moreover, our humanness must be sustained through social interaction, and fairly constantly so. When an association continues long enough for two people to become linked together by a relatively stable set of expectations, it is called a **relationship.**

People are bound within relationships by two types of bonds: expressive ties and instrumental ties. **Expressive ties** are social links formed when we emotionally invest ourselves in and commit ourselves to other people. Through association with people who are meaningful to us, we achieve a sense of security, love, acceptance, companionship, and personal worth. **Instrumental ties** are social links formed when we cooperate with other people to achieve some goal. Occasionally this may mean working with our enemies, as in the old political saying, "Politics makes strange bedfellows." More often, we simply cooperate with others to reach some end without endowing the relationship with any larger significance.

PRIMARY GROUPS
AND SECONDARY GROUPS

Sociologists have built on the distinction between expressive and instrumental ties to distinguish between two types of groups: primary and secondary. A **primary group** involves two or more people who enjoy a direct, intimate, cohesive relationship with one another (Cooley, 1909). Expressive ties predominate in primary groups; we view the people—friends, family members, and lovers—as ends in themselves and valuable in their own right. A **secondary group** entails two or more people who are involved in an impersonal relationship and have come together for a specific, practical purpose. Instrumental ties predominate in secondary groups; we perceive people as means to ends rather than as ends in their own right. Illustrations include our relationships with a clerk in a clothing store and a cashier at a service station. Sometimes primary group relationships evolve out of secondary group relationships. This happens in many work settings. People on the job often develop close relationships with coworkers as they come to share gripes, jokes, gossip, and satisfactions.

A number of conditions enhance the likelihood that primary groups will arise. First, group size is important. We find it difficult to get to know people personally when they are milling about and dispersed in large groups. In small groups we have a better chance to initiate contact and establish rapport with them. Second, face-to-face contact allows us to size up others. Seeing and talking with one another in close physical proximity makes possible a subtle exchange of ideas and feelings. And third, the probability that we will develop primary group bonds increases as we have frequent and continuous contact. Our ties with people often deepen as we interact with them across time and gradually evolve interlocking habits and interests.

We use the word "primary" in our daily conversations to refer to things that are essential and important. Clearly the term is appropriate for primary groups since they are fundamental to us and to society. First, primary groups are critical to the socialization process. Within them, infants and children are introduced to the ways of their society. Such groups are the breeding grounds in which we acquire the norms and values that equip us for social life. Sociologists view primary groups as bridges between individuals and the larger society because they transmit, mediate, and interpret a society's cultural patterns and provide the sense of oneness so critical for social solidarity.

Second, primary groups are fundamental because they provide the settings in which we meet most of our personal needs. Within them, we experience companionship, love, security, and an overall sense of well-being. Not surprisingly, sociologists find that the strength of a group's primary ties has implications for its functioning. For example, the stronger the primary group ties of troops fighting together, the better their combat record (Elder and Clipp, 1988; Copp and McAndrew, 1990). During World War II the success of German military units derived not from Nazi ideology, but from the ability of the German army to reproduce in the infantry company the intimacy and bonds found in civilian primary groups (Shils and Janowitz, 1948). What made the *Wehrmacht* so formidable was that, unlike the American army, German soldiers who trained together went into battle together. Additionally, American fighting units were kept up to strength through individual replacement, whereas German units were "fought down" and then pulled back to be reconstituted as a new group (Van Creveld, 1982). And the Israelis have found that combat units hastily thrown together without time to form close bonds perform more poorly in battle and experience higher rates of psychiatric casualties than do units with close bonds (Cordes, 1984; Solomon, Mikulincer, and Hobfoll, 1986).

Third, primary groups are fundamental because they serve as powerful instruments for social control. Their members command and dispense many of the rewards that are so vital to us and that make our lives seem worthwhile. Should the use of rewards fail, members can frequently win compliance by rejecting or threatening to ostracize those who deviate from the group's

"My people will get back to your people."

Drawing by Dedini; © 1991 The New Yorker Magazine, Inc.

norms. For instance, some religious cults employ "shunning" (a person can remain in the community, but others are forbidden to interact with him or her) as a device to bring into line individuals whose behavior goes beyond that allowed by the group's teachings. Even more importantly, primary groups define social reality for us by "structuring" our experiences. By providing us with definitions of situations, they elicit from us behavior that conforms to group-devised meanings. Primary groups, then, serve both as carriers of social norms and as enforcers of them.

IN-GROUPS AND OUT-GROUPS

It is not only the groups to which we immediately belong that have a powerful influence upon us. Often the same holds true for groups to which we do not belong. Accordingly, sociologists find it useful to distinguish between in-groups and out-groups. An **in-group** is a group with which we identify and to which we belong. An **out-group** is a group with which we do not identify and to which we do not belong. In daily conversation we recognize the distinction between in-groups and out-groups in our use of the personal pronouns "we" and "they." We can think of in-groups as "we-groups" and out-groups as "they-groups." In-groups typically provide us with our *social identities*—those aspects of our self-concept that we derive from a sense of belonging to groups and the feelings and emotional significance we attach to this belonging (Crocker and Luhtanen, 1990).

The concepts of in-group and out-group highlight the importance of *boundaries*—social demarcation lines that tell us where interaction begins and ends. Group boundaries are not physical barriers but rather discontinuities in the flow of social interaction. To one degree or another, a group's boundaries "encapsulate" people in a social membrane so that the focus and flow of their actions are internally contained. Some boundaries are based on territorial location, such as neighborhoods, communities, and nation-states. Others rest on social distinctions, such as ethnic group or religious, political, occupational, language, kin, and socioeconomic class memberships. Whatever their source, social boundaries face in two directions. They prevent outsiders from entering a group's sphere, and they keep insiders within that sphere so that they do not entertain rival possibilities for social interaction.

At times we experience feelings of indifference, disgust, competition, and even outright conflict when we think about or have dealings with out-group members. An experiment undertaken by Muzafer Sherif and his associates (1961) has shown how our awareness of in-group boundaries is heightened and antagonism toward out-groups is generated by competitive situations. The subjects were 11- and 12-year-old boys, all of whom were healthy, socially well-adjusted youngsters from stable, middle-class homes. The setting was a summer camp where the boys were divided into two groups.

During the first week at the camp the boys in each group got to know one another, evolved group norms, and arrived at an internal division of labor and leadership roles. During the second week, the experimenters brought the two groups into competitive contact through a tournament of baseball, touch football, tug-of-war, and treasure hunt games. Although the contest opened in a spirit of good sportsmanship, positive feelings quickly evaporated. During the third week, the "integration phase," Sherif brought the two groups of boys together for various events, including eating in the same mess hall, viewing movies, and shooting off firecrackers. But far from reducing conflict, these settings merely provided new opportunities for the two groups to challenge, berate, and harass one another. The experimenters then created a series of urgent and natural situations in which the two groups would have to work together to achieve their ends, such as the emergency repair of the conduit that delivered the camp's water supply. Whereas competition had heightened awareness of group boundaries, the pursuit of common goals led to a lessening of out-group hostilities and the lowering of intergroup barriers to cooperation.

REFERENCE GROUPS

More than a century ago, American writer Henry Thoreau observed: "If a man does not keep pace with his companions, perhaps it is because he hears a different drummer." Thoreau's observation contains an important sociological insight. We evaluate ourselves and guide our behavior by standards embedded in a group context. But since Americans are dispersed among a good many different groups—each with a somewhat unique subculture or counterculture—the frames of reference we use in assessing and fashioning our behavior differ. In brief, we have different **reference groups**—social units we use for appraising and shaping attitudes, feelings, and actions.

A reference group may or may not be our membership group. We may think of a reference group as a base we use for viewing the world, a source of psychological identification. It helps to account for seemingly contradictory behavior: the upper-class revolutionary, the renegade Catholic, the reactionary union member, the shabby gentleman, the quisling who collaborates with the enemy, the assimilated immigrant, and the social-climbing chambermaid. These individuals have simply taken as their reference group people other than those from their membership group (Hyman and Singer, 1968). The concept thus helps to illuminate such central sociological concerns as social networks, socialization, and social conformity.

Reference groups provide both *normative* and *comparative* functions (Felson and Reed, 1986). Since we would like to view ourselves as being members in good standing within a certain group—or we aspire to such membership—we take on the group's norms and values. We cultivate its lifestyles, political attitudes, musical tastes, food preferences, sexual practices, and drug-using behaviors. Our behavior is group-anchored. We also use the standards of our reference group to appraise ourselves—a comparison point against which we judge and evaluate our physical attractiveness, intelligence, health, ranking, and standard of living. When our membership group does not match our reference group, we may experience feelings of **relative deprivation**—discontent associated with the gap between what we have (the circumstances of our membership group) and what we believe we should have (the circumstances of our reference group). Feelings of relative deprivation often contribute to social alienation and provide fertile conditions for collective behavior and revolutionary social movements (see Chapter 12). The reference group concept, then, contains clues to processes of social change.

However, not all reference groups are positive. We also make use of negative reference groups, social units with which we compare ourselves to emphasize the differences between ourselves and others. For Cuban-Americans in Miami, Florida, the Castro regime functions as a negative reference group (Carver and Humphries, 1981). A good many of them fled their homeland after Castro came to power in the 1959 revolution. Militant opposition to the Castro regime helps the Cuban-Americans determine what they really believe in and decide who they really are. Of even greater significance, the negative reference group is a mechanism of social solidarity, an instrument by which the exile community binds itself together. It provides a common denominator for acceptance and ensures for members of the cause the benefits that accrue to true believers.

□ Group Dynamics

To understand groups is to understand much about human behavior. The reason is not difficult to come by since groups are the wellsprings of our humanness. Although we think of groups as things—distinct and bounded entities—it is not their static but their dynamic qualities that make them such a significant force. We need to examine what happens within groups.

GROUP SIZE

The size of a group is important because even though it is a structural component, it influences the nature of interaction. The smaller the group, the more opportunities we have to get to know other people well and to establish close ties with them. The popular adage "Two's company, three's a crowd" captures an important difference between two-person and three-person groups. Two-person groups—**dyads**—are the setting for many of our most intense and influential relationships, including that between parent and child and between husband and wife. Indeed, most of our social interactions take place on a one-to-one basis.

Sociologist John James (1951) and his students observed 7,405 informal interactions of pedestrians, playground users, swimmers, and shoppers and 1,458 people in a variety of work situations. They found that 71 percent of both the informal and work interactions consisted of 2 people, 21 percent involved 3 people, 6 percent included 4 people, and only 2 percent entailed 5 or more people. Emotions and feelings tend to play a greater part in dyads than they do in larger groups (Hare, 1976). But this factor also contributes to their relatively fragile nature: A delicate balance exists between the parties, and so if one of them becomes disenchanted, the relationship collapses. And contrary to what you might expect, 2-person relationships tend to be more emotionally strained and less overtly aggressive than other relationships (Bales and Borgatta, 1955; O'Dell, 1968).

The addition of a third member to a group—forming a **triad**—fundamentally alters a social situation. Coalitions become possible, with two members joining forces against a third member (Hare, 1976). With this arrangement, one person may be placed in the role of an "intruder" or "outsider." However, under some circumstances, the third person may assume the role of a "mediator" and function as a peacemaker.

One recurring question that has attracted the interest of sociologists is this: What is the optimum group size for problem solving? For instance, if you want to appoint a committee to make a recommendation, what would be the ideal size for the group? Small-group research suggests that five is usually the best size (Hare, 1976). With five members, a strict deadlock is not possible because there is an odd number of members. Further, since groups tend to split into a majority of three and a minority of two, being a minority does not result in the isolation of one person, as it does in the triad. The group is sufficiently large for the members to shift roles easily and for a person to withdraw from an awkward position without necessarily having to resolve the issue formally. Finally, five-person groups are large enough so that people feel they can express their emotions freely and even risk antagonizing one another, yet they are small enough so that the members show regard for one another's feelings and needs. As groups become larger, they become less manageable. People no longer carry on a "conversation" with the other members, but "address" them with formal vocabulary and grammar. As a result, they may come to share progressively less knowledge with one another, undermining group stability (Carley, 1991).

LEADERSHIP

Imagine a football team without a quarterback, an army without officers, corporations without executives, universities without deans, orchestras without conductors, and youth gangs without chiefs. Without overall direction, people typically have difficulty coordinating their activities. Consequently, in group settings some members usually exert more influence than others. We call these individuals *leaders.* Small groups may be able to get along without a leader, but in larger groups a lack of leadership leads to chaos.

Two types of leadership roles tend to evolve in small groups (Bales, 1970). One, a **task specialist,** is devoted to appraising the problem at hand and organizing people's activity to deal with it. The other, a **social-emotional specialist,** focuses on overcoming interpersonal problems in the group, defusing tensions, and promoting solidarity. The former type of leadership is *instrumental,* directed toward the achievement of group goals; the latter is *expressive,* oriented toward the creation of harmony and unity. In some cases, one person

assumes both roles, but usually each role is played by a different person. Neither role is necessarily more important than the other, and the situation does much to dictate the relative importance of each.

Leaders differ in their styles for exercising influence. Through the years, the classic experiments in leadership by Kurt Lewin and his associates (Lewin, Lippitt, and White, 1939; White and Lippitt, 1960) have generated considerable interest. In these pioneering investigations, adult leaders working with groups of 11-year-old boys followed one of three leadership styles. In the *authoritarian* style, the leader determined the group's policies, gave step-by-step directions so that the boys were certain about their future tasks, assigned work partners, provided subjective praise and criticism, and remained aloof from group participation. In contrast, in the *democratic* style, the leader allowed the boys to participate in decision-making processes, outlined only general goals, suggested alternative procedures, permitted the members to work with whomever they wished, evaluated the boys objectively, and participated in group activities. Finally, in the *laissez-faire* style, the leader adopted a passive, uninvolved stance; provided materials, suggestions, and help only when requested; and refrained from commenting on the boys' work.

The researchers found that authoritarian leadership produces high levels of frustration and hostile feelings toward the leader. Productivity remains high so long as the leader is present, but it slackens appreciably in the leader's absence. Under democratic leadership members are happier, feel more group-minded and friendlier, display independence (especially in the leader's absence), and exhibit low levels of interpersonal aggression. Laissez-faire leadership resulted in low group productivity and high levels of interpersonal aggression. However, it should be emphasized that the study was carried out with American youngsters accustomed to democratic procedures. Under other circumstances and in different cultural settings, an authoritarian leader may be preferred. The frequency of authoritarian leaders in developing nations has suggested to some sociologists that people may prefer a directed leadership style under highly stressful conditions (Bass, 1960). However, an equally plausible explanation is that it is easier for authoritarian leaders to seize and maintain leadership under these circumstances.

SOCIAL LOAFING

An old saying has it that "many hands make light the work." Yet the proverb falls short of the truth. For example, we might expect that three individuals can pull three times as much as one person can and that eight can pull eight times as much. But research reveals that whereas persons individually average 130 pounds of pressure when tugging on a rope, in groups of three they average 117 pounds each, and in groups of eight only 60 pounds each. One explanation is that faulty coordination produces group inefficiency. However, when subjects are blindfolded and *believe* they are pulling with others, they also slacken their effort (Ingham, 1974). Apparently when individuals work in groups, they work less hard than they do when working individually—a process called **social loafing** (Williams, Harkins, and Latané, 1981; Kameda et al., 1992; Karau and Williams, 1993).

When undergraduate men are asked to make as much noise as possible by shouting or clapping along with others, they produce only twice as much noise in groups of four and 2.4 times as much in groups of six as when alone (Latané, Williams, and Harkins, 1979). Presumably people slack off in groups because they feel they are not receiving their fair share of credit or because they think that in a crowd they can get away with less work. In comparable circumstances, Soviet peasants produced less when they worked on collective farms than when they cultivated a small plot of land for their own use. (Although the private plots occupied less than 1 percent of Soviet agricultural lands, some 27 percent of the total value of the nation's farm output was produced on

them.) We should not conclude from these findings that we can do away with work groups. Groups are essential to social life, and they can accomplish many things that individuals cannot. For instance, Alcoholics Anonymous, Parents Without Partners, Weight Watchers, Compulsive Shoppers, Parkinson's Support Group, and other self-help groups testify to the desirable influences and outcomes that can be associated with groups. Additionally, new research suggests that the loafing effect can be minimized by providing a standard against which members are asked to evaluate the group's performance (Harkins and Szymanski, 1989).

SOCIAL DILEMMAS

The social loafing effect suggests that there is an inverse relationship between group size and individual motivation. A closely related phenomenon is termed a **social dilemma**—a situation in which members of a group are faced with a conflict between maximizing their personal interests and maximizing the collective welfare (Komorita and Barth, 1985). The box provides one type of social dilemma: the prisoner's dilemma game. Garrett J. Hardin's (1968) "tragedy of the commons" illustrates another type of social dilemma in which the long-run consequences of self-interested individual choice result in social disaster. Hardin explored the situation in which a number of herders share a common pasture. Each person may reason that by putting another cow to graze, he or she will realize a benefit from it. But if each person follows this course, the commons will be destroyed and each will ultimately lose. Hardin was addressing the problem of population growth. The notion can be applied equally well to pollution, which is the reverse of the grazing problem; where grazing takes matter out of the commons, pollution puts matter in. Social dilemmas are encountered in many other spheres of life as well. Consider the choice confronting a soldier in a foxhole at the outset of a battle. The rational choice for each soldier would be to remain in the

Doing Sociology: The Prisoner's Dilemma Game

A social dilemma exists when behavior that is advantageous for one party leads to disadvantageous outcomes for others. An example is the problem of trust among intimates. One way social scientists have examined cooperative and competitive behaviors is by means of the *prisoner's dilemma game*. The game is based on a problem faced by two suspects held in police custody. Imagine for the moment that you and your partner have been taken to the police station on suspicion of having committed a crime. The police believe both of you are guilty, but they lack sufficient evidence to turn the case over to the district attorney for prosecution. The police officers place you and your partner in separate rooms. Using Figure 4.1 as your point of reference, consider the alternatives that confront you. You may confess or you may maintain your innocence. The police inform you that if both you and your partner remain silent, each of you will get off with 3-year sentences. If both of you confess, you each will serve 7 years. However, should you confess and implicate your partner while your coconspirator maintains his innocence, you will be released but your partner will receive a 15-year prison term. The situation will be reversed should you

maintain your innocence and your partner confesses. As you can gather, the prisoner's dilemma provides a mixed-motive situation in which players must choose between strategies of cooperation and competition.

What would you do under these circumstances? The "don't confess" option is the cooperative one. You show that you trust your partner not to take advantage of the situation by turning state's evidence. But you run the risk that your partner will confess and you will pay a heavy price. The "confess" option is the competitive one. You attempt to improve your situation by betraying your partner. But you also run the risk that your partner will take the same route, ensuring that you both will receive 7-year terms. In brief, what is the best strategy for you individually results in a particularly punishing outcome if you both select it.

Researchers find that what your opponent consistently does in early games influences how you subsequently respond. When your opponent is consistently (and even foolishly) cooperative, you are more likely to employ a competitive strategy in later games. Should your opponent reciprocate a cooperative move while remaining ready to compete if you do not reciprocate with cooperation, you become more inclined to cooperate. On the other hand, competition begets competition (Dixit and Nalebuff, 1991; Poundstone, 1992).

Robert Axelrod (1984) finds that the simplest and most effec-

tive strategy for playing the prisoner's dilemma game is one he calls "tit for tat." You cooperate on the first move. Thereafter you respond immediately and in kind to your partner's behavior, following a policy of strict reciprocity: a stringent eye-for-an-eye justice. The strategy seems to work because it combines four properties: It is nice, retaliatory, forgiving, and clear. It is *nice* because it avoids unnecessary conflict so long as the other party reciprocates. Tit for tat is *retaliatory* because it responds to provocation. When the other party makes an aggressive move, you immediately retaliate; any delay in retaliation would signal that competition can pay. The strategy is *forgiving* because it allows the other party to retreat following retaliation. So, should the other player resume cooperation after undertaking a competitive move, forgiveness results and cooperation can again ensue. Finally, tit for tat is *clear* and predictable. Clarity is essential so that the other party can grasp the consequences of his or her actions and thereby adapt new strategies that will promote long-term cooperation. Yet "tit for tat" does not always work. It is particularly vulnerable to cycles of recrimination that end up hurting both parties through relentless feuding (Kollock, 1993).

Business also has its prisoner's dilemmas. Should a business go for 65 percent of the market and risk a price war with its competitors? Or would it make more sense to go for 40 percent, allowing both sides to make money? More particularly, consider this example: If Pepsi lowers its price to gain market share from Coke, Coke will follow with a price cut. Neither company will gain new customers, but both firms will make considerably less money. Welcome to Individual Decision Making, a popular course at Yale's School of Organization and Management taught by Professor Barry Nalebuff. Nalebuff and his students attempt to design strategies that allow managers to look at a problem from two perspectives: your company's and your competitor's (yours and your coconspirator's perspectives in the crime example). It seems that in business, survival of the fittest and mutual cooperation are not necessarily contradictory but in fact complementary (Koselka, 1993).

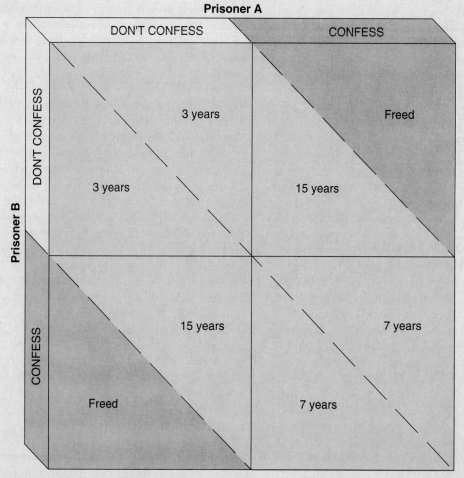

Figure 4.1   THE PRISONER'S DILEMMA GAME
The number in each of the cells shows the number of years each individual would spend in prison.

foxhole to avoid being killed, but if every soldier makes this choice, the battle will most certainly be lost and everyone in the unit will be killed (Kerr, 1983). In many social dilemmas there is a possibility that some other member of the group can and will provide the public good, making one's own contribution unnecessary—that is termed the "free-rider mechanism" (Petersen, 1992; Yamagishi and Cook, 1993).

What social mechanisms are available to influence individuals to act cooperatively rather than selfishly? One answer is social controls that restrict individual actions detrimental to the common good. (Macy, 1993). Government often serves this function by regulating access to various resources (see Chapter 8). Group norms frequently achieve the same end through informal sanctions (Messick et al., 1983). But there are also measures that induce people to act cooperatively and that elicit prosocial behaviors (Lynn and Oldenquist, 1986; Macy, 1990). Among these mechanisms are those that highlight group boundaries and foster a superordinate group identity (Kramer and Brewer, 1984; Brewer and Kramer, 1986). The findings of Muzafer Sherif and his associates (1961), discussed earlier in the chapter, provide a good illustration of circumstances in which the pursuit of common goals lowers barriers to cooperation. Moreover, where individuals are made to feel that they are being rewarded for their cooperative behavior (for instance, sharing in the profits or benefits equally), they are less likely to switch to self-centered, individualistic behavior (Komorita and Barth, 1985; Rapoport, 1988). Groupthink is another strategy, although it is one that can have disastrous outcomes, a matter that we now consider.

GROUPTHINK

In 1961 the Kennedy administration undertook the ill-fated Bay of Pigs invasion of Cuba. Nothing went right for the 1,400 Central Intelligence Agency (CIA)-trained Cuban invaders, most of whom were killed or captured by Castro's forces.

Not only did the invasion solidify Castro's leadership, it consolidated the Cuban-Soviet alliance and led the Soviet leadership to attempt to place nuclear missiles in Cuba. Later, President John Kennedy was to ask: "How could we have been so stupid?" Not only had the President and his advisers overlooked the size and strength of the Castro army, but in many instances they even had failed to seek relevant information.

Social psychologist Irving Janis (1972, 1982, 1989) suggests that the President and his advisers were victims of **groupthink**—a decision-making process found in highly cohesive groups in which the members become so preoccupied with maintaining consensus that their critical faculties are impaired. In groupthink, members share an illusion of invulnerability that leads to overconfidence and a greater willingness to take risks. Its victims believe unquestioningly in the rightness of their cause—in this case, the need to overthrow the communist Castro regime, which the American leaders perceived to be the essence of evil. Members of the group demand conformity and apply pressure to those who express doubts about a proposed course of action; they withhold dissent and exercise self-censorship. In fact, later evidence showed that Secretary of State Dean Rusk and Secretary of Defense Robert McNamara held widely differing assumptions about the invasion plan even though they had participated in the same meetings. Since groupthink entails concurrence-seeking that interferes with an adequate consideration of decision alternatives, it often leads to poor decisions ('t Hart, 1990). Even so, groupthink can sometimes produce a good outcome, just as high-quality decision-making procedures can occasionally result in a poor outcome (McCauley, 1989).

CONFORMITY

Groupthink research testifies to the powerful social pressures that operate in group settings and produce conformity. Although such pressures influence our behavior, we often are unaware of them. In a pioneering study, Muzafer Sherif (1936) demonstrated this point with an optical illusion. If people view a small, fixed spot of light in a darkened room, they perceive it as moving erratically in all directions. However, individuals differ in how far they think the light "moves." Sherif tested subjects alone and found their reference point. He then brought together in group settings people with quite different perceptions and asked them again to view the light and report aloud on their observations. Under these circumstances, their perceptions *converged* toward a group standard. Later, in solitary sessions, they did not return to the standard they had at first evolved but adhered to the standard of the group. Significantly, most subjects reported that they arrived at their assessment independently and that the group had had *no* influence on them.

Sherif presented subjects with an ambiguous situation; Solomon Asch (1952) asked subjects to match lines of the same length from two sets of cards displayed at the front of the room. He instructed the members of nine-person groups to give their answers aloud. However, all but one of the individuals were confederates of Asch, and they unanimously provided incorrect answers on certain trials. Despite the fact that the correct answer was obvious, nearly one-third of all the subjects' judgments contained errors identical with or in the direction of the rigged errors of the majority. Some three-fourths of the subjects conformed on at least one of the trials. Thus Asch demonstrated that some individuals conform to the false consensus of a group even though the consensus is contradicted by the evidence of their own eyes.

The case of Patricia Hearst, the daughter of a wealthy newspaper publisher, provides a good illustration of group conformity. As a 19-year-old student, she was kidnapped in Berkeley, California, in 1974 by members of the Symbionese Liberation Army. Although she loathed her captors, was forced to have sex with all three of the men, and was abused by the women, she did not escape even when they left her alone. She participated in bank robberies, even sometimes driving the get-away van. In her autobiography (1981), Patricia Hearst says she never believed in what the group was doing and that she was not indoctrinated by the Maoist lectures. Rather, she felt that she had been made a member of the team and wanted to perform as a team player. She asserts: "I felt I owed them something, something like loyalty." When individuals become totally dependent upon a group, they may surrender their autonomy and relinquish control over their bodies and destinies. The case of Patricia Hearst highlights the critical part groups play in our lives, particularly those groups from which we derive our identities and in which we embed ourselves in the course of our daily existence. As we will see shortly, such groups may function as total institutions.

□ Formal Organizations

As modern societies have become increasingly complex, so have the requirements of group life. As we noted in Chapter 2, the social organization of traditional societies revolves primarily around kin relations. The division of labor is simple, the people are culturally homogeneous, and there is no formal law. But contemporary societies composed of millions of people can no longer rely entirely on primary group arrangements to accomplish the tasks of social life. Food has to be produced, preserved, and transported over considerable distances to support large urban populations. The residents of large, anonymous communities can no longer count on family members and neighbors to enforce group norms and standards. Children can no longer be educated by the same "natural processes" by which parents teach them to walk and talk. And medical science in alliance with sophisticated technologies provides more effective treatments for illness than folk remedies do. For these and many other tasks, people require groups they can deliberately create for the achievement of specific objectives. Such groups are **formal organizations.**

In recent decades the United States has increasingly become a society of large, semiautonomous, and tightly knit formal organizations. Not only is there big government—extending from local municipal organizations to those of the federal government—but there are also big multinational corporations, big universities, big hospitals, big unions, and big farm organizations. Modern society is emerging as a web of formal organizations that appear, disappear, change, merge, and enter into countless relationships with one another. Although formal organizations have existed for thousands of years, dating back to ancient Mesopotamia, Egypt, and China, only in recent times have their scope and centrality become so pronounced. Not surprisingly, sociologist Robert Presthus (1978) calls modern society "the organizational society."

TYPES OF FORMAL ORGANIZATION

People enter formal organizations for a variety of reasons. Sociologist Amitai Etzioni (1964, 1975) classifies organizations on the basis of these reasons, identifying three major types: voluntary, coercive, and utilitarian. **Voluntary organizations** are associations that members enter and leave freely. Examples include the Parent-Teacher Association (PTA), a coin collectors' club, the League of Women Voters, the Girl Scouts, the local chapter of the National Association for the Advancement of Colored People, the auxiliary of a neighborhood church, and a bowlers' league. Members are not paid for participation. Individuals join voluntary organizations to fill their leisure time, to enjoy the company of like-minded people, to perform some social service, to advance some cause, or to seek self-help through organizations such as Alcoholics Anonymous (Woodard, 1987; Hurley, 1988; Gelman, 1991).

The fact that Americans join and support so many clubs and lodges has impressed foreign observers as one of the striking qualities of the nation's culture. Even in the 1830s, the French writer Count Alexis de Tocqueville noted: "Americans of all ages, all stations in life, and all types of disposition are forever forming associations." When voluntary organizations complete their goals, Americans often refashion them, finding new purposes to validate an enterprise. For example, once vaccines eliminated infantile paralysis, the March of Dimes organization reformulated its goals to embrace new health missions (Shills, 1957). In some cases program failure is essential because the effective solution of the problems the organizations address would eliminate the need for their existence. Skid row rescue missions provide a good illustration of this principle (Rooney, 1980).

People also become members of some organizations—**coercive organizations**—against their will. They may be committed to a mental hospital, sentenced to prison, or drafted into the armed forces. Sociologist Erving Goffman (1961b) has studied life in what he calls *total institutions*—places of residence where individuals are isolated from the rest of society for an appreciable period of time and where behavior is tightly regimented. In these environments the "inmates" or "recruits" are exposed to resocialization experiences that systematically seek to strip away their old roles and identities and fashion new ones. The induction process often includes **mortification.** Individuals are separated from families and friends who provide networks of support for old ways. They are made vulnerable to institutional control and discipline by being deprived of personal items, clothing, and accessories and are provided haircuts, uniforms, and standardized articles that establish an institutional identity. Often the new members are humiliated by being forced to assume demeaning postures, to engage in self-effacing tasks, and to endure insulting epithets (what sociologists term a *degradation ceremony*). These procedures leave individuals psychologically and emotionally receptive to the roles and identities demanded of them by the total institution.

Individuals also enter formal organizations formed for practical reasons—**utilitarian organi-**

zations. Universities, corporations, farm organizations, unions, and government bureaus and agencies are among the organizations people form to accomplish vital everyday tasks. Utilitarian organizations fall between voluntary and coercive organizations: Membership in them is neither entirely voluntary nor entirely compulsory. For example, we may not be compelled to secure employment with a corporation, but if we wish to support ourselves, doing so is an essential element of life.

BUREAUCRACY

So long as organizations are relatively small, they can often function reasonably well on the basis of face-to-face interaction. But if larger organizations are to attain their goals, they must establish formal operating and administrative procedures. Only as they standardize and routinize many of their operations can they function effectively. This requirement is met by a **bureaucracy,** a social structure made up of a hierarchy of statuses and roles that is prescribed by explicit rules and procedures and based on a division of function and authority. Sociologists use the concept in a way that differs sharply from the negative connotations "bureaucracy" has in popular usage. For instance, in everyday life we often employ the term to refer to organizational inefficiency. The bureaucrat is stereotyped as an officious, rule-conscious, responsibility-dodging clerk entangled in red tape and preoccupied with busywork.

Bureaucracy has developed over many centuries in the Western world (Bendix, 1977; Baron, Dobbin, and Jennings, 1986). It grew slowly and erratically during the Middle Ages and after. Only in the twentieth century has it fully flowered in response to the dictates of industrial society. As contemporary organizations have increased in size and complexity, more structural units and divisions have been required. In turn, some mechanism is needed for synchronizing and integrating the various activities. By providing for the performance of tasks on a regular and orderly basis, bureaucracies permit the planning and coordination of these activities in an efficient manner. Additionally, they aim to eliminate all unrelated influences on the behavior of their members so that people act primarily in the organization's interests. At the present time, most large, complex organizations in the United States are organized as bureaucracies.

WEBER'S ANALYSIS OF BUREAUCRACIES

German sociologist Max Weber (1946, 1947) was impressed by the ability of bureaucracies to rationalize and control the process by which people collectively pursue their goals. Although he was concerned about some of the negative consequences of bureaucracy, Weber contended that the needs of mass administration made bureaucracy an essential feature of modern organizational life. Weber dealt with bureaucracy as an *ideal type.* As pointed out in Chapter 1, an ideal type is a concept constructed by sociologists to portray the principal characteristics of a phenomenon. For example, sociologists can abstract common elements from a government agency, the Roman Catholic Church, the Teamsters' Union, IBM, and Yale University and arrive at a model for describing and analyzing organizational arrangements. But the model should not be mistaken for a realistic depiction of how real bureaucracies actually operate in the contemporary world.

The following are the major components of Weber's ideal bureaucracy—a sketch of a completely *rationalized* organization centered on the selection of the most appropriate means available for the achievement of a given goal:

1. Each office or position has clearly defined duties and responsibilities. In this manner, the regular activities of the organization are arranged within a clear-cut division of labor.
2. All offices are organized in a hierarchy of authority that takes the shape of a pyramid. Officials are held accountable to their superi-

"For all his brilliance, we're going to have to replace Trewell. He never quite seems able to reduce his ideas to football analogies."

Drawing by Ed Fisher; © 1991 The New Yorker Magazine, Inc.

ors for subordinates' actions and decisions in addition to their own.

3. All activities are governed by a consistent system of abstract rules and regulations. These rules and regulations define the responsibilities of the various offices and the relationships among them. They ensure the coordination of essential tasks and uniformity in performance regardless of changes in personnel.

4. All offices carry with them qualifications and are filled on the basis of technical competence, not personal considerations. Presumably trained individuals do better jobs than those who gain an office on the basis of family ties, personal friendship, or political favor. Competence is established by certification (for instance, college degrees) or examination (for example, civil service tests).

5. Incumbents do not "own" their offices. Positions remain the property of the organization, and officeholders are supplied with the items they require to perform their work.

6. Employment by the organization is defined as a career. Promotion is based on seniority or merit, or both. After a probationary period, individuals gain the security of tenure and are protected against arbitrary dismissal. In principle, this feature makes officials less susceptible to outside pressures.

7. Administrative decisions, rules, procedures, and activities are recorded in written documents preserved in permanent files.

Weber believed that bureaucracy is an inherent feature of modern capitalism. Yet he was equally insistent that a socialist society could not dispense with the arrangement. Indeed, Weber thought that socialism would see an increase, not a decrease, in bureaucratic structures. While recognizing the limitations of capitalism, he nonetheless felt it presented the best chances for the preservation of individual freedom and creative leadership in a world dominated by formal organizations (Ritzer, 1983). Some sociologists are not this optimistic. They have expressed concern that bureaucracies may pose an inherent challenge to human liberty by turning free people into "cogs" in organizational machines (Blau and Scott, 1962; Samuelson, 1987). Let us take a closer look at some of these matters.

DISADVANTAGES OF BUREAUCRACY

Weber's ideal form of bureaucracy—with its emphasis upon hierarchical order, line of command, and division of labor—proved popular among corporate executives who were schooled in the leadership model they learned in the infantry, on ships, and in the air during World War II. They fashioned bureaucracies built on command and control—a General George S. Patton mode with orders issued from above and followed by "grunts" at the bottom. Yet the Weber model is difficult to realize in practice. A number of forces undermine its operation (Perrow, 1979; Jaffee, 1993). First, human beings do not exist just for organizations. People track all sorts of mud from the rest of their lives with them into bureaucratic arrangements, and they have a great many interests that are independent of the organization. Second, bureaucracies are not immune to social change. When such changes are frequent and rapid, the pat answers supplied by bureaucratic regulations and rules interfere with rational operation. And third, bureaucracies are designed for the "average" person. However, in real life people differ in intelligence, energy, zeal, and dedication, so that they are not in fact interchangeable in the day-to-day functioning of organizations.

It may have occurred to you that Weber's approach to bureaucracy has a functionalist emphasis. He views the various components of his ideal type as a functional response to the requirements of large-scale organization. These properties permit a formal organization to achieve its goals in the fastest, most efficient, and most rational manner. Other social scientists have also pointed out that bureaucracies have disadvantages, or *dysfunctions* (see Chapter 1). There are those like political scientist Richard Rosecrance (1990) who believe that Americans in the post-World War II period came to embrace Weber's bureaucratic society with such a vengeance that our corporations became overstaffed, making the nation uncompetitive in world markets. In many organizations, management specialization—not production or meeting consumer needs—became the way to the top. Consequently, in the mid-1980s more than half of the typical American corporation consisted of workers uninvolved in operations or production. For example, at General Motors, 77.5 percent of the work force was white-collar and salaried; at Mobil Oil, 61.5 percent; at General Electric, 60 percent; and at AT&T, 42 percent. Rosecrance found that the ratio in Japanese corporations was about one-sixth of the American figure. Significantly, whereas Ford had twenty-two levels of management, its Japanese rival Toyota had five levels (Tiger, 1990). In order to become more competitive in the global economy, American firms have undertaken massive restructuring and downsizing (see Chapter 8). Added impetus was provided by the computer and telecommunications revolutions and the explosion of information which caused many companies to rethink their well-defined hierarchical arrangements and to substitute in their stead new structural arrangements, for instance, a network organization—a small hub at the center surrounded by a widely dispersed and elaborate array of resources (Wilke, 1993; Huey, 1994).

Other social scientists note other dysfunctions of bureaucratization. Let us consider a number of these problems.

Trained Incapacity. Social critic Thorstein Veblen (1921) pointed out that bureaucracies encourage their members to rely on established rules and regulations and to apply them in an unimaginative and mechanical fashion—a pattern he called **trained incapacity.** As a result of the socialization provided by organizations, individuals often develop a tunnel vision that limits their ability to respond in new ways when situations change. Government bureaucracies are especially risk-averse because they are caught up in such complex webs of constraint that any change is likely to rouse the ire of important constituencies (Wilson, 1990; 1993). Because of trained incapacity, bureaucracies are often inflexible and inefficient in times of rapid change. For example, for more than a decade the American automobile industry was unresponsive and uncreative in meeting the changing tastes of the American public and in confronting the inroads of foreign competitors in the American market. Its managers continued to build the same large and fuel-inefficient cars by the same manufacturing techniques, despite the superior quality and appeal of the Japanese products. Put another way, in real life bureaucracies lack effective performance appraisal even when people are inadequate or inefficient, contributing to a self-perpetuating organizational mediocrity. The way many bureaucracies respond to crises complicates such problems. Officials often take whatever measure will quickly erase the most visible part of the problem while letting someone else worry about the rest later.

Parkinson's Law. Weber viewed bureaucracy as a mechanism for achieving organizational efficiency. We gain a quite different picture from C. Northcote Parkinson (1962), who has gained renown as the author of **Parkinson's law:** "Work expands so as to fill the time available for its completion." Despite the tongue-in-cheek tone of his writing, Parkinson undertakes to show that "the number of the officials and the quantity of the work are not related to each other." He contends that bureaucracy expands not because of an increasing workload but because officials seek to have additional subordinates hired in order to multiply the number of people under them in the hierarchy. These subordinates in turn create work for one another, while the coordination of their work requires still more officials.

The relentless growth of bureaucracy is reflected in American government. When George Washington was inaugurated as president in 1790, there were 9 executive units and some 1,000 employees. A century later, over 150,000 civilians worked in the Harrison administration, a rate of growth ten times as fast as that of the population. And by 1980 nearly 3 million civil servants were employed by the executive branch. Whereas only 1 of 4,000 Americans were employed by the executive branch in 1790, the figure stood at 1 in 463 in 1891 and less than 1 in 75 by 1990. Of course factors other than those associated with Parkinson's law contributed to the growth in American government, including the expansion of government services. According to Robert Stone, the project director for the 1993 Gore Report (the *National Performance Review* designed to "reinvent government"), "As a rule, virtually any task being done by government[today] is being done by 20 or more agencies" (quoted by Church, 1993:27).

Oligarchy. Organizations, like all other groups, enjoy a formidable capacity for eliciting conformity. As we noted earlier, groups do not just control and dispense rewards and punishments. They also define social reality by structuring our experiences. Given the predominant role organizations have in contemporary life, some observers have expressed concern for the future of democratic institutions. They point out that all too often the needs of organizations take priority over those of individuals (Glassman, Swatos, and Rosen, 1987; Dandeker, 1990). Complicating matters, Robert Michels (1911/1966), a sociologist and friend of Weber, argued that bureaucracies contain a fundamental flaw that makes them undemocratic social arrangements: They invariably lead to oligarchy—the concentration of power in the hands of a few individuals who use their offices to advance their own fortunes and self-interests. He called this tendency the **iron law of**

"Does this mean I'm out of the loop?"

Drawing by Stevenson; © 1991 The New Yorker Magazine, Inc.

oligarchy—"Whoever says organization, says oligarchy" (p. 365).

Michels cites a variety of reasons for the oligarchical tendencies found in formal organizations. First, they have hierarchical structures with authority exercised downward from the top. Even when final authority is vested in the membership, the requirements of leadership and the dictates of overall administration make popular voting and related procedures inconsequential rituals. Second, officials have a great many advantages over their members. They have access to information that is unavailable to others, and they usually possess superior political skills and experience. Additionally, they control a variety of administrative resources, including communication networks, offices, and a treasury that can be used to carry out their official tasks or to ward off challengers. Moreover, they can use the rewards they control to coopt dissidents and rivals. And third, ordinary members tend to be uninterested in assuming leadership responsibilities and are apathetic toward the problems of the organization.

Michels points to the developmental course of European socialist parties and labor unions as evidence in support of his thesis that leaders seldom reflect the democratic aspirations of their organizations. Even so, not all organizations are oligarchic (Breines, 1980; Schwartz, Rosenthal, and Schwartz, 1981). For instance, the International Typographical Union (ITU), composed of typesetters, has maintained a democratic tradition by institutionalizing a "two-party system" (Lipset, Trow, and Coleman, 1956). Union elections are held on a regular basis, with the two parties putting up a complete slate of candidates. Where competing groups are active and legitimate, the rank-and-file have the potential for replacing leaders and introducing new policies. For instance, in 1964 rank-and-file Republicans nominated Barry Goldwater for president over the opposition of the established leadership, and in 1976 a political unknown and outsider, Jimmy Carter, got the Democratic party nomination.

So although the complexity of modern life requires large-scale formal organization, bureaucratic structures have their disadvantages and problems. There are limits to what large hierarchical organizations can accomplish (Stinchcombe, 1990; Wilson, 1990). Yet, as political scientist James Q. Wilson (1967:6) observes, we often lose sight of this fact:

If enough people don't like something, it becomes a problem; if the intellectuals agree with them it becomes a crisis; any crisis must be solved; if it must be solved, then it can be solved—and creating a new organization is the way to do it. If the organization fails to solve the problem (and when the problem is a fundamental one, it will almost surely fail), then the reason is "politics," or "mismanagement," or "incompetent people," or "meddling," or "socialization," or "inertia."

Hence, as Wilson points out, some problems cannot be solved, and some organizational and governmental functions cannot be performed well.

INFORMAL ORGANIZATION

The rules, regulations, procedures, and impersonal relationships prescribed by a bureaucracy only rarely correspond with the realities of organizational life for another reason. Formal organization breeds **informal organization**—interpersonal networks and ties that arise in a formal organization but are not defined or prescribed by it. Based on their common interests and relationships, individuals form primary groups. These informal structures provide means by which people bend and break rules, share "common knowledge," engage in secret behaviors, handle problems, and "cut corners." So work relationships are much more than the lifeless abstractions contained on an organizational chart that outlines the official lines of communication and authority.

The roots of informal organization are embedded within formal organization and are nurtured by the formality of its arrangements. Official rules and regulations must be sufficiently general to cover a great many situations. In applying general rules to a particular situation, people must use their judgment, and so they evolve informal guidelines that provide them with workable solutions. Additionally, in order to avoid bureaucratic "red tape," employees often arrive at informal understandings with one another. Indeed, if formal organization is to operate smoothly, it requires informal organization for interpreting, translating, and supporting its goals and practices. Thus people are tied to the larger group by their membership in primary groups that mediate between them and the formal organization. Further, the impersonality of bureaucratic arrangements distresses many people, and they search for warmth, rapport, and companionship in the work setting through informal relationships.

Factory workers typically evolve their own norms regarding what constitutes a "reasonable" amount of work, and these norms often do not conform with those of management (Roethlisberger and Dickson, 1939; Hamper, 1991). Sociologist Michael Burawoy (1979) studied informal organization among shop workers while working for a year as a machine operator at a large Chicago-area plant. He found that relations on the shop floor were dominated by "making out"—a competitive game the machine operators played by manipulating the rules and regulations governing their work. The workers did not passively conform to the dictates of management or to the technological aspects of their work but actively connived to put in place their own "shop-floor culture." A central theme of the culture revolved about maximizing their payoff from the firm's piecework bonus system while simultaneously holding up high piece rates through restriction of output.

Research has also shown the strong influence of the work group in regulating deviance and theft among individual workers. For instance,

Donald Horning (1970) studied blue-collar theft in a manufacturing plant and concluded that informal norms regulate both the type and the amount of property taken. Employee pilferage was a group-supported activity, even though the actual taking of property took place alone or in secret. And Gerald Mars (1974) reported in his study of dockworkers that materials in shipment were stolen according to the group-defined "value of the boat." In order for theft to go undetected by dock authorities, all members of a work group had to approve of and cooperate in the activity. Overall, American companies lose an estimated $50 billion a year to employee theft of cash or merchandise (Henry, 1990). In brief, formal organizations do not work strictly by the book.

ALTERNATIVE PERSPECTIVES

Until the past decade or so, Weber's approach to bureaucracy dominated American sociology. In large measure sociologists focused their attention on organizations as abstract social structures while often neglecting the behavior of the individuals who comprise them. Indeed, sociologists Peter M. Blau and Richard A. Schoenherr (1971:viii and 357) championed such an approach, observing:

Formal organizations, as well as other social structures, exhibit regularities that can be analyzed in their own right, independent of any knowledge about the individual behavior of their members . . . it is time that we "push men[and women] out" to place proper emphasis on the study of social structure in sociology.

Many sociologists studied formal organizations without noticing the processes by which social structures are produced and reproduced in the course of people's daily interactions. But much has changed in recent years as sociologists from differing perspectives have looked at the ways in which organizational reality is generated through the actions of people and groups of people (Benson, 1977; Zey-Ferrell, 1981; Hickson, 1987;

Romanelli, 1991). We will consider three of these approaches: the conflict, the symbolic interactionist, and the ethnomethodological.

The Conflict Perspective. Conflict theorists contend that organizational goals reflect the priorities of those who occupy the top positions. Viewed in this manner, organizations are not neutral social structures but arenas for conflicting interests in which the social issues and power relations of society are played out (Collins, 1975; Dandeker, 1990). Marxist social scientists have followed in the tradition of Karl Marx (1970), who saw bureaucracy as a manifestation of the centralizing tendencies of capitalism and an instrument of class domination. They analyze organizations within the context of the broader inequalities that operate within society and find that the distribution of power and the allocation of rewards within them mirror the larger society's class structure (Edwards, 1979; Burawoy, 1983).

In *Capital* (1867/1906) Marx claimed that the modern factory is a despotic regime made necessary by the competitive pressures of the market. These pressures compel technological innovation and work intensification, all of which rest on the availability of workers, who in order to survive must sell their labor power to capitalist employers. But as we will see in Chapters 5 and 7, Marx also viewed the factory as the crucible of revolution. The domination of the working class by capital would turn into its opposite, "the revolt of the working class."

More recent studies by Marxist social scientists suggest that bureaucratic mechanisms arose as much from the need of capitalists to impose labor discipline as from abstract notions of efficiency and rationality (Friedman, 1977; Edwards, 1978). Stephen Marglin (1974) shows that nineteenth-century British entrepreneurs established the hierarchical arrangement to guarantee themselves a central role in the production process. Katherine Stone (1974) finds that turn-of-the-century steel magnates established top-to-bottom chains of command and job ladders to isolate individual workers, break the power of skilled artisans, and combat growing labor militancy.

Marx thought that the bureaucratic structures inherited from capitalism would have to be altered and even eliminated by a revolutionary working class. He wrote (1867/1906:64): "The working class cannot simply lay hold of the ready-made state machinery and wield it for its own purposes." Instead, the workers would have to create a transitional bureaucracy that was representative of and responsive to their needs and goals. Marx chose as his model the short-lived Paris Commune of 1871. By establishing the conditions for the direct participation of workers in decision-making processes, the commune democratized the bureaucracy. However, as Marx's writings were interpreted and reformulated by Lenin and implemented by Stalin, the primary elements of Bolshevik policy in the former Soviet Union centered on the expansion of bureaucratic offices and the dominance of the state apparatus by a "new class" of Communist party officials (Djilas, 1957).

The Symbolic Interactionist Perspective. Critics of the structural or Weberian approach to organizations point out that people, not organizations, have motivations and goals. An organization's officers and managers can offer only incentives they believe will motivate employees to conform to goals that they define as paramount (Zey-Ferrell, 1981). Thus critics, particularly symbolic interactionists, contend that human beings are not spongelike, malleable organisms who passively absorb and adapt to their environments. Instead, they portray people as active agents who shape and mold their destinies and continually fashion new joint actions based on their definitions of the situation (Blumer, 1969). Organizational constraints only provide the framework within which people forge their actions as they appraise, choose, and decide on alternatives. In sum, symbolic interactionists portray organizational behavior as generated out of individual meanings that people translate into social realities (see Chapter 1).

And rather than depicting organizations in static terms, symbolic interactionists emphasize their dynamic and changing nature. This approach was taken by Anselm Strauss and his colleagues (1964) in their study of organizational behavior in two Chicago-area psychiatric hospitals. They treated a formal organization as a **negotiated order**—the fluid, ongoing understandings and agreements people reach as they go about their daily activities. To outsiders, the hospitals appeared to be tightly structured organizations that functioned in accordance with strict bureaucratic rules and regulations. However, the researchers found that in practice the hospitals operated quite differently. The organizations were simply too complex for a single set of rules to hold or for any one person to know all the rules, much less in exactly what situations they applied, to whom, in what degree, and for how long. Matters were complicated by constant turnover in staff and patients. Not only did people differ in their goals, they also differed in their conceptions of the nature, causes, and treatment of mental illness. Given these circumstances, most house rules served more as general understandings than as commands, and they were stretched, argued, reinterpreted, ignored, or applied as situations dictated. Individuals reached agreements with one another that provided a consensus for a time, but the understandings were subject to periodic modification and revision.

Chaos did not reign in the hospitals because the negotiations followed patterns that permitted some degree of predictability. Even so, Strauss and his colleagues concluded:

A skeptic, thinking in terms of relatively permanent or slowly changing structure, might remark that the hospital remains the same from week to week, that only the working arrangements change. . . . Practically, we maintain, no one knows what the hospital "is" on any given day unless he has a comprehensive grasp of the combinations of rules, policies, agreements, understandings, pacts, contracts, and other working arrangements that currently obtain. In a pragmatic sense, that combination "is" the hospital at the moment, its social order. Any changes that impinge upon this order—whether ordinary changes, like introduction of a new staff member or a betrayed contract or unusual changes, like the introduction of new technology or new theory—will necessitate renegotiation or reappraisal, with consequent changes in the organizational order. There will be a new order, not merely the re-establishment of an old order or reinstitution of a previous equilibrium. It is necessary continually to reconstitute the bases of concerted action, of social order. (1964:312)

Whether or not the negotiated order model of organizations is applicable to other kinds of settings is a matter for future research. But negotiations apparently do occur in many kinds of organizations, including factories, symphony orchestras, and political organizations (Lauer and Handel, 1983; Miner, 1991).

The Ethnomethodological Perspective. Since the 1940s, sociologist Harold Garfinkel and a number of his colleagues and students have undertaken to illuminate the commonplace, taken-for-granted activities that constitute our daily experience by an approach they call **ethnomethodology.** *Ethno,* borrowed from the Greek, means "people" or "folk," while *methodology* refers to procedures by which something is done or analyzed. Thus in its most literal sense "ethnomethodology" refers to the procedures—the rules and activities—that people employ in making social life and society intelligible to themselves and others (Garfinkel, 1974). Ethnomethodologists study the background understandings that constitute the "stuff" out of which stable social interaction emerges. And they investigate how people go about creating and sustaining for one another the *presumption* that there is an external social reality and order (Hilbert, 1992).

Sociologist Don H. Zimmerman (1971) applied the ethnomethodological perspective in examining the day-by-day operations of a large-scale organization, a public welfare agency. He studied how the receptionists went about processing applicants for public assistance and apportioning them among caseworkers. A cursory inspection suggested that the receptionists were governed by the "first-come, first-served" rule. But a deeper inspection revealed that they were also concerned with giving the *appearance* that applicants moved through the system in a sequential and orderly manner.

In order to do this, the receptionists had to deviate from the first-come, first-served rule. They did so on the basis of tacit understandings regarding the requirements of their work—certain assumptions regarding "what everyone who works here knows." For instance, receptionists would suspend the rule and switch the order of applicants when clients said they had a doctor's appointment or had to attend to some other urgent matter. Likewise, they would allow some applicants to request a particular social worker. And they routinely assigned "difficult" and "troublesome" applicants to a caseworker known to be good at handling "special problems."

Zimmerman concludes that as we go about our activities, we continually develop and interpret what a rule means. We do not mechanically follow rules like programmed robots. Instead, we invoke rationalizations that satisfy us and others that what we are doing constitutes "reasonable" compliance with a rule. In this sense, bureaucratic rules and regulations serve as a commonsense method by which we account for our behavior. We see and report patterning and stability in our lives because we go about "structuring" structure, collaboratively creating meanings and understandings of one another's activities. In grasping bureaucratic behavior, then, the relevant question is not What is the rule? but What has to be done? In practice, a rule may be employed or ignored depending on the context. But more importantly, it affords the members of an organization a convenient means to portray, explain, and justify their actions.

A Synthesis of Alternative Perspectives. Sociologist Charles Perrow (1982) joins threads from the conflict, symbolic interactionist, and ethnomethodological perspectives to argue that the notion of bureaucratic rationality masks the true nature of organizational life. He claims that our world is more "loosely coupled"—characterized by a substantial measure of redundancy, slack, and waste—than structural theories allow. Perrow says that organizations do not have goals, only constraints. Take the Sanitation Department of New York City:

To say its goal is to pick up the garbage—even to pick it up frequently, pick it all up, and do it cheaply—does not tell us much. These are not goals of that department but merely loose constraints under which those who use the organization must operate, and these are not really any more important than the following constraints: The cushy top jobs in the department can be used to pay off political debts; some groups can use the Sanitation Department as an assured source of employment and keep others out; upper management can use its positions as political jumping-off places or training spots; equipment manufacturers use it as an easy mark for shoddy goods; and, finally, the workers are entitled to use it as a source of job security and pensions and an easy way of making a living. (p. 687)

Perrow contends that private profit-making organizations are not much different. Lockheed has been described as a pension plan that makes missiles and planes on the side so that its pension plan can be funded. Steel plants are closed even though they make a respectable profit because they are worth more as tax writeoffs. The goal of making steel or even a profit does not pose a significant obstacle. Countless other organizations continue to exist even though they fail to provide decent mail service, prepare students for careers, or offer acceptable medical care. But should the organizations fail to satisfy some special-interest group that lives off them, then the consequences are defined as a major social problem.

Perrow concludes:

Do organizations have goals, then, in the rational sense of organizational theory? I do not think so. In fact, when an executive says, "This is our goal," chances are that he is looking at what the organization happens to be doing at the time and saying, "Since we are all very rational here,

and we are doing this, this must be our goal." Organizations, in this sense, run backward: The deed is father to the thought, not the other way around. (p. 687)

Perrow next links the conflict perspective to his analysis by arguing that social efforts at giving accounts and attributing rationality to organizations serve elites much more than they serve other people. These efforts create a world in which organizational hierarchy, technological requirements, and profit-making motives become legitimized.

HUMANIZING BUREAUCRACIES

Since large organizations play such a critical part in our daily lives, it may be well to conclude the chapter by asking, "Can we make bureaucracies more humane instruments for modern living?" If we value freedom and independence—if we are disturbed by the conformity of attitudes, values, and behavior that bureaucracies often induce—then we may wish to set up conditions that foster uniqueness, self-direction, and human dignity. Although affording no panaceas, a number of programs have been proposed that allow individuals greater range for developing their full capacities and potential in the context of organizational life. Let us briefly consider a number of these.

Employee Participation. About the same time that Japanese manufacturers vigorously entered American markets, American business leaders began a desperate search for remedies to try to breathe new life and competitive fire into their companies. Many became enamored with the highly touted fad known as "quality circles"—also called "participative management" and "working smarter"—an arrangement where a group of up to a dozen workers and one or two managers from the same department meet together on a regular basis to figure out ways of getting along better with each other, making work easier, raising output, and improving the quality of their products. Some 6,000 American companies, including General Motors, International Business Machines Corporation, and American Telephone and Telegraph, have instituted work reform programs at one time or another. In some cases workers are participating in high-level decisions dealing with how work should be organized, work hours, quality standards, and the hiring of subcontractors.

Although a good many companies have adopted employee participation programs, not all firms like them. A University of Michigan survey found that about 75 percent of the programs begun in the early 1980s failed (Saporito, 1986). Many of the programs were established for their publicity value or because managers wanted their employees to believe they were being consulted even though no real sharing of decision-making power actually occurred (Grenier, 1988). Indeed, a Gallup survey found that only 14 percent of corporate employees who worked for firms with quality-improvement and employee participation programs felt their companies gave them a chance to participate in decisions (Bennett, 1990). And few workers participate in their companies' most important decisions, such as product choice, plant location, and investment; the concept of participative management is typically confined to the shop floor and is not permitted to creep higher. Conflict theorists contend that workers win gains only through aggressiveness and that the relationship between management and labor is inherently adversarial. They claim that worker participation programs are simply cosmetic efforts that mask corporate attempts to scrap collective bargaining obligations. And union officials have been distrustful of quality circles because they fear that the circles will assume some of their functions as workers' representatives.

Proponents of the programs say that where management and workers are committed to them, absenteeism, tardiness, grievances, strikes, and labor costs are reduced. Moreover, product quality improves and pilferage lessens. For instance, General Motors plants that have the most intensive programs have better performance than automotive plants that lack the programs. Given these benefits, corporations continue to explore modified and revamped programs that center upon employee participation. One approach entails "self-managed teams," an arrangement in which workers largely operate without bosses. Employees set their own work schedules, prepare their own budgets, and receive group bonuses on the basis of the team's productivity. Managers, termed "coaches," function as advisors (Selz, 1994). Another approach builds on self-managing teams by breaking a firm into its major processes and then creating teams to perform an entire process (for instance, product development or sales generation). A company is limited to three or four layers of management between the chief executive officer and the multidisciplinary staffers who implement the process (Byrne, 1993).

Overall, new management strategies over the past decade have emphasized a lessening of hierarchy and authoritarianism and an increase in worker participation in workplace decision-making. They mark a departure from the theories of Frederick Winslow Taylor, which had dominated management philosophies since the 1920s. Taylor's system of "scientific management" held that production could be improved by rational, technology-centered organization and that workers could be pacified by providing them with adequate training and pay. But the changes should not be overestimated. When managers must make a tough decision, they often revert to the direct, authoritarian mode.

Small Work Groups. Some corporate officials find that small working groups are more productive for Americans than attempting to adopt Japanese management styles that depend on the Japanese worker's intense company loyalty. The approach appears highly adaptable within the computer industry, where small groups, given great freedom, can react quickly to abrupt technological change. Unlike other industries, where change is gradual, computer firms must regularly come up with new products or enhancements of the old, and at constantly lower prices.

Apple Computer turned to small groups to develop its Lisa and Macintosh computers. And even giant IBM has recognized the need for small groups, undertaking to reorganize itself into more autonomous operating units. IBM found that centralized organization interfered with innovation. One virtue of the small-group approach is that responsibility is lodged with the employees doing the actual work. And small groups can focus their energies on a single goal, foster creativity, and reward employees commensurate with their contributions.

Employee Ownership Plans. By 1990 nearly 10,000 companies in the United States shared some measure of ownership with more than 10 million employees. Workers owned the majority of the stock in some 1,000 companies, but the trend toward employee ownership has since slowed. Until recently, most employee ownership plans were management vehicles for sharing a piece of the pie and increasing worker productivity without fundamentally altering a company's structure. But newer arrangements entail employ-

ees actually taking over a firm. Many of the companies, such as Hyatt Clark Industries, Weirton Steel, and Rath Packing Company, were unprofitable, and the buyouts were a last resort to save a business and jobs for workers.

In many cases employee ownership has changed the way companies operate, including their labor-management relationships (Klein, 1987; Blasi, 1988). Greater employee initiative in the workplace has been found to cut costs. But much depends on a firm's profitability. When a company becomes profitable, differences tend to get smoothed over quickly. But when a firm continues to lose money, dissatisfaction mounts and difficulties deepen. For instance, the men and women at Weirton Steel have found that ownership does not always translate into power. They have taken pay cuts, accepted layoffs, and acquiesced as management spent $550 million to revamp the company's mill. After years of butting heads with management, the workers launched a battle in 1993 to gain actual control of the firm (Baker, 1993). So employee ownership does not guarantee labor peace.

Summary

1. Groups are not tangible things that have actual substance in the real world. Rather, they are products of social definitions—sets of shared ideas. As such they constitute constructed realities. We make groups real by treating them as if they are real, a clear application of the Thomas theorem.

2. Primary groups involve two or more people who enjoy direct, intimate, cohesive relationships. Expressive ties predominate in primary groups. Secondary groups entail two or more people who are involved in impersonal, touch-and-go relationships. Instrumental ties

predominate in secondary groups. Primary groups are fundamental to both us and society: They are critical to the socialization process; they provide settings in which most of our personal needs are met; and they are powerful instruments for social control.

3. The concepts of in-group and out-group highlight the importance of boundaries—social demarcation lines that tell us where interaction begins and ends. To one degree or another, a group's boundaries "encapsulate" people in a social membrane so that the focus and flow of their actions are internally con-

tained. Whatever their source, social boundaries face in two directions. They prevent outsiders from entering a group's sphere, and they keep insiders within the group's sphere so that they do not entertain rival possibilities for social interaction.

4. Reference groups provide the models we use for appraising and shaping our attitudes, feelings, and actions. A reference group may or may not be our membership group. We may think of a reference group as a base that we use for viewing the world, a source of psychological identification. It provides both normative and comparative functions.

5. The size of a group is of considerable importance because it influences the nature of our interaction. The smaller the group, the more opportunities we have to get to know other people well and to establish close ties with them. Emotions and feelings tend to assume a larger part in dyads than in larger groups. The addition of a third member to a group—forming a triad—fundamentally alters a social situation. In this arrangement, one person may be placed in the role of an outsider.

6. In group settings some members usually exert more influence than others. We call these individuals leaders. Two types of leadership roles tend to evolve in small groups: a task specialist and a social-emotional specialist. Leaders differ in their styles for exercising influence. Some follow an authoritarian style, others a democratic style, and still others a laissez-faire style.

7. When individuals work in groups, they work less hard than they do when working individually, a process termed social loafing. Presumably people slack off in groups because they feel they are not achieving their fair share of credit or because they think that in a crowd they can get away with less work.

8. In group settings, individuals may become victims of groupthink. Group members may share an illusion of invulnerability that leads to overconfidence and a greater willingness to take risks. Members of the group demand conformity and apply pressure to those who express doubts about a proposed course of action.

9. Groups bring powerful pressures to bear that produce conformity among their members. Although such pressures influence our behavior, we often are unaware of them. Solomon Asch shows that some individuals will conform to the false consensus of a group even though the consensus is contradicted by the evidence of their own eyes.

10. For a good many tasks within modern societies, people require groups they can deliberately create for the achievement of specific goals. These groups are formal organizations. People enter formal organizations for a good many reasons. Amitai Etzioni classifies organizations on this basis by identifying three types: voluntary, coercive, and utilitarian.

11. So long as organizations are relatively small, they can often function reasonably well on the basis of face-to-face interaction. If larger organizations are to attain their goals, they must establish formal operating and administrative procedures. This requirement is met by a bureaucracy, a social structure made up of a hierarchy of statuses and roles that is prescribed by explicit rules and procedures and based on a division of function and authority.

12. Max Weber approached bureaucracy as an ideal type. He sketched the following characteristics of a completely rationalized organization centered on the selection of the most appropriate means available for the achievement of a given goal: Each office has clearly defined duties; all offices are organized in a hierarchy of authority; all activities are governed by a system of rules; all offices carry with them qualifications; incumbents do not

own their positions; employment by the organization is defined as a career; and administrative decisions are recorded in written documents.

13. Bureaucracies also have disadvantages and limitations. These include the principle of trained incapacity, Parkinson's law, and the iron law of oligarchy. There are limits to what large hierarchical organizations can accomplish. The rules, regulations, procedures, and impersonal relationships prescribed by a bureaucracy only rarely correspond with the realities of organizational life.

14. Formal organization breeds informal organization. The roots of informal organization are embedded within formal organization and are nurtured by the formality of its arrangements. If formal organization is to operate smoothly, it requires informal organization for interpreting, translating, and supporting its goals and practices. People are tied to the larger group by their membership in primary groups that mediate between them and the formal organization.

15. Until the past decade or so, Weber's approach to bureaucracy dominated American sociology. Sociologists focused on organizations as abstract social structures while neglecting the behavior of the individuals who comprise them. But much has changed in recent years as sociologists from differing perspectives—particularly the conflict, symbolic interactionist, and ethnomethodological approaches—looked at the ways by which organizational reality is generated through the actions of people and groups of people.

16. Since large organizations play such an important role in our lives, we might ask how they can be made more humane. Among such programs are those that allow employee participation, small work groups, and employee ownership.

Glossary

bureaucracy A social structure made up of a hierarchy of statuses and roles that is prescribed by explicit rules and procedures and based on a division of function and authority.

coercive organization A formal organization that people become members of against their will.

dyad A two-member group.

ethnomethodology Procedures—the rules and activities—that people employ in making social life and society intelligible to themselves and others.

expressive ties Social links formed when we emotionally invest ourselves in and commit ourselves to other people.

formal organization A group people deliberately form for the achievement of specific objectives.

group Two or more people who share a feeling of unity and who are bound together in relatively stable patterns of social interaction.

groupthink A decision-making process found in highly cohesive groups in which the members become so preoccupied with maintaining group consensus that their critical faculties are impaired.

informal organization Interpersonal networks and ties that arise in a formal organization but are not defined or prescribed by it.

in-group A group with which we identify and to which we belong.

instrumental ties Social links formed when we cooperate with other people to achieve some goal.

iron law of oligarchy The principle that says that bureaucracies invariably lead to the concentration of power in the hands of a few individuals who use their offices to advance their own fortunes and self-interests.

mortification   A procedure in which rituals employed by coercive organizations render individuals vulnerable to institutional control, discipline, and resocialization.

negotiated order   The fluid, ongoing understanding and agreements people reach as they go about their daily activities.

out-group   A group with which we do not identify and to which we do not belong.

Parkinson's law   The principle that states that work expands so as to fill the time available for its completion.

primary group   Two or more people who enjoy a direct, intimate, cohesive relationship with one another.

reference group   A social unit we use for appraising and shaping our attitudes, feelings, and actions.

relationship   An association that lasts long enough for two people to become linked together by a relatively stable set of expectations.

relative deprivation   Discontent associated with the gap between what we have and what we believe we should have.

secondary group   Two or more people who are involved in an impersonal relationship and have come together for a specific, practical purpose.

social dilemma   A situation in which members of a group are faced with a conflict between maximizing their personal interests and maximizing the collective welfare.

social-emotional specialist   A leadership role that focuses on overcoming interpersonal problems in a group, defusing tension, and promoting solidarity.

social loafing   The process in which individuals work less hard when working in groups than they do when working individually.

task specialist   A leadership role that focuses on appraising the problem at hand and organizing people's activity to deal with it.

trained incapacity   The term Thorstein Veblen applied to the tendency within bureaucracies for members to rely on established rules and regulations and to apply them in an unimaginative and mechanical fashion.

triad   A three-member group.

utilitarian organization   A formal organization set up to achieve practical ends.

voluntary organization   A formal organization that people enter and leave freely.

Chapter 5

DEVIANCE

Most of us experience everyday life as having a good deal of order and regularity to it. Our interaction seems relatively patterned, producing flowing currents of activity that bind us within the larger social enterprise. Indeed, if we are to live with one another in a group environment, it is essential that we integrate and coordinate our actions. Whatever we want—food, clothing, sex, fame, football, a job, an education, or companionship—we must get it by working with and through other people. We must take up our positions in complex and organized groups and institutions—families, political parties, corporations, schools, churches, and ball teams (Cohen, 1966).

Clearly the work of the world gets done only as the actions of a great many people are fitted together. But if people are to fit their actions together, they must have common understandings about who is supposed to do what and when they are to do it. Some understandings may seem "better" than others in that they get the job done more effectively and efficiently. But the first requirement for organized social life is that there be some understandings, however arbitrary they may seem (Cohen, 1966). As we pointed out in Chapter 2, such understandings take the form of social expectations that are embedded in norms. Without norms for governing behavior, even interaction in a clique or family would be impossible. We would lack guideposts telling us what is permissible and what constitutes the outer limits of allowable behavior. If we lacked norms, interaction would be a real problem because we would never know what others might do (Sagarin, 1975).

Yet there is more to the story of norms (see Chapter 8). Norms have teeth, and teeth that can bite. Rewards and penalties are associated with them. In modern societies, the *state* is the mechanism by which a good many norms—*laws*—are enforced (see Chapter 8). Laws are not neutral: They tend to favor some group's interests, and they embody some group's preferred values. All this brings us to a consideration of deviance.

☐ The Nature of Deviance

In all societies the behavior of some people at times goes beyond that permitted by the norms. Norms only tell us what we are supposed to do or what we are not supposed to do; they do not tell us what people *actually* do. And what some of us actually do very often runs counter to what other people judge to be acceptable behavior. In brief, social life is characterized not only by conformity but by deviance. **Deviance** is behavior that a considerable number of people in a society view as reprehensible and beyond the limits of tolerance. We typically view behavior as deviant to the extent to which it is negatively valued and provokes hostile reactions.

SOCIAL PROPERTIES OF DEVIANCE

As viewed by sociologists, deviance is not a property *inherent* in certain forms of behavior (Erikson, 1962; Becker, 1963; Lemert, 1972); it is a property *conferred* upon particular behaviors by social definitions. In the course of their daily lives, people make judgments regarding the desirability or undesirability of this or that behavior. They then translate their judgments into favorable or unfavorable consequences for those who engage in the behavior. In this sense, then, deviance is what people say it is. You will find this idea clarified by reading and reflecting upon the material in the box dealing with the social construction of deviance. Then resume your consideration of deviance with the discussion below.

The Relativity of Deviance. Which acts are defined as deviant vary greatly from time to time, place to place, and group to group. For example, when ordinary people break into tombs, they are labeled looters. When archeologists break into tombs, they are hailed as scientists advancing the frontiers of knowledge. Yet in both cases burial sites are disturbed and items are carted away. For their part, Native Americans (Indians) contend that the activities of looters and archeologists are indistinguishable because both cases constitute religious and cultural sacrilege. Indeed, scientists and Native Americans differ sharply on whether deceased Indians are suitable objects for study and display. Archeologists say that even the crudest artifacts reveal much about early economic life, commerce, social organization, and religion. The pollen on buried objects yields insights about vegetation and climate, and skeletal remains tell volumes about health and disease. Such reasoning is incomprehensible to many Native Americans. "When an archeologist digs and he shakes the very roots of a living soul, it is wrong," says Maria Pearson, a Yankton-Sioux activist. "It is wrong for anybody to go into my grandmother's grave, my great-grandfather's grave, my great-great-grandfather's grave, because through all of this comes the mental security of my children, my grandchildren, and my great-grand-children" (quoted by Cowley, 1989:60). A federal law (the Native American Graves Protection and Repatriation Act) requires some 5,000 federally funded institutions and government agencies to return Native American skeletons, funerary and sacred objects, and items of profound cultural importance to American Indian tribes and native Hawaiians. However, not all Native American peoples plan to rebury all the returned material; many have opened or are planning to open museums of their own and much of it (aside from sacred objects) will be available to academic researchers (Morell, 1994).

These illustrations highlight the point that acts are not inherently deviant. A social audience decides whether or not some behavior is deviant. This is not to say that the acts we label homicide, stealing, sexual perversion, mental disturbance, alcoholism, gambling, and child abuse would not occur without social definitions. Rather, the critical issue is how people define behavior and the specific ways in which they react to it.

The Power to Make Definitions Stick. When people differ regarding their definitions of what is and is not deviant behavior, it becomes a question

Doing Sociology: The Social Construction of Deviance

To set the stage on the first day of class for their courses in introductory sociology and in the sociology of deviance, Professors John R. Brouillette and Ronny E. Turner of Colorado State University (1992) undertake an exercise that demonstrates the social construction of deviance. After outlining course procedures and content, one of the professor calls on a student to provide a small amount of saliva in a sterilized spoon. Somewhat embarrassed, the student provides the saliva. The professor thanks her and then he gives a brief lecture on the benefits and functions of saliva for the human body; for instance, saliva moistens the linings of the mouth and throat, aids in the prevention of infection, and facilitates digestion.

After discussing the benefits of saliva, the professor offers the student who initially provided the valuable body fluid an opportunity to take the spoon and return the saliva to her mouth. Invariably the student declines. The instructor comments that he has difficulty comprehending why someone would reject such a valued substance in the age of recycling. He then offers the contents of the spoon to a classmate. Some students respond by making gagging sounds. The professor expresses "surprise" since students often share a can of soda pop which also involves the sharing of saliva. The instructor then comments:

Not only that, but some students engage in a formerly criminal action, French kissing, which most couples consider intimate, loving, and appropriate. Actually, two people place their lips together, intermingle their tongues, and exchange or mix their saliva. Is this deviant? Certainly not! It's sexy . . . cool . . . and a "turn on."

Well, if you believe that's cool, picture this. A couple are parked at the top of Lookout Mountain, passionately embracing each other. The woman pulls a spoon from her purse, which she uses to

of which individuals and groups will make their definitions prevail. For example, in 1776 George Washington was labeled a traitor by the British. Twenty years later, he was the first president of the United States and beloved as "the father of his country." In the 1940s Menachem Begin was portrayed by British authorities in Palestine as a Zionist terrorist (he was the leader of the Irgun Zvai Leumi, the underground military organization so instrumental in forcing the British to give up their Palestinian mandate). Thirty years later, he was the popular head of the state of Israel. Had the Americans and Israelis lost their wars for independence, very likely both Washington and Begin would have been executed—or, at the very least, given long prison terms. In considerable measure, who is defined as deviant and what is defined as deviance depend on who is doing the defining and who has the power to make the definitions stick.

Some groups such as gays, lesbians, the disabled, and welfare mothers have entered the political arena and successfully challenged official definitions that portray them as "social problems." Indeed, individuals stigmatized and victimized by prevailing social definitions see their circumstances quite differently from those who enjoy power and enforce norms that embody their moral codes. We need only remind ourselves that not too long ago in colonial times the political and religious "establishment" of Salem, Massachusetts, was preoccupied with witches and

scrape some saliva from her mouth. To soothe her lover's raging hormones and to show her love for him, she offers him the spoon. Do you think it will turn him on to a point of no return? Probably not, unless he's into that kind of thing. Most likely the man would consider this a gross, disgusting offer and terminate the date much earlier than planned.

The professor next engages class members in a discussion of the difference between "saliva" and "spit." In the course of the discussion he introduces the students to the sociological concept of the social construction of reality:

There *is* a difference between spit and saliva. But no chemist will ever find it because the difference is not chemical. It's social. If people believe that spit and saliva are different, they are different. You had better know the difference or suffer the consequences. Spit is saliva in the wrong place or under the wrong circumstances. Nothing inherent in the mouth moisture itself necessitates a particular distinction between spit and saliva; no inherent change occurs. The difference is socially constructed. We social beings have drawn lines around behavior to demarcate deviant from normal, acceptable behavior.

The sociology professor then points out that "spit" and "saliva" are defined differently depending on who is engaging in a given behavior and on the social context in which the behavior occurs. Mothers are seen wiping dirt from an infant's face with moisture from the mouth. Jesus and other religious leaders reportedly used their "sputum" to cure the blind and the infirm. Moreover, males spit incessantly during athletic contests, a behavior typically deemed "inappropriate" for female athletes. For example, male marathon runners in the 1984 Summer Olympic Games were observed to spit constantly, whereas Joan Benoit, the winner of the gold medal in the women's marathon, apparently did not spit even once. In sum, deviance is *socially* defined behavior.

---

actively hunted them down. Some 200,000 to 500,000 people (85 percent of them women) were executed as witches in Europe between the fourteenth and seventeenth centuries (Ben-Yehuda, 1980).

Redefinitions of Normality and Deviancy. Within recent years, many behaviors Americans have traditionally judged to be deviant have undergone redefinition. Not too long ago compulsive gambling, alcoholism, drug addiction, and even many forms of mental illness were defined as evil and sinful. While such notions still persist, the view has increasingly gained currency that these behaviors are "medical problems." The "disorders" are considered "illnesses" analogous to physical ailments such as ulcers, diabetes, and high blood pressure. Their sufferers are placed in "hospitals" where they are called "patients" and given "treatment" by "physicians."

Some people, including sociologist and U.S. Senator Daniel Patrick Moynihan, believe that Americans are "defining deviancy down" so as to explain away and make "normal" what "a more civilized, ordered and healthy society" would and did label "deviant" not too many years ago. For example, Moynihan contends Americans have become progressively accustomed and hardened to levels of criminality that they once would have deemed intolerable. Homicide has come to be seen as merely a part of a social landscape that is as ineradicable as auto accidents. Likewise, the incidence of single parenthood has more than tripled since 1960 so that nearly 30 percent of all American youngsters are now born to unmarried mothers. According to Moynihan and others, fatherlessness and family breakup stand out as key variables associated with poverty, welfare dependency, crime, and other "social pathologies." Yet unmarried parenthood has been systematically redefined as merely another "lifestyle choice."

At the same time, many areas of behavior hitherto deemed benign have had their threshold radically "redefined upward." Old concerns like child abuse and family violence have become amplified in recent years. Simultaneously new areas of deviancy—including date rape and politically incorrect speech—have been discovered (Krauthammer, 1993). And smoking—not too long ago deemed an innocent vice—is coming under progressive regulation and even prohibition (smokers are now often depicted as mean-spirited or weak-willed people who insist on a "right" to pollute the air and puff their way to an early grave).

A Zone of Permissible Variation. In our daily lives we typically find that norms are not so much a point or a line as a zone (Williams, 1970). Even rather specific and strongly supported norms allow a zone of permissible variation. In actual practice, norms provide for bands of permissible behavior that may nonetheless depart from the strict letter of the law. For instance, professors are expected to conduct their classes with dignity and decorum. Yet one professor at a large midwestern university is known to stand on his desk or sit on a desk lectern in the course of the class period. Clearly, American culture does not define desks as appropriate for standing on or lecterns for sitting on. It is not surprising, therefore, that most students snicker and giggle when the professor steps up on the desk for his first lecture. And more than one student has wondered aloud what kind of "weirdo" is teaching the course. However, since the professor communicates well and is a recognized authority in his field, the vast majority of

students are quickly won over to his antics. In their course evaluations, the students usually comment that they were initially dismayed by the professor's informality but soon discovered that this style was an effective teaching technique. Hence a norm usually allows for *variant* behavior, new or at least different behavior that falls within the borders of the acceptable (Merton, 1968).

In sum, no behavior is deviant in itself; deviance is a matter of social definition. The same behavior may be viewed as deviant by one group but not by another. Further, much depends on the social context in which the behavior occurs. For instance, public drunkenness is frowned on in American life, yet it may be expected behavior at a New Year's Eve party.

SOCIAL CONTROL AND DEVIANCE

Our discussion so far has shown that if the work of the world is to get done, people must follow rules. Social order dictates that people have to be kept in line, at least most people, and that the line must be adhered to within allowable limits (Sagarin, 1975; Gibbs, 1989; Tyler, 1990). Without social order, interaction would be a real problem and expectations would be meaningless. Societies seek to ensure that their members conform with basic norms by means of **social control**, the methods and strategies that regulate behavior within society.

Functionalist and conflict theorists differ in how they view social control. As we will see in Chapter 8, functionalists see social control, particularly as it finds expression in the activities of the state, as an indispensable requirement for survival. If large numbers of people were to defy their society's standards for behavior, massive institutional breakdown and malfunctioning would result. Functionalists therefore see chaos as the alternative to effective social control. In contrast, as we will discuss at greater length in the chapter, conflict theorists contend that social control operates to favor powerful groups and to disadvantage others. They stress that no social arrangements

THE WALL STREET JOURNAL

*"Oh, I guess I was a nonconformist in college, but
I was just following the crowd."*

From *The Wall Street Journal*—Permission, Cartoon Features
Syndicate.

are neutral, and these theorists see their task as
disentangling and identifying the ways in which
institutional structures distribute the benefits and
burdens of social life unevenly while maintaining
these structures through the techniques and
instruments of social control.

There are three main types of social control
processes operating in social life: (1) those that
lead us to internalize our society's normative
expectations, (2) those that structure our world of
social experience, and (3) those that employ various formal and informal social sanctions. Let us
briefly consider each of these processes.

As we saw in Chapter 3, the members of a society undergo continuous *socialization,* a process by
which individuals acquire those ways of thinking,
feeling, and acting characteristic of their society's
culture. For infants and young children, conformity to the expectations of others is primarily a
product of external controls. As they grow older,
an increasing proportion of their behavior
becomes governed by *internal* monitors. These
internal monitors carry on many of the functions
earlier performed by external controls. In brief,
internalization occurs: Individuals incorporate
within their personalities the standards of behavior prevalent within the larger society. Such standards are often accepted without thought or questioning—indeed, we commonly experience them

as "second nature." As we immerse ourselves in
the life of a group, we develop self-conceptions
that regulate our conduct in accordance with the
norms of the group. By doing what group members do, we acquire our identities and a sense of
well-being. The group is *our* group, and its norms
are *our* norms. Social control thus becomes *self-
control.*

Our society's institutions also shape our experiences. In large part, we unconsciously build up
our sense of reality by the way our society orders
its social agendas and structures social alternatives. To the extent that we are locked within the
social environment provided by our culture, we
inhabit a somewhat restricted world. By virtue of
the biases in such arrangements, it usually does
not occur to us that alternative standards exist. In
this sense, we are *culture-bound.* Nonconformist
patterns do not come to our minds because the
alternatives are not known to our society.

Finally, we conform to the norms of our society because we realize that to do otherwise is to
incur punishment. Those who break rules are met
with dislike, hostility, gossip, and ostracism—
even imprisonment and death—while the conformist wins praise, popularity, prestige, and
other socially defined good things. It does not take
us long to appreciate that there are disadvantages
to nonconformity and advantages to conformity.

THE SOCIAL EFFECTS OF DEVIANCE

Not all behavior has a purpose or a use. And the
same is doubtless true for many instances of
deviance. Indeed, most of us think of deviance as
"bad"—as behavior that poses a "social problem."
Such a view is not surprising given the negative or
disruptive consequences of much deviance, or
what sociologists call *dysfunctions* (see Chapter 2).
But deviance also has positive or integrative consequences for social life, what sociologists call
functions. Sociologists such as Lewis A. Coser
(1962), Albert K. Cohen (1966), and Edward
Sagarin (1975) have contributed much to our
understanding in this area.

Dysfunctions of Deviance. Apparently most societies can absorb a good deal of deviance without serious consequences, but persistent and widespread deviance can impair and even undermine organized social life. Social organization derives from the coordinated actions of numerous people. Should some individuals fail to perform their actions at the proper time in accordance with accepted expectations, institutional life may be jeopardized. For instance, when a parent deserts a family, it commonly complicates the task of child care and rearing. And when in the midst of battle a squad of soldiers fails to obey orders and runs away, an entire army may be overwhelmed and defeated.

Deviance also undermines our willingness to play our roles and contribute to the larger social enterprise. If some individuals get rewards, even disproportionate rewards, without playing by the rules—for instance, "idlers," "fakers," "chiselers," "sneaks," and "deadbeats"—we develop resentment and bitterness. Morale, self-discipline, and loyalty suffer. Consider what your reaction would be if you knew that a good number of students in a particularly difficult course were getting the top grades by cheating on examinations. Your motivation to struggle with the material and to study long hours would undoubtedly be undermined.

Moreover, social life dictates that by and large we *trust* one another. We must have confidence that others will play by the rules. In committing ourselves to the collective enterprise, we allocate some resources, forgo some alternatives, and make some investment in the future. We do so because we assume that other people will do the same. But should others not reciprocate our trust—should they betray it—we feel that our own efforts are pointless, wasted, and foolish. We too often become less willing to play by the rules.

The Functions of Deviance. Although deviance may undermine social organization, it may also facilitate social functioning in a number of ways. First, it may promote conformity. Sociologist Edward Sagarin (1975:14) observes:

One of the most effective methods of keeping most people in line is to throw some people out of line. This leaves the remainder not only in better alignment but at the same time in fear of exclusion. . . . By reacting in a hostile manner to those who are not the good and the proper, a majority of the people or a powerful group may reinforce the idea of goodness and propriety and thus perpetuate a society of individuals who are conforming, more obedient, and more loyal to their ideology and rules of behavior.

Second, many norms are not expressed as firm rules or in official codes (see Chapter 2). Accordingly, as spelled out by Emile Durkheim (1893/1964), each time the members of a group censure some act as deviance, they highlight and sharpen the contours of a norm (Stevenson, 1991). Their negative reactions clarify precisely what behavior is disallowed by the "collective conscience." Sociologist Kai T. Erikson (1962) notes that one of the interesting features of agencies of control is the amount of publicity they usually attract. In earlier times, the punishment of offenders took place in the public market in full view of a crowd. Today we achieve much the same result through heavy media coverage of criminal trials and executions:

Why are these reports considered "newsworthy" and why do they rate the extraordinary attention they receive? Perhaps they satisfy a number of psychological perversities among the mass audience, as many commentators have suggested, but at the same time they constitute our main source of information about the normative outlines of society. They are lessons through which we teach one another what the norms mean and how far they extend. In a figurative sense, at least, morality and immorality meet at the public scaffold and it is during this meeting that the community declares where the line between them should be drawn. . . .[The trespasser] informs us, as it were, what evil looks like, what shapes the devil can assume. In doing so, he shows us the difference between kinds of experience which belong within the group and kinds of experience which belong outside it. (Erikson, 1962:310)

Third, by directing attention to the deviant, a group may strengthen itself. A shared enemy arouses common sentiments and cements feelings of solidarity. The emotions surrounding "ain't it awful" deeds quicken passions and solidify "our kind of people" ties. As we saw in Chapter 4, frictions and antagonisms between in-groups and out-groups highlight group boundaries and memberships. In the same way, campaigns against witches, traitors, perverts, and criminals reinforce social cohesion among "the good people." For instance, Erikson (1966) has shown that when the Puritan colonists thought their way of life was threatened, they created "crime waves" and "witchcraft hysterias" to define and redefine the boundaries of their community.

Fourth, deviance is a catalyst for change. Every time a rule is violated, it is being contested. Such challenges serve as a warning that the social system is not functioning properly. For instance, high robbery rates are not likely to suggest to a political elite that robbery should be legalized and the wealth of the society redistributed. But they do loudly proclaim that there are large numbers of disaffected people, that institutions for socializing youth are faltering, that power relations are being questioned, and that the moral structures of the society require reexamination. Thus deviance is often a vehicle for placing on a society's agenda the need for social repair and remedies. By the same token, the deviant way offers an alternative to existing ways. It is simultaneously a call for an examination of old norms and a new model (Sagarin, 1975). For instance, the Reverend Martin Luther King, Jr., and his supporters called the nation's attention to the undemocratic nature of southern segregation laws by disobeying them en masse. In due course, the civil rights movement led to these laws being changed.

□ Sociological Perspectives on Deviance

Deviance may have both positive and negative consequences for the functioning and survival of groups and societies. But why, we may ask, do people violate social rules? Why are some acts defined as deviance? Why are some individuals labeled deviants when they engage in essentially the same behaviors as other individuals who escape retribution and who may even enjoy acclaim? And why does the incidence of deviance vary from group to group and society to society? It is these types of questions that interest sociologists.

Other disciplines are also concerned with deviance, particularly biology and psychology. But they typically ask somewhat different questions, and they make somewhat different contributions to our knowledge. Whereas sociologists focus on social factors that generate deviance, biologists and psychologists typically look at the deviant actors and ask what is "wrong"—or at least different—about them. They seek to explain rule breaking in terms of the individuals themselves and their unique characteristics, such as a lack of self-control and an inability to delay gratification to pursue long-term goals (Gottfredson and Hirschi, 1990).

Here we will focus primarily on the questions posed by sociologists. Our doing so is not meant to ignore or disparage the insights of other disciplines. Take *schizophrenia*. Both biology and psychology have contributed a good deal to our understanding of the disorder—a severe form of mental illness characterized by such symptoms as hallucinations, disordered and illogical thinking, inappropriate emotional responses, personality deterioration, bizarre behavior, and gradual withdrawal from reality. Biologists and psychologists have shown that hereditary factors predispose individuals to some forms of schizophrenia. The hereditary component seems to derive from genes that code for proteins regulating brain activity, particularly neurotransmitters (chemicals released by nerve cells that determine the rate at which other nerve cells fire).

Yet an understanding of the biological and psychological factors involved in schizophrenia does not provide us with the full story. We need to take into account sociological factors as well.

Consider the following example. A man living in the Ozark Mountains has a vision in which God speaks to him. He begins preaching to his relatives and neighbors, and soon he has his entire community in a state of religious fervor. People say he has a "calling." His reputation as a prophet and healer spreads, and he attracts large audiences in the rural communities of Arkansas and Missouri. However, when he ventures into St. Louis and attempts to hold a prayer meeting—blocking traffic at a downtown thoroughfare during rush hour—he is arrested. The man tells the police officers about his conversations with God, and they take him to a mental hospital. Attending psychiatrists say he is "schizophrenic" and hospitalize him for mental illness (Slotkin, 1955). Thus we return full circle to sociological concerns. Again we are reminded that deviance is not a property inherent in behavior but a property conferred upon it by social definitions. Let us turn, then, to a consideration of four sociological approaches to deviance: the structural strain, cultural transmission, conflict, and labeling perspectives.

THE STRUCTURAL STRAIN PERSPECTIVE

As we noted earlier in the chapter, Emile Durkheim (1893/1964, 1897/1951) contended that deviance is functional for a society. He said that deviance and the punishment of the deviant reinforce the boundaries of acceptable behavior and serve as occasions on which people reaffirm their commitment to the society's moral order. Durkheim also made another contribution to our understanding of deviance with his idea of **anomie**—a social condition in which people find it difficult to guide their behavior by norms that they experience as weak, unclear, or conflicting. He pointed out that during times of rapid social change, people became unsure of what is expected of them and find it difficult to fashion their actions in terms of conventional norms. Old norms do not seem relevant, and emerging norms are still too ambiguous and poorly formulated to provide effective and meaningful guidelines for behavior. Under these circumstances, Durkheim believed that an upsurge in deviant behavior could be expected.

Robert K. Merton and Structural Strain. Sociologist Robert K. Merton (1968) has built on Durkheim's notions of anomie and social cohesion and linked them to American life. He says that for large numbers of Americans, worldly success—especially as it finds expression in material *wealth*—has become a cultural *goal*. However, only certain cultural *means*—most commonly securing a good education and acquiring high-paying jobs—are approved for achieving success. There might not be a problem if all Americans had equal access to the approved means for realizing monetary success. But this is not the case. The poor and minorities often find themselves handicapped by little formal education and few economic resources.

For those Americans who internalize the goal of material success—and not all individuals do—strong strains push people toward nonconformity and the use of unorthodox practices. They cannot achieve the culturally approved goals by using the culturally approved means for attaining them. One answer to this dilemma is to obtain the prestige-laden ends by any means whatsoever, including vice and crime. Contemporary professional criminals, members of organized crime, and drug dealers find much in common with Al Capone, the notorious bootlegger and mobster of the 1920s and early 1930s, who contended:

My rackets are run on strictly American lines and they are going to stay that way. . . . This American system of ours . . . call it Americanism, call it Capitalism, call it what you like, gives to each and every one of us a great opportunity if we only seize it with both hands and make the most of it. (Quoted by Cockburn, 1987:23)

But Merton emphasizes that a "lack of opportunity" and an exaggerated material emphasis are not enough to produce strains toward deviance. A society with a comparatively rigid class or caste

Modes of Adaption	Cultural Goals	Institutionalized Means
I Conformity	+	+
II Innovation	+	−
III Ritualism	−	+
IV Retreatism	−	−
V Rebellion	±	±

+ = Acceptance

− = Rejection

± = Rejection of prevailing values and substitution of new values

Figure 5.1 MERTON'S TYPOLOGY OF MODES OF INDIVIDUAL ADAPTATION TO ANOMIE

(SOURCE: Adapted with the permission of The Free Press, a Division of Simon & Schuster, Inc. from *Social Theory and Social Structure*, by Robert K. Merton. Copyright © 1949, 1957 by The Free Press; copyright renewed 1977, 1985 by Robert K. Merton.)

structure may lack opportunity and simultaneously extol wealth—the medieval feudal system being a case in point. It is only when a society extols *common* symbols of success for the *entire* population while structurally restricting the access of large numbers of people to the approved means for acquiring these symbols that antisocial behavior is generated.

Merton identifies five responses to the ends-means dilemma, four of them deviant adaptations to conditions of anomie (see Figure 5.1):

Conformity. Conformity exists when people accept both the cultural goal of material success and the culturally approved means to achieve the goal. Such behavior is the bedrock of a stable society.

Innovation. In innovation, individuals hold fast to the culturally emphasized goals of success while abandoning the culturally approved ways of seeking them. Such people may engage in prostitution, peddle drugs, forge checks, swindle, embezzle, steal, burglarize, rob, or extort to secure money and purchase the symbols of success.

Ritualism. Ritualism involves the abandoning or scaling down of lofty success goals while abiding compulsively by the approved means. For instance, the ends of the organization become irrelevant for many zealous bureaucrats. Instead, they cultivate the means for their own sake, making a fetish of regulations and red tape (see Chapter 4).

Retreatism. In retreatism individuals reject *both* the cultural goals and the approved means without substituting new norms. For example, skid row alcoholics, drug addicts, vagabonds, and derelicts have dropped out of society; they "are in society but not of it."

Rebellion. Rebels reject both the cultural goals and the approved means and substitute *new* norms for them. Such individuals withdraw their allegiance from existing social arrangements and transfer their loyalties to new groups with new ideologies. Radical social movements are a good illustration of this type of adaptation.

Merton's modes of individual adaptation deal with role behavior—not personality types. People may shift from one mode to another.

Applying Structural Strain Theory. A number of sociologists have applied structural strain theory to the study of juvenile delinquency. Albert Cohen (1955) suggests that lower-class boys are attracted to gangs because they are constantly being judged by a middle-class measuring rod. They find themselves failing in middle-class school environments that reward verbal skills, neatness, and an ability to defer gratification. The boys respond by banding together in juvenile gangs where they evolve "macho" standards rewarding "toughness," "street smarts," and "troublemaking"—standards that allow them to succeed. Indeed, Delbert S. Elliott (1966) finds that delinquent boys who drop out of school have a lower rate of juvenile court referrals after dropping out of school than when in school. Leaving school presumably provides a temporary solution to the frustrations they experience in meeting middle-class educational expectations.

Evaluating Structural Strain Theory. Merton's theory of structural strain draws our attention to those processes by which society generates deviance through the way it structures its culturally approved goals and means (Farnsworth and Leiber, 1989). In particular it tells us a good deal about monetary crime. His work sheds light on why there are crimes of profit and greed, white-collar and corporate crime, crimes of warmakers, and crimes of people in power and those searching for power (Sagarin, 1975).

However, critics point out that Merton overlooks the processes of social interaction by which people shape their definitions of the world about them and fashion their actions (Cohen, 1965). Merton portrays deviants as atomistic and individualistic beings—people more or less in a box

by themselves, working out solutions to stressful circumstances without regard to what other people are doing. Moreover, not all deviance stems from gaps between goals and means. Merton provides an image of American society in which there is a consensus on values and goals. But critics say that American society is pluralistic, with a good many subcultures (see Chapter 2). Numerous examples exist in American life of "deviant" behavior that can be explained as a failure to accept the same norms as are prevalent in most of the population: violations of fish and game laws among Native Americans, common-law marriage among some ethnic minorities, cockfighting among some groups with southern rural backgrounds, the producing of "moonshine" liquor among some Appalachian groups, and marijuana use among teenagers. In sum, the "problem" may not be that Americans suffer from a "poverty of values"; rather, Americans have a plethora of values, many of them in conflict with each other.

THE CULTURAL TRANSMISSION PERSPECTIVE

Structural strain theory provides us with insight into how society may unwittingly contribute to deviance by the way it structures its goals and opportunities. A number of other sociologists have emphasized the similarities between the way deviant behavior is acquired and the way in which other behavior is acquired (Schwendinger and Schwendinger, 1985). One of the first was French sociologist Gabriel Tarde (1843–1904), who in the late nineteenth century formulated a theory of imitation to explain deviance. Having spent a great part of his life as a provincial magistrate and later as director of criminal statistics for the French Ministry of Justice, Tarde was impressed by the significant part that repetition plays in human behavior. He contended that criminals, like "good" people, imitate the ways of individuals they have met, known, or heard about. But in contrast to law-abiding people, they imitate other criminals.

"We think he picked it up at the kennel."

Drawing by M. Twohy; © 1993 The New Yorker Magazine, Inc.

A number of decades later, during the 1920s and 1930s, sociologists at the University of Chicago were struck by the concentration of high delinquency rates in some areas of Chicago (Thrasher, 1927; Shaw, 1930; Shaw and McKay, 1942; Sampson and Groves, 1989). They undertook a series of investigations and found that in certain neighborhoods delinquency rates were stable from one period to another despite changes in ethnic composition. They concluded that delinquent and criminal behaviors are culturally transmitted from one generation to the next. From this viewpoint, it is "natural" that youths living in high-crime areas should acquire delinquent lifestyles. Moreover, as new ethnic groups enter a neighborhood, their children learn the delinquent patterns from the youth already there. Hence, the Chicago sociologists contended that youths become delinquent because they associate and make friends with other juveniles who are already delinquent.

Edwin H. Sutherland and Differential Association.
Edwin H. Sutherland (1939), a sociologist who was associated with the Chicago tradition of sociology, elaborated on these conclusions in developing his theory of **differential association.** This theory builds on the interactionist perspective and emphasizes the part social interaction plays in molding people's attitudes and behavior. Sutherland said that individuals become deviant to the extent to which they participate in settings where deviant ideas, motivations, and techniques are viewed favorably. For example, they may learn how to use and obtain illegal drugs, or how to steal and then sell stolen items. The earlier, the more frequent, the more intense, and the longer the duration of the contacts people have in such settings, the greater the probability that they too will become deviant. But more is involved than simply imitation. Deviant behavior is not only learned, it is also taught. The theory thus focuses on *what* is learned and from *whom* it is learned (Laub and Sampson, 1991).

The differential association theory provides a sophisticated version of the old adage that "good companions make good boys; bad companions make bad boys." When parents move to a new neighborhood to "get Mike away from his hoodlum friends," they are applying the principle of differential association. So are parole officers who try to restrict the associations of the paroled prisoners they supervise. By the same token, the theory suggests that imprisonment may be counterproductive when juveniles are incarcerated with experienced criminals.

Applying Cultural Transmission Theory. In pluralistic societies with multiple subcultures, groups differ in some of their values and expectations for behavior. Sociologist Walter B. Miller (1958, 1975) builds on this notion in his study of unlawful activity among lower-class juveniles. He sees their behavior as conformity to cultural patterns acquired through socialization in ghetto and inner-city settings. Lower-class culture, he says, attaches high value to a number of "focal concerns": *trouble*—welcoming "encounters" with police officers, school officials, welfare investigators, and other agents of the larger society; *toughness*—showing skills in physical combat and an ability to "take it"; *smartness*—being able to outwit, dupe, and outsmart others; *excitement*—seeking thrills, taking risks, and flirting with danger; *fate*—assuming that most of life's crucial events are beyond one's control and governed by chance and destiny; and *autonomy*—desiring to be free of external controls and coercive authority. Although these concerns are not inherently or necessarily delinquent, their pursuit creates situations in which unlawful activity is likely to emerge. For instance, an emphasis on toughness leads to verbal insult and physical attack, and the craving for excitement promotes auto theft.

Evaluating Cultural Transmission Theory. Cultural transmission theory shows that socially disapproved behaviors can arise through the same processes of socialization as socially approved ones (Kaplan, Johnson, and Bailey, 1987). It is a particularly useful tool for understanding why deviance varies from group to group and from society to society (Matsueda and Heimer, 1987;

Crane, 1991). However, the theory is not applicable to some forms of deviance, particularly those in which neither the techniques nor the appropriate definitions and attitudes are acquired from other deviants. Illustrations include criminal violators of financial trust; naive check forgers; occasional, incidental, and situational offenders; nonprofessional shoplifters; non-career-type criminals; and people who commit "crimes of passion." Further, deviants and nondeviants are often reared in the same environments—criminal behavior patterns are presented to two persons, but only one becomes a criminal. The individuals may be confronted with the same patterns but perceive them differently, producing different outcomes.

Cultural transmission theorists have traditionally stressed that delinquent youth learn crime from their friends. However, according to recent figures compiled by the Justice Department, more than half of all juvenile delinquents imprisoned in state institutions and more than a third of adult criminals in local jails and state prisons have immediate family members who have also been incarcerated. Indeed, the more chronic and serious the criminal behavior, the more likely it is to find that a person's relatives have spent time in jail. The figures do not answer the debate over whether it is the environment or genetic predisposition that fosters criminality. But the statistics do suggest that people typically learn delinquent behavior from their parents and siblings (Butterfield, 1992). Consequently, the focus of cultural transmission theory is shifting to the family unit.

THE CONFLICT PERSPECTIVE

Cultural transmission theorists emphasize that individuals who are immersed in different subcultures will exhibit somewhat different behaviors because they are socialized in different traditions. To this formulation conflict theorists respond:

True, groups have differing values and norms. But the question is "Which group will be able to translate its val-

ues into the rules of a society and make these rules stick?" Moreover, the institutional order generates clashing interests among major groups—classes, sexes, racial and ethnic groups, business organizations, labor unions, and farm associations. Accordingly, we need also ask, "Who reaps the lion's share of benefits from particular social arrangements?" Or, put another way, "How is society structured so that some groups are advantaged while other groups are disadvantaged and even stigmatized as deviant?"

Although in recent decades the conflict approach has taken many new directions (Colvin and Pauly, 1983; Hagan, 1989; Messner, 1989; Messner and Krohn, 1990), its early roots can be traced to the Marxist tradition (see Chapter 1). According to orthodox Marxism, a capitalist ruling class exploits and robs the masses, yet avoids punishment for its crimes. Individuals victimized by capitalist oppression are driven to commit acts in their struggle to survive that the ruling class brands as criminal (Bonger, 1936; Liska, 1987). Other types of deviance—alcoholism, drug abuse, family violence, sexual immorality, and prostitution—are products of the moral degeneration fostered by a social milieu founded on the unprincipled pursuit of profit and the subjugation of the poor, women, and African Americans, and other minorities. Mental and emotional problems also abound because people become estranged from one another and from themselves. Such estrangement resides in the separation of people from the means whereby they derive their livelihood—from the basis of their existence (see Chapter 8).

Richard Quinney: Class, State, and Crime.

One contemporary approach to deviance with strong Marxist components is that articulated by sociologist Richard Quinney (1974, 1980). Quinney says that the American legal system reflects the interests and ideologies of the ruling capitalist class. Law makes illegal certain behavior that is offensive to the morality of the powerful and that threatens their privileges and property:

Law is the tool of the ruling class. Criminal law, in particular, is a device made and used by the ruling class to pre-

serve the existing order. In the United States, the state—and its legal system—exist to secure and perpetuate the capitalist interests of the ruling class. (1974:8)

Quinney (1980:39) contends that if we are "to understand crime we have to understand the development of the political economy of capitalist society." Since the state serves the interests of the capitalist class, crime is ultimately a class-based political act embedded in capitalist social arrangements.

In striving to maintain itself against the internal contradictions eating away at its foundations, Quinney (1980:57) says that capitalism commits *crimes of domination.* Indeed, "one of the contradictions of capitalism is that some of its laws must be violated in order to secure the existing system." These crimes include those committed by corporations and range from price fixing to pollution of the environment. But there are also *crimes of government* committed by the officials of the capitalist state, Watergate being a well-publicized instance. In contrast, much of the criminal behavior of ordinary people, or *predatory crime*—burglary, robbery, drug dealing, and hustling of various sorts—is "pursued out of the need to survive" in a capitalist social order. *Personal crime*—murder, assault, and rape—is "pursued by those who are already brutalized by the conditions of capitalism." And then there are *crimes of resistance* in which workers engage in sloppy work and clandestine acts of sabotage against employers.

In sum, crime is endemic to capitalism: "When a society generates social problems it cannot solve within its own existence, policies for controlling the population are devised and implemented. Crime and criminal justice are thus integral to the larger issues of the historical development of capitalism" (Quinney, 1980:viii).

Applying Conflict Theory.

Conflict theory has led social scientists to investigate the ways in which the making and administration of law are biased by powerful interests. Numerous sociologists have noted that crime is defined primarily in terms of offenses against property (burglary, robbery, auto theft, and vandalism), whereas corporate crime is deemphasized (Sutherland, 1949; Coleman, 1985, 1987). Moreover, the penalty for crimes against property is imprisonment, whereas the most common form of penalty for business-related offenses is a monetary fine. Sociologist Amitai Etzioni (1985) found that between 1975 and 1984, 62 percent of the nation's largest corporations were involved in one or more illegal practices; 42 percent, in two or more; and 15 percent, in five or more. The offenses involved price fixing and overcharging, domestic and foreign bribes, fraud and deception, and patent infringements. Yet unlike robbers and muggers, corporations and their executives got off easy. And while the Federal Bureau of Investigation (FBI) keeps track of every murder, rape, assault, and auto theft reported in the United States, no agency keeps a record of crimes committed by corporations themselves.

Evaluating Conflict Theory. There is a good deal of truth in conflict theory (Schwendinger and Schwendinger, 1985). Indeed, it is obvious to most people that powerful individuals and groups make and administer the laws. In this sense, then, laws are not neutral but favor some group's interests and embody some group's values. Yet critics charge that such intuitive insights hardly satisfy the requirements of scientific inquiry (Hagan and Leon, 1977). For example, sociologist Stanton Wheeler (1976:527) says that while the emergence of conflict theory and the rediscovery of Marx have given new direction to our understanding of deviance, "it is my strong impression that the achievements have been more rhetorical than anything else."

Many conflict formulations need to be refined (Hawkins, 1987). For example, it is not always clear which specific individuals or groups are covered by such terms as "ruling elites," "governing classes," and "powerful interests." And conflict hypotheses need to be tested. For instance, William J. Chambliss and Robert Seidman (1971: 475) assert: "When sanctions are imposed, the most severe sanctions will be imposed on persons in the lowest social class." Yet research results are inconsistent. Some studies find few (Bernstein, Kelly, and Doyle, 1977) or no (Chiricos and Waldo, 1975) links between the status characteristics of criminal offenders and the sentences received; other studies find the relationship to be substantial (Lizotte, 1978; Bridges, Crutchfield, and Simpson, 1987); and still others find that the relationship depends on specific circumstances (Hagan, Bernstein, and Albonetti, 1980; Humphrey and Fogarty, 1987). And although corporations often seek to influence legislation and public policy, they do not necessarily predominate over other interest groups (Hagan, 1980, 1989). Clearly, additional research is needed. Conflict propositions cannot be accepted as articles of faith but require rigorous scientific investigation.

THE LABELING PERSPECTIVE

Conflict theorists contend that people often find themselves at odds with one another because their interests diverge and their values clash. Some people gain the power and ascendancy to translate their values and normative preferences into the rules governing institutional life. They then successfully place negative labels on violators of these rules. A number of sociologists have taken this notion and expanded on it. They are interested in the process by which some individuals come to be tagged as "deviants," begin to think of themselves as deviants, and enter on deviant careers.

Edwin Lemert, Howard S. Becker, and Kai T. Erikson: The Social Reaction to Deviance Approach. Proponents of the labeling perspective—sociologists such as Edwin M. Lemert (1951, 1972), Howard S. Becker (1963), and Kai T. Erikson (1962, 1966)—make a number of points. First, they contend that no act by itself is inherently criminal or noncriminal. The "badness" of an act does not stem from its intrinsic content but from the way other people define and react to it. Deviance is always a matter of social definition.

Second, labeling theorists point out that we all engage in deviant behavior by violating some norms. They reject the popular idea that human beings can be divided into those who are normal and those who are pathological. For instance, some of us exceed the speed limit, experiment with cocaine, shoplift, cheat on a homework assignment, sample homosexual publications, underreport our income to income tax authorities, swim in the nude, become intoxicated, commit vandalism in celebration of a football victory, trespass on private property, or "joyride" in a friend's car without permission. Labeling theorists call these actions **primary deviance**—behavior that violates social norms but usually goes unnoticed by the agents of social control.

Third, labeling theorists say that whether people's acts will be seen as deviant depends both on what they do *and* on what other people do about it. In short, deviance depends on which rules society chooses to enforce, in which situations, and with respect to which people. Not all individuals are arrested for speeding, shoplifting, underreporting income on their tax returns, trespassing, or the like. Blacks may be censured for doing what whites are "allowed" to do, women censured for doing what men are "allowed" to do, certain individuals censured for doing what their friends are also doing, and some may be labeled as deviants even though they have not violated a norm but simply because they are so accused (for instance, they appear "effeminate" and are tagged as "gay"). Of critical importance is the social audience and whether or not it *labels* the person a deviant.

Fourth, labeling people as deviants has consequences for them. It tends to set up conditions conducive to **secondary deviance**—deviance individuals adopt in response to the reactions of other individuals. In brief, labeling theorists contend that new deviance is *manufactured* by the hostile reactions of rule makers and rule abiders. An individual is publicly identified, stereotyped, and denounced as a "delinquent," "mental fruitcake," "forger," "rapist," "drug addict," "bum," "pervert," or "criminal." The label serves to lock the individual into an outsider status. Such a master status overrides other statuses in shaping a person's social experiences and results in a self-fulfilling prophecy. Rule breakers come to accept their status as a particular kind of deviant and organize their lives around this master status.

Fifth, people labeled "deviant" typically find themselves rejected and isolated by "law-abiding" people. Friends and relatives may withdraw from them. In some cases, they may even be institutionalized in prisons or mental hospitals. Rejection and isolation push stigmatized individuals toward a deviant group with other individuals who share a common fate. Participation in a deviant subculture becomes a way of coping with frustrating situations and for finding emotional support and personal acceptance. In turn, joining a deviant group solidifies a deviant self-image, fosters a deviant lifestyle, and weakens ties to the law-abiding community.

In sum, labeling theorists say that the societal response to an act, not the behavior itself, determines deviance. When the behavior of people is seen as departing from prevailing norms, it "sets off a chain of social reactions." Other individuals define, evaluate, and label the behavior. Norm violators then take these labels into account as they shape their actions. In many cases, they evolve an identity consistent with a label and enter on a career of deviance.

Applying Labeling Theory. Sociologist William J. Chambliss (1973) employed labeling theory to explain the differing perceptions and definitions that community members had of the behavior of two teenage gangs. At Hanibal High School, Chambliss observed the activities of the Saints, a gang of eight white upper-class boys, and the Roughnecks, a gang of six lower-class white boys. Although the Saints engaged in as many delinquent acts as the Roughnecks, it was the Roughnecks who were in "constant trouble" and universally considered to be "delinquent."

The Saints enjoyed an image as "good students" headed for college. Yet they were often truant from school and spent their weekends drinking, driving recklessly at high speeds, deliberately running red lights, shouting obscenities at women, vandalizing empty houses, removing warning signs from road repair sites, and erecting stolen barricades on highways where unsuspecting motorists would crash into them. But the Hanibal townspeople overlooked the Saints' high level of delinquency. They saw the Saints as law-abiding youths who simply went in for an occasional prank—"good boys sowing wild oats." After all, they were well dressed, displayed middle-class manners, and drove nice cars.

But it was otherwise for the Roughnecks. Everyone agreed that "the not-so-well-dressed, not-so-well-mannered, not-so-rich boys were heading for trouble." Their brawling and petty stealing were known throughout the community. Moreover, a high level of mutual distrust and hostility existed between the Roughnecks and the police. Several of the Roughnecks were arrested a number of times, and two of the boys were sentenced to 6 months in reform school. In sum, the community, the school, and the police related to the Saints as though they were good, upstanding youths with bright futures, but they treated the Roughnecks as young punks headed for trouble.

A number of factors contributed to the differential treatment given the two groups. For one thing, the Saints had access to automobiles and engaged in out-of-town escapades that were less visible to Hanibal citizens than those undertaken by the Roughnecks in the center of town. For another, when the Saints were confronted with an accusing police officer, they were apologetic and penitent, whereas the Roughnecks were hostile and belligerent. And finally, police officers knew that irate and influential upper-middle-class parents would come to the aid of their youngsters, whereas powerless lower-class parents would have to acquiesce in the law's definition of their son's behavior.

Chambliss (1973:30–31) concludes:

The community responded to the Roughnecks as boys in trouble, and the boys agreed with that perception. Their pattern of deviancy was reinforced, and breaking away from it became increasingly unlikely. Once the boys acquired an image of themselves as deviants, they selected new friends who affirmed that self-image. As that self-conception became more firmly entrenched, they also became willing to try new and more extreme deviances. With their growing alienation came freer expression of disrespect and hostility for representatives of the legitimate society. This disrespect increased the community's negativism, perpetuating the entire process of commitment to deviance.

Evaluating the Labeling Perspective. Unlike structural strain and cultural transmission theory, the labeling perspective does not focus on why some individuals engage in deviant behavior. Rather, labeling theory helps us to understand why the same act may or may not be considered deviant, depending on the situation and the characteristics of the individuals who are involved. In recent years, a number of labeling theorists have incorporated insights from conflict theory into their formulations. They have looked to societal inequalities and political processes to see how institutions are structured and how rules are made and enforced. For instance, between 1880 and 1920, unprecedented numbers of Americans were confined in mental asylums. Many contemporary observers concluded that the United States was experiencing an epidemic of madness. Instead, rather than an epidemic of mental illness, organizational and political forces were at work whereby state mental institutions were compelled to absorb increasing numbers of the aged poor and infirm who previously had been housed in city and county almshouses. At the same time, the construction and maintenance of asylums channeled jobs to political loyalists (Grob, 1983; Sutton, 1991).

But labeling theory also has its critics. For one thing, while labeling may help us understand how individuals become career deviants, it tells us little about what initially contributed to their deviant behavior. Indeed, in many forms of deviance it is the behavior or condition of the people themselves that is primarily responsible for their being labeled in the first place. Take mental illness. It seems that a vast majority of people who are hospitalized suffer acute disturbance associated with *internal* psychological or neurological malfunctioning (Gove, 1970). Their inner turmoil and suffering cannot be explained solely in terms of the reactions of other people. Yet even so, considerable evidence suggests that mental health professionals contribute to the social creation of mental disorders by their use of labeling systems and do not simply "discover" inner pathology or mental disease (Rosenhan, 1973; Eaton, 1986). And labels play an important role in how mental patients are perceived by others and by themselves (Link et al., 1989, 1991).

Likewise, deviance cannot be understood without reference to norms. If behavior is not deviance unless it is labeled, how are we to classify secret and undetected deviance, such as the embezzlement of funds, the failure to pay income taxes, and the clandestine sexual molestation of children? Moreover, many criminals pursue their deviant careers because they believe that crime *pays.* For instance, dealing drugs is a crime that offers potentially high returns (even small-time street dealers in Washington, D.C., gross on average $48,000 a year, netting $24,000 tax-free after paying for the drugs and runners) (Dumaine, 1991). Additionally, many street-level drug dealers in the District of Columbia hold legitimate jobs (such as delivery workers, office clerks, cooks, and construction laborers) and spend less than 4 hours a day hustling drugs (Treaster, 1990).

None of the sociological perspectives we have examined provides a complete explanation of deviant behavior. Each one highlights for us an important source of deviance. Deviant behavior takes a good many forms, and so we must approach each form in its own right to determine the specific factors involved. We turn next to a consideration of crime, a form of deviance that is particularly prevalent in modern societies.

□ Crime and the Criminal Justice System

Within modern societies, law is a crucial element in social control. Unlike informal norms such as folkways and mores, laws are rules enforced by the state. **Crime** is merely an act that is prohibited by law, and so not all deviant acts are crimes. For an act to be considered criminal, the state must undertake a political process of illegalizing—or *criminalizing*—it. Criminalization processes are encompassing growing spheres of American life, including environmental protection, government contracting, workplace requirements, male-female relationships (gender rights and sexual harassment), corporate management, family abuse, securities protection, banking regulation, and medical malpractice. The use of punitive measures to control vast areas of private life and economic activity takes many forms. For instance, landlords can lose their rental properties if their tenants deal in drugs, and auto dealers can be classified as money launderers for selling vehicles to drug dealers (DeLong, 1994).

The cost of crime is enormous. *U.S. News & World Report* (1994), on the basis of its consultations with economists and criminal justice experts, estimates that crime costs the United States $674 billion a year: costs associated with police protection, prisons, and the court system; the massive purchase by Americans of private protection; and health care costs and lost wages and productivity associated with homicide, rape, burglary, and assault.

What crimes have in common is not that they are necessarily acts we regard as immoral or wicked. For instance, a good many Americans consider it no more "evil" to cheat on their income taxes than did their parents or grandparents to purchase and consume illegal alcoholic beverages during Prohibition. Rather, the distinguishing property of crime is that people who violate the law are liable to be arrested, tried, pro-

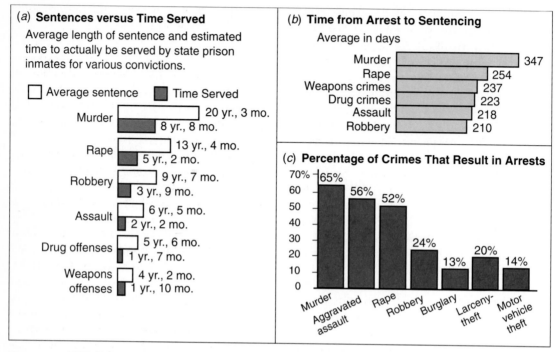

(a) Sentences versus Time Served

Average length of sentence and estimated time to actually be served by state prison inmates for various convictions.

☐ Average sentence ■ Time Served

Murder — 20 yr., 3 mo. / 8 yr., 8 mo.
Rape — 13 yr., 4 mo. / 5 yr., 2 mo.
Robbery — 9 yr., 7 mo. / 3 yr., 9 mo.
Assault — 6 yr., 5 mo. / 2 yr., 2 mo.
Drug offenses — 5 yr., 6 mo. / 1 yr., 7 mo.
Weapons offenses — 4 yr., 2 mo. / 1 yr., 10 mo.

(b) Time from Arrest to Sentencing

Average in days

Murder — 347
Rape — 254
Weapons crimes — 237
Drug crimes — 223
Assault — 218
Robbery — 210

(c) Percentage of Crimes That Result in Arrests

Murder 65%
Aggravated assault 56%
Rape 52%
Robbery 24%
Burglary 13%
Larceny-theft 20%
Motor vehicle theft 14%

Figure 5.2   THE OPERATION OF THE CRIMINAL JUSTICE SYSTEM IN THE UNITED STATES

(SOURCE: Copyright 1993, *USA Today,* December 29, 1993, p. 7A. Reprinted with permission. *The Wall Street Journal,* February 18, 1994, p. A14. Data are from the FBI's 1992 *Uniform Crime Report* and Bureau of Justice Statistics reports.)

nounced guilty, and deprived of their lives, liberty, or property. In brief, they are likely to become caught up in the elaborate social machinery of the **criminal justice system**—the reactive agencies of the state that include the police, the courts, and prisons. Let us briefly consider each of these components of the criminal justice system.

THE CRIMINAL JUSTICE SYSTEM

Judging by what they see on television, the American people are enamored with crime. The scenario of most television crime series invariably runs along these lines: A serious crime is committed; the police or detective hero sifts through the clues and tracks down the culprits; the prosecutor throws the book at them; judge and jury do their duty; and the criminals are sent to prison. In real

life, however, the picture is quite different. According to statistics from the Justice Department, of every 100 felonies committed in the United States, only 33 are reported to the police. Of these 33, only 6 are cleared by arrest. Of these 6 persons arrested, only 3 are prosecuted and convicted. Of these, only 1 is sent to prison; the other two cases are rejected or dismissed because of problems with the evidence or witnesses, or the perpetrators are diverted into treatment programs. Of those sent to prison, more than half receive a sentence of at least 5 years. However, the average inmate is released in about 2 years (see Figure 5.2).

The Police.   As of 1992, there were 748,830 full-time law enforcement officers in the United States, a rise of 40 percent since 1980. The police are a citizen's first link with the criminal justice system, and in many ways the most important one. When a crime occurs, the police are usually the first agents of the state to become involved.

Police officers are expected not only to collar lawbreakers but also to perform a variety of community roles, from being providers of emergency first aid to being dogcatchers, leading some police officers to call themselves "do-everything guys" (despite affirmative action programs, 95 percent of police officers are male). In towns of 50,000 population or more, on average only 45 officers are actually on patrol in the streets out of every 100 who are on duty at any given time. Indeed, police officers spend only about 15 percent of their time dealing with crime. Competing demands on their time vary from filling out reports and directing traffic to handling complaints about uncollected trash and responding to medical emergency calls.

In recent years many American communities have begun experimenting with what has been variously called "community-based policing" and "problem-oriented policing." The approaches seek to supplant negative and "hard skills" encounters with more personal and "soft skills" contacts centered on serving and protecting. Law enforcement agencies aim to forge partnerships with the communities they serve to reduce the massive alienation and distrust that permeates many inner-city neighborhoods. For instance, Detroit has established storefront mini police stations in congested neighborhoods in order to afford greater citizen access and input.

The Courts.   In the United States, the criminal justice system is an *adversary* system. The accused person—the *defendant*—is presumed to be innocent until proved guilty in a court of law by the representative of the state—the *prosecutor*. In many nations the questioning of witnesses is handled by judges, and guilt and innocence decided by a judge or panel of judges. But the American system assumes that justice is best served by pitting opposing lawyers against each other before a neutral judge and jury.

In practice, the fate of most of those accused of crime is determined by prosecutors. Prosecutors typically reject or reduce the severity of 50 to 80 percent of the charges filed by police. The reasons prosecutors cite range from case overload to police inefficiency in producing evidence. Of the some 2 million serious criminal cases filed each year in the United States, fewer than 1 in 5 goes to trial. The others end in dismissals or guilty pleas.

When prosecutors decide to take a case to trial, a number of matters confront judges. They must decide whether a defendant should be released on bail, how fast a case will come to trial, the legality of police and prosecution tactics, and, when the defendant is found guilty, the penalty. Should a defendant be sent to prison, the sentence can vary substantially depending on the judge and other factors. And once early releases granted by parole boards are factored in, disparities in time served can vary enormously. The average period spent in prison by convicted felons ranges from 13 months in South Dakota to 53 months in Massachusetts.

Prisons.   American prisons vary from dingy, fortresslike state penitentiaries built in the 1800s to ultramodern lockups. Yet the convict population is increasing more rapidly than the capacity of prisons. By 1992, there were 925,247 state and federal inmates (more than 180 percent higher than in 1980) and 444,584 local jail inmates (more than double the 1980 figure). California prisons have had an occupancy rate nearly double their design capacity (185 percent), followed by those in Massachusetts (170 percent), Vermont (157 percent), Pennsylvania (156 percent), and Ohio (155 percent). By 1990, more than 2 percent of the adult U.S. population was on probation, incarcerated, or on parole. As showed in Figure 5.3, the rate of imprisonment in the United States is the highest in the world. Unable to house the mounting flood of prisoners—while simultaneously confronting severe economic pressures

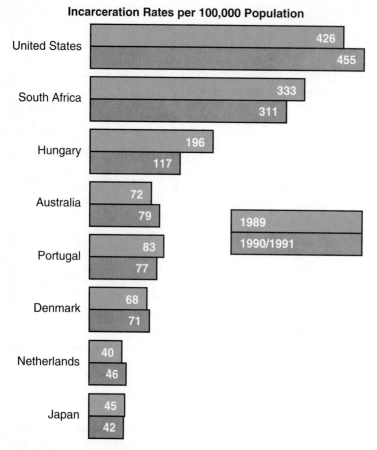

Incarceration Rates per 100,000 Population

United States	426 / 455	
South Africa	333 / 311	
Hungary	196 / 117	
Australia	72 / 79	
Portugal	83 / 77	
Denmark	68 / 71	
Netherlands	40 / 46	
Japan	45 / 42	

(Legend: 1989 / 1990/1991)

Figure 5.3   THE UNITED STATES IMPRISONS A LARGER SHARE OF ITS POPULATION THAN ANY OTHER NATION
According to a report by the Sentencing Project, a research group that promotes changes in sentencing, the high incarceration rate of the United States results from a crime rate higher than in most other nations and increasingly harsh criminal justice policies. (SOURCE: From *The New York Times,* February 11, 1992, p. C18. Reprinted by permission.)

in meeting local and state educational, health, and welfare needs—governments are looking for cheaper ways to deal with wrongdoers. Among these measures are suspended sentencing, expanded probation and parole programs, home confinement, halfway houses, and public-service requirements.

An increased likelihood that an arrest will lead to a prison sentence, not changes in sentencing laws or in the population, is primarily responsible for the nation's soaring prison population. Since 1973, average prison sentences have not lengthened, nor are inmates serving on average more time in prison. And although the pool of people considered most prone to be imprisoned—men (48 percent of the population and 95 percent of all prisoners), African Americans (11 percent of the population and 48 percent of prisoners), and individuals in their twenties (24 percent of the population but 50 percent of prisoners)—has increased since 1973, the prison population has grown four times as fast as the "prison-prone" pool. In sum, the United States has simply become more harsh in recent decades in its incarceration practices—a part of a "get tough on crime" policy (Langan, 1991). We will have more to say later in the chapter about the impact of prisons on inmates. But first, let us take a closer look at crime.

FORMS OF CRIME

Since a crime is an act prohibited by law, it is the state that defines crime by the laws it promulgates, administers, and enforces. Thus an infinite variety of acts can be crimes. In some nations, it is a crime to organize political parties in opposition to the established regime. In nations like Iran, it is a crime to belong to religious groups barred by the dominant religious authorities. In the United States, interracial marriages were barred by many states prior to a 1967 Supreme Court decision prohibiting such statutes. And Illinois requires dealers in marijuana, cocaine, and other illegal drugs to purchase tax stamps; a violator is subject to four times the amount of the tax, a $10,000 fine, and 3 years in prison. Since the list of possible acts falling under the heading of crime is inexhaustible, we cannot think of crime as something clearly defined as a unit. Instead, let us consider a number of forms of crime within the United States.

White-Collar and Corporate Crime. One type of crime that has been of particular interest to sociologists is **white-collar crime**—crime most commonly committed by relatively affluent persons, often in the course of business activities (Sutherland, 1949; Coleman, 1987, 1989). At the heart of much white-collar crime is a violation of a social relationship of trust (Shapiro, 1990). Included in white-collar crime are corporate crime, fraud, embezzlement, corruption, bri-

"The chairman of the board already wiped us out."

From *The Sunday Dispatch;* © 1991. Reprinted with special permission of North America Syndicate.

bery, tax fraud or evasion, stock manipulation, insider trading, misrepresentation of advertising, restraint of trade, and infringement of patents. Some estimates place the monetary cost of corporate crime at about twenty times that of all street crimes combined (Coleman, 1989).

The cost of public construction is increased between 10 and 50 percent because of bribery, kickbacks, and payoffs resulting in overcharges to taxpayers of more than $2 billion annually. In a "sting" operation conducted in the New York City area, undercover FBI agents offered or discussed bribes with municipal officials. On 105 of the occasions, the public officials accepted the bribes; the one official who turned down the bribe did so because he did not think the amount was enough (Blumenthal, 1987). Bank and insurance frauds are also commonplace. Indeed, recent experience has shown that the best way to rob a bank is to own one. The collapse of the nation's savings and loan industry is costing taxpayers hundreds of bil-

Table 5.1   PLEA BARGAINS BY MAJOR AMERICAN CORPORATIONS

Company	Accused of	Result
General Electric	Conspiracy, fraud, money laundering	Pleads guilty; pays $69 million in fines and restitution
United Technologies	Conspiracy, misuse of government information	Pleads guilty to four felony counts
Emerson Electric	Conspiracy, misuse of government information, false statements	Pleads guilty to three felony counts
Unisys	Conspiracy, misuse of government information, false claims	Pleads guilty to eight counts
Teledyne	False statements, conspiracy	Pleads guilty to three counts
Loral	Price gouging, fraud	Settlement, pays fine
Loral	Conspiracy, misuse of government information, false statements	Pleads guilty to three counts
Sundstrand	Conspiracy to overcharge and to provide illegal gifts	Pleads guilty to four counts
Textron	Making faulty engines	Pays fine, admits no wrongdoing
Salomon Brothers	Falsifying books, false bids, false tax losses	Agrees to Securities Exchange Commission settlement, pays $290 million fine
Rockwell International	Violations of environmental laws	Pleads guilty to ten counts, including five felonies

SOURCE: John Rothchild, "Sacred Cows," *Worth*, December/January, 1993, p. 56. Reprinted by permission of *Worth* magazine.

lions of dollars ($500 billion by some estimates, or $100 for every person on earth). Corruption, fraud, cronyism, and political bribery all contributed to what some have labeled "the greatest-ever bank robbery" (Mayer, 1990). Apparently Wall Street investment houses made the most off the swindle by selling mortgage-backed securities and stuffing savings and loans with junk bonds.

Corporations have been implicated in a variety of crimes, including overcharging the government on contracts, polluting the environment, short-changing consumers, violating employee privacy, price-rigging school milk contracts, disposing of hazardous waste in violation of the law, adulterating fruit juice, and engaging in accounting irregularities (Clinard, 1990; Rothchild, 1993). Table 5.1 provides a representative list of plea bargains entered into by major American corporations.

Nor have the nation's colleges and universities been spared from charges that they have engaged in abusive financial behavior. For instance, Stanford University refunded $924,517 to the federal government after having overcharged taxpayers by using research grants for such items as $5,500 to refurbish a piano and build a cedar-lined closet in the house of Donald Kennedy, Stanford's president at the time, and more than $1,000 for liquor served to guests at football-weekend receptions (Fenyvesi, 1991). The House Subcommittee on Oversight and Investigations cited the possibility that over a 10-year period Stanford overcharged the government $200 million for indirect research costs (De Witt, 1991). And Massachusetts Institute of Technology returned $731,000 that it had "inappropriately" charged for "research costs" between 1986 and 1990 (Begley, 1991).

The American criminal justice system is ill-equipped to deal with white-collar and corporate crime (Wheeler, Mann, and Sarat, 1988; Shapiro, 1990). Unlike a robbery, a stock or insurance fraud is typically complex and difficult to unravel. Local law enforcement officials commonly lack the skills and resources necessary to tackle crimes outside the sphere of street crime. Federal agencies will handle only the more serious white-collar and corporate crimes. In most cities, they will not investigate a bank embezzlement unless it exceeds $8,000 to $10,000 (in New York City, the cutoff is about $50,000). And the handful of white-collar criminals who are prosecuted and convicted are given a slap on the wrist. Street criminals who steal $100 may find their way to prison, while the dishonest executive who embezzles $1 million may receive a suspended sentence and a relatively small fine. Figures for the late 1970s show that embezzlers at banks stole an average of $23,000 each, but only 17 percent of them went to jail. Bank robbers, by comparison, stole only one-eighth as much, yet 91 percent ended up in jail (*U.S. News & World Report,* 1979:60).

Organized Crime. **Organized crime** refers to large-scale bureaucratic organizations that provide illegal goods and services in public demand. Such crime is likely to arise where the state criminalizes certain activities—prostitution, drugs, pornography, gambling, and loan-sharking—that large numbers of citizens desire and for which they are willing to pay. The most publicized crime organization has been an Italian-American syndicate, variously termed the Mafia or Cosa Nostra, which gained a substantial impetus from Prohibition. So much has been written about this group that it is difficult to separate myth from fact. However, it seems to be a loose network or confederation of regional syndicates coordinated by a "commission" composed of the heads of the most powerful crime "families" (Cressey, 1969; Roberts, 1984; Behar, 1990; Raab, 1990). The Mafia operates a vast system of political corruption and employs violence and intimidation against victims, rivals, and "renegades." Having piled up enormous profits from drug dealing and gambling, the Mafia has diversified into entertainment, labor unions, construction, trucking, vending machines, garbage carting, toxic waste disposal, banking, and insurance, as well as stock fraud and extortion. In recent years, however, the Mafia has been under siege: A series of federal trials has severely crippled its aging leadership, younger members are proving less dedicated than those of earlier generations, and foreign competition in narcotics has undercut Mafia operations (McFadden, 1987; Raab, 1990).

However, organized crime is hardly an Italian monopoly. Irish and Jewish crime figures have long cooperated with the Mafia. In New York and Philadelphia, African-American groups and the Mafia run gambling and narcotics operations in concert. In San Francisco and New York City, Chinese gangs shake down merchants and are involved in gambling, robberies, drug trafficking, loan-sharking, labor racketeering, and prostitution; the self-proclaimed Israeli Mafia extorts money in Los Angeles; and Colombian and Cuban drug rings have flooded Florida with their products.

Crime Committed by Government. Conflict theorists have drawn our attention to crime that is committed by governments (Barak, 1991). Nazi Germany provides a prime example in which more than 6 million Jews were murdered during the Holocaust of the Hitler years. The government of the United States participated in the massacre of countless Native Americans (even as late as 1890, U.S. Army forces armed with Hotchkiss machine guns mowed down nearly 300 Sioux at Wounded Knee, South Dakota). And in recent years, evidence has mounted that violence and racism are routine among the police departments of many large cities, including Los Angeles (Morrow, 1991; Mydans, 1991; Reinhold, 1991).

The Oval Office tapes of the Nixon White House reveal a president bent on using the powers of his office to victimize his enemies in ways counter to American law. For instance, on September 15, 1972, well into the cover-up of the Watergate break-in, Nixon mulls over the possibility of looking into the Internal Revenue Service's tax records of leading Democrats. "And there are ways to do it," says the President. "Goddamn it, sneak in in the middle of the night." On another occasion, Nixon suggests it might be a good idea to recruit "eight thugs" from the Teamsters' Union to attack antiwar protesters: "They've got guys who will go in and knock their heads off" (Perry, 1991). More recently, the Iran-contra scandal has shown that operatives of the nation's security organizations, including the Central Intelligence Agency and the National Security Council, engaged in secret arms shipments to the Nicaraguan contra rebels during the years that Congress barred aid to them.

Violent Crime. The Federal Bureau of Investigation annually reports on eight types of crime in its *Uniform Crime Reports.* These offenses are called **index crimes** and consist of four categories of violent crime against people—murder, rape, robbery, and assault—and four categories of crimes against property—burglary, theft, motor vehicle theft, and arson. It is these crimes that are covered widely by the news media, most feared by the public, and most denounced by political officials.

Annual FBI estimates of violent crime have tended to move up over the years, whereas reports from the Bureau of Justice Statistics (BJS) have shown the crime rate as typically constant or declining. The BJS data are based on national victimization surveys of the public, whereas the FBI statistics are based on crimes reported by police departments to the agency. When the first crime victimization surveys were undertaken in the early 1970s, it became clear that police records reflected only a small proportion of reported violent crimes. So over the years the FBI has worked with local police departments to improve the record keeping. Consequently, police reports to the FBI include crimes that often went

unrecorded in the past, imparting an upward bias to the FBI crime count. By contrast, the BJS victimization data show no clear trend in violent crime from 1973 to 1981, a decline in rates during most of the years intervening since 1981. Indeed, according to this survey, all crimes have declined by 6 percent since 1973, the first year the survey was conducted (although the actual number of victimizations has increased, the violent-crime rate has remained flat when population increases are taken into account). However, the media's preoccupation with violent crime, and some truly tragic incidents around the nation, have sent public concerns about crime soaring in recent years. Yet even the FBI's 1994 *Uniform Crime Reports* show violent crime edging lower, although the number of murders rose 3 percent from 1992. (We will have more to say on the measurement of crime later in the chapter.) Table 5.2 presents crime victimization rates for 1991.

Juvenile Crime. According to the FBI's *Uniform Crime Reports,* youngsters under 18 years of age accounted for 29 percent of those arrested for the most violent crimes between 1987 and 1992. A 1992 study by Northeastern University's College of Criminal Justice reports that between 1985 and 1991 the number of 17-year-olds arrested for murder increased by 121 percent, the number of 16-year-olds by 158 percent, the number of 15-year-olds by 217 percent, and the number of boys 12 years of age and under doubled. Schools also report a marked upsurge in violence. The National School Board Association says 82 percent of the more than 700 school districts it surveyed in September 1993 reported student involvement in assaults, fistfights, knifings, and shootings had "increased significantly" or "increased somewhat" in the preceding 5 years (Henry, 1994).

The prevailing juvenile justice system rests primarily upon a 1950s profile of the delinquent that was subsequently codified into law in the early 1960s. Its guiding idea is that youngsters who engage in antisocial behavior deserve another chance and can be reformed through the efforts of criminologists and social workers. Juveniles are provided with attorneys, and their names and records are kept confidential. Critics contend that the program has resulted in a revolving door that repeatedly sends dangerous youths back to the streets. They point to statistics by some researchers showing that about 7 percent of young offenders are responsible for up to three-quarters of the violent crimes committed by juveniles (Tracy, Wolfgang, and Figlio, 1990).

It is clear that the present system of juvenile justice has encountered substantial failures either in deterring violent crime by the young or in rehabilitating young criminals. Currently the agendas of many public prosecutors are headed by proposals to transfer violent juvenile recidivists to the adult system. Overall, the public also seems to be searching for responses that are both tough and humane.

Simultaneously, sociological work is being energized by recent ethnographies of poverty and crime (Hagedorn, 1988; Anderson, 1990; Padilla, 1992). We will return to these matters in Chapters 6 and 7. For now let us merely note that the problems of inner-city children and young people are compounded by a deindustrializing economy where well-paying, secure jobs are scarce. Attitudes of anger and defiance are readily transferred from school to the workplace in an environment of labor market marginality (Moore, 1991).

Victimless Crime. A **victimless crime** is an offense in which no one involved is considered a victim (Schur, 1965). These crimes include gambling, the sale and use of illicit drugs, and prohibited sexual relationships between consenting adults (such as prostitution and, in some states, homosexuality). Usually a crime has an identifiable victim who suffers as a result of the criminal behavior. But in victimless crime, only the offenders themselves are likely to suffer. The behavior is criminalized because society, or powerful groups within a society, defines the behavior as immoral. Paradoxically, then, the existence of a law can

Table 5.2   CRIME VICTIMIZATION RATES, 1991

	Victims per 1,000 Persons*
Gender	
Male	105
Female	80
Age	
12–15	164
16–19	185
20–24	189
25–34	106
35–49	76
50–64	45
65+	23
Race	
White	91
Black	106
Other	80
Ethnicity	
Hispanic	96
Non-Hispanic	92
Family income	
Less than $7,500	122
$7,500–$14,999	103
$15,000–$24,000	88
$25,000–$29,999	89
$30,000–$49,999	85
$50,000+	86
Residence	
Central city	119
Suburban	88
Nonmetropolitan	69
Region	
Northeast	70
Midwest	91
South	91
West	122

*Rates are calculated per 1,000 population ages 12 and older.

SOURCE: Lisa D. Bastian, "Criminal Victimization 1991," *Bureau of Justice Statistics Bulletin,* U.S. Department of Justice.

result in more crime than there would be in the absence of the law. A good example of the "law begets crime" principle is the Eighteenth Amendment to the U.S. Constitution; designed to prohibit alcoholic drink, the amendment contributed to a proliferation of gangster operations and webs of corruption throughout government (Woodiwiss, 1988).

In recent years there has been a movement to decriminalize many victimless crimes. Proponents of decriminalization argue that these crimes consume an inordinate amount of the time and money of the criminal justice system and clog already congested courts and jails. Additionally, when goods and services that many people desire and are willing to purchase are made illegal, a black market supplied by organized crime almost invariably develops. Complicating matters, victimless crimes are often related to the corruption of police officers and others in the criminal justice system who receive bribes and payoffs from illegal suppliers and practitioners. Finally, there are those who argue that victimless crime involves acts that are private matters and thus are not rightfully the concern of government or other people. Critics of decriminalization suggest that some acts are "inherently evil" and justify public action in the same manner that those opposed to rape, theft, murder, and incest undertake to impose their moral standards on society. So once again we find that deviance and crime are not matters on which all people can agree and arrive at a universal standard. Instead, competing groups seek to gain the support of the state for their own morality and values.

MEASURING CRIME

Statistics on crime are among the most unsatisfactory of all social data (Biderman and Lynch, 1991). Official crime records—such as the FBI's annual *Uniform Crime Reports* based on incidents filed with more than 15,000 law enforcement agencies—suffer from numerous limitations. For one thing, a large proportion of the crimes that are committed go undetected; others are detected but not reported; and still others are reported but not officially recorded when police officers and politicians manipulate their reports to show low crime rates for political purposes. For another, perceptions of crime vary from community to community; what is viewed as a serious crime by a citizen of a small town may be shrugged off by a big-city resident as an unpleasant bit of everyday life. (For instance, if someone steals a car and gets caught in most cities, it is called "vehicle theft"; in Philadelphia, police often call it "joyriding.")

When the *Uniform Crime Reports* are compared with victim-based measures of crime (based on survey samples of American households in which individuals are asked if they or any members of their household have been victims of a crime during the previous year), the rates of various crimes in the United States are substantially higher. Justice Department studies reveal that less than half of all crimes are reported to the police. What accounts for the public's apparent reluctance to report crime? Researchers find that the single most common reason for not reporting is that people feel the offense is not important enough to warrant police attention. The second most cited explanation is that the matter is too private or personal to share with a stranger. And many people have little faith in authorities, believing that "nothing can be done." Add to these a feeling of helplessness, fear of reprisal, police insensitivity, and an unwillingness to get caught up in the slow-moving machinery of the criminal justice bureaucracy, the reluctance of individuals to report crime becomes more understandable (Kidd and Chayet, 1984; Gest, 1989).

Self-report–based measures of crime, involving anonymous questionnaires that ask people which offenses they have committed, also reveal much higher rates of crime than those found in official crime statistics. For instance, studies of juvenile crimes show that a good many youngsters of all social classes break some criminal laws, the amount of unreported crime is enormous, and convicted offenders are highly unrepresentative of persons violating the criminal law (Thornberry and Farnworth, 1982; Steffensmeier and Streifel, 1991). Youths who are arrested and placed in juvenile facilities typically have limited resources or repeatedly commit serious offenses, or both.

The *Uniform Crime Reports* focus on crimes that are most likely to be committed by young people and individuals from lower socioeconomic backgrounds. Statistics on many categories of crime, such as white-collar crime and organized crime, are not routinely compiled. Many crimes committed by persons of upper socioeconomic status in the course of business are handled by quasi-judicial bodies, such as the Federal Trade Commission and the National Labor Relations Board, or by civil courts. As a result, many businesspeople are able to avoid being stigmatized as criminals. Additionally, in cases of some criminal offenses, such as income tax evasion and fraud, the crimes are unlikely to be reported in victimization studies.

DRUGS AND CRIME

A study undertaken by the National Institute of Justice (the research arm of the Justice Department) found that from one-half to three-fourths of the men arrested for serious crimes in twelve major American cities tested positive for recent drug use (Kerr, 1988a, b). Moreover, a significant proportion of violent offenders are either drug suppliers fighting over territorial rights or drug abusers desperately seeking the means to feed their habit. Another study of 254 hard-core juvenile crack and cocaine users in Miami revealed that the adolescents confessed to an average of 880 crimes each in the previous year (the average breaks down to 37 major felonies ranging from assault to burglary, 101 prostitution and other vice offenses, 205 petty property crimes such as shoplifting, and 538 drug sale and possession violations) (Columbus, Ohio, *Dispatch,* August 4, 1989:5A). Additionally, more women are held in jails across the United States on drug charges than on any other charges (one in four women commit crimes to support their drug habit) (Sanchez, 1992). Such findings have heightened interest among criminal justice officials, criminologists,

and sociologists concerning the complex relationship between drugs and crime. If drug abuse contributes to the nation's street crime, then perhaps fighting the drug problem may be a cheaper way of reducing the crime rate than placing people in prison. Until recently, many academics considered the study of the connections between crime and drug use as controversial and ideologically tinged. In the late 1960s and early 1970s, the issue of drug use divided conservatives and liberals. For instance, as late as 1974, Dr. Peter G. Bourne, who later became President Carter's top drug adviser, wrote that he believed cocaine was generally a "benign" drug. However, by the mid-1980s, a consensus had emerged among wide segments of American society that all drug use was detrimental and a dangerous sign.

Given the ties between drugs and crime, it is difficult to overlook the part that drug addiction plays in motivating criminal behavior. Clearly, programs dealing with crime problems will have to address drug problems. There are countless proposals for dealing with drug abuse, including continued prohibition, decriminalization, and legalization. Yet little consensus exists among either the lay public or professionals on the most effective strategies (MacCoun, 1993). Indeed, we can safely conclude that no single initiative will "solve" the crime problem or end the drug-crime relationship. People use drugs for a great many reasons, and obviously not all people who use drugs are street criminals. Moreover, as we pointed out earlier in this chapter, there are many factors that contribute to "criminal" behavior.

There are some, like medical historian David F. Musto (1987), who believe that the drug epidemic is slowing. As Musto sees it, the United States has tended to swing between periods of abstinence and tolerance for drug use. Cycles of use, abuse, reaction, and reuse stretch over so many decades that generations unknowingly adopt favorite addictions of their great-grandparents while deeming themselves to be wickedly modern. Since the Jamestown colonists first harvested tobacco in 1611, Americans have been afflicted by "drugs."

Musto finds the current pattern of drug use dating back to the 1960s (when the belief was popularized that one could be smarter, be sexier, and work better if one used drugs). But cocaine and heroin use also took root in the 1890s in an epidemic that did not end until the 1930s. Indeed, in 1910 President William Howard Taft told Congress: "The misuse of cocaine is undoubtedly an American habit, the most threatening of the drug habits that has ever appeared in this country." The earlier epidemic and the problems it spawned contributed to the prohibition movement and the constitutional ban on alcohol. Musto notes that the current antidrug movement is broader than just cocaine and also targets tobacco and alcohol. He believes that although it may take a number of years, Americans will beat the drug problem again. His work leads him to conclude that the first people to go on a drug are the avant-garde and the wealthy (with drug usage later migrating to the inner city), but the middle and upper classes are also the first to go off it. Significantly, researchers are finding that drug abuse is now on the decline in the United States. Even so, just as there will always be casualties with alcohol, so there will always be casualties with other drugs.

DIFFERING CONCEPTIONS OF THE PURPOSES OF IMPRISONMENT

Many Americans take a rather gloomy view of crime-fighting programs. They question whether anything works. More than one wag has cracked, "Crime should have been added to 'death and taxes' as inevitable facts of life." Complicating matters, a debate rages between "hardliners" and "softliners." Hardliners want tougher judges and unshackled police. Softliners see crime as the product of societal conditions, urge the police to work harder on "community relations," and emphasize rehabilitation over punishment. Criminology and penology also have been in flux, with the experts themselves unsure of the most effective methods for dealing with the prison population (Stephens, 1989; Morris and Tonry, 1990).

Let us explore these matters by considering four traditional purposes of imprisonment: punishment, rehabilitation, deterrence, and selective confinement.

Punishment. Prior to 1800 it was widely assumed that the punishment of deviants was required if the injured community was to feel morally satisfied. But toward the latter part of the eighteenth and the early part of the nineteenth centuries, the focus changed. The idea that prisons might rehabilitate criminals came to the forefront. The word "penitentiary" was coined to describe a place where a criminal might repent and then resolve to follow a law-abiding life.

In recent years there has been a renewed interest in punishment not to satisfy a desire for vengeance but to restore a sense of moral order. The argument runs like this: Certain acts are basically antisocial and heinous—for instance, murder, rape, genocide, and the sexual abuse of children—and ought to be punished. The community experiences a sense of moral outrage when behavior that is grossly immoral goes unpunished. This outrage can impair the social system because society operates with the tacit understanding that there is some measure of fairness and normal order to life. Punishment is essential to maintain people's commitment to social order and to basic values and norms. As the discerning reader probably has gathered, this approach draws on the functionalist perspective for support.

Rehabilitation. During the past century and a half, the concept of rehabilitation has dominated penal philosophy. It has drawn on a humanistic tradition that has pressed for the individualization of justice and has demanded the fair treatment of criminals. Viewed in this manner, crime resembles "disease," something foreign and abnormal to people. Inherent in the definition of a sick person is a presumption that individuals are not to blame for the disease and that we should direct our attention to curing them. To say, "It is not primarily the person's fault. He or she is sick,"

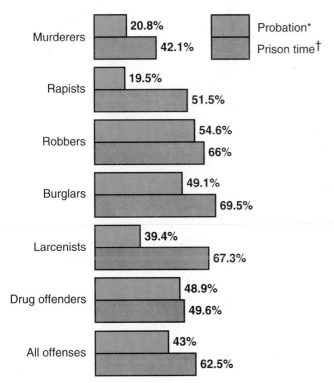

Murderers — 20.8% (Probation*), 42.1% (Prison time†)
Rapists — 19.5%, 51.5%
Robbers — 54.6%, 66%
Burglars — 49.1%, 69.5%
Larcenists — 39.4%, 67.3%
Drug offenders — 48.9%, 49.6%
All offenses — 43%, 62.5%

Probation*
Prison time†

* Includes only probation and probation with some jail time.
  Survey followed 79,000 felons from 1986 to 1989.
† Survey followed 108,850 state felons from 1983 to 1986.

Figure 5.4 RECIDIVISM
Percentage of felons who were arrested again within 3 years of receiving prison time or probation. (SOURCE: Data from Bureau of Justice Statistics. Adapted from *USA Today,* February 17, 1994, p. 2A. Copyright 1994, *USA Today.* Reprinted with permission.)

is to define the law violator as victim and not as victimizer.

Beginning in the 1960s, a number of criminologists began questioning the assumptions underlying rehabilitation strategies. And in recent years the chorus of critics has rapidly expanded. Critics of rehabilitation contend that education and psychotherapy cannot overcome or reduce the powerful tendency for some individuals to continue their criminal ways. They cite statistics on the high rate of *recidivism* (relapse into criminal behavior) to back up their argument (Martinson, 1974; Lipton, Martinson, and Wilks, 1975). Researchers typically find that the ultimate proba-

bility of recidivism for prison releases is about 50 percent (see Figure 5.4), and that the type of individual most likely to relapse is a young male who is a drug addict and/or an alcoholic with a large number of previous incarcerations, the last of which was a lengthy one for a crime against property (Schmidt and Witte, 1988). Critics of rehabilitation seek to show that rehabilitative efforts result in only limited reductions in criminality, and then only for some kinds of offenders and only under certain circumstances.

Deterrence. The notion of deterrence rests on assumptions about human nature that are

"So how are you doing with your community service?"

Drawing by Mort Gerberg; © 1991 The New Yorker Magazine, Inc.

difficult to prove. Even so, sociological studies seem to suggest that the *certainty* of apprehension and punishment does tend to lower crime rates (Waldo and Chiricos, 1972; Wolfgang, Figlio, and Sellin, 1972; Piliavin et al., 1986; Paternoster, 1989). Few studies, however, find an association between the *severity* of punishment and crime (Tittle and Logan, 1973; Gibbs, 1975; Grasmick and Bryjak, 1980; Paternoster and Iovanni, 1986; Bailey and Peterson, 1989; Paternoster, 1989). While sociologists recognize that the prospect of punishment has some deterrent effect under some circumstances, they have been more concerned with specifying the *conditions* under which punishment influences behavior (Brown, 1978; Erickson and Gibbs, 1978; Smith and Gartin, 1989). For instance, allegiance to a group and its norms typically operates as an even stronger force than the threat of societal punishment in bringing about conformity (Anderson, Chiricos, and Waldo, 1977; Meier and Johnson, 1977; Heckathorn, 1988, 1990). By the same token,

informal standards and pressures within delinquent subcultures may counteract the deterrent effects of legal penalties (Tittle and Rowe, 1974; Heckathorn, 1988, 1990).

Selective Confinement. There are those who argue, like Peter W. Greenwood (1982) of the Rand Corporation, that neither rehabilitation nor deterrence really works, and so it is useless to send people to prison with these goals in mind. However, imprisonment can be used to reduce crime rates (Blumstein and Cohen, 1987). If "hard-core" criminals are kept in prison and off the streets, they are not in a position to commit crimes (Justice Department figures reveal that nearly one out of five people arrested and charged with committing a felony are released from custody but rearrested for a similar felony offense before going to trial).

Greenwood (1982) developed a profile of the characteristics of individuals who are most likely to engage repeatedly in crime based on surveys of

2,200 inmates serving prison terms for robbery or burglary in California, Texas, and Michigan: imprisonment for more than half of the 2-year period preceding the most recent arrest, prior convictions for the same crime, a record that includes juvenile convictions before age 16, incarceration for a juvenile offense in a state or federal facility, heroin or barbiturate use as a juvenile, drug use during the 2 years prior to arrest, and unemployment during most of the period. Depending on the number of characteristics attributed to an individual, a subject is characterized as a low-, medium-, or high-rate offender. Greenwood asserts that incarcerating one robber who is among the top 10 percent in offense rates prevents more robberies than incarcerating eighteen offenders who are at or below the median.

Yet selective incarceration also poses difficulties. For instance, individuals who engage in robbery and burglary typically retire from these careers fairly early in life; hence the "out years" in a long sentence might represent a waste of prison capacity. There is also the legal and constitutional difficulty in a democratic nation in sentencing individuals on the basis of forecasts of their future behavior rather than on a verdict arising out of an actual crime. Further, comparable attempts by psychologists and psychiatrists to predict behavior on the basis of profile characteristics have been notoriously inaccurate (for instance, when they predict violence they seem to be wrong at least twice as often as they are right). Indeed, even according to Greenwood's own figures, only a little more than half the felons he places in the high-rate category belong there (Chaiken and Chaiken, 1982). Given these considerations, some sociologists simply conclude that the presence of a large proportion of law violators is probably inevitable, given the realities of contemporary social life (Martinson, 1974).

Summary

1. In all societies the behavior of some people at times goes beyond that permitted by the norms. Norms only tell us what we are supposed to do or what we are not supposed to do. They do not tell us what people actually do. And what some of us actually do very often runs counter to what other people judge to be acceptable behavior. In brief, social life is characterized not only by conformity but by deviance. Deviance is behavior that a considerable number of people view as reprehensible and beyond the limits of tolerance.

2. Implicit in a sociological definition of deviance is the notion that deviance is not a property inherent in certain forms of behavior; instead, it is a property conferred upon particular behaviors by social definitions. In this sense, deviance is what people say it is. Definitions as to which acts are deviant vary greatly from time to time, place to place, and group to group. When people differ regarding their definitions of what is and is not deviant behavior, it becomes a question of which individuals and groups will make their definitions prevail. Even so, in our daily lives we typically find that norms are not so much a point or a line but a zone.

3. Social order dictates that people, at least most people, have to be kept in line and that the line must be adhered to within allowable limits. Without social order, interaction would be a real problem and normative expectations would be meaningless. Accordingly, societies seek to ensure that their members conform with basic norms by means of social control.

Social control refers to the methods and strategies that regulate behavior within society. Three main types of social control processes operate within social life: (1) those that lead us to internalize our society's normative expectations, (2) those that structure our world of social experience, and (3) those that employ various formal and informal social sanctions.

4. It seems that most societies can absorb a good deal of deviance without serious consequences. But persistent and widespread deviance can be dysfunctional, impairing and even severely undermining organized life. It weakens people's willingness to play their roles and to obey the rules of society. But deviance may also be functional. It may promote social solidarity, clarify norms, strengthen group allegiances, and provide a catalyst for change.

5. According to the structural strain perspective, deviance derives from societal stresses. Robert K. Merton contends that American society sets forth goals of worldly success for the population at large but withholds the means for realizing these goals from significant segments of its population. He identifies five responses to the ends-means dilemma: conformity, innovation, ritualism, retreatism, and rebellion. Critics point out that the structural strain perspective overlooks those processes of social interaction by which people shape their definitions of the world about them and fashion their actions.

6. A number of sociologists have emphasized the similarities between the way deviant behavior is acquired and the way in which other behavior is acquired—the cultural transmission perspective. Edwin H. Sutherland elaborated on this notion in his theory of differential association. He said that individuals become deviant to the extent to which they participate in settings where deviant ideas, motivations, and techniques are viewed favorably. The earlier, the more frequent, the more intense, and the longer the duration of the contacts people have in deviant settings, the greater the probability that they too will become deviant. However, the theory is not applicable to some forms of deviance, particularly those in which neither the techniques nor the appropriate definitions and attitudes are acquired from other deviants.

7. Conflict theorists examine a variety of questions with respect to deviance. They ask, "Which group will be able to translate its values into the rules of a society and make these rules stick?" and "Who reaps the lion's share of benefits from particular social arrangements?" Marxist sociologists see crime as a product of capitalist laws that make behavior illegal that is offensive to the morality of the powerful and threatens their privileges and property. Critics charge that conflict formulations have given new directions to our understanding of deviance, but that the insights have been primarily rhetorical and require scientific inquiry.

8. Labeling theorists study the processes whereby some individuals come to be tagged as deviants, begin to think of themselves as deviants, and enter deviant careers. They say that the societal response to an act and not the behavior itself determines deviance. These sociologists point out that labeling people as deviants tends to set up conditions conducive to secondary deviance—deviance individuals adopt in response to the reactions of other individuals. Critics point out that labeling theory may help us understand how individuals become career deviants, but it tells us little about what contributed to their deviant behavior in the first place.

9. Crime is an act that is prohibited by law. The distinguishing property of crime is that people who violate the law are liable to be

arrested, tried, pronounced guilty, and deprived of their lives, liberty, or property. They become caught up in the elaborate social machinery of the criminal justice system—the reactive agencies of the state that include the police, the courts, and prisons. Within the United States, of every 100 felonies committed, only 33 are reported to the police. Of the 33 that are reported, only 6 are cleared by arrest. Of the 6 who are arrested, only 3 are prosecuted and convicted. Only 1 is sent to prison.

10. Since crime is an act prohibited by law, it is the state that defines crime by the laws it promulgates, administers, and enforces. An infinite variety of acts can be crimes. One type of crime that has been of particular interest to sociologists is white-collar crime—crimes committed by relatively affluent persons, often in the course of business activities. Another form of crime—organized crime—is carried out by large-scale bureaucratic organizations that provide illegal goods and services in public demand. Federal agencies keep records on index crimes—violent crimes against people and crimes against property. Still another type of crime is victimless crime—offenses in which no one involved is considered a victim.

11. Statistics on crime are among the most unsatisfactory of all social data. Official crime records suffer from numerous limitations. A large proportion of the crimes that are committed go undetected; others are detected but not reported; and still others are reported but not officially recorded. Official crime records are often supplemented by victim-based measures and self-report measures.

12. There have been four traditional purposes of imprisonment: punishment, rehabilitation, deterrence, and selective confinement. The rationale behind punishment is that it serves to restore a sense of moral order. Rehabilitation is premised on the notion that crime resembles disease and needs to be cured. Deterrence is based on the notion that if the price of crime is too high, people will not engage in it. And selective confinement suggests that crime rates can be reduced by keeping hard-core criminals in jail and off the streets.

Glossary

anomie A social condition in which people find it difficult to guide their behavior by norms they experience as weak, unclear, or conflicting.

crime An act prohibited by law.
criminal justice system The reactive agencies of the state that include the police, the courts, and prisons.

deviance Behavior that a considerable number of people in a society view as reprehensible and beyond the limits of tolerance.
differential association The notion that the earlier, the more frequent, the more intense, and the longer the duration of the contacts people have in deviant settings, the greater the probability that they too will become deviant.

index crimes Crimes reported by the Federal Bureau of Investigation in its Uniform Crime Reports. These offenses consist of four categories of violent crime against people—murder, rape, robbery, and assault—and four categories of crime against property—burglary, theft, motor vehicle theft, and arson.
internalization The process by which individuals incorporate within their personalities the standards of behavior prevalent within the larger society.

organized crime Large-scale bureaucratic organizations that provide illegal goods and services in public demand.

primary deviance Behavior that violates social norms but usually goes unnoticed by the agents of social control.

secondary deviance Deviance that individuals adopt in response to the reactions of other individuals.

social control Methods and strategies that regulate behavior within society.

victimless crime An offense in which no one involved is considered a victim.

white-collar crime Crime committed by relatively affluent persons, often in the course of business activities.

Chapter 6

SOCIAL
STRATIFICATION

Group living confers countless benefits on the members of society. Together they can accomplish a great many things that they could not otherwise achieve. But the advantages and disadvantages of the collective enterprise are not shared evenly. Most societies are organized so that their institutions systematically distribute benefits and burdens unequally among different categories of people. Sociologists call this structured system of inequality—the ranking or grading of individuals and groups into hierarchical layers—**social stratification**. Viewed in this manner, social arrangements are not neutral but serve and promote the goals and interests of some people more than they do those of other people.

The question of who gets what and why has intrigued humankind across the centuries (Lenski, 1966). The early Hebrew prophets who lived some 800 years before Christ—particularly Amos, Micah, and Isaiah—repeatedly denounced the rich and powerful members of their society. For example, Micah accused the leading citizens of his day of coveting and seizing their neighbors' fields and homes, being "full of violence," asking for bribes, and using dishonest and "deceitful" practices. Likewise, the classical Greek philosophers, including Plato and Aristotle, discussed at length the institution of private property and slavery. Writing in *The Republic* in 370 B.C., Plato observed: "Any city, however small, is in fact divided into two, one the city of the poor, the other of the rich; these are at war with one another." And in *The Laws of Manu*, compiled by Hindu priests about 200 B.C., we find an account of the creation of the world that portrays social inequalities as divinely ordained for the good of all. Indeed, as we will see later in the chapter, viewpoints regarding social stratification have tended to polarize. Some like Micah and Plato have criticized the existing distributive system, while others like the Hindu priests have supported it.

☐ Patterns of Social Stratification

Social stratification depends upon but is not the same thing as **social differentiation**—the process by which a society becomes increasingly specialized over time. Very early in their history, human beings discovered that a division of functions and labor contributed to greater social efficiency. Consequently, in all societies we find a separation of statuses and roles. This arrangement requires that people be distributed within the social structure so that the various statuses are filled and their accompanying roles performed. Nature helps to accomplish this task by dictating that only women should bear children, but nature does not go very much beyond this. Human beings have to figure out the rest for themselves.

Although the statuses that make up a social structure may be differentiated, they need not be *ranked* with respect to one another. For instance, within our society the statuses of infant and child are differentiated, but the one is not thought to be superior in rank to the other. They are merely different. Social differentiation sets the stage for—provides the social material that may or may not become the basis for—social ranking. In other words, whenever we encounter social stratification we find social differentiation, but not the other way around. Let us begin our consideration of social stratification by examining a number of different arrangements.

OPEN AND CLOSED SYSTEMS

Stratification systems differ in the ease with which they permit people to move in or out of particular strata (Wright and Cho, 1992). As we will see later in the chapter when we discuss social mobility, people often move vertically up or down in rank or horizontally to another status of roughly similar rank. Where people can change their status with relative ease, we refer to the arrangement as an **open system**. In contrast, where people have great difficulty in changing their status, we call the

arrangement a **closed system**. A somewhat similar distinction is conveyed by the concepts *achieved status* and *ascribed status* that we considered in Chapter 2. Achieved statuses are open to people on the basis of individual choice and competition, whereas ascribed statuses are assigned to people by their group or society.

Although there are no societies that are entirely open or entirely closed, the United States provides a good example of a relatively open system. The American folk hero is Abe Lincoln, the "poor boy who made good," the "rail-splitter" who through hard work managed to move "from log cabin to the White House." The American dream portrays a society in which all people can alter and improve their lot. Nearly two out of three Americans believe they have a good chance for getting ahead in the years to come. Today some 79 percent think they are more likely to succeed than their fathers, a figure up from 61 percent in 1939. And 66 percent now believe that the next generation's opportunities will be even better than theirs (Kraar, 1990).

The United States is founded not on the idea that all people should enjoy equal status, nor on the notion of a classless society. Rather, the democratic creed holds that all people should have an equal opportunity to ascend to the heights of the class system. In theory, the rewards of social life flow to people in accordance with their merit and competence and in proportion to their contribution to the larger social enterprise. However, in practice the ideal is not realized, since the American system places some measure of reliance on ascription, particularly in assigning statuses on the basis of gender, age, and race. We will examine these matters at greater length later in the chapter and in the chapter that follows.

When we think of a closed system, the Hindu caste arrangement often comes to mind, particularly as it operated in India prior to 1900. Under the traditional Hindu system, life was ordered in terms of castes in which people inherited their social status at birth from their parents and could not change it in the course of their lives. Historically there have been thousands of castes in India, although all of them have fallen into four major castes: the Brahmins, or priestly caste, who represent about 3 percent of the population; the Kshatriyas, allegedly descendants of warriors, and the Vaisyas, the traders, who together account for about 7 percent of Indians; and the Sudras, peasants and artisans, who constitute about 70 percent of the population. The remaining 20 percent are the Harijans, or Untouchables, who have traditionally served as sweepers, scavengers, leatherworkers, and swineherds.

Members of the lower castes were considered inferior, scorned, snubbed, and oppressed by higher-caste members regardless of personal merit and behavior. Rigid rules of avoidance operated within the system because contact with lower-caste members was believed spiritually to pollute and defile upper-caste members. Even today, caste still shapes behavior in some localities, especially in rural areas, setting the rules of courtship, diet, housing, and employment (Weisman, 1988; Crossette, 1991). The concept of *dharma* legitimates the system, establishing the idea that enduring one's lot in life with grace is the only morally acceptable way to live. But even at its zenith, the Hindu caste system never operated to foreclose mobility up and down the social ladder. Different birth and death rates among the castes, discontent among the disadvantaged and exploited, competition between members of different castes, the introduction of modern farming technologies, conversions to Buddhism and Islam, and other factors have operated against a completely closed system (Davis, 1949; Berreman, 1960; Gargan, 1992).

DIMENSIONS OF STRATIFICATION

We are indebted to Karl Marx and Max Weber for their insights that have helped us to unravel the nature of social stratification. Marx believed that the key to social stratification in capitalist societies is the division between those who own and control the crucial means of production—the oppressing capitalist class or bourgeoisie—and those who have only their labor to sell—the oppressed working class or proletariat. In Marx's view, these two groups and their conflicting interests provide the foundation for stratification in capitalist nations. For Marx, social stratification consists of a single dimension.

Weber (1946) felt that Marx provided an overly simplistic image of stratification. He contended that other divisions exist within society that are at times independent of the class or economic aspect. Consequently, he took a multidimensional view of stratification and identified three components: *class* (economic standing), *status* (prestige), and *party* (power). Each of these dimensions constitutes a distinct aspect of social ranking. Some statuses rank high in wealth, prestige, and power, such as that of most physicians. Yet the rankings of some statuses may be dissimilar. Some prostitutes and professional criminals enjoy economic privilege, although they possess little prestige or power. Members of university faculties and the clergy, while enjoying a good deal of prestige, typically rank comparatively low in wealth and power. And some public officials may wield considerable power but receive low salaries and little prestige. For the most part, however, these three dimensions hang together, feeding into and supporting one another (Wright, 1979, 1985). Let us examine each of them in turn.

Economic Standing. The economic dimension of stratification consists of wealth and income. **Wealth** has to do with what people own. **Income** refers to the amount of money people receive. Thus wealth is based on what people *have,* whereas income consists of what people *get.* For example, one individual may have a good deal of property but receive little income from it, such as people who collect rare coins, precious gems, or works of art. Another individual may receive a high salary but squander it on high living and have little wealth.

According to Federal Reserve Board and Internal Revenue Service data, the very rich in the

THE WALL STREET JOURNAL

"Actually, son, whether the glass is half full or empty isn't important—it's who owns the glass!"

From *The Wall Street Journal*—Permission, Cartoon Features Syndicate.

United States increased their share of the nation's total pool of privately held property during the economic boom of the 1980s. The richest 1 percent of U.S. households accounted for 37 percent of private net worth in 1989, up from 31 percent in 1983. By 1989, the top 1 percent (834,000 households with about $5.7 trillion of net worth) was worth more than the bottom 90 percent (84 million households, with about $4.8 trillion in net worth) (Nasar, 1992). See Figure 6.1. The surge in wealth at the top was accompanied by a sharp increase in the percentage of full-time workers who earn less than $12,195 annually ($6.10 an hour for someone working 40 hours a week, 50 weeks a year) from 12.1 percent of all full-time employees in 1979 to 18 percent by 1990 (DeParle, 1992).

Prestige. **Prestige** involves the social respect, admiration, and recognition associated with a particular social status. It entails a feeling that we are admired and thought well of by others. Prestige is intangible, something that we carry about in our heads. However, in our daily lives we commonly seek to give prestige a tangible existence through titles, special seats of honor, deference rituals, honorary degrees, emblems, and conspicuous displays of leisure and consumption. These activities and objects serve as symbols of prestige to which we attribute social significance and meaning. Much of our interaction with others consists of subtle negotiation over just how much deference, honor, respect, and awe we are to extend and receive. Even a simple conversation frequently involves a bargain that we will be attentive to what others say to us if they in turn will be attentive to what we say—a mutual exchange of "ego massages."

We show deference—behavior dramatizing and confirming a person's superior ranking—in a good many ways. In *presentation rituals* we engage in symbolic acts, such as revealing regard and awe by bowing, scraping, and displaying a humble demeanor. In *avoidance rituals* we achieve the same end by maintaining a "proper distance" from prestigious figures. Consider Theodore H. White's (1961:171) account of an incident that occurred in 1960 when John F. Kennedy's presidential nomination became a certainty. As Kennedy entered his "hideaway cottage," where a number of Democratic party leaders had assembled, he walked over to his brother Bobby and his brother-in-law Sargent Shriver:

The others in the room surged forward on impulse to join him. Then they halted. A distance of perhaps 30 feet separated them from him, but it was impassable. [After a few minutes, Shriver crossed the separating space and invited the leaders over.] First Averell Harriman; then Dick Daley; then Mike DiSalle; then, one by one, Kennedy let them all congratulate him. Yet no one could pass the little open space between him and them uninvited, because there was this thin separation about him, and the knowledge they were there not as patrons but as his clients. They could come by invitation only, for this might be a President of the United States.

Nearly a century ago, Thorstein Veblen (1899) highlighted the part that *conspicuous leisure* and *conspicuous consumption* play in revealing social ranking. He noted that in order to gain and hold prestige it is not enough merely to possess wealth

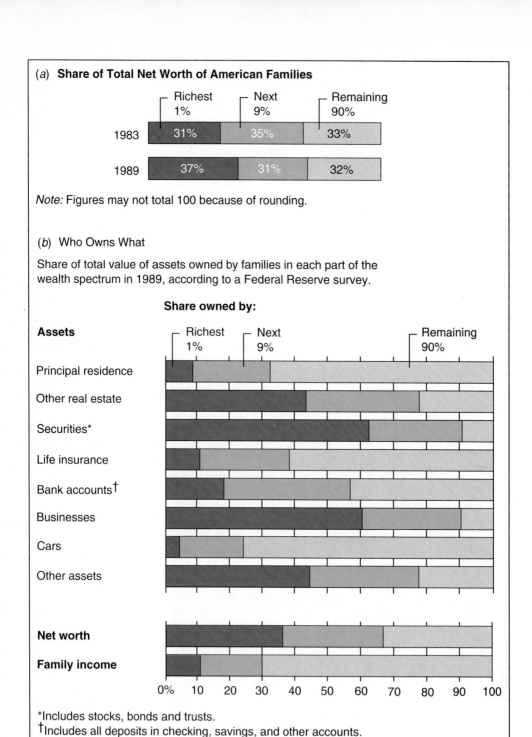

(a) **Share of Total Net Worth of American Families**

Richest 1% | Next 9% | Remaining 90%

1983: 31% | 35% | 33%

1989: 37% | 31% | 32%

Note: Figures may not total 100 because of rounding.

(b) **Who Owns What**

Share of total value of assets owned by families in each part of the wealth spectrum in 1989, according to a Federal Reserve survey.

Share owned by:

Assets — Richest 1% — Next 9% — Remaining 90%

Principal residence
Other real estate
Securities*
Life insurance
Bank accounts†
Businesses
Cars
Other assets

Net worth

Family income

0% 10 20 30 40 50 60 70 80 90 100

*Includes stocks, bonds and trusts.
†Includes all deposits in checking, savings, and other accounts.

Figure 6.1 THE CONCENTRATION OF U.S. WEALTH IN THE 1980s
(a) Federal Reserve Statistics report that between 1983 and 1989 the total net worth share of the richest 1 percent of the population grew by 6 percent. *(b)* A breakdown of the assets of the richest 1 percent of U.S. families shows that holdings in real estate, securities, and business account for the bulk of their assets. (SOURCE: Adapted from *The New York Times,* April, 21, 1992, p. A6. Copyright © 1992 by The New York Times Company. Reprinted by permission.)

and power. The wealth and power must be put on public view, for prestige is awarded only on evidence. It seems to help our self-esteem not only to know that we enjoy high status but to receive a reminder of it with some frequency (Faunce, 1989). One way we undertake to advertise high status is to lavish expenditure on clothing because we can size up one another's apparel at a glance. The requirement that people dress in the latest fashion, coupled with the fact that the accredited fashion changes from season to season, greatly increases the amount that must be spent on a wardrobe and hence enhances its symbolic significance. The automobile serves a similar purpose, particularly a very expensive one such as a Lexus, Lamborghini, Porsche, Bentley Continental, or Aston Martin. Veblen documents how relative success, tested by comparing one's own economic situation with that of others, becomes an established end. So comparisons find symbolic expression, since displaying one's bankbook or stock certificates would be impractical and considered in "poor taste."

The prestige of most Americans rests primarily on their income, occupation, and lifestyle (Coleman and Rainwater, 1978). Family background and wealth count for less than they did a generation or so ago. Simultaneously, an individual's "personality" and "gregariousness" have taken on greater importance. Although people still think that money is the most important thing, the lifestyle individuals project and the values they reflect now assume a critical part in determining their prestige (Jackman and Jackman, 1983).

Power.   Prestige typically leads others to conform to our wishes through voluntary compliance, deference, and acceptance. Not so with power. Power entails conduct by which we *compel* others to do what they do not wish to do (Kemper and Collins, 1990). As we will see in Chapter 8, power determines which individuals and groups will be able to translate their preferences into the reality of social life. **Power** refers to the ability of individuals and groups to realize their will in human affairs even if it involves the resistance of others. It provides answers to the question of whose interests will be served and whose values will reign. Wherever we look, from families to juvenile gangs to nation-states, we find that some parties disproportionately achieve their way. Even in such a simple matter as eye contact, we find the operation of power. Low-power people typically look less at an individual when they are speaking to a high-power person than when they are listening. In contrast, high-power people display nearly equivalent rates of looking while speaking and while listening (Ellyson et al., 1980). Not surprisingly, sociologist Amos Hawley (1963:422) observes: "Every social act is an exercise of power, every social relationship is a power equation, and every social group or system is an organization of power."

The bases of power fall into three categories. First, there are **constraints**—those resources that allow one party to add *new disadvantages* to a situation. People typically view constraints as punishments because they entail harming the body, psyche, or possessions of others (Molm, 1989). Second, there are **inducements**—those resources that allow one party to add *new advantages* to a situation. Individuals usually consider inducements to be rewards because they involve transferring socially defined good things—such as material objects, services, or social positions—in exchange for compliance with the wishes of the power wielder. Third, there is **persuasion**—those resources that enable one party to change the minds of other people *without* adding either advantages or disadvantages to a situation. By virtue of persuasion—based on one party's reputation, wisdom, personal attractiveness, or control of the media—individuals or groups are led to prefer the same outcomes the power wielder prefers.

Power affects the ability of people to make the world work on their behalf. To gain mastery of critical resources is to gain mastery of people. To control key resources is to interpose oneself (or one's group) between people and the means whereby people meet their biological, psychologi-

Doing Sociology: Stratification in Campus Life

Social stratification pervades all aspects of social life. It represents structured inequality in the allocation of rewards, privileges, and resources. Some individuals—by virtue of their roles or group memberships—are advantaged, while others are disadvantaged. College life is not exempt from these patterns, despite the fact that college communities are often portrayed as rather benign settings in which administration, faculty, and students are preoc-cupied with the pursuit of knowledge and human better-ment. Wherever one turns, social inequality confronts the members of the college community, a matter that two students discuss in the following observations:

Our math classroom is on the third floor of a building that overlooks the top floor of a parking ramp. At most three or four cars are parked up there, although it contains enough space for at least fifty cars. The lower levels of the ramp are also fairly empty. The ramp is only for the use of faculty. We students have to park some distance from campus and even then we have to get to school by 7:30 in the morning if we are to find a parking space. . . . The faculty enjoy many privileges. They have special offices; departmental chair-persons have more spacious offices; and deans and the university president have even more magnificent offices. The faculty have "fac-ulty restrooms" which are dis-tinct from those simply labeled "restroom." Each dean has his own private restroom. The faculty address us by our first names, whereas we have to call them "Doctor" and "Professor."

cal, and social needs. To the extent to which some groups command rewards, punishments, and per-suasive communications, they are able to dictate the terms by which the game of life is played. At times, to play the game "by the rules" means that it is no game at all—the deck is stacked, and so the outcome is a foregone conclusion.

☐ Explanations of Social Stratification

Throughout human history, the question of why social inequality and division should characterize the human condition has been a matter of lively concern (Lenski, 1966). And as with earlier philosophers, the issue has provided a central focus of the new science called sociology. Through the years, two strikingly divergent answers have emerged. The first—the conserva-tive thesis—has supported existing social arrange-ments, contending that an unequal distribution of social rewards is a necessary instrument for get-ting the essential tasks of society performed. In sharp contrast, the second view—the radical the-sis—has been highly critical of existing social arrangements, viewing social inequality as a dog-eat-dog and exploitative mechanism arising out of a struggle for valued goods and services in short supply. Contemporary theories of inequality fall broadly into one or the other tradition. Those with roots in the conservative tradition are labeled *functionalist* theories; those stemming from the radical tradition are called *conflict* theo-ries. Hence, as sociologists Seymour Lipset and Reinhard Bendix (1951:150) remarked over 40 years ago, "Discussions of different theories of class are often academic substitutes for a real conflict over political orientations."

I have been a college student now for three years. Time and again I hear it said that universities exist for students and that their primary purpose is to educate and enrich people's lives. I came to college quite idealistic, believing in its visionary commitment. But in the course of my campus experiences I have come to a quite different conclusion. Universities exist chiefly for university officials and the faculty. Student needs have minimal priority. As freshmen we are herded in mass lectures and recitation sections with little concern for our individual experiences, capabilities, or interests. We have little or no voice in what we are taught or who teaches us. These decisions are made in an authoritarian manner by others. It seems to matter little to the powers-that-be whether teaching is good, bad, or indifferent. Professors are ultimately judged on other attributes, most particularly their ability to bring research funds to the university and "knock out" publications. In fact, students are locked in an arrangement of structured inequality. Notice how the classroom is set up. We are placed in rows of undifferentiated seats that are usually bolted to the floor. The message is clear. Students are interchangeable with one another and count for little. In contrast, professors have about a fourth to a third of the classroom, a vast territory that they can freely roam about. Commonly a solid table or lectern sets the professor apart from the class, a physical barrier that symbolically underlines the social distance and status differential that separate us. The manner in which classroom seating is laid out bars egalitarian exchanges even were the professor disposed toward them. Thus students are continually reminded of their subordinate and disprivileged position.

THE FUNCTIONALIST THEORY OF STRATIFICATION

The functionalist theory of social inequality holds that stratification exists because it is beneficial for society. This theory was most clearly set forth in 1945 by Kingsley Davis and Wilbert Moore, although it has been subsequently modified and refined by other sociologists. Davis and Moore argue that social stratification is both universal and necessary, and hence no society is ever totally unstratified or classless. In their view all societies require a system of stratification if they are to fill all the statuses comprising the social structure and to motivate individuals to perform the duties associated with these positions. Consequently, society must motivate people at two different levels: (1) It must instill in certain individuals the desire to fill various positions, and (2) once the individuals are in these positions it must instill in them the desire to carry out the appropriate roles.

Society must concern itself with human motivation because the duties associated with the various statuses are not all equally pleasant to the human organism, are not all equally important to social survival, and are not all equally in need of the same abilities and talents. If social life were otherwise, it would make little difference who got into which positions, and the problem of social placement would be greatly reduced. Moreover, the duties associated with a good many positions are viewed by their occupants as onerous. Hence, in the absence of motivation, many individuals would fail to act out their roles.

On the basis of these social realities, Davis and Moore contend that a society must have, first, some kind of rewards that it can use as inducements for its members, and second, some way of distributing these rewards among the various statuses. Inequality is the motivational incentive that society has evolved to meet the twin problems of filling all the statuses and getting the occupants to enact the associated roles to the best of their abilities. Since these rewards are built into the social system, social stratification is a structural feature of all societies.

Employing the economists' model of supply and demand, Davis and Moore say that the positions most highly rewarded are those (1) that are occupied by the most talented or qualified incumbents (supply) and (2) that are functionally most important (demand). For instance, to ensure sufficient physicians, a society needs to offer them high salaries and great prestige. If it did not offer these rewards, Davis and Moore suggest that we could not expect people to undertake the "burdensome" and "expensive" process of medical education. So people at the top *must* receive the rewards they do. If they did not, the positions would remain unfilled and society would disintegrate.

This structure-function approach to stratification has been the subject of much criticism. For one thing, critics charge that people are *born* into family positions of privilege and disprivilege. As we will see later in our discussion of social mobility, where people end up in the stratification system depends in good measure on birth (Kim, 1987). Even in open class systems like the United States, the starting blocks in the competitive race are so widely staggered that the runners in the rear have only a remote chance of catching up with those ahead, while those starting ahead must virtually quit to lose ground. For instance, nearly two-thirds of the chief executive officers (CEOs) in 243 large American companies grew up in upper-middle- or upper-class families (Boone, Kurtz, and Fleenor, 1988). Such findings lead conflict theorists to contend that society is structured so that individuals *maintain* a ranking that is determined by birth and that is *irrespective* of their abilities.

Critics also point out that many of the positions of highest responsibility in the United States—in government, science, technology, and education—are not financially well rewarded (Bok, 1993). The officers of large corporations earn considerably more than presidents of the United States, cabinet members, and Supreme Court justices. For instance, in 1993, Michael Eisner, chairman of the Walt Disney Company, made $203.1 million (more than one-half million dollars a day for an entire year, or $78,081 an hour). Eisner earned the amount despite the fact that Disney's profit fell 63 percent in 1993 to $299.8 million (so Eisner's compensation equaled 68 percent of the amount of the company's earnings) (Byrne, 1994a). Figures for 1990 reveal that the average chief executive officer of a large American corporation received $1.9 million in total compensation—eighty-five times the average U.S. worker's pay (Hillkirk, 1991b). Additionally, one may ask whether garbage collectors, despite their lower pay and prestige, are more important to the survival of the United States than are top athletes who receive incomes in seven and even eight figures. Similarly, in 1993, Oprah Winfrey reportedly made $52 million, in part because her show is seen in 64 foreign markets (Samuelson, 1994). In sum, the notion that many low-paying positions are functionally less important to society than are high-paying positions is often difficult to support.

THE CONFLICT THEORY OF STRATIFICATION

The conflict theory of social equality holds that stratification exists because it benefits individuals and groups who have the power to dominate and exploit others. Whereas functionalists stress the common interests the members of society share, conflict theorists focus on the interests that divide people. Viewed from the conflict perspective, society is an arena in which people struggle for privilege, prestige, and power, and advantaged groups enforce their advantage through coercion (Grimes, 1991).

The conflict theory draws heavily on the ideas of Karl Marx. As discussed in Chapter 1, Marx believed that a historical perspective is essential for understanding any society. To grasp how a particular economic system works, he said that we must keep in mind the predecessor from which it evolved and the process by which it grows. According to Marx, the current state of technology and the method of organizing production are the primary determinants of the evolutionary direction of society. At each stage of history, these factors determine the group that will dominate the society and the groups that will be subjugated. For instance, under the feudal arrangement, the medieval lords were in control of the economy and dominated the serfs. Under the capitalist system, the manor lord has been replaced by the modern capitalist and the serf by the "free" laborer—in reality a propertyless worker who "has nothing to sell but his hands."

Marx contended that the capitalist drive to realize surplus value is the foundation of modern class struggle—an irreconcilable clash of interests between workers and capitalists. *Surplus value* is the difference between the value that workers create (as determined by the labor-time embodied in a commodity that they produce) and the value that they receive (as determined by the subsistence level of their wages). Capitalists do not create surplus value; they appropriate it through their exploitation of workers. Consequently, as portrayed by Marx, capitalists are thieves who steal the fruits of the laborer's toil. The capitalist accumulation of capital (wealth) derives from surplus value and is the key to—indeed, the incentive for—the development of contemporary capitalism. Marx believed that the class struggle will eventually be resolved when the working class overthrows the capitalist class and establishes a new and equitable social order.

Marx held that classes do not exist in isolation, independent of other classes to which they are opposed: "Individuals form a class only so far as they are engaged in a common struggle with another class" (quoted by Dahrendorf, 1959:14). Under capitalism, workers at first are blinded by a *false consciousness*—an incorrect assessment of how the system works and of their subjugation and exploitation by capitalists. But through a struggle with capitalists, the workers' "objective" class interests become translated into a subjective recognition of their "true" circumstances and they formulate goals for organized action—in brief, they acquire *class consciousness*. Hence, according to Marxists, if the working class is to take on its historical role of overturning capitalism, "it must become a class not only 'as against capital' but also 'for itself'; that is to say, the class struggle must be raised from the level of economic necessity to the level of conscious aim and effective class consciousness" (Lukacs, 1922/1968:76). It is not enough for the working class to be a "class in itself"; it must become a "class for itself."

Much of the appeal of Marx's work lies in its seemingly straightforward simplicity. He strips away the superficial verbiage and qualifications of which college professors seem so fond. But it is this very simplicity that is deceiving. Conflict is a pervasive feature of human life and is not restricted to economic relations. As Ralf Dahrendorf (1959:208) observes: "It appears that not only in social life, but wherever there is life, there is conflict." Dahrendorf holds that group conflict is an inevitable aspect of society, and he rejects Marx's view that the proletarian revolution will eliminate class conflict. Indeed, today sociological Marxism is encountering a crisis of confidence. Its credentials and prestige have been tarnished by the collapse of the Soviet regime and the slippage in the popularity of the social democratic Left in many Western nations. Marxist sociologists are responding by reconceptualizing many of their basic theoretical tenets (McNall, Levine, and Fantasia, 1991; Wright, Levine, and Sober, 1992).

Even in the realm of property, the Marxist dichotomy between the capitalist class and the working class hides or distorts other dynamic processes. Debtor and creditor have also stood against each other throughout history. For example, a dominant feature of nineteenth-century politics was the cheap-money cry of agrarians (the Greenback and Free Silver movements). Consumers and sellers have also confronted one another, a factor feeding the inner-city outbreaks

THE WALL STREET JOURNAL

"What's the point of having power if you can't occasionally get drunk with it?"

From *The Wall Street Journal*—Permission, Cartoon Features Syndicate.

of the 1960s. And divisions among racial and ethnic groups, skilled workers and unskilled laborers, and union organizations have been recurrent features of the American landscape.

Ownership of property in the form of the means of production—control over material facilities—constitutes only one source of power. Control over human beings—the possession of the *means of administration*—provides another (Giddens, 1985). Regimes in the pre-1991 Soviet Union and the nations of Eastern Europe provide a good illustration of this. More than 30 years ago, Milovan Djilas (1957, 1988), a Yugoslavian Marxist and one-time lieutenant of President Tito, pointed out that the "communist new class" was "made up of those who have special privileges and economic preference because of the administrative monopoly they hold" (1957:39). Long before the breakdown of the communist regimes, Djilas observed: "Power is an end in itself and the essence of contemporary Communism" (1957:169).

We also often overlook the fact that power flows from knowledge. More than 50 years ago the Austrian economist Joseph A. Schumpeter (1883–1950) emphasized that knowledge, technology, and innovation are the key cornerstones (more than price competition) for energizing economic life (Swedberg, 1991). For instance, within contemporary American life, engineers and technicians derive organizational and social power by virtue of their expertise. Indeed, some sociologists postulate the emergence of a "new middle class" in advanced industrial nations that is made up of professionals, semiprofessionals, and highly qualified craftsworkers who possess "skill and credential assets" and managers and supervisors who enjoy "organizational assets" (Collins, 1979; Kriesi, 1989).

Within the United States one can go a long way nowadays without property. As we will see in Chapter 8, a good deal of power derives from office rather than ownership in large multinational corporations. Not only do executives hold comparatively little in the way of property, but their influence lasts only as long as they hold their particular positions. Their hold on power is often tenuous, and they are easily replaceable. Much the same picture emerges from government. Neither Harry S. Truman, Dwight D. Eisenhower, Lyndon B. Johnson, Richard M. Nixon, Gerald Ford, nor Ronald Reagan launched his career from a base of financial, industrial, or landed property, yet each reached the pinnacle of power in the United States.

Recently Erik Olin Wright (1985, 1993; Steinmetz and Wright, 1989) has investigated class relations in the United States using Marx's idea that class must be defined in terms of people's relation to the means of production. He identifies four classes: capitalists, managers, workers, and the petty bourgeoisie (small entrepreneurs). Using samples of people in the labor force, Wright finds that these categories are about as good in explaining differences in income among people as are occupation and education. Even allowing for the effects on income of occupation, education, age, and job tenure, capitalists have higher incomes than do the other classes. Thus Wright concludes that being a capitalist makes a difference (Kamolnick, 1988).

A SYNTHESIS

Any number of sociologists have noted that both the functionalist and conflict theories have merit, but that each is better than the other in answering different questions (Sorokin, 1959; van den Berghe, 1963; Milner, 1987). For instance, Harold R. Kerbo (1983) observes that a supply and demand relation such as that proposed by structure-function theorists explains some of the distribution of rewards within the occupational structure. But he also notes that supply and demand is not free and unrestricted, the position taken by conflict theorists. Kerbo agrees with Marxian theorists that economic conflicts are among the most important sources of division in capitalistic societies, but not the only sources. He views stratification systems as socially evolved mechanisms—institutional arrangements—for reducing conflict over the distribution of valued goods and services in society.

Some sociologists such as Ralf Dahrendorf (1959) contend that society is basically "Janus-headed" and that functionalists and conflict theorists are simply studying two aspects of the same reality. Sociologist Gerhard E. Lenski (1966) builds on this observation and looks for ways of integrating the two perspectives to arrive at a workable synthesis. He tends to agree with functionalists that the chief resources of society are allocated as rewards to people who occupy vital positions and that stratification fosters a rough match between scarce talents and rewards. But as a society advances in technology, it becomes capable of producing a considerable surplus of goods and services. This surplus gives rise to conflicts over who should control it. Power provides the answer to the question of control and determines the distribution of the surplus. Consequently, with technological advance, an increasing proportion of the goods and services available to a society are distributed on the basis of power. In short, Lenski holds that both the functionalist and conflict positions are true, but that neither contains the whole truth.

□ The American Class System

Sociologists may disagree regarding the sources of social stratification. However, they agree that social inequality is a *structured* aspect of contemporary life. When sociologists say that social inequality is structured, they mean more than that individuals and groups differ in the privileges they enjoy, the prestige they receive, and the power they wield. Structuring means that inequality is hardened or institutionalized, so that there is a system for determining who gets what. Inequality does not occur in a random fashion but follows recurrent relatively consistent and stable patterns. Further, these inequalities are typically passed on from one generation to the next. Individuals and groups that are advantaged commonly find ways to ensure that their offspring will also be advantaged.

Sociologists have borrowed the term "stratification" from geology. However, it is important to realize that it is somewhat more difficult to classify individuals within strata than it is to categorize rocks. Geologists usually find it rather easy to determine where one stratum of rock ends and another begins. But social strata often shade off into one another so that their boundaries are dim and indistinct. All this raises the question of how we go about identifying classes.

IDENTIFYING SOCIAL CLASSES

In the course of our everyday conversations we talk about the "upper class," "middle class," and "lower class," referring to these social classes as distinct groups. Two views are found among sociologists concerning the accuracy of this popular conception (Lucal, 1994). The first view holds that classes are real, bounded strata that exist in conflicting relations with one another (the relational model). Although this position has been a central element in Marxist formulations (Marx and Engels, 1848/1955; Wright, 1985), it also

Table 6.1   IDENTIFYING SOCIAL CLASSES

Method	Advantages	Disadvantages
Objective	This is a clear-cut method for studying the correlates of social class. It is commonly the simplest and cheapest approach since data can usually be obtained from government sources.	The method often does not yield divisions that people themselves employ in their daily lives.
Self-placement	The method can be applied to a large population since survey techniques can be employed for securing the data. It is a useful method for predicting political behavior since who people think they are influences how they vote.	The class with which people identify may represent their aspirations rather than their current associations or the appraisals of other people.
Reputational	The method provides a valuable tool for investigating social distinctions in small groups and communities. It is especially useful for predicting associational patterns among people.	The method is difficult to use in large samples where people have little or no knowledge of one another.

emerges in the work of other sociologists who have identified a blue-collar/white-collar division in American life (Blau and Duncan, 1972; Vanneman and Cannon, 1987; Sobel, 1989). The second view portrays American society as essentially classless, one in which class divisions are blurred by virtue of their continuous and uninterrupted nature (the distributional model). Seen in this manner, "social classes" are culturally quite alike and simply reflect gradations in rank rather than hard-and-fast social groups (Hodge and Treiman, 1968; Eichar, 1989).

The differing conceptions derive in large measure from different approaches to identifying social classes: (1) the objective method, (2) the self-placement method, and (3) the reputational method. Although all the approaches produce some overlap in classes, there are appreciable differences in the results afforded by each (Kerbo, 1983). Moreover, each approach has certain advantages and disadvantages (see Table 6.1). Let us consider each method more carefully.

The Objective Method. The **objective method** views social class as a statistical category. The cat-

egories are formed not by the members themselves but by sociologists or statisticians. Most commonly people are assigned to social classes on the basis of income, occupation, or education (or some combination of these characteristics). The label "objective" can be misleading, for it is not meant to imply that the approach is more "specific" or "unbiased" than either of the others. Rather, it is objective in that numerically measurable criteria are employed for the placement of individuals. Figure 6.2 shows one way of depicting the distribution of Americans by family income.

The objective method provides a rather clear-cut statistical measure for investigating various correlates of class, such as life expectancy, mental illness, divorce, political attitudes, crime rates, and leisure activities. It is usually the simplest and cheapest approach since statistical data can be obtained from government agencies and the Census Bureau. But there is more to class than simply raw statistical data. In the course of their daily lives, people size one another up on a good many standards of excellence. Moreover, it is not only actual income, occupation, or education that matters but also the meanings and definitions

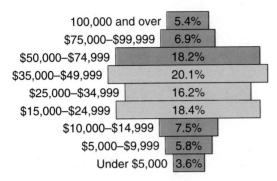

Figure 6.2 DISTRIBUTION OF FAMILIES, BY INCOME, 1990
(SOURCE: Data from U.S. Bureau of the Census. Adapted from "The Squeeze Is On," *Newsweek*, November 4, 1991, p. 24. Copyright 1991, Newsweek Inc. All rights reserved. Reprinted by permission.)

others assign to these qualities. For instance, a banker, while not falling below the middle class, is not necessarily accorded the highest social position in American communities (Warner and Lunt, 1941:82).

The Self-Placement Method. The **self-placement method** (also known as the subjective method) has people identify the social class to which they think they belong. Class is viewed as a social category, one in which people group themselves with other individuals they perceive as sharing certain attributes in common with them. The class lines may or may not conform to what social scientists think are logical lines of cleavage in the objective sense. Researchers typically ask respondents to identify their social class (see Figure 6.3).

Within American life a family's class position historically derived from the husband's position in the labor market. But long-term social and economic changes, particularly the movement of many women into the workplace and declining family size, seem to be altering the way many women assess their class identity (Baxter, 1994). The class identification of married men and women may be thought of as a continuum from "borrowing" (in which one's spouse's characteristics are more important than one's own) to "sharing" (in which equal weight is attached to one's own and one's spouse's characteristics) to "independence" (in which one's own characteristics outweigh those of one's spouse). Whereas in the 1970s, most employed women appraised their class position primarily in terms of the class position of their husbands, in the 1980s and 1990s employed women have moved toward a sharing model. Husbands also have moved in the direction of increasing independence. And single men and women now look increasingly to their own characteristics rather than those of their parents in assessing their class identities (Davis and Robinson, 1988). These trends seem linked to the growth of individualism that has permeated American life in recent years (Bellah et al., 1985).

The major advantage of the self-placement approach is that it can be applied to a large population, whereas, as we will shortly see, the reputational approach is limited to small communities. Table 6.2 shows how Americans rank the prestige of various occupations when asked to do so. The self-placement method is also an especially useful tool for predicting political behavior since who people *think* they are influences how they vote. However, the approach has its limitations. The class with which people identify may represent their aspirations rather than their current associations or the appraisals of other people. Further, when placing themselves in a national class structure, people commonly use fewer categories than they do when interacting with actual people and sizing them up in terms of subtle distinctions.

The Reputational Method. In the self-placement method people are asked to rank themselves. In the **reputational method** they are asked how they classify *other* individuals. This approach views class as a social group, one in which people share a feeling of oneness and are bound together in relatively stable patterns of interaction. Therefore class rests on the knowledge of who associates with whom. The approach gained prominence in

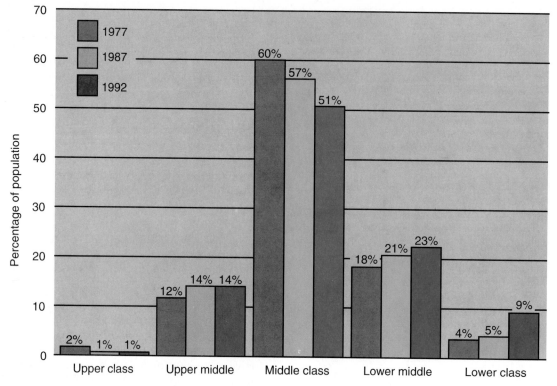

Figure 6.3 THE SELF-PLACEMENT FOR IDENTIFYING CLASS MEMBERSHIP
How Americans see themselves when asked to use one of four names for identifying their
social class. Young people ages 18 to 29 are the most pessimistic in defining their economic
class according to this Roper survey taken in June 1992. Those 60 and over are the most
optimistic. (SOURCE: From National Opinion Research Center, 1982.)

the 1930s when W. Lloyd Warner and his associates studied the class structure of three communities: "Yankee City" (Newburyport, Massachusetts), a New England town of some 17,000 people (Warner and Lunt, 1941, 1942); "Old City" (Natchez, Mississippi), a southern community of about 10,000 (Davis, Gardner, and Gardner, 1941); and "Jonesville" (Morris, Illinois), a midwestern town of about 6,000 (Warner, 1949). In Yankee City and Old City, Warner identified six classes: upper-upper, lower-upper, upper-middle, lower-middle, upper-lower, and lower-lower. In the more recently settled and smaller midwestern community of Jonesville he found five classes since individuals made no distinction between the

upper-upper and lower-upper classes (the former being an "old family" class representing "an aristocracy of birth and wealth" and the latter a class composed of the "new rich") (see Figure 6.4). Warner's sociological conception of the American class system was popularized by the media and gained considerable public appeal. Even today his formulations carry considerable weight in how the American public has come to view and think about social class in American life.

The reputational method is a valuable tool for investigating social distinctions in small groups and small communities. And it is particularly useful in predicting associational patterns among people. But it is difficult to use in large samples where people have little or no knowledge of one another.

Combining Approaches. Warner undertook most of his research prior to World War II. Recently sociologists Richard D. Coleman and Lee Rainwater (1978) have updated our understanding of the class structure of urban America by combining the self-placement and reputational methods. They interviewed residents of Kansas City and Boston, querying them about their perception of the levels of contemporary living. The urbanites ranked each other and themselves in the following manner:

1. *People who have really made it.* At the very top of the American class structure is an elite class of wealthy individuals. Some of these are old rich (the Rockefellers); others, the celebrity rich (Paul Newman); still others, the anonymous rich (a millionaire shopping center developer); and yet another group is made up of the run-of-the-mill rich (a well-heeled physician).

2. *People who are doing very well.* Corporate executives and professional people make up this class. These individuals reside in large, comfortable homes, belong to relatively exclusive country clubs, occasionally vacation in Europe and places known for their elite clientele, and send their children to private colleges or large, reputable state universities.

3. *People who have achieved the middle-class dream.* These individuals enjoy the "good life" as defined in material terms, but they lack the luxuries of those in the higher classes. More often than not they are subordinates who reside in a three-bedroom home with a family-TV room.

4. *People who have a comfortable life.* While enjoying a "comfortable" life, the members of this class have less money at their disposal than the people above them and they live in less fashionable suburbs.

Table 6.2 PRESTIGE RANKINGS OF OCCUPATIONS, 1972–1982

Occupation	Score
Physician	82
College teacher	78
Lawyer	76
Dentist	74
Bank officer	72
Airline pilot	70
Clergy	69
Sociologist	66
Secondary school teacher	63
Registered nurse	62
Pharmacist	61
Elementary school teacher	60
Accountant	56
Librarian	55
Actor	55
Funeral director	52
Athlete	51
Reporter	51
Bank teller	50
Electrician	49
Police officer	48
Insurance agent	47
Secretary	46
Mail carrier	42
Owner of a farm	41
Restaurant manager	39
Automobile mechanic	37
Baker	34
Salesclerk	29
Gas station attendant	22
Waiter and waitress	20
Garbage collector	17
Janitor	16
Shoeshiner	12

NOTE: Americans ranked a number of occupations in terms of prestige in national surveys conducted between 1972 and 1982. The highest possible score an occupation could receive was 90, and the lowest 10. The table shows the ranking of a number of the occupations.

SOURCE: National Opinion Research Center, 1982.

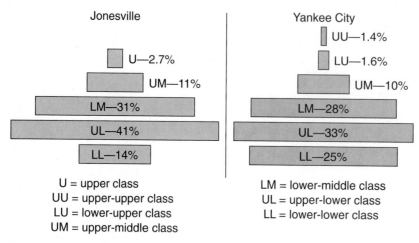

U = upper class
UU = upper-upper class
LU = lower-upper class
UM = upper-middle class

LM = lower-middle class
UL = upper-lower class
LL = lower-lower class

Figure 6.4 STRATIFICATION IN JONESVILLE AND YANKEE CITY
In Jonesville, a midwestern community, W. Lloyd Warner and his associates found five classes: one upper class, two middle classes, and two lower classes. In Yankee City, a considerably older eastern seaboard community, they identified six classes, the upper class being divided by an "old family"–"new family" chasm. Birth was crucial for membership in the "old family" (upper-upper) class. Its members could trace their lineage and wealth through many generations. In terms of wealth, the "new-family" (lower-upper) class could meet the *means* test, but its members failed to meet the *lineage* test so essential for upper-upper class membership. (SOURCE: Figure from *Democracy in Jonesville* by W. Lloyd Warner. Copyright 1949 by Harper & Brothers. Reprinted by permission of HarperCollins Publishers.)

5. *People who are just getting by.* Some Americans enjoy "respectable" jobs, but "the pay is not the greatest." The husband may be employed as a blue-collar worker and the wife as a waitress or store clerk. The couple may own or rent a small home, but they find that "getting by" puts a strain on their joint income.

6. *People who are having a difficult time.* Members of this group find "the going tough." Both the husband and the wife work (although periodically they may experience unemployment), but their income is low. Much of their leisure time is spent viewing television. They do, however, have one consolation: "They are not on welfare."

7. *People who are poor.* At the "bottom of the heap" are "people who are down and out." Many of them receive government assistance and benefits.

The Coleman-Rainwater divisions are somewhat unwieldy. For the most part, sociologists as well as laypeople find it easier to employ the labels "upper class," "middle class," "working class," and "lower class" (poor people) when considering class distinctions. Research suggests that these terms correspond reasonably well with objective class indicators such as income, education, occupational skill level, and manual versus nonmanual jobs (Kerbo, 1983). However, the terms mask important divisions and interests among groups in our society. Moreover, they do not necessarily correspond with self-placement identifications. Even so, these class terms remain useful both because they have the most meaning for the most people and because they are significantly related to major occupational and property divisions.

Recent changes in the economic and cultural fabric of the United States are blurring many old-time class distinctions. Even a decade ago America's class structure seemed a bit simpler than it does these days. Old socioeconomic rankings are giving way to an increasing segmentation of the nation's population. American society seems to be fragmenting into scores of distinct subcultures, each with unique tastes and yearnings of the type that once distinguished broad social classes. As a consequence, a good many Americans seem to be confused about just where they stand in the class hierarchy (Labich, 1994).

THE SIGNIFICANCE OF SOCIAL CLASSES

Few aspects of social life affect so strongly the way people behave and think as does social class. For one thing, it largely determines their **life chances**—the likelihood that individuals and groups will enjoy desired goods and services, fulfilling experiences, and opportunities for living healthy and long lives. Broadly considered, life chances have to do with people's level of living and their options for choice. For instance, the members of the higher social classes need to devote a smaller part of their resources to survival needs than do members of the lower social classes. Sociologist Paul Blumberg (1980) finds that Americans in the highest tenth of the class hierarchy spend about 11 percent of their income for food, as compared to over 40 percent for those in the lowest tenth. And the members of the higher classes also benefit in nonmaterial ways. Their children are more likely to go further in school and perform better than the children of parents who occupy lower socioeconomic positions (DiMaggio, 1982; Mickelson, 1990). Indeed, by 5 years of age, youngsters who have always lived in poverty have IQs on average 9 points lower than those who were never poor; this gap cannot be explained by differences in mothers' education, divorce rates, or race (Elias, 1994). Moreover, during the Vietnam war, some 80 percent of the 2.5 million men who served in Southeast Asia—out of 27 million men who reached draft age during the war—came from working-class and impoverished backgrounds (Appy, 1993).

Likewise, the infants of parents of the higher classes are more likely to survive than are infants of parents of the lower classes (Wicks and Stockwell, 1984; Wise et al., 1985). And among the elderly, the active life expectancy is greater for the nonpoor than for the poor (Katz, 1983; Otten, 1990). Education plays a particularly important role. The National Center for Health Statistics, drawing on a national survey of almost 50,000 households and 125,000 people, reports that almost one in four Americans with less than a high school education say they are in poor, or only fair, health, compared with a mere 3 percent of college graduates. And nearly 18 percent of those who have not finished high school are hospitalized each year, almost 2½ times the rate for college graduates (Otten, 1992). Moreover, according to the American Cancer Society, poor people have a higher risk of developing cancer and dying from it: Lower-income people have higher rates of lung, cervix, and esophagus cancers, in which lifestyle plays a critical role; about 37 percent of low-income people can expect to live 5 years after a cancer diagnosis, compared to about 50 percent of middle- and upper-income people (Findlay, 1986; Gaiter, 1991). And research consistently shows that those in the lower social classes have higher rates of mental illness (Williams, Takeuchi, and Adair, 1992; Link, Lennon, and Dohrenwend, 1993). Overall, higher-income people report greater satisfaction with their lives than do lower-income people (Opinion Roundup, 1987; Mirowsky and Ross, 1990).

Social class also affects people's **style of life**—the magnitude and manner of their consumption of goods and services. Convenience foods—TV dinners, potato chips, frozen pizza, and Hamburger Helper—are more frequently on the menus of lower-income than higher-income households. Lower-class families drink less vodka, scotch, bourbon, and imported wine but consume more beer and blended whiskey. Families in the middle and upper classes tend to buy living-room furniture one piece at a time from specialty stores; lower-class families are more likely to buy matched living-room sets from discount department stores or regular furniture stores. And lower-income families spend more of their leisure time watching television than do higher-income families (Bridgwater, 1982). By the same token, participation in health-club and gym activities rises with income and education (Waldrop, 1989).

Social class is similarly associated with various patterns of behavior. For instance, it influences political participation. Voting increases with socioeconomic status in most Western nations (Verba, Nie, and Kim, 1978; Zipp, Landerman, and Leubke, 1982; E. R. Smith, 1989). And class is an important determinant of sexual behavior (Weinberg and Williams, 1980). For example, the lower classes are more likely to experience sexual intercourse and other sexual behaviors at earlier ages than are the higher classes. In sum, one's social class leaves few areas of life untouched.

WHAT IS HAPPENING TO THE AMERICAN DREAM?

According to an increasing number of observers of the economic and social scene, growing numbers of Americans are losing the race for prosperity (Duncan, Smeeding, and Rodgers, 1992). Indeed, it seems that the American middle class is shrinking (see Figure 6.5). The Census Bureau found that in 1979, 12 percent of full-time, year-round workers earned low wages. By 1990, the share had risen to 18 percent. Workers ages 18 to 24 lost the most ground. In 1979, 23 percent of these younger workers earned low wages; by 1990, the share had risen to 43 percent. Those aged 25 to 34 fared little better. The share of full-time workers earning low wages in this group rose from 9 percent in 1979 to 18 percent in 1990.

Some economists like Frank Levy (1987, 1989; Levy and Michel, 1991) believe that members of the under-30 generation may never match their parents' living standards. However, it may be too early to conclude that those in the 20-something generation will not do as well as their parents. Labor shortages in the 1990s could force pay up. And the share of young families headed by college graduates will increase from 14 to 22 percent once the family heads complete their schooling (Bernstein, 1991a). Even so, many barometers suggest that U.S. living standards have been slipping in recent years (Uchitelle, 1990; Malabre, 1991; Pear, 1991).

The shrinking share of national income going to middle-income Americans has led some social scientists to express concern as to whether the American middle class is an endangered species (Thurow, 1987; Newman, 1993). As noted earlier in the chapter, Federal Research Board and Internal Revenue Service data suggest that the economic boom of the 1980s was associated with a growing concentration of wealth in the United States. These data and data showing a shrinking middle class suggest to some social scientists that the United States has moved in the direction of becoming a nation of "haves" and "have nots," with fewer people in between. These social scientists also point to the exodus of wealthy urban youth from the public school system and the "haves" abandonment of other public institutions (including the use of private overnight mail services, modems, and faxes to bypass the inadequacies of the U.S. Postal Service). The most severe gulf, they say, exists between the nation's privileged and residents of inner cities (see Chapter 11) (Bell, 1991).

Those who consider the middle class to be declining link the trend to industrial change in the United States that is eliminating high-paying jobs and replacing them with low-paying ones. Smokestack industries, like machine tools, autos, and steel, with their high-wage, skilled blue-collar workers, provide many middle-income jobs. Over the last decade, their share of total employment has fallen sharply. And when these industries shrink, the middle class shrinks with them. Also, corporate restructuring and layoffs have confronted many once-secure managers and profes-

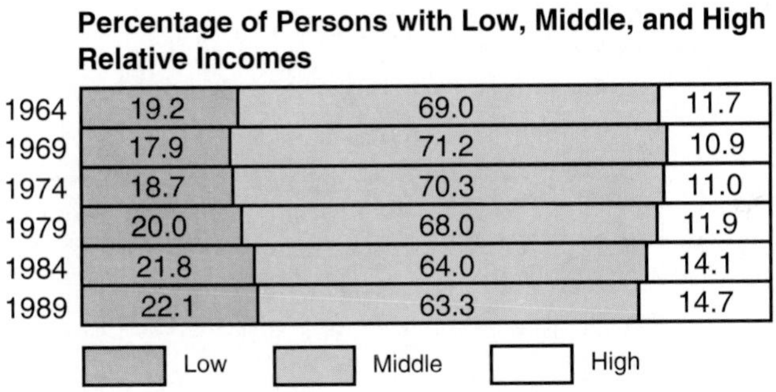

Percentage of Persons with Low, Middle, and High Relative Incomes

Year	Low	Middle	High
1964	19.2	69.0	11.7
1969	17.9	71.2	10.9
1974	18.7	70.3	11.0
1979	20.0	68.0	11.9
1984	21.8	64.0	14.1
1989	22.1	63.3	14.7

Low   Middle   High

Figure 6.5   U.S. MIDDLE CLASS IS SHRINKING
The percentage of Americans with middle incomes dropped from 71.2 percent in 1969 to 63.3 percent in 1989. High income in 1989 was over $74,304 for a family of four. Low income was below $18,576. (SOURCE: *U.S. News & World Report,* March 2, 1992, p. 12. Data from U.S. Census Bureau.)

sionals with the haunting specter of downward mobility. At the same time that jobs in manufacturing were declining over the past decade, nearly nine out of ten new jobs were created in the service and trade sectors of the economy (more than half of them in health, business services, finance, and eating and drinking places). From an employment viewpoint, large discount retailers, like Wal-Mart, Kmart, Target, Venture, and Home Depot, are becoming the "factories" of the 1990s. According to economists Barry Bluestone and Bennett Harrison (1982, 1987), it takes two department store jobs or three restaurant jobs to equal the earnings of one manufacturing job. Overall, service industries display a two-hump distribution in income—high and low. Other factors contributing to the rising inequality in the distribution of income are intense international competitive pressures and a rising proportion of lower-paid female workers.

Not everyone agrees that the middle class is in difficulty (Morris, Bernhardt, and Handcock, 1994). Political liberals have tended to accept the notion of a shrinking middle class. Other analysts, particularly those of more conservative convictions, have taken a more optimistic view (Nasar, 1987; Reynolds, 1992). For instance, Fabian Linden (1984, 1986, 1989) blames the statistics showing a shrinking middle class primarily on the postwar baby boom. As young baby boomers entered the work force in recent years, they swelled the ranks of low-income households. But as the baby boomers grow older, Linden says, their incomes will rise. He also points out that the second-fastest-growing age group in the United States has been people 65 and over. Thus, all told, some three-fifths of all homes with incomes under $15,000 consist of individuals under 35 or over 65. Simultaneously, with the increase in separations and divorces, families headed by women grew from 12 percent of all households in 1970 to 16 percent today. Linden concludes that the demise of the middle class is a "fiction" based on a misreading of the effects of large changes in the age and living arrangements of adult Americans.

Those who see the emergence of a bipolar income distribution and the eclipse of the middle class express concern for American democracy. According to conventional American sociological wisdom, a healthy middle class is essential for a healthy democracy. A society composed of rich and poor lacks a political and economic mediating group. This observation underlay Marx's prediction that revolution would ensue as the economy generated a bipolar income distribution consisting of rich and poor. In part Marx was

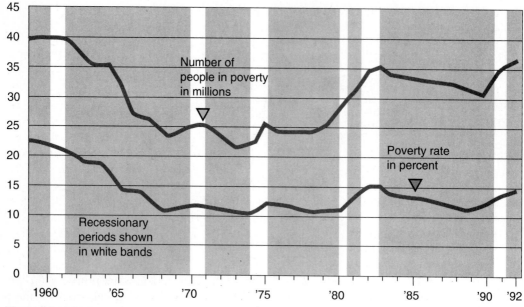

Figure 6.6 POVERTY IN THE UNITED STATES, 1960–1992
In 1992 the government classified a family of four as poor if it had cash income of less than $14,335. (SOURCE: Adapted from *The New York Times*, October 5, 1993, p. A8. Copyright © 1993 by The New York Times Company. Reprinted by permission. Data from Census Bureau, National Bureau of Economic Research.)

proved wrong because he did not foresee the rise of the middle class that had an interest in preserving capitalism and whose presence gave the poor hope that they too could escape poverty. But a shrinking middle class may now contribute to such a polarization. Downward social mobility for large numbers of a population can chill the soul and contribute to social meanness. All this brings us to the matter of poverty in the United States.

POVERTY IN THE UNITED STATES

Nearly 30 years after President Lyndon Johnson launched the Great Society, poverty remains an entrenched force in American life. Census Bureau statistics reveal that the percentage of Americans below the poverty line dropped from 22.2 percent in 1960 to a low of 11.1 percent in 1973. However, by 1983 the rate had risen to 15.2

percent. Since the mid-1980s, the poverty rate has hovered in the 13 percent range. However, it reached 14.5 percent in 1992, the highest since 1983 (see Figure 6.6).

Defining Poverty. The definition of poverty is a matter of debate. In 1795, a group of English magistrates decided that a minimum income should be "the cost of a gallon loaf of bread, multiplied by three, plus an allowance for each dependent" (Schorr, 1984). Today the Census Bureau defines the threshold of poverty in the United States as the minimum amount of money families need to purchase a nutritionally adequate diet, assuming they use one-third of their income for food. Liberals contend the line is too low because it fails to take into account changes in the standard of living (Ruggles, 1990). Conservatives say it is too high because the poor receive in-kind income in the form of public assistance, including food stamps, public housing subsidies, and health care (Kilpatrick, 1990; Rector, 1990).

Who Are the Poor?   About 62 percent of the nation's poor live in large cities, and their number is growing. Overall, poverty has become increasingly the lot of single and divorced mothers and their children (Polakow, 1993; Huston, McLoyd, and Coll, 1994). This trend has been termed the "feminization of poverty." Although fatherless families represent 16 percent of the nation's families, they constitute 46 percent of the households living in poverty. In 1992, 21.9 percent of all American children and 25 percent of those under age 6 were poor. Overall, the poverty rate for blacks was 33.3 percent, nearly three times the 11.6 percent rate for whites. The rate for Hispanic people was 29.3 percent, and for Asian Americans it was 12.5 percent.

The poverty rate for the elderly dropped from 35.2 percent in 1959 to about 12.4 percent in 1992. Federal outlays, including Social Security benefits indexed to the cost of living and Medicare benefits, have contributed to the economic gains of the elderly (even so, 20 percent of widowed and 24 percent of divorced older women remain impoverished. Farmers are more likely to be poor than their city cousins, with many compelled to supplement their incomes by involvement in the nonfarm labor force. Additionally, there are thousands of American farm workers who are poor, many of whom lack access to toilets and clean water at their work sites and suffer levels of parasitic illness rarely encountered in developed nations. And if individuals are handicapped, they are more than twice as likely as other workers to be poor. About 23 percent of working-age people who receive food stamps and 37 percent of Medicaid recipients are disabled.

An "Underclass"?   The term "underclass" has been applied by some social scientists to a population of people, concentrated in an inner city, who are persistently poor, unemployed, and dependent on welfare—with an emphasis on "persistently" (Coughlin, 1988). Initially, sociologist William Julius Wilson (1987) championed the concept to describe the plight of "the truly disadvantaged." But he and a number of other sociologists have since expressed concern that the term "underclass" is being misused by some journalists and political conservatives to argue that the poor have created their own plight and are to blame for their poverty. Moreover, the concept is frequently used to reinforce the view of white and middle-class "outsiders" that the inhabitants of inner-city neighborhoods are not only fundamentally different from mainstream Americans but violently dangerous and a nightmare threatening to engulf the American dream. In brief, "underclass" has become one more term used to label the black urban "other" as not fully human and not worthy of the opportunities and constitutional privileges accorded the population as a whole. Yet as historian Jacqueline Jones (1992) shows, the kind of poverty associated with contemporary urban ghettos has a long history dating back at least to the Civil War and has included white sharecroppers, Appalachian white migrants, and marginal white factory workers of the North.

Sociologist Christopher Jencks (1992) points out that people talk and write about the "underclass" in at least four different ways: income levels (the impoverished underclass), income sources (the jobless underclass), cultural skills (the educational underclass), and moral behaviors (a group that deviates from middle-class values and norms). Seen this way, Jencks says that the "underclass" is a much more heterogeneous group than the concept would suggest.

As discussed in Chapters 1 and 7, Wilson contends that the "underclass" exists mainly because of a sharp climb in inner-city joblessness by virtue of the elimination of hundreds of thousands of lower-skill jobs, the growing polarization of the labor market into low-wage and high-wage sectors, the relocation of manufacturing industries out of the central city, and periodic recessions. The problem, Wilson says, has been compounded

"This really gets you empathizing with those pickers."

Drawing by Wm. Hamilton; © 1991 The New Yorker Magazine, Inc.

by the concentration of the disadvantaged in inner-city ghettos and the isolation of these areas from more affluent communities. This social isolation leads to economic isolation and impoverishment.

Simply being poor, however, does not make a person a part of the "underclass." Indeed, the "underclass" constitutes a minority of the poor. The "underclass" is a core of inner-city poor, those individuals and families who are trapped in an unending cycle of joblessness and dependence on welfare or criminal earnings. Their communities are often plagued by drug abuse, lawlessness, crime, violence, and poor schools. Many "underclass" women were teenage mothers and high school dropouts who subsequently found themselves sidetracked without the resources or skills to escape a life of poverty. The rise of female-headed families is associated with the inability of

"underclass" men to find steady jobs (Wilson, 1987, 1991; Massey, 1990; Duncan and Rodgers, 1991; Jencks, 1992).

Some observers of the American scene have expressed concern that a "second nation"—a class of permanent have-nots—is emerging within American cities. Considerable controversy surrounds social programs for dealing with inner-city problems. Some argue that it is the economy, not the people, that requires reforming (more specifically, the provision of more well-paying, low-skill jobs). Others contend that welfare programs foster out-of-wedlock births, family breakdown, a reluctance to work, social demoralization, and dependence upon "societal handouts." Typically, liberals fault the social system while conservatives fault the individual. Let us examine these matters more closely by considering three major theories of poverty.

Theories of Poverty. Various theories have been advanced through the years to explain poverty. One approach looks to the characteristics of the poor to explain their difficulties. According to the **culture of poverty** thesis, the poor in class-stratified capitalist societies lack effective participation and integration within the larger society (Lewis, 1959, 1961, 1966). Clustered in large ghettos in cities such as New York, Mexico City, and San Juan, the poor develop feelings of marginality, helplessness, dependence, and inferiority. These circumstances allegedly breed weak ego structures, lack of impulse control, a present-time orientation characterized by little ability to defer gratification, and a sense of resignation and fatalism. The resulting lifeways are both an adaptation and a reaction of the poor to their disadvantaged positions. They become self-perpetuating patterns as the ethos associated with the culture of poverty is transmitted to successive generations (Murray, 1986; 1994). Political scientist Lawrence M. Mead (1992) recently offered a modified version of the theory, saying that the sources of contemporary poverty are essentially psychological and *not* cultural. He distinguishes his view from the earlier culture of poverty concept by arguing that the dependent poor share the values of the larger society but lack the confidence to try to live by them.

Many sociologists argue that the culture of poverty thesis has serious shortcomings (Valentine, 1968; Duncan, Hill, and Hoffman, 1988; Jaynes and Williams, 1989; Demos, 1990; Popkin, 1990). For instance, as we pointed out in Chapter 1, Elliot Liebow depicts the economically poor streetcorner men of Washington, D.C., as very much immersed in American life and not as carriers of an independent culture of poverty. They too want what other American men want, but they are blocked from achieving their goals by a racist social order. Significantly, a recent Louis Harris (1989) poll found that when members of the "underclass" are asked to name the most important changes that might improve their lives, they cite as their top three responses "better job opportunities," "more schooling available," and "more job training." When asked what they want most for their children, they list as their top four aspirations "learning to stay in school" (59 percent), "getting proper training to hold down good jobs" (58 percent), "earning enough money to be able to move into decent housing" (36 percent), and "being respected by other people" (28 percent).

Another view sees poverty as largely *situational* (Devine, Plunkett, and Wright, 1992; R. Stein, 1993). Research undertaken by the University of Michigan's Institute for Social Research (Duncan, 1984, 1987; Duncan, Hill, and Hoffman, 1988) portrays the poverty population as a kind of pool, with people flowing in and out. The findings are based on a survey of 5,000 American families chosen in 1968 and followed for a decade thereafter. The research casts doubt on the culture of poverty thesis that being poor at one time means being poor always. In the 10-year period, only 2.6 percent of the sample could be classed as persistently poor, as failing to meet the government's income standard for poverty in 8 or more of the 10 years. The 25 percent of the families in the sample who had received welfare at some time over the decade often received it for very short periods. Many people who slip into poverty do so for a limited time after major adverse events, such as divorce or illness. For many families, welfare serves as a type of insurance protection, something they use for a brief period but dispose of as quickly as they can.

Although women who were unmarried heads of households with children were somewhat more likely to be receiving welfare if they had come from welfare families, most women from welfare families did not receive welfare. The Michigan researchers found "little evidence that individual attitudes and behavior patterns affect individual economic progress." To a far greater extent, individuals "are the victims of their past, their environment, luck, and chance." Their findings support the view that the overwhelming majority of Americans, given any reasonable choice, would prefer to work to support themselves rather than live on welfare.

Still another view portrays poverty as a *structural* feature of capitalist societies. The cyclical movements between economic expansion and contraction—boom and bust—contribute to sharp fluctuations in employment. A century ago Marx contended that an *industrial reserve army* is essential for capitalist economies. The industrial reserve army consists of individuals at the bottom of the class structure who are laid off in the interests of corporate profits during times of economic stagnation and then rehired when needed for producing profits during times of economic prosperity. It is disproportionately composed of minorities, who traditionally have been the last hired and the first fired. Contemporary structuralists say that a "new industrial order" characterized by a significant shift from manufacturing to service-sector employment has produced massive vulnerability among all blue-collar workers. In sum, poverty derives from a lack of income-producing employment. And high inner-city rates of family disintegration, welfare dependency, drug abuse, and crime are additional outcomes of faulty economic organization (Marks, 1991; Jones, 1992).

Poverty Programs. "The poor you always have with you," says St. John's Gospel. But the poor have not always been treated in the same way. For much of Western history, assistance to the poor has taken the form of private almsgiving, sporadically augmented with public relief. Because of the holy merit in giving, charity served the dual purpose of improving the spiritual state of the almsgiver while relieving want. But government has also intervened, although not necessarily in a charitable manner. For instance, in eighteenth-century England, poor laws provided workhouses for the able-bodied indigent to discourage people from adding themselves to the ranks of paupers. Of interest, much of the eighteenth- and nineteenth-century debate surrounding definitions of poverty and its remedies is startlingly similar to that of today (Himmelfarb, 1984).

Within the United States, President Lyndon Johnson's Great Society produced a flurry of

social programs rivaling those of Franklin Roosevelt's New Deal. Some were later eliminated, while others were severely cut or revamped by the Reagan and Bush administrations. Many misconceptions prevail about welfare. For example, not everyone who is poor receives welfare: Only about 60 percent of the poor have received welfare benefits in recent years, and only about one-third have received cash welfare payments. And contrary to popular stereotype, whites use government safety-net programs more than African Americans and Hispanics do (even in urban areas, there are four poor whites for every three poor African Americans and every two poor Hispanics) (Usdansky, 1992). Additionally, although government spending on social programs has grown over the past 30 years, much of the growth has been for programs aiding the elderly regardless of economic status (O'Hare, 1987; Bernstein, 1991b).

As pointed out by economist David T. Ellwood (1988), welfare brings into conflict some of the nation's most precious values having to do with autonomy, responsibility, work, family, community, and compassion. The humanitarian provision of financial support to those in need often provides disincentives to work, provides incentives to change family structure, stigmatizes recipients, and isolates recipients from the mainstream. Social scientists are increasingly turning their attention to the development of programs that attempt to reconcile work incentives and financial assistance with proposals to get people off welfare altogether. They typically link work and other requirements with welfare payments to the employable poor, including single mothers. This emphasis parallels the "New Paternalistic" approach that has been gaining public favor: Large numbers of Americans want a welfare system that is simultaneously generous *and* demanding. The approach combines a strong moralistic helping ethos with strict accountability (relating to poor people much in the manner many American parents relate to a son or daughter who is in difficulty). Yet in many respects, "welfare" remains an intractable problem because under current labor market conditions, large numbers of unskilled workers cannot find "good jobs" and earn their way out of poverty (Jencks, 1992).

Two explanations have been advanced for the growth of welfare expenditures in contemporary Western nations. One view holds that relief institutions are a response to societal problems. As people's "needs" increase and the "capacity" of the economy grows, both consequences of industrialization and economic development, so do the responses of governmental relief-giving agencies. Seen in this fashion, the state is a "neutral arbiter" serving the common good. The other view portrays the state as an agency of ruling elites. The state is said to dole out welfare as a means of placating the rebellious poor and lessening popular opposition to existing social arrangements (Korpi, 1989; Steinmetz, 1990). Sociologists Larry Isaac and William R. Kelly (1981) looked into these matters, employing data from the African-American protest movement of the 1960s and early 1970s. While they found some support for both explanations, they found more support for the latter. As one observer (Kerbo, 1983:326) notes: "Hungry people in need don't bring more welfare; an angry poor who take their anger to the streets do."

□ Social Mobility

America has long been viewed as the "land of opportunity." Early in this century, the stories of Horatio Alger enjoyed wide appeal. The stories told of poor boys who "made good" in American life by reason of personal virtue, pluck, diligence, and hard work. More recently, best-selling books have described how individuals can achieve success by investing in real estate, bonds, collectibles, or the stock market, by dressing right, by intimidating others, by getting right with God, or by psyching themselves up. Underlying these notions is the assumption that individuals or groups can move from one level (stratum) to another in the stratification system, a process called **social mobility.** Whereas social inequality has to do with differences in the distribution of benefits and burdens and social stratification with a structured system of inequality, social mobility refers to the shift of individuals or groups from one social status to another.

There are at least two basic reasons why social mobility takes place within society. First, societies change, and whether change is rapid or slow, it leads to new circumstances. Social change alters the division of labor, introducing new positions, undermining old ones, and shifting the allocation of scarce, divisible resources. Additionally, the exclusion from high rank of capable members of the lower strata often contributes to social strains that lead them to challenge the established arrangement and overthrow it, modify it, or extract concessions from privileged groups. Second, shifts occur in the availability of different types of talent. Although elites may monopolize the opportunities for training and education, they do not control the natural distribution of talent and ability. Thus, very often people must be recruited from the lower ranks.

FORMS OF SOCIAL MOBILITY

Social mobility can take a number of forms. Mobility may be vertical or horizontal. **Vertical mobility** involves movement from one social status to another of higher or lower rank. As we saw in Table 6.2, Americans differ in the prestige ratings of various occupations. If an auto mechanic (prestige score 37) became a bank officer (score 72), this shift would constitute upward mobility. On the other hand, if the auto mechanic became a garbage collector (score 17), this change would involve downward mobility. If the auto mechanic took a job as a restaurant manager (score 39), this shift would represent horizontal mobility. **Horizontal mobility** entails movement from one social status to another that is approximately equivalent in rank.

Sociologists also distinguish between intergenerational and intragenerational mobility. **Intergenerational mobility** involves a comparison of the social status of parents and their children at some point in their respective careers (for example, as assessed by the rankings of their occupations at roughly the same age). Research shows that a large minority, perhaps even a majority of the American population, moves up or down at least a little in the class hierarchy in every generation. **Intragenerational mobility** entails a comparison of the social status of a person over an extended time period. Studies show that a large proportion of Americans have worked in different jobs and occupations in their lifetime (Sorensen, 1975; Duncan, 1984; Kurz and Muller, 1987). But there are limits to the variety of most people's mobility experience. Short-distance movements tend to be the rule, and long-distance movements the exception. Let us examine these matters more closely.

SOCIAL MOBILITY IN THE UNITED STATES

When sociologists talk about social mobility, they usually have intergenerational occupational mobility in mind. And given the traditional operation of sexism in the labor market, which until recent decades relegated women to the home or to low-paying jobs, much more is known about the mobility of men than of women. Perhaps the most impressive studies of social mobility in the United States have been undertaken by Peter M. Blau and Otis Dudley Duncan (1972), and more recently by David Featherman and Robert Hauser (1978). The Blau and Duncan study employed data collected by the Census Bureau in 1962 from a sample of over 20,000 men, while that of Featherman and Hauser consisted of a sample of over 30,000 men in 1973.

Summarizing the data from these and related studies, it seems that about 50 percent of American men are immobile, remaining in their father's stratum (Davis, 1982). About 25 percent are upwardly mobile, moving from farm or blue-collar jobs to white-collar jobs. Another 10 percent

are downwardly mobile, moving from white-collar to blue-collar jobs. And 15 percent move from farm to blue-collar positions.

There are two primary explanations for the higher rate of upward than downward intergenerational mobility in the United States. First, the *occupational structure* has been changing. With technological advances, more jobs were created toward the top of the occupational structure than toward the bottom. Consequently, more people were needed in top positions. Second, *fertility* plays a role, with white-collar fathers generating fewer sons than blue-collar fathers. Hence, with higher-occupation fathers producing fewer sons and the top of the occupational structure expanding, there is more room toward the top of the class hierarchy. Overall, more than twice as many men have moved into white-collar jobs as have moved out of them (Davis, 1982).

In Chapter 7 we will consider the special circumstances of African Americans and women in the United States and how racism and sexism have affected their mobility opportunities. However, it is important to point out here that the class system has proved to be much more rigid for African Americans than for the general population (Blau and Duncan, 1972; Featherman and Hauser, 1978b; Wright, 1978b, 1985; Pomer, 1986; Goldscheider and Goldscheider, 1991). Moreover, African-American fathers who have attained white-collar jobs have historically had greater difficulty than white fathers in passing their advantage to their sons. But this pattern may now be changing for those African Americans able to break into higher occupational positions (R. M. Clark, 1983). Research also shows that working women are less likely to be in an occupational status close to their fathers' than are men (Hauser and Featherman, 1977; Blossfeld and Huinink, 1991). Traditionally women have been concentrated in lower nonmanual and white-collar clerical jobs. Thus, regardless of whether their fathers are higher or lower in occupational rank, women are commonly pushed up to, or down to, the lower white-collar positions.

SOCIAL MOBILITY IN INDUSTRIALIZED SOCIETIES

Concern with social mobility has reflected interest in the extent to which various societies have realized the ideal of equality of opportunity. Sociological evidence reveals that no contemporary society comes close to allowing all its members the same chance to acquire desired statuses. In all industrial societies, a family's class position plays a large part in determining the status placement of offspring. But by the same token, no modern society denies its male members the opportunity to be upwardly mobile. In each nation for which data are available, a large proportion of men have moved up or down between generations (Lipset, 1982). In many nations, including the United States, France, Sweden, Hungary, and the Netherlands, relative intergenerational mobility chances have slowly but systematically increased since World War II (Ganzeboom, Treiman, and Ultee, 1991).

Overall there is little difference among various industrialized countries in the rates of occupational mobility between the blue-collar and white-collar classes (Erikson and Goldthorpe, 1992). The basic processes affecting rates of social mobility, once people of rural origin are set aside, appear to be structural—linked to the pace of economic development rather than to political or economic systems. Thus rates of mobility are comparable in socialist and capitalist nations. A comparison of social mobility during the period of communist regimes in six nations (Bulgaria, Czechoslovakia, Hungary, Poland, Romania, and Yugoslavia) and seven noncommunist ones (Australia, France, Italy, Norway, Sweden, the United States, and West Germany) revealed that blue-collar nonfarm sons (workers) were mobile into nonmanual jobs in 29.2 percent of the cases in the communist average and in 28.2 percent in the noncommunist sample (Connor, 1979). Although upward mobility may be somewhat higher in the United States than in most other countries, the United States does not appear to be significantly more open to mobility than other industrialized nations (Grusky and Hauser, 1984; Allmendinger, 1989; Ishida, Goldthorpe, and Erikson, 1991).

During the 1980s, the overall upward mobility of Americans appears to have slowed (Hout, 1988; Morris, Bernhardt, and Handcock, 1994). By the year 2000, it is likely that there will be even less overall upward social mobility (Krymkowski and Krauze, 1992). Although substantial numbers of low-income Americans moved up the income ladder in the 1980s, Treasury Department statistics suggest that those who started the decade at the very top tended to remain there (Wessel, 1992). Nearly half of those who were among the richest 1 percent of taxpayers in 1979 were still there a decade later. Most of those who fell out of the top 1 percent nonetheless managed to stay in the top 10 percent (only 2.2 percent had fallen to the bottom 20 percent). Some 0.3 percent of those in the bottom 20 percent had risen to the top 1 percent by 1988 (see Figure 6.7).

STATUS ATTAINMENT PROCESSES

In recent years, considerable sociological research has dealt with the factors underlying status transmission and attainment (Symposium, 1992). Blau and Duncan (1972) have developed a technique for studying the course of an individual's occupational status over the life cycle. Called the **socioeconomic life cycle,** it involves a sequence of stages that begins with birth into a family with a specific social status and proceeds through childhood, socialization, schooling, job seeking, occupational achievement, marriage, and the formation and functioning of a new family unit. The outcomes of each stage are seen as affecting subsequent stages in the cycle. In order to capture the specific contributions of each stage, Blau and Duncan (1972:163) analyze their data by means of a statistical procedure called *path analysis:*

We think of the individual's life cycle as a sequence in time that can be described, however partially and crudely, by a set of classificatory or quantitative measurements taken at

Status in 1988

	Top 1%	Top 2% to 20%	Next richest 20%	Middle 20%	Next poorest 20%	Poorest 20%
Top 1%	47.3%	38.6%	7.7%	3.8%	0.4%	2.2%
Top 20%	5.3	59.4	20.3	9.4	4.4	1.1
Next richest 20%	0.6	34.8	37.5	14.8	9.3	3.1
Middle 20%	0.4	14.6	32.3	33.0	14.0	5.7
Next poorest 20%	0.3	10.8	19.5	29.6	29.0	10.9
Poorest 20%	0.3	14.4	25.3	25.0	20.7	14.2

(left axis label: **Status in 1979**)

■ Upwardly mobile   ▨ Staying put   □ Downwardly mobile

Figure 6.7   INCOME-GROUP MOBILITY AS REFLECTED IN TAXPAYER DATA, 1979–1988 The Treasury Department study examined 14,351 taxpayers who filed returns in every year from 1979 to 1988 and compared their before-tax income at several points in the decade. Totals do not add to 100 because of rounding. (SOURCE: Adapted from *The Wall Street Journal*, June 2, 1992, A2. Reprinted by permission of *The Wall Street Journal*, © 1992 Dow Jones & Company, Inc. All rights reserved worldwide. Data from the Treasury Department.)

successive stages. . . . Given this scheme, the questions we are continually raising in one form or another are: how and to what degree do the circumstances of birth condition [determine] subsequent status? And how does status attained . . . at one stage of the life cycle affect the prospects for a subsequent stage?

Blau and Duncan conclude that the social status of a man's parents typically has little *direct* impact on his occupational attainment (the research was restricted to men). Instead, the primary influence of parental status is *indirect*, through its effect on level of schooling. (One of the virtues of path analysis is its ability to sort out direct from indirect effects.) Overall, education (years of schooling completed) is the fact that has

the greatest influence on a man's occupational attainment, both early and late.

Another factor that has a sizable effect is the level of the occupational status ladder at which a man starts his career. The lower he begins, the higher he has to rise and the less likely he is to reach the top positions. Entry into some positions is conditional on performance in temporally prior ones. All societies have ways of "remembering" socially relevant aspects of an individual's biography, and that information is employed to shape his current opportunities (Maddox and Wiley, 1976; Mare and Tzeng, 1989).

William Sewell and his associates have also investigated the status attainment process. They based their work on a survey of Wisconsin high school seniors conducted in 1957 and a follow-up study of one-third of them from 1964 through 1967. They conclude that educational and occupational attainments are the outcome of two related processes: those by which status aspirations are formed and those by which the aspirations become translated into an actual position in the status hierarchy. The Wisconsin data reveal that practically the entire effect of a family's socioeconomic status on a child's educational and occupational attainments is the result of the personal influences it exerts upon the child's status aspirations during adolescence. Other early factors that play a part are parental and teacher encouragement to attend college and the college plans of the adolescent's best friend. Then, too, advantaged families are better able to provide human and material resources that benefit the development of their children's academic skills.

But once these factors are controlled (statistically taken into account and allowed for), the effects of parental social status become insignificant and have no other direct influence upon status attainment. Rather, as Blau and Duncan also conclude, it is level of schooling that has the primary influence on subsequent occupational attainment. Overall, these sociological studies suggest that the contribution of schooling to father-son occupational inheritance consists of two separate steps: a relation between father's occupation and education, and a second relation between son's occupation and education.

Critics of status attainment research contend that it has an optimistic and functionalist bias (Coser, 1975; Horan, 1978; Knottnerus, 1987, 1991). Social positions are viewed as levels of performance, which are differentially evaluated and rewarded within a competitive market system. An underlying assumption is that the job market is fully open to individuals who acquire positions on the basis of competence. In contrast, conflict theorists argue that class categories are critical in determining the rewards Americans receive. Based on their ownership or nonownership of the

"Actually, Lou, I think it was more than just my being in the right place at the right time. I think it was my being the right race, the right religion, the right sex, the right socioeconomic group, having the right accent, the right clothes, going to the right schools . . ."

Drawing by W. Miller; © 1992 The New Yorker Magazine, Inc.

means of production, people are channeled into class positions. In sum, the attainment process is seen as differing substantially for the members of a capitalist society (Wright, 1978a, b, 1985; Smith, 1981). Additionally, although status attainment models have reasonably explained the outcomes of white males, they have been less effective in explaining the outcomes of African Americans and women (Persell, Catsambis, and Cookson, 1992; Winship, 1992). The box discusses some of these matters employing the playing cards metaphor.

Critics also contend that there are two sectors of the economy, or a **dual labor market**. The primary, or *core*, sector offers "good jobs" that provide high pay, security, and ample promotion possibilities. The other—the secondary, or *periphery*, sector—consists of "bad jobs" that provide low pay, poor working conditions, and little room for promotion. Recruitment to these two sectors varies, with African Americans and women found more often in the secondary, or periphery, sector (Beck, Horan, and Tolbert, 1978, 1980; Sakamoto and Chen, 1991). We will examine these matters at greater length in the next chapter.

Doing Sociology: The Playing Cards Metaphor

Professor Mark Abrahamson (1994) clarifies sociological concepts relating to social mobility for his students at the University of Connecticut by using an analogy: a "deck of playing cards." Although Abrahamson does not literally bring decks of cards to class, he points out that contemporary American cards are an amalgam of card games from Native Americans and from settlers across a broad panorama of countries. Games vary, even when similar cards are used. For instance, the relative rank of the cards may differ. In "Beat the Jack," all picture (royalty) cards and aces are of the same value and they are higher than all nonroyalty cards (which are of equal value to each other). In contrast, in "Bow to the King," aces are the lowest cards and a player who receives an ace is physically slapped by all the other players.

Abrahamson introduces the status attainment perspective by noting that the model tends to regard statuses as ranked in a continuous distribution. Viewed in this fashion, the principal statuses tend to be distributed in rank like the face values of cards in poker: jacks above tens, tens above nines, nines above eights, and so on. Status attainment models differ from conflict models like those of Karl Marx in which all royalty cards belong to the same "ruling class" and all nonroyalty cards belong to the "exploited classes." The game of "Beat the Jack" noted above best fits this model.

Abrahamson also notes that societies can be compared in terms of their "openness" and "closeness." In a completely open society, each generation's "cards" are removed from the game when they die, and so each new

Summary

1. Most societies are organized so that their institutions systematically distribute benefits and burdens unequally among different categories of people. Sociologists call the structured ranking of individuals and groups—their grading into horizontal layers or strata—social stratification. Social stratification depends upon but is not the same thing as social differentiation—the process by which a society becomes increasingly specialized over time.

2. Stratification systems differ in the ease with which they permit people to move in or out of particular strata. Where people can change their status with relative ease, sociologists refer to the arrangement as an open system. In contrast, where people have great difficulty in changing their status, sociologists term the arrangement a closed system.

3. Sociologists typically take a multidimensional view of stratification, identifying three components: economic (wealth and income), prestige, and power. The rankings of some statuses may be dissimilar. For the most part, however, these three dimensions hang together, feeding into and supporting one another.

4. The functionalist theory of social inequality holds that stratification exists because it is beneficial for society. According to sociologists Kingsley Davis and Wilbert Moore, society must concern itself with human motivation because the duties associated with the various statuses are not all equally pleasant to the

generation is dealt a hand of cards from a thoroughly shuffled fresh deck. In contrast, in a completely closed society, such as a traditional caste order, parents give "duplicates of their own cards to their children" and so no trading up or down of cards is permitted during the lifetime of the children. Abrahamson then asks students to build more complex models using the deck of cards metaphor. For instance, individuals may receive cards at birth on the basis of the social standing of their parents but then may trade cards up or down in conformity with certain rules.

Changes in occupational structure can also be illustrated by the metaphor. For instance, the generation of Americans who entered the labor force in the 30-year period following World War II experienced a good deal of upward intergenerational mobility. Abrahamson asks his students to imagine one generation being dealt from a master deck consisting of cards from a poker deck while the next generation is dealt from a master deck combining cards from poker and pinochle decks (a deck of pinochle cards is composed of forty-eight cards, most of which contain pictures and none of which has a face value less than 10). Consequently, regardless of the preparation and efforts of the second generation, invariably all its members will hold higher cards, on average, than will the preceding generation. However, should the overall amount of upward mobility decline by the year 2000, as many sociologists anticipate, the situation would be analogous to removing the high cards from the pinochle decks that were shuffled into the master deck during the 1960s and 1970s.

Abrahamson finds that his students periodically pleasantly surprise him by embellishing upon the deck of playing cards metaphor. Can you do likewise?

---

human organism, are not all equally important to social survival, and are not all equally in need of the same abilities and talents. Consequently, society must have, first, some things that it can use as inducements for its members, and second, some way of distributing these rewards differentially among the various statuses. Social stratification is the mechanism by which societies solve these twin problems.

5. The conflict theory of social inequality holds that stratification exists because it benefits individuals and groups who have the power to dominate and exploit others. The conflict perspective draws heavily on the ideas of Karl Marx. Marx contended that the capitalist drive to realize surplus value is the foundation of modern class struggle—an irreconcilable clash of interests between workers and capitalists. Initially workers are blinded by false consciousness, but through struggle with capitalists they evolve class consciousness.

6. Any number of sociologists have noted that both functionalist and conflict theories have merit, but that each is better than the other in answering different questions. They have sought a synthesis of the two positions. Thus Gerhard E. Lenski has looked for ways of integrating the two perspectives.

7. Three primary methods are employed by sociologists for identifying social classes. The objective method views social class as a statistical category. People are assigned to social

classes on the basis of income, occupation, or education (or some combination of these characteristics). The self-placement method has people identify the social class to which they think they belong. Class is viewed as a social category, one in which people group themselves with other individuals they perceive as sharing certain attributes in common with them. The reputational method asks people how they classify other individuals. This approach views class as a social group.

8. Few aspects of social life affect so strongly the way people behave and think as does social class. For one thing, it largely determines their life chances—the likelihood that individuals and groups will enjoy desired goods and services, fulfilling experiences, and opportunities for living healthy and long lives. Social class also affects people's style of life—the magnitude and manner of their consumption of goods and services.

9. Controversy surrounds the issue of whether or not the American middle class is an endangered species. Those who consider the middle class to be declining link the trend to industrial change in the United States that is eliminating high-paying jobs and replacing them with low-paying ones. Others see the demise of the middle class as a "fiction" based on a misreading of the effects of large changes in the age and living arrangements of adult Americans.

10. The Census Bureau defines the threshold of poverty in the United States as the minimum amount of money families need to purchase a nutritionally adequate diet, assuming they use one-third of their income for food. Children and the elderly account for nearly half of all Americans living in poverty. Three theories predominate regarding poverty. One explains the difficulties of the poor as stemming from a culture of poverty. Another view sees poverty as largely situational. Still another view portrays poverty as a structural feature of capitalist societies.

11. Social mobility takes a number of forms. It may be vertical or horizontal. And it may be intergenerational or intragenerational. When sociologists talk about social mobility, they usually have intergenerational occupational mobility in mind. Although upward mobility may be somewhat higher in the United States than in most other countries, the United States does not appear to be significantly more open to mobility than other industrialized nations.

12. Sociologists see education as a critical factor in the social mobility of individuals in the United States. It seems that education has the greatest influence on occupational attainment. William Sewell and his associates contend that educational and occupational attainments are the outcome of two related processes: those by which status aspirations are formed and those by which the aspirations become translated into an actual position in the status hierarchy. Critics of status attainment research contend that it has a functionalist bias.

Glossary

closed system   A stratification system in which people have great difficulty changing their status.

constraints   Those resources that allow one party to add new disadvantages to a situation.

culture of poverty   The view that the poor possess self-perpetuating lifeways characterized by weak ego structures, lack of impulse control, a present-time orientation, and a sense of resignation and fatalism.

dual labor market An economy characterized by two sectors. The primary, or core, sector offers "good jobs," and the secondary, or periphery, sector offers "bad jobs."

horizontal mobility Movement from one social status to another that is approximately equivalent in rank.

income The amount of money people receive.

inducements Those resources that allow one party to add new advantages to a situation.

intergenerational mobility A comparison of the social status of parents and their children at some point in their respective careers.

intragenerational mobility A comparison of the social status of a person over an extended period of time.

life chances The likelihood that individuals and groups will enjoy desired goods and services, fulfilling experiences, and opportunities for living healthy and long lives.

objective method An approach to the identification of social classes that employs such yardsticks as income, occupation, and education.

open system A stratification system in which people can change their status with relative ease.

persuasion Those resources that enable one party to change the minds of other people without adding either advantages or disadvantages to the situation.

power The ability of individuals and groups to realize their will in human affairs even if it involves the resistance of others.

prestige The social respect, admiration, and recognition associated with a particular social status.

reputational method An approach to identifying social classes that involves asking people how they classify others.

self-placement method An approach to identifying social classes that involves self-classification.

social differentiation The process by which a society becomes increasingly specialized over time.

social mobility The process in which individuals or groups move from one level (stratum) to another in the stratification system.

social stratification The structured ranking of individuals and groups; their grading into horizontal layers or strata.

socioeconomic life cycle A sequence of stages that begins with birth into a family with a specific social status and proceeds through childhood, socialization, schooling, job seeking, occupational achievement, marriage, and the formation and functioning of a new family unit.

style of life The magnitude and manner of people's consumption of goods and services.

vertical mobility Movement of individuals from one social status to another of higher or lower rank.

wealth What people own.

Chapter 7

INEQUALITIES
OF RACE, ETHNICITY,
AND GENDER

Stratification contains the answer to the question of *who gets what, when, and how.* As a consequence, a society's "good things"—particularly income, wealth, prestige, and power—are distributed unevenly. So are the burdens and unpleasant chores. In sum, stratification represents institutionalized inequality in the distribution of social rewards and burdens. People are locked into an arena of social relationships in which they differ sharply in their life chances and styles of living. In Chapter 6 we examined the class system of stratification. In this chapter we turn our attention to two additional systems of stratification, race and/or ethnicity and gender.

Within the United States, African Americans, Hispanics, Native Americans (Indians), Asian Americans, and Jews have been the victims of prejudice and discrimination. Throughout much of the nation's history, they have been confined to subordinate statuses that have not been justified by their individual abilities and talents. The same has held true for women. Traditionally men have gotten the best jobs, have been exempt from menial household chores, have enjoyed the top political offices, and have had the prerogative of initiating sexual activity. These dimensions of stratification—class, race, and gender—combine and intersect in different ways, producing complex, joint effects (Mutchler and Burr, 1991; Kane, 1992).

Social scientists have noted many similarities between the status of African Americans and that of women within the United States (Myrdal, 1944; Hacker, 1951, 1974; Smith and Steward, 1983). Take racist and sexist stereotypes. Both African Americans and women have been portrayed as intellectually inferior, emotional, irresponsible, dependent, and childlike. The rationalization for their subordination has been similar—the myth of "contented African Americans who know their place" and the notion that "women's place is in the home." Recent generations of both African Americans and women have challenged those stereotypes by participating in social movements for equal rights.

□ Racial and Ethnic Stratification

Although racial and ethnic stratification is similar to other systems of stratification in its essential features, there tends to be one major difference. Racial and ethnic groups often have the *potential* for carving out their own independent nation from the existing state. Political separatism may offer racial and ethnic groups a solution that is not available to disadvantaged class and gender groups. Class and gender groups typically lack the potential for becoming self-sufficient political states because they do not function as self-sufficient social or economic groups.

Although separatist tendencies and their chances for success vary enormously among nations, the underlying potential for such movements exists in most nations with diverse racial and ethnic groups. Unlike class stratification, the issue is not replacement of one elite by another or even a revolutionary change in the political system. Instead, the question is one of whether the racial or ethnic segments of the society will be willing to participate within the existing nation-state arrangement (Lieberson, 1970). Class conflicts threaten governments, but they rarely pose alternative definitions of the territorial boundaries of the nation (Geertz, 1963). Examples abound in the contemporary world of separatist movements, including the Palestinians in the Middle East, the Irish Catholics of Northern Ireland, the Ibo of Nigeria, the Tamil minority in Sri Lanka, the various Muslim and Christian factions in Lebanon, and the Sikhs in India's Punjab.

MINORITIES

Societies throughout the world contain peoples with different skin colors, languages, religions, and customs. These physical and cultural traits, by providing high social visibility, serve as identifying symbols of group membership. In turn, individuals are ascribed statuses in the social structure based on the group to which they belong (see Chapter 2). Many of the same principles we will consider in this chapter also apply to what are variously termed *socially marginalized groups*—vulnerable and frequently victimized populations who typically have little economic, political, and social power, including cancer and acquired immunodeficiency syndrome (AIDS) patients, the elderly, children, and lower-level employees.

Races. People in various parts of the world differ in certain hereditary features, including the color of their skin, the texture of their hair, their facial features, their stature, and the shape of their heads. But by the same token, the features that humans everywhere share are substantially larger and of considerably greater importance than their differences. Even so, we readily recognize that *groups* of Norwegians, Chinese, and Ugandans differ in their physical characteristics. The concept of **race** is used to refer to this fact. Biologists typically view races as populations that differ in the incidence of various hereditary traits (more narrowly, they conceive of a race—or subspecies—as an inbreeding, geographically isolated population that differs in distinguishable hereditary traits from other members of the species).

Although we readily recognize that populations differ in physical appearance, scientists have considerable difficulty identifying races and categorizing people in terms of them. For the most part, races are not characterized by fixed, clear-cut differences but by fluid, continuous differences. It is often next to impossible to tell where one population ends and another begins. For instance, where and among what people in Africa or Europe can one say with certainty that here and among these people individuals of white ancestry cease, and there and among those people individuals of black ancestry start? With respect to skin color, hair form, stature, and head shape, populations grade into one another. Additionally, peoples differ in a great many ways, and these variations occur independently of one another. Hence, classifications based on skin color do not necessarily yield the same results as those based on some other characteristic. For example, extremely kinky hair is found among the moderately pigmented San of the Kalahari Desert (South Africa), and straight or wavy hair among some dark-pigmented peoples of southern India (Barnicott, 1964; Zuckerman, 1990).

Because human beings do not lend themselves readily to cut-and-dried "racial" classifications, scientists are far from agreement in dividing human populations into "races." But what interests us here is the social significance people attach to various traits. By virtue of individuals' social definitions, skin color or some other trait becomes a "sign" or "mark" of a social status (Denton and Massey, 1989).

Race, then, is a social construct, not an absolute (Davis, 1991). The matter is highlighted by the more than 1.1 million "interracial" married couples in the United States. The children of these couples pose a challenge to the Census Bureau and others who would classify them. Before 1989, the National Center for Health Statistics (NCHS) tabulated the race of American children from data about the races of the parents on birth certificates. A child born to a white and a nonwhite parent was assigned to the nonwhite group. When neither parent was white, the child was assigned the father's race. Beginning in 1989, the NCHS no longer looked to the father's race and assigned the mother's race to the child (Crispell, 1993a).

Ethnic Groups. Groups that we identify chiefly on cultural grounds—language, folk practices, dress, gestures, mannerisms, or religion—are called **ethnic groups.** Within the United States, Jewish Americans, Italian Americans, and Hispanics are examples of ethnic groups. Ethnic groups often have a sense of peoplehood, and to one degree or another many of them deem themselves to be a nation (Stack, 1986).

Ethnic identities are often "constructed" by their bearers. For instance, an Asian-American consciousness has arisen among many disparate Asian nationality groups in the United States (Espiritu, 1992). The new identity arose in part as a response to political expediency. Native-born Americans several generations removed from China, Korea, and Japan recognized that it was to their advantage to have larger numbers. The adoption of a "panethnic" identity is not limited to Asian Americans. Political mobilization has contributed to a "supratribal" identity among many Native Americans (Nagel, 1994).

The tendency of ethnic groups to band together deliberately into larger ethnic grouping is but one example of the construction of ethnic identities. Individuals at times also select from an "ethnic menu." Many white Americans of European descent—often the offspring of several intermarriages—consciously "choose" an ethnic identity among the several in their background (Lieberson and Waters, 1993). Much in this manner 4.5 million Irish immigrants became 40 million Irish Americans (Hout and Goldstein, 1994).

We often confuse nationalism (a feeling of loyalty to a nation or an ethnic group) with a feeling of loyalty to the state (a political unit). Yet a nation and a state are distinctive social entities. Consider Europe. Virtually every territory of Europe has combined at some time or other with almost every one of its neighbors. In fact, the territories covered by European political states have never been, and could not possibly be, exactly the same as the territories inhabited by various ethnic groups. Very often ethnic groups occupy small pieces of territory or are dispersed by residence and place of occupation throughout a territory. Thus political self-determination for one ethnic nationality is often incompatible with political self-determination for another. Many European political states contain multiple nationality groups: Great Britain (English, Scottish, Welsh, Northern Irish), Belgium (Flemings and Walloons), former Czechoslovakia (Czechs and Slovaks), and Switzerland (Germans, French, and Italians). The consequence is that many political states periodically experience ethnic strife and even violence that derive from the minority status of some groups. A case in point is the tragedy surrounding the recent breakup of the Yugoslavian multinational state and its replacement by open hostilities and warfare among rival ethnic groups (Sekulic, Massey, and Hodson, 1994).

Between the end of World War II and the late 1980s, issues of political self-determination went largely into eclipse, especially in Europe, as the Cold War split much of the world between two armed ideologies—led, respectively, by the United States and the Soviet Union. But with the fading of the Cold War and the collapse of the communist bloc, ideological hatreds have tended to give way to ethnic, racial, and religious hatreds. The lifting of ideological repression in Eastern Europe (including Yugoslavia) and the old Soviet empire has released pent-up national and ethnic aspirations deeply rooted in people's social memories and history. The evaporation of the Cold War has meant that superpower restraints no longer hold national and tribal antagonisms in check. From South Africa to Sri Lanka, from Israel to India, and from Angola to Trinidad, separatist movements are once again tearing nations apart. In sum, the cessation of ideological warfare does not mean the end of social conflict. Indeed, as Cold War tensions subside, the world appears bent on entering a possibly more dangerous era of ethnic, racial, and religious warfare (Moynihan, 1993).

Properties of a Minority Group. Sociologists commonly distinguish five properties as characteristic of minority groups (Wagley and Harris, 1964; Vander Zanden, 1983):

1. A minority is a social group whose members experience discrimination, segregation, oppression, or persecution at the hands of another social group, the *dominant group.* As a result of the power differential between the two groups, the members of a minority are disadvantaged. Equally important, they are the source of the dominant group's advantages since the oppression of one people confers privilege and status on another.

2. A minority is characterized by physical or cultural traits that distinguish it from the dominant group. By virtue of these traits, its members are lumped together and "placed" in less desirable positions in the social structure.

3. A minority is a self-conscious social group characterized by a consciousness of oneness. Its members possess a social and psychological affinity with others like themselves, providing a sense of *peoplehood.* This consciousness of oneness is accentuated by the members' common suffering and burdens.

4. Membership in a minority group is generally not voluntary. It is an ascribed position since an individual is commonly born into the status. Thus a person does not usually choose to be black or white.

5. The members of a minority, by choice or necessity, typically marry within their own group (endogamy). The dominant group strongly discourages its members from marrying members of the minority group and usually scorns those who do. The minority may encourage its members to marry among themselves to preserve their unique cultural heritage.

We may define a **minority group** as a racially or culturally self-conscious population, with hereditary membership and a high degree of ingroup marriage, that suffers oppression at the hands of a dominant segment of a nation-state (Williams, 1964).

PREJUDICE AND DISCRIMINATION

Prejudice and discrimination are so prevalent in contemporary life that we often assume they are merely "part of human nature." Yet this view ignores the fact that individuals and societies vary enormously in levels of prejudice and discrimination. Even in Hitler's Germany, some "Aryans" opposed anti-Semitism and helped Jews flee the Nazi Holocaust. And whereas Asians have found acceptance in Hawaii and have prospered there, on the West Coast and in British Columbia they have had a long history of persecution (Glick, 1980). Similarly, whites held a positive image of blacks in the ancient world, a situation in sharp contrast with recent history (Snowden, 1983).

Prejudice.   **Prejudice** refers to attitudes of aversion and hostility toward the members of a group simply because they belong to it and hence are presumed to have the objectionable qualities ascribed to it (Allport, 1954; Devine, 1989). As such, prejudice is a state of mind—a feeling, opinion, or disposition. Sociologist Herbert Blumer (1961) notes that four feelings typically characterize dominant group members; (1) a sense that they are superior to members of the minority group; (2) a feeling that minority members are by their nature different and alien; (3) a sense that dominant group members have a proprietary claim to privilege, power, and prestige; and (4) a fear and suspicion that members of the minority have designs on dominant group benefits. In this respect, prejudice frequently reflects a "sense of group position."

A number of sociologists detect the emergence in recent years of a new form of prejudice against African Americans among affluent, suburban whites. They label it **symbolic racism.** Symbolic racism is not the racism of the Old South, with its doctrines of racial inferiority and legal segregation (Kluegel and Smith, 1982; Killian, 1990; Kluegel, 1990). Instead, it is a new form of racism in which three components converge. First, there is the feeling among many whites that African Americans have become too demanding, too pushy, and too angry, and that they are getting more than they rightly deserve. Second, there is the belief that African Americans do not play by "the rules of the game," typified by the traditional American values of hard work, individualism, and delay of gratification. And third, many whites stereotype blacks in the imagery of welfare mothers, crime in the streets, and quota systems. Such secret attitudes lead whites to vote against political candidates who

support antipoverty programs, to move to the suburbs to escape school desegregation, and to consider "racism" as "somebody else's" problem (Katz and Hass, 1988; Raymond, 1991). Much of this sentiment is rooted in white self-interest; many white Americans are unwilling to support programs from which they do not see tangible self-benefit and which may impose costs and taxes upon them (Bobo and Kluegel, 1993).

Discrimination.   Whereas prejudice is an attitude or a state of mind, discrimination is action. **Discrimination** involves the arbitrary denial of privilege, prestige, and power to members of a minority group whose qualifications are equal to those of members of the dominant group. Prejudice does not necessarily coincide with discrimination—a one-to-one relationship does not inevitably hold between attitudes and overt actions. Sociologist Robert K. Merton (1968) identifies four relationships between prejudice and discrimination and adds folk labels to the types of individuals so described:

1. *The all-weather liberal*—the unprejudiced person who does not discriminate.
2. *The reluctant liberal*—the unprejudiced person who discriminates in response to social pressures.
3. *The timid bigot*—the prejudiced person who does not discriminate in response to social pressures.
4. *The all-weather bigot*—the prejudiced person who unhesitatingly acts on the beliefs he or she holds.

Merton points out that equal opportunity legislation has the greatest impact on the reluctant liberal and the timid bigot.

Since World War II, public opinion surveys show a steady but gradual shift toward greater liberalism on race issues among whites. The greatest change took place between 1970 and 1972. Much of the long-term change derives from individuals born after 1940, who are typically less prejudiced than those born earlier in the century (Steeh and Schuman, 1992). Similarly, since World War II, whites have shifted from more blatant forms of discrimination to more subtle forms. Even so, when in 1990 researchers with the Urban Institute sent carefully matched pairs of young black and white men to apply for the same 476 entry-level jobs advertised in the *Washington Post* and the *Chicago Tribune,* in one out of every five cases the black man did not get as far as his equally qualified white counterpart (the black man did not get an application form, was not given an interview, or did not receive a job offer when the white man did) (Wessel, 1991).

Institutional Discrimination. Discrimination is not practiced just by individuals. In their daily operation, the institutions of society also systematically discriminate against the members of some groups in what is called **institutional discrimination.** Civil rights activist Stokely Carmichael and political scientist Charles Hamilton (1967) have shown that businesses, schools, hospitals, and other key institutions need not be staffed by prejudiced individuals in order for discrimination to occur. Take employment. Employers often specify the qualifications candidates must have in order to be considered for particular jobs. Usually the qualifications have to do with prior job-related experience and some measure of formal education. The standards appear nondiscriminatory because they apply to all individuals regardless of race, creed, or color. But when members of some racial and ethnic groups lack equal opportunities to gain job experience and to receive college and professional degrees, they enter the job market at disadvantage (Braddock and McPartland, 1987; Tienda and Lii, 1987).

African Americans have been particularly victimized by institutional discrimination. For centuries they have been the victims of inequality and low status. At each point along the road toward building a satisfying career—from job candidacy, to job entry, to performance evaluation and pro-

"Well, it all depends. Where are these huddled masses coming from?"

Drawing by Handelsman; © 1992 The New Yorker Magazine, Inc.

motion—African Americans must overcome greater obstacles than those encountered by whites (Braddock and McPartland, 1987; Pettigrew and Martin, 1987). Moreover, as we will see later in the chapter, the handicaps associated with poverty, an absence of skills, inadequate education, and low job seniority have been left largely untouched by civil rights legislation. Indeed, low status has self-perpetuating qualities. Some 30 years ago, President Lyndon B. Johnson made this point in his June 1965 commencement address at Howard University. He asserted:

Doing Sociology: Institutional Discrimination

The institutions of modern societies are often structured in ways that deny equal opportunities to the members of some ethnic and racial groups. Students in introductory sociology classes at Ohio State University have examined a number of ways in which institutional discrimination has operated to restrict the entrance of African Americans to major state universities. For instance, although African Americans comprise about 10 percent of the population of Ohio, they represent less than 5 percent of the students enrolled on the Columbus campus of Ohio State University (4.8 percent of undergraduates, 4.9 percent of graduate students, and 3.8 percent of students in the professional colleges). Despite the fact that the university has inaugurated a variety of programs and scholarships to attract African-American students, the proportion of African-American students has fallen in recent years. African Americans are also vastly underrepresented in premed, engineering, and accounting programs, majors that afford career lines to the most prestigious and remunerative professions and occupations.

Examining their own backgrounds, students point out that a selective process already at work in the elementary and middle school years shaped their later academic opportunities. Suburban school systems, overwhelmingly white in composition, provide solid preparation in mathematics. Students from these schools are given the training essential for attacking premed, engineering, and accounting courses. In many cases, the students were tested in the seventh grade, and those who showed superior aptitude in mathematics were placed in advanced courses. These students had a head start—they could master introductory algebra in eighth grade and take calculus in twelfth grade. In contrast, students in inner-city schools with large African-American enrollments typically have had access to less rigorous programs in mathematics. Consequently, many African-American youth are less adequately prepared for college curriculums, and disproportionate numbers of African-American students find themselves in remedial math programs at the university. Thus the differences in education provided to white and black youngsters affect later performance in college.

You do not take a person who for years has been hobbled by chains and liberate him, bring him up to the starting line of a race and . . . say, you're free to compete with all the others and still justly believe that you have been completely fair.

In brief, equality of opportunity, even if realized in American life, does not necessarily produce equality of outcome: On the contrary, to the extent that winners imply losers, equality of opportunity almost ensures inequality. Consequently, African Americans and many other minorities have concerned themselves not merely with removing the barriers to full opportunity but with achieving the fact of *equality of outcome*—parity in family income, in housing, and in the other necessities for keeping families strong and healthy. It has been this sentiment that has propelled proponents of affirmative action programs.

One mechanism by which institutional discrimination is maintained is **gatekeeping**—the decision-making process whereby people are admitted to offices and positions of privilege, prestige, and power within a society. Generally gatekeepers are professionals with experience and credentials in the fields they monitor—for example, individuals in personnel, school admission, and counseling offices. Although in theory they

Although African-American students are underrepresented at Ohio State University and in programs leading to the most prestigious and remunerative professions and occupations, the same cannot be said for the football and basketball programs. At a major state university like Ohio State, the athletic program is a "big business," with an annual budget in excess of $20 million. Sports programs are major vehicles for winning financial support for the institution from state legislators, alumni, and corporate contributors. As a result, universities feel it necessary to field winning football and basketball teams. Significantly, the football and basketball programs—the two principal and most financially remunerative sports—are carried disproportionately by African-American youth (in contrast, swimming, golf, and tennis—"country-club" type sports—are dominated by whites). However, participation in "big-time" sports is exceedingly time-consuming, and students have difficulty combining participation with more rigorous academic programs like premed, engineering, and accounting. Thus football and basketball players are more apt to pursue majors in education and communications, occupations that usually do not provide a "fast track" to economic success. Plus, there are jobs for fewer than 5,000 professional athletes.

Although basketball and football may provide opportunities for black youth, sports are hardly color-blind. For the most part, coaches are white. Further, African Americans are more likely to play peripheral positions in football that are away from the decisions of play, including wide receiver, running back, and defensive back. Few African Americans play quarterback, center, or middle linebacker. Similarly, in basketball white players are more apt to fill the play-making guard position, the leadership position on the court. And in baseball, African Americans are more likely to be fielders than they are to be catchers or pitchers. Thus although sports allow select African-American youth entrance to a university, they limit their chances to enter more remunerative professions. And if they are fortunate enough to join professional teams, their positions will probably be limited. Institutional arrangements thus structure the opportunities available to youth and contribute to the perpetuation of social inequalities.

assess candidates on the basis of merit, skills, and talents—and not in terms of race, ethnicity, class, family, or religion—their decisions have been biased (Pettigrew and Martin, 1987; Chase and Bell, 1990; Farkas et al., 1990; Karen, 1990). Merit, skills, and talent are relative matters. The issue of which group's *values* will be used for judging who is "capable," "bright," "conscientious," and "resourceful" comes to the forefront. Will the standards of excellence be those of the white middle class? the African Americans? Puerto Rican? or Chinese-American community? And which group's members will be the *judges* who determine the people who meet the qualifications? Historically, gatekeepers have been white and male, and they have selected candidates who have resembled themselves in family patterns, dress, hairstyle, personal behavior, and the ownership and use of property.

Another mechanism of institutional discrimination is called **environmental racism**—the practice of deliberately locating incinerators and other types of hazardous waste facilities in or next to minority communities. For instance, Houston's African American neighborhoods are more likely than white ones to be the location of a hazardous waste facility. One researcher found that twenty-one of the city's twenty-five legally operating incinerators, mini incinerators, and landfills were in predominantly African-American neighborhoods (Horowitz, 1994).

DOMINANT GROUP POLICIES

Dominant groups have pursued a variety of policies toward minorities. At times these policies may parallel those of the minority; at other times they run counter to minority group aims. Sociologists George E. Simpson and J. Milton Yinger (1972) identify six major types of policies: assimilation, pluralism, legal protection of minorities, population transfer, continued subjugation, and extermination. Let us examine each of these more closely.

Assimilation. One way that dominant groups seek to "solve" a minority group "problem" is to eliminate the minority by absorbing it through assimilation. **Assimilation** refers to those processes whereby groups with distinctive identities become culturally and socially fused. Minorities may also prefer this method, as have many immigrant groups in the United States. However, dominant groups and minority groups often approach assimilation differently. Within the United States, two views toward assimilation have dominated. One—the "melting pot" tradition—has seen assimilation as a process whereby peoples and cultures would fuse within the nation to produce a new people and a new civilization. The other—the "Americanization" tradition—has viewed American culture as an essentially finished product on the Anglo-Saxon pattern and has insisted that immigrants promptly give up their cultural traits for those of the dominant American group.

Pluralism. Some minorities do not wish to be assimilated. They value their separate identities and customs, and they prefer a policy of **pluralism**—a situation in which diverse groups coexist side by side and mutually accommodate themselves to their differences. The groups cooperate when this is essential to their well-being, particularly in political and economic matters. Switzerland provides a good illustration of pluralism. Historically, the Swiss nation arose from the desire of heterogeneous communities to preserve their local independence through a system of mutual defense alliances. There is no Swiss language. Instead, the Swiss speak German, French, or Italian, with all federal documents translated into the three "official languages." The various cantons, in addition to their language differences, also have somewhat different cultural patterns. And while the majority of Swiss are Protestant, there is a sizable Catholic population. Although religious and ethnic prejudices are by no means absent, the Swiss have learned to live harmoniously with their differences.

As we shall note shortly, the United States is emerging as a multicultural society. In California, for instance, the most populous state with 31 million inhabitants, the Euro-American population will cease to be the majority group around 1997; Latino, Asian, and African-American groups make up the state's "emergent majority."

Legal Protection of Minorities. Closely related to pluralism is the legal protection of minorities through constitutional and diplomatic means. In some nations, significant segments of the population reject coexistence with minorities on equal terms. Under these circumstances, the government may make legal provision for the protection of the interests and rights of all individuals. The Thirteenth, Fourteenth, and Fifteenth Amendments to the U.S. Constitution, although not pluralistic in intent, have attempted to protect the rights of minorities, especially those of African Americans. Recent civil rights legislation has had a similar objective.

Population Transfer. At times dominant groups have resorted to population transfer to reduce the presence of the minority. This approach matches the secessionist aim of some minorities—both hope to reduce intergroup difficulties through physical separation. At times the migration is forced. For instance, the separation of Pakistan from India after World War II was accompanied by the migration of more than 12 million Muslims and Hindus, in part induced by terrorism and in part arranged under government auspices. People may also flee before invaders. In recent times the Kurds of Iraq, Iran, and Turkey have sought to flee across the borders of one or more of these neighboring nation-states as Iraqi, Iranian, or Turkish military units undertake periodic campaigns against them.

Continued Subjugation. The policies just discussed attempt to incorporate minorities into a society or to drive them out. Often, however, the dominant group prefers to retain its minorities, although it seeks to keep them "in their place"—subservient and exploitable. This approach often finds expression in "internal colonialism." For example, South African whites historically sought *apartheid* arrangements that allow for the political and economic subjugation of blacks and other non-Europeans. Although in 1994 the black majority moved from repression into the halls of South African government, more problematic and enduring is the subjugation that derives from institutional arrangements embedded in the nation's social structure. Likewise, it has been difficult to enforce laws restricting the migration of Mexicans into the United States because powerful business groups in the Southwest and elsewhere want an exploitable minority.

Extermination. Intergroup conflict may become so intense that the physical destruction of one group by the other becomes the overriding goal. History abounds with examples of **genocide**—the deliberate and systematic extermination of a racial or ethnic group. North American whites destroyed more than two-thirds of the Native American population. The Boers of South Africa looked upon the Hottentots as scarcely more than animals and hunted them ruthlessly.

And between 1933 and 1945, the Germans murdered 6 million Jews and 500,000 Gypsies. It should be emphasized that these policies are not mutually exclusive, and several may be practiced simultaneously.

THE FUNCTIONALIST AND CONFLICT PERSPECTIVES

Functionalist and conflict theorists take differing views of racial and ethnic stratification. Yet as we noted in Chapters 1 and 6, the perspectives complement each other. Each draws our attention to aspects of social life that the other tends to overlook.

The Functionalist Perspective. Functionalists conceive of society as resembling a living organism in which the various parts of a system contribute to its survival. Accordingly, they look to the functions and dysfunctions associated with given social patterns. Although at first sight racial and ethnic conflict would seem to impair social solidarity and stability, functionalists point out that conflict may nonetheless be functional for a society (Coser, 1956). First, conflict promotes group formation, and groups are the building blocks of a society. It facilitates a consciousness of kind—an awareness of shared or similar values. The distinction between "we," or the in-group, and "they," or the out-group, is established in and through conflict (see Chapter 4). Groups in turn bind people together within a set of social relationships. And they define the statuses people occupy in the social structure, particularly positions that are ascribed.

Second, not only is a group defined and its boundaries established through conflict, but conflict also promotes group cohesion. It makes group members more conscious of their group bonds and may increase their social participation. Some social scientists have pointed out that anti-Semitism and antiblack sentiment may be functional in that they provide dominant group members who lack a sense of cohesion within the society with an anchor—with a sense of group membership (Ackerman and Jahoda, 1950; Adorno et al., 1950; Bettelheim and Janowitz, 1950). It highlights their racial and ethnic membership, providing them with a means of identification in an uncertain, alienated world.

Third, ethnic and racial conflict may function as a safety valve for the society as a whole (Hepworth and West, 1988; Berkowitz, 1989). Prejudice provides for the safe release of hostile and aggressive impulses that are culturally tabooed within other social contexts. By channeling hostilities from within family, occupational, and other crucial settings onto permissible targets, the stability of existing social structures may be promoted. This is the well-known *scapegoating* mechanism.

And fourth, functionalists point out that a multiplicity of conflicts between large numbers of differing groups within a society may be conducive to a democratic as opposed to a totalitarian order. The multiple group affiliations of individuals contribute to a variety of conflicts crisscrossing society. The groups thus operate as a check against one another. A person's segmental participation in numerous groups, rather than total absorption by one group, results in a kind of balancing mechanism and prevents deep cleavages along one axis (for instance, it prevents cleavage along rigid class lines that results in class struggle). In contrast, in totalitarian societies, there is a maximum concentration of power in one institution—the monolithic state.

The dysfunctions of racial and ethnic conflict are often more readily apparent than its functions. Conflict may reach a frequency and intensity that imperils a larger social system, as has occurred with the collapse of the central regimes in Yugoslavia, the Soviet Union, and Lebanon. Further, energy and resources are drained and dissipated by friction that might otherwise be directed within more productive channels and cooperative activities. Fears and expectations of conflict may lead to an inefficient and ineffective employment of human resources and individual talents.

The Conflict Perspective. Whereas functionalists emphasize social stability and the mechanisms that promote or interfere with it, conflict theorists see the world as in continual struggle. Conflict theorists contend that prejudice and discrimination can best be understood in terms of tension or conflict among competing groups. They point out that three ingredients commonly come into play in the emergence and initial stabilization of racism (Noel, 1972; Vander Zanden, 1983): ethnocentrism, competition, and unequal power.

As we noted in Chapter 2, *ethnocentrism* involves the tendency to judge the behavior of other groups by the standards of one's own. Individuals assume that it is the nature of things that all people should be organized according to the same assumptions that characterize their own group. When individuals are strongly ethnocentric, they find it easy to perceive the out-group as an object of loathing—as a symbol of strangeness, evil, and even danger. Ethnocentrism provides a fertile soil for prejudicial attitudes and stereotypes.

Competition intensifies ethnocentric sentiments and may lead to intergroup strife (Olzak, 1992). In human affairs, conflict theorists point out that people typically seek to improve their outcomes with regard to those things—particularly privilege, prestige, and power—that they define as good, worthwhile, and desirable. When they perceive their group outcomes as mutually exclusive and legitimate, so that each group can realize its goals only at the expense of the other, intergroup tensions are likely to mount (Beck and Tolnay, 1990; Olzak, 1990; Belanger and Pinard, 1991). For the most part, the attitudes people evolve toward out-groups tend to reflect their perceptions of the relationships they have with the groups. Where the relations between two groups are viewed as competitive, negative attitudes—prejudice—will be generated toward the out-group. The boys' camp experiment undertaken by Muzafer Sherif and his associates (1961) and described in Chapter 4 documents this process.

Competition provides the motivation for systems of social inequality, and ethnocentrism channels competition along racial and ethnic lines, but power determines which group will subordinate the other (Noel, 1972). Without power, prejudices cannot be translated into discrimination, and groups cannot turn their claims on scarce resources into institutional discrimination. In brief, power is the mechanism by which domination and subjugation are achieved.

Marxist-oriented theorists take the conflict thesis even further. They say that racial prejudice and exploitation arose in the Western world with the rise of capitalism (Cox, 1948; Szymanski, 1976, 1978; Geschwender, 1978). These sociologists link American race and ethnic relations to world colonization processes and argue that prejudice, discrimination, and racism are rooted in the very structure of society itself—in a distinctive legal and normative code that sanctifies domination and discrimination by whites. Marxist theorists have traditionally contended that racist notions serve the economic interests of the capitalist class in four ways. First, ideologies of racial superiority make colonialism and racist practices palatable and acceptable to the white masses. Second, racism is profitable, since capitalists can pay minority workers less and thus generate greater profits for themselves. Third, racist ideologies divide the working class by pitting white workers and minority workers against one another—a tactic of "divide and conquer." And fourth, capitalists require minority workers as an industrial reserve army that can be fired during times of economic stagnation and rehired when needed for producing profits during times of prosperity (see Chapter 6).

Marxists blame capitalists for generating racism, but sociologist Edna Bonacich (1972, 1975; Cheng and Bonacich, 1984) says that economic competition within a **split labor market** underlies the development of tensions among ethnic groups. A split labor market is an economic arena in which large differences exist in the price of labor at the same occupational level. Bonacich notes that when a group sells its labor at rates sub-stantially lower than the prevailing ones, higher-paid labor faces severe competition to maintain its advantage. When the cheaper labor is of a differing racial or ethnic group, the resulting class antagonism takes the form of racism. The antagonism focuses on racial or ethnic issues, although the source of the conflict is one of class.

Bonacich contends that the more expensive labor resists displacement through exclusion or a caste system. The anti-Chinese movement, which flourished in California in the 1870s, illustrates an exclusion strategy. White workers sought to drive the Chinese from their communities through harrassment and violence and to shut off the entry of new immigrants. The racial caste system was the strategy employed in the post–Civil War period. White labor erected social and legal barriers—Jim Crow segregation arrangements—to avoid competition with black workers.

Regardless of the precise form that conflict theories take, and they do differ substantially from one another, they nonetheless contrast sharply with functionalist theories that look to the forces that contribute to stability rather than those that divide.

RACIAL AND ETHNIC GROUPS IN THE UNITED STATES

We have considered the nature of minority groups, prejudice, discrimination, and institutional discrimination and discussed the functionalist and conflict perspectives. Let us now turn to an examination of the circumstances of a number of groups within the United States (total population of 254.9 million in 1992): African Americans (30.4 million), Hispanics (24 million), Native Americans (Indians) (2 million), and Asian Americans (7.9 million). However, before doing so, it is worth reminding ourselves that the United States is undergoing a transition from a predominately white society rooted in Western European culture to a global society composed of diverse racial and ethnic groups. By the year 2050, according to Census Bureau pro-

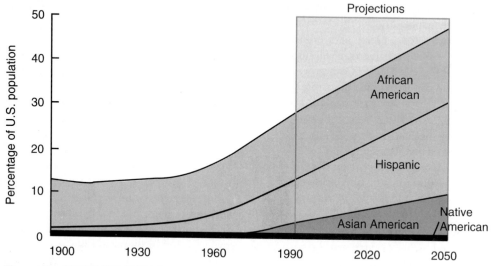

Figure 7.1   SHARE OF MINORITIES IN THE POPULATION OF THE UNITED STATES, 1900–2050
The figures for the post-1990 period represent population projections by the Census Bureau.
(SOURCE: Adapted from William P. O'Hare, "America's Minorities—The Demographics of Diversity," *Population Bulletin,* Vol. 47, No. 4, 1992, figure 1, p. 9. Reprinted by permission of Population Reference Bureau, Inc.)

jections, today's minorities will comprise nearly one-half of the American population (O'Hare, 1992; Pear, 1992). For instance, Hispanic Americans are expected to grow from 9 percent of the population to 14 percent in 2010 and 23 percent in 2050 (rising to 81 million in 2050). The Asian-American population is expected to grow to 12 million in the year 2000 and 41 million in 2050 (from 3 percent to 10 percent of the total population at midcentury). By contrast, the Census Bureau estimates that the African-American population will nearly double in 60 years, to 62 million in 2050 (from 12 percent today to just over 13 percent in 2010 and 16 percent in 2050). Native Americans will remain about 1 percent but will double in numbers to 4.3 million. Overall, the U.S. population is projected to stand at 393 million by the year 2050. See Figure 7.1.

African Americans. It is very likely that the first African American came to the New World with Columbus. However, African-American settle-

ment in the New World did not begin until 1619, when English colonists at Jamestown, Virginia, purchased twenty Africans from a Dutch man-of-war. It seems that the blacks were accorded the status of indentured servants, much in the fashion of whites. But in the 1660s legal recognition was given to the enslavement of African Americans for life, and the first law was passed banning interracial sexual relations. The subjugation of African Americans was well rooted in the British colonies, and the tradition was carried on by the new American nation. At the Constitutional Convention of 1787, southerners succeeded in winning additional representation in Congress on the basis of slavery, in securing federal support for the capture and return of fugitive slaves, and in preventing the closing of the African slave trade before 1808. In point of fact, the American nation arose as a Greek-style democracy, one in which democracy was extended only to the male, white population. The doctrine of black inferiority or "differences" placed African Americans beyond the pale of the American democratic creed. Although American mythology says that the Civil War was fought to free the slaves, historians agree that the political struggle that unfolded between the North and the South was primarily a contest between a southern plantation elite and northern industrial, mercantile, and agrarian interests.

During Reconstruction, the Radical Republicans were in part motivated by the abolitionist argument that a legalized caste system was not compatible with American institutions. But they were also concerned lest the southern states reenter the Union with the old planter elite still in control. Indeed, the North's lack of commitment to African-American rights doomed Reconstruction. However, the institution of Jim Crow— legalized segregation—did not follow automatically on the overthrow of the Reconstruction regimes (Woodward, 1966). The principle of hard-and-fast segregation did not become the rule until the 1890s. Before this time, African Americans still voted in substantial numbers and received equal treatment on common carriers, trains, and streetcars. Even so, blacks and whites attended separate schools, and whites did not accept African Americans as social equals. It was during the 1890s and early 1900s that lynching attained its most staggering proportions and that Jim Crow laws mandating segregation were passed throughout the South.

With World War II came a new era of change in the South. Major assaults were directed against segregation from a good many quarters. The stage was set for even more drastic change when the Supreme Court ruled on May 17, 1954, that mandatory school segregation was unconstitutional. In the years that followed, the Supreme Court moved toward outlawing legalized segregation in all areas of American life. Simultaneously, the civil rights movement of the 1960s galvanized popular support for the enactment of new civil rights legislation, particularly the Civil Rights Acts of 1964, 1965, and 1968. However, as the United States entered the 1970s, resistance mounted among segments of the white community to addi-

tional programs and to affirmative action measures. By the 1980s, under the Reagan administration, the nation began moving down a road that has involved the dismantling of the War on Poverty and various federal programs for minorities and the poor. Budget cutting and budget balancing have taken a severe toll on social programs.

In recent years a debate has raged over the question of whether opportunities for African-American economic advancement are affected more by race or by class position (Omi and Winant, 1987; Feagin, 1991a; Willie, 1991). Sociologist William Julius Wilson (1978, 1987; Wilson and Aponte, 1985) believes that racial discrimination has become less important than social class in influencing the life chances of African Americans. He says that civil rights legislation and affirmative action programs have substantially lifted the cap historically imposed on African-American social mobility by segregation, resulting in greater educational, income, and occupational differentiation: African Americans with good educations and job skills rapidly moved into the American middle class; African Americans with limited educations and job skills became the victims of soaring joblessness and welfare dependency. Structural factors—the disappearance over the past quarter-century of hundreds of thousands of low-skill jobs, mainly involving physical labor—have meant that inner-city African Americans have become a severely disadvantaged class. These patterns are most evident in large American cities where smokestack industries once attracted young men with few or no skills to jobs that nonetheless paid well enough to support wives and children. Now poor urban African Americans find themselves relegated to all-black neighborhoods where they are socially isolated from mainstream American life. Complicating the problem, many middle-class African Americans have moved out of the inner city, no longer sustaining its churches, schools, recreational facilities, and stores or providing role models that help keep alive the perception that securing an education is worthwhile. Wilson says that racism created a large African-American lower class that contemporary changes in the economy and job trends perpetuate. A recent examination of Census Bureau figures undertaken by the Population Reference Bureau (1991) also suggests that the gap between poor and affluent African Americans is growing, reflecting not only the economic success of a rising African-American middle class but the increasing isolation and despair among African Americans who have fallen further out of the economic mainstream.

But not all sociologists agree with Wilson's views regarding "the declining significance of race" (Collins, 1983; Pomer, 1986; Feagin, 1991b). Sociologist Charles V. Willie (1979, 1991) argues that discrimination and racist practices still persist in American life and confront all African Americans regardless of their social class. He interprets income, education, and housing data as revealing that blacks and whites with similar qualifications are treated unequally in the marketplace—evidence of a "racial tax" levied on African Americans for not being white. Considerable differences are also found in measures of psychological well-being between blacks and whites regardless of social class, suggesting that psychological costs are also associated with being an African American in the United States (Thomas and Hughes, 1986).

Still other sociologists find evidence suggesting that both racial and class factors are important in shaping the current African-American experience (Allen and Farley, 1986; Farley and Allen, 1987). A 608-page report issued in 1989 by the National Research Council (Jaynes and Williams, 1989), an arm of the National Academy of Sciences, concluded that although blacks have made important economic and social gains over the past 50 years, they still lag significantly behind whites—indeed, a "great gulf" separates the two races. It attributed the low relative status of African Americans to a combination of broad-based economic factors and persistent racism. The report found that the expected lifetime earnings of black men relative to those of white men rose over four decades but then leveled off in the 1980s (hovering at about 57

percent of those of white men during the 1980s). Housing segregation also remains substantial, with African Americans more likely to be excluded from renting or buying in many residential areas, to be quoted higher prices and rents, and to be "steered" to neighborhoods that already have high African-American concentrations (1990 census data reveal that more than 9 million African Americans live in neighborhoods that are at least 90 percent black). Overall, the National Research Council report suggests that the full integration of African Americans into a "color blind society is unlikely in any foreseeable future," primarily because of continuing social and economic barriers and low rates of interracial marriage. Figure 7.2 provides data on the persistence of the gap between African Americans and whites.

African-American young males face particularly difficult problems. As shown in Figure 7.3, they confront grim job prospects. Moreover, the leading cause of death among African-American youth is homicide (accidents are second, suicide is third). Indeed, African-American young men in New York City's Harlem are less likely to reach the age of 40 than are young men in Bangladesh. One in every four African-American men aged 20 through 29 are in prison, on parole, or on probation (more than the total number of African-American men in college).

Sociologist Elijah Anderson (1978, 1990, 1994) has devoted much of his career to the study of inner-city problems. In the 1970s he studied the streetcorner patrons of Jelly's, a bar and liquor store located in a run-down building on Chicago's South Side. He later studied two Philadelphia neighborhoods. His work takes us inside the world of inner-city African-American young men and portrays the havoc that interpersonal violence and aggression brings to their lives. He finds that violent inclinations spring from the frustrations and alienation associated with the lack of good jobs, the stigma of race, and the fallout from drug use and trafficking.

Despair is so pervasive that it has spawned an "oppositional culture" governed by what Ander-

Education

Persons, 25 years and older, with 4 years of college or more, by percentage of their racial group

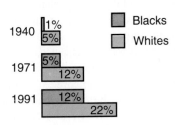

■ Blacks
□ Whites

1940
1% / 5%

1971
5% / 12%

1991
12% / 22%

Occupation

Employed civilians, 1992, by percentage of their racial group in specific jobs

Professional/ managerial — 17% / 28%

Technical/sales/ administrative — 28% / 32%

Service occupations — 24% / 12%

Construction/ repairs — 8% / 12%

Laborers/ operators — 22% / 14%

Family Income

Percentage of racial group by total income; 1992 dollars

$50,000 to $74,999

1982
9% / 19%

1992
11% / 21%

$75,000 to $99,999

1982
2% / 7%

1992
3% / 8%

$100,000 and over

1982
1% / 5%

1992
2% / 7%

Figure 7.2   AFRICAN-AMERICAN PROGRESS IN THE UNITED STATES: A MIXED MESSAGE Although African Americans have made some gains in American life, the stubborn persistence of race problems endures. The United States has not become an integrated society despite the expansion of the African-American middle class. (SOURCE: Data from U.S. Bureau of Census. Adapted from *Newsweek,* November 15, 1993, p. 54. © 1993, Newsweek Inc. All rights reserved. Reprinted by permission.)

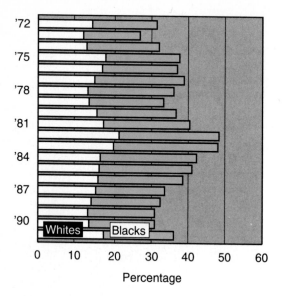

Figure 7.3 GRIM PROSPECTS CONFRONTING AFRICAN-AMERICAN YOUTH
Seasonally adjusted jobless rate among 15- to 19-year-old men. (SOURCE: Data from U.S. Labor Department. Reprinted by permission of *Investor's Business Daily,* July 24, 1992. © 1992, Investor's Business Daily Inc.)

son calls the "code of the streets." At the heart of this code is a reverence for respect—being treated "right" and accorded the deference one deserves. Because they are buffeted by so many forces beyond their comprehension and control, inner-city youth find "respect" to be an illusive and problematic commodity. Anderson portrays the code of the streets as a cultural adaptation to a profound lack of faith in the police and the criminal justice system. Ultimately each individual must fall back upon his or her own resources. Young children find in the course of their play that they will be constantly tested and that they must fight back in response to the pushing and shoving they experience from their peers. Mothers, fathers, brothers, sisters, cousins, neighbors, and friends verbalize and reinforce the message: "Watch your back." "Protect yourself." "Don't let someone 'dis'[mess with] you." "If someone messes with you, you got to pay them back."

Central to the code of the streets is the presentation of self (see Chapter 3): One's bearing must convey the subtle message that one can take care of oneself and be capable of violence should the situation require it. The craving for respect (or "juice" as it is sometimes called) turns into a thin-skinned quest to prove one's "manhood" and invariably leads to violence. A "real man" cannot allow himself to be diminished by another and under the code of the streets must show his "nerve"—if need be by throwing a punch, "getting in someone's face," or pulling a trigger. Many hard-core, street-oriented youth view the risk of a violent death as preferable to being "dissed" (disrespected) by another. Such unflappable posturing may insulate the youth from an otherwise overwhelming social reality.

Anderson contends that a paucity of good jobs plays a large role in urban ills. Finding themselves unable to support a family financially, many young men choose to wield their sexual prowess as evidence of manhood. Their legacy is often babies who in turn are doomed to equally troubled lives. So-called "decent families" encounter considerable difficulty transmitting conventional mainstream values to their offspring in an environment saturated with the frustrations of joblessness, poverty, drugs, and self-destructive behaviors.

On an optimistic note, although one in four young African-American males are in the criminal justice system, three out of four are not. The picture is not as devastating if one includes all African-American males, although if one focuses simply on inner-city youth the problem is appreciable.

In sum, the gap between many blacks and whites remains substantial. Class, then, is not replacing race as a significant factor in the African-American experience. Rather, class is interacting with race to produce the social cleavages that remain a continuing feature of American life (Colasanto and Williams, 1987).

Hispanics. Hispanics are people who were born in or whose ancestors were born in Spain or

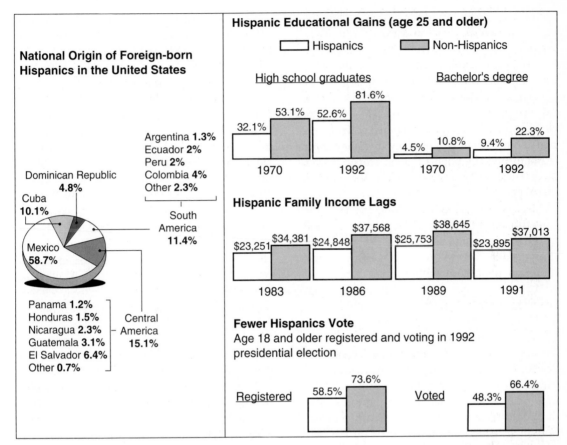

Figure 7.4 HISPANICS IN THE UNITED STATES
Mexican Americans constitute by far the largest Hispanic group in the United States. Cuban Americans have the highest income and the most education. (SOURCE: Data from U.S. Bureau of Census. Adapted from *USA Today,* July 16, 1993, p. 10A.) Copyright 1993 *USA Today.* Reprinted with permission.)

in Latin American nations. Until recently, "Hispanic" did not exist as a self-designation for most peoples of Spanish-speaking ancestry in the United States; it was primarily a term of convenience for administrative agencies and scholarly researchers. Some people of Spanish descent, particularly younger people, find "Hispanic" archaic, if not downright offensive. They prefer instead to identify themselves as "Latino" or by their own ethnic group: Cuban, Nicaraguan, Guatemalan, Colombian, Dominican, Puerto Rican, or just plain American. Some Mexican

Americans like the name "Chicano." In sum, the nation's Hispanic population is not a consolidated minority (see Figure 7.4). Beyond a common language heritage and some shared cultural threads, the groups have different histories, distinct concentrations in different areas of the United States, and substantially different demographic and socioeconomic characteristics (Bean and Tienda, 1987; Portes and Truelove, 1987; Vega, 1990).

Over the past four decades, the Hispanic population of the United States has grown rapidly. California and Texas account for more than half the nation's Hispanics, primarily Mexican Americans. Puerto Ricans are the predominant Hispanics in New York City, where about half of mainland Puerto Ricans reside; Cubans are the largest Hispanic group in Florida, where about 60 percent of Cuban-origin Hispanics live. Some 92 percent of all Hispanics live in cities, compared with 80 percent of other ethnic groups. They are also younger than the total U.S. population, on average, with a median age of 23, as contrasted to the national median of 32.9.

Mexican Americans have a long history in the United States that stretches back to the period before New England was colonized. Many of them trace their ancestry to the merging of the Native American population with Spanish settlers. In 1821 Mexico secured its independence from Spain, and shortly thereafter a substantial portion of the new Mexican nation became part of the United States (resulting from the annexation of Texas, the conquest of northern Mexico, and the Gadsden Purchase). Like African Americans and Native Americans, people of Mexican ancestry did not originally become a part of American society through voluntary immigration. With the exception of the American Indians, they are the only American minority to enter the society through the conquest of their homeland.

In recent decades the Spanish-speaking population of the United States has grown substantially through immigration. Persons of Hispanic origin now account for about half the legal immigration into the United States. Additionally, vast numbers enter the United States illegally. An increasing number are Salvadorans and other Central Americans fleeing guerrilla war, political oppression, and economic deprivation. But the largest group continues to be Mexicans who see little chance of earning a satisfactory living in their crowded nation (Vernez and Ronfeldt, 1991). *Maquiladoras* (U.S. factories built in Mexican border towns) have contributed to the influx. The *maquiladoras* have drawn many individuals from the Mexican interior to border communities. When they can-

not find jobs there, they cross the Rio Grande, often illegally, in search of work in the United States (Frey and O'Hare, 1993).

Many Hispanics are falling behind other segments of the population in climbing the educational ladder. According to the Census Bureau, Hispanics as a group are nearly three times more likely to drop out of school than are either blacks or whites; by the age of 17, nearly one in five Hispanics has dropped out, compared with about one in sixteen blacks and one in fifteen whites. According to the National Council of La Raza, an umbrella organization for 120 Hispanic groups, at each grade level a larger percentage of Hispanic children than white or black youngsters are enrolled below grade level. An estimated 56 percent of Hispanic adults are functionally illiterate. Among Hispanics age 25 and older, only 9.9 percent have completed college, compared with 21.9 percent of other Americans (Cook, 1990; Kantrowitz, 1991).

Hispanics have traditionally also earned less than have non-Hispanics. About 30 percent of male Hispanic workers are concentrated in lower-paying jobs as laborers or assembly-line workers, compared with 19.5 percent of non-Hispanic male workers. About 10.7 percent of Hispanic men are in managerial and professional jobs, a rate less than half that of non-Hispanic men (27.4 percent). Hispanic women, like their non-Hispanic counterparts, are clustered in technical, sales, and support jobs or in the service sector. But in these groups they are represented in lower proportions than their non-Hispanic counterparts. In 1990, the Census Bureau reported that 23.4 percent of Hispanic families were living in poverty (compared with a 9.2 percent rate of poverty among non-Hispanic families) (Barringer, 1991a). And whereas in 1979 the income of the typical Hispanic family was 71 percent of that of the average non-Hispanic family, the figure had fallen to 64 percent by 1992. Communities along the Rio Grande Valley (strung in pearl-like fashion along Highway 83 from Mission to Harlingen) rank as the poorest metropolitan areas in the

United States (including McAllen, Laredo, and Brownsville, Texas).

Native Americans (Indians). The 1990 census counted nearly 2 million Native Americans (Indians, Eskimos, and Aleuts) within the United States, represented by 542 tribes (since the Census Bureau does not require proof of heritage, it is impossible to know how many Americans now find it fashionable to be Indian and so falsely assert an Indian background). The tribes or nations vary in size from those with some 44 members (the Siuslaw) to those with more than 308,132 members (the Cherokee). An additional 50 or more tribes have vanished through massacres by whites, disease, destruction of their economic base, or absorption by other groups. Overall, Native-American peoples vary substantially in their history, lifestyles, kin systems, language, political arrangements, religion, economy, current circumstances, and identities.

Estimates vary widely as to how many Native Americans were found in the area north of the Rio Grande in 1492 (Denevan, 1992; Verano and Ubelaker, 1992). Some anthropologists place the figure as low as 700,000, and others as high as 15 million. Contrary to popular mythology, most nations were not nomadic hunting peoples but farming and fishing peoples with relatively stable communities. Initially the European powers treated the Native-American groups as alien nations that could be enemies or allies against their European adversaries. But as time passed, the tribal territories of the Native Americans were appropriated and their inhabitants either annihilated or driven inland.

After the Revolutionary War, the American government followed a policy of negotiating treaties of land cession with the Native Americans. When the Native Americans failed to agree, they were confronted with military force. The 1830 Removal Act provided for the relocation of all eastern tribes to lands west of the Mississippi River. This forced migration is widely regarded as one of the most dishonorable chapters in American history and is known as "the Trail of Tears." At least 70,000 people were removed, of whom more than 20,000 died en route. West of the Mississippi, the tragedies of defeat and expropriation were repeated. The federal government merely extended to the western Indians the system of treaties and reservations it had used to dispossess the Indians of the East. When the Native Americans resisted, they were systematically slaughtered (Josephy, 1991).

Until 1871, the United States treated the Native-American tribes as sovereign yet dependent domestic nations with whom it entered into "treaties." But in the 1870s it shifted its policy to one making Native Americans "wards" of the federal government. The new policy had as its aim forced assimilation. This policy had a devastating impact on the Native Americans and their cultures. And it created massive poverty and appalling health problems. In 1929 the government reversed its policy and encouraged Native Americans to retain their tribal identifications and cultures. But during the Eisenhower administration the federal government returned to assimilationism, encouraging Native Americans to leave the reservations and settle in urban areas. Then, during the 1970s, the goal of national policy was again reversed, as the government sought to strengthen Native Americans' control over their own affairs without cutting them off from federal concern and support. The course of governmental policy toward Native Americans shifted repeatedly, oscillating between separatist and assimilationist extremes.

Native Americans have paid dearly for these inconsistencies and vacillations. About 25 percent of Native Americans live on reservations, which cover 52.4 million acres in twenty-seven states. The largest reservation, the Navajo in Arizona, New Mexico, and Utah, is 15 million acres. Forty-one percent of those on reservations live below the poverty level (almost 70 percent of Navajos are still without electricity despite the fact that high-voltage wires run like silver threads across the vast Arizona tracts of the Navajo Nation to the

"Kemo sabe, I want you to be official greeter at my new casino."

Drawing by Mankoff; © 1994 The New Yorker Magazine, Inc.

Pacific Ocean). Overall, unemployment among males 20 to 64 years old is about 60 percent; it ranges from 23 percent on the Pimas Salt River reservation to 82 percent on the Sioux Rosebud reservation in South Dakota (Valente, 1991; Kilborn, 1992). Native Americans are the most severely disadvantaged of any population within the United States (Snipp, 1989; Visgaitis, 1994). Life expectancy in some tribes is 45 years. By adolescence, Indian children show high rates of suicide, alcoholism, and drug abuse: The suicide rate among young people is often more than ten times the national average, and nearly 50 percent of all young Native Americans have serious alcohol or drug problems. Diabetes and the complications of alcoholism are the sources of the greatest disability among adults. Rates are highest in dislocated tribes where traditional lifestyles have been severely disrupted (Yates, 1987; Egan, 1988). On some reservations, 25 percent of the children suffer the harsh symptoms of fetal alcohol effect (because their mothers drank heavily during

pregnancy, the children experience mental retardation and severe behavior problems). It is hardly surprising that many Native-American leaders look upon alcohol as an especially devastating problem, one that over time confronts their people with "genocide without firing a single bullet" (Huntley, 1983). Complicating the health problems are other issues: Tribes across the United States are grappling with some of the nation's worst pollution problems—uranium tailings, land and water contamination, chemical lagoons, and illegal dumps (Satchell, 1993). And of concern to some health officials is the fact that in recent years the federal government has granted many tribes the right to operate gambling operations, including casinos and high-stakes bingo parlors, as a means of raising money for economic development (Clines, 1993; Eckholm, 1994).

Asian Americans. Asian Americans total 7.3 million Americans. Of these, about 1.6 million are Chinese, 1.4 million Filipinos, 615,000 Vietnamese, 800,000 Koreans, 847,000 Japanese, 815,000 Asian Indians, 149,000 Laotians, 147,411 Cambodians, 91,000 Thais, 90,000 Hmong, and 81,000 Pakistanis. Almost 40 percent of all Asian Americans, or 2.4 million people, live in California, while New York and Hawaii each have slightly more than 9 percent (Barringer, 1991; Barringer, Gardner, and Levin, 1993).

It was during the gold rush period in California that the first large-scale immigration of Chinese to the United States took place. At first the Chinese were welcomed as a source of cheap labor. But when the speculative gold bubble burst, whites faced competition with Chinese workers. The cry became "The Chinese must go." In the post–Civil War period, the Chinese were the victims of mob violence, bloodshed, pillage, and incendiarism. California led the nation in the passage of anti-Chinese laws, many of which remained in effect until the 1950s (for instance, the California state constitution provided that corporations could neither directly nor indirectly employ Chinese and empowered cities and towns to remove Chinese from within city limits). Although some Chinese responded to this persecution by returning to China, most dispersed eastward. They took up residence in Chinatowns, ghettos made up of Chinese.

By the end of World War II, except for a few large cities, Chinatowns had largely disappeared from the American scene. But in recent years the Chinatowns of New York City, San Francisco, and a few other large cities have obtained a new lease on life and have expanded as a result of sharp increases in immigration from Hong Kong and Taiwan (made possible by the passage of new immigration legislation in 1965 that did away with the old quota system, under which only 105 Chinese were allowed entry each year). Above the gaudy storefronts of the nation's Chinatowns, Chinese families are jammed into tiny flats (more than 60 percent of current Chinese-Americans were born overseas, and the figure climbs to more than 80 percent in an area like New York City's Chinatown). In some cities, including San Fran-

cisco, more than a quarter of the residents of Chinatown live below the poverty level (Loo, 1991). In recent years, New York City's Chinatown has become the center of the city's apparel industry, which is second only to the restaurant business as the chief source of employment for Chinese immigrants.

The Japanese have also been victims of prejudice and discrimination. On two occasions the government launched an effort to exclude them from American life. In 1907 President Theodore Roosevelt reached an agreement with Japan to limit the immigration of Japanese to the United States. Later, during World War II, the government placed some 120,000 Japanese (two-thirds of whom were American citizens) in ten concentration camps. The action had more to do with racism than with national security, since none of the nation's other so-called enemies in residence (Germans and Italians) were subjected to internment—and not one Japanese American was ever convicted of spying.

In recent years the nation's media have heralded Asian Americans as "the model minority" and "a superminority." They now enjoy the highest median family income of the nation's ethnic groups ($42,250 in 1991, largely because Asian households are more likely to have multiple wage earners). Yet Asian Americans are a varied group, with considerable contrasts and diversity. Some Asian Americans, such as Japanese Americans, have comparatively high incomes, while the earnings of Laotians, Cambodians, and Vietnamese are quite low (especially among recent refugees who typically have come from rural areas and who possess few marketable skills) (Dunn, 1994). Through thrift, strong family ties, and hard work, many Asian Americans have managed to achieve upward mobility. Recent immigrants have included a high proportion of doctors and engineers, and fully 33 percent of Asian adults have completed college (compared with 17.5 percent of whites). The National Center for Education Statistics finds that Asian-American students are more likely than other students to enroll in college preparatory programs (47 percent take the academic program, compared with 37 percent of whites, 29 percent of African Americans, and 23 percent of Hispanics). They also take more math and science courses and spend more time on homework than other students do (Zigli, 1984; Butterfield, 1986). But Asian-American leaders also point out that the "model minority" myth obscures such problems as crime, high suicide rates, mental disorders, and disintegrating families among poor refugees and immigrants who have difficulty coping with a strange, new society (Lee, 1990). A 1989 study by the U.S. Department of Health and Human Services found that the suicide rate among Chinese Americans 15 to 24 years old was 36 percent higher than the national average for this age group; the rate for Japanese Americans was 54 percent higher (Rigdon, 1991). While two out of every five Asian Americans aged 25 and older have had at least 4 years of college, nearly double the non-Hispanic white figure, one in five has not completed high school, about the same as the non-Hispanic white proportion (Otten, 1991). And although many Asian-American youths enjoy remarkable academic success, evidence suggests that they may be encountering discrimination when they apply to the nation's most prestigious universities (Lindsey, 1987; Bunzel, 1988). On the job, too, Asian-American workers face widespread discrimination and are often the victims of racially motivated harassment and violence (Dugger, 1992; Mura, 1992). By the same token, Asian Americans find that they soon "top out," reaching positions beyond which their employers fail to promote them (the median salary of Asian male college graduates is $37,550, about 90 percent of the median salary of white male college graduates, $41,660) (Barringer, 1992).

☐ Gender Stratification

Men and women differ in their access to privilege, prestige, and power. The distribution problem of who gets what, when, and how has traditionally been answered in favor of males. Throughout the world, human activities, practices, and institutional structures are ordered in terms of differentiations between men and women—in brief, by *gender*. For the most part, the state, the law, politics, religion, higher education, and the economy are institutions that have been historically developed by men, that are currently dominated by men, and that are symbolically interpreted from the standpoint of men. As such they are "gendered institutions." The only major institution in which women have had a central, defining role, although a subordinate one, has been the family (Acker, 1992).

Until relatively recently, Americans did not conceive of women as a subordinate group. It is true, of course, that women do not reside in ghettos, although this is increasingly the fate of single-parent African-American women. Even though prestigious Ivy League institutions and medical, engineering, law, and business schools traditionally catered to male students, women have not been segregated in inferior schools. Moreover, they freely interact with—even live with—men, the presumed dominant group. How then can they be viewed as a minority? Let us return to the five properties of a minority group we considered earlier in the chapter.

1. Historically, women have encountered *prejudice and discrimination*. We will examine this matter at greater length later in the chapter.

2. Women possess *physical and cultural traits* that distinguish them from men, the dominant group.

3. Through the efforts of the women's liberation movement and consciousness-raising groups, women have increasingly become a *self-conscious social group* characterized by an awareness of oneness.

4. *Membership is involuntary* since gender is an ascribed status that is assigned to a person at birth.

5. Only the fifth characteristic does not apply to women, since *endogamy* (in-group marriage) is not the rule.

It is clear that women and other minority groups share many characteristics in common. Noting that sexism pervades the social fabric, sociologist Jessie Bernard observes:

[Sexism is] the unconscious, taken-for-granted, assumed, unquestioned, unexamined, unchallenged acceptance of the belief that the world as it looks to men is the only world, that the way of dealing with it which men have created is the only way, that the values which men have evolved are the only ones, that the way sex looks to men is the only way it can look to anyone, that what men think about what women are like is the only way to think about what women are like. (Quoted in Gornick and Moran, 1971:xxv)

Before examining these matters in greater detail, let us turn to a consideration of gender roles and identities.

GENDER ROLES AND CULTURE

It seems that all societies have seized on the anatomical differences between men and women to assign **gender roles**—sets of cultural expectations that define the ways in which the members of each sex should behave. Anthropological evidence suggests that gender roles probably represent the earliest division of labor among human beings. Consequently, we are all born into societies with well-established cultural guidelines for the behavior of men and women.

Anthropologist George P. Murdock (1935) finds in his cross-cultural survey of 224 societies that vast differences exist in the social definitions of what constitutes appropriate masculine and feminine behavior. Indeed, as shown in Table 7.1, the allocation of duties often differs sharply from that of our own society. For instance, for generations American communities have had laws restricting the weights that a working woman is permitted to lift. Moreover, women have been excluded from many jobs because the men who control these jobs define women as "stupid," "delicate," and "emotional." Yet among the Arapesh of New Guinea, the women were assigned the task of carrying heavy loads because their heads were believed to be harder and stronger than those of men. Among the Tasmanians of the South Pacific, the most dangerous type of hunting—swimming out to remote rocks in the sea to stalk and club sea otters—was assigned to women. Moreover, women formed the bodyguard of Dahomeyan kings because they were deemed to be particularly fierce fighters. And although most peoples believe that it is the men who should take the initiative in sexual matters, among the Maori and the Trobriand Islanders this prerogative falls to women (Ford and Beach, 1951).

The great variation in the gender roles of men and women from one society to another points to a social foundation for most of these differences (Bernard, 1987; South and Trent, 1987; Intons-Peterson, 1988). So do the changes observed from one time to another in sex-linked behavior patterns within the same society. Not too long ago in Western history, the dashing cavalier wore long curls and perfume; he had a rapier and a stallion; and he also employed powder and lace and soft leather boots that revealed a well-turned calf. In the 1950s men who wore long hair were labeled "sissies" and "queers." But in the 1960s long hair came into style, and today more intermediate hairstyles are in vogue. All this suggests that gender roles are largely a matter of social definition and socially constructed meanings.

GENDER ROLES AND BIOLOGY

When a baby is born, the first thing people want to know is whether it is a boy or a girl. The biological aspects of gender consist of the physical differences between men and women: Women have the capacity to menstruate, carry a fetus until delivery, and provide it with milk after birth; men have the ability to produce and transmit sperm. But beyond these matters, the role biology plays in

Table 7.1   THE DIVISION OF LABOR BY SEX IN 224 SOCIETIES

Activity	Number of Societies and Sex of Person by Whom the Activity Is Performed				
	Men Always	Men Usually	Either Sex	Women Usually	Women Always
Hunting	166	13	0	0	0
Trapping small animals	128	13	4	1	2
Herding	38	8	4	0	5
Fishing	98	34	19	3	4
Clearing agricultural land	73	22	17	5	13
Dairy operations	17	4	3	1	13
Preparing and planting soil	31	23	33	20	37
Erecting and dismantling shelter	14	2	5	6	22
Tending and harvesting crops	10	15	35	39	44
Bearing burdens	12	6	35	20	57
Cooking	5	1	9	28	158
Metalworking	78	0	0	0	0
Boat building	91	4	4	0	1
Working in stone	68	3	2	0	2
Basket making	25	3	10	6	82
Weaving	19	2	2	6	67
Manufacturing and repairing of clothing	12	3	8	9	95

SOURCE: Reprinted by permission from *Social Forces,* May 15, 1937. "Comparative Data on the Division of Labor by Sex," by George P. Murdock. Copyright © The University of North Carolina Press.

producing behavioral differences between men and women is shrouded in controversy. Until relatively recently, it was generally believed that two quite separate gender roads exist, one leading from XX chromosomes at conception to womanhood and the other from XY chromosomes to manhood. But medical researchers at Johns Hopkins Medical Center are finding that there are not two roads, but one road with a number of forks where each of us turns in either a male or female direction. In other words, it appears that we become male or female by stages (Ehrhardt and Meyer-Bahlburg, 1981; Money, 1987).

In the early weeks following conception, XX and XY embryos proceed along a sexually neutral course. Around the sixth week, the Y chromosome sends a message to the two gonads to become testes. Apparently at this point the neutral and female roads converge. Likewise, at later forks in the road, without a push in the male direction, the fetus takes a female turn. Other important points in shaping gender occur with the secretion of sex hormones and the fashioning of sex organs. When the developmental process goes awry at one or more critical junctions, individuals develop reproductive organs of both sexes. Individuals whose reproductive structures are sufficiently ambiguous that it is difficult to define them exclusively as male or female are called **hermaphrodites.**

The Johns Hopkins Medical Center researchers find that social definitions play a crucial role in influencing the gender identities of hermaphrodites. At birth the child is classed as a boy or a girl, and a whole series of environmental forces then come into play (Money and Tucker, 1975:86–89):

The label "boy" or "girl" . . . has tremendous force as a self-fulfilling prophecy, for it throws the full weight of society to one side or other as the newborn heads for the gender fork [in the road], and the most decisive sex turning point of all. . . . [At birth you were limited to] something that was ready to become your gender identity. You were wired but not programmed for gender in the same sense that you were wired but not programmed for language.

Some researchers suggest that the human embryo has a bisexual potential. It seems that biological factors do not themselves produce differences in male or female behavior but affect the threshold for the elicitation of such behavior. Hormonal differences may "flavor" a person for one kind of gender behavior or another. But even so, hormones do not dictate that the behavior be learned. Rather, hormones make it easier for a person to learn certain gender-related behaviors. And these behaviors are constantly being shaped and modified by the environment (Scarf, 1976; Imperato-McGinley et al., 1979; Money, 1987; Mitchell, Baker, and Jacklin, 1989).

On the basis of a survey of over 2,000 books and articles on sex differences, psychologists Eleanor E. Maccoby and Carol N. Jacklin concluded in 1974 that there are four fairly "well-established" differences between boys and girls:

1. Beginning about age 11, girls show greater verbal ability than boys.
2. Boys are superior to girls on visual-spatial tasks in adolescence and adulthood, although not during childhood.
3. At about 12 or 13 years of age, boys move ahead of girls in mathematical ability.
4. Males are more aggressive than females.

Rather than settling controversies as to the "essential" or "basic" nature of men and women,

"Are you the opposite sex or is it ME?"

Used by permission of Hank Ketcham and © by North America Syndicate.

the Maccoby-Jacklin findings intensified them. Other psychologists promptly launched new surveys of the literature of gender differences and came to quite different conclusions (Halpern, 1992). For instance, Janet Shibley Hyde (1991) looked at the evidence for the alleged cognitive differences (verbal ability, visual-spatial ability, and mathematical ability). She concluded that the magnitude of the differences is at best quite small. In the years that have intervened since the original Maccoby-Jacklin survey, the gap between male and female performance on standardized tests has disappeared on verbal tests and narrowed on mathematics tests; only among highly precocious math students does the disparity between males and females remain large (Hyde, Fennema, and Lamon, 1990). One explanation for the narrowing of the gender gap in mathematics is that the sexual revolution has made contemporary girls and young women more confident about their mathematical talents and capabilities than were previous generations. But even more important, a close connection exists between the future educational and economic opportunities for women and their performance as youngsters in school: Equality in opportunities for adults yields parity among males and females in earlier preparatory and mathematical performances (Baker and Jones, 1993).

Yet much bias remains. Research reveals that girls are still treated differently in school than boys are and that parents, teachers, and peers hold higher academic expectations for boys than for girls (American Association of University Women, 1992; Sadker and Sadker, 1994). Other disparities also persist. A 1988 survey by the College Board found that 59 percent of college-bound male seniors, contrasted with 52 percent of female seniors, had taken trigonometry. The comparable figures for calculus were 21 percent for boys and 15 percent for girls. And whereas 51 percent of the boys had taken physics, only 35 percent of the girls had done so (Berger, 1989). Not surprisingly, in 1993 boys had higher scores on 11 of 14 subjects covered by the Scholastic Aptitude Test (SAT) (young women had a narrow lead only in English, German, and literature), and 18,000 boys—but only 8,000 girls—were eligible for National Merit Scholarships. In sum, it seems that many factors continue to weigh against women in math and science (significantly, math functions as a "career filter" not only for technical fields but also for most professions).

The matter of gender differences in aggression is also controversial. Psychologist Todd Tieger (1980), based on his survey of the literature, says that such differences become observable in children's spontaneous behavior only at about 5 years of age. During these early years, social factors foster the differential learning and expression of aggression by boys and girls. Whereas adults encourage boys to display aggression, girls are pressured to inhibit it. From boyhood scuffles and sporting events onward, men learn to view aggression in much the manner Karl von Clausewitz saw war—as an instrument to attain respect, status, and power. Whether the stakes be a handful of marbles or a nation's grandeur, males use aggression because it works. In contrast, females learn from their parents, the media, and "cooperative girls' games" that they must control their aggressive impulses and revile them as a character flaw (Campbell, 1993). However, Maccoby has seen little reason to alter her earlier conclusions (Maccoby and Jacklin, 1980; Maccoby, 1990). Nevertheless, she does emphasize that aggressiveness is less a trait of individuals than it is behavior that characterizes people in some kinds of situations. Women, like men, can be expected to exhibit aggression where the norms support such displays, and inhibit it in other domains (Hyde, 1984; Perry, Perry, and Rasmussen, 1986). In sum, it seems that there is little that is psychologically either male or female, although our cultural definitions often make it appear so.

ACQUIRING GENDER IDENTITIES

Gender identities are the conceptions we have of ourselves as being male or female. As such they are invisible, something that cannot be established by appearance. For most people, there is a good fit between their anatomy and their gender identity. Boys generally come to behave in ways their culture labels "masculine," and girls learn to be "feminine." But there are some individuals for whom this is not the case. The most striking examples are *transsexuals*—individuals who have normal sexual organs but who psychologically feel like members of the opposite sex. In some cases, as with Jan Morris, Christine Jorgensen, Renee Richards, and Roberta Cowell, medical science has found a way, through surgery and hormones, to reduce the incompatibility by modifying the person's anatomy to conform with the gender identity.

As we have noted in our discussion of culture and biology, learning plays a key part in the acquisition of gender identities. However, the exact nature of this learning has been the subject of considerable debate. According to Sigmund Freud and his followers, gender identity and the adoption of sex-typed behaviors are the result of an *Oedipus conflict* that emerges between the ages of 3 and 6. During this period, children discover the genital differences between the sexes. According to Freudians, this discovery prompts children to see themselves as rivals of their same-sex parent for the affection of the parent of the other sex. Such desires and feelings give rise to considerable anxiety. Freud said the anxiety is resolved through complicated psychological maneuvers in which children come to identify with the parent of the same sex. By virtue of this identification, boys acquire masculine self-conceptions and girls learn feminine self-conceptions. However, research that has tried to test Freud's theory has been either inconclusive or at odds with it. Additionally, cross-cultural research suggests that the Oedipus conflict does not occur among all peoples, including the Trobriand Islanders of the South Pacific (Malinowski, 1929).

Unlike Freud and his followers, *cultural-transmission* theorists contend that the acquisition of gender identities and behaviors is not the product of an Oedipus conflict but rather is a gradual process of learning that begins in infancy (Bandura, 1971, 1973; Fagot, Leinbach, and O'Boyle, 1992). They suggest that parents, teachers, and other adults shape a child's behavior by reinforcing responses that are deemed appropriate to the child's gender role and discouraging inappropriate ones. Moreover, children are motivated to attend to, learn from, and imitate same-sex models because they think of same-sex models as more like themselves (Mischel, 1970). Children are given cues to their gender roles in a great variety of ways. Parents often furnish boys' and girls' rooms differently, decorating those of boys with animal motifs and those of girls with floral motifs, lace, fringe, and ruffles (Rheingold and Cook, 1975; Lobel and Menashri, 1993). The toys found in the rooms also differ. Boys are provided with more vehicles, military toys, sports equipment, toy animals, and mechanical toys, and girls with more dolls, doll houses, and domestic toys (Caldera, Huston, and O'Brien, 1989; Lawson, 1989).

Cultural-transmission theory draws our attention to the part socialization plays in shaping the sex-typed behavior of children. However, the image we gain from the theory is one of essentially passive individuals who are programmed for behavior by adult bearers of culture. *Labeling theory* (also called cognitive-developmental theory) provides a corrective to this perspective by calling our attention to the fact that children actively seek to acquire gender identities and roles. According to developmental psychologist Lawrence Kohlberg (1966, 1969; Kohlberg and Ullian, 1974), children come to label themselves as "boys" or "girls" when they are between 18 months and 3 years of age. Once they have identified themselves as males or females, they want to adopt behaviors consistent with their newly discovered status. This process is called *self-socialization*. According to Kohlberg, children form a stereotyped conception of maleness and femaleness—an oversimplified, exaggerated, cartoonlike image. Then they use this stereotyped image in organizing behavior and cultivating the attitudes and actions associated with being a boy or a girl.

Both the cultural-transmission and labeling theories of gender-role learning have received research support (Maccoby and Jacklin, 1974; Bem, 1981; Serbin and Sprafkin, 1986; Martin and Little, 1990). Increasingly, social and behavioral scientists are coming to the view that any full explanation of gender-role acquisition must incorporate elements from both theoretical approaches.

THE FUNCTIONALIST AND CONFLICT PERSPECTIVES ON GENDER STRATIFICATION

The functionalist and conflict perspectives offer interpretations of gender stratification that resemble and parallel their positions on class and racial or ethnic stratification. Functionalists suggest that a division of labor originally arose between men and women because of the woman's role in reproduction. By virtue of the fact that women were often pregnant or nursing, preindustrial societies assigned domestic and childrearing tasks to them. In contrast, by virtue of their larger size and greater muscular strength, men were assigned hunting and defense tasks. Functionalists contend that a gender division of labor promoted the survival of the species and therefore was retained.

Sociologists Talcott Parsons and Robert Bales (1955) have built upon principles derived from the study of the dynamics of small groups in refining the functionalist position. They argue that two types of leaders are essential if a small group is to function effectively (see Chapter 4). *Instrumental leaders* (task specialists) devote their attention to appraising the problem at hand and organizing people's activity to deal with it. *Expressive leaders* (social-emotional specialists) focus on overcoming interpersonal problems in the group, defusing tensions, and promoting solidarity. Parsons and Bales suggest that families are also organized along instrumental-expressive lines. Men specialize in instrumental tasks (particularly roles associated with deriving a livelihood), and women in expressive tasks (nurturing roles that are allegedly an extension of their reproductive and nursing functions).

Conflict theorists reject functionalist arguments as simply offering a rationale for male dominance. They contend that a sexual division of labor is a social vehicle devised by men to ensure themselves of privilege, prestige, and power in their relationships with women. By relegating women to the home, men have been able to deny women those resources they need to succeed in the larger world. More particularly, conflict theorists have advanced a number of explanations for gender stratification (Collins, 1975; Vogel, 1983; Collier, 1988; Bradley, 1989; Chafetz, 1990). Some argue that the motivation for gender stratification derives from the economic exploitation of women's labor. Others say that the fundamental motive is men's desire to have women readily available for sexual gratification. And still

others emphasize that the appropriation of women is not for copulation but for procreation, especially to produce male heirs and daughters who can be used as exchanges in cementing political and economic alliances with other families.

Sociologist Joan Acker (1992) suggests that in industrial capitalist societies, production is privileged over reproduction. Whereas business, commerce, and industry are viewed as an essential source of well-being and wealth, childrearing, child care, and elder care are seen as secondary and wealth-consuming. Although "the family" is enshrined and idealized, reproduction (the domain of women) is shrouded in societal shadows and devalued. But should "the family" fail to function according to the idealized stereotype, it is widely portrayed as in decline and peril (see Chapter 9).

In order to appraise the matters raised by functionalist and conflict theorists, let us examine gender globally and in the United States.

THE GLOBAL PLIGHT OF WOMEN

In 1994, for the first time, the U.S. State Department focused attention in its annual human rights report on the treatment of women. The findings from 193 nations portray a grim picture of day-to-day discrimination and abuse. In Zaire, school-age girls spend one-third as much time in school as boys do, and they are responsible for most of the heavy farm work. In the Republic of the Congo, adultery is illegal for women, although not for men. Indonesian women are reluctant to go out alone at night because men widely view them as fair game for sexual attack. Governments typically turn a blind eye to the abuse of women, and in many nations the state is a major institutional source of discrimination. In Morocco, for instance, the law excuses a man for killing his wife if she is caught in the act of adultery, but it does not condone a wife's killing of her husband under similar circumstances. In many cases, brothels pay off local officials and the police—indeed, one human rights group reported that Thai police regularly drive Burmese women into Thailand and deliver them to brothels (Greenhouse, 1994).

A 1993 United Nations Human Development Report found that there still is no nation that treats its women as well as its men. Islamic militants have been crusading against Western-style women's rights and have been making considerable headway in Middle Eastern countries. The collapse of the Soviet regime has thrown Russian women out of work in disproportionate numbers (70 percent of those laid off in the first two postcommunist years). Most of the workers in sweatshops helping to boom the Chinese economy are women. Worldwide, half a million women annually die from pregnancy-related problems, including botched abortions. And in China, India, and some other nations where sons are valued more highly than daughters, traditional methods of female infanticide and modern sex-selective abortions provide the means for disposing of unwanted baby girls (China and India together have 75 million fewer women than they should have according to demographic calculations) (MacFarquhar, 1994).

Throughout the world women are sexually victimized. An estimated 85 to 114 million women, mostly Muslims in Africa, the Middle East, and Southeast Asia, have endured some form of "female genital mutilation" (a procedure typically undertaken to "ensure" virginity and eliminate sexual sensation, thereby making women "more marriageable") (Kaplan, 1993). And alas for women, mass rape and sexual sadism in war is not uncommon—an instrument not only of sexual violence but a vehicle to demean an enemy's national pride and honor. Men frequently deem rape during war to be an act of winners. They see women as "property," and so violating them is a way for victors to show who now "controls" that property.

Two-thirds of the world's illiterates are female, 600 million women cannot read, and 90 million girls are not in school. As teenagers, many youngsters are forced into marriage and sometimes bought and sold for prostitution and slave labor.

As wives and mothers, women are often treated little better than farmhands and baby machines. And should they outlive their husbands, they may be denied an inheritance, banished from their homes, and forced to live out their lives as beggars. In sum, worldwide social attitudes, norms, and institutions deem women to be inferior—and discrimination tends to start at birth. A 1993 International Labor Organization report, on the basis of a forty-one-nation survey, concluded that women will need another 1,000 years to match the political and economic clout of men (Sanchez, 1993).

GENDER ROLES IN THE UNITED STATES

The gender roles defined by a society have profound consequences for the lives of its men and women. They constitute master statuses that carry primary weight in people's interactions and relationships with others (see Chapter 2). In doing so, they place men and women in the social structure, establishing where and what they are in social terms. Thus gender roles establish the framework within which men and women gain their identities, formulate their goals, and carry out their training. Additionally, gender roles are a major source of social inequality. Just as our society structures inequalities based on race and ethnic membership, so it institutionalizes inequalities based on gender.

The Family. In large measure, sexual inequality has historically been sustained by assigning the economic-provider role to men and the childrearing role to women. The division between the public and domestic spheres has been a compelling one. Labor in the public sphere has been rewarded by money, prestige, and power, whereas labor in the domestic sphere has been typically isolated and undervalued (Daniels, 1987; Ferree, 1990; Kessler-Harris, 1990). Gender stereotypes arise in response to a gender division of labor and then serve to rationalize it by attributing to the sexes

THE WALL STREET JOURNAL

"I've just figured how much I'm worth as a housewife. The only trouble is that it's more than you earn."

From *The Wall Street Journal*—Permission, Cartoon Features Syndicate.

substantially different personality characteristics and traits (Hoffman and Hurst, 1990). The result is that the male experience becomes "privileged" and the female experience is "otherized" (Bem, 1993).

Across the years the gender division of labor has operated to bind women to their reproductive function. Until recent decades, motherhood has been central to American definitions of the female role. Each woman has been expected to raise one man's children in an individual household viewed as private property and private space. Male dominance implied the notion that men "owned" a woman's sexuality. Women were viewed as providing a man with sexual and domestic services in exchange for his financial support. Within this arrangement, a sexual double standard prevailed that permitted men, but not women, considerable sexual freedom and adventure. Until the twentieth century, English and American common law viewed women as undergoing "civil death" upon marriage. Women lost their legal identity when they married and, in the eyes of the law, became "incorporated and consolidated" with their husbands. A wife could not own property in her own right or sign a contract. And a husband could require his wife to live wherever he chose and to submit to sexual intercourse against her will.

Although American men, particularly younger men, are shifting their views on doing housework, the burden still falls primarily upon women (South and Spitze, 1994). Whether or not they work outside the home, wives do about 80 percent of the shopping, laundry, and cooking, and about two-thirds of the housecleaning, dishwashing, child care, and family paperwork. However, men typically do more yardwork and home maintenance than women. Although husbands among highly educated couples take on 80 percent more chores than do husbands among couples with only grammar school education, children with highly educated parents do less housework. Consequently, increasing education primarily shifts the responsibility for helping the wife or mother from the children to the husband (Otten, 1989). Despite their greater household responsibilities, women allocate just as much effort on paid jobs as do men—and indeed some research suggests they work harder in the workplace (Bielby and Bielby, 1988). It should come as little surprise, therefore, that a Gallup poll found that three out of four American women—age 18 to 54—reported they experienced stress in trying to be everything to everyone (Peterson, 1988). Not surprisingly, when women assume overwhelming responsibility for household duties, their satisfaction with the family division of household labor is low and their dissatisfaction impacts adversely upon their marital happiness (Suitor, 1991; Piña and Bengtson, 1993).

Today marriage and family have become less of an organizing force in the lives of contemporary American women. Over the last three decades, younger-generation women have come to experience and lead dramatically different lives than those of their older counterparts. Work outside the home is no longer limited by obligations that traditionally bound women to husbands and children. Although they still place a high value on marriage and the family, younger women are now more likely to delay marriage and childbearing (see Chapter 9). Women in the younger generations are taking greater control of their lives and are more independently integrating labor-force participation and family responsibilities than did their older counterparts (McLaughlin et al., 1988).

The Workplace. Married women's labor-force participation in the United States over the past 200 years is represented by a U-shaped curve, with relatively high participation rates in the 1790s, declining rates accompanying industrialization during the nineteenth century, and rising rates after the beginning of the twentieth century (mounting substantially after 1960). Although married women's participation in the labor force fell during the nineteenth century, single women entered the labor force in increasing numbers throughout that period. In recent decades, lower fertility and changing social attitudes contributed to the jump in the labor-force participation of women, while higher rates of divorce impelled more women to join the work force. African-American women have always worked for pay in larger proportions than have white women (Herring and Wilson-Sadberry, 1993).

In the United States, some 58 percent of adult women are now in the paid labor force (the proportion of men is 76 percent). This figure compares with 50 percent of women in Germany, 53 percent in France, 54 percent in the United Kingdom, and 72 percent in Denmark. Since 1950, the number of American mothers employed outside the home has tripled. About 59 percent of the nation's estimated 52 million children under age 15 have mothers who are working outside the home (57 percent of women with children under age 6 and 51 percent with children under age 1). Women have gained ground by moving into higher-paying fields traditionally dominated by men (for instance, today women make up 30 percent of residents in medical programs and 43 percent of law students). More and more women are also training for higher-paying jobs. [The Department of Education (1989) predicts that by the year 2000 women will be earning more doctoral degrees than men do.]

Despite these changes, many of the current figures on the employment of women bear a striking resemblance to those of previous decades. There was little substantial change in the gender segregation of occupations between 1900 and 1970. Since then gender segregation has shown only a slow decline (Tienda, Smith, and Ortiz, 1987; Zimmer, 1988; Jacobs, 1989; DiPrete and Grusky, 1990; Reskin and Roos, 1990). The increase in female employment has come largely through the displacement of men by women in some low-paying categories and through the rapid expansion of "pink-collar" occupations. Women fill more than 90 percent of all secretarial, bookkeeping, and receptionist positions. The "sticky floor" is an apt metaphor for the occupational frustrations experienced by the bulk of the nation's working women. Consider, for example, that hundreds of thousands of American women find themselves trapped in low-wage, low-mobility jobs in state and local government (55 percent of the 3 million or so women in state and local government jobs across the nation work in the lowest-paying employment categories; only a quarter of all men—and merely a fifth of white men—work in these categories). These are the workers who dispense driver's licenses, care for the mentally ill, and move the ceaseless paperwork (Noble, 1992).

Positions at the top still elude women executives, who find that they crash into what has been labeled the "glass ceiling." And if the invisible barriers associated with "glass ceilings" do not stop them, "glass walls" do (barriers that prevent

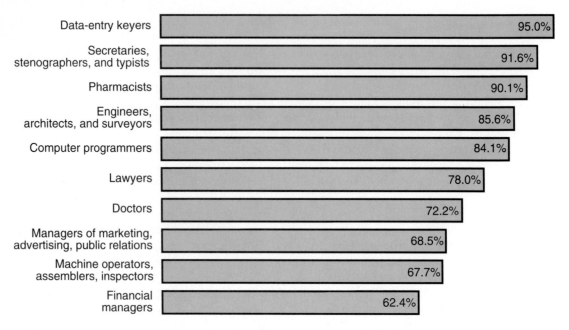

Figure 7.5 WOMEN'S WAGES REMAIN BELOW PARITY
Women's median wages for selected jobs in 1992 as a percentage of men's median wages for the
same jobs. (SOURCE: Data from U.S. Bureau of Labor Statistics. From *The Wall Street Journal,* June 9, 1993,
p. B1. Reprinted by permission of *The Wall Street Journal,* © 1993 Dow Jones & Company, Inc. All rights
reserved worldwide.)

women from moving laterally in corporations
and thus gaining the supervision experience they
need to advance vertically) (Lopez, 1992). In
1992, women still held less than a third of the
managerial jobs in some 38,059 U.S. firms, and
among 200 of the nation's largest companies, they
held only one-fourth of the jobs classified as
"officials and managers" (Sharpe, 1994). Less than
7 percent of top executives are women. In 1990,
when *Fortune* magazine sifted through the names
of the highest-paid officers and directors at the
799 public companies on its list of the 1,000
largest American industrial and service companies, only 19 of the 4,012 top positions were held
by women (less than one-half of 1 percent) (Fierman, 1990). A 1992 poll of 201 chief executives of
the nation's largest companies revealed that only
16 percent believed it "very likely" or "somewhat
likely" that they could be succeeded by a female
CEO within the next decade (Fisher, 1992). And

as of early 1993, women accounted for only 6.2
percent of the 11,715 directors (721 board seats)
of the nation's biggest 500 industrial and 500 service companies (Dobrzynski, 1993).

Women also earn less than men do. Overall, a
woman now earns just 71 cents for each dollar
earned by her male counterpart (Otten, 1994).
Some nations do better in gender pay comparisons. For instance, by the late 1980s, the ratio of
female-to-male weekly wages ranged from 80 to
90 percent in Australia, Denmark, France, New
Zealand, Norway, and Sweden (Clark, 1993).
Although the gap between the earnings of American men and women closed in the 1980s,
significant disparities remain (see Figure 7.5). The
disparity reaches into all spheres of American
life, including the scientific community (see Figure 7.6).

Economist Barbara R. Bergmann (1987) calcu-
lates that discrimination accounts for about half

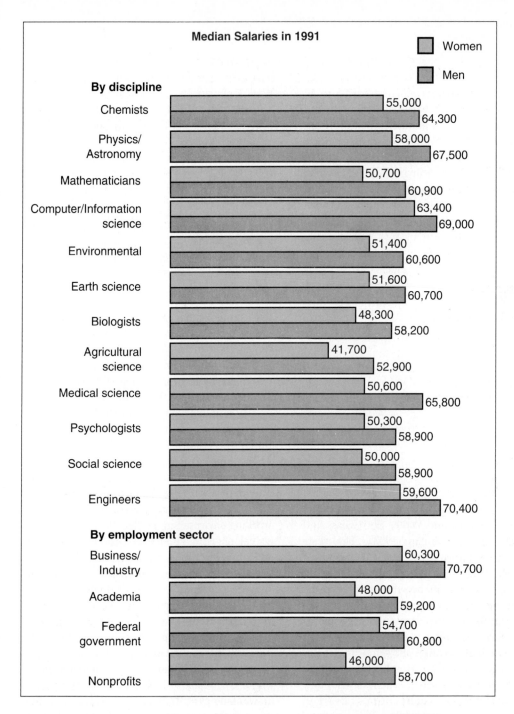

Figure 7.6 THE OUTER CIRCLE: U.S. SCIENCE PENALIZES ITS FEMALE SCIENTISTS
Women's median salaries lagged behind those of men in 1991 by at least $5,000. The most
dramatic differences occur in medical science. (Reprinted with permission from *Science*, vol. 261,
September 24, 1993. Copyright 1993 American Association for the Advancement of Science.)

of the wage gap; differences in work experience, training, and related factors account for the other half. The Census Bureau estimates that 35 to 40 percent of the gap in earnings for men and women derives from gender discrimination (Pear, 1987). Overall, the earnings of contemporary women still seem to be determined by the Old Testament rule, as stated in Leviticus 27:3–4: "A male between 20 and 60 years old shall be valued at 50 silver shekels. . . . If it is a female, she shall be valued at 30 shekels."

Overall, the career patterns of women are quite different from those of men. Given our contemporary family and work arrangements, the economic advancement of women is complicated by the social organization of child care. Economist Sylvia Ann Hewlett observes (quoted by Castro, 1991:10):

In the U.S. we have confused equal rights with identical treatment, ignoring the realities of family life. After all, only women can bear children. And in this country, women must still carry most of the burden of raising them. We think that we are being fair to everyone by stressing identical opportunities, but in fact we are punishing women and children.

All too often we overlook the fact that women who have children encounter a substantial career disadvantage (Desai and Waite, 1991; Glass and Camarigg, 1992; Tilghman, 1993). The years between 25 and 35 are critical in the development of a career. During this phase of the life span, lawyers and accountants become partners in the top firms, business managers make it to the fast track, college professors secure tenure at good universities, and blue-collar workers find positions that generate high earnings and seniority. Yet it is this time when women are most likely to leave the labor force to have children. When they do, they suffer in their ability to acquire critical skills and to achieve promotions. Even when new mothers return to work within a few months, male managers typically conclude that the women are no longer free to take on time-consuming tasks and pass them over for promotion (Wadman, 1992). Equal opportunity for women in public spheres remains substantially frustrated by gender-role differentiation within the family. Sociologist Mirra Komarovsky (1991:23) observes:

[I]n order to provide real options for men and women we shall have to reorganize economic and other institutions in a profound way, more profound in my opinion, than would be necessary, for example, to solve the problems of the black minority in the United States. . . . Social investments in child care, maternity and paternity leaves, flexible work hours, job sharing, and other changes will be required to balance the private and public worlds for both men and women.

Even though many companies are now attempting to appear "family-friendly," family issues still impede women's careers (Shellenbarger, 1992).

Sexual harassment also remains a common workplace hazard for women (Fitzgerald, 1993). While insufficient to deny Clarence Thomas a seat on the Supreme Court, Anita Hill's allegations in 1991 marked a watershed in the nation's perception of the seriousness of sexual harassment. The Equal Employment Opportunity Commission defines sexual harassment as "unwelcome" sexual attention, whether verbal or physical, that affects an employee's job conditions or creates a "hostile" working environment (Adler, 1991). Examples of sexual harassment include unsolicited and unwelcome flirtations, advances, or propositions; graphic or degrading comments about an employee's appearance, dress, or anatomy; the display of sexually suggestive objects or pictures; ill-received sexual jokes and offensive gestures; sexual or intrusive questions about an employee's personal life; explicit descriptions of a male's own sexual experiences; abuse of familiarities such as "honey," "baby," and "dear"; unnecessary, unwanted physical contact such as touching, hugging, pinching, patting, or kissing; whistling and catcalls; and leering. We do not have precise statistics on the actual incidence of sexual harassment.

However, a 1991 *New York Times*/CBS News poll found four of ten women indicating that they had encountered some form of what they regarded as sexual harassment at work, and five of ten men said that at some point while on the job they had said or done something that could have been construed by a female colleague as harassment (Kolbert, 1991).

Politics and Government.   In 1984, for the first time in American history, a woman was named to the presidential ticket of a major political party. Geraldine Ferraro became the Democratic party's vice-presidential candidate. Many political analysts thought that Ferraro's selection would contribute to more women running for national public office. However, Ferraro's experience—particularly the embarrassment the public limelight caused her family—may have dampened the enthusiasm of many women to undertake the run for high office. Democratic Congresswoman Patricia Schroeder of Colorado caught an old political chestnut in 1987, when she was exploring a bid for the presidency: "Are you running as a woman?" she was asked. "Do I have an option?" Representative Schroeder shot back. In due course she scrapped her 1988 run for the presidency, saying she was under too much pressure to change her style and was expected to give up too much of herself. When it comes to the presidency, a 1937 Gallup survey revealed that 65 percent of Americans said they would not vote for a woman for president even if she were qualified. By 1987 the figure had dropped to 12 percent, although a differently worded Roper question in 1992 showed a 32 percent rejection. The United States might have been expected to break the barrier before conservative and Catholic Ireland elected Mary Robinson president in 1990 despite her support of abortion rights and outspoken feminism. Even three Muslim nations—Turkey, Pakistan, and Bangladesh—have overcome strong religious reservations to female leadership. As of early 1994, the list of nations that had or had had a woman prime minister or president included Western nations (Great Britain, France, Canada, Ireland, Portugal, and Iceland), an Asian nation (the Philippines), Latin American nations (Argentina, Bolivia, and Nicaragua), an Eastern European nation (Poland), Middle Eastern nations (Israel and Turkey), almost the entire subcontinent region (India, Pakistan, Bangladesh, and Sri Lanka), and West Indian nations (Haiti, Dutch Antilles, and Dominica) (Harwood and Brooks, 1993).

Political success has not come easily to American women (Witt, Paget, and Matthews, 1993). Men still dominate American political life, but their monopoly on office is threatened. In 1992, propelled in part by outrage over Anita Hill's treatment at the Clarence Thomas confirmation hearings the previous year, women ran for Congress in record numbers. In the elections, women increased their numbers in the U.S. Senate from 2 to 6, and their representation in the House of Representatives from 29 to 48. The year 1992 may turn out to be a landmark year. Women now constitute a majority of voters, and thousands of women have entered politics at the local and state levels over the last two decades, enlarging the pool of candidates for higher office.

The Women's Movement.   Over the past 30 years, no social movement has had a more substantial impact on the way Americans think and act than the women's movement. Such movements have arisen throughout human history, particularly within the context of social revolutions and movements for national independence. Initially women get caught up in the same broad currents that engulf a nation. But then they begin to extend the ideology of social justice and equality to their circumstances. The suffragist movement of the 1830s developed out of the abolitionist movement when women discovered strong parallels between their conditions and those of African Americans. In the 1960s, the women's movement built upon earlier movements while gaining new impetus from the involvement of women in the civil rights movement (Taylor, 1989; Buechler, 1990; Simon and Danziger, 1991). Cross-national research suggests that the "first wave" (1800–1950) of women's movements focused primarily on legal equality, including the pursuit of suffrage, or the right to vote; the "second wave" (since the 1960s) has centered primarily on social equality, particularly in jobs and education (Chafetz and Dworkin, 1986).

The revival of feminist activity in the 1960s was spearheaded by a variety of groups. Some, such as the National Organization for Women (NOW), were organized at the national level by well-known women. Others were grassroots groups that engaged in campaigns for abortion reform or welfare rights, consciousness-raising rap sessions, or promotion of the interests of professional or lesbian women. After nearly 30 years of feminist activism, a 1992 *Time*/CNN survey found that only 5 percent of American women think the women's movement had not improved their lives, and 57 percent indicated they thought there is still a need for a strong women's movement (Blackman, Painton, and Taylor, 1992).

Persistence and Change. As we will discuss at greater length in Chapter 9, traditional family roles are in a state of flux. The image of the nuclear family with a breadwinning male and a full-time female homemaker represents only 12 percent of American households. In more than 60 percent of families, both husband and wife work. Some 66 percent of women who are single parents are in the work force. And 33 million children have mothers who work full time. Increasingly the dilemma posed for women is how to balance a job with marriage and motherhood.

Recent polls show that the majority of American men and women have adopted a number of "liberated" beliefs about women. However, many Americans, particularly men, remain reluctant to abandon traditional notions of "women's work" when it comes to housekeeping and rearing children (Townsend and O'Neil, 1990; Davis and Robinson, 1991; Grigsby, 1992). Whereas men are more able to pursue their careers single-mindedly, women feel that they must try to balance their responsibilities on the job with their duties at home. As we noted earlier in the chapter, household and child-care responsibilities still fall disproportionately upon women. One woman, commenting upon this "gendering" in American family life, says: "Some things are done so many times a day and for so many years that it is difficult to assess my true reaction to having to do them. They are taken for granted and done without thinking about them" (Berk, 1985:207). Given these realities, nearly half (49 percent) of adults surveyed by the Gallup Organization in 1989 said that, all things considered, American men have a better life than American women. In 1975, only 32 percent of adults agreed with the same statement. Some 22 percent of Americans said that women had it better than men in 1989, a figure down from 28 percent in 1975. Women who came of age since the 1960s are most inclined to see it as a man's world: 63 percent of women age 18 to 49 believe that men have it better, compared with 40 percent of older women. Sixty percent of women and 53 percent of men say that marriage is most satisfying when both partners have jobs. But 76 percent of Americans say it is now harder for marriages to be successful, and 66 percent say that it is now harder for women to combine jobs and family (Gallup Organization, 1990). In sum, both persistence and change characterize the status of women in American life.

Summary

1. Stratification represents institutionalized inequality in the distribution of social rewards and burdens. People are locked within an arena of social relationships in which they differ sharply in their life chances and styles of living. In Chapter 5 we examined the class system of stratification; in this chapter we turned to two additional systems of stratification, race and/or ethnicity, and gender.

2. Although racial and ethnic stratification is similar to other systems of stratification in its essential features, there is one overriding difference. Racial and ethnic groups have the potential to carve their own independent nation from the existing state. Unlike class stratification, the issue is not replacement of one elite by another or even a revolutionary change in the political system. Instead, the question is one of whether the racial or ethnic segments of the society will be willing to participate within the existing nation-state arrangement.

3. Racial groups are populations that differ in the incidence of various hereditary traits. Ethnic groups are identified on the basis of distinctive cultural backgrounds. Racial and ethnic groups are often minority groups. Five properties characterize a minority: (1) Its members experience discrimination, segregation, oppression, or persecution at the hands of a dominant group; (2) it is characterized by physical or cultural traits that distinguish it from the dominant group; (3) it is a self-conscious social group; (4) membership in a minority is generally involuntary; and (5) the members of a minority, by choice or necessity, typically marry within their own group.

4. Prejudice is a state of mind—a feeling, opinion, or disposition. In contrast, discrimination is action, what people actually do in their daily activities. Discrimination is not practiced just by individuals. In their day-to-day operation, the institutions of society also systematically discriminate against the members of some groups—a process called institutional discrimination. Gatekeeping is one mechanism by which institutional discrimination occurs.

5. Dominant groups have pursued a variety of policies toward minorities. At times these policies may parallel those of the minority; at other times they run counter to minority group aims. The chapter examined six types of dominant group policies: assimilation, pluralism, legal protection of minorities, population transfer, continued subjugation, and extermination.

6. Functionalist and conflict theorists take differing views of racial and ethnic stratification. Functionalists look to the functions and dysfunctions it has for the survival of the social system and its parts. They note that conflict promotes group formation and solidarity. Simultaneously, conflict may imperil the larger social system. Conflict theorists contend that prejudice and discrimination can best be understood in terms of tension or conflict among competing groups. Often three ingredients come into play in the emergence and stabilization of racism: ethnocentrism, competition, and unequal power.

7. Within the United States African Americans, Hispanics, Native Americans (Indians), and Asian Americans have been the victims of prejudice and discrimination. The subjugation of African Americans extends to the period of exploration and colonialization. Like African Americans, people of Mexican heritage and Native Americans did not origi-

nally become a part of American society through voluntary immigration. Both Native Americans and Mexicans entered the society through conquest of their homeland. Asian Americans have also encountered considerable difficulty in the United States, but in recent decades the circumstances of many of them have greatly improved.

8. Men and women differ in their access to privilege, prestige, and power. The distribution problem of who gets what, when, and how has traditionally been answered in favor of males. Women exhibit four of the five properties commonly associated with a minority group. Apparently all societies have seized on the anatomical differences between men and women to assign gender roles—sets of cultural expectations that define the ways in which the members of each sex should behave.

9. The biological aspects of gender consist of the physical differences between men and women: Women have the capacity to menstruate, carry a fetus until delivery, and provide it with milk after birth; men have the ability to produce and transmit sperm. But beyond these matters, the role biology plays in producing behavioral differences between men and women is shrouded in controversy. Some researchers suggest that the human embryo has a bisexual potential. It seems that biological factors do not themselves produce differences in male or female behavior but affect the threshold for the elicitation of such behavior.

10. Gender identities are the concepts we have of ourselves as being male or female. Three theories seek to account for the process by which children acquire their gender identities. According to Freudians, the adoption of sex-typed behaviors is the result of an Oedipus conflict that emerges between the ages of 3 and 6. Cultural-transmission theorists draw our attention to the part socialization plays in the process. Labeling theories examine the process whereby children come to label themselves as "boys" or "girls" and cultivate the appropriate gender-related behaviors.

11. The functionalist and conflict perspectives offer interpretations of gender stratification that resemble and parallel their positions on class and racial or ethnic stratification. Functionalists suggest that families are organized along instrumental-expressive lines, with men specializing in instrumental tasks and women in expressive tasks. Conflict theorists contend that a sexual division of labor is a social vehicle devised by men to ensure themselves of privilege, prestige, and power in their relationships with women.

12. The gender roles defined by a society have profound consequences for the lives of its men and women. They constitute master statuses that carry primary weight in people's interactions and relationships with others. In so doing, they place men and women in the social structure, establishing where and what they are in social terms. Thus gender roles set the framework within which men and women gain their identities, formulate their goals, and carry out their training. Additionally, gender roles are a major source of social inequality.

Glossary

assimilation Those processes whereby groups with distinctive identities become culturally and socially fused.

discrimination The arbitrary denial of privilege, prestige, and power to members of a minority group whose qualifications are equal to those of members of the dominant group.

environmental racism The practice of deliberately locating incinerators and other types of hazardous waste facilities in or next to minority communities.

ethnic group A group identified chiefly on cultural grounds—language, religion, folk practices, dress, gestures, mannerisms.

gatekeeping The decision-making process whereby people are admitted to offices and positions of privilege, prestige, and power within a society.

gender identities The conceptions we have of ourselves as being male or female.

gender roles Sets of cultural expectations that define the ways in which the members of each sex should behave.

genocide The deliberate and systematic extermination of a racial or ethnic group.

hermaphrodites Individuals whose reproductive structures are sufficiently ambiguous that it is difficult to define them exclusively as male or female.

institutional discrimination Systematic discrimination against the members of some groups by the institutions of society in their daily operation.

minority group A racially or culturally self-conscious population, with hereditary membership and a high degree of in-group marriage, which suffers oppression at the hands of a dominant segment of a nation-state.

pluralism A situation where diverse groups coexist side by side and mutually accommodate themselves to their differences.

prejudice Attitudes of aversion and hostility toward the members of a group simply because they belong to it and hence are presumed to have the objectionable qualities ascribed to it.

races Populations that differ in the incidence of various hereditary traits.

split labor market An economic arena in which large differences exist in the price of labor at the same occupational level.

symbolic racism A form of racism in which whites feel that blacks are too aggressive, do not play by the rules, and have negative characteristics.

Chapter 8

POLITICAL
AND
ECONOMIC POWER

Power pervades all aspects of social life. It furnishes the resources to get things done—to provide the direction essential for coordinating and integrating individual activity so that collective goals can be achieved. And it determines which individuals and groups will be able to translate their preferences into the reality of day-to-day social organization. *Power,* as we noted in Chapter 6, refers to the ability of individuals and groups to realize their will in human affairs even if it involves the resistance of others. By virtue of power, change is brought about in one party—in attitude, behavior, motivation, or direction—that would not have occurred in its absence.

Power is institutionalized in a patterned, recurrent manner and hence is embedded in social arrangements. It gives direction to human affairs, channeling people's actions along one course rather than another. Yet power entails not only the ability to get things done but to get them done in the way that one party prefers they be done. Alexander Hamilton alluded to this attribute of power when he wrote in *The Federalist* in 1788: "In the general course of human nature, a power over a man's subsistence amounts to a power over his will." The power that makes a real difference in the way social life works is the power that flows from the dominant organizations and institutions. This chapter examines "power that makes a real difference." It focuses on economic and political institutions.

☐ Power, Authority, and the State

Because the collective enterprise—group life—makes us mutually dependent on one another, we can achieve many of our goals only by influencing other people's behavior. As we pointed out in discussing social stratification in Chapter 6, power affects the ability of people to make the world work on their behalf. Those individuals and groups who control critical resources—rewards, punishments, and persuasive communications—

are able to dictate the way social life is ordered. To command key organizations and institutions is to command people. Indeed, power is the bedrock of social organization (Bierstedt, 1950). It contributes to the creation and perpetuation of social groups and institutions. The state is such an organization and institution.

THE STATE

The **state**—the political institution—is an arrangement that consists of people who exercise an effective monopoly in the use of physical coercion within a given territory. In the final analysis the state rests on **force**—power whose basis is the threat or application of punishment. Clearly the ability to take life and inflict suffering affords a critical advantage in human affairs. In effect, force constitutes a final court of appeals; there is usually no appeal to force except the exercise of superior force. For this reason, sovereign nations restrict, and even prohibit, the independent exercise of force by their subjects. If it were otherwise, governments could not suppress forceful challenges to their authority (Lenski, 1966; Lehman, 1988). But even though force is ultimately the basis of the state, it is only in unusual situations that societal power actually takes this form.

The state is a relatively recent institution. Changes in subsistence patterns that permitted the production of a *social surplus*—goods and services over and above those necessary for survival—provided the foundations for the state (see Chapter 2). External factors also played a part. A state typically arose as part of a larger social arrangement or system of states called *nation-states*. The nation-state arrangement legitimates sovereignty, state purposes, a military, and territorial jurisdiction (Thomas and Meyer, 1984; Giddens, 1985).

Within Western nations, the domain of the state has expanded across time. A growing number of activities—touching many spheres of social life including education, medicine, the family, religion, working conditions, and technology—

have become incorporated within its "general welfare" function (Skocpol and Amenta, 1986). The public welfare expenditures of Western capitalist democracies rapidly increased after World War II, but the pace has slackened since the late 1970s. In some nations, especially those like Sweden with social democratic governments, social programs were transformed into comprehensive systems of universal benefits that guaranteed the citizenry a basic standard of living—what has been called the *welfare state*. During the New Deal years and through the 1960s, the United States also followed the conventional welfare-state path with the state directly financing and providing a variety of social services. But beginning in the 1970s, the nation shifted the focus of its public activity increasingly toward the managing and financing of various medical and elderly benefits through the private market (privatized, commercial, and for-profit business activity) by means of tax incentives, state-established business standards, and policies stressing business responsibilities (Gilbert and Gilbert, 1989). As the state has taken on more and more activities, its role has become increasingly rationalized through the introduction of explicit rules and procedures based on a division of function and authority that Max Weber called a *bureaucracy* (Bourdieu, 1994) (refer back to Chapter 4).

Two views have prevailed regarding the state. Functionalists depict the state as an essential social institution that evolved as societies moved from traditional to modern ways. This image of the state predates contemporary sociological theory. It found expression in the social contract perspective that was articulated by seventeenth- and eighteenth-century social philosophers such as Thomas Hobbes (1588–1679). Hobbes contended that human beings were "naturally" a perverse and destructive lot. He conjectured that early in history human beings had voluntarily entered into a social agreement providing for central authority and collective defense as a measure to rid themselves of rampant brutality, violence, and chaos. But other philosophers such as Jean

Jacques Rousseau (1712–1778) disagreed. According to Rousseau, private property was the root of human social evils. Once private property was established, the state followed as an institution to define and defend property rights. In their original "state of nature," Rousseau said, human beings were "noble savages"—spontaneous, outgoing, loving, kind, and peaceful. The advent of private property ended this idyllic existence, bringing with it corruption, oppression, and obedience to a privileged class. Rousseau's approach foreshadowed the modern conflict perspective on the state. Let us examine the functional and conflict views more carefully.

THE FUNCTIONALIST PERSPECTIVE ON THE STATE

Functionalists contend that there is a good reason why the state arose and why it has assumed a dominant position in contemporary life. They say that society must maintain order and provide for the common good. More particularly, they point to four primary functions performed by the state.

Enforcement of Norms. It is easy to take the state for granted. Yet the eminent anthropologist George Peter Murdock (1950a:716) tells us:

[F]or 99 percent of the approximately one million years that man has inhabited this earth, he lived, thrived, and developed without any true government whatsoever, and . . . as late as 100 years ago half the people of the world— not half the population but half the tribes or nations— still ordered their lives exclusively through informal controls without benefit of political institutions.

As we pointed out in Chapter 2, where people lack a formal political institution, they enforce their folkways and mores through the spontaneous and collective action of community members. Thus the Native-American Crow subjected violators of community mores to scathing ridicule. But in modern, complex societies characterized by a preponderance of secondary relationships, these arrangements are no longer adequate. A special body or organization is required to ensure law and order—the state.

Planning and Direction. Rapid social change dictates that people can no longer rely on the gradual, more-or-less spontaneous evolution of folkways and mores to provide guidelines for daily life. New norms become indispensable. Such norms—*laws*—result from conscious thought, deliberate planning, and formal declaration. And laws have an added advantage: They can be changed more easily than folkways and mores. By way of illustration, the folkways of fairness that regulated traffic in horse-and-buggy days are no longer adequate for the congested conditions of the nation's highways. Nor are the laws governing automobiles suitable for handling congested air traffic over airports.

In addition, the complexity and scope of many activities require overall coordination and integration. Under contemporary urban conditions, people find that personal and informal arrangements no longer suffice to provide highways, fire and police protection, public sanitation, safeguards to public health, and assistance to the poor and infirm. These and many other activities dictate central direction. Similarly, in times of war, financial panic, or natural disaster, people often cannot cope with the magnitude of the crisis through independent and individual actions. The efficient and effective coordination and channeling of the human endeavor requires planning and direction. This task can be performed by only one or at most a few individuals. And these individuals must have the power and authority to implement their plans (Davis, 1949).

Arbitration of Conflicting Interests. Because many resources are scarce and divisible—particularly privilege, prestige, and power—people find themselves in conflict as they pursue their goals. If no bonds other than the pursuit of immediate self-interest were to unite people, society would quickly degenerate into a Hobbesian nightmare in which "war against all" comes to prevail. If conflicts among different social strata, races, religions, and special-interest groups were to become deep and intense, the entire social fabric would be imperiled. Some agency is required that is sufficiently strong to contain conflict within tolerable limits—and that agency is the state (Goode, 1972).

Protection Against Other Societies. Throughout human history, societies have felt it necessary to protect their members and interests against outside groups and to advance their fortunes through acts of aggression against other groups. Two primary means for achieving these ends have been war and diplomacy. However, both war and diplomacy call for centralized control and mobilization if a people are to maximize their position relative to their adversaries. The state meets this requirement. Indeed, sociologist Charles Tilly (1990) surveys European history and concludes that states are shaped primarily by the need to prepare for and wage war. In modern nations the classic dividing line between foreign and domestic policy has become increasingly blurred. For instance, within the United States, the dictates of Cold War global commitments and the expenditure of enormous funds on the military have enabled the Pentagon to give substantial direction and shape to the nation's post–World War II industrial policy and growth (Hooks, 1990a).

In sum, functionalists view the state much in the fashion of social contract philosophers. They deem it to be a social mechanism—a necessary institution—that evolved as societies moved from more traditional to modern ways of life (see Chapter 2).

THE CONFLICT PERSPECTIVE ON THE STATE

Functionalists see the state as a rather benign institution. Not so conflict theorists! They contend that the state is a vehicle by which one or more groups impose their values and stratification system upon other groups. As they

"This should jump-start the economy."

Drawing by Bernard Schoenbaum; © 1991 The New Yorker Magazine, Inc.

view the matter, the state has its origin in the desire of ruling elites to give permanence to social arrangements that benefit themselves. More fundamentally, they depict the state as an instrument of violence and oppression. Conflict sociologist Randall Collins (1975:351–352) asserts:

What we mean by the state is the way in which violence is organized. The state consists of those people who have the guns or the other weapons and are prepared to use them; in the version of political organization found in the modern world, they claim monopoly on their use. The state is, above all, the army and the police, and if these groups did not have weapons we would not have a state in the classical sense. This is a type of definition much disputed by those who like to believe that the state is a kind of grade-school assembly in which people get together to operate for their common good. . . . [However, the basic question is] who will fight or threaten whom and who will win what?

Conflict theorists see the state arising in history with the production of a social surplus—

goods and services over and above what is necessary for human survival. In hunting and gathering societies, land is communally owned, and the members of the community share the food derived from it. Agricultural societies are less egalitarian than hunting and gathering groups (see Chapter 2). Intensive agriculture produces food surpluses, and so it is no longer essential that every human hand be employed in subsistence activities. Some individuals can apply their talents and abilities to new occupations, such as pottery, masonry, and weaving. Of equal significance, some members of society can live off the surplus produced by others—elites who become the beneficiaries of privilege (Lenski, 1966). Political scientists Kenneth Prewitt and Alan Stone (1973:12–13) observe:

If craftsmen produce artifacts and ornaments, these status symbols become the possessions of the ruling class. If warriors venture forth to conquer and return with slaves and women, the slaves will serve in the fields and kitchens of the ruler and the women will be placed in their harems. If the productive labor of society is used to build palaces, temples, and monuments, these edifices will be inhabited by or dedicated to the members of the ruling class. It has been a constant fact of history that much more than an equal share of the social surplus is retained by the rulers for private pleasures.

Anthropologists Charles Wagley and Marvin Harris (1964:242) also point out that the rise of the state had other social consequences. It gave rise to subject peoples (dominant-minority group relationships):

Only with the development of the state did human societies become equipped with a form of social organization which could bind masses of culturally and physically heterogeneous "strangers" in a single social entity. Whereas primitive peoples derive their cohesion largely from a common culture and from kinship and other kinds of personal ties, state societies are held together largely by the existence of a central political authority which claims a monopoly of coercive power over all persons within a given territory. Theoretically, with a sufficiently strong development of the apparatus of government, a state soci-

ety can extend law and order over limitless subgroups of strangers who neither speak the same language, worship the same gods, nor strive for the same values.

A good example is the Soviet Union, which, prior to its collapse in 1991, had come to comprise one-sixth of the world's landmass, 289 million people, and more than 130 nationalities and ethnic groups, including Armenians, Ingush, Chechens, Tatars, Volga Germans, Kalmucks, Uzbeks, Jews, Yakuts, Russians, and Ukrainians. The problem dates back to the old czarist Russian Empire. Now, out from under the old Russian and Soviet orders, a host of peoples are pursuing long-repressed yearnings for nationhood. Similarly, the crumbling of the Yugoslavian state has unleashed a nasty civil war among Serbs, Croats, Slovenes, Bosnian Muslims, and Albanians.

There is a difference of opinion among conflict theorists regarding the nature of the state. Marxist controversies have given impetus to the debate and have prompted sociological researchers to pursue their own explorations. Some theorists (*instrumental theorists*) have taken literally the *Communist Manifesto*'s dictum that "the executive of the modern state is but a committee for managing the common affairs of the whole bourgeosie." Seen in this manner, the state is an instrument that is manipulated, virtually at will, by the capitalist class (Beirne, 1979). As we will see later in the chapter, several studies seek to show that economic power inheres in the ownership or control of the means of production (factories, banks, and large farms) and is typically transformed into political influence (Kolko, 1962; Miliband, 1969; Domhoff, 1970, 1983). Capitalists, it is alleged, accomplish this transformation through lobbying, campaign financing, intermarriage within the capitalist class, and the corruption by business of the judiciary and federal and state legislatures.

Other conflict theorists (*structural theorists*) contend that the state apparatus exercises "relative autonomy" in its relationship with the capitalist class. They say that state structures do not simply reflect dominant class interests but rather have their own structures and capacities that affect society (Skocpol, 1980; Quadagno, 1984; Hooks, 1990b). The state, then, is conceived as an actor with interests of its own that often reflect neither those of a particular class nor those of the larger society (Barkey and Parikh, 1991). According to this view, relentless class war between capitalists and workers, boom and bust economic cycles, and intercorporate conflict place constraints on the ability of the capitalist class to manipulate political institutions at will. Although the state may promote a climate favorable to capitalist enterprise, it must also legitimate the sanctity of the social order and maintain internal peace (O'Connor, 1973). By virtue of this latter requirement, the state routinely pursues policies that are at variance with the interests of *some* capitalists. For instance, it enacts welfare legislation that supports unemployed and nonproductive workers, places restrictions on rent that inhibit the ability of landlords to receive open market rentals, passes and enforces antitrust legislation, and imposes taxes on corporations (Beirne, 1979). Accordingly, the state apparatus is seen as standing above the individual elements of the economy, even though in its basic orientation it promotes a social environment conducive to capitalist arrangements. In this fashion the unity of the capitalist class is maintained (Poulantzas, 1973; Block, 1987; Jessop, 1985, 1990).

The collapse of communism in much of the world has diminished the appeal of Marxist explanations of the state (van den Berg, 1988). Yet current research on social policy and the welfare state and comparative-historical studies of state formation owe much to sociological interest generated by Marxist debates (Jenkins and Brents, 1989, 1991; Tilly, 1990; Gilbert and Howe, 1991; Carruthers, 1994).

LEGITIMACY AND AUTHORITY

Both functionalist and conflict theorists see force as the foundation of sovereignty. But as we pointed out earlier in the chapter, they disagree on the ends served by the state's use of force. Functionalists see force as restraining those who would put their self-interests above the public good, whereas conflict theorists see force as an instrument of subjugation and exploitation. In Chapter 1 we noted that a number of sociologists have sought to reconcile the two positions by emphasizing that consensus and coercion give a Janus-headed character to society: Both consensus and conflict are seen as central elements of social life.

Although force may be an effective means for seizing power, and though it remains the ultimate foundation for the state, it is not the most effective means for political rule (Lenski, 1966). As officials of the Soviet and Eastern European communist regimes discovered, force is both inefficient and costly. Now the ex-Soviet Empire is in a tangle of crises: social, economic, political, and national. Moreover, honor, normally a prized possession, is denied to those who rule by force alone. And finally, if an elite is inspired by revolutionary visions for building a new social order, the ideals remain unfulfilled unless the masses come to embrace the new order as their own. The English leader and orator Edmund Burke (1729–1797) captured the essence of these matters when he noted that the use of force alone is but temporary: "It may subdue for a moment; but it does not remove the necessity of subduing again; and a nation is not governed, which is perpetually to be conquered."

All this highlights the importance of the distinction that sociologists make between power that is legitimate and power that is illegitimate. Legitimate power is **authority.** When individuals possess authority, they have a recognized and established *right* to determine policies, pronounce judgments, settle controversies, and, more broadly, act as leaders. Legitimacy—the social justification of power—takes a number of forms (Lipset, 1994; Stryker, 1994). Sociologist Max Weber (1921/1968) has suggested a threefold classification of authority based on the manner in which the power is socially legitimated: legal-rational, traditional, and charismatic.

Weber's interest in authority derived from his broader political interests. Indeed, Weber has often been called the "bourgeois Marx" because of the similarities in the two men's intellectual interests and the differences in their political orientations. Although critical of modern capitalism, Weber did not advocate revolution, preferring instead gradual change. Let us consider Weber's three bases of authority.

Traditional Authority. In **traditional authority,** power is legitimated by the sanctity of age-old customs. People obey their rulers because "this is the way things have always been done." Additionally, they may perceive a ruler's power as eternal, inviolable, and sacred. Many Roman Catholics invest the pope with infallibility deriving from divine guidance when he acts in matters pertaining to the Church. Similarly, medieval kings and queens ruled in the name of "a divine right" ordained by God. It was this type of authority that Emperor Hirohito enjoyed until the American occupation authorities imposed a legal-rational system on Japan following World War II. A good deal of moral force stands behind traditional authority. Often the claim to such authority rests on birthright; it is generally inherited, since royal blood is thought to be somehow different from and superior to the blood of commoners.

Legal-Rational Authority. In **legal-rational authority,** power is legitimated by explicit rules and rational procedures that define the rights and duties of the occupants of given positions. It is this type of authority that Weber depicted as prevailing in his ideal-type bureaucracy, discussed in Chapter 4. Under this arrangement, officials claim obedience on the grounds that their commands fall within the impersonal, formally defined scope of their office. Obedience is owed not to the person but to a set of impersonal principles that have been devised in a rational manner.

In the United States, the authority of government leaders is accepted because Americans accept the premise that the law is supreme. Americans accept the exercise of power because they have come to believe that policies and orders are formulated in accordance with rules to which they subscribe. They accept the authority of a newly elected president even when the election campaign was waged in bitterness and anger. The system would crumble were a large number of Americans to reject these "rules of the game." In fact, this occurred in 1861 when southern states rejected the election of Abraham Lincoln and federal authority, seceding from the Union and initiating the Civil War. And it was the perception by Americans that President Richard M. Nixon had failed to abide by the rules in the Watergate case that led to his downfall in the 1970s. Ideally, then, legal-rational authority is "a government of laws, not of people."

Charismatic Authority. In **charismatic authority,** power is legitimated by the extraordinary superhuman or supernatural attributes people attribute to a leader. Founders of world religions, prophets, military victors, and political heroes commonly derive their authority from charisma (meaning literally "gift of grace"). Miracles, revelations, exceptional feats, and baffling successes are their trademarks. They are the Christs, Napoleons, Caesars, Hitlers, Castros, Joan of Arcs, and Ayatollah Khomeinis who dot the pages of history. At times such leaders have a sense of being "called" to spread the new word. They communicate a sense that the past is decadent but that a new day awaits people who follow them, as symbolized in Christ's injunction, "It is written . . . , but I say unto you . . . ."

Weber viewed each of these three bases of authority as ideal types. As we noted in Chapter 1, *ideal types* are concepts sociologists construct to portray the principal characteristics of a phenomenon. Hence, in practice, any specific form of authority may involve various combinations of all three. For example, Franklin Delano Roosevelt gained the presidency through legal-rational principles. By the time he was elected president for the fourth time, his leadership had a good many traditional elements to it. And many Americans viewed him as a charismatic leader.

☐ Economic Power

All societies confront three basic economic problems. *What* goods and services should they produce and in what quantities? *How* should they employ their limited resources—land, water, minerals, fuel, and labor—to produce the desired goods and services? And for *whom* should they produce the goods and services? The manner in which they answer these questions has profound consequences for the nature and the structure of the societies. For instance, if they decide to produce guns and weaponry in large quantities, their citizens' standard of living will be lower than if they emphasize the satisfaction of consumer needs. How they go about producing the desired goods and services shapes the world of work, how it is organized, the satisfactions it provides, and the status it accords. And decisions regarding the "for whom" question influence the distribution of wealth, income, and prestige. Clearly the answers to these questions derive from the structuring of power within societies.

As we pointed out in Chapter 2, people have responded somewhat differently over the course of human history to the dictates posed by economic survival. Hunting and gathering economies were the earliest form of organized social life. Horticultural, agrarian, and industrial modes of production followed. And some social analysts say that advanced nations are currently moving in the direction of postindustrial social organization. Changes in the way people produce, distribute, and consume goods and services result in strong pressures for change in other institutional arrangements as well.

In recent decades, two fundamentally different types of economic systems have competed for people's allegiance. One has been characterized by a capitalist market economy, and the other by a socialist command economy. Each has taken a quite different approach to economic power. And each has had substantially different social and political implications. Let us examine these matters more carefully.

COMPARATIVE ECONOMIC SYSTEMS

Modern economic systems differ from one another in two important aspects. First, they provide different answers to the question, How is economic activity organized—by the market or by the plan? Second, they provide different answers to the question, Who owns the means of production—individuals or the state? However, these questions do not demand an "either-or" answer. Each question allows for a range of choice, with a great many gradations in between. And no contemporary nation falls totally at one or the other pole, although the United States and the pre-1991 Soviet Union typically supplied opposite answers to both questions.

In practice, we commonly merge the two features and talk about contrasting economic systems. We think of **capitalist economies** as relying heavily on free markets and privately held property, and **socialist economies** as relying primarily on state planning and publicly held property. Yet the two characteristics are not necessarily equivalent. For instance, in Nazi Germany the government controlled and planned the economy, although ownership remained mainly in private hands. And in pre-1991 Yugoslavia the means of production were socially owned, although the economy was largely organized by markets.

Market and Command Economies. In a market economy, consumers determine which goods and services should be provided and in what quantities by registering their dollar votes. Those things that they do not want, or that are overproduced, fall in price. Items that are in short supply rise in price. Price movements act as signals to profit-making individuals and firms. They cut back on goods with falling prices and increase the production of goods with rising prices. Economists call this mechanism *consumer sovereignty.* Underlying this approach is the ideological notion that if each economic unit is allowed to make free choices in pursuit of its own best interests, the interests of all will be best served. However, many social reformers fault consumer sovereignty for promoting such ills as violence in television programming and high-sugar, low-nutrient breakfast cereals. In command economies, the state or central planning authority determines the items that will be produced and their quantities. The problem with this arrangement is highlighted by the pre-1991 Soviet Union, where there were fewer automobiles and more copies of Lenin's books than consumers desired. A command economy is often very good in moving a peasant society toward industrialization by mobilizing the masses to build miles of railroad and large dams. But a command economy finds it difficult to produce a complex array of consumer goods in the absence of market signals.

Free-market and command economies also differ in how they go about allocating their available resources to various productive activities. Ideally, societies allocate their resources to productive activities and use known productive techniques in such a way that no reallocation of resources or change of technique would yield more of any good without yielding less of another. For instance, if we try to grow oranges in South Dakota and wheat in Florida, we are unlikely to have as much success as if we reverse these land utilization patterns. In free-market economies, competition among suppliers of goods and labor services is thought to ensure the most efficient and productive use of resources. Command economies, in contrast, are based on the assumption that rational decision-making affords better results than the haphazard operation of market forces.

Finally, market and command economies differ in how they handle the "for whom" issue—how income is distributed. Market economies rely on the same price system that determines wages, interest rates, and profits for determining the distribution of income among people in the society. Historically, one of the major criticisms of the market system (especially when embedded in a type of market arrangement that some have labeled "buccaneer capitalism") has been that it does not distribute income in an equitable manner. Income payments go in substantial amounts to private owners of physical capital—capitalists. And critics allege that the economic and political power held by capitalists limits the government in working toward a more just and equal social system. They say that while economic growth is a legitimate societal goal, fairness and justice are also essential. Moreover, they contend that some problems like the ecology crisis and the absence of jobs for young inner-city African Americans are not readily amenable to laissez-faire solutions (see Chapter 6). Accordingly, they say that different standards are called for in mature industrial societies like the United States where free markets and social welfare must be balanced (Heilbroner, 1993). Indeed, in truth the American economy is not simply a freestanding system driven by human beings dispassionately detached from social values and concerns who calculate their best interests. Other impulses and goals, such as sharing income with the poor, training unskilled workers, organizing low-cost health care, excelling at technology, and competing effectively with Japan and Europe, also shape American capitalism (Uchitelle, 1991a).

Disillusionment with Command Economies. For nearly a half-century following World War II, many peoples looked for their social salvation in political formulas with a strong collectivist bent. But in recent years this faith has been evaporating. In the Soviet Union and the Eastern European "people's democracies," the citizenry witnessed "rational planning" degenerate into economic chaos and utopian dreams turn into police-state nightmares. Critics of command economies point to Germany and Korea, each of which was split into two parts following World War II and each pair of which began at roughly the same economic starting point with similar histories and cultural heritages. At the time of their reunification in 1990, East Germany's per capita gross domestic product was less than half that of West Germany (the East German economy had been considered by many to be "the jewel of the Soviet bloc"). The disparity was even greater in the Koreas, where in 1992 the per capita gross domestic product of North Korea was less than one-sixth that of South Korea (Oliver, 1994).

During the 1980s, many of the social democratic economies of Western Europe encountered mounting difficulty in paying for their welfare programs and so sought to reduce the public spheres of their economies while expanding the market sectors. For instance, by the 1990s, Sweden—which for decades had been held up as a model of how to maintain a vigorous capitalist sector while simultaneously sustaining a substantial social welfare system—had come to experience economic stagnation and mounting unemployment (Keatley, 1994). Even so, except for many former communist nations, there has not been a wholesale dismantling of social service programs in Western nations. For example, despite the efforts of Sweden's conservative prime minister, Carl Bildt, Sweden's public sector has been reduced only slightly, from about 70 percent of the gross domestic product in 1990 to about 67 percent in 1992. Many governments have simply looked less to general political solutions to their societal problems and instead have tended to focus their attention upon specific remedies for narrowly defined problems. It seems that while capitalism may have difficulty coexisting with the welfare state, it also has difficulty existing without social programs that manage the hardships produced by the unbridled operation of market processes (Skocpol, 1992; Amenta, 1993; Orloff, 1993).

Misunderstandings Surrounding the Welfare State. Few people really like welfare programs. If nothing else, "welfare" implies that some

From *The Wall Street Journal*—Permission, Cartoon Features Syndicate.

human beings are unable to care for themselves and so are unable to achieve personal self-actualization and self-sufficiency on the basis of their own resources. Even so, welfare is an enduring reality. At least four conceptions of purpose have coexisted in the design of American social welfare programs: (1) *behaviorist*—making the poor behave in a manner more acceptable to dominant groups, (2) *residualist*—providing a social "safety net" for disadvantaged populations, (3) *social insurance*—affording universal protection against life's reversals and misfortunes, and (4) *egalitarian populist*—creating social equality (Marmor, Marshaw, and Harvey, 1990). These rationales, to one degree or another, underlie the nation's various welfare programs. Simultaneously, as economist Herbert Stein (1993) observes, the United States has two "welfare states." As far as federal expenditures are concerned, the welfare state for the nonpoor is five times as large as that for the poor. The welfare state includes Medicare and Social Security benefits, farm subsidies, and college tuition grants for the nonpoor.

Mixed Economies. When we look at the contemporary world, we are hard pressed to find a pure form of a capitalist market economy. Even the United States in the early nineteenth century, which many economic historians deem to be as close to an example of pure capitalism as one can find, had government subsidies for railroads and canals. And the former Soviet Union had its black markets (an "underground market economy") while a disproportionate share of its agricultural output came from small private plots of land. Indeed, to one degree or another, most nations are characterized by mixed economies. For instance, in the contemporary United States the nation's tax laws influence investment decisions by providing tax incentives and shelters for investors in real estate and mineral exploration. Regulatory agencies impose pollution controls, standards for work conditions, rates for electrical utility companies, and licensing of prescription drugs. Additionally, some enterprises, such as the Tennessee Valley Authority (TVA), the Postal Service, Amtrak, and Conrail, operate as publicly owned agencies.

The Many Faces of Capitalism. With the triumphal ascendancy of capitalism in the 1990s, more and more analysts are noticing that capitalism is not a monolith—any more than communism was. And with their communist adversaries consigned to history, capitalist nations are beginning to skirmish over the relative merits of their approaches. They are jockeying to sell their particular mode to the emerging economies of Russia, Eastern Europe, Latin America, and Asia (Neff, 1994).

Most prominently, the dynamic Asian nations do not view U.S.-style laissez-faire as an economic model. In Japan, Singapore, Hong Kong, South Korea, and Taiwan, government has intervened massively in economic life and fostered a "government-business symbiosis" quite different from the situation in Europe and North America (Scott, 1991). These nations have forged strong business-government links, have subsidized capital investment, have fostered large conglomerates, and have

resisted imports. Indeed, Japanese economic arrangements "break so many rules of capitalism" that some economists question whether it is "really capitalism or an entirely different breed of economic cat" (Blinder, 1990). Sociologist Peter L. Berger (1986) finds that East Asian versions of capitalism emphasize group solidarity and respect for tradition rather than individual achievement—what he terms "communal capitalism." Berger concludes that a high degree of state intervention in an economy is quite compatible with successful capitalism development. In brief, laissez-faire capitalism—"let the state leave business alone"—is only one version of capitalism.

☐ Transition from a Command to a Market Economy

The transition from a command to a market economy in Eastern Europe, the former Soviet Union, and China is often portrayed as one in which an old communist edifice has crumbled, setting the stage for a social restructuring along capitalist lines. As portrayed in the Western media, the collapse of the one-party state has left these societies disordered and paralyzed without viable institutions. Such views are simplistic. They fail to grasp the plurality of transitions and transformations that are leading to a multiplicity of distinctive paths, differing in kind from one country to the next and leading in each nation to asynchronous and disharmonious processes and patterns (Stark, 1992). For instance, the Russians have been involved in at least three simultaneous transitions: (1) the transition from a planned economy to a free-market economy, (2) the transition from an authoritarian state to a democracy, and (3) the transition from a vast, old-style colonial empire to a single nation-state. All the while, China has attempted a seemingly more cautious route of grafting a free-market economy onto the established planned economy under an authoritarian regime.

The far-reaching marketization and privatization of former communist economies is proceeding slowly, and social uncertainty is extraordinarily high. In September 1993, Polish voters returned former communists to power. And in May 1994, Hungarian voters gave former communists more votes and parliament seats than they gave rival political parties. The architects of capitalist "shock therapy" had assumed that there would be victims in their game plan—pensioners, unskilled young people, and middle-aged workers made redundant by privatization—but gambled that the march to a full market economy would not stall. Instead, some 40 years of communism ingrained in the populace expectations of social care and security that the capitalist-oriented parties failed to meet (Goldfarb, 1992; Perlez, 1993). The Hungarian politician and writer Gáspár M. Tamás (1992:73) characterizes the persistence of old mind-sets and institutions in these terms:

All the surveys and polling data show that public opinion in our region rejects dictatorship, but would like to see a strong man at the helm; favors popular government, but hates parliament, parties, and the press; likes social welfare legislation and equality, but not trade unions; wants to topple the present government, but disapproves of the idea of a regular opposition; supports the notion of the market (which is a code word for Western-style living standards), but wishes to punish and expropriate the rich and condemns banking for preying on simple working people; favors a guaranteed minimum income, but sees unemployment as an immoral state and wants to punish or possibly deport the unemployed.

Western political leaders—and academic economists—have typically assumed that the superior efficiency and performance of capitalist institutions would allow for their simple transplantation to other nations. Yet experience is showing that these institutions cannot be replicated according to instructions—indeed, the failure of socialism derived from the attempt to organize economic life according to a grand design. By contrast, the origins of capitalism in Western nations did not develop by either blueprint or conscious design

(Stark, 1992). Moreover, many of the legal and monetary institutions that make privatization possible—the rule of law, the enforceability of contracts, an independent judiciary, and a stable currency—are as yet in their infancy.

The outcomes of the transitions and transformations occurring in much of the former communist world are far from certain. Some, like Zbigniew Brzezinski (1993), best known as President Jimmy Carter's national security adviser, worry that the former communist societies, without a compelling alternative, will lose themselves in unrealistic expectations of material progress. When they cannot meet these expectations, Brzezinski says, these nations may turn in envy and frustration to new doctrines of hate and aggression. In any event, the exodus from Leninism gives much evidence of leading not to the promised land but to much wandering in the wilderness. In most cases, cumbersome and ineffective bureaucracies, unable to achieve sustained, dynamic economic growth and system integration, confront weak civil societies without political organizations strongly rooted in the citizenry. Yet at the same time, many parallel structures and evolving organizational forms are combining with older institutional arrangements in new and novel adaptations, rearrangements, permutations, and reconfigurations (Burawoy and Krotov, 1992; Stark, 1992).

In reflecting on these matters, it is worth noting that many of us have a habit of viewing Russia and non-Western nations through the prism of a Western democratic ideology. For decades, we saw an alien "totalitarianism" and "communism." Now we scrutinize these same nations from the vantage point of standards and institutions rooted in a "free market" and a "democratic" society (see the discussion of ethocentrism in Chapter 2).

CORPORATE CAPITALISM

The government is an important participant in the American economy, but the primary productive role is played by private business. Although most of the more than 20 million businesses in the United States are small, large corporations have a substantial impact on the economy.

The Power of National Corporations. When you drive a car, operate a computer, replace a light bulb, purchase gasoline, or eat a breakfast cereal, you are using products manufactured by an oligopoly. An **oligopoly** is a market dominated by a few firms. When we look at such giants of American business as General Motors, IBM, and General Electric, we find oligopolies. General Motors must compete with Ford, Chrysler, Toyota, and Honda; IBM with Apple, Control Data, and Hewlett-Packard; and General Electric with Westinghouse (in the electric generator market) and with Pratt and Whitney (in the jet engine market).

Such gigantic firms exercise enormous power in American life. The decisions made by their officials have implications and ramifications that reach throughout the nation. Take the restructuring and downsizing of large American corporations that has occurred over the past decade. By one estimate, America's 500 largest companies have shed 4 million jobs since 1980 (Melloan, 1993). Clearly, today's corporation is no longer a secure or stable workplace. In a quest for efficiency, firms have been charging billions of dollars off their earnings in order to lay off hundreds of thousands of workers (Byrne, 1994b).

Corporate executives contend that large-scale staff reductions are essential if the companies are to maintain competitiveness in a fast-changing global marketplace. Yet considerable evidence suggests that companies slashing jobs often end up with more problems than profits. A 1991 survey examined more than 850 downsized corporations and found that only 41 percent met the profitability goals they had set for themselves. Restructuring seemingly gains some ground for a firm in the short run, but in the long term a company needs products and services whose sales grow. A major roadblock that stands in the way of profit growth from downsizing is sagging employee morale. Workers began to ask, "Am I going to have a job?" rather than, "This is a great place to work; how can I make it better?" In an attempt to head off a calamitous drop in morale, many companies offer their older employees early retirement. But some 90 percent of all companies offering early retirement programs find they lose people they consider necessary and good performers. Complicating matters, firms commonly make the mistake of eliminating workers but not the work, so that the surviving employees typically have to labor faster or more hours merely to keep up. Invariably the consequences are employee burnout and work left undone or the ratcheting up again of costs by rehiring (Boroughs, 1992).

The U.S. economy has long been in flux. According to a study conducted for the Census Bureau, from 1972 to 1988 roughly one in ten manufacturing jobs were created annually, while another one out of ten were destroyed. In brief, one in five manufacturing jobs shifted about in the economy each year. Even so, some industries now appear to have stabilized. For instance, although the number of Americans employed in steel production shrank by nearly three-fourths from 1951 to 1986, the industry has since maintained a level of about 170,000 workers (Dentzer, 1993). Overall, the productivity of American labor has been steadily rising. The watershed year was 1981. Total productivity growth in the nation's manufacturing sector more than doubled after 1981, to 3.3 percent a year in the 1981–1990 period from 1.4 percent a year in the 1950–1981 period. Nominal unit labor costs stopped their 17-year rise, while real unit labor costs declined 25 percent (Jensen, 1994). On the global scene the United States seems to be keeping and regaining customers in key industries, including motor vehicles, semiconductors, and computers (Faltermayer, 1994). But the costs associated with the obsolescence of human and physical capital have often been high and have generated considerable hardship in many sectors of American life (for instance, see the discussion of the plight of African-American youth in Chapter 7).

The Power of Multinational Corporations. The rise of multinational corporations and the growing internationalization of the world economy have given a new dimension to economic power (Szymanski, 1981; Fennema, 1982; Biersteker, 1987; Barnet and Cavanagh, 1994). **Multinational corporations** are firms that have their central office in one country and subsidiaries in other countries. Throughout the world, companies are shedding the banner of a national identity and proclaiming themselves to be global enterprises whose fortunes no longer depend on the economy of one nation. "The United States does not have an automatic call on our resources," says Cyrill Siewert, chief financial officer at the Colgate-Palmolive Company, a firm that now sells more toothpaste, soaps, and other toiletries outside the United States than inside. "There is no mind-set that puts this country first" (Uchitelle, 1989:1). Many executives say their global strategy supersedes preferential treatment for American employees. Robert H. Galvin, Motorola's chairperson, whose firm makes telephone pagers in both Florida and Malaysia, says: "We need our far Eastern customers, and we cannot alienate the Malaysians. We must treat our employees all over the world equally" (Uchitelle, 1989:1).

Multinational corporations are playing a growing role in the structuring of the division of labor within the world economy. The economic integration of less developed nations into the structures of a world economy can be traced to European exploration and colonization beginning in the fifteenth century. The arrangement has been characterized by the differentiation of core and periphery regions (Wallerstein, 1974a, 1980, 1989; Shannon, 1989). **Core regions** consist of geographical areas that dominate the world economy and exploit the rest of the system; **periphery regions** consist of those areas that provide raw materials to the core and are exploited by it. At first the peripheral areas exported spices, coffee, tea, and tobacco to Europe. Later, they became suppliers of agricultural and mineral raw materials, while their advantaged classes provided mar-

kets for industrial goods from Europe (Boswell, 1989; Chase-Dunn, 1989). Today the annual income from sales of the largest corporations exceed the gross national products of most countries in which they do business. In fact, about half of the largest economic units in the world are not nations but multinational corporations.

But multinational firms do not only rival nations in wealth. They also frequently operate as "private governments," pursuing their worldwide interests by well-developed "foreign policies." In some instances, multinational corporations have posed a threat to the sovereignty of the nations in which they operate. For instance, International Telephone and Telegraph (ITT) flagrantly intervened in Chile's domestic political life in the early 1970s when it assisted the opponents of Salvador Allende. When Allende, a Marxist, was elected president of Chile, ITT worked with the Central Intelligence Agency to overthrow his legally constituted government by a coup that installed a military dictatorship. Nor have developed nations been exempted. In an attempt to secure foreign military contracts, Lockheed made payments to politically influential people in a number of countries. Among those touched by the scandal were a former Japanese prime minister and a member of the Dutch royal family. Since their operations extend across a great many national boundaries, a government has difficulty holding multinational firms accountable to its laws. And the governments of host countries find it more difficult to deal with a multinational corporation than with a domestic firm because the multinational corporation can exercise the option of leaving a nation to carry out business elsewhere.

Companies become multinational for a variety of reasons. The traditional answer has been that they go abroad to develop a source of cheap raw materials. But in recent years they have also gone abroad in search of lower wages. For instance, textile, shoe, and electronic firms have opened factories in Hong Kong, Taiwan, and South Korea to produce labor-intensive products. American multinationals have a major stake in keeping

"Hey, this says 'Made in Japan.'"

Drawing by Stevenson; © 1992 The New Yorker Magazine, Inc.

much of their production overseas. They manufacture and sell nearly three times as much abroad as they make in and export from the United States. Likewise, multinational firms import to the United States parts they use in manufacturing that can be made more cheaply by foreign suppliers. Multinationals are not only the biggest exporters in the United States; they also are the nation's biggest importers, often bringing more into the United States than they ship out. The Big Three automakers were net importers of about $6 billion in 1988 (Nussbaum, 1988).

Multinational companies are increasingly taking on a *transnational* character. Although few companies are totally untethered from their home countries, the globalization of economic activity is fostering a trend toward a form of "stateless" corporation (Sklair, 1991). A one-world market exists for products ranging from consumer electronics to carbonated drinks to automobiles. In the emerging global economy, it is becoming increasingly difficult to say what is an "American," "Japanese," or "Swedish" product. For instance, in some cases, vehicles sold in the United States are built in twelve countries, with parts coming from all over the world. If saving American jobs is your goal, should you buy a Toyota Camry made in

Kentucky or a Mercury Tracer made in Mexico? A Mazda MX-6 made in the United States or a Pontiac LeMans made in Korea? In fact, it is now impossible to purchase a completely American-made vehicle.

If a large corporation like General Motors, IBM, or AT&T is to maintain a leadership position in the United States, it must also attain and hold leadership positions in all developed markets worldwide (for instance, IBM picks up more than 62 percent of its sales abroad; even the Coca-Cola Company, the quintessential American soft-drink firm, takes in better than 80 percent of its operating income from outside the United States). It has to have the ability to do research, design, engineer, and manufacture in any part of the developed world and to export from one country to another.

There is considerable controversy regarding the impact multinational corporations have on less developed or peripheral nations in the Third World. One view, associated with mainstream Marxism, asserts that international capitalism has transformed the economies of precapitalist countries, made them capitalist, and established the foundation for worker-led socialist revolutions. Sociologist Albert Szymanski (1981) contends that prior to the 1960s, Western colonialism posed obstacles to Third World industrialization. But he says that in recent decades imperialist obstacles have been removed and capital has flowed to low-wage areas. The contrasting view argues that Third World nations have been capitalist for centuries, have de-developed in the face of the onslaught from advanced capitalist nations, and continue to be exploited (Baran and Sweezy, 1966; Wallerstein, 1974a, 1980). Other sociologists claim that foreign investment in a country creates dependencies that have a long-term negative effect on the nation's rate of economic growth (Bornschier and Chase-Dunn, 1985; London and Williams, 1988). Moreover, they find that the penetration of multinational corporations weakens the power of labor and middle-class groups and strengthens the hand of traditional power holders (Rubinson, 1976).

It is difficult to arrive at overall generalizations regarding the economic impact of multinational corporations on Third World nations because the impact often differs from corporation to corporation, from one time to another, and from country to country (Newman, 1979; Evans, 1981; Leisinger, 1988). Some multinationals export high technology to the Third World to promote development, while others refuse to do so. Some nations, such as South Korea, Taiwan, Hong Kong, and Singapore, have used multinational firms as organizational vehicles to begin raising their populations out of poverty. But in many other cases, trade and investment by multinational firms have made jobs disappear. For example, the introduction of machinery has often led to a loss of agricultural jobs. Moreover, the economies of Third World nations frequently become tied to a single industry, increasing dependence on foreign investors, distorting patterns of national economic development, and rendering the nations especially vulnerable to bust and boom economic cycles (Noble, 1989; Stokes and Anderson, 1990).

The Control of Corporations. We have seen that the decisions made by corporations have vast consequences not only for the citizens of one country but also for the global community. They have a substantial impact upon employment opportunities, economic conditions (depression and inflation), consumer choices, and political authority. All this raises the question of who controls corporations—who are their decision makers? In 1932 Adolph Berle, Jr., and Gardiner C. Means published *The Modern Corporation and Private Property,* a book that has had a profound impact on scholarly thought on the matter. They said that corporate power resides with chief executives, who themselves have little financial stake in the firms they manage. The logic of their argument rested on the assertion that the stock of most large corporations is widely dispersed. Consequently, no shareholders possess a sufficient block of stock to impose corporate policy on the managers who make the day-to-day decisions for their firms. This state of affairs has been labeled "the managerial revolution" (Burnham, 1941).

Some critics see the managerial revolution as the source of many of America's current economic problems. They say that corporations pile rewards on executives who display impressive short-term results. Consequently, managers show an excessive concern for short-run profits. Fearing a dip in today's profits, American executives keep research and technology on short rations and skimp on the investment needed to ensure competitiveness in the future. They manage their businesses like investment portfolios, with the various units or divisions viewed as investment opportunities competing for scarce funds. All units are held strictly accountable by a common yardstick—the return they immediately yield from the resources they consume. Since research and technology and long-term capital expenditures do not produce short-term profits, these areas receive minimal resources.

Critics also charge that managers have turned from making goods to making money by means other than production. They contend that American industries are managed by persons increasingly oriented toward realizing profits by financial stratagems, commodity speculation, and fast-return investments. Large investors and speculators—called corporate raiders—have found that they can make a good deal of money by buying and selling companies. They view a corporation primarily as a salable bundle of assets rather than as a producer of goods and services. During the "deal decade" of the 1980s, buyers shelled out an astounding $1.5 trillion, plus billions more in defensive maneuvers, in corporate mergers and acquisitions (including highly leveraged buyouts, recapitalizations, and takeovers) (Faltermayer, 1991). One example of this trend has been corporate mergers that have given rise to **conglomerates**—companies that operate in a variety of completely different markets and produce unrelated products. For instance, in the early 1980s Beatrice Foods pursued an aggressive acquisitions strategy that steadily transformed the Chicago concern into a $10-billion-a-year conglomerate with fifty companies selling everything from cosmetics to luggage to orange juice. However, in the mid-1980s, very focused companies—those having a limited range of diversification—became the stock-market favorites. So Beatrice Foods was taken over by a new group of investors who promptly sought to recoup their investment and make a substantial profit by breaking up the company and selling off various units.

Critics also say that top executives are slow to innovate while shunning risk. And they adopt strategies that allow substantial expense accounts and high salaries for themselves. For instance, in 1990, the average chief executive officer (CEO) of 365 large American firms received $1.9 million in total compensation—eighty-five times the average U.S. worker's pay. In contrast, the average Japanese CEO makes only seventeen times the earnings of the average Japanese worker; the average CEO in Germany makes twenty-three times the pay of the average worker there (Hillkirk, 1991a). However, others contend that the objective of any pay program is for rewards to correlate with results. Assessed by the standard of profit performance, the system seems to work (James and Soref, 1981; Byrne, 1984). Although in the

past corporate boards may have sat passively while chief executives performed below par, today the boss is at substantial risk (consider, by way of example, the fate of Robert C. Stempel of General Motors, John Akers of IBM, Anthony D'Amato of Borden, Kay Whitmore of Eastman Kodak, John Sculley of Apple Computer, Paul Lego of Westinghouse Electric, and James Robinson, III, of American Express) (Linden and Rotenier, 1994).

The managerial perspective, with its emphasis on leadership discretion, has largely dominated the thinking of American sociologists and economists since the 1930s. However, over the past decade a growing chorus of social scientists has advanced the view that important constraints operate on managers in discharging their responsibilities (Mintz and Schwartz, 1985; Fligstein, 1990; Fligstein and Brantley, 1992). For one thing, suppliers of raw materials and customers for finished products place limits on the maneuverability of corporate executives. Even greater constraints are imposed by large banks (eight major New York City commercial banks are responsible for making over 50 percent of all industrial bank loans). Through their control of capital resources, major corporate lenders can decide which projects will be pursued and which will remain unfunded. Overall, their control of strategic financial resources allows banks to constrain managerial choices (Mintz and Schwartz, 1985; Loomis, 1988).

Other constraints also operate. Large institutional investors—mutual, trust, and pension funds—now control nearly half of all corporate stock in the United States and are assuming a greater voice in how companies are run. For instance, in recent years California's influential public pension fund (California Public Employees Retirement System—Calpers) has turned up the heat on major corporations (including giants like IBM, Time Warner, and Polaroid) to heed shareholders' interests by threatening to vote against the reelection of their directors (Stevenson, 1992). Moreover, at least 80 percent of all the stock traded on the nation's stock exchanges is controlled by institutional investors. Large institutions buy and sell large blocks of stock, with enormous consequences for corporate affairs. For instance, when they sell in tandem, they can squelch financing and expansion plans and undermine a firm's morale. Similarly corporate policies can be established through intercorporate ownership (Clawson and Neustadtl, 1989; Baker, 1990). And **corporate interlocks**—networks of individuals who serve on the boards of directors of multiple corporations—also place constraints on what the managers of one firm can undertake without reference to the needs and requirements of other firms. And interlocks are a way for firms to gather the strategic information their officials need to make corporate decisions (Mintz and Schwartz, 1985).

In sum, it is clear that professional managers exercise considerable authority in corporate decision-making. But even though they may own little or none of a corporation's stock, executive officers continue to be governed by the requirement that they optimize profits. The ascendance of corporate managers has not freed corporations to pursue goals and policies that consistently run counter to profit maximization. The vision of a "soulful corporation" has not been realized. Rather, an arrangement characterized by a "constrained management" has evolved. While in many cases the separation of ownership from control has given managers greater range for autonomy, it has also rendered managers subservient to the constraints of an institutionalized system of rational profit seeking (Herman, 1981; Zeitlin, 1989). The dictates of the drive for profits limit and circumscribe managerial discretion by tying managerial compensation and promotion to investors' rate of return. Hence, corporations remain fundamentally capitalist in goal and in practice.

WORK AND THE WORKPLACE

Power extends into the workplace. Among other things, it determines whether or not work will be available, how work will be organized, and the manner in which work will be remunerated. In a capitalist market economy, such as that found in the United States, the problem of organizing economic activity begins with a system of property rights involving the uses of resources and a structure of authority for mobilizing these resources. Property rights consist of the claims individuals or groups have on objects; conversely, they define the conditions under which some individuals or groups are excluded from the use or enjoyment of these objects. As we noted earlier in the chapter, under a capitalist market economy the means by which people secure their livelihoods (the factories, mines, offices, and farms) are privately owned and oriented to the production of profits.

The work experience of Americans has undergone significant change over the past 160 years and, as shown in Table 8.1, continues to undergo change. Although more than 70 percent of the labor force worked on the farm in 1820, by 1910 only 31 percent of Americans were engaged in agriculture. Today the number of individuals employed in the service industries is approaching the same 70 percent as the proportion involved in farming a century and a half ago (with 2 percent of the labor force in agriculture and about 28 percent in blue-collar jobs and manufacturing). These changes have been accompanied by a shift from a nonindustrial to an industrial society. In nonindustrial societies, the family overshadows and dominates other institutional spheres. Working (earning a living) is not readily distinguishable from other social activities. The situation is quite different in industrial societies (Dubin, 1976). First, the workplace is physically segregated from the home. Second, working time is temporally separated in the daily cycle from leisure time. Third, specialized organizational structures—complex authority hierarchies—take over the management of work activities (Stinchcombe, 1983). And finally, the economic institution increasingly becomes the focus of other institutions, with the family, government, religion, and education accommodating to its requirements.

Table 8.1 FUTURE WORKERS: THE WORK FORCE OF THE FUTURE WILL BE OLDER AND MORE DIVERSE*

	1990		2005		Percent Change in Labor Force 1990–2005
	Participation Rate	Labor Force	Participation Rate	Labor Force	
Total aged 16 and older	66.4	124,787	69.0	150,732	20.8%
Men, total	76.1	68,234	75.4	79,338	16.3
Aged 16 to 24	71.5	11,157	73.1	12,564	12.6
Aged 25 to 54	93.5	48,258	92.4	54,780	13.5
Aged 55 and older	39.3	8,818	41.8	11,994	36.0
Women, total	57.5	56,554	63.0	71,394	26.2
Aged 16 to 24	63.1	10,096	66.0	11,484	13.8
Aged 25 to 54	74.1	39,882	82.3	49,782	24.8
Aged 55 and older	23.0	6,577	28.7	10,128	54.0
White	66.8	107,177	69.7	125,785	17.4
Black	63.3	13,493	65.6	17,766	31.7
Asian and other races	64.9	4,117	66.4	7,181	74.4
Hispanic[†]	67.0	9,576	69.9	16,790	75.3

*Labor force participation rates by sex, age, and race; civilian labor force in thousands; and projected percentage change, 1990–2005.
†Hispanics may be of any race.

SOURCE: *Monthly Labor Review,* November 1991, Bureau of Labor Statistics. Adapted from *American Demographics,* May 1992, p. 59. Reprinted with permission.

Significantly, economist Juliet B. Schor (1993) finds that over the past 20 years the time Americans spend on the job has been rising. In the years immediately following World War II, the United States had the shortest work time of all the advanced industrial nations. Today, only Japanese workers put in more time (see Figure 8.1). In 1969 the average working American put in 1,786 hours on the job; by 1989 the figure had risen to 1,924 hours—adding nearly a thirteenth month of work to the year. Schor (1992) contends that Americans are working longer to achieve a 1970 standard of living. Rather than trading productivity gains for leisure time, Americans have been putting in more time at work.

The Significance of Work. People work for a good many reasons. "Self-interest" in its broadest sense, including the interests of family and friends, is a basic motivation for working in all societies. But self-interest need not involve just providing for subsistence or accumulating wealth. For instance, among the Maori, a Polynesian people of the South Pacific, a desire for approval, a sense of duty, a wish to conform to custom and tradition, a feeling of emulation, and a pleasure in craftsmanship are additional reasons for working (Hsu, 1943). Even within the United States, we cannot understand work as simply a response to economic necessity. Surveys reveal that 74 percent of American men and 72 percent of American women say they would continue to work even if they were to get enough money to live as comfortably as they would like to for the rest of their lives (survey by the Gallup Organization, July 25–28, 1991). When asked to choose whether they enjoy work or their free time more, over 60 percent of employed Americans say they enjoy both equally or that they cannot choose between the two (Robinson, 1989).

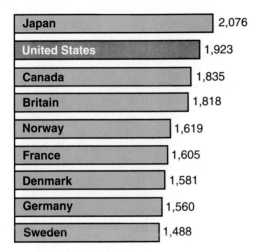

Japan	2,076
United States	1,923
Canada	1,835
Britain	1,818
Norway	1,619
France	1,605
Denmark	1,581
Germany	1,560
Sweden	1,488

Figure 8.1 COMPARATIVE WORKLOADS IN ADVANCED INDUSTRIAL COUNTRIES Hours worked by manufacturing workers in selected industrial nations in 1991. The data exclude vacations and holidays. A person who works 40 hours a week without any vacations or holidays would put in 2,080 hours a year on the job. (SOURCE: Adapted from *The New York Times,* August 29, 1993, p. F9. Data from U.S. Bureau of Labor Statistics.)

Work has a good many social meanings (Levinson, 1964). When individuals work, they gain a contributing place in society. The fact that they receive pay for their work indicates that what they do is needed by other people and that they are a necessary part of the social fabric. Work is also a major social mechanism for placing people in the larger social structure and affording them identities. Much of who individuals are, to themselves and others, is interwoven with how they earn their livelihood. In the United States it is a blunt and ruthlessly public fact that to do nothing is to be nothing and to do little is to be little. Work is commonly seen as the measure of an individual's worth.

Work affects an individual's personal and family life in many ways (Small and Riley, 1990). Jobs that permit occupational self-direction—initiative, thought, and independent judgment in work—foster people's intellectual flexibility. So

individuals with such jobs become more open in approaching and weighing evidence on current social and economic issues. The effects of occupational self-direction also generalize to other nonwork settings. Individuals who enjoy opportunities for self-direction in their work are more likely to become more self-confident, less authoritarian, less conformist in their ideas, and less fatalistic in their nonwork lives than other individuals. In turn, these traits lead, in time, to more responsible jobs that allow even greater latitude for occupational self-direction. Moreover, a variety of workplace conditions—the restriction of opportunity to exercise self-direction, work overload, poor quality of interpersonal relations on the job, few opportunities for cooperative problem-solving, job insecurities, job loss, and low earnings—have emotional repercussions that are associated with negative family interaction (Menaghan, 1991). So the job affects the person and the person affects the job in a reciprocal relationship across the life course (Kohn and Schooler, 1982, 1983; Miller, Slomczynski, and Kohn, 1985; Kohn et al., 1990). In sum, our work is an important socializing experience that influences who and what we are.

Satisfaction and Alienation in Work. Sociologists find that individuals in occupations that combine high economic, occupational, and educational prestige typically show the greatest satisfaction with their work and the strongest job attachment (Kohn and Schooler, 1973, 1982; Hartman and Pearlstein, 1987). However, the prestige factor partly subsumes a number of other elements, including the amount of control and responsibility that goes with an occupation. The opportunity to exercise discretion, accept challenges, and make decisions has an important bearing on how people feel about their work (Stroud, 1990; Keita and Sauter, 1992; Lawler, 1992). The most potent factors in job satisfaction are those that relate to workers' self-respect, their chance to perform well, their opportunities for achievement and growth, and the chance to contribute something personal and quite unique.

opinion polls show that on the whole the vast majority of Americans (at least 85 percent) are satisfied with the work they are doing (surveys by the National Opinion Research Center, February–April of 1985–1990). Even so, only about 40 percent would keep their present jobs if they had the opportunity to choose some other job.

When individuals fail to find their work fulfilling and satisfying, they may experience **alienation**—a pervasive sense of powerlessness, meaninglessness, normlessness, isolation, and self-estrangement (Seeman, 1959). One expression of alienation is *job burnout*—individuals no longer find their work fulfilling and satisfying; this leads to a sense of boredom, apathy, reduced efficiency, fatigue, frustration, and despondency. In burnout, individuals complain that they feel drained and used up and that they have nothing more to give to their work. They become cynical, callous, and insensitive toward the people they encounter in the work setting. Frequently, victims of burnout are highly efficient, competent, energetic individuals with high ideals and expectations. Indeed, "in order to burn out, a person needs to have been on fire at one time" (Pines and Aronson, 1988:11). Nurses, teachers, and police officers seem to be particularly prone to burnout.

Two somewhat different perspectives on alienation are provided by Karl Marx and Emile Durkheim (Lukes, 1977). Marx saw alienation as rooted in capitalist social arrangements. For Marx, work is our most important activity as human beings. Through work we create our world and ourselves. The products of our labor reflect our nature and form the basis for our self-evaluations. Further, through work we experience ourselves as active beings who shape the world about us. But according to Marx (1844/1960:500), individuals in capitalist societies lose control of their labor and become commodities, objects used by others:

Labor . . . is external to the worker, i.e., it does not belong to his essential being; . . . in his work, therefore, he does not affirm himself but denies himself. . . . His labor is . . . merely a means to satisfy needs external to it. . . . It belongs to another; it is the loss of self.

Thus Marx portrayed workers under capitalism as alienated from productive activity, the products of their labor, their coworkers, and their own human potential. Rather than being a process that is inherently satisfying, work becomes an unfulfilling activity that simply produces a subsistence wage. Workers sell their labor to capitalists who use the workers in any manner they see fit. As a result, human beings are reduced to little more than beasts of burden or inanimate machines. Under capitalism, then, work violates people and deadens the human spirit.

Marx saw alienation as the outcome of social forces that inhere in capitalist arrangements and separate human beings from meaningful, creative, and self-realizing work. In contrast, Durkheim depicted alienation as arising from the breakdown of the cohesive ties that bind individuals to society.[1] For Durkheim, the central question was whether or not people are immersed in a structure of group experiences and memberships that provide a meaningful and valued context for their behavior. A group either coheres and makes life comprehensible and viable for individuals or it fails to do so, engendering pathology (akin to what we called *anomie* in Chapter 5). Whereas Marx emphasized freedom from social constraint as the source of human happiness, Durkheim stressed that human happiness depends on a society that provides people with rules. Rules, said Durkheim, integrate individuals into cohesive social groups and give direction and meaning to their activity.

Both Marx and Durkheim identify forces that can result in alienation. Since much of life is spent at work, people's work experiences profoundly affect how they come to think about themselves and the satisfactions they realize. Yet, by the same token, group bonds are also associated with human happiness. However, individuals show considerable differences in their reactions to their work and group experiences. What one person finds a challenge, another may view as an unendurable pressure. Even assessments of monotony vary widely. In fact, almost any job will seem boring to some people (Stagner, 1975). And we need hardly be reminded that people differ enormously in what they view as adequate or inadequate contact with other people and in their requirements for formal rules and direction (Lowenthal, 1964).

☐ Political Power

Controlling the means of economic production is one resource for exercising power. But it is not the only one. Modern societies contain a rather wide array of fairly distinct dimensions of power, including those found in religion, science, the arts, medicine, education, and the media. Sociologist Suzanne Keller (1963) suggests that each of these spheres can have its own set of powerful individuals and groups—what she terms **strategic elites.** These elites—people with significant power—operate primarily in their own rather specialized domains.

But, as we pointed out earlier in the chapter, the state assumes a particularly critical role in contemporary life. It seems that some form of centralized government is indispensable to modern society. Possession of the means of administration is, as Max Weber contended, an alternative to possession of the means of production as a basis of social power (see Chapter 6). Of course, power in one sphere can also be employed to achieve power in other spheres. Within the United States, economic power is often converted into political power (the Kennedy family provides a classic illustration of the process). By the same token, political power can be used to advance one's economic status (the "poor boy–successful politician" syndrome reflected in the career of Lyndon B. Johnson is a good example). Let us explore the matter of political power at greater length.

TYPES OF GOVERNMENT

Government entails those political processes that have to do with the authoritative formulating of rules and policies that are binding and pervasive throughout a society. In contemporary nations, the decisions made by government profoundly affect the everyday lives of their citizens, and very often the citizens of other nations as well. Policies relating to the state of the economy, the direction of economic development, military expenditures, issues of war and peace, drug trafficking, education, health care, social welfare, and environmental issues leave no individual untouched by their consequences and ramifications. In dealing with these matters, three quite different types of government have competed in recent generations for people's allegiance: totalitarianism, authoritarianism, and democracy. Each can be considered an ideal type, for in practice many nations have regimes with mixtures of totalitarian, authoritarian, and democratic elements.

Totalitarianism. It is exceedingly difficult for most of us to maintain value neutrality in considering totalitarianism since this type of government runs counter to many of our fundamental values. **Totalitarianism** is a "total state," one in which the government undertakes to control all parts of the society and all aspects of social life. Those individuals and groups (elites) who dominate the state apparatus seek to control all subordinate governmental units, all institutions (including the economy, education, religion, medicine, the arts, science, and communication), all associations (labor unions, churches, occupational and professional organizations, special-interest associations, and youth groups), and even individual families and cliques. All organizations become an extension of the state and act as its agent. The hallmark of totalitarianism is its power structure, not its economic order. The two major prototypes of totalitarianism—Nazi Germany under Hitler and communist Russia under Stalin—remind us that this form of government can incorporate either a capitalistic or a socialistic economy.

A totalitarian society typically has three characteristics: a monolithic political party, a compelling ideology, and pervasive social control. One political party is permitted, and it brooks no opposition. Only a small proportion of the population are party members, although party membership is a requisite for all important social positions. A totalitarian ideology proclaims the official values of the entire society, is utopian in nature, pertains to all areas and aspects of life, and establishes universal goals. It stipulates grandiose schemes for social reconstruction and societal betterment that provide the moral basis for the extension of state power. To enforce its power and propagate its ideologies, a totalitarian regime employs every available means of social control. It uses the educational and communications networks, while simultaneously exercising terror by a secret police.

Authoritarianism. **Authoritarianism** is a political system in which the government tolerates little or no opposition to its rule but permits nongovernmental centers of influence and allows debate on some issues of public policy. Many African and Latin American countries ruled by military regimes are authoritarian. Similarly, following Stalin's death in 1953 and until its disintegration in 1991, the Soviet Union progressively took on the properties of an authoritarian, as opposed to a totalitarian, state. Repression became more selective, and the range of permissible discussion and debate broadened. During the years between 1985 and 1991, when he headed the Soviet state, Mikhail Gorbachev followed a degree of structural change that had been unprecedented in Soviet history. His decisions and proposals were intended to galvanize his nation's lethargic economy, ease the grip of the state, and improve the country's international image. Censorship in theaters and the press was relaxed. In August 1991, old-guard communist *apparatchiks* staged a 3-day putsch intended to forestall further change

and to restore authoritarian obedience. The failure of the coup speeded the discrediting of the Communist party and the disintegration of the Soviet central government. History offers few precedents for so abrupt a collapse of an empire. The Ottoman Empire slowly degenerated, the Third Reich fell in war, and Great Britain gradually withdrew from its global empire. But the Soviet empire simply crumbled as its ideology ceased to hold and the costs of a ponderous state bureaucracy and massive instruments of security overwhelmed its economy (Schmemann, 1993). When totalitarian and authoritarian systems fail, democratic ones do not automatically rise up in their place. The outcome in the former Soviet Union remains in doubt.

Democracy. **Democracy** is a political system in which the powers of government derive from the consent of the governed and in which regular constitutional avenues exist for changing government officials. It is an arrangement that (1) permits the population a significant voice in decision-making through the people's right to choose among contenders for political office, (2) allows for a broad, relatively equal citizenship among the populace, and (3) affords the citizenry protection from arbitrary state action. Quite clearly, democratic governments are not distinguished from totalitarian or authoritarian regimes by the absence of powerful officials. And for the most part democracy is not characterized by the rule of the people themselves. Only in relatively rare instances, such as the New England town meeting of colonial times, do we encounter *direct democracy*—face-to-face participation and decision-making by the citizens. Rather, most democratic nations are characterized by *representative democracy*—officials are held accountable to the public through periodic elections that confirm them in power or else replace them with new officials.

A number of sociologists have undertaken a search for those factors that promote a social climate favorable to a stable democracy (Kornhauser, 1959; Lindblom, 1990; Patterson, 1991; Lipset, 1994). One factor they identify is the existence of conflict and cleavage associated with a competitive struggle over positions of power, challenges to incumbents, and shifts in the parties holding office. Many well-organized but countervailing interest groups serve as a check against one another. Each group is limited in influence because, in the process of governing, officials must also take into account the interests of other groups as well. Simultaneously, interest groups provide independent power bases from which citizens can interact with government. Consequently, the citizenry enjoys the protection of many groups and institutions against the encroachment of any one of them. No group or institution can attain a monopoly of power. A strong **civil society**—a social realm of mediating groups, networks, and institutions that sustains the public life outside the worlds of the state and the economy—is conducive to democratic life (Cohen and Arato, 1992). This state of affairs is in sharp contrast to totalitarian societies, where isolated and vulnerable individuals confront an omnipotent state. However, competition and conflict can get out of hand in democratic societies: Sharp social polarization that derives from substantial income inequality may bring democratic institutions into question and undermine popular commitment to them (Muller, 1988; Bollen and Jackman, 1989).

Relatively stable economic and social conditions also seem to favor a democratic order (Neuhouser, 1992). Significant institutional failure confronts people with stressful circumstances that can make them vulnerable to extremist social movements (see Chapter 12). For example, Germany underwent ruinous inflation and economic dislocation in the 1920s that made the middle classes susceptible to Nazism. In this economic and social environment, the middle classes felt their status eroding and their financial fortunes collapsing before the onslaught of large-scale capitalist enterprise and a powerful labor movement.

Finding themselves precariously situated in a world that seemed increasingly incomprehensible and that was swallowing them up in a torrent of social change, they turned to Nazism as the road to salvation. The result was the death knell of Germany's fragile democratic institutions. In somewhat like fashion, the chaos and social breakdown accompanying their defeat in war made the Russian people susceptible to the revolutionary slogans of communism in 1917.

Finally, a stable democracy benefits from an underlying consensus among the populace that a democratic government is desirable and valid. The various groups accord legitimacy to the political institution. They believe they can realize their goals within the existing organizational framework because they enjoy "fair play" access to the seats of power. As we will see, voting is a key mechanism for achieving consensus. For instance, although Americans wage their election campaigns with great fury and fervor, once the election returns are in, the candidates and parties accede to the results. The losers recognize the legitimacy of the process and do not resort to extralegal and violent remedies. Rather, they criticize the incumbent officials and prepare to "throw the rascals out" at the *next* election.

These formulations, however, are not accepted by all sociologists. As we will note later in the chapter, many conflict theorists reject the pluralistic model of American society these formulations imply. Instead, they contend that the United States is governed by a "power elite." For instance, although acknowledging that political parties, labor unions, and other voluntary and occupational associations have an impact on the "middle levels" of power, sociologist C. Wright Mills (1956) contends that a "power elite" uses these organizations as administrative vehicles for carrying out predetermined policies and as mechanisms for controlling the rest of society. But before turning to these matters, let us look more generally at political power in the United States.

POLITICAL POWER IN THE UNITED STATES

Both totalitarian and democratic governments are marked by competition for political positions. But what distinguishes democracies and the American system is that the contest for positions of power is legitimized—norms define political competition and opposition as expected and appropriate. Free and competitive elections, the right to form opposition parties, freedom to criticize those in power, freedom to seek public office, and popular participation are among the commonly accepted hallmarks of democratic procedures. Central to the process are political parties, popular electoral participation, interest-group lobbying, and the mass media.

Political Parties. A **political party** is an organization designed to gain control of the government by putting its people in public office. It is not the same thing as an interest group, an organization that undertakes to affect policy without assuming the responsibilities of running the government. Members of an interest group seek control over government decisions as a means to an end. But a political party pursues the control of government as an end. Thus mass-based political parties tend to abandon or modify policy views that interfere with their gaining or maintaining political office. Political parties are major mediating institutions between the citizenry and the state (Lipset, 1993).

Within American life, the major political parties function as brokers or intermediaries between the people and the government. The relatively pragmatic nature of the parties reflects this fact, as do the structural peculiarities of a two-party system. In order to win control of the government, each party must shape itself to afford the widest possible appeal to the electorate. This requirement tends to pull each party to a centrist position, leaving the more extreme elements at the fringes. In close elections, both the Republican and Democratic parties strive for the support of the same uncommitted, often middle-of-the-road, voters. In many respects, then, they end up resembling one another. Occasionally one of their more extreme factions gains control of the presidential nominating machinery. But then they commonly suffer electoral disaster, the fate of the Goldwater Republican right in 1964 and the McGovern Democratic left in 1972. Critics of the American system say that centrist forces and pressures result in the voters not getting a real choice. But proponents point out that what is really happening is that the parties are performing one of their chief functions: compromising different and conflicting points of view prior to the election (Olson and Meyer, 1975).

Electoral Participation and Voting Patterns. The American political system is rooted in the participation of its citizenry in the governmental process through periodic elections. The principle that each person has one vote is seen as a basic mechanism for offsetting the inequalities that otherwise abound in the society by virtue of class, gender, and racial inequalities. Yet many Americans do not vote. Over the past 55 years, between 50 and 64 percent of the electorate has voted in presidential elections (in contrast, in 1876, when memories of the Civil War were still fresh, 82 percent of eligible voters—mostly limited to white males—cast ballots). Nonvoters are likely to be younger, less educated, and poorer than those who do vote. Even so, more and more Americans no longer feel they can affect the political process on the national level. A 1990 study found that "cynicism toward the political system in general is growing as the public in unprecedented numbers associates Republicans with wealth and greed and Democrats with recklessness and incompetence" (Oreskes, 1990b). For their part, politicians are showing less and less interest in involving voters directly in the political process (for instance, in recent elections to the U.S. House of Representatives, the average incumbent has won election by nearly 75 percent of the vote). And indeed, politicians spend considerable time building up a vast array of incumbent protections designed to squeeze out their political competition (Ginsberg and Shefter, 1990).

The turnout rate in presidential elections is typically 25 to 30 percent lower in the United States than in most Western European nations. Political scientists estimate that at least 9 percentage points of the difference is attributable to American personal registration statuses (Glass, Squire, and Wolfinger, 1984). In Western Europe, Canada, Australia, and New Zealand, it is the responsibility of the state to compile and maintain electoral registers. The United States is the only nation where the entire burden of registration falls on the individual rather than the government. Additionally, many nonvoters view their success or lack of success in life as a matter of "luck" and hence not as something that can be influenced by political participation (Hadley, 1978). Generally speaking, higher-status people see a relationship between politics and their own lives. But many lower-status people do not see the political system as offering them anything, or anything they can relate to effectively.

As reflected in Table 8.2, there are also important differences in how various segments of the population vote. As a general rule, voters who are better off do tend to support Republican candidates and those who are less well off tend to support Democratic candidates. Even so, Democrats still receive a significant proportion of their votes from higher-status people, and the Republican Ronald Reagan did well among blue-collar workers. Prior to the 1930s African-American voters tended to support the party of Abraham Lincoln and African-American emancipation, but since Franklin D. Roosevelt and the New Deal they have overwhelmingly voted Democratic. Although the voting patterns of men and women have not traditionally differed, in recent years women have been more likely to support the Democratic party than have men. Overall, there is a persistence of voter identifications with particular parties. Nonetheless, changes do occur, although not as precipitously as is commonly imagined (Smith, 1989; Alwin and Krosnick, 1991).

Interest-Group Lobbying. People who share common concerns or points of view are called **interests,** and the groups that organize them are called **interest groups.** One distinction that is often made is between special-interest groups and public-interest groups. **Special-interest groups** are interest groups that primarily seek benefits from which their members would derive more gains than the society as a whole. Examples include chambers of commerce, trade associations, labor unions, and farm organizations. **Public-interest groups** are interest groups that pursue policies that presumably would be of no greater benefit to their members than to the larger society. Consumer protection organizations are good illustrations of public-interest groups.

Among special-interest groups that have attracted considerable controversy are **political action committees** (PACs), interest groups that are set up to elect or defeat candidates, but not through the organization of a political party. PACs were specifically authorized by the 1971 Federal Election Campaign Act, but they had existed before then as well. Money is important in an era of multimillion-dollar campaigns, especially for purchasing media advertising. Political action committees typically base their contributions less on ideological or geographical factors than on whether the recipient sits on a congressional committee that can help them (Berke, 1990d). And many political action committees hedge their bets by contributing to both candidates in a campaign, ensuring that they later will have access to the winner. Even so, incumbents get the greater share of the monies (in recent elections, political action committees have donated twelve times as much to incumbents as to challengers in congressional elections) (Berke, 1990c). Moreover, more than half the senators seeking reelection to the U.S. Senate typically finance their campaigns primarily from contributions acquired from outside their home states as opposed to contributions made chiefly by their constituents (Berke, 1990b). It seems that the members of Congress do not sell their votes

Table 8.2 VOTING BY GROUPS IN RECENT PRESIDENTIAL ELECTIONS*

Percent of 1992 total		1976		1980			1984		1988		1992		
		Carter	Ford	Reagan	Carter	Anderson	Reagan	Mondale	Bush	Dukakis	Clinton	Bush	Perot
	Total vote	50	48	51	41	7	59	40	53	45	43	38	19
46	Men	50	48	55	36	7	62	37	57	41	41	38	21
54	Women	50	48	47	45	7	56	44	50	49	46	37	17
87	Whites	47	52	56	36	7	64	35	59	40	39	41	20
8	Blacks	83	16	11	85	3	9	90	12	86	82	11	7
3	Hispanics	76	24	33	59	6	37	62	30	69	62	25	14
1	Asians	—	—	—	—	—	—	—	—	—	29	55	16
22	18–29 years old	51	47	43	44	11	59	40	52	47	44	34	22
38	30–44 years old	49	49	55	36	8	57	42	54	45	42	38	20
24	45–59 years old	47	52	55	39	5	60	40	57	42	41	40	19
16	60 and older	47	52	54	41	4	60	40	50	49	50	38	12
6	Not a high school graduate	—	—	46	51	2	50	50	43	56	55	28	17
25	High school graduate	—	—	51	43	4	60	39	50	49	43	36	20
29	Some college education	—	—	55	35	8	61	38	57	42	42	37	21
40	College graduate or more	—	—	52	35	11	58	41	56	43	44	39	18
24	College graduate	—	—	—	—	—	—	—	62	37	40	41	19
16	Postgraduate education	—	—	—	—	—	—	—	50	48	49	36	15
49	White Protestant	41	58	63	31	6	72	27	66	33	33	46	21
27	Catholic	54	44	50	42	7	54	45	52	47	44	36	20
4	Jewish	64	34	39	45	15	31	67	35	64	78	12	10
17	White born-again Christian	—	—	63	33	3	78	22	81	18	23	61	15
14	Family income under $15,000	58	40	42	51	6	45	55	37	62	59	23	18
24	$15,000–$29,999	55	43	44	47	7	57	42	49	50	45	35	20
30	$30,000–$49,999	48	50	53	39	7	59	40	56	44	41	38	21
20	$50,000–$74,999	36	63	59	32	8	66	33	56	42	40	42	18
13	$75,000 and over	—	—	63	26	10	69	30	62	37	36	48	16

*1992 data were collected by Voter Research and Surveys based on questionnaires completed by 15,490 voters leaving 300 polling places around the nation on election day. 1976 data were based on a survey conducted by CBS News with questionnaires from 15,300 voters. Data for other years were based on surveys of voters conducted by *The New York Times* and CBS News: 15,201 in 1980; 9,174 in 1984; and 11,645 in 1988. Those who gave no answer are not shown. Dashes indicate that a question was not asked or a category was not provided in a particular year. Family income categories in 1976: under $8,000, $8,000–$12,000, $12,001–$20,000, and over $20,000. In 1980: under $10,000, $8,000–$14,999, $15,000–$24,999, $25,000–$50,000, and over $50,000. In 1984: under $12,500, $12,500–$24,999, $25,000–$34,999, $35,000–$50,000, and over. "Born-again Christian" was labeled "born-again Christian/fundamentalist" in 1992 and "fundamentalist and evangelical Christian" in 1988. Male and female college graduates include those with postgraduate education. In 1976 and 1980, "occupation" referred to the head of the household. Family financial situation is compared to 1 year ago in 1984 and 1992; 4 years ago in 1976 and 1980; 1976 and 1984 numbers from NBC News.

SOURCE: *The New York Times*, November 5, 1992, p. B9. Copyright © 1992 by The New York Times Company. Reprinted by permission.

for PAC contributions. Rather, contributions are the way interest groups gain access to legislators to plead their cases and obtain special favors for given pieces of legislation (Clawson, Neustadtl, and Scott, 1992).

The Mass Media. The **mass media** consist of those organizations—newspapers, magazines, television, radio, and motion pictures—that undertake to convey information to a large segment of the public. Whereas earlier generations of Americans depended primarily on newspapers for their political information, recent generations have depended chiefly on television. Studies show that two-thirds of Americans get most of their news from television, and over half get *all* their news in this manner (Shea, 1984). The public secures information about candidates from television through news broadcasts and paid advertising. Often the media's main role is that of "agenda setting": Media coverage places an issue or problem foremost on the public's agenda, where it can become a central factor influencing the public's perception of an incumbent's or challenger's performance (Iyengar, 1991). Although there is little credible evidence that the television networks knowingly favor particular presidential candidates, they do influence public attitudes by their selection of news events. They slant their programs toward the exciting, the provocative, the timely, and the unusual, which encourages candidates to make "news" and provide good "visuals."

For example, Jimmy Carter and his advisers correctly judged that the winner of the Iowa caucuses, the first real events of the 1976 campaign season, would emerge as the "front runner." Accordingly, beginning in 1974, and for 2 years thereafter, the Carter campaign concentrated its efforts on Iowa. Even though Carter did not really win Iowa (he finished second to "uncommitted"), the media portrayed him as the state's winner and he quickly became the center of media attention. One month earlier only 3 percent of the American public had known who Jimmy Carter was (a former governor of Georgia). The rest is history.

More and more campaigns are being turned over to high-powered professionals who advise candidates on every detail, ranging from which issues they should tackle to the images they should project in their media appearances. Increasingly physical appearance and "good looks" are surfacing as paramount matters in an era when packaging candidates for the media is so critical. Moreover, TV advertising, for which candidates spend nearly half their campaign funds, gives greater emphasis to style and personality over substance. Professionals cite evidence showing that a colorful event in which a candidate utters a few catchy one-liners wins more votes than an earnest discussion of the issues. Computer technology is also being employed to target specific voter groups and then bombard them with TV advertising and direct-mail appeals specifically tailored to their interests. And campaign managers are employing public opinion polls not only to find out how voters perceive their candidates but to determine what voters want to hear their candidates say (Altschiller, 1988; Oreskes, 1990a). These matters raise the question, How does the political system actually operate, and who makes it run? Different answers have been proposed.

MODELS OF POWER IN THE UNITED STATES

One of the longest running debates in the social sciences has to do with the nature of power in the United States. Is power concentrated in the hands of the few or distributed widely among various groups within American life? What is the basis of power? Is the exercise of power in the United States unrestricted or is it limited by the competing interests of numerous groups? Social scientists have supplied quite different answers to these questions, represented by three theoretical perspectives: the Marxist (or ruling class), the elitist, and the pluralist.

The Marxist Perspective. Marxist theory has had a profound impact on sociological thinking about power and social organization. Not only has it influenced the work of conflict sociologists, but it has provided a backdrop—even a target—in terms of which non-Marxist sociologists have formulated their rival interpretations (see Chapter 1). Sociologists following in the Marxist tradition, such as J. Allen Whitt (1979, 1982), hold that political processes must be understood in terms of the institutional structure of society as it is shaped by underlying class interests and conflict.

Whitt contends that the ways in which the major social institutions (especially the economic institution) are organized have critical implications for how power is exercised. Rather than focusing primarily upon the individuals who control the seats of power (as do power elite theorists), Whitt looks to the *biases* inherent in social institutions as shaping political outcomes. He portrays society as structured in ways that place constraints on decision makers and render their formulation of policy largely a foregone conclusion. Given the capitalist logic of institutions in Western nations, the ruling class usually need not take direct action to fashion outcomes favorable to its interests. The political outcomes are built within the capitalist ordering of affairs by the way agendas are set and alternatives are defined.

The Elitist Perspective. The elitist perspective found early expression in the ideas of several late-nineteenth- and early-twentieth-century European sociologists such as Vilfredo Pareto, Gaetano Mosca, and Robert Michels. They undertook to show that the concentration of power in a small group of elites is inevitable within modern societies (Olsen, 1970). These theorists rejected Marx's idealistic vision of social change that would bring about a classless and stateless society. Instead, they depicted all societies past the bare subsistence level—be they totalitarian, monarchical, or democratic—as dominated by the few over the many. The masses, they held, cannot and do not govern themselves. Even so, change occurs across time through the gradual circulation of elites—one group of elites comes to replace another.

Within the United States, elitist theory has taken a somewhat different course, particularly as it is formulated in the work of sociologist C. Wright Mills (1956). Mills contends that the major decisions affecting Americans and others—especially those having to do with issues of war and peace—are made by a very small number of individuals and groups whom he terms the "power elite." The real rulers of the United States, says Mills, come from three groups: corporation executives, the military, and high-ranking politicians. They are the ones who made such fateful decisions as those surrounding the Bay of Pigs invasion of Cuba, the bombing of North Vietnam, the supplying of military assistance to pro-American elements in Central America, and the procurement of major weapon systems.

The elitist model depicts elites as unified in purpose and outlook because of their similar social backgrounds, their dominant and overlapping positions in key social institutions, and the convergence of their economic interests (Domhoff, 1983, 1990; Zeitlin, 1989; Akard, 1992; Greider, 1992). For instance, sociologist Michael Useem (1983) contends that an "inner circle" of interconnected corporate officers and directors assumes the stewardship of American political and social affairs. He finds that inner-group members are more likely to belong to exclusive social clubs, have upper-class parents, participate in major business associations, serve on government advisory boards, belong to the upper levels of nonprofit and charitable organizations, gain media coverage for themselves, maintain informal contacts with government leaders, and prefer one another's company. According to elitist theorists, elites invariably get their way whenever important public decisions are at stake. They manage conflicts in the larger society in such a way as to produce outcomes favorable to themselves. Their power is pervasive; it leaves few areas of social life untouched and results in a relatively stable distribution of power.

"But how do you know for sure you've got power unless you abuse it?"

Drawing by Mankoff; © 1992 The New Yorker Magazine, Inc.

The Pluralist Perspective. The pluralist perspective sharply contrasts with both the power elite and Marxist models. Pluralist theorists start with interest groups as the basic feature of organized political life. They say that no one group really runs the government, although many groups have the power to veto policies that run counter to their interests (Riesman, 1953; Dahl, 1961). Important decisions are made by different groups depending on the institutional arena—business organizations, labor unions, farm blocs, racial and ethnic associations, and religious groups. When their interests diverge, the various interest groups compete for allies among the more-or-less unorganized public. But the same group or coalition of groups does not set broad policies. Instead, group power varies with the issue. A mounting body of sociological research reveals that politics in the United States typically proceeds within many relatively self-contained policy domains, each operating more or less independently with its own issues, actors, and processes (Burstein, 1991a).

Most groups remain inactive on most issues and mobilize their resources only when their interests are immediately at stake. Viewed in this fashion, the resulting distribution of power tends to be unstable because interests and alliances are typically short-lived and new groups and coalitions are always being organized as old ones disintegrate. Moreover, government achieves substantial autonomy by operating as a broker or balancing agent among competing interest groups.

Some pluralists say that so many interest groups have sprung up in the United States in recent years, each demanding special attention to its own concerns, that government has become paralyzed. All too often it is unable to respond effectively and efficiently in dealing with major problems (Shea, 1984). Stalemate results when powerful and nearly equal opposing interests confront one another on an issue. Policymakers also become preoccupied with certain highly focused and emotional issues and ignore the less dramatic but vital ones. Whether it is abortion, gun control, pollution, nuclear power, or tax deductions for business lunches, increasing numbers of groups are single-mindedly pursuing their narrow interests. Such outcomes tend to go with single-issue politics.

Conclusions.   What conclusions can we draw from the contending models of power? At the outset, it should be stressed that elitist theorists such as Mills and even Marxian-oriented theorists do not argue that a power elite or governing class dominates American society. Given the many interest groups in the United States, no one group can achieve complete dominance. Even so, when important decisions are made—especially on the critical issues of war and peace and on matters fundamentally affecting the economy—some corporate and political power centers clearly have greater input than other groups.

Yet given the divisions within the highest echelons of American government on levels of welfare and defense spending and tax policies, it is exceedingly difficult to make a convincing case for a unified power elite. At the same time, it is hard to deny that major corporate, military, and political interests have a common stake in preserving existing institutional arrangements. And it is also true, as structural Marxists remind us, that the political and economic institutions seem to gain an existence separate from the specific individuals who have ownership or positions of authority within them. Thus the question is not only, Who runs America? but also, What runs America? In sum, each model contains a kernel of truth, and a synthesis of the formulations seems at present to afford the most satisfactory approach (Campbell, 1987; McNamee, 1987; Burris, 1988).

Summary

1. Power pervades all aspects of social life. It furnishes the resources that provide direction essential for coordinating and integrating individual activity so that collective goals can be achieved. And it determines which individuals and groups will be able to translate their preferences into the reality of day-to-day social organization. Social interaction is the essence of power because power always exists within social relationships.

2. The state—the political institution—is an arrangement that consists of people who exercise an effective monopoly in the use of physical coercion within a given territory. In the final analysis the state rests on force—power whose basis is the threat or application of punishment. Two views have prevailed regarding the state. Conservatives see government as employing force as an instrument of right to restrain and rebuke those who would place their self-interest above the common good. In contrast, radicals maintain that the state employs force to suppress right and defend selfish interests. The conservative view sees the state as a social contract; the radical view, as an organization of violence that serves the interests of elites.

3. Functionalists contend that there is a good reason why the state arose and why today it has assumed a dominant position in contemporary society. They point to four primary functions performed by the state: the enforce-

ment of norms, overall social planning and direction, the arbitration of conflicting interests, and the protection of a society's members and interests against outside groups.

4. Conflict theorists contend that the state is a vehicle by which one or more groups impose their values and stratification system upon other groups. As they view the matter, the state has its origin in the desire of ruling elites to give permanence to social arrangements that benefit themselves. More fundamentally, they depict the state as an instrument of violence and oppression.

5. Although force may be an effective means for seizing power, and though it remains the ultimate foundation of the state, it is not the most effective means for political rule. Accordingly, sociologists distinguish between power that is legitimate and power that is illegitimate. Legitimate power is authority. Sociologist Max Weber suggests that power may be legitimated by traditional, legal-rational, and/or charismatic means.

6. Modern economic systems tend to differ from one another in two important respects. First, they provide a different answer to the question of how economic activity is organized—by the market or by the plan. Second, they provide a different answer to the question of who owns the means of production—individuals or the state. In practice, we commonly merge the two features and talk about contrasting economic systems. We think of capitalist economies as relying heavily on free markets and privately held property, and socialist economies as relying primarily on state planning and publicly held property.

7. The government is an important participant in the American economy. But the primary productive role is played by private business. Large corporations exercise enormous power in American life. The decisions made by their officials have implications and ramifications that reach throughout the nation. The rise of multinational corporations and the growing internationalization of the world economy have given economic power a new dimension. Such firms rival nations in wealth and frequently operate as private governments pursuing their worldwide interests by well-developed foreign policies. Some social scientists say that a managerial revolution has separated ownership and effective control in corporate life. But other social scientists point to the institutional constraints that operate on corporate decision makers. Hence, corporations remain fundamentally capitalist in goal and in practice.

8. Power extends into the workplace. It determines whether or not work will be available, how work will be organized, and the manner in which work will be remunerated. People work for a good many reasons in addition to "self-interest." And work has many social meanings, especially those that define a person's position in the social structure. Individuals in occupations that combine high economic, occupational, and educational prestige typically show the greatest satisfaction with their work and the strongest job attachment. When individuals fail to find their work satisfying and fulfilling, they may experience alienation. Marx saw alienation as the outcome of social forces that inhere in capitalist arrangements and separate human beings from meaningful, creative, and self-realizing work. Durkheim depicted alienation as arising from the breakdown of the cohesive ties that bind individuals to society.

9. Government entails those political processes that have to do with the authoritative formulating of rules and policies that are binding and pervasive throughout a society. Totalitarianism is a "total state"—one in which the government undertakes to extend control over all parts of the society and all aspects of social life. A totalitarian society typically has three characteristics: a monolithic political party, a com-

pelling ideology, and pervasive social control. Authoritarianism is a political system in which the government tolerates little or no opposition to its rule but permits nongovernmental centers of influence and allows debate on some issues of public policy. Democracy is a political system in which the powers of government derive from the consent of the governed and in which regular constitutional avenues exist for changing government officials. A number of factors promote a social climate favorable to a stable democracy: countervailing interest groups, multiple loyalties, stable economic and social conditions, and an underlying political consensus.

10. A constitutional system of government defines and prescribes the boundaries within which political power is pursued in the United States. Central to American political processes are political parties, popular electoral participation, interest-group lobbying, and the mass media. Political parties are organizations designed to gain control of the government by putting their people in public office. They operate in a political environment in which the citizenry participates in the governmental process through periodic elections. Additionally, people who share common concerns or points of view form interest groups to advance their concerns. Since the mass media are the chief source of people's political information, political parties and interest groups are increasingly tailoring candidates and issues in ways that capture media attention.

11. One of the longest running debates in the social sciences has to do with the nature of power in the United States. Marxist theory holds that political processes must be understood in terms of the institutional structure of society as it is shaped by underlying class interests and conflict. The elitist model depicts major decisions as being made by a power elite who constitute the real rulers of the United States. The pluralist perspective contends that no one group really runs the government because interest groups constitute countervailing and balancing political forces. Each model contains a kernel of truth, and a synthesis of the formulations seems at present to afford the most satisfactory approach.

Glossary

alienation A pervasive sense of powerlessness, meaninglessness, normlessness, isolation, and self-estrangement.

authoritarianism A political system in which the government tolerates little or no opposition to its rules but permits nongovernmental centers of influence and allows debate on issues of public policy.

authority Legitimate power.

capitalist economy An economic system relying primarily on free markets and privately held property.

charismatic authority Power that is legitimated by the extraordinary superhuman or supernatural attributes people attribute to a leader.

civil society A social realm of mediating groups, networks, and institutions that sustains public life outside the worlds of the state and the economy.

conglomerates Companies that operate in completely different markets and produce largely unrelated products.

core regions Geographical areas that dominate the world economy and exploit the rest of the system.

corporate interlocks Networks of individuals who serve on the boards of directors of multiple corporations.

democracy A political system in which the powers of government derive from the consent of the governed and in which regular constitutional avenues exist for changing government officials.

force Power whose basis is the threat or application of punishment.

government Those political processes that have to do with the authoritative formulating of rules and policies that are binding and pervasive throughout a society.

interest groups Organizations of people who share common concerns or points of view.

interests People who share common concerns or points of view.

legal-rational authority Power that is legitimated by explicit rules and rational procedures that define the rights and duties of the occupants of given positions.

mass media Those organizations—newspapers, magazines, television, radio, and motion pictures—that undertake to convey information to a large segment of the public.

multinational corporations Firms that have their central office in one country and subsidiaries in other countries.

oligopoly A market dominated by a few firms.

periphery regions Geographical areas that provide raw materials to the core and are exploited by it.

political action committees Interest groups set up to elect or defeat candidates, but not through the organization of a political party.

political party An organization designed to gain control of the government by putting its people in public office.

public-interest groups Interest groups that pursue policies that presumably would be of no greater benefit to their members than to the larger society.

socialist economy An economic system relying primarily on state planning and publicly held property.

special-interest groups Interest groups that primarily seek benefits from which their members would derive more gains than the society as a whole.

state An arrangement that consists of people who exercise an effective monopoly in the use of physical coercion within a given territory.

strategic elites Powerful individuals and groups who exercise significant power in their own rather specialized domains.

totalitarianism A "total state"—one in which the government undertakes to control all parts of the society and all aspects of social life.

traditional authority Power that is legitimated by the sanctity of age-old customs.

Chapter 9

THE FAMILY

We hear a good deal nowadays about "the crisis of the American family" and even about its impending death. "Pessimists" believe that the state of marriage has undergone a grave loss over the past 40 years. They cite easy divorce, the postponement of marriage, a rise in the proportion of the never-married, and the ready availability of contraception as forces that have eroded the family and compromised its "ultimate function"—the licensing of reproduction. Indeed, they are appalled by the proliferation of family types and forms in the late twentieth century: never-married mothers, single-parent families, stepfamilies, cohabiting couples, and gay and lesbian families. And they note with alarm many signs that they take as evidence of decay and disintegration: Divorce rates soared during the 1960s and 1970s (although they slowed during the 1980s); birth and marriage rates have fallen; the proportion of unwed mothers has increased; single-parent households have proliferated; mothers of infants and young children have entered the labor force in large numbers; and the elderly are placing growing reliance on the government rather than the family for care in their later years.

"Optimists," in contrast, believe the family is not declining but merely revealing its flexibility and resilience. They say that traditional family forms are no longer appropriate for contemporary times—indeed, the structures were flawed as conformity-ridden and male-dominated. Optimists readily admit that the meaning of marriage has been changing and with it the family institution. But they claim that pronouncements concerning the death of the family, or at least its impending doom, are greatly exaggerated.

In the political realm, pessimistic conservatives typically decry what they portray as the lack of traditional family values and issue urgent calls for their revival. At the same time, optimistic liberals endorse the proliferation and flexibility in family structures and call for new government assistance programs. As sociologist and U.S. Senator Daniel Patrick Moynihan (1985) has observed, conservatives—fearing government interference—prefer to talk about family values but not new governmental initiatives. Liberals, fearing a "blaming the victim" mentality, like to talk about public policy initiatives but not family values. Taking a more centralist position, Dennis A. Ahlburg and Carol J. De Vita (1992:39) observe:

Valuing the family should not be confused with valuing a particular family form. . . . Social legislation (or "pro-family" policies) narrowly designed to reinforce only one model of the American family is likely to be shortsighted and have the unintended consequence of weakening, rather than strengthening, family ties. Recognizing the diversity of American families and addressing the complexity of their needs must lie at the heart of the policy debates on family issues.

A word of caution is also in order: Much of the debate over the family may be misguided because it uses the stereotypical white, middle-class family of the 1950s as a point of departure for either praise or criticism of subsequent changes (less informed by reality than by old television series like "Leave It to Beaver," "Ozzie and Harriet," and "The Donna Reed Show") (Kain, 1990; Skolnick, 1991). In any event, whether the American family is "disintegrating" or merely "changing," widespread behavioral changes are occurring throughout Western societies. Table 9.1 compares the circumstances of American children in 1990 with those in 1960. And Figure 9.1 reveals substantial shifts in American family arrangements.

While its obituary continues to be written, the family itself has held on and, if you literally believe what Americans say, it may actually be flourishing (almost two-thirds of married Americans rate their own marriages as "very happy"). Researchers have been asking Americans about their families for over 50 years, and Americans consistently reply that the family takes priority over everything else in their lives. In survey after survey, respondents identify traditional relationships among parents, children, and siblings as the most important aspect of life. They view families as more important than work, recreation, friend-

Table 9.1 A COMPARISON OF THE STATE OF AMERICAN CHILDREN, 1960 AND 1990

1960		1990
5%	Children born to unmarried mothers	28%
7%	Children under 3 living with one parent	27%
90%	Children under 3 living with both parents	71%
2%	Children under 3 living with a divorced parent	4%
17%	Mothers returning to work within 1 year of a child's birth	53%
10%	Children under 18 living in a one-parent family (approx.)	25%
28/1,000	Infant mortality (deaths before first birthday)	9/1,000
27%	Children under 18 living below the poverty line	21%
18.6%	Married women with children under 6 years old in labor force	60%

SOURCE: Carnegie Corporation Report; U.S. Census Bureau; The Urban Institute; the National Center for Children in Poverty. Adapted from The *New York Times*, April 12, 1994, p. A11. Copyright © 1994 by The New York Times Company. Reprinted by permission.

ships, or status. Yet surveys also show that most people put their jobs, possessions, and personal freedom before their family responsibilities. Moreover, many of their attitudes have changed. For instance, there has been a substantial decline in the ideal of marital permanence (the percentage of women who say that parents who do not get along should split up rather than stay together for the sake of the children rose from 51 percent in 1962 to 82 percent in 1985). The goal of "having a happy marriage" currently ranks well above "being married to the same person for life" and even farther above merely "being married" (Glenn, 1992).

Laments about the current condition of the family imply that at an earlier time in history the family was more stable and harmonious than it

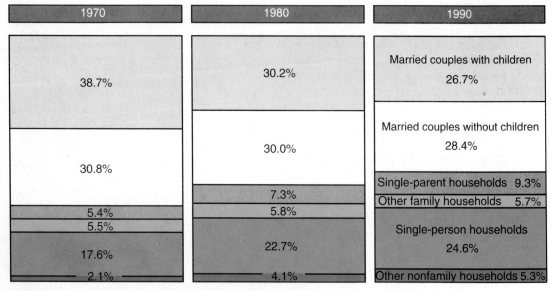

| 1970 | 1980 | 1990 |

Figure 9.1 TODAY'S FAMILIES DIFFER FROM THOSE OF AN EARLIER GENERATION
The U.S. Census Bureau defines a family household as two or more people related by blood, marriage, or adoption. By this definition, families now account for a smaller share of U.S. households (70.2 percent in 1992) than they did in 1970 (81.2 percent). (SOURCE: The U.S. Census Bureau. Adapted from *American Demographics* magazine, July 1992, p. 2. Reprinted with permission.)

currently is. Yet, despite massive research, historians have not located a "golden age of the family" (Flandrin, 1979; Degler, 1980; Coontz, 1992). For instance, the marriages of seventeenth-century England and New England were based on family and property needs, not on choice by affection. Families were often devastated by desertion and death. Loveless marriages, the tyranny of husbands, high death rates, and the beating and abuse of children add up to a grim image (Shorter, 1975). Indeed, concerns about the family have a long history (Hareven, 1987; Mintz and Kellogg, 1988; Coontz, 1992). Educators of the European medieval and Enlightenment periods were worried about the strength and character of the family. In colonial and frontier times people expressed anxiety about the disruption of family life. And in the nineteenth and early twentieth centuries, worry about the family was cloaked in recurrent public hysteria regarding the "peril" posed to the nation's Anglo-American institutions by the arrival of immigrant groups with "alien cultures."

In sum, the "family question," despite its many guises, is not new. So, given the lesson of history and the certainty that families will continue to adapt in unforeseen ways, it is safe to assume that debate will continue.

□ Structure of the Family

What is the family? Although we all use the term and doubtless have a clear idea of what we mean by it, the "family" is an exceedingly fuzzy concept that is difficult to define. When we set about separating families from nonfamilies, we encounter all sorts of problems (Stephens, 1963). Many of

"You have a right to know—I've been married occasionally."

Drawing by P. Steiner; © 1991 The New Yorker Magazine, Inc.

us think of the family as a social unit consisting of Mom, Pop, and the kids, living alone in a comfortable home of their own (the image conveyed by a "Kodak family" about to open gifts under a Christmas tree). But as we will see in the course of the chapter, such a definition is too restrictive. Even in the United States, the "Ozzie and Harriet" model of the family—a married couple, breadwinner husband and homemaker wife, raising children—now comprises only one in five families. Moreover, in many societies it is the kin group, and not a married couple and their children, that is the basic family unit. And with so many Americans living in single-parent households, stepparent households, childless households, gay and lesbian households, and unmarried cohabiting male and female households, a number of sociologists suggest that it would be better to dispense with the concept of "family" altogether and focus instead upon "sexually bonded primary relationships" (Scanzoni et al., 1989).

Sociologists have traditionally viewed the **family** as a social group whose members are related by ancestry, marriage, or adoption and live together, cooperate economically, and care for the young (Murdock, 1949). But there are those who are unhappy with this definition, arguing that psychological bonds are what families are all about; they see the family as a close-knit group of people who care about and respect each other. A recent poll found that many Americans are now willing to accept alternatives to traditional notions of the family. Indeed, 77 percent of Americans thought that "a man and a woman who live together for a long time, are not married, but are raising children" are a "family"; roughly 27 percent also placed a gay or lesbian couple raising children in this category; and 21 percent regarded two homosexuals "committed to each other and living together" as a "family" (Roper Organization, Roper Reports 92-3, February 1992). Broadly considered, then, many Americans deem that long-term relationships, heterosexual or homosexual, should be considered as families. And a 1990 poll found that only 22 percent of randomly selected American adults picked the legalistic definition for "family" ("a group of people related by blood, marriage, or adoption"), whereas three-quarters chose instead a much broader and more emotional description ("a group of people who love and care for each other") (Seligmann, 1990). The family, then, is a matter of social definition. Because the family is a social construct, family ties are often independent of legal or kin status (Gubrium and Holstein, 1990).

Clearly, defining the family is not simply an academic exercise. How we define it determines the kinds of families we will consider normal and the kinds we will consider deviant, and what rights and obligations we will recognize as legally and socially binding. A growing number of judges and legislators are now expanding to qualifying domestic partners some of the benefits traditionally accorded married heterosexuals, including health benefits, property and life insurance, bereavement leave, and annuity and pension rights.

FORMS OF THE FAMILY

As we look about the world, and even in our own society, we encounter a good many differences in the ways in which families are organized. Families vary in their composition and in their descent, residence, and authority patterns.

Composition. Social relationships between adult males and females can be organized within families by emphasizing either spouse or kin relationships. In the **nuclear family** arrangement, spouses and their offspring constitute the core relationship; blood relatives are functionally marginal and peripheral. In contrast, in the **extended family** arrangement, kin—individuals related by common ancestry—provide the core relationship; spouses are functionally marginal and peripheral. The nuclear family pattern is the preferred arrangement among most Americans. In the course of their lives, Americans typically find themselves members of two nuclear families. First, an individual belongs to a nuclear family that consists of oneself and one's father, mother, and siblings, what sociologists call the **family of orientation.** Second, since over 90 percent of Americans marry at least once, the vast majority of the population are members of a nuclear family that consists of oneself and one's spouse and children, what sociologists call the **family of procreation.**

Extended families are found in numerous forms throughout the world. In one case, that of the Nayar—a soldiering caste group in the pre-British period of southwestern India—spouse ties were virtually absent (Gough, 1959; Dumont, 1970; Fuller, 1976). When a woman was about to enter puberty, she was ritually "married" to a man chosen for her by a neighborhood assembly. After three ceremonial days, she was ritually "separated" from him and was then free to take on a series of "visiting husbands" or "lovers." Although a woman's lovers gave her regular gifts on prescribed occasions, they did not provide support. When a woman had a child, one of the men—not necessarily the biological father—paid a fee to the midwife and thus established the child's legitimacy. However, the man assumed no economic, social, legal, or ritual rights or obligations toward the child. It was the mother's kin who took responsibility for the child.

For some time, sociologists assumed that industrialization undercut extended family patterns while fostering nuclear family arrangements. For instance, William J. Goode (1963) surveyed families in many parts of the world and concluded that industrialization weakens extended family patterns. For one thing, industrialism requires that people move about in search of new job and professional opportunities, weakening kin obligations that depend on frequent and intimate interaction. For another, industrialism substitutes nonkin agencies for kin groups in handling such common problems as police protection, education, military defense, and moneylending. However, in recent years sociologists have taken a new look and have found that industrialization and extended family arrangements are not necessarily incompatible (Smelser, 1959; Cherlin, 1983). By virtue of high mortality rates, the nuclear family had come to prevail in England before industrialization got under way (Laslett, 1974, 1976; Stearns, 1977; Quadagno, 1982). And when Tamara K. Hareven (1982) examined family life in a textile community of New Hampshire in the nineteenth century, she discovered that industrialism promoted kin ties. Not only did different generations often reside together in the same household, but they provided a good deal of assistance to one another. Indeed, economic dislocations and the increased availability of nonnuclear kin may actually have encouraged the formation of extended family households in the early industrialization of England and the United States (Ruggles, 1987). Overall, a growing body of research suggests that differences in household forms do not correspond neatly with differences in economic arrangements. Throughout the world considerable diversity characterizes household patterns, suggesting that a large number of factors—in addition to the nature of the political economy—interact with one another to produce the contours of family life (Kertzer, 1991).

Descent.   Societies trace descent and pass on property from one generation to the next in one of three ways. Under a **patrilineal** arrangement, a people reckon descent and transmit property through the line of the father. Under a **matrilineal** arrangement, descent and inheritance take place through the mother's side of the family. The Nayar were a matrilineal people. A child owed allegiance to the mother's brother and not the father. Property and privileged positions passed from maternal uncle to nephew. Under the **bilineal** arrangement, both sides of an individual's family are equally important. Americans are typically bilineal, reckoning descent through both the father and the mother (however, the surname is transmitted in a patrilineal manner).

Residence.   Societies also differ in the location where a couple take up residence after marriage. In the case of **patrilocal** residence, the bride and groom live in the household or community of the husband's family. The opposite pattern prevails in **matrilocal** residence. For example, among the Hopi, a Southwest Pueblo people, the husband moves upon marriage into the dwelling of his wife's family, and it is here that he eats and sleeps. In the United States, newlyweds tend to follow **neolocal** patterns in which they set up a new place of residence independent of either of their parents or other relatives.

Authority.   Although the authority a man or woman enjoys in family decision-making is influenced by their personalities, societies nonetheless dictate who is expected to be the dominant figure. Under **patriarchal** arrangements, it is usually the eldest male or the husband who fills this role. The ancient Hebrews, Greeks, and Romans and the nineteenth-century Chinese and Japanese provide a few examples. Logically, the construction of a **matriarchal** family type is

very simple and would involve the vesting of power in women. Yet true matriarchies are rare, and considerable controversy exists as to whether the balance of power actually rests with the wife in any known society (Stephens, 1963). Even though matriarchies may not be the preferred arrangement in most societies, they often arise through default upon the death or desertion of the husband. In a third type of family, the **egalitarian** arrangement, power and authority are equally distributed between husband and wife. This pattern has been on the increase in recent years in the United States, where marriage is changing from a one-vote system in which men make the decisions to a system in which the couple sort out choices jointly.

FORMS OF MARRIAGE

The fact that the parties to a marriage must be members of two different kin groups has crucial implications for the structuring of the family. Indeed, the continuity, and therefore the long-term welfare, of any kin group depends on obtaining spouses for the unmarried members of the group from other groups. By the same token, a kin group has a stake in retaining some measure of control over at least a portion of its members after they marry (Lee, 1977). Accordingly, we need to take a closer look at marital arrangements, particularly marriage. **Marriage** refers to a socially approved sexual union between two or more individuals that is undertaken with some idea of permanence.

Exogamy and Endogamy.   All societies regulate the pool of eligibles from which individuals are expected to select a mate. A child's kin generally have more in mind than simply getting a child married. They want the child married to the *right* spouse, especially where marriage has consequences for the larger kin group. Two types of marital regulations define the "right" spouse: *endogamy* and *exogamy*. **Endogamy** is the requirement that marriage occur within a group. Under these circumstances, people must marry within their class, race, ethnic group, or religion. **Exogamy** is the requirement that marriage occur outside a group. Under these circumstances, people must marry outside their kin group, be it their immediate nuclear family, clan, or tribe.

Regulations relating to exogamy are based primarily on kinship and usually entail **incest taboos,** rules that prohibit sexual intercourse with close blood relatives. Such relationships are not only prohibited but also bring reactions of aversion and disgust. Incest taboos were once singled out by social scientists as the only universal norm in a world of diverse moral codes. But sociologist Russell Middleton (1962) found that brother-sister marriage was not only permitted but frequently practiced by the ancient Egyptians. He speculates that brother-sister marriage served to maintain the power and property of a family and prevented the splintering of an estate through inheritance. A similar arrangement apparently also occurred among the royal families of Hawaii, the Inca of Peru, and the Dahomey of West Africa. Additionally, the degree of kinship covered by incest varies from society to society. For example, in colonial New England it was incestuous if a man married his deceased wife's sister. But among the ancient Hebrews, the custom of the levirate required that a man had to marry his deceased brother's widow under some circumstances. In the contemporary world, in mainly Muslim countries of northern Africa and western and southern Asia, marriages contracted between persons who are related as second cousins or closer account for between 20 and 55 percent of the total (Bittles et al., 1991).

There have been numerous attempts to account for both the existence and the prevalence of incest taboos. Anthropologist Claude Levi-Strauss (1956) suggests that incest taboos promote alliances between families and reinforce their social interdependence (the Zulu have a saying: "They are our enemies, and so we marry them."). Anthropologist George Peter Murdock (1949) says that incest taboos prevent destructive

sexual jealousies and rivalries within the family. Sociologist Kingsley Davis (1960) contends that incestuous relationships would hopelessly confuse family statuses (for example, the incestuous male offspring of a father-daughter union would be the son of his own sister, a stepson of his own grandmother, and a grandson of his own father). And sociobiologists, noting the children raised together on Israel's kibbutzim seldom marry each other, argue that this behavior is prewired by genes (Wilson, 1975; Lumsden and Wilson, 1981). Admittedly, these matters remain unresolved, and social scientists continue to find themselves perplexed about the real basis of incest taboos (Arens, 1986).

Types of Marriage. The relationships between a husband and wife may be structured in one of four ways: **monogamy,** one husband and one wife; **polygyny,** one husband and two or more wives; **polyandry,** two or more husbands and one wife; and **group marriage,** two or more husbands and two or more wives. Monogamy appears in all societies, although other forms may not only be permitted but preferred. It was the preferred or ideal type of marriage in less than 20 percent of 862 societies included in one cross-cultural sample (Murdock, 1967).

Polygyny has enjoyed a wide distribution throughout the world, with 83 percent of 862 societies permitting husbands to take plural wives. The Old Testament, for example, records polygynous practices among the Hebrews: Gideon had many wives, who bore him 70 sons; King David had several wives; King Solomon reportedly had 700 wives and 300 concubines; King Solomon's son Rehoboam had 18 wives and 60 concubines; and Rehoboam's sons in turn had many wives.

The lot of husbands with several wives rarely if ever conforms to the Hollywood image of the Arabian sheik whose harem is ready and waiting to provide him every pleasure. Indeed, anthropologist Ralph Linton (1936:183–184) believes that the polygynous husband should be pitied, not envied, by other men:

[T]here are few polygynous societies in which the position of the male is really better than it is under monogamy. If the plural wives are not congenial, the family will be torn by feuds in which the husband must take the thankless role of umpire, while if they are congenial he is likely to be confronted by an organized female opposition.

Although Linton overstated the case, his point is worth considering. And generally, it is only the economically advantaged males who can afford to have more than one wife (for example, in China, India, and the Islamic countries, polygyny has usually been the privilege of the wealthy few). Polygyny involves far more than sex; it is closely tied to economic production and status considerations (Heath, 1958). The arrangement tends to be favored where large families are advantageous and women make substantial contributions to subsistence.

Although polygyny has a wide distribution, polyandry is exceedingly rare. Polyandry usually does not represent freedom of sexual choice for women; often, it involves the right or the opportunity of younger brothers to have sexual access to the wife of an older brother. If a family cannot afford wives or marriages for each of its sons, it may find a wife for the eldest son only. Anthropologist W. H. R. Rivers (1906:515) studied polyandrous practices among the Todas, a non-Hindu people in India, and observed:

The Todas have a completely organized and definite system of polyandry. When a woman marries a man, it is understood that she becomes the wife of his brothers at the same time. When a boy is married to a girl, not only are his brothers usually regarded as also the husbands of the girl, but any brother born later will similarly be regarded as sharing his older brother's right. . . . The brothers live together, and my informants seemed to regard it as a ridiculous idea that there should even be disputes or jealousies of the kind that might be expected in such a household. . . . Instead of adultery being regarded as immoral

. . . according to the Toda idea, immorality attaches rather to the man who grudges his wife to another.

Social scientists are far from agreement on whether group marriage has ever existed as a cultural norm. There is some evidence that it did occur among the Kaingang of the jungles of Brazil, the Marquesans of the southern Pacific, the Chukchee of Siberia, and the Todas of India. At times, as among the Todas, polyandry appears to slip into group marriage, where a number of brothers share more than one wife (Stephens, 1963).

THE FUNCTIONALIST PERSPECTIVE ON THE FAMILY

As we have noted in other chapters, functionalist theorists stress that if a society is to survive and operate with some measure of effectiveness, it must guarantee that certain essential tasks are performed. The performance of these tasks—or *functions*—cannot be left to chance (see Chapter 2). To do so would be to run the risk that some activities would not be carried out, and the society would disintegrate. Although acknowledging that families show a good deal of variation throughout the world, functionalists seek to identify a number of recurrent functions families typically perform (Davis, 1949).

Reproduction. If a society is to perpetuate itself, new members have to be created. Sexual drives do not necessarily take care of the matter because many people are aware that they can satisfy their sexual needs in the absence of procreation. For instance, the "pill," coitus interruptus, intrauterine devices (IUDs), condoms, abortion, infanticide, the rhythm method, and countless other techniques allow couples to separate sexual enjoyment from reproduction. Consequently, societies commonly motivate people to have children. Among peasant peoples, children are often defined as an economic asset. Likewise, religious

Doing Sociology: Family Statuses and Roles

A number of instructors find that family relationships afford an unusually useful vehicle for sensitizing their students to the key sociological concepts of *status* and *role*. You will recall from our discussion in Chapter 2 that a status is a position within a group or society—a location in a social structure. A role is a set of expectations (rights and duties) that define the behavior people view as appropriate and inappropriate for the occupant of a status (the incumbent of a position). The difference between a status and a role is that we *occupy* a status and *play* a role.

Professor Mary Minard Moynihan (1989) of Assumption College in Worcester, Massachusetts, asks each of her students to imagine that "you are about to be married." As an out-of-class writing assignment, Moynihan has each student draw up a "marriage contract" that indicates the "reciprocal obligations you expect from yourself and your partner for the long term as well as for everyday life."

You may also wish to prepare a "contract" for a long-term relationship with a partner (of the same or different gender). Remember from the discussion in Chapter 2 that rules impinge on us as sets of norms that define our *duties*—the actions others can legitimately insist that we perform—and our *rights*—the actions we can legitimately insist that others perform. Since every role has at least one reciprocal role attached to it, the rights of one role are the duties of the other role, and vice versa. In drawing up such a contract, would you notice any potential sources of *role strain*—a situation in which individuals find the expectations of a single role incompatible so that they have difficulty performing the role (see the discussion in Chapter 2)? What contractual mechanisms can you suggest for dealing with these potential difficulties?

Professor David S. Adams (1993) of Ohio State University at Lima takes a somewhat differ-

considerations may operate (in precommunist China, where ancestor worship provided the foundation for religious life, one's comfort in the hereafter could be ensured only by having numerous sons). And in the United States, many Americans still define marriage and children as affording the "good life"; in fact, the absence of children is often viewed as a misfortune (Pebley and Bloom, 1982).

Socialization. At birth, children are uninitiated in the ways of culture, and thus each new generation subjects society to a recurrent "barbarian invasion" (see Chapter 3). Most infants are fairly malleable in that within broad limits they are capable of becoming adults of quite different sorts. It is urgent, therefore, that they become the "right" kind of adults. Through the process of socialization, children become inducted into their society's ways, and it is the family that usually serves as the chief culture-transmitting agency. The family functions as an intermediary in the socialization process between the larger community and the individual.

Care, Protection, and Emotional Support. Whereas the offspring of lower animals can survive independently of their parents within a matter of days or weeks, this is not true of human children. Their prolonged dependency dictates that they be fed, clothed, and provided with shelter well into puberty. Throughout the world, the family has been assigned the responsibility for shielding, protecting, sustaining, and otherwise

ent tack in his introductory sociology classes, employing a kinship example. Adams begins the discussion by distributing a handout to each student that contains a diagram of the kin of an idealized family: a married couple with one female and one male offspring. He asks the students to identify on the diagram individuals falling within such kinship categories as "siblings," "parents," "uncles," "aunts," "nieces," "nephews," "grandparents," "grandchildren," and "cousins."

Adams's primary interest, however, is the distinction between "first cousins" and "second cousins." Among the social expectations associated with the status of first cousin is the norm that first cousins must not marry (incest taboos apply). Adams asks his students, "Who are your second cousins?" Invariably students respond that their second cousins are their parents' first cousins and their own first cousins' children. Adams then explains to the students that, strictly speaking, these individuals are not their second cousins. He reminds them that cousins, like siblings, are all members of one's own generation.

Adams next asks the class how many of them know their second cousins by name. Few students raise their hands. Adams then asks, "If siblings have parents in common and first cousins have grandparents in common, what do second cousins have in common?" Looking at the kinship diagram, students discover that *second cousins are all those members of a generation who have great-grandparents in common.* (Can you figure out the definition of third cousins?) The students quickly discover that, by this definition, they have a good many more second cousins than they had realized. In concluding, Adams points out that one reason why we are so clear about the identity of our first cousins and typically unclear about our second cousins is that we must be able to identify our first cousins lest we, unsuspecting, marry one of them (violate incest taboos). In contrast, although we are not encouraged to marry second cousins, we do not encounter legal obstacles barring us from doing so.

---

maintaining children, the infirm, and other dependent members of the community (Rossi and Rossi, 1990). Moreover, since people are social beings, they have a variety of emotional and interpersonal needs that can be met only through interaction with other human beings. The family provides an important source for entering into intimate, constant, face-to-face contact with other people. Healthy family relationships afford companionship, love, security, a sense of worth, and a general feeling of well-being.

Assignment of Status. Societies constantly confront a continual stream of raw material in the form of new infants who must be placed within the social structure (see the box, Family Statuses and Roles). This function can be accomplished by assigning some statuses to an individual on the basis of family membership, what sociologists call *ascribed statuses* (see Chapter 2). The family confers statuses that (1) orient a person to a variety of interpersonal relationships, including those involving parents (parent-child), siblings (brothers and sisters), and kin (aunts, uncles, cousins, and grandparents), and that (2) orient a person to basic group memberships, including racial, ethnic, religious, class, national, and community relationships.

Regulation of Sexual Behavior. As we noted earlier in the chapter, a society's norms regulate sexual behavior by specifying who may engage in sexual behavior with whom and under what circumstances. In no known society are people given total freedom for sexual expression. Although some 70 percent of the world's societies permit some form of sexual license, even those societies typically do not approve of childbirth out of wed-lock—this is the **norm of legitimacy** (like other norms, this one is occasionally violated, and those who violate it are usually punished). Legitimacy has to do with the placement of a child in a kin-ship network that defines the rights the newborn has to care, inheritance, and instruction (Goode, 1960; Malinowski, 1964). A great many social complications result when this norm is violated.

In sum, the functionalist perspective draws our attention to the requirements of group life and to the structural arrangements whereby these requirements are met. But critics point out that these tasks can be performed in other ways. Indeed, by virtue of social change, many of the economic, child-care, and educational functions once performed by the family have been taken over by other institutions. Even so, the family tends to be the social unit most commonly responsible for reproduction, socialization, and the other functions we considered.

THE CONFLICT PERSPECTIVE ON THE FAMILY

Functionalists spotlight the tasks carried out by the family that serve the interests of society as a whole. Many conflict theorists have seen the fam-ily as a social arrangement benefiting some people more than others. Friedrich Engels (1884/1902), Karl Marx's close associate, viewed the family as a class society in miniature, with one class (men) oppressing another class (women). He contended that marriage was the first form of class antago-nism in which the well-being of one group derived from the misery and repression of another group. The motivation for sexual domi-nation was the economic exploitation of a woman's labor.

Sociologist Randall Collins (1975, 1988a) says that historically men have been the "sexual aggres-sors" and women the "sexual prizes for men." He traces male dominance to the greater strength, size, and aggressiveness of men. Women have been victimized by their smaller size and their vulnerability as childbearers. Across an entire spectrum of societies women have been seen as sexual property, taken as booty in war, used by their fathers in economic bargaining, and consid-ered as owned by their husbands. Collins (1975:232) says that "men have appropriated women primarily for their beds rather than their kitchens and fields, although they could certainly be pressed into service in the daytime too."

According to Collins, men have ordered society so that women are their sexual property. They claim exclusive sexual rights to a woman much in the manner that they determine access to eco-nomic property like buildings and land. Marriage becomes a socially enforced contract of sexual property. Hence, within Western tradition, a mar-riage was not legal until sexually consummated, sexual assault within marriage was not legally rape, and the principal ground for divorce was sexual infidelity. A woman's virginity was seen as the property of her father, and her sexuality as the property of her husband. Thus rape has often been seen less as a crime perpetrated by a man against a woman than as a crime perpetrated by one man against another man.

In recent years, however, economic and politi-cal changes have improved women's bargaining position. When they were no longer under the control of their fathers, they became potentially free to negotiate their own sexual relationships. But women often found that within the free mar-riage market, they had to trade their sexuality for the economic and status resources of men. Collins suggests that in an economic world dominated by men, the most favorable female strategy became one in which a woman maximized her bargaining power by appearing both as sexually alluring and as inaccessible as possible. She had to hold her sexuality in reserve as a sort of grand prize that she exchanged for male wealth and status, stabi-lized by a marriage contract. Under such an arrangement, femininity and female virginity came to be idealized, and women were placed on a pedestal so that an element of sexual repression was built into courtship. But as women have increased their economic opportunities, freeing themselves from economic dependence on men, they have gained the resources to challenge the "double standard" of sexuality. The sexual bargains they strike can focus less on marriage and more on immediate pleasure, companionship, and sexual gratification.

Although conflict theory reverberates with the seminal ideas of Friedrich Engels and Karl Marx, other social scientists have approached the issue of conflict somewhat differently. At the turn of the century, psychoanalyst Sigmund Freud (1930/1961) and sociologist Georg Simmel (1908/1955, 1908/1959) also advanced a conflict approach to the family. They contended that intimate relationships inevitably involve antagonism as well as love. More recently, sociologists like Jetse Sprey (1979) have developed these ideas and suggest that conflict is a part of all systems and interactions, including the family and marital interactions. They see family members as confronting two conflicting demands: to compete with one another for autonomy, authority, and privilege, and simultaneously to share one another's fate in order to survive and even flourish. Viewed in this fashion, the family is a social arrangement that structures close interpersonal relationships through ongoing processes of negotiation, problem solving, and conflict management. This view is quite compatible with the interactionist perspective.

THE INTERACTIONIST PERSPECTIVE ON THE FAMILY

As we saw in Chapters 2 and 3, symbolic interactionists emphasize that human beings create, use, and communicate with symbols. They interact through role taking, a process of reading the symbols used by others and attributing meaning to them. Interactionists portray humans as a unique species because they have a mind and a self. The

mind and self arise out of interaction and provide the foundation for enduring social relationships and group life. Thus when they enter interactive situations, people define the situation by identifying the expectations that will hold for themselves and others. They then organize their own behavior in terms of these understandings.

One way in which families reinforce and rejuvenate their bonds is through the symbolic mechanism of rituals. Social scientists find that household rituals like gathering for meals are a hidden source of family strength. Indeed, it seems that when families preserve their rituals, their children fare better emotionally, even when the family faces other disruptive problems like alcoholism. This understanding has led some therapists to help families establish rituals as a means to heal family stresses and tensions (Goleman, 1992).

The symbolic interactionist perspective is a useful tool for examining the complexities of a relationship. Thus, should the roles of one family member change, invariably there are consequences for the other family members as well. For example, later in the chapter we will see that parenthood alters the husband-wife relationship by creating new roles and increasing the complexity of the family unit. Likewise, family life is somewhat different in homes where a mother is in the paid labor force or where an economic provider is unemployed. And the loss of critical family roles, such as occurs at the time of divorce, has vast implications for family functioning. The symbolic interactionist perspective draws our attention to the complex interconnections that bind people within relationships. We encounter individuals as active beings who evolve, negotiate, and rework the social fabric that constitutes the mosaic of family life (Gubrium and Holstein, 1990).

In sum, functionalist theorists focus on the structural properties and functions of family systems. Conflict theorists portray the family as a system of perpetual "give and take" and conflict regulation (Dahrendorf, 1965). And symbolic interactionists see the family as a dynamic entity through which people continually fashion ongoing relationships and construct a group existence. Although each perspective yields differing insights, each offers a complementary lens through which to view institutional life.

□ Marriage and the Family in the United States

The issues that divide functionalist and conflict theorists are also encountered among the American public. Indeed, the family has become such a debated topic that sociologists Brigitte Berger and Peter L. Berger (1983) title their recent book *The War over the Family*. To its critics on the political left and among some feminists, the nuclear family is the source of many modern woes. To political conservatives, the family is the last bastion of morality in a world that is becoming increasingly decadent. And to the army of helping professionals, the family is a problem, an institution in grave difficulty. Let us see what we can make of all this by taking a closer look at marriage and the family in American life.

CHOOSING A MARRIAGE PARTNER

Since marriage brings a new member into the inner circle of a family, a child's relatives have a stake in the person who is to be the spouse. Random mating might jeopardize these interests. If children were permitted to "fall in love" with anybody, they might choose the *wrong* mate. Although love has many meanings, we usually think of the strong physical and emotional attraction between a man and a woman as **romantic love.** The ancient Greeks saw such love as a "diseased hysteria," an overwhelming force that irresistibly draws two people together and leads them to become passionately preoccupied with one another.

The Social Regulation of Love. Although most societies recognize that some people may be "smitten" by love, Americans have capitalized on such feelings and elevated them to an exalted position in national life (Hendrick and Hendrick, 1992). Many other peoples have viewed romantic love quite differently (Xiaohe and Whyte, 1990). Consider these words of the elders of an African tribe who, in discussing the problems of "runaway" marriages and illegitimacy, complained in the 1883 Commission on Native Law and Custom: "It is all this thing called love. We do not understand it at all . . ." (quoted by Gluckman, 1955:76). The elders saw romantic love as a disruptive force. Given their cultural traditions, marriage did not imply a romantic attraction toward the spouse-to-be, marriage was not the free choice of partners, and considerations other than love determined the selection of a mate.

Sociologist William J. Goode (1959) finds that romantic love is given more emphasis in some societies than in others. At one extreme, societies view marriage without love as mildly shameful; at the other, they define strong romantic attachment as a laughable or tragic aberration. The American middle class falls toward the pole of positive approval; the nineteenth-century Japanese and Chinese fell toward the pole of disapproval; and the Greeks after Alexander and the Romans of the empire took a middle course.

Societies undertake to "control" love in a variety of ways. One approach is *child marriage*. This pattern was employed at one time in India. A child bride went to live with her husband in a marriage that was not physically consummated until much later. Another approach involves the *social isolation* of young people from potential mates. For instance, the Manus of the Admiralty Islands secluded their young women in a lodge built on stilts over a lagoon. Still another approach entails the *close supervision* of couples by chaperons, an arrangement found among seventeenth-century Puritans. And finally *peer and parental pressures* may be brought to bear to ensure that youngsters "go with the right people." For example, in the United States parents often threaten, cajole, wheedle, and bribe their children

"Love comes and goes, Janet, but this is true co-dependency!"

Drawing by M. Twohy; © 1993 The New Yorker Magazine, Inc.

to limit their social contacts to youths with "suitable" ethnic, religious, and educational backgrounds. Regardless of the arrangement employed, the net result is the same—a person's range of choice is narrowed by social barriers.

Factors in Mate Selection. Given a field of eligible mates, why do we fall in love with and marry one person and not another? A variety of factors seem to be at work. One is **homogamy,** the tendency of like to marry like. People of similar age, race, religion, nationality, education, intelligence, health, stature, attitudes, and countless other traits tend to marry one another to a degree greater than would be found by chance. The principle holds even for illegal drug use (Yamaguchi and Kandel, 1993). Although homogamy seems to operate with respect to social characteristics, the evidence is less clear for such psychological factors as personality and temperament.

Physical attractiveness also plays a part in mate selection. On the whole, Americans share similar standards for evaluating physical attractiveness (Udry, 1965). Moreover, we prefer the compan-

ionship and friendship of attractive people to that of unattractive people (Feingold, 1990). When talking on the telephone to a man they believe to be physically attractive, women are more poised, more sociable, and more vivacious than when they talk to a man they believe to be physically unattractive (Brody, 1981). However, since the supply of unusually beautiful or handsome partners is limited, in real life we tend to select partners who have a degree of physical attractiveness similar to our own (Murstein, 1972, 1976; White, 1980; Feingold, 1988). According to the **matching hypothesis,** we typically experience the greatest payoff and the least cost when we follow this course since individuals of equal attractiveness are the ones most likely to reciprocate our advances.

Still another factor operates in choosing a mate. We feel most comfortable with people who have certain personality traits, while those with other traits "rub us the wrong way." Sociologist Robert F. Winch (1958) has taken this everyday observation and formulated a theory of **complementary needs.** This concept refers to two different personality traits that are the counterparts of each other and that provide a sense of completeness when they are joined. For instance, dominant people find a complementary relationship with passive people, and talkative people find themselves attracted to good listeners. Complementary needs may play an important part in *codependency*. For instance, researchers find that having learned to obtain approval and self-esteem by conforming to the demands of an exploitive person, women with alcoholic parents continue to seek opportunities to help such people, including "Mr. Wrong" (Lyon and Greenberg, 1991). Roles also complement one another (Murstein, 1976). By way of illustration, a bedroom athlete is likely to be attracted to a lusty, passionate partner rather than a cold, cerebral one with little "animal" sensuousness. Thus interpersonal attraction also depends on how well each partner fulfills the role expectations of the other and how mutually gratifying they find their "role fit" (Bluhm, Widiger, and Miele, 1990; Collins and Read, 1990).

Exchange theory provides a unifying link among these three factors. It is based on the notion that we like those who reward us and dislike those who punish us (Blau, 1964; Molm, 1991; Lawler and Yoon, 1993). Many of our acts derive from our confidence that from them will flow some benefit—perhaps a desired expression of love, gratitude, recognition, security, or material reward. In the course of interacting with one another, we reinforce the relationship by rewarding each other. Thus people with similar social traits, attitudes, and values are mutually rewarded by validating one another's lifestyle and supporting it at very low cost. In selecting partners of comparable physical attractiveness, we minimize the risk of rejection while maximizing the profit from such a conquest. And the parties in complementary relationships offer each other high rewards at low cost to themselves. In sum, exchange theory proposes that people involved in a mutually satisfying relationship will exchange behaviors that have low cost and high reward.

MARRIED COUPLES

Most adult Americans hope to establish an intimate relationship with another person and make the relationship work. This finding underlies a study of American couples undertaken by sociologists Philip Blumstein and Pepper Schwartz (1983). They investigated the experiences of four types of couples: married, cohabiting, homosexual male, and lesbian. The study centered on New York City, Seattle, and San Francisco, where the researchers secured 12,000 completed questionnaires. From these, Blumstein and Schwartz selected 300 couples for in-depth interviews. Eighteen months later, they sent half the couples a follow-up questionnaire to determine if they were still living together. As with most volunteer samples, the survey was not wholly representative, since it was weighted toward white, affluent, well-educated Americans. The researchers believe that any bias is toward the liberal side and that the nation is probably even more conservative in its family patterns than their results show.

Blumstein and Schwartz had expected American couples to be less conventional than they were. Take work. Although 60 percent of the wives were employed outside the home, only 30 percent of the men and 39 percent of the women believed that both spouses should work. Even when the wives had full-time jobs, they did the greater part of the housework. Whereas 59 percent of the women contributed eleven or more hours a week to household chores, only 22 percent of the men contributed this amount of time. Indeed, husbands so objected to doing housework that the more they did of it, the more unhappy they were, the more they argued with their wives, and the greater were the chances the couple would divorce. In contrast, if a man did not contribute what a woman felt to be his fair share of the housework, the relationship was not usually jeopardized.

American men seem preoccupied with dominance and power. In fact, they could take pleasure in their partner's success only if it was not superior to their own. In contrast, women were found to be happier and relationships were more stable when the male partners were ambitious and successful. Most married couples pooled their money. However, regardless of how much the wife earned, they measured their financial success by only the husband's income.

Most of the married couples had sexual relations at least once a week. People who had sex infrequently were just as likely to have a long-lasting relationship as those who had sex often. While couples were happier when the opportunity to initiate and refuse sex was shared equally by the partners, in more than half of the cases the husbands were still the primary initiators. But whereas the women tended to link sex and love, men often did not. Less than a third of the couples engaged in extramarital activities. Husbands were more often repeatedly unfaithful than wives, but their transgressions did not necessarily represent dissatisfaction with either their partner or the relationship as a whole. Women, in contrast, often strayed just once, mostly out of curiosity; but for them, infidelity was more likely to blossom into a full-fledged love affair.

Early in the marriage men were more likely than women to feel encroached upon by the relationship and to complain that they needed more "private time." But in long-standing marriages, it was the wives who more often complained that they did not have enough time by themselves. Further, women were more likely than men to say they were the emotional caretakers of the family, although 39 percent of the men indicated that they focused more on their marriage than they did on their work. In about a quarter of the marriages, both partners claimed they were relationship-centered.

Like Blumstein and Schwartz, Theodore Caplow and his colleagues (1982) expected to find the American nuclear family in trouble when they undertook a restudy of "Middletown," a pseudonym for Muncie, Indiana. Robert S. and Helen Merrill Lynd (1929, 1937) had made Middletown into a leading sociological laboratory in their celebrated 1920s study. Sociologists generally agree that the Lynds' research represents one of the best large-scale uses of anthropological methods in the study of an American community. The Lynds portrayed Middletown as a small city whose residents were straining to enter the twentieth century but who nevertheless clung to a nineteenth-century faith in the value of work, church, family, and country.

On the surface, much seems to have changed in Middletown in the intervening 50 years. High school students wear blue jeans and T-shirts to classes; mothers leave their children at day-care centers and take jobs; there is bloodshed on television and graphic sex in the movies; and some junior high school girls visit the Planned Parenthood center to get their birth control pills. But Caplow and his associates conclude that the doomsayers are wrong and that the family has not lost its attractiveness. They observe (1982:323):

Tracing the changes from the 1920s to the 1970s, we discovered increased family solidarity, a smaller generation gap, closer marital communication, more religion, and less mobility. With respect to the major features of family life, the trend of the past two generations has run in the opposite direction from the trend nearly everyone perceives and talks about.

They say their findings were as surprising to them "as they may be to our readers." Other researchers have come to essentially similar conclusions (Whyte, 1990).

Although divorce rates have soared, the research described and other studies reveal that Americans have not given up on marriage. Public opinion surveys confirm that Americans depend very heavily on marriage for their psychological well-being (Glenn and Weaver, 1981). Moreover, one of the most consistent findings in health research is that married people typically enjoy better health than the nonmarried (Kitson and Morgan, 1990; Sherbourne and Hays, 1990; Zick and Smith, 1991; Wandycz, 1993).

Table 9.2 MOST AMERICANS MARRY BY AGE 65: BUT NEVER-MARRIEDS ARE INCREASING*

| | *1992* | | | | *2010* | | | |
	Total	*Never married (%)*	*Married, spouse present (%)*	*Other[†] (%)*	*Total*	*Never married (%)*	*Married, spouse present (%)*	*Other[†] (%)*
Men								
15 and older	93,760	30.2	57.1	12.7	117,134	32.1	54.0	13.9
15 to 24	17,180	89.4	9.1	1.5	22,219	92.8	6.1	1.1
25 to 34	21,125	38.6	51.8	9.6	19,654	50.3	41.5	8.1
35 to 44	19,506	14.1	70.1	15.8	19,805	18.0	64.3	17.8
45 to 54	13,114	7.3	75.9	16.8	21,741	8.8	72.7	18.5
55 to 64	10,036	5.6	79.0	15.4	17,129	5.3	77.6	17.1
65 and older	12,800	4.2	73.8	22.0	16,586	4.1	71.7	24.2
Women								
15 and older	101,483	23.0	52.7	24.2	125,209	25.2	50.5	24.3
15 to 24	17,235	79.6	16.9	3.4	21,663	85.9	11.8	2.3
25 to 34	21,368	25.6	59.4	15.0	20,300	33.1	54.1	12.8
35 to 44	20,065	10.6	69.0	20.4	20,552	14.9	65.7	19.3
45 to 54	13,910	5.3	69.0	25.7	22,722	6.4	67.8	25.8
55 to 64	11,114	4.0	66.3	29.7	18,539	3.7	66.1	30.3
65 and older	17,790	4.9	39.8	55.3	21,433	4.7	39.7	55.5

*Number in thousands and percentage distribution of civilian noninstitutionalized population aged 15 and older by marital status, sex, and age, 1992 and 2010.
[†]Includes married, spouse absent; divorced; and widowed.
SOURCE: Census Bureau and *American Demographics* projections. Adapted from *American Demographics*, June 1994, p. 59.

As Table 9.2 shows, most people try marriage by age 65 (less than 5 percent of Americans never marry). However, American men and women are marrying later than they have in recent history. The median age of first marriage for U.S. men rose to 26.5 years in 1992 from a low of 22.6 years in the mid-1950s (the previous peak in median age had been 26.1 years in 1890, the first year the information was gathered). For American women the figure rose to 24.4 years in 1992, up from a low of 20.2 years, also in the mid-1950s (in 1890, half of all women were married by the age of 22). Although people are postponing marriage, by their early forties, 91 percent of men and 92 percent of women have been married at least once.

Additionally, increasing numbers of Americans no longer view marriage as a permanent institution but rather as something that can be ended and reentered. The proportion of men who are divorced and have not remarried peaks at 12 percent in the 40- to 44-year age group. For women, the peak is 16 percent, in the 45- to 54-year range.

PARENTHOOD

Nuclear families that are not disrupted by divorce, desertion, or death typically pass through a series of changes and realignments across time, what sociologists call the **family life cycle** (Hill, 1964; Copeland and White, 1991; White, 1991). These changes and realignments are related to the altered expectations and requirements imposed on a husband and wife as children are born and grow up. The family begins with the husband-wife pair and becomes increasingly complex as members are added, creating new roles and multiplying the number of relationships. The family then stabilizes for a time, after which it begins shrinking as each of the adult children is launched. Finally, it returns once more to the husband-wife pair, and eventually terminates with the death of a spouse. Of course, many individual and family behaviors do not occur at the usual ages or in the typical sequence assumed by the family life cycle model. At times decisive economic, social, political, or military events intervene to alter the normal course of events (Elder, 1983).

Each modification in the role content of one family member has implications for all the other members. The arrival of the first child compels the reorganization of a couple's life since living as a trio is more complicated than living as a pair. Parents have to juggle their work roles, alter their time schedules, change their communication patterns, and relinquish some privacy. And parenthood competes with the husband or wife role. Women with a first child are more likely than childless women to report that their husbands are not paying enough attention to them (Ryder, 1973). Moreover, marital adjustment ratings typically fall after the birth of a first child (Belsky and Rovine, 1990). Overall, it seems that although their initial encounter with parenthood may be stressful, most couples do not find it sufficiently stressful to warrant calling the experience a crisis (McLaughlin and Micklin, 1983; Ruble et al., 1988). Contemporary parents appear to have a less romantic and more realistic view of the probable effects of children on their lives than did earlier generations of parents. And despite the changes a child brings to their lives, most couples report enormous satisfaction with parenthood.

As a couple have additional offspring, their children are also affected. An only child, an oldest child, a middle child, and a youngest child all experience a somewhat different world because of the different social webs that encompass their lives. For instance, research suggests that first-born children are fortune's favorites (Cicirelli, 1978). First-borns are overrepresented in college populations, at the higher IQ levels, among National Merit and Rhodes scholars, in *Who's Who in America*, among American presidents (52 percent), among men and women in Congress, and in the astronaut corps. One explanation is that the first-born plays a parent surrogate role in dealing with later-born siblings. The eldest child functions as a sort of intermediary between later-borns and the parents, encouraging the development of the older child's verbal, cognitive, and leadership skills. Later children tend to be more relaxed and gregarious and less inhibited than the eldest child because parents are typically more relaxed in their parenting than they are with first-borns (Brooks, 1984). Another explanation—the **resource dilution hypothesis**—says that in large families resources get spread thin, to the detriment of all the offspring. Family resources include such things as parental time and encouragement, economic and material goods, and various cultural and social opportunities (music and dance lessons and travel at home and abroad). Sociologists frequently employ the resource dilution hypothesis to explain the relationship they find between the number of siblings and educational attainment: Increases in the number of siblings are associated with the completion of fewer years of schooling and the attainment of fewer educational milestones (positions in student government, on the school newspaper, in drama groups, and so on). In brief, families with few children can offer greater educational advantages to their offspring than can families with large numbers of children (Blake, 1989).

Clinical psychologists and psychiatrists have stressed the problem parents face when their children leave home. Dissatisfaction is most common among couples who had used their children's presence to disguise the emptiness of their own relationship. But most couples do not experience difficulty with the "empty-nest" period; the majority view this stage as a time of "new freedoms." Indeed, national surveys show that middle-aged women whose children have left home experience greater general happiness and enjoyment of life, in addition to greater marital happiness, than middle-aged women with children still living at home (White and Edwards, 1990; Vander Zanden, 1993).

EMPLOYED MOTHERS

As we pointed out in Chapter 7, sexual inequality has been sustained historically by assigning the economic provider role to men and the childrearing role to women. However, over the past several decades, increasing numbers of mothers with children have found employment outside the home. More than half of all mothers with children under 6 years of age are now in the work force. In 1950, only one in eight were working. Fifty-one percent of married women whose youngest child has not yet reached its first birthday are currently at work, twice the proportion in 1970. Figure 9.2 provides data on working mothers.

Serious concern is frequently voiced about the future of the nation's children as more and more mothers enter the work force. Many people fear that the working mother represents a loss to children in terms of supervision, love, and cognitive enrichment. Research findings are contradictory regarding the effects of maternal employment during a child's first year, with some studies reporting negative cognitive and social outcomes (Baydar and Brooks-Gunn, 1991) and others finding only minimal negative outcomes (Parcel and Menaghan, 1994). For older youngsters, however, an accumulating body of research suggests that there is little difference in the development of children whose mothers work and that of children whose mothers remain at home (Hoffman, 1989; Scarr, Phillips, and McCartney, 1989; Hofferth and Phillips, 1991). In fact, many psychologists and sociologists are no longer asking whether it is good or bad that mothers work. Instead, they are finding that a more important issue is whether the mother, regardless of employment, is satisfied in her situation (Hoffman, 1989; Hock and DeMeis,

1990; MacEwen and Barling, 1991). The working mother who gets personal satisfaction from employment, who does not feel excessive guilt, and who has adequate household arrangements is likely to perform as well as or better than the nonworking mother. Women who are not working and would like to, and working mothers whose lives are beset by harassment and strain, are the ones whose children are most likely to display maladjustment and behavior problems. Overall, much depends on the family's socioeconomic circumstances, the father's role, the attitudes of other family members, and the availability of support systems ranging from child-care facilities to helpful friends and relatives. Yet we would do well to remind ourselves that women are unlikely to achieve equality and peace of mind in the workplace until fathers also bear an equal burden for childrearing and care. So long as the matter remains strictly a "women's issue," we will be constrained by inherently imperfect alternatives.

With the entry of women into the labor force, arrangements for child care are shifting from care in the home to care outside the home. According to a 1990 Census Bureau study, American families spend an estimated $15.5 billion annually on child care. Families in which the employed mother lives in poverty spend about 25 percent of their income for child-care services; better-off families pay about 6 percent of their family income on child care. Of those working mothers who use child-care arrangements for their children under age 5, 29.9 percent make provision for care in their own home, another 35.6 percent secure care in someone else's home, 24.4 percent use organized child-care facilities, and 8.9 percent of the mothers care for the child at work (Trost, 1990). Additionally, no one knows how many American children function as guardians for younger brothers and sisters while their parents are at work. Estimates of the number of latchkey youngsters range from 2 to 15 million (or from 7 to 45 percent of all elementary school children). A 1990 national survey by the U.S. Department of Education found that 44 percent of 5- to 12-year-

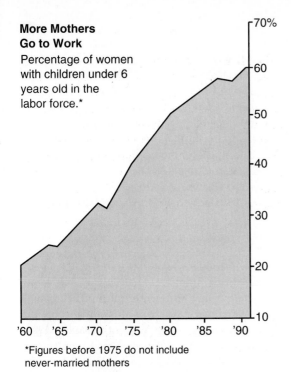

More Mothers Go to Work

Percentage of women with children under 6 years old in the labor force.*

*Figures before 1975 do not include never-married mothers

Mothers of Infants: Who Works?
Women who had a child in the last year and their percentage in the labor force by marital status and education, as of June 1990.

Married, husband present	56.6%
Widowed, divorced or separated	50.5%
Never-married	40.2%

College, 4 or more years	68.0%
College, 1 to 3 years	62.8%
High school, 4 years	52.0%
Less than high school	30.0%

Figure 9.2   MOTHERS WHO WORK
More and more American mothers are entering the paid labor force. (SOURCE: Bureau of Labor Statistics and the U.S. Census Bureau. Adapted from *The New York Times,* October 4, 1992, p. 18. Copyright © 1992 by The New York Times Company. Reprinted by permission.)

olds whose mothers were employed were left home alone without adult care (Creighton, 1993).

For significant portions of the day or night, many working parents are unable to care personally for their children, and they lack relatives or friends to whom they can turn for reliable babysitting. One answer to this problem is day care. But the quality of the day care currently available and affordable leaves many people dissatisfied (child-care workers rank among the lowest 10 percent of wage earners in the United States). Ralph Nader, the consumer activist, describes some centers as "children's warehouses." And sex-abuse scandals at centers from California to New York have terrified a good many parents. Additionally, low-quality facilities are more likely to spread a variety of diseases, especially colds, diarrhea, and dysentery.

The United States is one of the few industrialized nations that does not have a comprehensive day-care program. European nations—particularly Sweden—have established nationally subsidized support systems. Only 2 percent of U.S. business and government employers sponsor day-care centers for their workers' children. Child-care advocates warn that failure to develop a national policy toward child care will result in "a generation of neglected children." Unfortunately, much of the day care currently available to North American parents is of poor quality. Researchers find that in centers where group size is large, the ratio of caretakers to children is low, and the staff is untrained or poorly supervised, a child's well-being is compromised (Belsky, 1990).

There is, however, one encouraging note. Most child psychologists agree that high-quality day care and preschools provide acceptable child-care arrangements (Kagan, Kearsley, and Zelazo, 1978; MacKinnon and King, 1988; Field, 1991). Such programs are characterized by small group size, high staff-child ratios, well-trained staffs, good equipment, and attractive and nurturing environments. Most children show remarkable resilience. Throughout the world, children are raised under a great variety of conditions, and the day-care arrangement is just one of them. The effects of day care depend to some extent on the amount of time a child spends at a center and on the quality of parent-child interaction during the time the family is together (Stith and Davis, 1984). Moreover, working mothers provide a somewhat different role model for their children that is associated with less traditional gender-role concepts and a higher evaluation of female competence (Hoffman, 1989; Debold, Wilson, and Malave, 1993).

TWO-INCOME FAMILIES

Nearly 34 million working wives in the United States bring home 31 percent of the family income (women who work full-time bring home more than twice the share of family income that part-timers do, at 38 percent) (Krafft, 1994). Although more than 65 percent of American married couples are dual-earner pairs, women still continue to shoulder the primary responsibility for household tasks and child care (two-thirds of dual-earning couples have children at home). Mothers are more likely than fathers to take time off if children are sick or if problems with child care arise. For the most part, American couples still see career as "more" primary for husbands, and family as "more important" for wives (the prevailing ideology continues to define men primarily as breadwinners and women as homemakers) (Silberstein, 1992). Although most women benefit from their participation in the paid labor force, they bear the primary costs of carrying a double workload (Lewis, Izraeli, and Hootsmans, 1992). The result is that overwhelming numbers of working women report they do not have enough time to meet their home and work responsibilities (General Mills, 1981). When women are expected to contribute more than men to the household division of labor, they may be less effective on the job than they otherwise might be and they may not realize their true career potential. Alternatively, they may fall victim to the "superwoman" syndrome and attempt to excel both on the job and at home.

In two-income families, the man typically has a larger voice in major household decisions than the woman does. Junior-senior relationships commonly operate, with the wife usually secondary. For instance, should a husband be offered a better position in another area of the country, the wife typically makes the move regardless of the effect the transfer will have on her career (Bielby and Bielby, 1992). According to the Employee Relocation Council, women accounted for about 18 percent of corporate moves in 1992, up from 5 percent in 1980. By the year 2000, some experts predict that a third of transferees will be female, and one in four trailing spouses will be men (up from 15 percent in 1990 and about 7 percent in 1985) (Lublin, 1993). Moreover, some wives fear that should they take over responsibility for their own finances, their husbands will feel that their masculinity is threatened. However, if they relinquish control of their income to the husband, they often experience resentment and bitterness. Consequently, many couples maintain separate accounts or pool only a portion of their incomes.

Scheduling time together is a frequent source of tension for dual-career couples (Moore, 1984; Kingston and Nock, 1987). But the conflict often masks problems of commitment, lack of intimacy, and divergent goals. Arguments over work schedules usually have more to do with "how much does he or she care" than with the amount of time the couple actually spends together. Another source of tension derives from income differences. In nearly one-fifth of dual-career couples, the wife earns more than the husband. Men often feel their self-esteem threatened in this situation, and such couples run a high risk of psychological and physical abuse, marital conflict, and sexual problems (Kessler and McRae, 1981; Rubenstein, 1982; Hays, 1987). Yet the difficulties are not insurmountable, provided couples can come to terms with old expectations and new realities and learn what works best for them. Women are growing more confident of their knowledge and abilities, while increasing numbers of men are learning to share family responsibility and power. The dynamics of family decision-making are currently in transition as many dual-income couples evolve new patterns and traditions for family living (Guelzow, Bird, and Koball, 1991; Vannoy and Philliber, 1992).

FAMILY VIOLENCE, CHILD ABUSE, AND INCEST

Mounting evidence suggests that family violence, child abuse, and incest are much more common than most Americans had suspected. The expression "coming out of the closet" is an apt one when applied to battered women and victims of child abuse and sexual molestation. They have been as reluctant to reveal their plight as gay persons have been to reveal their sexual preferences. Traditionally, they have attempted to keep the indignities they have experienced locked inside the family home.

Estimates of family violence vary widely. Estimates based on probability samples suggest that minimally from 2 to 3 million American women are assaulted by male partners each year (Browne, 1993). A representative 1985 survey of couples found that nearly one-eighth of the husbands had carried out one or more acts of physical aggression against their wives during the preceding 12 months (Straus and Gelles, 1990). And the Centers for Disease Control and Prevention estimate that at least 6 percent of pregnant women are battered by their spouses or partners (Hilts, 1994). At least one in ten married women have experienced marital rape (Gelles and Cornell, 1985; Straus and Gelles, 1986, 1989). Although both men and women engage in violence, men typically do more damage than their female partners (Walker, 1989; Alexander, Moore, and Alexander, 1991). Some men find it easier to control the weaker members of the family by force because it does not require negotiation or interpersonal skills. Women put up with battering for a variety of reasons (Strube and Barbour, 1983; Simons, Johnson, Beaman, and Conger, 1993). For one thing, the fewer the resources a wife has in the way of education or job skills, the more vulnerable she is in the marriage. For another, Americans place the burden of family harmony on women, with the implication that they have failed if the marriage disintegrates. Moreover, many women become "entrapped" in abusive relationships, a process whereby they escalate their commitment to a previously chosen but failing course of action in order to justify or "make good" on their prior investments (the women come to believe that they have "too much invested to quit") (Strube, 1988). Finally, the more a wife was abused by her parents and witnessed violence in her childhood home, the more likely she is to remain with an abusive husband.

Children also suffer abuse and neglect. One need spend only an hour or so in a supermarket or a shopping mall to observe instances of children being physically or verbally abused. Such public behavior is but the tip of the iceberg (a 1994 USA Today/CNN/Gallup Poll found that 67 percent of American adults agree that "a good, hard spanking" is sometimes necessary in discipling a child, down from 84 percent in 1986). Neglect of children is a closely related problem. The recent epidemic of cocaine and crack use has contributed to a substantial increase in the incidence of child abuse and neglect, placing growing demands on the child-welfare system. A great many factors are related to abuse and violence. Researchers find that social stress, including the loss of a job or divorce, is associated with the maltreatment of children (Steinberg, Catalano, and Dooley, 1981; Fiala and LaFree, 1988). Moreover, families that are socially isolated and outside neighborhood support networks are more at risk for child abuse than families with rich social ties (Garbarino and Sherman, 1980; Trickett and Susman, 1988). Additionally, abusive parents are themselves likely to have been abused when they were children (Widom, 1989a,b; Dodge, Bates, and Pettit, 1990; Simons et al., 1991).

Although incest has been called the last taboo, its status as a taboo has not kept it from taking place but merely from being talked about. Indeed,

most people find it so offensive that parents may be sexually attracted to their children they prefer not to think about it. Probably the best available figures on sexual abuse come from a national survey of more than 2,000 adults undertaken in 1985 for the Los Angeles Times by psychologist David Finkelhor and his colleagues. They found that 27 percent of the women and 16 percent of the men disclosed a history of some sort of sexual abuse during their childhood (Darnton, 1991). The perpetrator is commonly the father, uncle, or other male authority figure in the household. In cases of father-daughter incest, the fathers are typically "family tyrants" who employ physical force and intimidation to control their families (Finkelhor, 1979; Herman and Hirschman, 1981). The mothers in incestuous families are commonly passive, have a poor self-image, and are overly dependent on their husbands, much the same traits found among battered wives. The victims of molestation are usually shamed or terrified into treating the experience as a dirty secret. The sexual abuse of children often leads to behavior problems, learning difficulties, sexual promiscuity, runaway behavior, drug and alcohol abuse, gastrointestinal and genitourinary complaints, compulsive rituals, clinical depression, low self-esteem, and suicidal behavior. Victimized women tend to show lifetime patterns of psychological shame and stigmatization (Kendall-Tackett, Williams, and Finkelhor, 1993; Malinosky-Rummell and Hansen, 1993).

Over the past decade, the problems of family violence, child abuse, and incest have emerged as major issues. Even so, considerable ambivalence still exists on these subjects. Much needs to be done to assist the victims. Social service agencies need to be restructured so that battered family members can find real help. Remedial laws need to be enacted. Some—but not all—researchers find that the arrest of offenders is the most effective means for preventing new incidents of wife battery (Berk and Newton, 1985; Sherman et al., 1992). Perhaps of even greater importance, a cultural revolution of attitudes and values is required to eradicate the abuse of women and children (Gelles, Straus, and Harrop, 1988; Buzawa and Buzawa, 1990).

DIVORCE

Although divorce rates have been on the upswing in recent decades, they stabilized and even slowly declined in the 1980s as Americans became more conservative and more realistic in their marital expectations. Decades ago, when today's elderly were establishing families, divorce was relatively infrequent. In 1980, only 15 percent of Americans aged 65 to 74 reported that their first marriage had ended in divorce. By contrast, roughly half of those aged 25 to 35 in 1980 had either ended their first marriage in divorce or expected to do so before they reached age 75 (Glick, 1984). Yet rising divorce rates tell us little about the level of marital satisfaction or even stability. Changes in official divorce statistics do not inform us about unofficial separation or the proverbial poor family's divorce—desertion. Moreover, the current rate of marital breakup through divorce is approaching the level of marital breakup through death in earlier centuries. Indeed, by adding desertion to death, a greater proportion of middle-aged couples in the nineteenth century suffered marital dissolution than do their contemporary counterparts (Skolnick, 1981; Riley, 1991).

With the number of divorced people in the population having increased over the past 20 years and young people delaying the formation of new unions, the number of divorced people per 1,000 married people has tripled in the past two decades; there are now 142 divorced people for every 1,000 married people. More than half of the couples who divorce have children. Researchers find that the households of divorced mothers and fathers are substantially more disorganized than those of intact families, with the children more likely to evidence behavioral and academic problems (Amato and Keith, 1991; Mulkey, Crain, and Harrington, 1992; Amato, 1993). The first 2 years after a divorce are especially difficult. Divorced

THE WALL STREET JOURNAL

"Full disclosure laws require me to inform you that you have a 40% chance of divorce within five years."

From *The Wall Street Journal*—Permission, Cartoon Features Syndicate.

parents do not communicate as well with their children, are less affectionate, and are more inconsistent discipliners than are parents in intact families (Wallerstein and Blakeslee, 1989). Divorced mothers with teenage sons find their situation particularly stressful, in part because they have greater difficulty establishing control and authority (Hetherington, 1989). Financial problems complicate the difficulties of many women. Only half of divorced mothers receive any money at all from their children's fathers, and this is seldom much. Moreover, divorce is not the end of family changes but often the beginning. As we will note shortly in our discussion of stepfamilies, most divorced parents remarry, and since the rate of divorce among remarriages is greater than among first marriages, many children experience complex family lives (Furstenberg and Cherlin, 1991).

The notion that divorce has adverse consequences for children influences many couples to remain unhappily married until their youngsters reach adulthood. However, a mounting body of evidence suggests that staying together for the sake of the children is not necessarily helpful if the marriage is marred by conflict, tension, and discord. Many of the emotional, behavioral, and academic problems children exhibit after their parents divorce are apparent before the time of the actual breakup of the family. The difficulties appear to be more a product of stressful marriages than of divorce itself (Cherlin et al., 1991; Furstenberg and Cherlin, 1991; Cherlin, 1992).

Although divorce may be more commonplace today, it is no more a routine experience for adults than it is for children. In many cases, divorce exacts a greater emotional and physical toll than almost any other type of stress, including widowhood (Kitson and Holmes, 1992). Separated and divorced people are overrepresented in mental institutions; more likely to die from cardiovascular disease, cancer, pneumonia, and cirrhosis of the liver; and more prone to die from accidents, homicides, and suicides. Middle-aged and elderly women are especially devastated by divorce. These women—called *displaced homemakers*—have often dedicated themselves to managing a home and raising children and then find themselves jettisoned after years of marriage. Within the United States, some 100,000 people over the age of 55 divorce each year. Many of the women find themselves ill-equipped to deal with the financial consequences. Frequently they have not worked outside their homes since they were married some forty or more years earlier. And the women are cut off from their ex-husbands' private pension and medical insurance plans.

Most divorced people remarry. About five of every six divorced men and three of every four divorced women marry again. Divorced men are more likely to remarry than women. For one thing, divorced men are more likely to marry someone not previously married. For another, because men usually marry younger women, divorced men have a larger pool of potential partners to choose from. Should the divorced remarry, they are more likely to divorce again than are individuals in first marriages. If current projections hold, about 61 percent of men and 54 percent of women in their thirties who remarry will undergo a second divorce. It seems that individuals drag into the new marriage many of the insecurities and personality problems that disrupted the pre-

vious one. And with one divorce under their belt, they are less hesitant about securing a second one should trouble appear.

STEPFAMILIES

Remarriage frequently results in stepfamilies (also termed "reconstituted" and "blended" families). Because more than half of remarried persons are parents, for better or worse, their new partners become stepparents. So remarriage means having to accommodate "strangers in the home" (Beer, 1989). One in six American families are stepfamilies; 35 million Americans live in one, including 20 percent of the nation's children under age 18 (about 40 percent of remarriages unite two divorced persons; half of them are a first marriage for one member of the couple; and in 11 percent of remarriages, one or both members of the couple have been widowed).

Most stepparents attempt to re-create a traditional family because it is the only model they have. But a stepfamily functions differently than the traditional nuclear family (Pill, 1990; Larson, 1992). For one thing, the stepparent role does not necessarily approximate that of a biological parent, particularly in authority, legitimacy, and respect. For another, the family tree of a stepfamily can be very complex and convoluted, populated not only by children of both spouses but by six sets of grandparents, relatives of former spouses, relatives of new spouses, and the people former spouses marry. The more complex the social system of the remarriage, the greater the ambiguity about roles within the family and the greater the likelihood of difficulties (Clingempeel, 1981). Matters are further complicated because stepparents and stepchildren do not have a mutual history or have not had a previous opportunity to bond.

Stepfamilies often start on a highly idealistic note. But as the months go by, their outlook on the family changes, and individuals gain a more realistic view. Misunderstandings in stepfamilies take many forms. Most often, they are caused by conflicting family traditions, unfulfilled expectations, financial pressures, loyalty conflicts, unresolved power struggles, and ill-defined behavior standards for the children. Discipline is a frequent problem because children often see the stepparent as an intruder. Society also lacks a clear picture of how members should relate to one another; for instance, how should a son relate to his stepparent, and vice versa, and how should the custodial stepparent relate to the former spouse?

Most resident stepparents are stepfathers (nine out of ten stepchildren live with their biological mothers and stepfathers). Stepfathers usually underrate their parenting skills and their contributions to the lives of their stepchildren. Indeed, their stepchildren and spouses give them higher marks than they give themselves (Bohannan and Erickson, 1978). Children living with stepfathers apparently do just as well, or just as poorly, in school and in their social lives as children living with natural fathers. And children with stepfathers on the whole do better than children from father-absent homes (Beer, 1988; Fine and Kurdek, 1992).

The stepfamily must adjust to many types of challenges not encountered by most natural families. In order to succeed, the stepfamily must loosen the boundaries that encapsulated the two previous biological families and structure a new social unit (Whiteside, 1989; Coleman and Ganong, 1990). As old arrangements "unfreeze," members must evolve a oneness that allows the new family to act together for common ends. Most workable solutions leave some of the "old" ways of doing things intact while fashioning new rituals, expectations, and rules. When the restructuring is successful, the members no longer need to give constant attention to relationships and can relate to one another spontaneously and comfortably.

CARE FOR THE ELDERLY

Despite the significant changes that have occurred in family roles in recent decades, it is grown children who still bear the primary responsibility for their aged parents. The sense of obligation is strong even when the emotional ties between the parent and child are weak (Baumann, 1991; Whitbeck, Hoyt, and Huck, 1994). In 80 percent of the cases, any care an elderly person requires is provided by his or her family. This assistance supplements what the elderly receive from savings, pensions, Social Security, Medicare, and Medicaid. Additionally, a survey sponsored by the National Center for Health Statistics found that some 85 percent of Americans aged 80 and older saw or spoke to their children two to seven times a week; only 3 percent spoke to or saw their children just a few times a year (Kolata, 1993).

Some 52 percent of Americans between the ages of 53 and 61 and 44 percent of those between the ages of 58 and 66 have at least one living parent. Social scientists call middle-aged adults the *sandwich generation* because they find themselves with responsibilities for their own teenage and college-age children and for their elderly parents. Care for the elderly falls most often on daughters and daughters-in-law. These women have historically functioned as our society's "kin-keepers" (Brody, 1990; Brody et al., 1994). Despite the changing roles of women, when it comes to the elderly, the old maxim still applies: "A son's a son till he takes a wife, but a daughter's a daughter for the rest of her life." Indeed, daughters are three times more likely to provide parental care than are sons (Dwyer and Coward, 1991). Yet 61 percent of the women also work (although the average care giver is 45 years old, female, and married, 35 percent of caregivers to the elderly are themselves older than 65 years of age, and 10 percent are older than 75). Although being employed substantially reduces the hours of assistance that sons provide their elderly parents, it does not have an appreciable effect on the amount of time provided by daughters (Stoller, 1983). Not surprisingly, women of the sandwich generation are subjected to role overload stresses that are often compounded by their own age-related problems, including lower energy levels, the onset of chronic ailments, and family losses (Brody, 1990; Schulz, Visintainer, and Williamson, 1990). The women must juggle competing role demands of employed worker, homemaker, wife, mother, grandmother, and caregiving daughter. Indeed, caring for a dependent adult has become for many women a second full-time job (Spitze and Logan, 1990; Stoller and Pugliesi, 1990).

The motivations, expectations, and aspirations of the middle-aged and the elderly at times differ because of their different positions in the life cycle. Intergenerational strain is usually less where financial independence allows each generation to maintain separate residences. Both the elderly and their adult offspring seem to prefer intimacy "at a distance" and opt for independent households as long as possible. Adult day-care centers, which provide supervision in a group setting for aged or disabled people living at home, have multiplied tenfold in the past decade to 3,000, and the trend is accelerating (Shellenbarger, 1994). Elderly parents who call upon their children for assistance are more likely to be frail, severely disabled, gravely ill, or failing mentally. When middle-aged adults fail to take responsibility for an ailing parent, it may reflect not "hardheartedness" but a realization that the situation is more stressful than they can cope with. But to do so commonly produces strong feelings of guilt (Dressel and Clark, 1990).

☐ Alternative Lifestyles

Despite popular perceptions that the American family is a dying institution, the evidence we have reviewed in this chapter suggests that the family tree is as deeply rooted as ever in the social landscape. It is, however, sprouting varied branches. Family relationships are becoming more tangled as a result of people living longer and occasionally changing mates to suit the seasons of their lives. Increasing numbers of children are growing up with several sets of parents and an assortment of half brothers and sisters and stepbrothers and -sisters. Simultaneously, by virtue of the rapid expansion in lifestyle options, Americans now enjoy more alternatives in tailoring their relationships to individual choice. A **lifestyle** is the overall pattern of living people evolve to meet their biological, social, and emotional needs. Let us examine a number of lifestyle options.

SINGLEHOOD

Despite our couples-oriented society, single-person households are outpacing the growth of most other household types. The number of Americans living alone has increased 90 percent since 1970, much faster than the 12 percent growth in married couples. By 1990, nearly 23 million Americans were living alone, so roughly one of every four occupied dwelling units had only one person in it. Yet singles are hardly a monolithic group, with the divorced (11.5 million), widowed (12.7 million), and never-married (45.7 million) constituting distinct groups of those aged 15 and older. The high incidence of divorce, the ability of the elderly to maintain their own homes alone, and the deferral of marriage among young adults have contributed to the high rate of increase in the number of nonfamily households. Additionally, more than half of young adults between 18 and 24 years of age are living with their parents (one in nine adults between 25 and 34 also live in a parent's home).

Figure 9.3 shows the percentage of men and women who live alone by age category. The percentage of young people 25 to 29 who have never married is more than double the 1970 rate. More liberal sex standards, the high divorce rate, money woes, and the pursuit of education and careers have spurred young adults to marry later than at any time since the Census Bureau started keeping track in 1890. Although many men and women have postponed marriage, recent changes suggest that a growing proportion of Americans will simply elect never to marry at all. Overall, rates of nonmarriage increase as education increases, par-

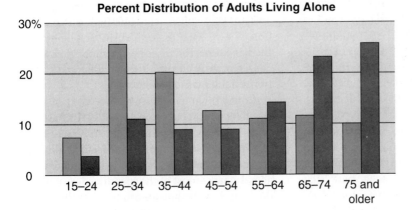

Percent Distribution of Adults Living Alone

■ Men ■ Women

Figure 9.3 LIVING ALONE, BY GENDER, 1990
Adult men are more likely than women to live alone, but women live longer than men.
(SOURCE: U.S. Bureau of the Census, *Current Population Reports,* Series P-20, No. 450.)

ticularly for women (in 1990, 25 percent of men and 17 percent of women age 30 to 34 had never married, nearly triple the 1970 rate). Even so, the population remaining single today is smaller than it was at the turn of the century, when fully 42 percent of all American adult men and 33 percent of adult women never married (Kain, 1984).

There are degrees of singleness. A person may be single, then choose to cohabit or marry, and perhaps decide later to divorce and become single again. Singlehood is a reclaimable status. As sociologist Roger W. Libby (1977:49–50) points out, singlehood as a lifestyle for younger Americans is quite varied:

Between the extreme images of the swinging and always elated single and the desperately lonely, suicidal single lies a continuum of single people with joys and sorrows similar to those of people electing other life-styles. . . . We are left, then, with the impression that singlehood (like marriage) is not a lifelong commitment for most people. Choices are usually replaced by new choices.

In recent years, the notion that people must marry if they are to achieve maximum happiness

and well-being has been increasingly questioned. A good many Americans no longer think of singlehood as a residual category for the unchosen and lonely. Overall, singles are benefiting from a decrease in the social stigma attached to flying solo. Indeed, singles have found that as their numbers have grown, a singles subculture is available to them in most metropolitan areas. They can move into a singles apartment, go to a singles bar, take a singles vacation, join a singles consciousness-raising group, and so on. And if they wish, they can lead an active sex life without acquiring an unwanted mate, child, or reputation. However, there has been a marked decrease in casual sex in the United States in recent years, in part a response to fears surrounding such diseases as acquired immune deficiency syndrome (AIDS).

UNMARRIED COHABITATION

The number of adults who share living quarters with an unrelated adult of the opposite sex has increased in recent decades (marriage is differentiated from other types of intimate relationships by its institutionalized status). Only 2 percent of American women born between 1928 and 1932 cohabited before marrying or attaining age 30; 40 percent of those born between 1958 and 1962 did so (Schoen and Weinick, 1993). Cohabiting before marriage has become quite prevalent, with some 58 percent of recently married couples having done so (Otten, 1988). The high proportion of married couples who live together prior to marriage suggests that premarital cohabitation may become institutionalized as a new step between dating and marriage. By the same token, however, the rise in cohabitation is associated with the decline in marriage (Bumpass, Sweet, and Cherlin, 1991). Changes in the economy, including the increase in the labor-force participation of women and the decline in the relative importance of the family in the transmission of power and wealth have contributed to the growing social acceptance of cohabitation (Parker, 1990).

Although the media often label cohabiters "unmarried marrieds" and their relationships "trial marriages," the couples typically do not see themselves this way. Nor does research support the notion that cohabitation before marriage is associated with later marital success. It seems that the "kinds of people" who choose to flout convention by cohabiting are the same kinds of people who flout traditional conventions regarding marital behavior, have a lower commitment to marriage as an institution, and are more likely to disregard the stigma of divorce (Glenn, 1990; DeMaris and Rao, 1992). College students commonly define cohabitation as part of the courtship process rather than as a long-term alternative to marriage. One study of students in the Boston area found cohabiting couples to be no less likely to marry, and no more likely to break up, than noncohabiting students who were "going together" (Risman et al., 1981). Although about a fourth to a third of students at major universities had cohabiting experiences in the mid-1970s

(Macklin, 1974, 1978), the pattern reversed in the 1980s. Many college students look on cohabitation as a restricting and demanding lifestyle. At the same time, there has been a shift toward more conservative values and stronger religious conviction among many students.

Couples living together but not married are far less liberated about money, sex, and housework than their nontraditional living arrangement might suggest. Like married men, cohabiting men are more likely to be the ones who initiate sexual activity, make most of the spending decisions, and do far less of the housework than do their working women partners (Blumstein and Schwartz, 1983; South and Spitze, 1994). Cohabiting couples experience many of the same sorts of problems as married couples (Gross, 1977). However, unmarried couples see themselves as less securely anchored than married couples and accordingly feel more tentative about their ability to endure difficult periods. The average cohabitation lasts only about 12 months; some are more a matter of convenience than anything else (cheaper rent and food) (Larson, 1991). Perhaps the insecurities associated with cohabitation contribute to the higher incidence of interpersonal violence among cohabiting couples (Yllo and Straus, 1981).

SINGLE PARENTHOOD

One American youngster in four lives with just one parent (see Figure 9.4). Of all such children, 86 percent live with their mothers. However, men raising children on their own have climbed from 10 percent of single parents in 1980 to nearly 15 percent in 1992 (some two-thirds of single fathers are divorced; roughly 25 percent are among the never-married; and only 7.5 percent are widowers). The largest share of youngsters in single-parent homes—38.6 percent—are living with a divorced parent, and 30.6 percent are living with a parent who has never married (others reside with a parent who is married but separated or are offspring of a widowed parent).

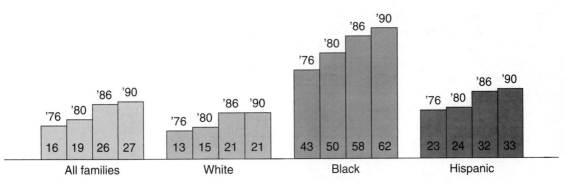

Figure 9.4   SINGLE-PARENT FAMILIES AS A PERCENTAGE OF FAMILIES
WITH CHILDREN, 1976–1990.
(SOURCE: U.S. Bureau of the Census.)

As we pointed out in Chapter 6, female-headed households are likely to be low-income households. In the case of divorce, marital separation frequently produces a precipitous and sustained decline in household income for the mother and child (in contrast, marital dissolution often leads to an improvement in the economic standard of living for men) (Holden and Smock, 1991). The reduction of income for divorced women and their dependent children is not compensated for by a corresponding reduction in expenditures for food, housing, and other items, and so the drop in living standards persists indefinitely. Unwed motherhood is also on the increase. According to the Census Bureau, nearly a quarter of the nation's unmarried women now become mothers, an increase of nearly 60 percent over the past decade (Bachu, 1993). See Figure 9.5. The increase has been especially steep among educated and professional women who are choosing to become mothers.

There is a critical difference between the married poor with children and the single-parent poor: On average the married poor move out of poverty; the single-parent poor do not (Weiss, 1984). The Census Bureau reports that in 1992 some 47 percent of the families headed by single mothers lived below the poverty level, as against 8.3 percent of the families headed by two parents.

About 18 percent of the families headed by a single father live in poverty.

Women heading a single-parent family typically experience greater stress than women in two-parent families (Fassinger, 1989; Simons, Beaman, Conger, and Chao, 1993). For one thing, lack of job training, loss of skills during the childbearing years, and discriminatory hiring and promotion patterns often mean that single mothers work for low wages. Female family heads report much lower self-esteem, a lower sense of effectiveness, and less optimism about the future than their counterparts in two-parent settings. Many single-parent mothers complain of a lack of free time, spiraling child-care costs, loneliness, and unrelenting pressures associated with the dual demands of home and job. Although many women do not choose single parenting, most are proud of their ability to survive under adverse circumstances (Richards, 1989).

Single fathers also encounter many of the same problems. Juggling work and child care poses a good deal of difficulty, especially for fathers with preschool youngsters. Many fathers first attempt to have someone come into their homes and care for the children there while they are at work. But the vast majority find that this arrangement does not work out. Many fathers then gravitate toward

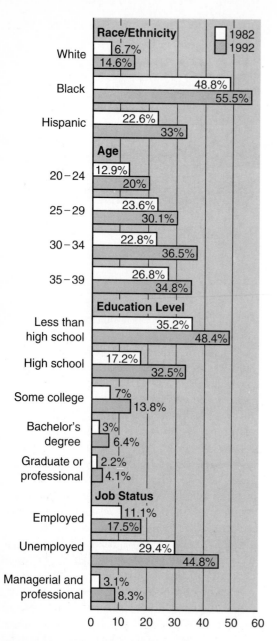

Figure 9.5 CHANGE SWEEPING AMERICAN FAMILY LIFE: SHARP INCREASE AMONG NEVER-MARRIED MOTHERS

Census Bureau data reveal a substantial rise in the percentages of never-married women, 18 to 44 years of age, who have children. The statistics challenge stereotypes that have tied out-of-wedlock births primarily to women who are poor and uneducated, although women in these categories still remain much more likely than other women to become single mothers. Among white women and women who attended college, the percentage who became mothers without marrying more than doubled. For women with managerial or professional jobs, it nearly tripled. (SOURCE: U.S. Department of Commerce and the Bureau of the Census as appeared in *Newsweek,* July 26, 1993, p. 53. © 1993, Newsweek, Inc. All rights reserved. Reprinted by permission.)

Drawing by Koren; © 1992 The New Yorker Magazine, Inc.

day-care centers and nursery schools where they feel that the staff has a professional commitment to children (Mendes, 1976). Once the children start elementary school, fathers usually allow them to stay alone after school. Many single fathers report that their greatest difficulty in making the transition to single parenthood is losing their wife's help and companionship; they say that it is more difficult for them to become single than to become a single parent (Smith and Smith, 1981). Overall, the single father is neither the extraordinary human being nor the bumbling "Mr. Mom" depicted in many popular stereotypes (Greif, 1985).

Many families headed by single parents survive their hardships with few ill effects—some even blossom as a result of the spirit of cooperation brought out by their difficulties. However, a dis-turbing number of children and their parents are saddled with problems. Some studies show that juvenile delinquency is twice as likely to occur in a single-parent home as in a two-parent home. Lack of parental supervision and persistent social and psychological strains are usually complicated by problems of poverty (Mann, 1983; Bank et al., 1993). Moreover, children living in single-parent families are much more likely to be enrolled below the grade that is modal for their age than children living with both parents (Bianchi, 1984). In sum, single parents are in need of a variety of services not currently available in most communities. These services include day-care facilities that are affordable and convenient to home or work, various forms of counseling, child-care enrichment, after-school programs, and parent education.

GAY AND LESBIAN COUPLES

Few people in the history of Western society have been more scorned, feared, and stigmatized than gays and lesbians.

Americans still evidence considerable ambiguity about where they stand on issues of gay rights. In 1993, a poll sponsored by *U.S. News & World Report* found that 65 percent of Americans say they want to ensure equal rights for gays (Shapiro, 1993). Yet at the same time, fully half opposed extending current civil rights laws to include the gay population (44 percent said that extending civil rights laws to homosexuals would end discrimination; 43 percent expressed concern that it would amount to endorsing the gay lifestyle). Most Americans still view homosexuality as a "lifestyle" choice rather than a matter of civil rights (46 percent believe that homosexuals choose to be gay or lesbian, and this group tends to oppose civil rights for gays; however, 32 percent believe that gays "are born that way"). It seems that a good many Americans do not want to appear bigoted, but at the same time they do not want to seem too tolerant either. Although gays and lesbians have won a number of important victories in their drive to prohibit discrimination on the basis of sexual orientation, many realms of equality still elude them and preclude their freedom in practicing an open homosexual lifestyle in all spheres of American life (Ingrassia, 1993; Shilts, 1993; Woods, 1993).

Homosexuality is a preference for an individual of the *same* sex as a sexual partner. Estimates vary from one survey to another on the proportion of the adult population that is predominantly homosexual in orientation. A 1948 Alfred C. Kinsey report estimated that 10 percent of white males were more or less exclusively gay. Most current estimates of the exclusively homosexual population range from 1 to 2 percent of adults (Barringer, 1993; Crispell, 1993b). However, since there are so many gradations in sexual behavior and preferences, many sociologists and psychologists take the view that there are heterosexual or homosexual *practices* but not homosexual *individuals* (Bell, Weinberg, and Hammersmith, 1981). In brief, "homosexuality" and "heterosexuality" are terms that describe behavior, not the identity of a person. A person with a gay or lesbian orientation may or may not elect to engage in homosexual behavior. Further, gays and lesbians are a varied group (Bell and Weinberg, 1978). They are found in all occupational fields, political persuasions, religious faiths, and racial and ethnic groups. Some are married, have children, and lead lives that in most respects are indistinguishable from those of the larger population. Others enter homosexual unions that are relatively durable.

Researchers at the Kinsey Institute (Bell and Weinberg, 1978:216) have concluded that "homosexual adults who have come to terms with their homosexuality, who do not regret their sexual orientation, and who can function effectively sexually and socially, are no more distressed psychologically than are heterosexual men and women." Their research shows that lesbians tend to form more lasting ties than do gays. However, whereas lesbian and heterosexual couples place considerable emphasis on fidelity, gay couples tolerate outside sexual relations quite well (Blumstein and Schwartz, 1983). About 90 percent of gays with established partners engage in sexual relations with other men. On the whole, the men define fidelity not in terms of sexual behavior but in terms of each individual's commitment to the other. Gays are more likely to break up over money issues and other incompatibilities than over sexual faithfulness. Compared to married couples, gay and lesbian couples are more likely to split up household tasks so that each partner performs an equal number of different tasks (however, lesbian couples tend to share more tasks, whereas gay couples are more likely to have one or the other partner perform the tasks) (Kurdek, 1993).

Summary

1. When we set about separating families from nonfamilies, we encounter all sorts of problems. The way in which we define the family is not simply an academic exercise. It determines the kinds of families we will consider to be normal and the kinds we consider to be deviant, and what rights and obligations we will recognize as legally and socially binding. For our purposes in the chapter, we view the family as a group of people the members of a community define as a household unit. Typically these individuals are related by blood, adoption, or marriage and cooperate economically. Viewed in this fashion, the family is an institution.

2. As we look about the world, and even in our own society, we encounter a good many differences in the ways families are organized. Families vary in composition and in descent, residence, and authority patterns. Social relationships between adult males and females can be organized within families by emphasizing either spouse or kin relationships. In the nuclear family arrangement, spouses and their offspring constitute the core relationship; blood relatives are functionally marginal and peripheral. In the extended family arrangement, kin provide the core relationship; spouses are functionally marginal and peripheral.

3. The fact that the parties to a marriage must be members of two different kin groups has crucial implications for the structuring of the family. The continuity, and therefore the long-term welfare, of any kin group depend on obtaining spouses for the unmarried members of the group from other groups. By the same token, a kin group has a stake in retaining some measure of control over at least a portion of its members after they marry. All societies regulate the pool of eligibles from which individuals are expected to select a mate. They also structure the relationship between a husband and wife in one of four ways: monogamy, polygyny, polyandry, and group marriage.

4. Functionalist theorists stress that if a society is to survive and operate with some measure of effectiveness, it must guarantee that essential tasks are performed. The performance of these tasks—or functions—cannot be left to chance. Although acknowledging that families show a good deal of variation throughout the world, functionalists identify a number of functions families typically perform: reproduction; socialization; care, protection, and emotional support; assignment of status; and regulation of sexual behavior.

5. Functionalists spotlight the tasks carried out by the family that serve the interests of society as a whole. Conflict theorists have seen the family as a social arrangement benefiting some people more than others. Friedrich Engels viewed the family as a class society in miniature, with one class (men) oppressing another class (women). Randall Collins sees the family as an instrument for maintaining male claims to women as sexual property. Other conflict sociologists say that intimate relationships inevitably involve antagonism as well as love.

6. Societies undertake to regulate the process whereby young people choose a marriage partner. Romantic love is given more emphasis in some societies than in others. Societies "control" love in a variety of ways, including child marriage, social isolation of young people, close supervision of couples, and peer and parental pressures. A variety of factors operate in the selection of a mate:

homogamy, physical attractiveness, and complementary needs. Exchange theory provides a unifying link among these factors. It proposes that people involved in a mutually satisfying relationship will exchange behaviors that have low cost and high reward.

7. Most adult Americans hope to establish an intimate relationship with another person and make the relationship work. Despite the considerable change in family patterns in recent decades, American couples remain rather conventional in their marital relationships. Divorce rates have soared, but Americans have not given up on marriage. However, increasing numbers of Americans no longer view marriage as a permanent institution but rather as something that can be ended and reentered.

8. Nuclear families that are not disrupted by divorce, desertion, or death typically pass through a series of changes and realignments across time, what sociologists call the family life cycle. These changes and realignments are related to the altered expectations and requirements imposed on a husband and wife as children are born and grow up. Each modification in the role content of one family member has implications for all the other members.

9. Increasing numbers of mothers are working. Many social scientists are no longer asking whether it is good or bad that mothers work. Instead, they are finding that a more important issue is whether the mother, regardless of employment, is satisfied in her situation. Two-income couples are also on the increase. Even so, women still continue to shoulder the primary responsibility for household tasks and child care.

10. Mounting evidence suggests that family violence, child abuse, and incest are much more common than most Americans had suspected. These patterns appear to be transmitted through socialization processes from one generation to another. Divorce is also on the upswing in American life. Although it may be more commonplace, it is hardly a routine experience; it exacts a considerable emotional and physical toll from all family members. Most divorced people remarry, and remarriage frequently results in stepfamilies. Despite the significant changes that have occurred in family roles in recent decades, it is grown children who still bear the primary responsibility for their aged parents.

11. By virtue of the rapid expansion of lifestyle options, Americans now enjoy more alternatives in tailoring their relationships to individual choice. A lifestyle is the overall pattern of living people evolve to meet their biological, social, and emotional needs. Among the varying lifestyle options for Americans are singlehood, unmarried cohabitation, single parenthood, and gay and lesbian relationships.

Glossary

bilineal An arrangement based on reckoning descent and transmitting property through both the father and the mother.

complementary needs Two different personality traits that are the counterparts of each other and that provide a sense of completeness when they are joined.

egalitarian An arrangement in which power and authority are equally distributed between husband and wife.

endogamy The requirement that marriage occur within a group.

exchange theory The view that proposes that people

involved in a mutually satisfying relationship will exchange behaviors that have low cost and high reward.

exogamy　The requirement that marriage occur outside a group.

extended family　A family arrangement in which kin—individuals related by common ancestry—provide the core relationship; spouses are functionally marginal and peripheral.

family　Traditionally defined as a social group whose members are related by ancestry, marriage, or adoption and who live together, cooperate economically, and care for the young.

family life cycle　Changes and realignments related to the altered expectations and requirements imposed on a husband and a wife as children are born and grow up.

family of orientation　A nuclear family that consists of oneself and one's father, mother, and siblings.

family of procreation　A nuclear family that consists of oneself and one's spouse and children.

group marriage　The marriage of two or more husbands and two or more wives.

homogamy　The tendency of like to marry like.

homosexuality　A preference for an individual of the same sex as a sexual partner.

incest taboos　Rules that prohibit sexual intercourse with close blood relatives.

lifestyle　The overall pattern of living that people evolve to meet their biological, social, and emotional needs.

marriage　A socially approved sexual union between two or more individuals that is undertaken with some idea of permanence.

matching hypothesis　The notion that we typically experience the greatest payoff and the least cost when we select partners who have a degree of physical attractiveness similar to our own.

matriarchial　A family arrangement in which power is vested in women.

matrilineal　An arrangement based on reckoning descent and inheritance through the mother's side of the family.

matrilocal　The residence pattern in which a bride and groom live in the household or community of the wife's family.

monogamy　The marriage of one husband and one wife.

neolocal　The residence pattern in which newlyweds set up a new place of residence independent of either of their parents or other relatives.

norm of legitimacy　The rule that children not be born out of wedlock.

nuclear family　A family arrangement in which the spouses and their offspring constitute the core relationship; blood relatives are functionally marginal and peripheral.

patriarchal　A family arrangement in which power is vested in men.

patrilineal　An arrangement based on reckoning descent and inheritance through the father's side of the family.

patrilocal　The residence pattern in which a bride and groom live in the household or community of the husband's family.

polyandry　The marriage of two or more husbands and one wife.

polygyny　The marriage of one husband and two or more wives.

resource dilution hypothesis　The thesis that in large families resources get spread thin, to the detriment of all the offspring.

romantic love　The strong physical and emotional attraction between a man and a woman.

Chapter 10

RELIGION, EDUCATION, AND MEDICINE

Institutions are a central component of social structure (see Chapter 2). They are strategic instruments through which human life is patterned, stabilized, and made predictable. Because of institutions, we feel there is an appreciable element of regularity, efficiency, and certainty in our daily activities. Indeed, we organize our relationships with other people and carry out the essential tasks of group life within the context of institutions. So there is a vital link between a society's institutional arrangements and the private experiences of its members.

In Chapter 8 we considered the political and economic institutions, and in Chapter 9 the family institution. In this chapter we turn our attention to the religious, educational, and medical institutions. Each of these institutions is focused on the solution to a set of problems encountered in social living (see Chapter 2). As we will see in the pages that follow, religious, educational, and medical institutions have evolved to meet basic social needs and to keep society going.

☐ Religion

Religion has to do with those socially shared ways of thinking, feeling, and acting that have as their focus the realm of the supernatural or "beyond." As Emile Durkheim (1912/1965) points out, religion is centered in beliefs and practices that are related to *sacred* as opposed to *profane* things. The **sacred** involves those aspects of social reality that are set apart and forbidden. The **profane** has to do with those aspects of social reality that are everyday and commonplace. The sacred, then, is extraordinary, mysterious, awe-inspiring, and even potentially dangerous—it "sticks out" from normal, routine life (Berger, 1967). The same object or behavior can be profane or sacred depending on how people define it. A wafer made of flour when seen as bread is a profane object, but it becomes sacred to Catholics as the body of Christ when it is consecrated during the Mass. Because the sacred is caught up with strong feelings of reverence and awe, it can usually be approached only through **rituals**—social acts prescribed by rules that dictate how human beings should comport themselves in the presence of the sacred. In their religious behavior, human beings fashion a social world of meanings and rules that govern what they think, feel, and act, in much the same way that they do in other realms of life.

VARIETIES OF RELIGIOUS BEHAVIOR

Religious behavior is so varied that we have difficulty thinking about it unless we use some classificatory means for sorting it into relevant categories. Although no categories do justice to the diversity and richness of the human religious experience, sociologist Reece McGee (1975) provides us with one scheme that is both insightful and manageable: simple supernaturalism, animism, theism, and a system of abstract ideals.

Simple supernaturalism is prevalent in preindustrial societies. It entails the notion of **mana,** a diffuse, impersonal, supernatural force that exists in nature for good or evil. With mana people do not entreat spirits or gods to intervene on their behalf. Rather, they *compel* a superhuman power to behave as they wish by manipulating it mechanically. For instance, the act of carrying a rabbit's foot is thought to bring the bearer good luck; the capacity to bring good luck is as much an attribute of the rabbit's foot as is its color or weight. One need not talk to the rabbit's foot or offer it gifts, but only carry it. Similarly, the act of uttering the words "Open, sesame" serves to manipulate impersonal supernatural power. Many athletes use lucky charms, elaborate routines, and superstitious rituals to ward off injury and bad luck in activities based on uncertainty. Similarly, many American hotels and office and apartment buildings have thirteen floors, but few have a floor labeled 13 (in Taiwan, Hong Kong, and some parts of China, the pronunciation for the number 4 is similar to that of the word for death, and so many apartment buildings in these societies do not have a fourth floor). Mana is usually employed to reach "here-and-now" goals—control of the weather, assurance of a good crop, cure of an illness, good performance on a test, success in love, or victory in battle. It functions much like an old-fashioned book of recipes or a home medical manual.

Animism involves a belief in spirits or otherworldly beings. People have seen spirits throughout nature—in animals, plants, rocks, stars, rivers, and at times in other individuals. Since spirits are personified and are believed to act on the basis of associated motives and emotions, individuals customarily employ techniques in dealing with them similar to those they employ in their human relationships. Love, punishment, reverence, and gifts have all been used to deal with superhuman spirits. And cajolery, bribery, and false pretenses may be seen to be as effective as awe. Additionally, in animism, as with mana, supernatural power is often harnessed through rituals that compel a spirit to act in a desired way.

In **theism** religion is centered in a belief in gods who are thought to be powerful, to have an interest in human affairs, and to merit worship. Judaism, Christianity, and Islam are forms of **monotheism,** or belief in one god. They all have established religious organizations, religious leaders or priests, traditional rituals, and sacred writings. Ancient Greek religion and Hinduism (practiced primarily in India) are forms of **polytheism,** or belief in many gods with equal or relatively similar power. Hindu gods are often tribal, village, or caste deities associated with a particular place—a building, field, or mountain—or a certain object—an animal or a tree.

Finally, some religions focus on a set of abstract ideals. Rather than centering on the worship of a god, they are dedicated to achieving moral and spiritual excellence. Many of the religions of Asia are of this type, including Taoism, Confucianism, and Buddhism. Buddhism is directed toward reaching an elevated state of consciousness, a method of purification that provides a release from suffering, ignorance, and selfishness. In the Western world, humanism is based on ethical principles. Its adherents discard all theological beliefs about God, heaven, hell, and immortality, and substitute for God the pursuit of good in the here and now. Heaven is seen as the ideal society on earth and hell as a world in which war, disease, and ignorance flourish. The soul is the human personality, and immortality is deeds that live on after death for good or evil in the lives of other people.

RELIGIOUS ORGANIZATIONS

Norms, beliefs, and rituals provide the cultural fabric of religion. But there is more to the religious institution than its cultural heritage. As with other institutions, there is also the structural mosaic of social organization whereby people are bound together within networks of relatively stable relationships. We need to examine not only the religious customs of a people but the ways in which people organize their religious life.

Sociologists distinguish among four ideal types of religious organization: churches, denominations, sects, and cults (Niebuhr, 1929; Troeltsch, 1931; Iannaccone, 1988). Whereas churches and denominations typically exist in accommodation with the larger society, sects and cults often find themselves at odds with established social arrangements and practices. Cults differ from sects in that they are viewed by their members as being pluralistically legitimate, providing one among many alternative paths to truth or salvation. In this respect, cults resemble denominations. In contrast, the sect, like the church, defines itself as being uniquely legitimate and possessing exclusive access to truth or salvation. This model is depicted in Figure 10.1.

The Church. The **church** is a religious organization that considers itself uniquely legitimate and typically enjoys a positive relationship with the dominant society. It usually operates with a bureaucratic structure and claims to include most of the members of a society. In fact, members are

	Positive relationship with society	Negative relationship with society
Claims lone legitimacy	CHURCH	SECT
Accepts pluralistic legitimacy	DENOMI-NATION	CULT

Figure 10.1 TYPES OF RELIGIOUS ORGANIZATIONS
(SOURCE: Adapted from Roy Wallis, *Sectarianism: Analyses of Religious and Non-Religious Sects.* New York: Wiley, 1975, p. 41. Reprinted by permission of Peter Owen Ltd.)

born into the church if their parents are affiliated with it; they do not have to *join* the church. The aim of the church is professedly universal. Its message is *Extra ecclesiam nulla salus*—"Outside the church there is no salvation." Its response to competing groups is to suppress, ignore, or coopt them (see Table 10.1).

The church typically makes its peace with the secular aspects of social life. It tends to be a conservative body and allies itself with the advantaged classes. For the most part, it does not champion new causes or social reform but accepts the dominant goals and values of society. It also frequently looks back to an earlier way of life. When groups within the church attempt to give it new directions, church officials frequently attempt to block the changes (Seidler and Meyer, 1989; Burns, 1990). A good illustration of this is the opposition Vatican leaders have posed to the theology of liberation that has gained strength in Latin America. The theology of liberation is a body of teachings that draws on Marxist analysis in emphasizing the special commitment of Roman Catholics to the poor. The Vatican has condemned the theology of liberation as endangering "the healthy doctrine of the faith" and leading to "the destruction of the authentic sense of the sacraments and the word of faith."

Table 10.1   TYPES OF RELIGIOUS ORGANIZATION

Characteristic	Church	Denomination	Sect	Cult
Size	Large	Moderate	Small	Small
Relationship with secular world	Affirms prevailing culture and social arrangements	Supports current culture and social arrangements	Renounces or opposes prevailing culture and social arrangements	Although critical of society, focuses on evil within each person
Relationship with other religious groups	Claims lone legitimacy	Accepts pluralistic legitimacy	Claims lone legitimacy	Accepts pluralistic legitimacy
Religious services	Formal services with minimal congregational participation	Formal services with limited congregational participation	Informal services with high degree of congregational participation	Informal meetings that draw upon the participation of adherents
Clergy	Specialized; professional; full-time	Specialized; professional; full-time	Unspecialized; little formal training; part-time	Charismatic; founder or leader has little formal training
Doctrines	Literal interpretations of scriptures	Liberal interpretation of scriptures	Literal interpretation of scriptures	New and independent tradition with a rather secularized view of the divine
Social class of members	All social classes	Middle and upper	Primarily disadvantaged	Chiefly middle and educated
Sources of members	Born into the faith; seeks universal membership	Often requires later validation of membership acquired from parents	Voluntary confessional membership	Often lacks formal membership
Emphasis	Religious education and transmission of religion to the children of members	Religious education and transmission of religious values to youth	Evangelism and adult membership	Living one's life in accordance with basic tenets
Church property	Extensive	Depends on affluence of members	Little	None or limited

SOURCE: Adapted from Glen M. Vernon, *Sociology of Religion*, New York: McGraw-Hill, 1962, p. 174.

The church attaches considerable importance to the means of grace that it administers, to a system of doctrine that it has formulated, and to the administration of rituals that it controls through an official clergy. It strives to dominate all aspects of social life—to teach and guide the members of society and dispense saving grace. The church type is exemplified by the Roman Catholic Church of thirteenth-century Europe and the Theravada Buddhism of feudal Southeast Asia. Vestiges of the church arrangement are found in contemporary nations with mandated "official" religions, including the Islamic Shiites of Iran; the Catholic Church of Italy, Monaco, and Spain; the Lutherans of Denmark, Iceland, Norway, and Sweden; the Hindus of Nepal; the Jews of Israel; the Buddhists of Burma; the Greek Orthodox Church of Greece; and the Church of England.

The Sect. The **sect** is a religious organization that considers itself uniquely legitimate but is at odds with the dominant society. It usually consists of a small, voluntary fellowship of converts, most of whom are drawn from disadvantaged groups. The sect does not attempt to win the world over to its doctrines but instead practices exclusiveness; it follows literally the phrase, "Come out from among them and be ye separate." It is often founded by individuals who break away from a church and claim that they represent the true, cleansed version of the faith from which they split (Stark and Bainbridge, 1979; Wilson, 1990). Members who entertain heretical opinions or engage in immoral behavior are subject to expulsion. Occasionally group pressures can be so powerful—as in the cases of the Reverend Jim Jones (the People's Temple in Guyana) and David Koresh (the belief that Armageddon was coming to the Mount Carmel compound near Waco, Texas)—that self-destructive practices and even suicide may not be an individual option but a group requirement. The sect thinks of itself as an elect—a religious elite. Sect members believe that other religious interpretations are in error, and they portray the larger society as decadent and

THE WALL STREET JOURNAL

"Fred, do you want to join a cult?"

From *The Wall Street Journal*—Permission, Cartoon Features Syndicate.

evil (see Table 10.1). It is often a form of social dissent, exemplified by the Anabaptists of Reformation times and the Mormons, Shakers, and Quakers of the eighteenth and nineteenth centuries. Some new religions such as the Children of God and the Reverend Sun Myung Moon's Unification Church are also sectlike.

Most sects are small, and many of them fail to grow larger. Their high state of tension with the larger society serves to cut them off from potential recruits (Stark and Bainbridge, 1981). Should they survive and gain adherents, they tend to become more churchlike. A number of factors seem to be at work (Niebuhr, 1929). For one thing, the problem of training the children of the original members almost inevitably causes some compromise to be made in the rigid requirements for membership evolved in the sect's early years. The Presbyterians, for instance, inaugurated the Half-Way Covenant so that children whose "calling and election" was not yet sure could be held within the fold. For another, as a sect gains adherents and the promise of success, it begins to reach out toward greater influence within the society. In the process it gradually accommodates itself to the larger culture it is attempting to conquer and attracts an increasing number of persons who enjoy social and economic privileges. Finally, the nature of the religious impulse renders it difficult to sustain. Fervor begins to be replaced with reasoned faith and bureaucratic structures.

The Denomination. The **denomination** accepts the legitimacy claims of other religions and enjoys a positive relationship with the dominant society. In many cases it is a sect in an advanced stage of development and adjustment to the secular world. The membership of the denomination comes largely from the middle class. The moral rigor and religious fervor of the sect are relaxed. It usually has an established clergy who have undergone specialized training to prepare for their positions at a theological seminary. Although conversions provide one source for new members, most individuals are born into the group. Accordingly, church officials are particularly concerned with developing a training program to prepare the children of members to become adult adherents of their faith.

Members often define churchgoing as one of the duties of upstanding members of the community and as an integral part of involvement in the "okay world." The denomination is content to be one organization among many, all of which are deemed acceptable in the sight of God. Examples of denominations include most of the major religious groups in the United States: Presbyterians, Baptists, Congregationalists, Methodists, Unitarians, Lutherans, Episcopalians, Roman Catholics, and Reform and Conservative Jews.

The Cult. The **cult** accepts the legitimacy of other religious groups but finds itself at odds with the dominant society. Like the denomination, the cult does not lay claim to *the* truth, but unlike the denomination it tends to be critical of society. The cult does not require its members to pass strict doctrinal tests but instead invites all to join its ranks. It usually lacks the tight discipline of sects whose rank-and-file members attempt to hold one another "up to the mark." And unlike the sect, it usually lacks prior ties with an established religion, constituting instead a new and independent religious tradition (Stark and Bainbridge, 1979). The cult frequently focuses on the problems of its members, especially those who are confronted with loneliness, fear, inferiority, tension, and similar problems. Some cults are built about a single function, such as spiritual healing or spiritualism. Others, like various New Thought cults, seek to combine elements of conventional religion with ideas and practices that are essentially nonreligious. Still others direct their attention toward the pursuit of self-awareness, self-realization, wisdom, or insight, such as Vedanta, Soto Zen, the Human Potential Movement, and Transcendental Meditation.

THE FUNCTIONALIST PERSPECTIVE ON RELIGION

Functionalist theorists look to the contributions religion makes to society's survival. They reason that if every known society seems to have something called religion, its presence cannot be dismissed as a social accident (Davis, 1951). If religion were not adaptive, societies would long since have evolved without it. Accordingly, they ask what functions are performed by religion in social life.

Durkheim: Religion as a Societal Glue. In *The Elementary Forms of Religious Life* (1912/1965), the last of his major works, Emile Durkheim brought his concern with group forces to an analysis of the functions of religion. He selected for his study the Arunta, an Australian aboriginal people. The Arunta practice **totemism,** a religious system in which a clan (a kin group) takes the name of, claims descent from, and attributes sacred properties to a plant or animal. Durkheim says that the totem plant or animal is not the

Doing Sociology: Intercollegiate Rivalries

Emile Durkheim contended that religious rituals function as an important source for creating, reinforcing, and maintaining social solidarity. Observations by students in introductory sociology classes at Ohio State University suggest that intense intercollegiate rivalries serve a similar function, particularly traditional, season-concluding football games such as those between Ohio State and The University of Michigan. The sociology students point out that American colleges and universities recruit students from a great many differing backgrounds and with diverse affiliations, allegiances, interests, and traditions. Given the influx of large numbers of new students each year, how are colleges and universities to instill in the new arrivals a consciousness of oneness and a sense of belonging to a common group? One particularly potent mechanism is a rivalry between the in-group and an out-group, especially an intercollegiate game. Such encounters afford a powerful device for highlighting the boundaries of a group, fostering "we-group" sentiments, and cementing bonds among group members. Thus traditional games provide occasions for the members of a college community to engage in a variety of activities that have symbolic significance in promoting their collective consciousness.

Durkheim pointed to the part that a totem ancestor played among the Arunta in symbolizing their society. The college mascot performs a somewhat similar function for the college community—the Badger, the Gopher, the Tiger, the Wolverine, the Trojan, and so on. The "totem" of Ohio State University is Brutus Buckeye. The significance of this symbol was highlighted before a recent Ohio State–Michigan football game when the "head" of Brutus Buckeye was stolen. The thief demanded a ransom for its return, and the story quickly became the focus of local media attention. Ohio State football fans felt an emptiness and loss—a sense that the absence of Brutus Buckeye at the game would create a void and perhaps even mystically result in "bad luck" for the team. Although the thief was never apprehended, the head was found in a dumpster before game time and the finder received a reward of $2,000.

The Arunta inhabit a semi-desert region in central Australia. They are a hunting and gathering

source of totemism but a stand-in for the real source, society itself. He contends that religion—the totem ancestor, God, or some other supernatural force—is the symbolization of society. By means of religious rituals, the group in effect worships itself. Society harnesses the awesome force inherent in people's perception of the sacred for animating a sense of oneness and moral authority. The primary functions of religion are the creation, reinforcement, and maintenance of social solidarity and social control. (See "Doing Sociology.")

Durkheim observes that if we are left to ourselves, our individual consciousnesses—our inner mental states—are closed to one another. Our separate minds cannot come in contact and communicate except by "coming out of themselves." Consequently, social life dictates that the internal be made external—the intangible, tangible. Our inner consciousness is transformed into a *collective* consciousness through the symbolic device of religious rituals. By uttering the same cry, pronouncing the same word, or performing the same gesture, we inform one another that we are united

people who range over a vast area in small bands of two or three families each. Their religious ceremonies provide occasions when the nearly 2,000 members get together and renew their societal ties. In a somewhat similar fashion, big games like that between Ohio State and Michigan afford occasions when alumni and long-term Ohio State supporters assemble to reestablish and heighten their sense of oneness and to reaffirm their allegiance to the university. (The point is not lost on Ohio State University's president, Gordon Gee, who observes, "Athletics is an issue that is important to a lot of universities in this country. Any university president that denies that is not dealing with reality. People attend a football game brunch or whatever that might not be able to come here otherwise. . . . We're going to make sure the people take away a

message. That's the value of having strong athletics. It also raises the level of visibility of the institution" (Stephens, 1990:1A). Gee might also have mentioned that winning football programs afford many other benefits, not the least of which is financial support.)

The Arunta engage in elaborate ceremonials in which members dress in ritual garments, dance, and recall myths telling of the heroic deeds of their totemic ancestors. Again, sociology students note many parallels with the Ohio State–Michigan game. The football players, cheerleaders, and band members outfit themselves in distinctive uniforms, and fans wear the unique scarlet and gray colors of Ohio State. Radio and television stations carry special programs recalling previous Ohio State–Michigan games, presenting gridiron stars of earlier years and interviewing current

players and coaches. Campus-area stores display Ohio State slogans, souvenirs, and memorabilia. Students and alumni attend a gigantic pep rally the evening before the game. At game time the university band plays rousing songs such as the "Buckeye Battle Cry" and "Carmen Ohio" to fire the enthusiasm of the crowd. Cheerleaders and Brutus Buckeye orchestrate chants that build collective excitement. On the field, the football players become the symbolic embodiment—a tangible expression—of the university and its community. What is otherwise rather ill-defined and indistinct—a gigantic university with over 50,000 students, thousands of faculty and staff, and countless alumni—becomes in the course of a Saturday football afternoon a living and profoundly meaningful social reality—indeed, a distinctive social entity.

---

in a shared state of mind. Simultaneously, we mentally fuse ourselves within a social whole. We generate a sort of electricity or collective euphoria that lifts us to an intense state of exaltation that overrides our individual beings. Religious rituals thus operate in two ways: First, they provide vehicles by which we *reveal* to one another that we share a common mental state; second, they *create* among us a shared consciousness that contributes to a social bonding.

Durkheim emphasizes the similarity in our attitudes toward society and toward God. Society

inspires the sensation of divinity in the minds of its members because of its power over them. Moreover, society, like God, possesses moral authority and can inspire self-sacrifice and devotion. And finally, religion is capable of endowing individuals with exceptional powers and motivation. Accordingly, Durkheim says that the religious person is not the victim of an illusion. Behind the symbol—religion—there is a real force and reality: society. Durkheim concludes that when religion is imperiled and not replaced by a satisfying substitute, society itself is jeopardized: Individuals pursue their private interests without regard for the dictates of the larger social enterprise.

Additional Functions. Durkheim draws our attention to how religion functions as a "societal glue" that contributes to social cohesion and solidarity by integrating and unifying the members of a community. Moreover, when a society links its morality to religion, social control may be furthered. The enforcement of norms is greatly enhanced if recourse can be had to priests, the unknown, the divine, idealism, and supernatural agents.

Sociologists have shown that religion may perform other functions as well. For one thing, it helps people in dealing with life's "breaking points." Much of the human experience is uncertain and insecure. Humankind is recurrently confronted with crises and haunting perplexities—floods, epidemics, droughts, famines, wars, accidents, sickness, social disorder, personal defeat, humiliation, injustice, the meaning of life, the mystery of death, and the enigma of the hereafter. Religion deals with these ultimate problems of life, provides "answers," and often offers the prospect of hope through magical control or spiritual intercession. Moreover, it assists people in the transitional stages of life. Most religions celebrate and explain the major events of the life cycle—birth, puberty, marriage, and death—through *rites of passage* (ceremonies marking the transition from one status to another).

Religion may also be an impetus to social change (Warner, 1993). For instance, African-American churches have historically made a significant contribution to the mobilization of protest, as was evident in the civil rights movements of the 1950s and 1960s. The African-American ministers of Montgomery, Alabama, organized a bus boycott in 1955 and 1956 that was instrumental in bringing about desegregation of the city's buses after Rosa Parks was arrested for violating a local bus segregation ordinance. And

the Southern Christian Leadership Conference (SCLC), led by the Reverend Martin Luther King, Jr., and other African-American ministers, was at the forefront of the African-American protest movement of the 1960s. African-American churches provided the civil rights movement with an established mass base, a leadership structure that for the most part was economically independent of the white power structure, meeting places for the organization of protest activities, and a viable financial foundation. Currently, African-American churches are a major force in the economic development and revitalization of inner-city neighborhoods. Similarly, the gay liberation movement has practiced the art of church-based mobilization. The Metropolitan Community Church in New York City was at the organizational center of the movement to legitimate gay culture in the United States.

THE CONFLICT PERSPECTIVE ON RELIGION

From the writings of functionalist theorists we gain a view of religion as a vital source for social integration and solidarity. We derive a quite different image from conflict theorists. Some of them depict religion as a weapon in the service of ruling elites who use it to hold in check the explosive tensions produced by social inequality and injustice. Others see religion as a source of social conflict and point to the religious wars of the Middle Ages and to present-day religious strife in the Middle East, India, and Ireland. Still others see religion as a source of social change.

Marx: Religion as the Opium of the People. The stimulus for many of the contributions made by conflict theorists comes from the work of Karl Marx. Marx (1844/1960:43–44) portrayed religion as a painkiller for the frustration, deprivation, and subjugation experienced by oppressed peoples. He said it soothes their distress but that any relief it may provide is illusory because religion is a social narcotic:

Religious suffering is at the same time an expression of real suffering and a protest against real suffering. Religion is the sigh of the oppressed creature, the sentiment of a heartless world, and the soul of soulless conditions. It is the opium of the people.

Marx saw religion as producing an otherworldly focus that diverts the oppressed from seeking social change in this world. It leads people to project their needs and desires into the realm of make-believe and obscures the real source of social misery and class conflict. More particularly, religion engenders a false consciousness among the working class that interferes with its attainment of true class consciousness. A Marxist reading of English history suggests that the development of Methodism in nineteenth-century England prevented revolution by redirecting workers' discontent and fervor into a religious movement (McGuire, 1981). And the Russian revolutionary Leon Trotsky was so aware of the similarity of revolutionary Marxism to religious sectarianism that in the late 1890s he successfully recruited the first working-class members of the South Russian Workers' Union among adherents of religious sects.

Marx viewed religion as an expression of human alienation. People shape social institutions with the expectation that they will serve their needs but find instead that they themselves become the servants of the institutions they have created. Social institutions, rather than providing for the wants and enriching the lives of the entire community, are taken over by the ruling class and used to oppress and victimize people. Thus people fashion gods, lose their knowledge that they have done so, and then find themselves having to live their lives at the behest of these same gods. As with the economic, family, and legal institutions, people no longer see themselves as the authors of their own products but as part of an encompassing natural order that dominates and directs them. Hence, in much the manner that they are alienated from their labor (see Chapter 8), the members of the working class are alienated from

the larger social environment: "The more powerful becomes the world of objects which they create . . . , the poorer they become in their inner lives, and the less they belong to themselves. It is just the same as in religion. The more of themselves humankind attributes to God, the less they have in themselves" (Marx, 1844/1960:122).

Any number of sociologists have agreed with Marx that there is an inherently conservative aspect to religion (Glock, Ringer, and Babbie, 1967; Hannigan, 1991). The sense of the sacred links a person's present experience with meanings derived from the group's traditional past. Religious beliefs and practices provide taken-for-granted truths that are powerful forces militating against new ways of thinking and behaving. Practices handed down from previous generations, including institutional inequalities and inequities, become defined as God-approved ways and highly resistant to change. For instance, American slavery was justified as part of God's "natural order." In 1863, the Presbyterian Church, South, met in General Synod and passed a resolution declaring slavery to be a divine institution ordained by God. More recently segregation was justified on similar grounds. Said Louisiana State Senator W. M. Rainach in defending segregation in 1954: "Segregation is a natural order—created by God, in His wisdom, who made black men black and white men white" (*Southern School News,* 1954:3). Likewise, the Hindu religion threatens believers who fail to obey caste rules with reincarnation (rebirth) at a lower caste level or as an animal.

Religion may also legitimate changes favoring powerful and wealthy groups. Imperialism has often been supported by religious or quasi-religious motivations and beliefs. In the 1890s President William McKinley explained his decision to wage the expansionist war against Spain and seize Cuba and the Philippines as follows (quoted by McGuire, 1981:188):

I am not ashamed to tell you, gentlemen, that I went down on my knees and prayed to Almighty God for light and guidance more than one night. And one night late it came to me this way. . . . There was nothing left for us to do but to take them all and to educate the Filipinos and uplift and civilize and Christianize them and by God's grace do the very best we could by them, as our fellow men for whom Christ also died.

Religion, then, can be a potent force in the service of the established order. Religious organizations themselves are frequently motivated to legitimate the status quo because they also have vested interests to protect, including power, land, and wealth (Collins, 1981).

Religion and Social Change. A number of conflict theorists have recently taken a new look at the relationship between religion and social change (McGuire, 1981). They see religion not as a passive response to the social relations of production but as an active force shaping the contours of social life. Thus it can play a critical part in the birth and consolidation of new social structures and arrangements. While acknowledging that some aspects of religion inhibit change, they point out that others challenge existing social arrangements and encourage change (Billings, 1990). Under some circumstances religion can be a profoundly revolutionary force that holds out a vision to people of how things might or ought to be. So religion is not invariably a functional or conservative factor in society, but often one of the chief, and at times the only, channel for bringing about a social revolution.

Throughout history, religion has provided an unusually effective vehicle for change because of its ability to unite people and their social lives. American history has been no exception. The religious movements associated with the Great Awakening in the late eighteenth and early nineteenth centuries were an important impetus to the abolitionist movement and later to the temperance and prohibition movements. They also had an impact on the democratization of the American political system, promoting popular participation in what was largely an oligarchy of the economically privileged. The civil rights and peace movements of

recent decades have likewise drawn strength from religious motivations and the resources of religious organizations. The same observation currently holds true in the movement to empower women (Warner, 1993).

Sociologist Peter L. Berger (1979) suggests that in the clash between traditional and modern social arrangements, religious sentiments and organizations can be used in three contrasting ways. First, religion can be mobilized in opposition to modernization and for the reaffirmation of traditional authority. This is the route taken by Ayatollah Khomeini and his Shiite followers in Iran. Second, religion can adapt to the secular world and harness religious motivations for secular purposes. This is the path taken by John Calvin and his Protestant followers. And third, religion can retain its fundamental roots while applying them to contemporary concerns. This is the road taken by the fundamental revivalist movement in the United States. Let's examine each of these alternatives in turn.

REAFFIRMING TRADITION: THE IRANIAN ISLAMIC REVOLUTION

In February 1979, Ayatollah Khomeini returned to Iran from exile in Paris and led a revolution that toppled Shah Mohammed Riza Pahlavi. The Iranian monarchy was replaced by a theocratic regime rooted in Islamic traditions and anti-Western fervor. Nine months later, a militant crowd seized control of the U.S. Embassy in Teheran and launched 444 days of tension that appreciably affected the 1980 American presidential election. In subsequent years, the new Islamic state has weathered a power struggle and the purging of many of the revolution's prominent figures, a campaign of bombings and assassinations by internal enemies, severe economic difficulties, and a war with neighboring Iraq.

A number of forces converged to produce the Iranian revolution (Fischer, 1980; Abrahamian, 1989; Foran, 1993a). For one thing, the Islamic clergy, or mullahs, found their authority and wealth severely eroded as the shah sought to modernize and secularize the nation. The shah's policies tightened the cohesiveness of the clergy and transformed the mullahs into a revolutionary force. Although weakened, the clergy retained control of the religious institution and used the network provided by mosques as a power base to attack the shah's order and ultimately to bring the state apparatus under clerical domination. The rural migrants who were flooding Iranian cities—the "disinherited," as they were called by anti-shah activists—steadfastly supported the Islamic clergy. From them, the mullahs recruited and organized the Revolutionary Guards, the paramilitary force that served as the foot soldiers of the revolution. The clergy rallied the Iranian masses against the decadence and degradation they perceived in Iranian life, against Western practices and fashions, and against rampant materialism and modernization. Religion thus became an idiom for political and nationalistic expression.

In the face of intense foreign pressures and destabilizing internal conditions and tensions, the beleaguered masses took refuge in religion. Resentment against persistent Western dominance and the imposition of Western ways fed revolutionary fervor. Young people rediscovered their grandparents' traditions as they sought a religious source for their social and cultural identities. The new power that oil conferred and the West's insatiable dependence on it made defiance seem feasible. The oil boom had also enriched a privileged class, brought accusations that the money had not been spent for the good of the people, and upset traditional economic and social patterns. Complicating matters, the brutality of the shah's secret police alienated Westernized intellectuals, students, civil servants, technical experts, and traditional merchants of the bazaar.

In the decade following the revolution, the mullahs secured political dominance by filling nearly all the seats in parliament through their Islamic Republican party. The local mosques served as the building blocks of power, functioning as an amalgam of political clubhouse, government office, police station, and educational center. A system of Islamic law and justice came to supersede secular law and a formal judiciary. A systematic campaign was undertaken to purge Western ways, alcohol, gambling, prostitution, and pornography from Iranian life. Women had to wear head scarves, and those who neglected to do so were often sent to a "reeducation center." And during its early years, the regime felt it to be a religious duty to export revolution so that an Islamic empire would come into being, stretching from the Persian Gulf to the Mediterranean and beyond.

Islamic fundamentalism gained additional impetus during the early 1990s. The trend was most notable in regions that historically had been part of the Islamic world. Islamic fundamentalists have challenged several governments in North Africa and the Middle East that in recent years have been secular in their orientation, including those in Algeria, Tunisia, Egypt, Saudi Arabia, Jordan, and the once Soviet Asia. With the worldwide decline of communism and the demise of the Soviet Union (long foes of Islamic fundamentalism), many Muslim peoples began to look to their earliest Islamic roots, and they have used the tools of the modern nation-state to reinforce an Islamic agenda. In addition, as in Iran, they have viewed an Islamic resurgence as a defensive measure against the intrusions of Western society (Miller, 1992). In sum, Islamic fundamentalism has proven itself to be less reactionary than reactive: Its leaders have typically "reached back" to some presumed "fundamentals" in order to power their resistance against outside forces, modernity, relativism, pluralism, and compromisers within their tradition (Marty and Appleby, 1992). Even so, Muslims are hardly a monolithic group either religiously or politically (Esposito, 1992).

PROMOTING SECULAR CHANGE: THE PROTESTANT ETHIC

People's orientations to their gods and the supernatural can inhibit secular change and modernization. But their religious beliefs and practices can also promote socioeconomic change. Max Weber (1904/1958, 1916/1964, 1917/1958) studied several world religions in order to discern how a religious **ethic**—the perspective and values engendered by a religious way of thinking—can affect people's behavior. He suggests that there are periods in historical development when circumstances push a society toward a reaffirmation of old ways or toward new ways. At such critical junctures, religion—by supplying sources of individual motivation and defining the relationship of individuals to their society—can be a source of historical breakthrough. While a religious ethic does not mechanically determine social action, it can give it impetus by shaping people's perceptions and definitions of their material and ideal interests.

In *The Protestant Ethic and the Spirit of Capitalism* (1904/1958), Weber turned his sociological eye to one historic breakthrough—the development of capitalism. He sought a link between the rise of the Protestant view of life and the emergence of capitalist social arrangements in Western society. He maintained that the development of capitalism depended upon the creation of a pool of individuals who had the attitudes and values necessary to function as entrepreneurs. Once capitalism is established, it carries on in a self-perpetuating fashion. The critical problem, Weber said, is to uncover the origin of the motivating spirit of capitalism in precapitalist society. He believed that Protestantism, particularly Calvinism, was crucial to, but not the only factor in, the rise of this spirit. Calvinism is based on the teachings of the French theologian and reformer John Calvin (1509–1564) and found expression in a variety of religious movements including Puritanism, Pietism, and Anabaptism.

Weber noted that Protestantism and modern capitalism appeared on the historical scene at roughly the same time. There were other links as well. First, capitalism initially attained its highest development in Protestant countries, particularly the United States and England, whereas Catholic nations like Spain and Italy lagged behind. Second, in nations with both Protestant and Catholic regions, such as Germany, it seemed to be the Protestant regions that pioneered in capitalist development. And third, Weber marshaled evidence that suggested it was by and large the Protestants, not the Catholics, who became the early capitalist entrepreneurs. Based on these observations, Weber (1904/1958:64) concluded that the **Protestant ethic,** particularly as it was embodied in Calvinist doctrine, instilled an "attitude which seeks profit rationally and systematically."

The Calvinist ethos had other elements that fed capitalist motivation, particularly its *doctrine of predestination.* Calvin rejected the idea prevalent in Catholicism of the Middle Ages that a person's status in the afterlife is determined by the way he or she behaves here on earth. Instead, Calvin taught that at birth every soul is predestined for heaven or hell. This notion was especially disquieting since people did not know whether they were among the saved or the damned. According to Weber, Calvin's followers, in their search for reassurance, came to accept certain earthly signs of **asceticism** as proof of their salvation and genuine faith: hard work, sobriety, thrift, restraint, and the avoidance of fleshly pleasures. As people are wont to do, the Calvinists, preoccupied with their fate, subtly began to cultivate these very behaviors. More important, self-discipline and a willingness to delay gratification are qualities that lead people to amass capital and achieve economic success. Capitalist entrepreneurs could ruthlessly pursue profit and feel that they were fulfilling their Christian obligation. Thus the Calvinist ethos took the spirit of capitalism out of the realm of individual ambition and translated it into an ethical duty.

A good many scholars since Weber have raised serious questions regarding his hypothesis (Tawney, 1926; Robertson, 1933; Samuelsson, 1961; Cohen, 1980). They have looked to other factors in explaining the origins of capitalism, including a surge in commerce during the fifteenth and sixteenth centuries, technological innovations, the influx of capital resources from New World colonies, unrestrained markets, and the availability of a free labor force. Further, sociologist Randall G. Stokes (1975) has shown that the beliefs comprising the Protestant ethic do not necessarily lead people to engage in entrepreneurial activities. Calvinism did not produce capitalist outcomes when it was transplanted by Dutch and French Huguenot settlers (Afrikaners) to South Africa. Although Afrikaner Calvinism was theologically identical to European Calvinism, it has a conservative rather than an innovative economic impact. It is worth noting that *The Protestant Ethic and the Spirit of Capitalism* was one of Weber's earlier works. In lectures given shortly before his death, Weber incorporated many new elements in his analysis of the origins of large-scale capitalism (Collins, 1980). Even so, his early work, although not necessarily accurate in all its particulars, remains a sociological landmark. It demonstrates the impact religion can have on human affairs in producing outcomes that are not necessarily intended or foreseen by its adherents.

ADAPTING TRADITION: RELIGION IN CONTEMPORARY LIFE

We have seen that religion may be a conservative force, impeding modernization and reaffirming traditional authority, as in contemporary Iran. It may also be a powerful agent for social change, creating a perception of the world that gives an impetus to innovation and rationalized economic activity, as in the case of Calvinism. Finally, religion may draw upon people's spiritual yearnings and adapt them to modern life. Many Western intellectuals had anticipated that processes of rationalization would lead to the gradual withering away of religious ideas and institutions. This view found expression in the **secularization thesis,** the notion that profane (nonreligious) considerations gain ascendancy over sacred (religious) considerations in the course of social evolution (Herberg, 1955; Lechner, 1991; Chaves,

1994). In much the manner that industrialization, urbanization, bureaucratization, and rationalization have been equated with modernization, so secularization has been widely assumed to accompany the transformation of human societies from simple to complex forms.

Some evidence seemingly supports the secularization thesis. The Gallup polling organization has been questioning Americans since 1937 on their religious practices. In 1993 some 40 percent of the adult population *said* they had attended a church or synagogue in the 7-day period preceding the time of the interview (claims of membership have ranged from a high of 76 percent in 1947 to a low of 65 percent in 1990, with membership in 1993 standing at 69 percent of the adult population) (Princeton Religion Research Center, 1994). However, *actual head counts* at selected churches reveal that only 20 percent of Protestants and 28 percent of Catholics show up for Sunday services (Hadaway, Marler, and Chaves, 1993). It seems that most people believe that going to church is a good thing to do and so they tell pollsters they have gone to church when in fact they have not done so. Moreover, members of the baby-boom generation abandoned their traditional religious loyalties in large numbers during the 1960s and 1970s, and although they are more religious now than they were as adolescents and young adults, they still seem to be exploring spiritual questions in a highly individualistic way. Denominational loyalties are weak among most baby boomers—many say that one should "explore many different religious traditions" rather than "stick to a particular faith" (Roof, 1992).

Yet despite what may seem to be low turnouts for worship services, very little sociological evidence supports the notion that secularization is taking place in American life (Hadden, 1987b; Cornwall, 1989; Greeley, 1989). For one thing, sociologists Roger Finke and Rodney Stark (1992) show that America's pious past is a nostalgic illusion. In 1776—at the time of the American Revolution—only 17 percent of the population held membership in a church (on any given Sunday morning there were at least as many people recovering from late Saturday nights in the taverns as were in church). By 1860, the rate of religious membership had increased to 37 percent, to 53 percent in 1916, and to 59 percent in 1952. Today's religious adherents top 62 percent of the population, a historical high.

The secularization thesis also ignores high levels of contemporary religiosity in American life. Religion remains a powerful force despite having dramatically changed in response to challenges posed by the state (for instance, the assumption of many services historically provided by religious organizations), the mass media (for example, the rise of televangelism and the media airing of the sexual and financial scandals associated with a number of television ministries), and higher education (for instance, the transformation of many public attitudes, including a decline in religious prejudice among denominations and a decline in the saliency of denominational affiliation for personal identity) (Wuthnow, 1988, 1989). The vast majority of Americans still say they believe in the existence of God and life after death (significantly, the proportion of Americans professing belief in God has not dipped below 94 percent over the past half-century) (Princeton Religion Research Center, 1994). A recent national survey of 113,000 Americans found that only 7.5 percent of the population said they had no religious affiliation (Goldman, 1991). Indeed, in recent years, the nation has undergone a fundamentalist and evangelical revival that has represented an attempt to capture the roots of religious inspiration and shape them to the contemporary world (Hunter, 1983, 1987; Ammerman, 1987; Poloma, 1989; Johnson, 1990).

Fundamentalism is a Protestant movement that opposes "modernist" theology and seeks to conserve the basic principles underlying traditional Christianity; it views the Bible as the literal and unerring word of God. *Evangelicalism* is a "glad tidings" movement whose members profess a personal relationship with Jesus Christ; adherents

believe that the Bible provides the only authoritative basis for faith, stress the importance of personal conversion, and emphasize the importance of intense zeal for Christian living. Although the public often lumps fundamentalists and evangelicals together, they are far from a monolithic, unified, conservative movement. Indeed, their differences are every bit as great as those dividing Catholics, Episcopalians, Methodists, and Baptists (Hadden and Shupe, 1988).

Fundamentalists and evangelicals have undertaken to shape their Christian faith to contemporary concerns, simultaneously absorbing and resisting change (Hunter, 1983, 1987, 1988). Conservative Christians have poured enormous energy into constructing and expanding a vast edifice of "parallel institutions" for preserving their way of life and achieving their vision of truth: a publishing industry, missionary and social outreach agencies, and some 18,000 elementary and secondary schools accounting for nearly 2.5 million students. Many religious conservatives have also entered the political arena (although the Christian Coalition—founded in 1989 from the remnants of the Pat Robertson presidential campaign—is currently the largest group, there is not a single Christian Right but an assortment of organizations, constituencies, and leaders who share traditional family values, oppose abortion and gay rights, and favor school prayer) (Wilcox, 1992). A 1992 survey found that 55 percent of evangelicals—and 78 percent of the regular churchgoers among them—say that faith is an important factor in their political decisions (this compares with about 30 percent among mainline Protestants and Catholics) (Guth, 1993).

According to Finke and Stark (1992), religions that gain members in the religious "marketplace" are the hardline ones. They portray religious groups as functioning much in the manner of "firms" competing for souls in a "divine economy" [Peter L. Berger (1969:138) also uses economic imagery in which he depicts religious institutions as "marketing agencies" and religious traditions as "consumer commodities"]. Competition fosters religious vitality, while monopoly breeds religious stagnation. Finke and Stark find that the "winners" have historically been "upstart sects," groups that today include Pentecostal, Holiness, and Fundamentalist sects. In Colonial times the established denominations went into decline when confronted with competition from Baptist and Methodist sects. In turn Methodism went into decline when its circuit-rider clergy dismounted and became professionalized, its hellfire and brimstone theology cooled, and its rustic camp meetings became "respectable middle-class summer resorts." The "winners" in the religious marketplace evidence entrepreneurial energy, organizational flexibility, and a dynamic clergy who know the needs and speak the language of ordinary people. High-cost faiths—those that impose sacrifices and even stigmas on their members—consistently outperform their more respectable counterparts (hardline religious groups also get rid of "free riders" who dilute the congregation's solidarity by using it for weddings, funerals, and an occasional spiritual boost without affording much in return). There seems to be an indissoluble link between how much a religion demands and how much its members feel it can offer in return. The "losers" are the "mainline denominations," especially the Congregationalists, Presbyterians, and Episcopalians, who have evolved a well-educated, seminary-trained clergy.

The difficulties the United States has experienced in recent years have contributed to the resurgence of conservative Christianity. Domestic and international developments have sorely tested the American character. As a nation we seem to have stumbled, experiencing the disgrace of failed leadership at home and the humiliation of impotence abroad. Despite great strides to erase social inequalities and new technological breakthroughs, poverty persists and drug abuse and crime seem out of control. Historically we have thought of ourselves as a good, God-fearing people, who, with the helping hand of God, had the ability to control our destiny. Given these circumstances, conservative Christianity has offered an old diagnosis: Our problems are of our own making; we must repent and make things right with God before we can again assume our role in the divine plan (Hadden, 1987a).

STATE-CHURCH ISSUES

The First Amendment to the U.S. Constitution states: "Congress shall make no law respecting an establishment of religion, or prohibiting the free exercise thereof. . . ." While this prohibition applies only to Congress, the Supreme Court has held it applicable to the states by virtue of the due process clause of the Fourteenth Amendment. It has provided the foundation for the principle of the separation of church and state, by which organized religion and government have remained substantially independent of each other. Compared with many other nations, the United States has maintained a remarkably hands-off attitude toward religion. Some sociologists believe that the absence of a coerced monopoly has compelled American religious institutions to operate in a pluralistic environment comparative to a market economy (Warner, 1993). Even so, in a number of cases, laws have been enacted and upheld by the Supreme Court that have impinged upon religious practices, including those against polygamy among Mormons and against snake-handling by charismatic Christians.

The separation of church and state has not denied a religious dimension to the American political scene (Wills, 1990; Williams and Demerath, 1991). Although most Americans deem an individual's religious beliefs and practices to be a strictly private matter, there are nonetheless certain common elements of religious orientation most Americans share. These religious dimensions are expressed in a set of beliefs, symbols, and rituals that sociologist Robert Bellah (1970; Bellah and Hammond, 1980) calls **civil religion.** Its basic tenet is that the American nation is not an ultimate end in itself but a nation under God with a divine mission. Although religious pluralism prevents any one denomination from supplying all Americans with a single source of meaning, civil religion compensates by providing an overarching sacred canopy. President Reagan captured this sentiment when he observed at a Dallas prayer breakfast in August 1984: "I believe that faith and religion play a critical role in the political life of our nation, and always has, and that the church—and by that I mean all churches, all denominations—has had a strong influence on the state, and this has worked to our benefit as a nation."

Civil religion finds expression in the statements and documents of the Founding Fathers, presidential inaugural addresses, national holidays, historic shrines, mottos, and patriotic expressions in times of crisis and peril. There are four references to God in the Declaration of Independence. Every president has mentioned God in his inaugural address (except George Washington in his second inauguration). Thanksgiving is a national holiday celebrated as a day of public thanksgiving and prayer. And the government engages in many religious practices, from the phrase "In God We Trust" on its currency to the prayers said in Congress. Significantly, both sides of American electoral politics (for instance, Reverends Jesse Jackson and Jerry Falwell) employ civil religion to interpret and legitimate their places and agendas within national life (Williams and Demerath, 1991).

Throughout American history, the influence of religion on secular politics and government has remained strong. As noted earlier in the chapter, religion has historically played a major role in a good many American social movements. Today groups armed with moral agendas are also seeking to gain public support for their programs. For instance, liberal religious organizations and the nation's Catholic bishops are pushing a set of issues that includes disarmament and improved social services for the disadvantaged. The Christian right has likewise come to the fore with an appeal to recover the Christian roots, heritage, and values of an older America. The result has been a reopening of the debate over the role religion should play in public policy (Olson and Carroll, 1992). At issue is not the right of religious activists to enter the political arena and lobby for laws consistent with their beliefs. Rather, the issue has been one of defining the place a religiously defined morality has in a pluralist society. The main controversies have resided in those areas in which private morality and public policy overlap. Abortion provides a good illustration. There are those who insist that abortion is a private moral choice and that the state has no right to make the practice illegal. Others, particularly antiabortion groups, contend that abortion is no more a matter of private moral choice than slavery was and that the state has an obligation to stop it. Other equally emotional issues have related to prayer in public schools, pornography, and the rights of gays and lesbians.

The current debate suggests that religion remains a powerful moving force in American life. In some respects, Americans are no closer to resolving how to relate people's religious lives to their civil lives than was the case in the days of Thomas Jefferson and James Madison. Clearly the issue is not one to be decided once and for all. Each generation of Americans must tackle its own version of the church-state question. The strength of the nation's pluralistic system has historically resided in a built-in check in which a backlash or countermovement sets in when any one group pushes too hard for its religious values.

☐ Education

Controversy also envelops the educational institution. This fact is hardly surprising since in modern societies few individuals and groups do not have a substantial stake in the educational enterprise. The reason is not difficult to discern: Learning is a fundamental process in our lives. It allows us to adapt to our environment by building on previous experience. Through our successes and failures in coping with our life circumstances, we derive an accumulating body of information that serves as a guide to decisions and actions. Social scientists view **learning** as a relatively permanent change in behavior or capability that results from experience. Since learning is so vital to social life, societies do not usually leave it to chance. Societies may undertake to transmit particular attitudes, knowledge, and skills to their members through formal, systematic training—what sociologists call **education.** Education is one aspect of the many-sided process of socialization by which people acquire behaviors essential for effective participation in society (see Chapter 3). It entails an explicit process in which some individuals assume the status of teacher and others the status of student and carry out their associated roles.

THE FUNCTIONALIST PERSPECTIVE ON EDUCATION

Schools initially came into existence several thousand years ago to prepare a select few for a limited number of leadership and professional positions. However, in the past century or so public schools have become the primary vehicles by which the members of a society are taught the three Rs, affording them the literacy skills required by large-scale industrial and bureaucratic organizations. The curricula of schools—such "core" subject areas as mathematics, natural science, and social science—are remarkably similar throughout the world. Standardized models of mass education apparently arose cross-culturally in conjunction with the diffusion of standardized models of the nation-state, which were closely linked to goals of national development, economic progress, and the formal integration of individuals within a larger social collectivity (Benavot et al., 1991; Meyer, Ramirez, and Soysal, 1992). Viewed from the functionalist perspective, the schools make a number of vital contributions to the survival and perpetuation of modern societies.

Completing Socialization. Many preliterate and peasant societies lack schools. They socialize their youngsters in the same "natural" way that parents teach their children to walk or talk. Consider the following account of the Copper Eskimos by anthropologist Diamond Jenness (1922: 170, 219):

A girl . . . is encouraged to make dolls and to mend her own clothing, her mother teaching her how to cut out the skins. Both boys and girls learn to stalk game by accompanying their elders on hunting excursions; their fathers make bows and arrows for them suited to their strength. One of their favourite pastimes is to carry out, in miniature, some of the duties they will have to perform when they grow up. Thus little girls often have tiny lamps in the corners of their huts over which they will cook some meat to share with their playmates. . . . The children naturally have many pastimes that imitate the actions of their elders. . . . Both boys and girls play at building snow houses. In summer, with only pebbles to work with, they simply lay out the ground plans, but in winter they borrow their parents' snow-knives and make complete houses on a miniature scale.

The content of culture among the Copper Eskimos is quite similar for everyone, and people acquire it mostly in an unconscious manner through daily living. Unlike the Copper Eskimos, adults in modern societies cannot afford to shape their children in their own image. Too often parents find themselves with obsolete skills, trained for jobs that are no longer needed. The knowledge and skills required by contemporary living cannot be satisfied in a more or less automatic and "natural" way. Instead, a specialized educational agency is needed to transmit to young people the ways of thinking, feeling, and acting mandated by a rapidly changing urban and technologically based society.

Social Integration. Functionalists say that the education system functions to inculcate the dominant values of a society and shape a common national mind. Within the United States students learn what it means to be an American, become literate in the English language, gain a common heritage, and acquire mainstream standards and rules. In this fashion youngsters from diverse ethnic, religious, and racial backgrounds are immersed within the same Anglo-American culture and prepared for "responsible" citizenship (see Chapter 7). Historically, the nation's schools have played a prominent part in Americanizing the children of immigrants (Dunn, 1993). Likewise, the schools are geared to integrating the poor and disadvantaged within the fabric of dominant, mainstream institutions. How well the educational institution performs these functions is a debatable matter. As we will note later in the chapter, conflict theorists see educational activities directed toward these ends as serving the interests of elite classes and groups.

Screening and Selecting. As we noted in Chapter 2, all societies ascribe some statuses to individuals independent of their unique qualities or abilities. Other statuses are achieved through choice and competition. No society ignores entirely individual differences or overlooks individual accomplishment and failure. Modern societies in particular must select certain of their youth for positions that require special talents. The educational institution commonly performs this function, serving as an agency for screening and selecting individuals for different types of jobs. By conferring degrees, diplomas, and credentials that are prerequisites for many technical, managerial, and professional positions, it determines which young people will have access to scarce positions and offices of power, privilege, and status. For many members of modern society, the schools function as "mobility escalators," allowing able, gifted individuals to ascend the social ladder (Krymkowski, 1991). Again, as we will see later in the chapter, conflict theorists contest this point and allege instead that the schools serve to guarantee that the sons and daughters of the elite—having acquired the "proper" credentials—are able to secure the best positions.

Research and Development. For the most part, schools are designed to produce people who fit into society, not people who set out to change it. However, schools, particularly universities, may not only transmit culture; they may add to the cultural heritage. Contemporary American society places a good deal of emphasis on the development of new knowledge, especially in the physical and biological sciences, medicine, and engineering. In recent decades, the nation's leading universities have increasingly become research centers. Indeed, by virtue of their research roles, 88 colleges and universities are among the top 500 contractors for the U.S. Department of Defense. (Massachusetts Institute of Technology and Johns Hopkins University rank among the top 20 contractors.) This emphasis on research has led universities to judge professors not primarily in terms of their competence as teachers but as researchers. Promotions, salary increases, and other benefits are usually contingent on grant procurement, research, and publication. Critics contend that academic success is most likely to come to those who have learned to "neglect" their teaching duties to pursue research activities (a survey of tenure-track faculty members at 4-year institutions reveals that the more hours an instructor spends in class per week, the lower the pay; faculty who teach only graduate students get paid the most; and the more time faculty members spend on research, the higher the compensation) (Jacobson, 1992). But defenders say that even when students are not themselves involved in research projects, they benefit from the intellectual stimulation a research orientation brings to university life. Critics also contend that large universities like MIT and Stanford have profited enormously from Pentagon- and Cold-War-related federal funding and that the "price of success" has been their shaping of many academic programs to the requirements of the national security state (Leslie, 1993).

THE CONFLICT PERSPECTIVE ON EDUCATION

Conflict theorists see the schools as agencies that reproduce and legitimate the current social order through the functions they perform. By reproducing and legitimating the existing social order, the educational institution is seen as benefiting some individuals and groups at the expense of others (Collins, 1977, 1979, 1988b).

Reproducing the Social Relations of Production.

Some conflict theorists depict American schools as reflecting the needs of capitalist production and as social instruments for convincing the population that private ownership and profit are just and in the best interests of the entire society (Apple, 1982; Apple and Weis, 1983). In *Schooling and Capitalist America* (1976), Samuel Bowles and Herbert Gintis set forth the **correspondence principle**—that the social relations of work find expression in the social relations of the school. They say that the schools mirror the workplace and hence on a day-to-day basis prepare children for adult roles in the job market. The authoritarian structure of the school reproduces the bureaucratic hierarchy of the corporation, rewarding diligence, submissiveness, and compliance. The system of grades employed to motivate students parallels the wage system for motivating workers. In short, the schools are seen as socializing a compliant labor force for the capitalist economy.

If indeed the educational system is to prepare youth for the workplace, many educators, economists, and politicians are saying that "traditional schools" are failing to teach what students will need to know to support themselves in the "real world." A Labor Department commission recommended in 1992 that America's schools be "reinvented" so that every student gets "workplace know-how" for the high-tech job market (Secretary's Commission on Achieving Necessary Skills, 1992). Often "a high school diploma is little more than a certificate of attendance," the report said. It went on to observe that employers know this and so they discount the diploma. High school students who do not anticipate going to college also know it and "similarly devalue their education, questioning its 'relevance' because it prepares them for no particular future." Observers of American life express concern that an increasingly diverse work force that lacks the proper skills will make it more difficult for American firms to survive against Japanese and German competition. And by failing to provide sufficient economic growth, the federal government will have a more difficult time maintaining Social Security and Medicare benefits at current levels for Americans who retire in the next century.

Control Devices.

Conflict theorists agree with functionalist theorists that schools are agencies for drawing minorities and the disadvantaged into the dominant culture. But they do not see the function in benign terms. Sociologist Randall Collins (1976) contends that the educational system serves the interests of the dominant group by defusing the threat posed by minority ethnic groups. In large, conflict-ridden, multiethnic societies like the United States, the schools become instruments to Americanize minority people. Compulsory education erodes ethnic differences and loyalties and transmits to minorities and those at the bottom of the social hierarchy the values and lifeways of the dominant group. Schools, then, are viewed as control devices employed by established elites.

Productive Capital.

Conflict theorists see the research and development function of the universities quite differently than do functionalist theorists. For instance, Michael W. Apple (1982) gives a Marxist twist to the functionalist argument by contending that the educational institution produces the technical and administrative knowledge necessary for running a capitalist order. Viewed in this manner, education is part of the system of production. It not only reproduces existing social arrangements but develops the know-how needed by capitalists to fuel the economy and gain competitive advantage in world markets (Barrow, 1990).

Credentialism.

Collins (1979) also downplays the functionalist argument that schools serve as

Money and SAT Scores

Family Income	SAT Averages	
	Verbal	Math
Less than $10,000	353	415
$10,000–$20,000	379	434
$20,000–$30,000	404	452
$30,000–$40,000	418	466
$40,000–$50,000	430	480
$50,000–$60,000	440	491
$60,000–$70,000	449	500
$70,000 or more	469	528

Figure 10.2   FAMILY INCOME AND SCHOLASTIC APTITUDE TEST SCORES
The figure shows the relationship between scores on the SAT and the family income for 1991 college-bound high school seniors. (SOURCE: Data from The College Board. Adapted from *U.S. News & World Report.* Copyright, September 9, 1991, p. 10. Reprinted by permission.)

Average Monthly Earnings

Professional $4,961
Doctorate $3,855
Master's $2,822
Bachelor's $2,116
Associate $1,672
Vocational $1,237
Some college $1,280
H.S. graduate $1,077
No H.S. diploma $492

Figure 10.3   THE FINANCIAL VALUE OF A POSTSECONDARY EDUCATION
The Census Bureau, on the basis of surveys of 23,000 households in the spring of 1990, reports that those with post-high school degrees earned an average of $2,231 monthly, compared with $1,077 for those with a high school disploma and just $492 for those who lack a high-school diploma (the figure shows the average monthly earnings, by educational level). On average, however, African Americans earned less than whites did at each educational level, with the exception of those with master's degrees. For instance, African Americans with bachelor's degrees earned an average of $1,814 a month, compared with $2,149 for whites. (SOURCE: U.S. Census Bureau. Adapted from *USA Today.* Copyright, January 28, 1993, D-1. Reprinted by permission.)

mobility escalators. He cites evidence that students acquire little technical knowledge in school and that most technical skills are learned on the job. Although more education is needed to obtain most jobs, Collins says that this development is not explained by the technical requirements of the job. The level of skills required by typists, receptionists, salesclerks, teachers, assembly-line workers, and many others is not much different than it was a generation or so ago. Collins calls these tendencies **credentialism**—the requirement that a worker have a degree for its own sake, not because it certifies skills needed for the performance of a job. Since education functions as a certification of class membership more than of technical skills, it functions as a means of class inheritance. Figure 10.2 shows the relationship between family income and Scholastic Aptitude Test (SAT) scores; SAT scores play a particularly important role in determining acceptance or rejection by the nation's elite colleges and universities (approximately 84 percent of all U.S. 4-year colleges use the SAT for admissions purposes).

Whereas at one time a college degree brought an elite occupational status with elite pay, today it brings a middle-class status with middle-class pay. Even so, a degree after high school seemingly affords financial benefits (see Figure 10.3). A recent study—unusual in that it compares data from identical twins to distinguish the impact of nurture from that of nature—estimates that, on average, each year of education (from grade school through graduate school) adds 16 percent to a person's lifetime earnings (Passell, 1992). Moreover, the gap between those with more and less education appears to be increasing. Indeed, some economists say that the United States is moving to a two-tiered society, with education levels explaining much of the division (Freadhoff, 1992).

THE INTERACTIONIST PERSPECTIVE ON EDUCATION

In their own right classrooms are self-contained "little worlds" teeming with behavior. It is these little worlds nested in schools that symbolic interactionists undertake to capture in their work. These sociologists no longer view the school as a "black box" in which something goes in and something comes out. Rather, they are interested in the processes occurring in schools. Consider communication, the heart of classroom life. Philip W. Jackson (1968) estimates from his observations in several elementary classrooms that teachers average over 200 interpersonal exchanges every hour of the school day. Much of the communication is one-way, with the teacher *telling* and students *listening*. Indeed, since the teacher functions as the communication "gatekeeper," students are often frustrated in taking the initiative in communicative interaction. Additionally, the physical arrangement of the traditional classroom—with students seated in rows facing the teacher—effectively channels most communication flows through the teacher. One consequence of these procedures and arrangements is that they tend to produce individuals who are programmed for input and not communication output.

Classroom research also sheds provocative insights on social inequality (Mehan, 1992). Many data suggest, for instance, that schools perform relatively well with upper- and middle-class youngsters. We would expect this would be the case, for the schools are staffed by middle-class teachers, the school's structure is modeled after middle-class life, and better school facilities are provided for these youngsters (our big-city schools, which have the poorest youngsters with the most difficult problems, get the least money, while our suburban schools, which have the wealthiest youngsters from the best educated homes, get the most money). Consider the **hidden curriculum.** The hidden curriculum consists of a complex of unarticulated values, attitudes, and behaviors that subtly mold children in the image preferred by the dominant institutions. Teachers model and reinforce traits that embody middle-class standards—industry, responsibility, conscientiousness, reliability, thoroughness, self-control, and efficiency. Even when teachers are originally from another social class, they still view their role as one of encouraging the development of a middle-class outlook on such matters as thrift, cleanliness, punctuality, neatness, ambition, sexual morality, and respect for property and established authority. Children learn to be quiet, to be on time, to line up, to wait their turn, to please their teachers, and to conform to group pressures. In some cases middle-class teachers, without necessarily being aware of their bias, find inner-city and minority children unacceptable—indeed, different and depressing. Their students tend to respond by taking the attitude, "If you don't like me, I won't cooperate with you." The net result is that the youngsters fail to acquire basic reading, writing, and math skills.

Educational self-fulling prophecies, or *teacher-expectation effects*, also victimize inner-city and minority children. The children fail to learn because those who are charged with teaching them do not believe that they will learn, do not expect that they can learn, and do not act toward them in ways that help them to learn (Clark, 1965). Researchers find that teachers' assessments of students are affected by the stereotypes the teachers hold of various social classes and racial groups. On the whole, white teachers rate white students higher than either their African-American or their Hispanic counterparts (Jensen and Rosenfeld, 1974). According to a survey conducted by the College of Education at Ohio State University, more than one-third of its student teachers do not feel they are competent to teach youngsters of different races, cultures, or income levels (Hanley, 1988). Among inner-city and minority youngsters, negative teacher-expectation effects breed student alienation and school failure, encourage oppositional forms of behavior designed to undermine the school's control strategies, and foster attitudes that lead to the mocking, taunting, and ostracism of children who do their homework and strive toward academic excellence (Solomon, 1992).

THE BUREAUCRATIC STRUCTURE OF SCHOOLS

Until a few generations ago, schooling in the United States usually took place in a one-room schoolhouse. One teacher taught all eight grades, with the more advanced and older students helping the less capable and younger students with their lessons. So long as the schools remained relatively small, they could operate on the basis of face-to-face interaction. But like hospitals, factories, and businesses, schools grew larger and more complex. In order to attain their goals, they had to standardize and routinize many of their operations and establish formal operating and administrative procedures. In brief, they turned to a bureaucratic arrangement, a social structure made up of a hierarchy of statuses and roles prescribed by explicit rules and procedures and based on a division of function and authority (see Chapter 4).

Like other complex organizations, schools do not exist in a social vacuum but are tightly interlocked with other institutions. At the very top of this organizational arrangement is the federal government, which through a variety of agencies, including the Department of Education and the federal court system, profoundly influences educational life. Consider, for instance, court rulings in desegregation cases and recent policies mandating practices relating to the education of handicapped children. State educational authorities also provide encompassing standards and regulations, like those setting the number of days in a school year, and they allocate state monies for specified programs.

The formal organization of American schools and colleges typically consists of four levels: (1) the board of education or trustees, (2) administrators, (3) teachers or professors, and (4) stu-

"It's nothing personal against you, Mrs. Gruber—I just don't trust people who work for the government."

From *The Wall Street Journal*—Permission, Cartoon Features Syndicate.

dents. The control of most schools and colleges is vested in an elected or appointed board of laypeople. It generally appoints and assigns administrators and teachers, decides on the nature of educational programs, determines building construction, and approves operational budgets. The administrators—superintendents, principals, presidents, chancellors, and deans—are responsible for executing the policies of the board. Although in theory the board determines policy, in actual practice many policy questions are settled by administrators. Teachers are the immediate day-to-day link between the larger system and individual students, the latter occupying the lowest position in the school bureaucracy. Elementary and secondary teachers usually enjoy less authority in decision-making than their counterparts in higher education. In sum, the school system is characterized by a chain of command, a network of positions functionally interrelated for the purpose of accomplishing educational objectives.

By virtue of bureaucratic arrangements, school environments are remarkably standardized in both their physical and their social characteristics. Physical objects, social relations, and major activities remain much the same from day to day, week to week, and even year to year. These patterns are most apparent at the elementary and secondary school levels. For instance, time is highly formalized. The pledge of allegiance is followed by math at 8:35, which is followed by reading at 9:10, which is followed by recess, and so on over the course of the day. The music teacher comes for 50 minutes on Tuesday afternoons, and children go to gym on Wednesday and Friday mornings at 10:20. There is almost a holy aura about the "daily grind" as mandated by the schedule.

Individual behavior is rigidly governed by sets of rules—no loud talking during seat work, raise your hand to talk during discussions, keep your eyes on your paper during tests, and no running in the halls. The physical layout of the school and the omnipresent symbols of adult authority emphasize and reinforce the subordinate status of the pupils. Cloakrooms and lunchrooms have a special space reserved for the teachers and a separate space for children. The teacher has a special desk in a special part of the classroom. Although the teacher may inspect a child's desk and possessions at will, the child is denied a similar right. It is a system that encourages student passivity and makes the school a relatively uninteresting place, resembling in many ways what sociologist Erving Goffman (1961b) has called a *total institution* (see Chapter 4).

THE EFFECTIVENESS OF SCHOOLS

In a clarion call to Americans to awaken to the abject state of their educational system, the National Commission on Excellence in Education said in 1983 that we are a "nation at risk" because of a "rising tide of mediocrity" in the schools. In the years since the publication of *A Nation at Risk,* new reports show that the achievement levels of primary and secondary students remain "low" and are "not improving." Indeed, according to the Department of Education, fewer than 10 percent of the nation's high school seniors have the skills necessary to perform demanding jobs or do college work (Center for Education Statistics, 1990).

The reports mention many of the same indicators, including poor achievement test scores, a a long-term slippage in college entrance test scores (see Figure 10.4), declines in both enrollments and achievement in science and mathematics, the generally poor performance of American students on international tests (see Figure 10.5), the high cost incurred by business and the military for remedial and training programs, and the substantial levels of functional illiteracy found among American adults and children.

Psychologist Harold W. Stevenson and his colleagues (1992, 1993) have spent more than 15 years in cross-cultural studies of American, Chinese, and Japanese educational practices and school experiences. They find that American schoolchildren lag behind schoolchildren in Japan and Taiwan from the day they enter school. The poorer performance of American youngsters seems to be related to the way American schools manage instruction. For one thing, the average school year is shorter in the United States—180 days versus 240 in Japan and Taiwan—and the school day is a half hour to 2 hours shorter. For another, American children spend less than half as much time as Taiwanese and less than two-thirds as much time as the Japanese on academic activities (and spend considerably more time viewing television than do Taiwanese and Japanese youngsters). Finally, cultural differences also appear to affect performance. Japanese and Taiwanese parents seem to place greater emphasis than their American counterparts on the importance of children's working hard at school and on homework. Indeed, Asian parents believe—and their youngsters are expected to understand—that academic learning is their primary responsibility. Both Japanese and Chinese parents think achievement is directly related to hard work and effort. In contrast, American parents—despite the old adage depicting Americans as confirmed believers in hard work—rate innate ability as a stronger factor than effort in their children's school success. Parents who believe success depends more upon ability than effort are less likely to require

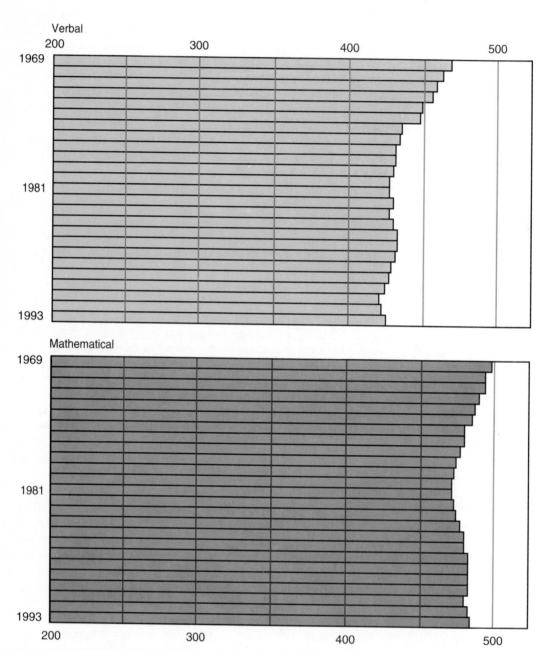

(a) SAT Scores, 1969–1993

Verbal

Mathematical

Figure 10.4 SCHOLASTIC APTITUDE TEST (SAT) SCORES, 1969–1993
Scores on both the verbal and mathematics sections of the SAT rose in 1993 for the second year in a row. However, women's average scores continue to lag behind men on both sections of the test: Men averaged 428 on the verbal section and 502 on the math section; women averaged 420 and 457, respectively. (SOURCE: College Board. Adapted from *The Chronicle of Higher Education*, September 1, 1993, A46. Reprinted by permission.)

(b) SAT Averages by Ethnic Group, 1992–1993

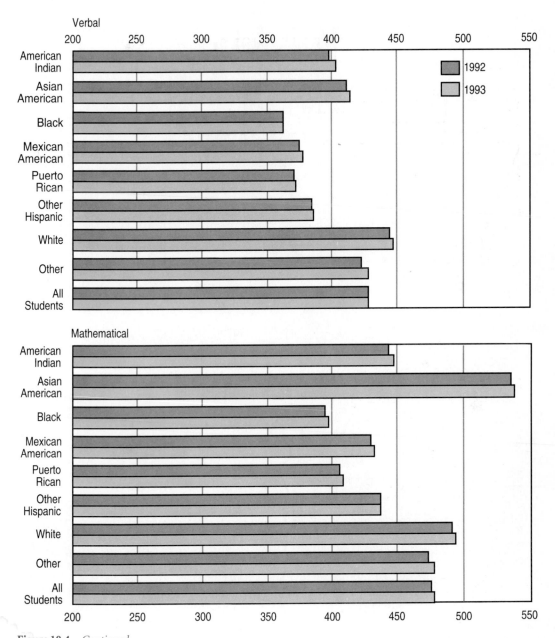

Figure 10.4   *Continued*

(a) Who Spends the Most

Total spending from government and private sources for each student, calculated as a percentage of per capita gross domestic product, 1991.

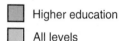

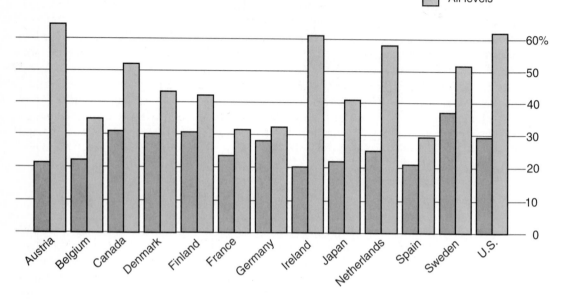

(b) Achievement: A Comparison

Average achievement in reading and math for 14- and 13-year-olds, respectively, in each country, 1991.

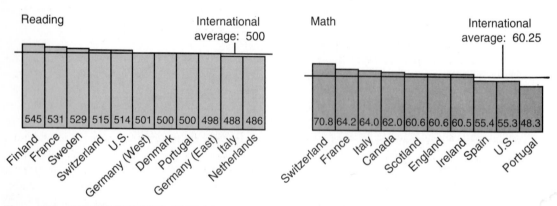

Figure 10.5   HOW THE UNITED STATES COMPARES ON EDUCATION WITH OTHER WESTERN NATIONS
The figure provides data released in December 1993 by the Organization for Economic Cooperation and Development, based in Paris. (SOURCE: Organization for Economic Cooperation and Development. Adapted from The *New York Times,* December 9, 1993, p. A8. Copyright © 1993 by The New York Times Company. Reprinted by permission.)

their children to work hard at learning than are parents who value effort. American parents are also more likely to be satisfied with their children's achievement and schools than are their Asian counterparts.

Social scientists have examined what makes a school effective. Child psychiatrist Michael Rutter (1979) led a University of London team in a 3-year study of students entering twelve London inner-city secondary schools. The researchers found that schools only a scant distance apart and with students of similar social backgrounds and intellectual abilities had quite different educational results. The critical element distinguishing the schools was their "ethos" or "climate." The successful schools fostered expectations that order would prevail in the classrooms, and they did not leave matters of student discipline to be worked out by individual teachers for themselves. As a result, it was easier to be a good teacher in some schools than in others. Additionally, the effective schools emphasized academic concerns—care by teachers in lesson planning, group instruction, high achievement expectations for students, a high proportion of time spent on instruction and learning activities, the assignment and checking of homework, and student use of the library. The researchers also found that schools that fostered respect for students as responsible people and held high expectations for appropriate behavior achieved better academic results. In the more successful schools, many students assumed responsibilities as group captains or as participants in school assemblies. However, there was no relationship between the size and age of the school building and student discipline or achievement.

Other research supports the conclusion that successful schools foster expectations that order will prevail and that learning is a serious matter (Winn, 1981; Lee and Bryk, 1989). Much of the success enjoyed by private and Catholic schools has derived from their ability to provide students with an ordered environment and strong academic demands (Coleman, Hoffer, and Kilgore, 1982a; Coleman and Hoffer, 1987; Flanigan, 1991;

Putka, 1991). Academic achievement is just as high in the public sector when the policies and resulting behavior are like those in the private sector (Coleman, Hoffer, and Kilgore, 1982b). In sum, successful schools possess "coherence": Things stick together and bear predictable relationships with one another (Coleman and Hoffer, 1987). It seems that a growing number of American parents are looking for many of these qualities in their youngsters' schooling. So "fed up" with public schools, some parents are turning to home schooling (in 1994 nearly 400,000 school-aged children were learning at home), evangelical schools, and private-tuition schools.

THE AVAILABILITY OF EDUCATION

Higher education in the United States is big business—a $100 billion business representing 2.7 percent of the gross national product. In recent years the cost of higher education has outpaced the growth in family income and is nearly triple the rate of inflation. The price of an undergraduate education at many top universities exceeded $100,000 in 1995, and the tab is expected to climb an additional $70,000 or more by the year 2000. There are a good many reasons why a college education is costly. For one thing, education is a labor-intensive industry, with about three-quarters of a college's budget going for faculty and staff salaries. Even so, faculty salaries were stagnant during the early 1990s (38 percent of all faculty members are part-timers and more than half the faculty at fast-growing, 2-year community colleges work only part time; on average, part-timers earn $6,300 a year, with pay ranging from $900 to $3,000 per course at most schools). At the same time, however, the number of administrators—deputy provosts and assistant deans—has been growing rapidly (including specialists in student services, student placement, and auditing to deal with new government regulations and fund raising) (Honan, 1994). Other costs have also mounted. College utility bills have doubled over the past decade. And years of deferred maintenance have meant growing costs in keeping buildings functional.

Even with substantial increases, tuition does not cover the real costs of educating a student. On average, tuition at private colleges covers three-fourths of the cost (private gifts and investment income provide the rest), whereas at lower-priced public institutions it covers about 25 percent (public institutions are subsidized by state taxes). The cutback in federal subsidies is complicating the educational cost crunch (between 1980 and 1990, the cost of higher education went up 126 percent, while federal financial aid rose 47 percent). A report by the American College Testing Program concluded that inadequate financial aid, poor academic preparation, and low college retention rates are responsible for the continuing gaps in college-completion rates between wealthier and poorer students and between white and minority students (Mortenson and Wu, 1991). In 1970, a student from the top quarter of the nation's income distribution was nearly six times as likely to earn a bachelor's degree as was a student from the bottom quarter of the distribution. In 1979, the wealthier student was only four times as likely to earn a degree, but by 1989 the wealthier student's chance of securing a degree had increased to twelve times that of the poorer student (only 20 percent of the nation's undergraduates are young people between 18 and 22 years of age who are pursuing a parent-financed education; two-fifths of all students are part-timers; and more than a third of all undergraduates are over age 25).

The likelihood that an African-American person age 25 to 29 had a bachelor's degree in the 1960s was two-fifths of that for a white person of the same age (Mortenson and Wu, 1991). African Americans were half as likely as whites to have had a bachelor's degree in the 1970s, and their progress has since stalled. A Hispanic person age 25 to 29 was less than one-third as likely as a same-age white person to have a bachelor's degree in the mid-1970s. The figure improved to about two-fifths in 1989. A good many factors make it difficult for minority youth to gain entrance to and then remain in college. First, many of the students secure weaker academic preparation in elementary and secondary schools than do white students. Second, most campuses lack a "critical mass" of minority students and faculty who can serve as role models and make new students feel at home. And third, many minority students are first-generation collegians, and they do not secure the emotional or financial support from home that second- and third-generation collegians receive (Johnson, 1988).

□ Medicine

Like the educational institution, the functions now carried out by the medical institution were once embedded in the activities of the family and religious institutions. Only in relatively recent times has **medicine** emerged as a distinct institution, providing an enduring set of cultural patterns and social relationships responsible for problems of health and disease. The World Health Organization defines **health** as "a state of complete physical, mental, and social well-being and not merely the absence of disease or infirmity." We usually assess people's health by how well they are able to function in their daily lives and adapt to a changing environment. Health, then, has a somewhat different meaning for a soldier, a nursing home resident, an airline pilot, a steel worker, a high school football player, a presidential candidate, and a computer programmer. In contrast to health, most of us think of disease as an undesirable, serious, and limiting circumstance. **Disease** is a condition in which an organism does not function properly because of biological causes. The problems may result from microbial infection, dietary deficiency, heredity, or a harmful environmental agent. The functionalist, conflict, and interactionist perspectives provide us with valuable insights regarding medicine and health care.

THE FUNCTIONALIST PERSPECTIVE ON MEDICINE

Functionalists note that health is essential to the preservation of the human species and organized social life. If societies are to function smoothly and effectively, there must be a reasonable supply of productive members to carry out vital tasks. Where large numbers of people are ill or physically unfit (as in some developing nations where malaria is widespread), low vitality, low productivity, and poverty abound as major social problems. Moreover, community personnel, resources, facilities, and funds must be withdrawn from other essential activities to care for the nonproducing sick (Hertzler, 1961).

Functionalists say the medical institution evolved across time to deal with problems of health and disease. More specifically, they see the medical institution performing a number of key functions in modern societies. First, it treats and seeks to cure disease. Second, the medical institution attempts to prevent disease through health maintenance programs, including vaccination, health education, periodic checkups, and public health and safety standards. Third, it undertakes research in the prevention, treatment, and cure of health problems. And fourth, it serves as an agency of social control by defining some behaviors as "normal" and "healthy" and others as "deviant" and "unhealthy."

Sociologist Talcott Parsons (1951) expands upon the functionalist position in his analysis of the **sick role**—a set of cultural expectations that define what is appropriate and inappropriate behavior for people with a disease or health problem (also see Turner, 1987). He says one way societies contain the negative effects of health problems is through institutionalizing illness in a special role, one having the following characteristics:

□ Sick people are exempt from their usual social roles and responsibilities. They need not attend school or go to work, and other people will not censure them for doing so.

□ Sick people are not thought to be at fault for their condition. Being sick is a physical matter, not a moral one.

□ Sick people have the duty to get well and "not enjoy themselves too much." Because being sick is an undesirable state, sick people are obligated to seek competent help from medical practitioners.

□ Sick people should cooperate with medical practitioners and follow their instructions.

Like other functionalists, Parsons assumes illness must be socially controlled lest it impair societal functioning.

THE CONFLICT PERSPECTIVE ON MEDICINE

Implicit in the functionalist image of the sick role is the assumption that health care services are impartially and equally available to all members of a society regardless of class, race, age, gender, or creed. This image is challenged by conflict theorists (Waitzkin, 1983). They say that people of all societies prefer health to illness. Yet some people achieve better health than others because they have access to those resources that contribute to good health and to recovery should they become ill.

Conflict theorists point out that the higher our social class, the more likely we are to enjoy good health, receive good medical care, and live a long life. Poor people experience more disability and lower levels of health than do affluent people. Even though access to health care among the poor has improved in recent years, when level of disability is taken into account, the poor receive less care for their illnesses than the nonpoor (Wallace, 1990; Gibbons, 1991; Stein, Fox, and Murata, 1991). Overall, the American health care system reflects the needs of the affluent more than those of the poor. Some 28 million Americans—12 percent of the population—have problems that hinder their access to the health care system. And some 40 million Americans live in federally designated areas with a shortage of primary medical care, a disproportionate percentage of whom are poor and members of minority groups (Walmer, 1990, 1991). Overall, physicians tend to be scarce in poverty areas, and travel difficulties are often complicated by inadequate public transportation.

In practice American medical care has traditionally operated as a dual system in which the poor have utilized public sources—hospital outpatient departments, emergency rooms, and public clinics—while middle- and upper-income Americans use private sources—physicians in private or group practice. Patients using public sources must often maneuver between multiple clinics to obtain their services, and the services are usually disease-oriented rather than preventive. In addition, the atmosphere in these institutions is often dehumanizing. Since African Americans, Hispanics, and Native Americans (Indians) are more likely to be poor than are whites, these groups also experience higher rates of disease and shorter life expectancies (Friend, 1990; Leary, 1991). For instance, African American and other minority women are 2.7 times as likely to die of pregnancy-related complications as white women (DeChick, 1988). The diabetes rate is 33 percent higher among African Americans as among whites, and African Americans have twice the level of infant mortality (Lee, 1989). Hispanics suffer from an excessive incidence of cancers of the stomach, esophagus, breast, pancreas, and cervix and of tuberculosis and cirrhosis (Altman, 1991).

THE INTERACTIONIST PERSPECTIVE ON MEDICINE

Symbolic interactionists view "sickness" as a condition to which we attach socially devised meanings. By way of analogy, consider the blight that attacks potatoes and corn. "Blight" is merely a humanly fashioned construct: If we wished to cultivate parasites, rather than potatoes or corn, we would not view the condition as "blight." In like manner, the invasion of an individual's body by cholera germs no more carries with it the stamp

of "sickness" than does the souring of milk by other forms of bacteria. For a condition to be interpreted as a sickness, the members of a society must define it as such. Indeed, in your daily life you often "negotiate" the definitions (C. Clark, 1983). When something seemingly goes amiss with your health, you may attempt to "validate" your interpretation of the symptoms by checking with others: "Dad, do you think this rash is hives?" or "Doctor, do I have a sore throat?" Your father may reply, "It looks to me like a couple of mosquito bites," and your physician may respond, "Your throat doesn't *look* too bad to me, but how does it *feel*? When you swallow, does it hurt?"

Some conditions are so prevalent among a population that people typically do not consider them as "unusual" or "symptomatic." Among many Hispanics in the Southwest, diarrhea, sweating, and coughing are "taken-for-granted," everyday occurrences. Similarly, lower-back pain is a common condition experienced by many lower-class American women, who often view it not as a product of disease or disorder but as an integral part of their day-to-day lives. By the same token, many people are medically "suggestible." For instance, three researchers at Baylor College of Medicine recently recruited 100 volunteers, attached each one by electrodes to a stimulator, and told them that they might experience a headache from the electric current. The volunteers did not know that the stimulator was a sham and incapable of producing a painful sensation. Even so, 50 percent reported pain (Shorter, 1991).

For its part, the medical profession frequently defines certain conditions as diseases even though there is little evidence that the conditions have biological causes or respond to medical treatment. For example, prior to 1973 the American Psychiatric Association included homosexuality in its manual of mental illnesses. By the same token, federal agencies have engaged in a long debate as to whether the definition of AIDS should be expanded since the criteria for AIDS-related disability benefits are hampered by the complexity of defining a disease that has no symptoms of its own (Navarro, 1992). In a like manner, medical "remedies" often need to be negotiated. For instance, at San Francisco General Hospital's bustling refugee clinic, a Haitian man refuses a blood test, fearing that the blood, which holds a "portion of the soul," could be used for sorcery, and a Vietnamese patient cuts his medication in half, convinced that American drugs, meant for large people, will be too powerful (Goode, 1993).

In some cases, a medical treatment is discovered *before* the condition is seen as a medical one. The discovery that the amphetamine Ritalin has a calming effect on some youngsters led to the conclusion that their disruptive behavior, short attention span, temper tantrums, fidgeting, and difficulty in learning is a disorder—"attention-deficit hyperactivity disorder" (ADHD) (the designation employed by the American Psychiatric Association). Previously, the youngsters were defined as "bad," and parents and teachers responded to their "misbehavior" with punishment (Conrad and Schneider, 1980). Today, an increasing number of behaviors that earlier generations defined as being immoral or sinful are coming to be seen as forms of sickness, a process sociologists call the **medicalization of deviance.** Drug abuse, alcoholism, and child abuse are regarded in many quarters as psychological difficulties that are "medical" problems requiring treatment by physicians, especially psychiatrists. At the present time controversy surrounds the issue as to whether incest, murder, and rape should be viewed as "crimes" that are best handled by jailers or as "sicknesses" best treated by medical practitioners. These considerations bring us to an examination of the American health care delivery system.

THE AMERICAN HEALTH CARE DELIVERY SYSTEM

Many societies have evolved one or more "specialist" positions to deal with sickness (Hughes, 1968). Curers, shamans, physicians, nurses, and other practitioners are relied upon to explain illness and to offer means for eliminating or controlling it. Drugs, poultices, surgery, bone setting, confinement, acupuncture, electric shock, leeching, talking, ritual, magic, and appeal to the supernatural are techniques used by medical practitioners in one or more societies. Additionally, medical practitioners serve as gatekeepers who legitimately channel people into the sick role. And in modern societies physicians certify that people have been born, have died, are fit to work, are eligible for disability benefits, are entitled to accident claims, and are at a danger to themselves or society.

Any number of observers of the American scene have pointed out that the United States truly does not have a "health care system" but rather a "disease cure system" (Konner, 1993; Spiegel, 1994). The public believes, and a good many physicians behave as if, most illnesses are curable. Americans typically view the body as if it were a machine with replaceable parts: Defects can be identified, removed, and replaced through medical treatment, be it via drugs, surgery, organ transplants, or gene therapy. In much the manner they take their automobiles to mechanics for 10,000- and 20,000-mile checkups, so many Americans take their bodies to physicians for annual physical checkups (the notion "Pay now or pay later").

The expectation of cure in the American system has generated an explosion of invasive, expensive, and often risky medical interventions. The emphasis falls on disease and not on the people who have the diseases. Most Americans die of chronic and progressive illnesses like cancer, stroke, and heart disease. Cure is the exception and not the rule. For instance, most clinicians and researchers in the field of coronary artery disease concentrate on ways to clear out fatty plaque buildups in arteries or to replace clogged arteries surgically. These techniques do not cure the disease, work less often than we wish, are done at great risk to patients, and cost a colossal amount of money. Yet much evidence suggests that behaviors such as eating a diet low in saturated fat and cholesterol, avoiding smoking, and getting moderate exercise can both prevent and reverse much heart disease. Indeed, in some respects, the nation's "health crisis" is, as sociologist and U.S. Senator Daniel Patrick Moynihan observes, a "social crisis" (social pathologies such as drug and alcohol abuse and poor health practices such as the lack of exercise and unhealthy diets have nothing to do with flaws in the medical system, yet they nonetheless show up in medical costs) (Kuttner, 1994).

American medical practice is enamored with technology. Indeed, many people look to legal documents like living wills to ensure that they will not confront death in a vegetative state hooked up to life-support systems. In keeping with a high-tech emphasis, medical care is highly specialized. Health economists say that a medical system should have about 50 percent of its doctors practicing primary care (family practice, internal medicine, and pediatrics). Yet in 1992, only a third of the nation's physicians were in primary care and less than 15 percent of medical students had decided to go into general medicine, an all-time low (Rosenthal, 1993).

From a virtual cottage industry dominated by individual physicans and not-for-profit hospitals, health care is evolving into a network of corporations running everything from hospitals and home health care services to retirement homes and health spas. By 1995, Americans were spending an estimated $1 trillion a year on health care. These expenditures account for nearly 15 percent of the nation's gross domestic product, a proportion up from 5.9 percent in 1965. In contrast, only about 10 percent of the gross domestic product of Canada, and less than 7 percent of that of Japan and the United Kingdom, goes to health care, although these nations provide universal coverage. So formidable has the medical care industry become that some critics have labeled it "the medical-industrial complex."

Hospitals. Separate facilities for the ill came into existence among the ancient Greeks. But it was not until the Middle Ages in western Europe that the hospital movement began in earnest. By 1450, there were some 600 hospitals in England alone. Most hospitals were run by Catholic religious orders because healing and health care were deemed to be the province of religion. The hospitals also cared for the poor, the disabled, and the itinerant. The linking of the medical and social functions had grave health consequences. Travelers housed with sick people in one hospital would then carry germs to the next hospital, readily infecting people whose resistance to disease was already low. Toward the end of the 1600s and during the 1700s, financial abuses and the mismanagement of funds by some religious orders led local governments to take on greater responsibility for the management of hospitals. About the same time, care of the indigent was physically segregated in facilities separate from the ill (Rosen, 1963).

By the late 1800s, hospital services were improving. Advances in medical research, especially bacteriology, provided a stronger scientific basis for treatment and the control of infection. New diagnostic tools, such as X-rays, and advances in surgical procedures made many diseases, injuries, and deformities more amenable to medical operations. By the turn of the century, the trustees of charity hospitals began to woo doctors who cared for well-to-do patients at home. More and more charity hospitals refurbished their rooms and advertised their amenities. In the process, the hospitals ceded considerable control to private physicians, who were more concerned with making the hospital a workshop for the treatment of paying patients than a center for administering charitable care. Hospitals became businesses governed by commercial incentives. As insurance developed first for hospital bills and later for physicians' bills, the hospital industry and the medical profession flourished. By 1965, Congress had established Medicare to pay some of the health care costs of the elderly, and Medicaid for those of the "deserving" poor. By the mid-1960s, then, hospitals, physicians, private insurers, and the government had devised a system for financing health care that was ripe for big business and the emergence of for-profit hospital chains (Gray, 1991; Lindorff, 1992).

Physicians. Sociologist Paul Starr (1982) has traced the transformation of health care from a household service to a market commodity and the rise of the private medical practice. He shows that well into the nineteenth century, most American doctors eked out scant incomes. However, - following the Civil War, a contracting household economy, a growing urban population, and more efficient transportation and communication expanded the market for medical services. By the turn of the twentieth century, doctors were well on the road to endowing their profession with a "cultural authority" sufficient to justify claims to self-regulation, state protection, client deference, and control of the means of work. In turn, doctors capitalized on these gains to develop medical specialities and mutual networks that decreased competition and increased their economic and political power. By the 1930s, private practitioners had acquired sufficient influence and prestige to establish themselves as virtually the sole arbiters of medicine in the United States. They dominated hospitals, medical technology, and other health practitioners, including nurses and pharmacists. Additionally, doctors institutionalized their authority through a system of medical education and standardized educational licensing.

Medicine is increasingly becoming a corporate undertaking. Many physicians have set up professional corporations to achieve the benefits of group practice and to take advantage of special tax-sheltering provisions. Walk-in clinics—quick-treatment centers that do not require an appointment—are being established in countless communities. Private corporations like Humana hire physicians for their health care clinics. And man-

"Hi! My name is Kevin, and I'll be your doctor today."

Drawing by M. Stevens; © 1994 The New Yorker Magazine, Inc.

aged care arrangements, such as health maintenance organizations (HMOs) and preferred provider organizations (PPOs), are winning growing numbers of patients. Under these latter arrangements an employer or an insurer typically contracts with a network of physicians to provide its employees or members with health care for a fixed sum of money each year. Although many physicians complain that joining health care networks appreciably lessens their autonomy and incomes, the economic dictates of contemporary private practice often lead them to take this route. At the same time critics worry that the financial incentives associated with HMOs and PPOs are skewed toward the pretense of health care delivery and that there is a disincentive to provide patients with quality care.

Interaction between a physician and patient was traditionally governed by inequality. Like other professionals, doctors derived their power from their command of an esoteric body of knowledge acquired through academic training and leavened by a service orientation toward the client. The "competence gap" justified both the physician's assumption of authority and the client's trust, confidence, and compliance. However, a good many Americans are no longer willing to accept a boorish bedside manner. Indeed, a 1991 survey conducted by the American Medical Association found considerable disenchantment: 63 percent of the American public agreed that "Doctors are too interested in making money"; only 42 percent agreed that "Doctors usually explain things well to their patients"; and only 31 percent agreed that "Most doctors spend enough time with their patients" (Nazario, 1992). Consequently, a new type of relationship is emerging between many physicians and their patients that is based on consumerism. It focuses on the purchaser's (the patient's) rights and the seller's (the physician's) obligations. In a consumer relationship, the seller lacks authority because the buyer can make the decision to buy or not to buy. With many patients coming to view doctors as self-interested vendors of their services, the practice of medicine is becoming customer-driven. These and other factors have fostered the growth of alternative therapies, including chiropractic, acupuncture, biofeedback, homeopathic medicine, herbalism, and reflexology (a third of the population today consults alternative healers) (Eisenberg et al., 1993). At the same time, the ethical practice of medicine has come under growing scrutiny, especially situations that pose conflicts of interest (for example, physicans who refer patients to medical facilities in which they own an interest or from whom they receive a percentage of the fees in return for referrals) (Rodwin, 1993).

The Nursing Profession. The nursing profession grew out of the religious and charitable activities of early hospitals. Religious orders of nuns took on the care of the sick and the poor. By the latter half of the 1800s, however, increasing numbers of nonreligious personnel were employed to perform various custodial functions in hospitals. Since the jobs required no formal training and were deemed to be menial labor, many poor and uneducated women entered the field. This her-

itage has contributed to the undeservedly low prestige that the profession of nursing has long endured (Mauksch, 1972; Baer, 1991). Additionally, wages in nursing, like those in other fields with a large concentration of women, remain low even today.

The professionalization of nursing—the emergence of professional standards, education, and nursing organizations—received impetus from the activities of Florence Nightingale and her organization of nurses during the Crimean War (an 1853–1856 war with Great Britain, France, and Turkey on one side and Russia on the other). Nightingale sought to strengthen cooperative ties between physicans and nurses in the care of patients. Although her efforts carved out a special niche in patient care for nurses, it had the side effect of establishing nursing as a profession under the jurisdiction of physicians. By World War I, most nurses were educated in 2- or 3-year nursing programs with a hospital apprenticeship. Today, most nurses earn a bachelor of science degree in nursing in a 4-year college degree program, and many go on to secure master's degrees in specialized areas.

Through the years nursing has remained almost exclusively female—some 94.5 percent of America's 1.7 million nurses (see Table 10.2). About 60 percent of all registered nurses work in hospitals, where they serve simultaneously as managers of hospital wards and assistants to physicians. These dual functions often place nurses in situations of role conflict because they are responsible to both administrative and medical authorities. And in an era of high medical technology and intensive-care units, nurses have had to assume more responsibilities, leading many to experience role overload. At the same time, nurses have been steadily acquiring more autonomy in health care. In recent years they have boldly moved into territory previously controlled by physicians, including delivering primary health care on their own (primary care refers to the initial care a patient receives before being referred, if necessary, to a specialist) (Herbert, 1993).

Table 10.2 EMPLOYED CIVILIANS, 16 AND OVER, IN HEALTH OCCUPATIONS, 1990

Occupation	Number	Women (%)	African-American (%)	Hispanic (%)
Administrators	175,000	66.5	7.5	2.9
Professionals				
Doctors and dentists	871,000	17.8	3.0	3.7
Registered nurses	1,673,000	94.5	7.4	2.5
Pharmacists	171,000	37.2	4.1	4.1
Dieticians	83,000	95.0	20.1	3.5
Therapists	325,000	76.6	6.0	2.9
Doctors' assistants	67,000	39.6	6.4	5.2
Technical				
Licensed practical nurses	443,000	96.3	17.6	3.8
Laboratory technologists and technicians	297,000	76.3	15.1	4.1
Dental hygienists	87,000	99.1	2.5	3.0
Health record technicians	69,000	94.0	15.4	8.1
Radiologic technicians	123,000	76.4	12.8	4.8
Service				
Nursing aides, orderlies and attendants	1,452,000	90.8	30.7	6.5
Other aides, non-nursing	448,000	84.5	21.0	5.6
Dental assistants	187,000	98.7	5.6	7.4

SOURCE: Bureau of Labor Statistics. Adapted from *The New York Times,* September 5, 1991, p. A10. Copyright © 1991 by The New York Times Company. Reprinted by permission.

FINANCING HEALTH CARE

The nation's health expenditures have steadily increased in recent decades (medical costs soared from $75 billion in 1970 to an estimated $1 trillion by 1995). A number of forces have pushed costs up. First, the classical rules that govern marketplace exchanges have not been applied to the health industry. The sellers—doctors and hospitals—have traditionally determined the price and product options; the buyers—patients—rather than shopping around, have bought what the sellers have ordered. And since doctors and hospitals have been paid for what they do, regardless of whether the care actually benefits the patient, they have had few incentives not to use every medical service and technique available. Second, labor costs have risen sharply (since 1950 the number of hospital workers per bed has more than tripled). Simultaneously, administrative costs—personnel for such activities as billing, accounting, and institutional planning—have grown three times faster since 1970 than costs for health care personnel. Third, the continual upgrading in the scope and intensity of medical services is costly. Technological advances include such accepted practices as hip replacement and coronary-bypass surgery, new therapies such as liver and heart transplantation, and new diagnostic techniques such as computerized axial tomography (CAT) and magnetic resonance imaging (MRI) devices. Fourth, our population is getting larger and older, and this fact alone contributes about 1 percentage point a year to the increase in real costs. More and more Americans are living beyond age 85. It is this age group in which chronic diseases and disorders of

THE WALL STREET JOURNAL

*"George, buy me a thousand shares in the drug
company that makes XPG-94."*

From *The Wall Street Journal*—Permission, Cartoon Features
Syndicate.

aging take their main toll. Fifth, modern medicine
does not reduce the percentage of sick people. It
actually increases it by keeping more people alive,
although not cured. And sixth, we have expanded
our concept of health to encompass mental and
psychological difficulties and "conditions" like
infertility that people once were expected to "live
with."

Soaring health care costs have led to new
arrangements for financing health care. The new
arrangements have developed piecemeal over the
past 15 years. Their theme is "competition"—the
notion that physicians, hospitals, and other health
providers should compete for patients in a price-
sensitive market, not unlike the markets for other
goods and services. The air of competition is
changing the ways Americans use and pay doctors
and hospitals. It is also reshaping financial incentives that have encouraged unnecessary care.
Another approach to holding down costs is to
keep people out of the hospital. Increasingly, hospitals and independent medical companies are
setting up satellite outpatient surgical centers,

mobile diagnostic laboratories, hospices, and
walk-in clinics for routine care. At the same time,
government, in seeking to cut costs, has become
progressively more involved in regulating the
activities of both hospitals and physicians. Sociologist Mary Ruggie (1992) terms this "step-by-
step" growth of government regulation in a political climate that endorses private enterprise and
marketplace rate setting "the paradox of liberal
intervention." The cost of government health care
spending has simultaneously mounted (in 1960,
the federal government paid only 9 percent of the
nation's health care costs; today, it picks up more
than 30 percent of the tab).

Widespread dissatisfaction with the U.S. health
care system had led some American leaders to
contend that the United States should provide all
its citizens, as an entitlement, with the essentials
of adequate health care, regardless of their ability
to pay, as is done in Canada. In 1971, the Canada
Health Act mandated that the government pay for
all medically necessary physician and hospital services. It allowed the eleven provinces and two territories to administer their own programs, negotiate doctors' fees, and set hospital budgets. In 1994
the United States devoted at least 40 percent more
of its gross domestic product to health care than
Canada did. The lower Canadian costs are due to
lower physician and hospital costs (physician fees
are 2.4 times higher and hospital fees nearly 3
times higher in the United States than in Canada)
and a slower rate in the introduction of new,
expensive technology. Administration costs are
also lower in Canada, where paperwork and
administration absorb about 11 percent of the
nation's health care spending (in the United
States, some 24 percent goes to paperwork and
administration). Of interest, infant mortality
rates are 20 percent less in Canada than in the
United States and Canadian life expectancy is a
year longer. Moreover, death rates in U.S. and
Canadian hospitals are similar for a variety of
procedures. Significantly, on a per capita basis,
U.S. citizens receive only about three-quarters of
the doctors' services that Canadians do. It seems

that by capping fees for procedures, Canadians have increased rather than limited access to care because the arrangement has induced doctors to do more procedures to maintain their incomes. But the Canadian government-sponsored health care system is not without its critics. Critics point to long waits for some medical procedures and services (the wait for a cataract or a lens replacement operation is about 3 months, while that for a coronary bypass is 3 to 6 months). More recently, shrinking government revenues caused by Canada's economic recession during the early 1990s, combined with exploding medical costs, have forced cutbacks in services and hospital beds (Farnsworth, 1991).

A single-payer system, or Canadian-style, solution to health care reform would decimate the American health insurance industry in one swift stroke. Moreover, the Congressional Budget Office estimates that it would require a $556 billion increase in federal spending by 1998, by far the biggest increase in history. The government would very likely gain vast new powers over what services would be covered and which facilities would be expanded or shut down. However, a single-payer system would tend to preserve the traditional bedrock of American medicine: the freedom to choose one's own physician (with the proliferation of managed-care plans, this freedom is increasingly being constrained) (Symonds, 1994).

Summary

1. Religion is centered in beliefs and practices that are related to sacred as opposed to profane things. The sacred is extraordinary, mysterious, awe-inspiring, and even potentially dangerous. The same object or behavior can be profane or sacred, depending on how people define it. Because the sacred is caught up with strong feelings of reverence and awe, it can usually be approached through rituals.

2. Religious behavior is so varied that we have difficulty thinking about it unless we use some classificatory means for sorting it into relevant categories. One scheme distinguishes between simple supernaturalism, animism, theism, and a system of abstract ideals. Simple supernaturalism entails the notion of mana—a diffuse, impersonal, supernatural force that exists in nature for good or evil. Animism involves a belief in spirits or otherworldly beings. Theism is a religion centered in a belief in gods who are thought to be powerful, to have an interest in human affairs, and to merit worship. And finally, some religions focus on a set of abstract ideals that are oriented toward achieving moral and spiritual excellence.

3. Sociologists distinguish among four ideal types of religious organization: churches, denominations, sects, and cults. Whereas churches and denominations exist in a state of accommodation with the larger society, sects and cults find themselves at odds with established social arrangements and practices. Cults differ from sects in that cults are viewed by their members as being pluralistically legitimate, providing one among many alternative paths to truth or salvation. In this respect, cults resemble denominations. In contrast, the sect, like the church, defines itself as being uniquely legitimate and possessing exclusive access to truth or salvation.

4. Functionalist theorists look to the contributions religion makes to societal survival. According to Emile Durkheim, religion—the

totem ancestor, God, or some other supernatural force—is the symbolization of society. By means of religious rituals, the group in effect worships itself. Viewed in this manner, the primary functions of religion are the creation, reinforcement, and maintenance of social solidarity and social control. In addition, religion helps people in dealing with life's "breaking points." And it may be an impetus to social change.

5. Some conflict theorists depict religion as a weapon in the service of ruling elites who use it to hold in check the explosive tensions produced by social inequality and injustice. Karl Marx portrayed religion as a painkiller for the frustration, deprivation, and subjugation experienced by oppressed peoples. Other conflict theorists see religion not as a passive response to the social relations of production but as an active force shaping the contours of social life. It can play a critical part in the birth and consolidation of new social structures and arrangements.

6. Sociologist Peter L. Berger suggests that religion can be employed in three contrasting ways. First, it can be mobilized in opposition to modernization and as a reaffirmation of traditional authority. This is the route taken by Ayatollah Khomeini and his Islamic Shiite followers in Iran. Second, religion can adapt to the secular world and harness religious motivations for secular purposes. According to Max Weber, this is the path taken by John Calvin and his Protestant followers. Third, religion can retain its fundamental roots while applying them to contemporary concerns. This is the road taken by the fundamental revivalist movement in the United States.

7. Education is one aspect of the many-sided process of socialization by which people acquire behaviors essential for effective participation in society. It entails an explicit process in which some individuals assume the status of teacher and others the status of student and carry out their associated roles.

8. Viewed from the functionalist perspective, schools make a number of vital contributions to the survival and perpetuation of modern societies. A specialized educational agency is needed to transmit the ways of thinking, feeling, and acting mandated by a rapidly changing urban and technologically based society. The educational system serves to inculcate the dominant values of a society and shape a common national mind. It functions as an agency for screening and selecting individuals for different types of jobs. And schools, particularly universities, may add to the cultural heritage through research and development.

9. Conflict theorists see schools as agencies that reproduce and legitimate the current social order through the functions they perform. By reproducing and legitimating the existing social order, the educational institution is seen as benefiting some individuals and groups at the expense of others. Some conflict theorists depict American schools as reflecting the needs of capitalist production and as social instruments for convincing the population that private ownership and profit are just and in the best interests of the entire society.

10. Symbolic interactionists see classrooms as "little worlds" teeming with behavior. They seek to capture the processes occurring in schools, no longer viewing the school as a "black box" in which something goes in and something comes out. Their work sheds provocative insights on social inequality. They see American schools primarily benefiting advantaged youngsters and alienating disadvantaged youngsters through the hidden curriculum and educational self-fulfilling prophecies (negative teacher-expectation effects).

11. So long as the schools remained relatively small, they could operate on the basis of face-to-face interaction. But like hospitals, facto-

ries, and businesses, schools grew larger and more complex. In order to attain their goals, they had to standardize and routinize many of their operations and establish formal operating and administrative procedures. Like other complex organizations, schools do not exist in a social vacuum but are tightly interlocked with other institutions. The formal organization of American schools and colleges typically consists of four levels: (1) the board of education or trustees, (2) administrators, (3) teachers or professors, and (4) students.

12. Social scientists have examined what makes a school effective. Successful schools foster expectations that order will prevail and that learning is a serious matter. Much of the success enjoyed by private and Catholic schools has derived from their ability to provide students with an ordered environment and strong academic demands.

13. Like those of the educational institution, the functions now carried out by the medical institution were once embedded in the activities of the family and religious institutions. Functionalists say the medical institution

evolved across time to deal with problems of health and disease. They note that health is essential to the preservation of the human species and organized social life. Implicit to the functionalist image of society is the assumption that health care services are impartially and equally available to all members of a society regardless of class, race, age, gender, or creed. Conflict theorists challenge this view. They note that some people achieve better health than others because they have access to those resources that contribute to good health and recovery should they become ill. Interactionist theorists view "sickness' as a condition to which we attach socially devised meanings. They look to the processes and structures these definitions produce.

14. Many societies have evolved one or more "specialist" positions to deal with sickness. In recent decades the medical care industry has grown appreciably larger, consuming about 15 percent of the nation's gross domestic product. Hospitals, physicians, and nurses comprise central roles in the health care delivery system. Soaring health costs have led to new arrangements for financing health care.

Glossary

animism   A belief in spirits or otherworldly beings.

asceticism   A way of life characterized by hard work, sobriety, thrift, restraint, and the avoidance of earthly pleasures.

church   A religious organization that considers itself uniquely legitimate and enjoys a positive relationship with the dominant society.

civil religion   Elements of nationalism and patriotism that take on the properties of a religion.

correspondence principle   The notion set forth by Samuel Bowles and Herbert Gintis that the social rela-

tions of work find expression in the social relations of the school.

credentialism   The requirement that a worker have a degree that does not provide skills needed for the performance of a job.

cult   A religious organization that accepts the legitimacy of other religious groups but finds itself at odds with the dominant society.

denomination   A religious organization that accepts the legitimacy of other religious groups and enjoys a positive relationship with the dominant society.

disease   A condition in which an organism does not function properly because of biological causes.

education   The transmission of particular attitudes, knowledge, and skills to the members of a society through formal, systematic training.

educational self-fulfilling prophecies   (also called *teacher-expectation effects*) The fact that many children fail to learn, especially inner-city and minority young-sters, because those who are charged with teaching them do not believe that they will learn, do not expect that they can learn, and do not act toward them in ways that help them to learn.

ethic   The perspective and values engendered by a religious way of thinking.

health   As defined by the World Health Organization, "a state of complete physical, mental, and social well-being and not merely the absence of disease or infirmity."

hidden curriculum   A complex of unarticulated val-ues, attitudes, and behaviors that subtly fit children in the image of the dominant institutions.

learning   A relatively permanent change in behavior or capability that results from experience.

mana   The notion that there is in nature a diffuse, impersonal, supernatural force operating for good or evil.

medicalization of deviance   An increasing number of behaviors that earlier generations defined as being immoral or sinful are coming to be seen as forms of sickness.

medicine   An institution providing an enduring set of cultural patterns and social arrangements responsible for problems of health and disease.

monotheism   The belief in one god.

polytheism   The belief in many gods with equal or relatively similar power.

profane   Those aspects of social reality that are every-day and commonplace.

Protestant ethic   The Calvinist ethos that embodied the spirit of capitalism.

religion   Those socially shared ways of thinking, feel-ing, and acting that have as their focus the realm of the supernatural or "beyond," and that are centered in beliefs and practices that are related to sacred things.

rituals   Social acts prescribed by rules that dictate how human beings should comport themselves in the presence of the sacred.

sacred   Those aspects of social reality that are set apart and forbidden.

sect   A religious organization that considers itself uniquely legitimate but is at odds with the dominant society.

secularization thesis   The notion that profane (non-religious) considerations gain ascendancy over sacred (religious) considerations in the course of social evolu-tion.

sick role   A set of cultural expectations that define what is appropriate and inappropriate behavior for people with a disease or health problem.

theism   A religion centered in a belief in gods who are thought to be powerful, to have an interest in human affairs, and to merit worship.

totemism   A religious system in which a clan (a kin group) takes the name of, claims decent from, and attributes sacred properties to a plant or animal.

Chapter 11

THE HUMAN
ENVIRONMENT

Sociology highlights for us the critical part the social component plays in the human experience. But since humans are also physical beings, their very nature dictates that they be located within space in some sort of habitat. Accordingly, human populations must achieve a working relationship with their environment. The **environment** consists of all the surrounding conditions and influences that affect an organism or a group of organisms. Like other forms of life, human beings confront their environment not so much as individuals but as units in cooperative association. Among their chief adaptive mechanisms are social organization and technology. As we noted in Chapter 2, the subsistence strategy a population employs—hunting and gathering, horticulture, agriculture, or industrialism—has critical implications for its culture and social structure.

One way of viewing the environment is as an **ecosystem**—a relatively stable community of organisms that have established interlocking relationships and exchanges with one another and their natural habitat. Consider, for instance, the links that bind together fish, a marine environment, and a small hunting and gathering population. In surface waters fish excrete organic waste that is converted by marine bacteria to inorganic products; the latter serve as nutrients for algal growth; the algae are eaten by the fish; human beings consume fish; human waste products decompose and provide nutrition for plants; plants assist in oxygenating the atmosphere, which is essential for sustaining the marine bacteria, algae, fish, and human beings. In brief, all components are caught up in a complex and delicately balanced cycle of life.

The process achieves self-purification of the environment. Wastes produced in one step in the cycle become the necessary raw materials for the next step. We gain an appreciation for the efficiency of the arrangement when things go wrong. If the marine environment is overloaded with sewage and industrial effluents, the amount of oxygen required to support waste decomposition by the bacteria of decay may be insufficient.

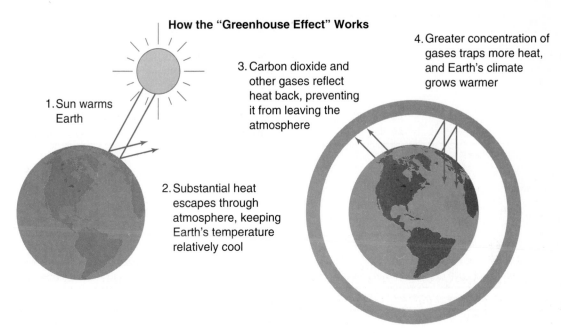

How the "Greenhouse Effect" Works

1. Sun warms Earth

2. Substantial heat escapes through atmosphere, keeping Earth's temperature relatively cool

3. Carbon dioxide and other gases reflect heat back, preventing it from leaving the atmosphere

4. Greater concentration of gases traps more heat, and Earth's climate grows warmer

Figure 11.1   THE THEORY OF HOW THE GREENHOUSE EFFECT WORKS
(SOURCE: From *USA Today,* June 28, 1988. Copyright 1988, *USA Today.* Reprinted with permission.)

Lacking the necessary oxygen, the marine bacteria and fish die, and the entire cycle is halted. In this fashion countless streams, rivers, and lakes have become devoid of life and human beings have lost a vital resource. So each component in the ecosystem is tied to others in an astonishingly complex web involving the circular flow of energy and materials within the living and nonliving environment. Indeed, one intriguing but controversial theory—the Gaia hypothesis—suggests that living things and inanimate forces constitute a unified system so that planet Earth functions as a superorganism in which plant and animal life interact with geophysical and chemical processes to maintain conditions suitable for life (for instance, living things stabilize the atmosphere, temper the climate, and maintain atmospheric oxygen through a complex set of feedback relationships with the physical world).

A particularly graphic but disconcerting example of ecosystem linkages is the issue of global warming associated with the *greenhouse effect hypothesis*—carbon dioxide and other pollutants spewed into the air by industrial societies are believed to trap heat in the earth's atmosphere and warm the planetary climate (see Figure 11.1). The United States is the world's biggest emitter of carbon dioxide, the principal human-made atmospheric gas among several that trap the earth's heat (see Table 11.1). After examining results from various computer models, a scientific advisory committee to the United Nations concluded in 1990, and again in 1992, that a doubling of atmospheric carbon dioxide—which is projected to occur by the year 2100 in the absence of remedial action—will raise the average global temperature by 3 to 8 degrees Fahrenheit. In comparison, the earth has warmed by some 5 to 9 degrees since the last ice age. Should global warming of 8 degrees occur, some computer projections show sea levels rising 4 feet as water expands and polar ice caps melt. Coastal areas where tens

Table 11.1 A COMPARISON OF GASES AND THEIR SOURCES

Potency

Carbon dioxide is the most abundant human-made "greenhouse" gas. But others trap more heat per molecule. Over 100 years, for example, 1 ton of methane can cause 21 times as much warming as 1 ton of carbon dioxide.

Gas	Estimated Lifetime	Global Warming Potential		
		20 Years	100 Years	500 Years
Carbon dioxide	—	1	1	1
Methane	10	63	21	9
Nitrous oxide	150	270	290	190
CFC-11	60	4,500	3,500	1,500
CFC-12	130	7,100	7,300	4,500

A Look at Various Nations

Carbon dioxide emissions for selected countries are expressed below in total metric tons, metric tons per capita and metric tons per $1,000 of gross national product. The United States emits more, in total, than any other country.

Country	1988 Total	Per Capita	Emissions/GNP Ratio
East Germany	327.4	19.8	6.01*
United States	**4,804.1**	**19.4**	**3.60**
Canada	437.8	16.9	2.77
Czechoslovakia	233.6	15.0	2.66*
Australia	241.3	14.7	2.52
Soviet Union	3,982.0	13.9	2.05*
Poland	459.4	12.1	1.90*
West Germany	669.9	11.0	1.74
United Kingdom	559.2	9.9	1.50
Romania	220.7	9.5	1.19*
South Africa	284.2	8.4	1.00
Japan	989.3	8.1	0.98
Italy	359.7	6.2	0.98
France	320.1	5.9	0.80
Korea	204.6	4.8	0.63
Spain	187.7	4.8	0.56
Mexico	306.9	3.7	0.55
China	2,236.3	2.1	0.43
Brazil	202.4	1.5	0.35
India	600.6	0.7	0.34

*The emissions/GNP is likely to be underestimated for centrally planned economies.

SOURCES: *Environmental Protection Agency; "Policy Implications of Greenhouse Warming,"* National Academy of Sciences; and *The New York Times,* September 10, 1991. Copyright © 1991 by The New York Times Company. Reprinted by permission.

of millions of people reside would be inundated. Some areas of the world, such as Canada and Siberia, could benefit from the change. But across the U.S. farm belt, dry summers and mild winters would mean that drought would become the rule rather than the exception. Although leading experts in the field have consistently found merit in the global warming theory, the issue is far from settled and critics continue to attack the model's predictions on a variety of grounds (for instance, the model cannot be trusted because it fails to reproduce the exact pattern of warming that the globe actually experienced over the last century) (Stevens, 1993).

☐ The Ecological Environment

Ecology is the study of the interrelations between the living and nonliving components of an ecosystem. Sociologists are particularly interested in the human environment. One way of viewing the human ecological complex is to examine the relationships among population (P), organization (O), environment (E), and technology (T), the so-called POET complex. Take the matter of air pollution in Los Angeles (Duncan, 1959, 1961). Residents of Los Angeles experience periodic episodes of bluish-gray haze in the atmosphere that reduces visibility and irritates the eyes and the respiratory tract (E → P). The smog also damages plants (E → E) and erodes a variety of metals (E → T). Through the years, Los Angeles residents have organized various civic movements to deal with the problem and have secured the enactment of a variety of regulatory measures (E → O). Among other things, industrial plants have been required to install pollution-abatement devices (O → T).

Meanwhile, chemists have confirmed the "factory in the sky" theory of smog formation—combustion and related processes release unburned hydrocarbons and oxides of nitrogen into the atmosphere that, when subjected to strong sunlight, form smog (T → E). Also implicated in the problem is the frequent occurrence of temperature inversion in the Los Angeles area, which keeps polluted air from rising very far above ground level (E → E). The problem has intensified with the growth in the population, leading residents to spread out over a wide territory (P → E) and heightening dependence on the automobile as the principal means of transportation (T → O). Duncan (1961:146) notes the following paradox: "Where could one find a more poignant instance of the principle of circular causation . . . than that of the Los Angelenos speeding down their freeways in a rush to escape the smog produced by emissions from the very vehicles conveying them?"

THE FUNCTIONALIST PERSPECTIVE ON THE ENVIRONMENT

Functionalist theorists approach the ecological environment by examining the interconnections among the various parts composing the ecosystem (Faia, 1986, 1989). They see the ecosystem as exhibiting a tendency toward equilibrium, in which its components maintain a delicately balanced relationship with one another. The notion of equilibrium implies that the system, despite internal changes and the impingement of external forces, remains on a relatively even keel. The perspective is nicely captured by the notion of Spaceship Earth—the idea that our planet is a vessel in the void of the universe, a closed system with finite resources that, if destroyed or depleted, cannot be replaced. Life exists only in the biosphere, a thin skin of air, soil, and water on the surface of the planet. The earth's biosphere has served humankind well. We have multiplied to nearly 6 billion people and expanded almost to all corners of the globe. In large part our remarkable access has derived from our ability to alter the environment and take from it the resources we need. But functionalists stress that our survival depends on our ability to maintain a precarious balance among the living and nonliving components

*"They're such cute little animals I hate to hunt them.
But if we don't thin out their numbers they'll simply starve themselves
out of existence!"*

Drawing by Ed Fisher; © 1992 The New Yorker Magazine, Inc.

comprising the biosphere. They fear that our pollution of the environment and our depletion of the earth's natural resources are jeopardizing the very environment that is the basis for life.

A graphic example of the reciprocal ties that bind human beings and their physical environment is provided by the sub-Saharan region of Africa. The tragedy of the region has been captured in recent years by television portrayals of the massive sufferings of its people. The scenes are familiar: pale deserts haunted by starving people, infant bellies swollen by want, and dead cattle. An estimated 35 million people in Africa live on the interfaces of deserts and arable land and are threatened by hunger. The overworking of marginal lands for crops, grazing, and firewood has resulted in "desert creep." Much of this "desertification" is not attributable to basic climatic change. Rather, the introduction of Western techniques, such as irrigation, deep plowing, and the use of chemical fertilizers has served to compound the region's problems (Cowell, 1984a; Press, 1988; Tucker, Dregne, and Newcomb, 1991). For instance, irrigated land became waterlogged, accumulated too much salt, and became useless. And the wells dug in arid regions led to people and cattle congregating in the vicinity of the wells, with the herds overgrazing the pastures and trampling the ground with their hoofs. Thus a vicious circle has been at work in which people intensify their exploitation of the land in order to compensate for desert creep, only to complicate their problems as this misuse in turn feeds new desert expansion. Functionalists emphasize that human beings must become more sensitive to both the manifest and latent consequences of their actions on the environment in order to avoid this type of damage to the ecosystem.

THE CONFLICT PERSPECTIVE ON THE ENVIRONMENT

As is true on many other issues, the conflict perspective does not offer a unified point of view on environmental matters. Some conflict theorists depict environmental problems as due more to the distribution of the world's resources than to a limited amount of resources available in the world. They say that the basic issue is not how much is available but rather one of which individuals and groups will secure a disproportionate share of what is available. Hence, the critical decisions that affect the environment are made not in the interests of present and future generations but in the interests of those groups that can impose their will on others. Conflict theorists also point out that people tend to be separated into two camps on environmental issues. On the one side there are those who favor economic development and growth even if it results in some measure of environmental damage. On the other side there are those who see environmental preservation as their primary goal and believe that the environment must take precedence over economic goals. The two groups are at odds and contest each other in the political arena.

Conflict theorists see many of the same circumstances in Africa as do the functionalists, but come to somewhat different conclusions. They point out, using International Monetary Fund figures, that the foreign debt of the forty-four sub-Saharan countries was nearly twenty-five times higher in 1987 than it was in 1970, increasing from $5.7 to $138 billion. This growing indebtedness exerted pressure on African governments to promote cash crops for export rather than food crops for their people (according to the World Bank, from 1980 to 1987 African farmers increased their food output by only 1.3 percent, less than half the rise in population). Simultaneously, commodity prices have fallen on the world market. Consequently, the African nations cannot repay their debts, nor can they afford to purchase food from other nations. Complicating matters, much of the money provided by Western aid agencies was diverted to highly visible projects, such as roads, port facilities, airports, and office buildings. Thus the aid money was recycled to Western corporations, while small African farmers were neglected. Moreover, when Western nations have provided food to African governments, they have found an outlet for surplus food in need of a market and have benefited American and European farmers. Finally, assistance is often rendered to African governments that are friendly toward the donor nations, in the process stabilizing the existing regimes (Cowell, 1984b; Farnsworth, 1990).

THE INTERACTIONIST PERSPECTIVE ON THE ENVIRONMENT

Symbolic interactionists give environmental issues a somewhat different twist, focusing their sociological eye upon "people behaviors." They are interested in what the public has to say about the environment and what they are prepared to do about it. Apparently most Americans believe that they are a people who are devoted to preserving the environment. But Americans are deeply divided over how to do it and at what cost to taxpayers, businesses, and national economic interests. Recent public opinion polls reveal that 94 percent of Americans consider protecting the environment a very important issue, and 63 percent support stronger laws and regulations to get the job done. Yet fewer than half of all Americans (48 percent) are willing to "go full speed ahead" in "spending money to clean up the environment," while 47 percent say that given the nation's other problems, it would be best to "go slow." Eight of ten Americans say protecting the environment is generally more important than keeping prices down. But only 67 percent would be willing to pay 15 to 20 cents a gallon more for gasoline that causes much less pollution, and only 27 percent favor a 25-cent gasoline tax increase to encourage less driving, more conservation, and less dependence on foreign energy sources (69 percent oppose such a tax) (Linden, 1990; Gutfeld, 1991).

Interactionists have also provided significant insight on the socially constructed understandings and myths people have about the environment. For instance, a considerable gap often exists between public and expert perceptions of risk. Indeed, many experts believe that the American public preoccupies itself with relatively modest environmental threats while neglecting bigger threats that could unleash catastrophe (Stevens, 1991). Public opinion surveys show that oil spills, hazardous waste, underground storage tanks, and releases of radioactive materials arouse high public emotions. But in terms of the actual magnitude of the risk they pose, scientists advising the Environmental Protection Agency rate these threats near the bottom. By contrast, global warming and the destruction and alteration of natural habitats rank relatively low in public concerns, but scientists place them among the top risks because their long-term potential consequences seem so damaging and their effects so widespread and difficult to reverse (see Table 11.2).

Scientists provide quantitatively measured assessments of risk, what are called "risk hazard" factors. We should not conclude that the public necessarily disregards such assessments. Rather, people use the information in combination with information about the social, political, and ethical characteristics of a risk to make decisions about its acceptability, what have been called "risk outrage" factors. For example, given two risks of equal magnitude, a risk that is voluntary (under individual control, like skiing) is more acceptable than one that is involuntary (under governmental or corporate control, like food preservatives); one that seems fairly distributed among the population is more acceptable than a risk that seems unfairly distributed; a natural risk (like radon found naturally in the soil) is more acceptable than an artificial one (like the same amount of radon in radioactive mine tailings); a risk that is detectable is more acceptable than one that is undetectable; and a familiar risk (like a train wreck) is more acceptable than an exotic risk (like a hypothetical accident involving recombinant DNA). The public's *perception* of risk, then, is as important as is the *reality* of risk, an insight Perrier astutely grasped. Finding benzene, a carcinogen, in Perrier bottled water, the firm undertook an expensive campaign to regain the confidence of the public and restore Perrier's image of credibility (the pristine reputation of the bubbly mineral water—"It's perfect. It's Perrier.") (Wandersman and Hallman, 1993).

In sum, symbolic interactionists point out that environmental issues qualify for the adjective "social" because they involve human judgments, decisions, and choices. "Risks" are identified and decisions made about their management in a social context. Environmental issues are also social issues because they entail the exercise of power. As we pointed out in Chapter 7, the poor and minorities are much more exposed to the dangers of natural and technological hazards than are other citizens, what is termed *environmental racism.* Indeed, much risk is actually politically negotiated—a network of government agencies, corporations, and public-interest groups grapple daily with selected hazards as diverse as bovine growth hormone in milk and explosive decompression in commercial aircraft (Cvetkovich and Earle, 1992; Dake, 1992).

Table 11.2   WHAT'S A SERIOUS HAZARD?

Experts Rank Risks*	The Public Perceives Risks[†]

Relatively high-risk ecological problems:
    Habitat alteration and destruction (soil erosion, deforestation, etc.)
    Species extinction and overall loss of biological diversity
    Stratospheric ozone depletion
    Global climate change (greenhouse warming)
	Ranked as very serious risks by at least 20 percent of people polled, in descending order:
	
	Hazardous waste sites (in use)
	
	Hazardous waste sites (abandoned)
	
	Worker exposure to toxic chemicals

Relatively high risks to human health:
    Outdoor air pollutants
    Worker exposure to chemicals in industry and agriculture
    Air pollution indoors
    Pollutants in drinking water
	Destruction of protective ozone layer
	
	Radiation from nuclear power plant accident
	
	Industrial accidents releasing pollutants into air, water, or soil

Relatively medium-risk ecological problems:
    Herbicides and pesticides
    Pollution of surface water
    Acid deposition (acid rain, etc.)
    Airborne toxic substances
	Radiation from radioactive wastes
	Underground storage tanks leaking gasoline and other substances
	Pesticides harming farmers, farm workers, and consumers who work with them

Relatively low-risk ecological problems:
    Oil spills
    Groundwater pollution (hazardous wastes, underground tanks, etc.)
    Escape of radioactive materials
    Acid runoff to surface waters
    Thermal pollution
	Pesticide residue on foods eaten by humans
	The greenhouse warming effect
	Nonhazardous wastes, like trash disposal
	Radiation from X-rays

SOURCES: *Science Advisory Board, Environmental Protection Agency; [†]The Roper Organization. Adapted from *The New York Times,* January 29, 1991. Copyright © 1991 by The New York Times Company. Reprinted by permission.

THE FUTURE: PESSIMISTIC AND OPTIMISTIC SCENARIOS

Disagreement exists within the expert community about the future. Are environmental conditions likely to get better or worse? And what are the likely long-term effects of economic growth and development? Some experts take a pessimistic view on these matters, while others find considerable room for optimism (Logan, 1993).

The Pessimistic Scenario. Many authorities express grave concern about the prospects for the earth. Some, like sociologist William R. Catton (1980; Catton, Lenski, and Buttel, 1986), say that capitalist and socialist nations alike have committed themselves to policies of economic growth that disregard the pollution of the biosphere and the rapid consumption of nonrenewable resources (also see Ehrlich and Ehrlich,

1990). Catton contends that we are not "approaching" a resource limit but have already exceeded the earth's carrying capacity for human beings. He estimates that more than 90 percent of our species is sustained by energy resources that are not replenishable. As these energy resources become exhausted and pollution systematically undermines the environment, a "crash" or decrease in population is inevitable. The situation is like a population of yeast cells feeding on a vat of freshly pressed grape juice. The large supply of sugar allows exuberant growth until the resource is exhausted and the concentration of alcohol (pollution) it produces becomes too great. The yeast population then becomes extinct. The world's problems are complicated by the fact that three-quarters of the earth's population uses about 25 percent of the resources; the other 75 percent are consumed by the affluent, industrialized quarter of humanity. Catton suggests the possibility that various social antagonisms and ills, including racism, social inequalities, nazism, war, and student unrest, may result from population pressure in an environment with too few resources.

Sobering conclusions are also contained in *The Global 2000 Report to the President,* issued in 1980 by the Council on Environmental Quality. It insists that because the earth is of finite weight and the population is ever-increasing, we soon will be running out of natural resources. The report's main conclusion is that "the world in 2000 will be more crowded, more polluted, less stable ecologically, and more vulnerable to disruption than the world we live in now. Serious stresses involving population, resources and environment are clearly visible ahead." The report contends that the world is likely to be confronted with substantially higher prices for food, oil, minerals, and fertilizer. In less developed countries, it sees increasing soil erosion, little room for the expansion of cropland, water shortages, deforestation, loss of species, more overcrowding, and more pollution. It concludes that the world's people will be "poorer in many ways" and life will be

"more precarious" by the year 2000 "unless the nations of the world act decisively to alter current trends." The only way out, the report says, would be centralized government planning, controls on the allocation of scarce resources, and internationalism. Through the years Lester R. Brown and his associates (Brown, Flavin, and Postel, 1990, 1991) at the Worldwatch Institute and ecologists Paul R. Ehrlich and Anne H. Ehrlich (1970, 1990, 1991) have also been strong proponents of the pessimistic scenario.

The Optimistic Scenario. The pessimistic scenario seems intuitively convincing: We live in a finite world, and so things must necessarily run out. The optimistic scenario is not nearly as intuitively convincing. It generally raises a simple question: Why have things not as yet run out (Bovard, 1989; Tierney, 1990)? It is this question that economist Julian L. Simon and the late futurist Herman Kahn (1984) ask. Indeed, they explicitly contradict the wording in *Global 2000,* saying: "If present trends continue, the world in 2000 will be less crowded (though more populated), less polluted, more stable ecologically, and less vulnarable to resource-supply disruption than the world we live in now. Stresses involving population, resources, and environment will be less in the future than now." On the basis of historical trends, they predict declining scarcity, falling prices for raw materials, and increased wealth. Given time to adjust to shortages with known methods and new inventions, Simon and Kahn say that free people create additional resources. For instance, plastics were originally developed as substitutes for elephant ivory in billiard balls after tusks began to grow scarce. And the Greeks made the great transition from the Bronze Age to the Iron Age 3,000 years ago when the supply of tin needed to make bronze was disrupted by wars in the eastern Mediterranean. Thus an actual or perceived shortage eventually leaves us better off than if the shortage had never arisen, thanks to resulting new techniques. The free play of market forces is fundamental to the vision of Simon and Kahn, who place considerable faith in human ingenuity and the rate of technological advance. They view government intervention in the market as more often the cause of, rather than a solution to, the problems of the world. Hence, contrary to the pessimistic scenario, which portrays the planet as a closed ecosystem, the optimistic scenario depicts it as a flexible marketplace.

Pessimists look at the economic resources already discovered in the world and conclude that the rest will be more difficult to find and more expensive to extract. But Simon (1981) says cost is not a function of scarcity but of technology. He notes that once upon a time ships were dispatched to kill whales for their oil. Then resourceful individuals began to spread blankets on the surface of oily pools and wring them out by hand to extract the petroleum. Next human beings turned to drilling holes in the ground to get oil. Overall, he finds that the history of raw materials and energy is one of steadily declining prices.

Simon rejects the warnings of those who talk about "nonrenewable resources" in a "finite world," noting that our Spaceship Earth is a body of 260 billion cubic miles of material. Nor does he accept the specter of environmental ruin. He argues that pollution was far worse in nineteenth-century cities, with coal dust, horse manure, and human excrement posing serious health hazards. Simon looks for proof that the environment is improving in data showing lower age-specific death rates and increased life expectancies. He rejects claims that we are destroying our "delicately balanced" ecology, noting that ecologists once pronounced Lake Erie to be "eternally dead," yet today it is teeming with fish. And he finds fault with forecasts of global famine, citing statistics to show that throughout the world people are eating better than ever because the amount of cropland and yields per acre are increasing. According to Simon (1989, 1990), people who are engaged in work and creating knowledge are "the ultimate resource." Wealth, rather than being a fixed quantity, is produced by people. And so Simon believes that new

immigrants to the United States are to be welcomed as affording beneficial outcomes. In sum, Simon would leave the world more or less to its own devices, especially to the operation of unimpeded market forces, a point of view many ecologists dismiss as naive or foolhardy.

The ability of pessimists and optimists to use the *identical* data to arrive at diametrically opposite conclusions leads us again to the insight supplied by symbolic interactionists that social problems (as well as environmental problems) are matters of social definition. Even more crucially, the question becomes one of which individuals and groups will be able to translate their vision of reality into official public policy.

THE EFFECTS OF CROWDING

We commonly think that crowding is bad for people. Popular belief holds that it breeds family breakdown, mental illness, suicide, alcoholism, crime, and violence. The notion has found support in research which shows that population buildup has bad effects on deer, rats, and a variety of other organisms (Christian, 1963). For instance, John Calhoun (1962) studied overcrowding among Norway rats and found that high population densities led to the disintegration of family life, high infant mortality rates, small litters, inadequate nest building, abandonment of the young, cannibalism, and sadism. Calhoun labeled the situation a "behavioral sink."

In contrast, the impact of crowding on human behavior is more complex, and it does not invariably result in pathology (Choldin, 1978; Jain, 1989). Take crime. Implausible as it may seem, over the past 30 years American urban density and household crowding have declined sharply, while crime rates have soared. Additionally, crowded cities, including Tokyo, London, Buffalo, and Providence, have low crime rates, whereas relatively uncrowded cities, including Los Angeles, Houston, and New Orleans, are characterized by high crime rates. Likewise, in

New York City no relationship has been found between neighborhood crowding and the crime rate. When the economic level of neighborhoods is equated, population density is not associated with the crime rate or any other type of social, mental, or physical pathology. Likewise, contrary to commonsense notions, low density and high suicide rates go together (the highest suicide rates are in Nevada and New Mexico; the lowest suicide rates are in New Jersey and New York) (Frankel and Taylor, 1992). And although researchers have attempted to link crowding to aggression, studies typically show that there is no significant independent association between the two factors (Sundstrom, 1978). Such findings seemingly suggest that the source of social pathology must be elsewhere.

We would be amiss, however, to conclude that crowding has no impact on human behavior. It does. Social scientists distinguish between density and crowding. **Density** has to do with the physical compactness of people in space. **Crowding** is the perception people have that too many other individuals are present in the situation. Crowding, then, is not a product of absolute numbers but of people's social definitions. Thus architectural designs—the arrangement of doors, windows, partitions, and other dividers—that give people a greater sense of privacy lead them to feel less crowded even though the density remains the same. Similarly, the sense of crowding that students often experience in long-corridor dormitories can be lessened by modifying the hallways so as to cluster the residents into suites with fewer than twenty members (Baum and Davis, 1980).

A good many factors influence whether or not people define a situation as being crowded (Sundstrom, 1978; Jain, 1989). Duration is one factor. For instance, people typically find it easier to tolerate a brief exposure to high-density conditions such as a ride on a crowded elevator than prolonged exposure on a cross-country bus. A second factor is predictability. People typically find crowded settings even more stressful when they

are unable to predict them. A third factor has to do with frame of mind. There are times when individuals welcome solitude and other times when they prefer the presence of others. A fourth factor involves the environmental setting. People generally report that they can tolerate crowding better in impersonal settings such as a shopping center or an airline terminal than they can in more personal settings like their home or apartment. Finally, crowding seems to intensify people's definition of a situation (Freedman, 1975). If people are fearful and antagonistic—or excited and friendly—crowding tends to intensify the feelings. Crowding makes a doctor's waiting room and a subway car all the more unpleasant, whereas it makes a football game and a party all the more enjoyable. And even though a crowded New York subway car turns people off, a crowded San Francisco cable car, crammed with people hanging over the sides, is defined as a "tourist attraction."

☐ Population

It is difficult to consider the human environment without turning rather quickly to a discussion of the world's population. **Demography** is the science dealing with the size, distribution, composition, and changes in population. Demographic data show that population growth is at once both awesome and sobering. The U.S. Census Bureau placed the world population at 5.6 billion in 1994 and projected it will grow to 7.9 billion by 2020. More than half the people in the world live in six nations: China, India, the United States, Indonesia, Brazil, and Russia. However, world population growth has slowed to about 1.5 percent a year after peaking at 2 percent in the 1960s. Even so, the earth gains 3 new human beings every second, 180 each minute, 10,800 each hour, and 259,200 each day. Between 90 and 100 million people—roughly equivalent to the population of Eastern Europe or Central America—are added each year. As we go back in time, population statistics

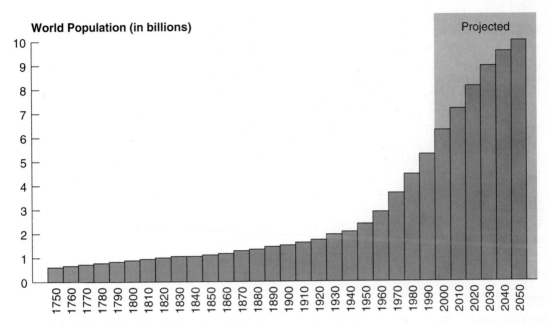

Figure 11.2 WORLD POPULATION GROWTH
World population was estimated to have reached 5 billion on July 11, 1987. It is expected to
double to 10 billion people by the year 2050. (SOURCE: Data from Population Reference Bureau.
Adapted from *Columbus Dispatch,* July 11, 1991. Reprinted, with permission, from *The Columbus* (Ohio)
Dispatch, July 11, 1991.)

become increasingly fragmentary and unreliable, so that the earliest figures represent at best informed guesses. It is estimated that some 40,000 years ago the world population stood at about 3 million. At 8000 B.C., the dawn of agriculture, it was 5 million. At the time of Christ, it was 200 million, an estimate believed to have a fair degree of accuracy. By 1650, it had climbed to 500 million, and by 1830, to 1 billion. At the end of World War II and the advent of the nuclear age, it stood at 2.3 billion. Thus it took millions of years for humankind to reach 1 billion in number, but within a century it had reached 2 billion, and within an additional quarter-century, 4 billion (see Figure 11.2).

ELEMENTS IN POPULATION CHANGE

All population change within a society can be reduced to three factors: the birth rate, the death rate, and the migration rate into or out of the society. In 1994 the population of the United States stood at 260.8 million, with a projected population of 300.4 million in 2010 and 338.3 million in 2025 (Population Reference Bureau, 1994).

Birth Rate. The **crude birth rate** is the number of live births per 1,000 members of a population in a given year. In 1994 the crude birth rate for Americans was 16 per 1,000, substantially lower than that of Nigeria in western Africa with a crude birth rate of 54 per 1,000 and Uganda in eastern Africa with a crude birth rate of 51. The measure is called "crude" because it obscures important differences among races, ethnic groups, classes, age groups, and other categories within the population by lumping all births within a single figure. The **general fertility rate** indicates the annual number of live births per 1,000 women age 15 to 44. Between 1970 and 1973 the U.S. general fertil-

Curve (scale at left) shows
total births each year (millions)

Bars (scale at right) show children per
each woman of childbearing age (15–44)

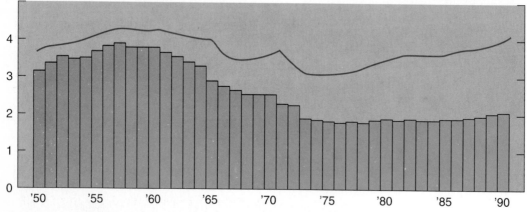

Figure 11.3   THE NUMBER OF BABIES BORN IN THE UNITED STATES
(SOURCE: U.S. Bureau of the Census.)

ity rate hurtled downward from 88 births to 69 births and stayed in that vicinity for 15 years. Then, from 1988 to 1990, it shot up from 67 to 71 births per 1,000 women of childbearing age. Demographers also calculate **age-specific fertility,** or the number of live births per 1,000 women in a specific age group, such as 25 to 29 or 30 to 34. Fertility rates provide us with information regarding the *actual* reproductive patterns of a society. By contrast, the potential number of children that could be born if every woman of childbearing age bore all children she possibly could is called **fecundity.**

As shown in Figure 11.3, the annual number of births among American women fell from just over 4 million in 1964 to 3.1 million in 1973 and then began rising again in the late 1970s. In 1990, 4,179,000 babies were born in the United States, but the figure fell to 4,039,000 in 1993. The reason the number of births was rising is that the number of women of childbearing age had increased as the large generation born during the baby boom of the 1950s reached adulthood. However, the average number of children born to women of childbearing age in recent years has been nearly half of what it was three decades earlier. Childbearing is also up

sharply among women in their thirties who postponed having babies until their schooling was completed and their careers were begun.

It takes an average of 2.1 children per woman of childbearing age for a modern population to replace itself without immigration; this is the level of **zero population growth** (ZPG). As shown in Figure 11.3, for the first time since 1971, births in the United States in 1990 surpassed the population-replacement rate of 2.1. However, if everything went as planned, the nation's low birth rates would be even lower. Some 35 percent of all births to currently and formerly married women are unintended. Twenty-five percent are "mistimed" or wanted at a later date.

Death Rate.   The **crude death rate** is the number of deaths per 1,000 members of a population in a given year. In 1994 the crude death rate for Americans was 9 per 1,000, substantially lower than that of Sierra Leone in western Africa with a crude death rate of 22 per 1,000 (Population Reference Bureau, 1994). As in the case of birth rates, demographers are interested in **age-specific death rates,** or the number of deaths per 1,000 individuals in a specific age group. Such data can be quite revealing. For instance, at ages 24 to 45, the disparity in death rates between minorities and whites is highest: 2.5 times greater in African Americans, 1.8 times higher in American Indians, and 1.25 times greater in Hispanics (the major reason is that homicide and accidental death rates are substantially higher for these minorities than for whites).

The **infant mortality rate** is the number of deaths among infants under 1 year of age per 1,000 live births. In 1994 the infant mortality rate in the United States was 8.3 per 1,000 (approximately 7.3 deaths per 1,000 live births for whites versus 17.6 deaths for African Americans). Many industrialized nations report even lower infant mortality rates than this: Iceland, 3.9; Finland, 4.4; Sweden, 4.8; and Norway 5.8. In contrast, Guinea in western Africa and Mozambique in eastern Africa have a rate of 147 for every 1,000 infants born (Population Reference Bureau, 1994).

The life expectancy of Americans reached 75.7 years in 1992. White men born in 1992 can expect to live 73.2 years; African-American men have a life expectancy of 65.5 years. White women born in 1992 have a life expectancy of 79.7 years; African-American women, 73.9 years (National Center for Health Statistics, 1993). Overall, human life expectancy is nearly twice as long as it was in 1840. The United States ranks seventeenth in average life expectancy on a list of thirty-three developed nations, while Japan holds the lead. As a result of the greater longevity of women, there are currently in the United States three women for every two men over the age of 65; in the over-85 bracket, the margin is better than two to one. Genetic differences may play a part in these sex differences (Epstein, 1983; Holden, 1987). Women appear to be more durable organisms because of an inherent sex-linked resistance to some types of life-threatening disease. For instance, the female hormone estrogen is a protective factor against cardiovascular disease. Lifestyle differences also seem to play a part. Smoking and job hazards are higher for men than for women (Verbrugge, 1988, 1989). But with the rising incidence of smoking among teenage girls, women may lose some of their statistical advantage in the years ahead.

Migration Rate. The **net migration rate** is the increase or decrease per 1,000 members of the population in a given year that results from people entering (immigrants) or leaving (emigrants) a society. Migration is the product of two factors. There are those forces—*push* factors—that encourage people to leave a habitat they already occupy. And there are those forces—*pull* factors—that attract people to a new habitat. Before people actually migrate, they usually compare the relative opportunities offered by the present and the anticipated habitats. If the balance is on the side of the anticipated habitat, they typically migrate unless prevented from doing so by a Berlin Wall, immigration quotas, lack of financial resources, or some other compelling reason. In the 1840s the push of the potato famine in Ireland and the pull of employment opportunities in the United States made this country appear attractive to many Irish people. Likewise, the push resulting from the failure of the 1848 revolution and the pull of American political freedom led many Germans to seek their fortunes in this country. At the present time, both push and pull factors are contributing to the entry into the United States of large numbers of illegal aliens from Mexico. Low agricultural productivity and commodity prices in Mexican agriculture have served as a push factor, and high American wages have served as a pull factor (see Chapter 7).

Noneconomic considerations also influence migration patterns. For instance, the American military presence in Korea and the Philippines has meant that potential immigrants from these nations have been partially Americanized even before leaving their homeland; successful immigrants in turn pave the way for additional arrivals by supplying them with information, employment, and financial assistance (Suro, 1991). Movement of people from one nation to another is called **international migration**. There were about 100 million people "living outside their countries of birth or citizenship" in the mid-1980s. Although the numbers may seem large, only a small minority of the world's population ever moves across national boundaries. In only a few nations, including Cuba, Afghanistan, Haiti, and El Salvador, have as much as one-tenth of a national population emigrated in recent decades (Kalish, 1994).

People also move about within a nation—**internal migration**. Data from the census taken in the United States every 10 years reveal the impact of changing migration patterns. The 1980 census showed a historical first: A majority of the American population resided in the South and West. During the 1980s the trend continued, with California, Texas, and Florida accounting for 52 percent of the nation's population growth. Although the boom in the fastest-growing states is fueled by births, migration (both international and national) is a bigger factor. Boom states gain political clout nationally because congressional seats are allocated on the basis of population. And although rapid population growth often fuels economic growth, it simultaneously strains municipal and state services.

Growth Rate. The **growth rate** of a society is the difference between births and deaths, plus the difference between immigrants and emigrants per 1,000 population. In recent years the United States has had a growth rate of roughly 1 percent (each day the U.S. population grows by about 6,300 people; of this number, 4,400 represent the surplus of births over deaths, with the remainder coming from immigration). The highest annual population growth rate is 11.3 percent, in the United Arab Emirates. The growth rate of the pre-1991 Soviet Union was roughly comparable to that of the United States. However, a number of nations, including Germany and Hungary, have negative annual growth rates, which means that without immigration they will lose population. If we consider merely the difference between the birth and death rates (the rate of natural increase), it takes a population with an annual

rate of increase of 1 percent 69 years to double its population; a 4 percent annual rate increase leads to a doubling of the population in 17 years.

POPULATION COMPOSITION

Births, deaths, and migration affect population *size*. Sociologists are also interested in the *composition* or characteristics of a population. Among these characteristics are gender, age, rural or urban residence, race, religion, national origin, marital status, income, education, and occupation. The sex composition of a population is of particular significance. It is measured by the *sex ratio*—the number of males per 100 females. At birth, there are roughly 105 males for every 100 females. But around age 21 or so, women begin to outnumber men, and the rate accelerates as people grow older. Typically, frontier, mining, cattle-raising, and lumbering areas attract a disproportionate number of males (so does Silicon Valley, California, where men outnumber women, 166 to 100). Females, in contrast, are found in greatest numbers in cities that concentrate on commercial and clerical activities (for instance, Hartford, Connecticut, and Washington, D.C.).

Another important population characteristic is its age composition. A population heavily concentrated in the 20- to 65-year range has a large labor force relative to its nonproductive population. Its dependency burdens tend to be light. In contrast, a population concentrated at either extreme of the age distribution—either under 20, over 65, or both—has a heavy dependency ratio (a large number of nonproductive individuals relative to its productive population). We can gain an appreciation for the social significance of these matters by examining population pyramids.

Population Pyramids. The age and sex composition of a population can be portrayed by a **population pyramid,** often called the "tree of ages" (see Figures 11.4 and 11.5). It is based either on absolute numbers or on proportions. Age groupings are placed in order on a vertical scale, with

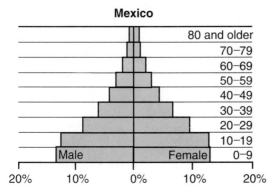

Mexico

	80 and older
	70–79
	60–69
	50–59
	40–49
	30–39
	20–29
	10–19
Male Female	0–9

20%   10%   0%   10%   20%

Figure 11.4 POPULATION PYRAMID OF
MEXICO, 1990
The pyramid reflects a young and growing population
composed primarily of youngsters and teenagers.
(SOURCE: 1990 Mexican Census. Adapted from *American
Demographics*, 14 (September, 1992, p. 9.)

the youngest age group located at the bottom and
the oldest age group at the top of the diagram. On
the horizontal axis are plotted the numbers or
proportions that each specified age group represents of the total, with the sum or portion corresponding to the male segment placed to the left of
the central dividing line and that comprising the
female segment placed to the right of it. The pyramid itself represents the entire population.
Demographers use population pyramids to visualize age and gender distributions. Sociologists
use them to analyze trends in fertility, mortality,
and migration. Businesses often use them to gain
a better understanding of their markets.

The 1990 Mexican population pyramid shown
in Figure 11.4 has the shape of a true pyramid. It
is typical of a population that is growing by virtue
of a high birth rate and a declining death rate. The
American pyramids shown in Figure 11.5 reveal a
quite different picture. Figure 11.5 traces the projected shape of the age structure of the United
States from 1960 through 2040 as the baby-boom
generation ages (the size of future cohorts can
only be estimated since they cannot be predicted
with complete accuracy). The 1960 population
pyramid reveals a narrow portion that consists of

the 1930s Great Depression cohort who were 20
to 29 years of age. By the year 2000, this cohort
will be ages 60 to 69 (at all ages it is smaller than
either its predecessor or its successor cohorts).

The baby-boom cohort (born 1946–1964)
stands out in all the pyramids. Demographers
liken its progress through the population pyramid
to that of a watermelon swallowed by a python. In
1960, the cohort forms the base of the pyramid;
by 1990, it extends across the middle section (ages
25 to 44); and by 2040, it constitutes the protrud-
ing bands of individuals aged 75 and older. It is a
generation that has had an enormous impact
upon American life. In the 1950s the baby
boomers made the United States a child-oriented
society of new schools, suburbs, and station wag-
ons. They provided the nation with Davy Crockett
and rock and roll, went to Woodstock and Vietnam, and fueled the student, civil rights, and
peace movements of the 1960s and early 1970s.
Baby boomers are currently emerging as the
"power generation" in major political and economic institutions. By the year 2030, one out of
every five Americans will be 65 or older and
dependent on a Social Security and Medicare system that must be supported by the smaller generations behind them. The Social Security dependency ratio—the number of workers compared
with the number of recipients—was five to one in
1965 but will drop to two to one by 2035.

The baby-bust cohort (born in the 1970s)
stands in sharp relief to the baby boomers (represented by the pinched-in base of the 1980
pyramid). It in turn is succeeded by the baby-
boom-echo generation (born during the 1990s).
Not until 2020 does the echo cohort catch up to
the baby-boom cohort in size, when a rising
mortality rate takes its toll of baby boomers. Following the baby-boom echo is the baby-bust
echo. As you may have noted, the population
projections contained in Figure 11.5 presume
fluctuating fertility patterns characterized by
"booms" and "busts" (the complicating ramifications of immigration are typically considered
in advanced courses).

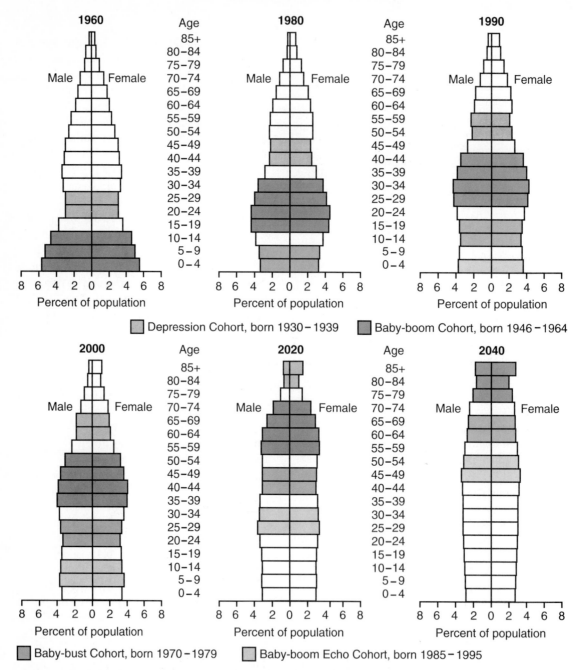

U.S. Population Pyramids, 1960–2040

Depression Cohort, born 1930–1939   Baby-boom Cohort, born 1946–1964

Baby-bust Cohort, born 1970–1979   Baby-boom Echo Cohort, born 1985–1995

Figure 11.5 POPULATION PYRAMIDS, UNITED STATES, 1960–2040
The pyramids trace the demographic impact of the Great Depression cohort (born, 1930–1939), the baby-boom cohort (born, 1946–1964), the baby-bust cohort (born, 1970–1979), and the baby-boom echo cohort (born, 1985–1995). (SOURCE: U.S. Bureau of the Census and Population Reference Bureau projections. Adapted from Leon F. Bouvier and Carol J. De Vita, "The Baby Boom—Entering Midlife," *Population Bulletin*, Vol. 46, No. 3, 1991, figure 3, pp. 10–11.)

"They're baby boomers—like, you know, really old."

Drawing by Weber; © 1994 The New Yorker Magazine, Inc.

Much of the demographic theory dealing with American fertility levels has been stimulated by the work of Richard A. Easterlin (1961, 1987) who has charted regular cycles that rise and fall about every 20 years. He suggests that small generations typically produce large ones and large generations produce small ones. Easterlin conjectures that smaller cohorts have less competition for jobs as they enter the work force, thereby encouraging early marriage and childbearing. So birth rates rise, producing a baby boom. Large generations confront the opposite situation when they reach adulthood. They delay marriage and have fewer children, contributing to a baby bust. Easterlin focuses attention upon social and economic factors, but other factors may intervene to short-circuit the cycles and produce differing outcomes (Pampel, 1993). In any event, the periodic rise and fall of births in the United States creates waves of people who move through the age groups, alternately building up and eroding major institutional arrangements and changing the social landscape.

MALTHUS AND MARX

The relationship between population growth and the level of a nation's welfare has long been a central concern for those interested in population problems. The concern has been especially pronounced since 1798, when the English historian and political scientist Thomas Robert Malthus (1766–1834) first published his *Essay on the Principle of Population*. Many of the issues he raised are still being debated today. Malthus took an extremely pessimistic view, asserting that human populations tend to increase at a more rapid rate than the food supply needed to sustain them. Human beings, Malthus said, confront two unchangeable and antagonistic natural laws: (1) the "need for food" and (2) the "passion between the sexes." He contended that, whereas agricultural production tends to increase in arithmetic fashion (1-2-3-4-5-6-7-8), population has a tendency to increase in geometric fashion (1-2-4-8-16-32-64-128). Based on this formulation, Malthus took a dim view of the future, for if populations always increase to the ultimate point of subsistence, progress can have no lasting effect. Population will invariably catch up and literally "eat" away the higher levels of living. He considered famine, war, and pestilence to be the chief deterrents to excessive population growth. But Malthus also recognized that preventive checks might reduce the birth rate—what he called "moral restraint." But since he was also an ordained minister, either it did not occur to him that people might use birth control, or he viewed birth control as a sin and beneath human dignity.

Many questions have since been raised regarding the Malthusian thesis. For one thing, Malthus failed to appreciate the full possibilities of the Industrial Revolution and its ability to expand productive capacities to an extent unknown in his time. Additionally, there is no clear evidence that food always and everywhere can increase only in arithmetic ratio. For example, within the United States the application of technology—farm machinery, irrigation, fertilizers, pesticides, and hybrid plants and animals—has resulted in subsistence growing as fast and even faster than population. Indeed, a growing body of evidence indicates that demographic pressure stimulates technological evolution, leading to more productive agricultural techniques (Boserup, 1965; Cohen, 1977). And as previously noted, Malthus did not foresee the possibility of new birth control methods or their application within the context of a value system favoring small families.

In some respects, Malthus may be seen as an intellectual predecessor of the political conservatives of the present (Dupaquier, Fauve-Chamoux, and Grebenik, 1983). When governments attempt to do good (providing social welfare programs), Malthus thought that they end up doing evil. By fostering early marriage, he contended, the English Poor Law that subsidized the incomes of workers with families merely increased the numbers of the poor. Even so, Malthus did encourage public policies that would lead people to consider rationally the future consequences of their actions.

Karl Marx (1867/1906) took issue with many Malthusian notions and formulations. He insisted that an excess of population, or more particularly of the working class, depends on the availability of employment opportunities, not a fixed supply of food. Marx believed that a deepening crisis of the capitalist system would inevitably force increasing numbers of workers into the ranks of the unemployed, leading some individuals to conclude that society is overpopulated. Thus he traced the problems associated with population growth to capitalist society and sought cures in a fundamental restructuring of the social and economic order.

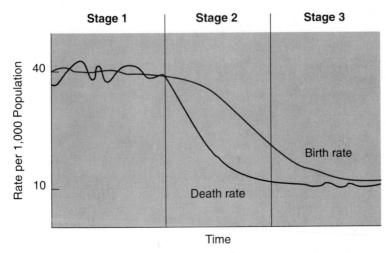

Figure 11.6 TRENDS IN BIRTH AND DEATH RATES ACCORDING TO THE THEORY OF DEMOGRAPHIC TRANSITION

Viewed in this fashion, population is always relative to the *social structure.* In sum, whereas Malthus looked primarily to the individual to restrain population growth through self-control, Marx looked to collective action to refashion institutional life. Many of the issues raised by Malthus and Marx continue to be debated today, particularly as they have come to be expressed in the debate between advocates of the pessimistic and optimistic ecological scenarios discussed earlier in the chapter.

DEMOGRAPHIC TRANSITION

A number of social scientists have employed the idea of demographic transition to map out the population growth characteristic of the modern era (Davis, 1945; Notestein, 1945; Chesnais, 1992). Viewed as history, the notion seeks to explain what has happened in European nations over the past 200 years. Viewed as theory, it has been used to predict what will happen in developing nations in the future. **Demographic transition theory** holds that the process of modernization is associated with three stages in population change (see Figure 11.6).

Stage 1: High potential growth. Societies untouched by industrialization and urbanization are characterized by a high birth rate and a high death rate. As a result, the population remains relatively stable. The stage is described as having "high potential growth" because once the societies gain control over their death rates, their growth is likely to be rapid.

Stage 2: Transitional growth. Modernization has its initial impact on mortality levels. Improved housing, better levels of nutrition, and improvements in health and sanitary measures bring about a steady decline in death rates. Since a decisive reduction in the death rate has traditionally been associated with a marked drop in the infant mortality rate, a larger proportion of the huge yearly crop of babies survives and in time themselves become parents. Thus a drop in the death rate, while the birth rate of a population remains unchanged, results in a marked increase in the rate of population growth. But as time passes, couples begin to realize that with lower infant mortality rates, fewer births are required to produce the same number of surviving children, and they adjust their fertility accordingly. Moreover, the costs and benefits associated with children change as modernization progresses, making small families economically advantageous. The second stage ends when the birth rate sinks to meet the death rate.

Stage 3: Population stability. Modernization allows couples to gain control of their fertility through effective birth control techniques while simultaneously undermining religious proscriptions against their use. The result, according to demographic transition theorists, is that modern societies come to be characterized by low mortality and low fertility, a situation approximating zero population growth.

Social scientists have debated whether modernization produces these stages in a reliable, regular way (Eberstadt, 1981; Coale and Watkins, 1986). For one thing, they are not sure that the stages represent an accurate portrayal of European demographic history. For instance, demographer William Petersen (1960) finds that the Netherlands followed a quite different demographic course than that suggested by the theory. In the modern era, the Netherlands underwent a more-or-less continuous growth in population, although its death rate did not decline until the twentieth century. Indeed, in the period between 1750 and 1850, the death rate apparently rose. Dutch population growth was a product of a rise in fertility that followed the breakdown of traditional inhibitions against procreation. Likewise, the transition process in many other European nations did not follow the scenario outlined by proponents of the theory. Nor does demographic transition theory apply directly to the poor countries of today's world. For example, in some nations, such as Jamaica, fertility has actually gone up in recent decades as an initial response to economic advance (Tilly, 1978b). Other theories fare little better. For example, the French experience does not lend support to conflict and Marxist theories contending that specific modes of production are associated with particular demographic patterns (McQuillan, 1984). Apparently, a great many variables come to bear in quite different interrelationships to produce widely different demographic outcomes (Knodel, 1988; Bogue and Hartmann, 1990).

POPULATION POLICIES

There are three basic schools of thought relating to fertility reduction policies. The first approach involves *family planning.* Its proponents contend that if contraceptives are made readily available and information regarding the value and need for birth planning is disseminated throughout a society, people will reduce their fertility. In turn, a reduction in fertility will allow investment in economic development. Contemporary Bangladesh provides a good illustration of a nation that is cutting its birth rate significantly by aggressively promoting the adoption of modern contraceptive methods—without first waiting for the reduction that customarily comes with higher living standards. The South Asian nation, one of the world's poorest and most densely populated, has a traditional economy in which a good many families rely on children for economic security. Even so, Bangladeshi fertility rates declined by 21 percent between 1970 and 1991, from 7 to 5.5 children per woman. During this time frame, the use of contraception among married women of reproductive age rose from 3 percent to 40 percent. However, the program was quite expensive, and in some localities individual women were visited 300 times by caseworkers (Passell, 1994; Stevens, 1994).

It is also easy to fall into the "technological fallacy"—adopting a blind faith in the gadgetry of contraception—without fully appreciating the *social* changes that may first be required. Even the best technique will not be employed unless people want to use it. For instance, while modern contraception makes it easier for Kenyans to limit family size, they have not responded (Passell, 1994). The simple truth is that people in many parts of the world do *not* want to limit their number of children. Chinese women want 4.1 children on average, and Malay women want 4.7. In Liberia, women from the Mandingo tribe want 6.9 children, and those from the Lorma tribe want 5.1 (Hardee-Cleaveland, 1989). For many individuals, children are their chief protection against the buffetings of life, providing care when they are unemployed, sick, or elderly. Birth rates come down when people are motivated to lower their fertility, whether or not they have modern contraceptives available to them. Throughout human history, people have been quite enterprising in separating sexual enjoyment from procreation.

A second approach entails a *developmentalist* strategy. According to this school of thought, fertility is a pattern of behavior tied closely to the institutional and organizational structure of society. "Development is the best contraception" was a popular slogan of the 1970s. Although modernization has often been associated with a decline in fertility, as our discussion of the demographic transition theory reveals, the relation is not clear-cut enough to justify a simple causal link between industrialization and smaller families.

A third approach involves a *societalist* perspective. The government fashions policies designed to produce changes in demographic behavior. Demographer Kingsley Davis (1971:403) suggests a number of social reforms that would reduce fertility by rewarding low fertility and penalizing high fertility:

[T]he most effective social changes would be those that offer opportunities and goals that compete with family roles. For instance, giving advantages in housing, taxes, scholarships, and recreation to single as compared to married people, would discourage early marriage. Giving special educational and employment opportunities to women would foster career interests and therefore lessen motherhood as a woman's sole commitment. . . . Discontinuing the custom of family names, giving more complete control over children to nursery and elementary schools while holding parents responsible for the costs. . . . As for methods of birth control, including abortion, these could be provided free of charge.

A number of nations have used coercion to reduce fertility. For a period in the 1970s, India inaugurated a program of forced sterilization that resulted in just under 1 million vasectomies being performed each month (Kaufman, 1979). And in recent years China has instituted harsh methods to curb population growth, including punishing couples who have two or more children and fining a woman pregnant with a second child 20 percent of her pay if she refuses to have an abortion (in 1986, according to Chinese officials, there were 53 abortions to every 100 births) (WuDunn, 1991; Tien, 1992). Such programs have aroused considerable indignation among many citizens in Western nations.

For the most part population planners have focused on how to keep the world's poorest women from having more babies. Vast programs in Asia, Africa, and Latin America have been geared to sterilizing women, implanting them with intrauterine devices, handing out contraceptives, and imposing quotas on family size. Some women's groups contend that these traditional methods are demeaning and coercive and that a dramatic shift in emphasis is required. They call for the expansion of health services to include prenatal care, the education of girls and young women, and the promotion of women's equality. The proponents of these measures argue that birth rates in poorer nations will decline only after the status, health, education, and economic opportunities for women improve—in brief, when women gain more control over their lives (Chira, 1994a). Overall, it is clear that programs for reducing fertility remain quite controversial, both in terms of their effectiveness and their morality.

Concern about population *growth* is giving way to a new worry in some nations, population *loss*. Some governments are becoming increasingly concerned about the low level of births in their countries. For instance, in Spain and Italy, traditionally nations of large families, the birth rate has fallen to 1.3 (well below the population replacement level of 2.1). In the European Community as a whole the average is only 1.58. In Japan the rate is 1.57 (the world average is 3.3). A number of governments, including those in France and the French-speaking province of Quebec, have offered cash bonuses in recent years to women for having babies. However, it may be easier to bring down fertility in developing nations than to raise it in developed ones.

Economic hardships have taken a telling toll on the former communist nations of Eastern Europe and the Soviet Union. The crisis and fall of communist rule has precipitated plummeting birth and marriage rates and soaring death rates from Leipzig to Vladivostok. From 1989 to the first half of 1993, the birth rate fell more than 20 percent in Poland, 25 percent in Bulgaria, 30 percent in Estonia and Romania, 35 percent in Russia, and more than 60 percent in eastern Germany (Eberstadt, 1993, 1994). As we pointed out in Chapter 8, the transition from a command to a market economy is proving to be a traumatic social undertaking.

□ The Urban Environment

We have seen that both population size and composition have a great many ramifications for all phases of social life. The distribution of a population in space also assumes critical significance. The "where" may be an area as large as a continent or as small as a city block. Between these extremes are world regions, nations, national regions, states, cities, and rural areas. Changes in the number and proportion of people living in various areas are the cumulative effect of differences in fertility, mortality, and net migration.

One of the most significant developments in human history has been the development of cities. Although many of us take cities for granted, they are one of the most striking features of our modern era. A **city** is a relatively dense and permanent concentration of people who secure their livelihood chiefly through nonagricultural activi-

ties. The influence of the urban mode of life extends far beyond the immediate confines of a city's boundaries. Many of the characteristics of modern societies, including the problems, derive from an urban existence. Perhaps we can gain a better appreciation for these matters by first considering the origin and growth of cities.

THE ORIGIN AND EVOLUTION OF CITIES

Cities constitute a relatively recent development in human history. Not until the Neolithic period did conditions become ripe for the existence of large settlements of people. The domestication of plants and the husbandry of animals were critical innovations that allowed human beings to become a partner with nature rather than a parasite on nature. In contrast with their hunting and gathering ancestors, human beings now achieved the ability to "produce" food, allowing for population expansion in settled communities (Childe, 1941, 1942).

Preindustrial Cities. Early Neolithic communities were more a matter of small villages than of cities. A number of innovations had to be added to the Neolithic complex before towns evolved. Between 6000 and 4000 B.C., the invention of the ox-drawn plow, the wheeled cart, the sailboat, metallurgy, irrigation, and the addition of new plants—when taken together—afforded a more intensive and productive use of Neolithic innovations. When this enriched technology came to be applied in locales where climate, soil, water, and topography were most favorable, the result was a sufficiently productive economy to permit the concentration in one place of people who did not grow their own food. These favoring conditions were found in broad river valleys with alluvial soil that was not exhausted by successive use, with a dry climate that minimized the leaching of soil, with ample days of sunshine, and with a nearby river that afforded a supply of water for irrigation.

Among the early centers of urban development were Mesopotamia, the Nile Valley of Egypt, the

Indus Valley of India, and the Yellow River Basin of China (Davis, 1955, 1967). Yet by itself a productive economy was not sufficient to allow for the growth of cities. Rather than providing food for a surplus of city dwellers, cultivators can, at least in theory, multiply on the land until they end up producing just enough to sustain themselves. New forms of social organization were also required. Bureaucratic structures and stratification systems arose that enabled government officials, religious personnel, merchants, and artisans to appropriate for themselves part of the produce grown by cultivators (see Chapters 4 and 5).

For the most part, preindustrial cities did not exceed 10 percent of the population of an area. Cities of 100,000 or more were rare, although under favorable social and economic conditions some cities surpassed this size. Rome in the second century A.D., Constantinople as the political successor to Rome, Baghdad before A.D. 1000, the cities of Sung China between A.D. 1100 and 1300, and Tokyo, Kyoto, and Osaka in seventeenth- and eighteenth-century Japan all had populations well above 100,000, and in some cases, possibly even a million (Sjoberg, 1960). However, the size of preindustrial cities was restricted by a variety of factors. First, the roads and vehicles could not accommodate the transportation of bulky materials for long distances. And the preservation of perishable commodities, including foodstuffs, was difficult. Second, early cities had trouble securing the hinterlands. Their inhabitants were constantly threatened and often conquered by neighboring cities and nonurban peoples. Indeed, in time even mighty Rome succumbed to foreign invaders. Third, the absence of modern medicine and sanitation meant that urban living was frequently deadly. The water supply was often polluted by sewage, and as commercial centers, cities attracted transients who served as carriers of contagious diseases. Finally, serf, slave, and caste arrangements bound the peasantry to the land and prevented rural-urban migration. These and other factors made early cities primarily small affairs (Davis, 1955).

Industrial-Urban Centers. Urbanization has proceeded quite rapidly during the past two centuries. In 1800 there were fewer than fifty cities in the world with 100,000 or more population. And by 1900, only one in twenty earthlings lived in a city with a population of at least 100,000. Today, one in five people live in a center with at least 100,000 people. And there are 321 cities around the world with populations of at least 1 million or more people (140 in Asia; 53, Europe; 43, North America; 42, Latin America; 37, Africa; and 6, Oceania) (Schwartz, 1990). Most early urban communities were city-states, and many modern nations have evolved from them. Even where the nation became large in both size and land area, the city has remained the focus for political and economic activities, and the core and magnet of much social life. To people of other nations, the city often represents the nation, and this tradition survives in the modern use of a city, such as Washington, London, and Moscow, as a synonym for a nation.

Both social factors and technological innovations contributed to the acceleration of urban growth. Organizational changes permitted greater complexity in the division of labor (see Chapter 4). Simultaneously the events labeled the Industrial Revolution allowed human beings to use steam as a source of energy, reinforcing those forces promoting the widespread use of machines.

Power-driven machines accelerated social trends that were drawing manufacturing out of the home to a centralized factory. As the factory system expanded, increasing numbers of workers were needed. People flocked to the factories, attracted not only by the novelty of urban life but by the opportunity to realize greater economic rewards. In Europe city growth was also stimulated by the demise of feudal systems and the emergence of nation-states. Under the impetus of nationalism, large geographic areas were consolidated, enlarging internal markets, integrating transportation systems, providing for common coinage and weights, and abolishing internal duties on goods.

Metropolitan Cities. Industrial-urban centers have typically been geographically scattered, and although dominating their hinterlands, have had only tenuous economic and social relations with them. More recently, metropolitan cities have emerged. This phase in urban development does not represent a sharp break with the industrial-urban tradition but rather a widening and deepening of urban influences in every area of social life. Increasingly cities have become woven into an integrated network. The technological base for the metropolitan phase of urbanism is found in the tremendous increase in the application of science to industry, the widespread use of electric power (freeing industry from the limitations associated with steam and belt-and-pulley modes of power), and the advent of modern forms of transportation (the automobile and rapid transit systems have released cities from the limitations associated with foot and hoof travel, which had more or less restricted growth to a radius of 3 miles from the center).

Steam and belt-and-pulley power techniques had produced great congestion in urban areas by the beginning of the twentieth century. But a number of factors have increasingly come to the foreground and bucked earlier centripetal pressures, including rising city taxes, increased land values, traffic and transportation problems, and decaying and obsolescent inner zones. These and other forces have accelerated the centrifugal movement made technologically possible by electric power, rapid transit, the automobile, and the telephone. The result has been the development of satellite and suburban areas, broad, ballooning urban bands linked by beltways that constitute cities in their own right. In population, jobs, investment, construction, and shopping facilities, they rival the old inner cities. They are the sites of industrial plants, corporate offices and office towers, fine stores, independent newspapers, theaters, restaurants, superhotels, and big-league stadiums.

The conventional distinction between cities and rural areas is eroding in many Western societies as the world is becoming, in Marshall McLuhan's oft-quoted phrase, a "global village." In many cases, the rural interstices between metropolitan centers have filled with urban development, making a "strip city" or **megalopolis.** The northeastern seaboard is a good illustration of this process. A gigantic megalopolis lies along a 600-mile axis from southern New Hampshire to northern Virginia, encompassing 10 states, 117 counties, 32 cities larger than 500,000 people, and embracing nearly a fifth of the U.S. population. Urban projections suggest that by the year 2050, if not sooner, another urbanized strip will extend from New York State through Pennsylvania, Ohio, northern Indiana and Illinois to Green Bay, Wisconsin, and Minneapolis–St. Paul (see Figure 11.7).

Global Cities. Sociologist and urban planner Saskia Sassen (1991) contends that changes in the world economy are transforming major urban centers into what she calls the "global city." As factories, offices, and corporate headquarters have moved out of major cities over the past two decades, other economic players have moved in. Major urban centers are now central marketplaces for financial trading and investment banking and the kind of higher value-added activities (legal and accounting firms, advertising agencies, and management consultants) upon which contemporary corporations rely. In sum, the "things" a global city makes are services and financial goods. New York, London, and Tokyo are prime examples of the global city—Amsterdam, Hong Kong, Sao Paulo, Sydney, and Toronto are others.

The critical processes fostering the development of the global city are dispersal and concentration. Advanced technology and telecommunications facilitate the decentralization of economic functions and the transfer of routine jobs to low-wage areas of the world. Simultaneously, the worldwide dispersal of production and manufacturing require the centralization of a variety of managerial and financial operations and services. These functions tend to cluster in big cities, and the cities in turn become centers for control and

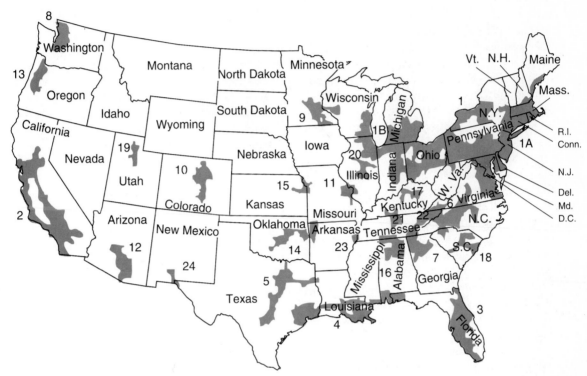

Figure 11.7 MEGALOPOLISES IN THE YEAR 2000
Projections suggest that the heavily urban shaded areas on the map will characterize many sections of the United States by the year 2000. The megalopolitan areas shown here are numbered in order of population size. (SOURCE: Adapted from *Population Growth and American Future*. Washington, D.C.: U.S. Government Printing Office.)

1. Metropolitan Belt
1A. Atlantic Seaboard
1B. Lower Great Lakes
2. California Region
3. Florida Peninsula
4. Gulf Coast
5. East Central Texas–
   Red River
6. Southern Piedmont
7. North Georgia–
   South East Tennessee
8. Puget Sound
9. Twin Cities Region
10. Colorado Piedmont
11. St. Louis
12. Metropolitan Arizona
13. Willamette Valley
14. Central Oklahoma–
    Arkansas Valley
15. Missouri–Kaw Valley
16. North Alabama
17. Blue Grass
18. South Coastal Plain
19. Salt Lake Valley
20. Central Illinois
21. Nashville Region
22. East Tennessee
23. Memphis
24. El Paso–
    Ciudad Juarez

coordination of the global economy. Sassen looks at the global city as the "brain" of the world economy—an actual production site—as if it were a complex of factories.

Clustered in big cities are "transnational spaces"—the locations of high-rolling finance and service corporations—that to one degree or another are outside the purview of any state or national government (see the discussion of multinational and transnational corporations in Chapter 8). They have evolved a kind of "global culture" that creates a transterritorial economic space for communication so that the airports, hotels, restaurants, and high-price, high-prestige

Concentric Zone Theory

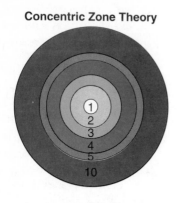

Sector Theory

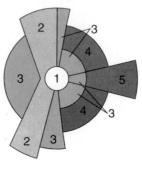

Multiple Nuclei Theory

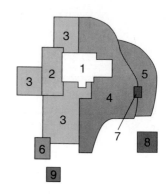

1. Central Business District
2. Wholesale Light Manufacturing
3. Low-Class Residential

4. Medium-Class Residential
5. High-Class Residential
6. Heavy Manufacturing

7. Outlying Business District
8. Residential Suburb
9. Industrial Suburb
10. Commuters' Zone

Figure 11.8 THEORETICAL PATTERNS OF URBAN STRUCTURE
(SOURCE: Reprinted from "The Nature of Cities" by Chauncey D. Harris and Edward L. Ullman from *The Annals of the American Academy of Political and Social Science,* vol. 242, 1945. Reprinted by permission.)

locations are more or less alike from one global city to another.

According to Sassen, the global economy and its cities have contributed to the emergence of a new urban class structure. The growth of transnational financial and service sectors has created a class of highly paid managers and professionals. But their success relies on a large, low-wage, insecure labor force (for instance, the cleaning crew that comes in after hours and the truck drivers who deliver the office supplies). So the high-tech companies that service the new economy create conditions for urban poverty and bring a polarization of incomes and jobs. The global city becomes the terrain of the affluent and the poor, with the middle class all but disappearing. Within the United States, Miami is rapidly emerging as a global city, a center for firms whose operations extend to Latin America and the Caribbean (Sassen and Portes, 1993).

PATTERNS OF CITY GROWTH

A good deal of the sociological enterprise is directed toward identifying recurrent and stable patterns in people's social interactions and relationships (see Chapter 2). In like fashion, sociologists are interested in understanding how people order their relationships and conduct their activities in space. They provide a number of models that attempt to capture the ecological patterns and structures of city growth (see Figure 11.8).

Concentric Circle Model. In the period between World Wars I and II, sociologists at the University of Chicago viewed Chicago as a social laboratory and subjected it to intensive study. The **concentric circle model** enjoyed a prominent place in much of this work (Park, Burgess, and McKenzie, 1925). The Chicago group held that the modern city assumes a pattern of concentric circles, each with distinctive characteristics. At the center of the city—*the central business district*—are retail stores, financial institutions, hotels, theaters, and businesses that cater to the needs of downtown shoppers. Surrounding the central business district is an area of residential deterioration caused by the encroachment of business and industry—*the zone in transition.* In earlier days these neighborhoods had contained the pretentious homes of wealthy and prominent citizens. In later years they became slum areas and havens for marginal business establishments (pawnshops, secondhand stores, and modest taverns and restaurants). The zone in transition shades into the *zone of working-men's homes* that contains two-flats, old single dwellings, and inexpensive apartments inhabited largely by blue-collar workers and lower-paid white-collar workers. Beyond the zone occupied by the working class are *residential zones* composed primarily of small business proprietors, professional people, and managerial personnel. Finally, out beyond the area containing the more affluent neighborhoods is a ring of encircling small cities, towns, and hamlets, *the commuters' zone.*

The Chicago group viewed these zones as ideal types since in practice no city conforms entirely to the scheme. For instance, Chicago borders on Lake Michigan, so that a concentric semicircular rather than a circular arrangement holds. Moreover, critics point out that the approach is less descriptive of today's cities than cities at the beginning of the twentieth century. And apparently some cities such as New Haven have never approximated the concentric circle pattern (Davie, 1937). Likewise, cities in Latin America, Asia, and Africa exhibit less specialization in land use than those in the United States.

The Sector Model. Homer Hoyt (1939) has portrayed large cities as made up of a number of sectors rather than concentric circles—the **sector model** (see Figure 11.8). Low-rent districts often assume a wedge shape and extend from the center of the city to its periphery. In contrast, as a city grows, high-rent areas move outward, although remaining in the same sector. Districts within a sector that are abandoned by upper-income groups become obsolete and deteriorate. Thus, rather than forming a concentric zone around the periphery of the city, Hoyt contends that the high-rent areas typically locate on the outer edge of a few sectors. Furthermore, industrial areas evolve along river valleys, watercourses, and railroad lines rather than forming a concentric circle around the central business district. But like the concentric circle model, the sector model does not fit a good many urban communities, including Boston (Firey, 1947).

The Multiple Nuclei Model. Another model—the **multiple nuclei model**—depicts the city as having not one center but several (Harris and Ullman, 1945). Each center specializes in some activity and gives its distinctive cast to the surrounding area. For example, the downtown business district has as its focus commercial and financial activities. Other centers include the "bright lights" (theater and recreation) area, "automobile row," a government center, a wholesaling center, a heavy-manufacturing district, and a medical complex. Multiple centers evolve for a number of reasons. First, certain activities require specialized facilities—for instance, the retail district needs to be accessible to all parts of the city, the port district requires a suitable waterfront, and a manufacturing district dictates that a large block of land be available near water or rail connections. Second, similar activities often benefit from being clustered together—for instance, a retail district profits by drawing customers for a variety of shops. Third, dissimilar activities are often antagonistic to one another—for example, affluent residential development tends to be incompatible with industrial development. And finally, some activities cannot afford high-rent areas and hence locate in low-rent districts—for instance, bulk wholesaling and storage. The multiple nuclei model is less helpful in discovering universal spatial patterns in all cities than in describing the unique patterns peculiar to particular communities.

ECOLOGICAL PROCESSES

The structural patterning of cities derives from a number of underlying ecological processes. As we have seen, people relate to one another and undertake their activities in ways that result in geographic areas taking the form of **natural areas** with distinctive characteristics. One process by which natural areas are formed is **segregation**—a process of clustering wherein individuals and groups are sifted and sorted out in space based on their sharing certain traits or activities in common. This clustering takes place voluntarily when people find that close spatial proximity is advantageous. For instance, the multiple nuclei model of city growth suggests that certain similar activities profit from cohesion provided by a segregated district. Likewise, some nationality and cultural groups prefer to live in close proximity to one another. This arrangement (ethnic enclaves) facilitates communication, understanding, and rapport and fosters we-group identification and loyalties (Bonacich and Modell, 1980; Aldrich, Zimmer, and McEvoy, 1989). Additionally, a segregated neighborhood protects against the intrusion of strange values, norms, and beliefs, while simultaneously providing political leverage with City Hall through bloc voting. Of course segregation may also be involuntary. Residential neighborhoods frequently attempt to exclude incompatible commercial and industrial activities through zoning ordinances. And as we noted in Chapter 7, ethnic and racial groups may systematically exclude from their neighborhoods other groups, including African Americans, Hispanics, and Jews. A recent housing discrimination study (conducted by the Urban Institute and Syracuse University for the Department of Housing and Urban Development) found that more than 50 percent of African Americans and Hispanics trying to rent or to buy a home face biased treatment

as compared with whites (Yinger, 1991). The survey consisted of 3,800 audits, or paired tests, in 25 metropolitan areas. White testers posed as housing customers with similar incomes and schooling as African-American or Hispanic testers, and their treatment was then compared. In some cases, minority applicants were told a unit had already been rented or sold. In others, they were shown only one unit, often in a less desirable location, and were not informed about the availability of others. In still other instances, they were "steered" to apartments or properties in predominantly minority neighborhoods.

Invasion and succession are also critical ecological processes. **Invasion** takes place when a new type of people, institution, or activity encroaches on an area occupied by a different type. Should the invasion continue until the encroaching type displaces the other, **succession** is said to have occurred. When people with quite different backgrounds come to share or compete for urban neighborhoods, issues of race, class, and culture often become highlighted and lead to social conflict (Winnick, 1991; Wysocki, 1991). Although a neighborhood's ecological function may remain unchanged (for instance, residential), it typically becomes a less desirable place to live or work. Yet the reverse process also takes place. Georgetown, in Washington, D.C., was an abject slum in the 1920s. More recently, private individuals have restored many of the crumbling pre–Civil War mansions, providing expensive and attractive housing in which government, business, and professional leaders reside. **Urban gentrification**—the return of the middle class, usually young, white, childless professionals (sometimes called *yuppies,* for "young urban professionals"), to older neighborhoods—is happening in large cities throughout the United States (Haight-Ashbury in San Francisco, Queen Village in Philadelphia, Mount Adams in Cincinnati, New Town in Chicago, German Village in Columbus, Ohio, and Brooklyn Heights in New York). The process typically culminates in the displacement of the poor and minorities from these neighborhoods by upwardly mobile whites with financial resources and clout. Many older cities are counting on urban gentrification to counteract their eroding population and tax bases. However, even though the "back-to-city" movement has transformed some neighborhoods, it has hardly been a panacea for urban ills (indeed, it may compound the ills when the poor are displaced and pushed into adjoining neighborhoods). Moreover, urban gentrification appears to have slowed in recent years.

URBAN CRISES AND THE FUTURE OF AMERICAN CITIES

Looking out over Chicago from the ninety-fourth-floor observatory of the John Hancock building, one sees a city that resembles an old Oriental rug: It is bright and vital in some places and worn and bare in others. The bare spots on the face of Chicago and older American cities began to appear in the mid-1950s, and by the 1970s the exodus of residents and corporations had become a serious problem. Left behind were vast areas of abandoned houses, apartment buildings, neighborhood stores, and factories. St. Louis, Cleveland, Pittsburgh, and Detroit suffered population declines of 13 percent or more in the 1970s. During the 1980s several large northeastern and midwestern metropolitan areas, including New York, Philadelphia, St. Louis, and Milwaukee, gained back some of the ground they had lost in the 1970s. Others, like Detroit (which has lost half its population since 1950), Cleveland, Pittsburgh, Buffalo, and New Orleans, continued to decline. Overall, the 1990 census found that more than half of all Americans—50.2 percent—now live in thirty-nine large metropolitan areas (up from 45.9 percent in 1980), each with a population of more than 1 million.

The "doughnut structure" is an apt description of the course of metropolitan development in many American cities since World War II. The hole in the doughnut is the decaying central city, and the ring is a prosperous and growing suburban and exurban region. In some cases, such as New York City's Manhattan, the hole is a core area that is being revitalized, and the ring is a surrounding part of the city that is becoming progressively blighted. A number of trends have contributed to the phenomenon. For one thing, since World War II, the suburbs and exurbs of most American cities have grown more rapidly than the cities themselves. For another, urban growth returned to coastal regions in the United States in the 1980s. People tend to follow jobs and migrate to areas where they believe there are better employment opportunities. Additionally, cities are less likely to lose population to their suburbs if both the city and the suburbs are comparable in public services and costs (Bradbury, Downs, and Small, 1982).

Urban decline is both descriptive and functional. *Descriptive decline* has to do with the loss of population or jobs. *Functional decline* refers to a deterioration in city services and the social amenities of urban life. Descriptive decline occurs as people who have the resources to leave the city do, while those who are poor have little choice but to remain (22.2 percent of the housing of Philadelphia, 19.5 percent of that of Detroit, and 18.4 percent of the housing of Washington is "boarded-up"—vacant homes and apartments that provide a vacuum often filled by crime and drugs). The proportion of poor residents increases as their number is swelled by recent migrants who are also poor. Urban ills are aggravated and require an increasing share of a city's resources. Life in the city then becomes less agreeable and more costly for middle- and upper-income residents, who move out of the city. This reinforcing pattern hurts the city and complicates its ability to be responsive to people's needs. All this means that American cities are less able to fulfill one of their historical functions—namely, helping society assimilate and integrate the poor and immigrants (Bradbury, Downs, and Small, 1982). Cities require sustained infusions of resources from the outside, particularly the federal government, at the very time that deficit cutting and austerity are curtailing federal urban programs.

Functional decline is reflected in the decay in older industrial cities of the urban infrastructure—the network of roads, bridges, sewers, rails, and mass transit systems. Currently half of all American communities cannot expand because their water treatment systems are at or near capacity (according to the Environmental Protection Agency, more than 10,800 wastewater facilities have water quality or public health problems; additionally, some cities lose as much as 30 percent of their daily water supply as a result of leaky pipes). Many roads and bridges are bearing far greater burdens than they were designed to accommodate. Some projections suggest that traffic congestion could increase over the next 20 years by more than 400 percent on the nation's freeways and over 200 percent on nonfreeways (Schwartz, 1989). Additionally, many roads and bridges are deteriorating. For instance, nearly 70 percent of New York City's 2,027 bridges are no longer able to carry the loads for which they were designed—indeed, the Federal Highway Administration reports that 68.2 percent of the bridges in New York State are either structurally deficient or functionally obsolete (*New York Times,* 1991). Overall, more than half of the most heavily traveled roads in the United States—1,068,227 miles that connect urban areas and intracity areas—are in poor or fair condition (Howlett, 1992).

In response to the fiscal crises of recent decades, many local and state officials have balanced budgets by canceling preventive maintenance and deferring necessary repairs of public works. One major obstacle to infrastructure maintenance is the diversity and multiplicity of responsibility, which falls upon more than 100 federal agencies, not to mention 50 states, more than 3,000 counties, and thousands of local agencies. In addition, corruption on the part of construction firms, labor unions, public officials, and organized crime has wastefully dissipated public funds.

"*I say move the inner cities out to the suburbs like everything else!*"

From *The Columbus Dispatch;* © 1992. Reprinted with special permission of North America Syndicate.

SPRAWLING URBAN GROWTH

A new form of urban organization is emerging in the United States, but as yet sociologists and demographers have not coined an accepted name for it. Growing American metropolitan areas are sprouting multiple "outer cities," "minicities," or "edge cities" (Suro, 1990; Garreau, 1991). Whereas several decades ago a central city was relatively compact, now everything is spread over a much larger crescent of development. The broad, multi-lane beltways and expressways that ring most large cities have made an interlinked metropolis possible. The transition has been facilitated by the development of a service-based economy in which telecommunications—telephones, faxes, and electronically linked computers—allow service-sector firms to locate anywhere. Residents use these "outer" communities collectively as a city—a centerless city. They often live in one suburb, work in another, shop in still another, and go to a physician in yet another (between 1960 and 1990, the number of workers in the United States increased 78 percent—twice as fast as the population as a whole; simultaneously, the number of Americans who commute to other counties to work virtually tripled, from 9 million to more than 27 million).

These new urban centers include the area around Route 128 and the Massachusetts Turnpike in the Boston region; the Perimeter Center area at the northern tip of Atlanta's beltway; Irvine, in Orange County, south of Los Angeles; and Fairfax County across the Potomac from Washington. In population, investment, construction, jobs, and stores they rival the old inner cities. However, community life and institutions of the sort that once characterized the central city and its "downtown" are often lacking in these outer-belt communities. Shopping malls or clusters of office buildings, warehouses, or factories are scattered around at interchanges along the broad, ballooning bands of interlinked beltways. These centers of development—perhaps a collection of computer companies, a regional medical center, or a recreation complex—generate other development. The typical dwelling units are the condominium, the large apartment complex, and the celebrated suburban home.

In most cases, government structures and policies have yet to adapt to the new patterns of growth. Regional approaches are required to deal with issues like taxation, highways, parks, water, and waste disposal. Moreover, many new information-processing types of jobs are moving to outer-belt communities where they are effectively out of reach for many city dwellers. The trend may be increasing the racial polarization of American society and worsening the crisis in the nation's central cities. Census data reveal that the suburbs are becoming more riven by class, with blue-collar suburbs tending to decline (edge cities seldom grow near blue-collar suburbs) and white-collar suburbs blossoming (Glastris, 1992). Today's hard choices—or social drift and inattention—will determine the shape of urban life for decades to come.

Summary

1. Since humans are physical beings, their very nature dictates that they be located within space in some sort of habitat. Accordingly, human populations must achieve a working relationship with their environment. One way of viewing the environment is as an ecosystem—a relatively stable community of organisms that have established interlocking relationships and exchanges with one another and their natural habitat. Sociologists find it useful to study the relationships among population (P), organization (O), environment (E), and technology (T), the POET complex.

2. Functionalist theorists approach the human environment by examining the interconnections among the various parts comprising the ecosystem. They see the ecosystem as exhibiting a tendency toward equilibrium in which its components maintain a delicately balanced relationship. The perspective is nicely captured by the notion of Spaceship Earth—the idea that our planet is a vessel in the void of the universe, a closed system with finite resources that, if destroyed or depleted, cannot be replaced.

3. Some conflict theorists depict environmental problems as due more to the distribution of the world's resources than to a limited amount of resources available in the world. They say that the basic issue is not how much

is available but rather which individuals and groups will secure a disproportionate share of what is available. The critical decisions that affect the environment are made not in the interests of present and future generations but in the interests of those groups that can impose their will on others. Conflict theorists also point out that people tend to be separated into two camps on environmental issues. On the one side there are those who favor economic development and growth even if it results in some measure of environmental damage. On the other side there are those who see environmental preservation as their primary goal and believe the environment must take precedence over economic goals.

4. Experts are in disagreement regarding the long-term effects of economic growth and development. Many authorities express grave concern about the prospects for the planet. They say that capitalist and socialist nations alike have committed themselves to policies of economic growth that disregard the pollution of the biosphere and the rapid consumption of nonrenewable resources. Other authorities take a more optimistic view. They look to technology to save us. The free play of market forces is fundamental to their vision.

5. Population buildup has bad effects on deer, rats, and a variety of other organisms. In contrast, the impact of crowding on human behavior is more complex and does not invariably result in pathology. Social scientists distinguish between density and crowding. Density has to do with the physical compactness of people in space. Crowding is the perception people have that too many other individuals are present in the situation. Crowding, then, is not a product of absolute numbers but of people's social definitions.

6. All population change within a society can be reduced to three factors: the birth rate, the death rate, and the migration rate into or out

of the society. The number of children born in recent years in the United States has risen to near the baby-boom highs of the late 1950s. The reason the number of births has risen is that the number of women of childbearing age has increased as the large generation born during the baby boom of the 1950s has reached adulthood. Even so, young American women say they want so few children that, if they have the children they say, their generation will not replace itself. The life expectancy of Americans has now reached a high of 75 years 5 months. Migration is the product of two factors. There are those forces—push factors—that encourage people to leave a habitat they already occupy. And there are those forces—pull factors—that attract people to a new habitat.

7. Birth, death, and migration affect population size. Sociologists are also interested in the composition or characteristics of a population. They are particularly interested in the sex ratio (the number of males per 100 females) and age composition. A population pyramid is a useful tool for analyzing population change and discerning population trends.

8. Thomas Robert Malthus held that, whereas agricultural production tends to increase in arithmetic fashion, population has a tendency to increase in geometric fashion. Based on this formulation, Malthus took a dim view of the future. For if populations always increase to the ultimate point of subsistence, progress can have no lasting effect. However, Malthus failed to appreciate the full possibilities of the Industrial Revolution and its ability to expand productive capacities to an extent unknown in his time. Additionally, there is no clear evidence that food always and everywhere can increase only in an arithmetic ratio. Karl Marx took issue with Malthus, insisting that an excess of population is related to the availability of

employment opportunities, not to a fixed supply of food.

9. A number of social scientists have employed the idea of demographic transition to map out the population growth characteristic of the modern era. Viewed as history, the notion seeks to explain what happened in European nations over the past 200 years. Viewed as theory, it has been used to predict what will happen in developing nations in the future. Demographic transition theory holds that the process of modernization is associated with three stages in population change: stage 1, high potential growth; stage 2, transitional growth; and stage 3, population stability.

10. There are three basic schools of thought relating to fertility reduction policies. The first approach involves family planning. Its proponents contend that if contraceptives are made readily available and information regarding the value and need for birth planning is disseminated throughout a society, people will reduce their fertility. A second approach entails a developmentalist strategy. It holds that modernization automatically decreases fertility. A third approach involves a societalist perspective. The government fashions policies designed to produce changes in people's demographic behavior.

11. Cities constitute a relatively recent development in human history. Not until the Neolithic period did conditions become ripe for the existence of large settlements of people. Preindustrial cities were primarily small affairs. Urbanization has proceeded rapidly during the past 180 years, resulting in industrial-urban centers. More recently, metropolitan cities have emerged. This phase in urban development does not represent a sharp break within the industrial-urban tradition but rather a widening and deepening of urban influences in every area of social life. In many cases, the rural interstices between metropolitan centers have filled with urban development, making a "strip city" or megalopolis. Currently, the world economy is transforming some major urban centers into global cities—central marketplaces for financial trading and investment banking and the kind of higher value-added activities that contemporary corporations require.

12. Sociologists are interested in understanding how people order their relationships and conduct their activities in space. They provide a number of models that attempt to capture the ecological patterns and structures of city growth: the concentric circle model, the sector model, and the multiple nuclei model.

13. The structural patterning of cities derives from a number of underlying ecological processes. People relate to one another and undertake their activities in ways that result in geographic areas taking the form of natural areas with distinctive characteristics. One process by which natural areas are formed is segregation. Invasion and succession are also critical ecological processes.

14. Urban decline in many American cities has been both descriptive and functional. Descriptive decline has to do with the loss of population or jobs. Functional decline refers to a deterioration in city services and the social amenities of urban life. Descriptive decline occurs as people who have the resources to leave the city do, while those who are poor have little choice but to remain. Functional decline is reflected in the decay in older industrial cities of the urban infrastructure—the network of roads, bridges, sewers, rails, and mass transit systems.

Glossary

age-specific death rate   The number of deaths per 1,000 individuals in a specific age group.

age-specific fertility   The number of live births per 1,000 women in a specific age group.

city   A relatively dense and permanent concentration of people who secure their livelihood chiefly through nonagricultural activities.

concentric circle model   The approach to city growth that says that the modern city assumes a pattern of concentric circles, each with distinctive characteristics.

crowding   The perception that people have that too many other individuals are present in a situation.

crude birth rate   The number of live births per 1,000 members of a population in a given year.

crude death rate   The number of deaths per 1,000 members of a population in a given year.

demographic transition theory   A view of population change that holds that the process of modernization passes through three stages: high potential growth, transitional growth, and population stability.

demography   The science dealing with the size, distribution, composition, and changes in population.

density   The physical compactness of people in space.

ecology   The study of the interrelations between the living and nonliving components of an ecosystem.

ecosystem   A relatively stable community of organisms that have established interlocking relationships and exchanges with one another and their natural habitat.

environment   All the surrounding conditions and influences that affect an organism or group of organisms.

fecundity   The potential number of children that could be born if every woman of childbearing age bore all the children she possibly could.

general fertility rate   The annual number of live births per 1,000 women age 15 to 44.

growth rate   The difference between births and deaths, plus the difference between immigrants and emigrants per 1,000 population.

infant mortality rate   The number of deaths among infants under 1 year of age per 1,000 live births.

internal migration   Population movement within a nation.

international migration   Population movement among nations.

invasion   A new type of people, institution, or activity that encroaches on an area occupied by a different type.

megalopolis   A strip city formed when the rural interstices between metropolitan centers fill with urban development.

multiple nuclei model   The approach to city growth that assumes a city has several centers, each of which specializes in some activity and gives its distinctive cast to the surrounding area.

natural areas   Geographic areas with distinctive characteristics.

net migration rate   The increase or decrease per 1,000 members of the population in a given year that results from people entering (immigrants) or leaving (emigrants) a society.

population pyramid   The age and sex composition of a population as portrayed in the tree of ages.

sector model   The approach to city growth that assumes that large cities are made up of sectors—wedge-shaped areas—rather than concentric circles.

segregation   A process of clustering wherein individuals and groups are sifted and sorted out in space based on their sharing certain traits or activities in common.

succession   Invasion that continues until the encroaching type of people, institution, or activity displaces the previous type.

urban gentrification   The return of the middle class—usually young, white, childless professionals—to older urban neighborhoods.

zero population growth   The point at which a modern population replaces itself without immigration—2.1 children per woman.

Chapter 12

SOCIAL
CHANGE

Social life is not a material or substance to be molded: rather, it is an ongoing process constantly renewing, remaking, changing, and transforming itself. Indeed, life is never static but always in flux. In nature there are not any fixed entities, only transition and transformation (Whitehead, 1929; Sheldon, 1954). According to modern physics, the objects you normally see and feel consist of nothing more than patterns of energy that are forever moving and altering. Conceptions of "stuff," mass in the old sense of quantity or matter, have largely been displaced by more dynamic notions of process. Atoms, once supposedly fixed and solid, have broken down into protons, neutrons, and electrons, and these in turn have been broken down into energy and motion. From electrons to galaxies, from amoebas to humans, from families to societies, every phenomenon exists in a state of continual "becoming."

The dynamic quality of life often eludes us by virtue of our perceptual and conceptual limitations. Our thinking apparatus demands that we be furnished with discrete and identifiable "things." For instance, we "benchmark" time in seconds, minutes, hours, days, weeks, and years and, as we have done repeatedly in this text, capsulate epochs in such statements as "since World War II" and "the 1960s." Structure-function approaches help us to partition social life into discrete structures, including statuses and institutions. They allow us to place a "handle" on the fluid quality of life so that we may grasp, describe, and analyze it, making it understandable and intelligible. But as many conflict and symbolic interactionist theorists emphasize, the dichotomy between structure and process gives birth to problems that are frequently unnecessary. For one thing, the dichotomy produces difficulty in handling change. Indeed, the word "change" itself is saturated with certain nonprocess connotations, implying a shift from one static and relatively stable "state" to another. Admittedly, the English language does not help us in formulating these matters since the nouns that provide the subjects of most of our sentences chiefly refer to static objects, not to ongoing process. Given these problems and limitations, in this chapter we will address social change and process, the dynamic quality of social life.

□ A World of Change

Sociologists refer to fundamental alterations in the patterns of culture, structure, and social behavior over time as **social change.** It is a process by which society becomes something different while remaining in some respects the same. The impact of social change is strikingly apparent when we reflect on events that influenced our parents' and grandparents' lives and realize how distant the events seem to us. Consider the enormous transformations that have taken place across American life over the past 60 years. We have restyled many of our most basic values and norms. As the author William Manchester (1993) notes, racial upheaval, a sexual revolution, computer and communications breakthroughs, and a new national identity as a world power have remolded our national life. In the early 1930s, the U.S. population was half its present size, yet in the depth of the Great Depression more than 15 million men were out of work. Rural America lacked electricity, and its roads were dirt. In foreign affairs, we were an insular, second-class power, although Americans themselves were an ardently patriotic people. Welfare and divorce were shameful. Pregnancy made even married women uncomfortably self-conscious, and maternity clothes were designed to "keep your secret." Manliness was prized, and patriarchal authority was vested in men as heads of families. Homosexual men were deemed "sex perverts," and millions of Americans had never heard of lesbians. Had there been a watchword then, it would have been "duty." Today it would more likely be "rights": civil rights, women's rights, gay rights, welfare rights, children's rights, animal rights, the right to life, the right to choose, the right to protect, and the rights of the disabled. Given the impact that social change has on our lives, let us begin our discussion by examining some of its sources.

SOURCES OF SOCIAL CHANGE

Social change confronts people with new situations and compels them to fashion new forms of action. A great many factors interact to generate changes in people's behavior and in the culture and structure of their society. Sociologists identify a number of particularly critical factors, the impact of which differs with the situation and the time and place.

The Physical Environment. As we saw in Chapter 11, humans are physical beings who are located in some sort of habitat. If they are to survive, they must achieve a working relationship with their environment. Among the chief adaptive mechanisms available to a population are social organization and technology. But the social organization and technology that are adaptive to one environment are not necessarily adaptive to another. Hunting and gathering, horticultural, agricultural, and industrial societies all present different types of adaptations. Should the environment change for any reason, those who have evolved a given type of adaptation must respond by making appropriate institutional changes, fashioning new forms of social organization and new technologies. Droughts, floods, epidemics, earthquakes, and other forces of nature are among the ever-present realities that compel people to alter their lifeways. Additionally, as we noted in Chapter 11, human beings also have a substantial impact on their physical environment. Hazardous-waste dumps, acid rain, pollution of the water and air, overtaxing water resources, erosion of topsoil, and desertification result from human damage to the ecosystem. Thus human beings are tied to their environment in a chain of complex interchanges.

Population. Changes in the size, composition, and distribution of a population also affect culture and social structure. In Chapter 11 we saw the impact that the baby-boom generation is having on American life as the large "bulge" of persons born after World War II makes its way through the age groups. Already they have left their mark on musical tastes and the political climate. And what some have called the "narcissism of the '70s" appears to be on the wane as maturing members of the baby-boom generation look for close relationships and commitments. Likewise, the graying of the American population is having vast social ramifications. It is a principal factor in the nation's soaring Social Security, Medicaid, and health care costs (those 85 and over are the fastest growing part of the population). The graying of the society is also posing thorny dilemmas in the workplace as large numbers of middle-aged workers jockey for advancement. Increasing numbers of people are lining up for promotion, but there are fewer slots opening up than there are people willing to fill them. This situation can lead to frustration and an increase in midlife career changes, although people may also respond by pouring more of their energies into hobbies or family and community pursuits.

Clashes over Resources and Values. As we have repeatedly noted in this text, conflict is a form of interaction in which people are involved in a struggle over resources or values. Individuals and groups find themselves at odds; they feel separated by incompatible objectives. Not surprisingly, conflict is a basic source of social change. Members of a group must marshal their resources for competition. For instance, during wartime they must alter their customary ways of ordering their daily lives, and they may invest greater authority in military leaders. Of course, conflict also often involves negotiation, compromise, or accommodation. The swirling currents produced by these dynamic processes result in new institutional arrangements. Yet history demonstrates that the outcome of such interaction is rarely total fulfillment of the goal or goals of the parties involved. Most commonly, the end result is not a simple quantitative mixing of aspects of the opposing programs, but a completely new qualitative entity. Who could have foretold in 1870 the South that eventually emerged from the contest between the reconstructionists and their opponents? In 1918, the Europe and Russia that arose following a war "to end all wars" and "to make the world safe for democracy"? In 1933, the economic and social America that developed from the struggle between Roosevelt supporters and anti-New Dealers? In 1965, the nation that would emerge 30 years later after a decade of social turbulence? Or today, the societies that will arise in Eastern Europe and the former Soviet empire with the collapse of communism? Thus old orders continually erode and new ones arise.

Supporting Values and Norms. A society's values and norms act as "watchdogs" or "censors" permitting or inhibiting certain innovations. They may also serve as "stimulants." It is interesting to compare our readiness to accept technological innovations with our resistance to changes in economic theory, religion, or the family. Our use of the word "inventor" reflects this cultural bias. The inventor is one who innovates in material things, whereas the inventor of intangible ideas is often called a "revolutionary" or "radical," words with odious connotations. Among Samoans, considerable allowance is made for innovation in decorative arts, yet this freedom is negated by the culture's failure to give the innovator much recognition. Contrast this outlook with that of the Israelites of the eighth and seventh centuries B.C. who felt a strong need for spiritual interpretation and thus gave honor and followership to prophets who could find new ways of interpreting the will of God in the interests of the society (Herskovits, 1945).

Innovation. A **discovery** represents an addition to knowledge, whereas an **invention** uses existing knowledge in some novel form. Thus a discovery constitutes the perception of a relationship or fact that had not previously been recognized or

THE WALL STREET JOURNAL

DAVE CARPENTER...

"Great little product, but liability could eat you up."

From *The Wall Street Journal*—Permission, Cartoon Features Syndicate.

understood. Einstein's theory of relativity and Mendel's theory of heredity were discoveries. In contrast, an invention involves a new combination of old elements. The automobile was composed of six old elements in a new combination: a liquid gas engine, a liquid gas receptacle, a running-gear mechanism, an intermediate clutch, a driving shaft, and a carriage body.

Innovations—both discoveries and inventions—are not single acts but a cumulative series of transmitted increments plus a series of new elements. Consequently, the greater the number of cultural elements on which innovators may draw, the greater the frequency of discovery and invention. And just as a prolific couple gives birth to descendants who may multiply geometrically, so a pregnant invention may bring forth a geometrically increasing number of progeny. For example, glass gave birth to lenses, costume jewelry, drinking goblets, windowpanes, test tubes, X-ray tubes, light bulbs, radio and television tubes, mirrors, and many other products. Lenses in turn gave birth to eyeglasses, magnifying glasses, telescopes, cameras, searchlights, and so on. Such develop-

ments reflect the *exponential principle*—as the cultural base increases, its possible uses tend to grow in geometric ratio.

Diffussion. **Diffusion** is the process by which culture traits spread from one social unit to another. Diffusion is a people process and hence is expedited or hindered by the social environment. Simply because a trait is functionally superior does not necessarily ensure that individuals will adopt it. Much depends upon the network of relationships that tie people together in patterns of meaningful communication and influence (Strang and Tuma, 1993). For instance, researchers typically find that physicians who are the most involved in interpersonal relations with their colleagues introduce a new drug or procedure into their practices sooner than do their relatively isolated colleagues. When positioned in uncertain and unfamiliar medical terrain, doctors often look to their colleagues to confirm their own judgments and to share responsibility should a new drug or procedure prove to be wrong. So, even though medical breakthroughs are reported in the mainstream press as routinely as local murders, patients often find that their doctors are not familiar with the details of a new treatment or decline to use it. Take the case of streptokinase, a clot-dissolving drug for saving the lives of people having heart attacks. Some 15 years after the introduction of the drug and its favorable review in the medical literature, two-thirds of American heart-attack patients still do not receive the clot-dissolving drug.

Significantly, each culture or subculture contains a minimum of traits and patterns unique to or actually invented by it. It is easy, for instance, for Americans to minimize their debt to other peoples. We point with pride to what other societies have acquired from us, yet we often neglect to note what we have gained from them. As an illustration, consider the following account of the cultural content in the life of a "100 percent" American written as satire by anthropologist Ralph Linton (1937:427–429):

Doing Sociology: The Un-TV Experiment

Sociologist Bernard McGrane (1993b) of Chapman University in Orange, California, asks his students to "watch television" for the purpose of "seeing" television, in don Juan's sense: "Thus, as a teacher . . . don Juan's . . . contention was that he was teaching me how to 'see' as opposed to merely 'looking,' and that 'stopping the world' was the first step to 'seeing'" (Castaneda, 1972:ix). In what McGrane terms "our un-TV experiment," the students engage in "stopping the world" by "stopping the televi-

sion." As you may have already inferred, McGrane uses this technique as one means to demonstrate to his students how we go about the "social construction of reality."

In one exercise, the students are instructed to count "technical events" for 10 minutes on television. Anything other than "pure television" is a "technical event." Pure television consists of the type of images we see depicted on stationary TV cameras in banks, pawn shops, and jewelry stores—in short, a visual recording of what is before the equipment. Technical events include a TV camera zooming downward, a visual switch from one person to another, and an image of a car traveling down a road accompa-

nied by musical sounds. The students count the number of times they see or hear a "cut," "zoom," "superimposition," "voice-over," "fade in/out," and the like. The number of technical events that the students typically report range from about 90 to more than 180.

This counting exercise takes on extraordinary significance when we realize that we commonly take "technical events" for granted. We do not actually notice the events nor do we appreciate the frequency with which they occur. One student observed that he previously had not realized that television comes in "bits and pieces." In short, we have all watched television on countless occasions,

---

[D]awn finds the unsuspecting patriot garbed in pajamas, a garment of East Indian origin; and lying in a bed built on a pattern which originated in either Persia or Asia Minor. He is muffled to the ears in un-American materials: cotton, first domesticated in India; linen, domesticated in the Near East; wool from an animal native to Asia Minor; or silk whose uses were first discovered by the Chinese. . . .

If our patriot is old-fashioned enough to adhere to the so-called American breakfast, his coffee will be accompanied by an orange, domesticated in the Mediterranean region. He will follow this with a bowl of cereal made from grain domesticated in the Near East. . . . As a side dish he may have the egg of a bird domesticated in Southeastern Asia or strips of the flesh of an animal domesticated in the same region. . . .

In sum, a great number of social forces are at work, making for a continual process of social change.

The Mass Media. Diffusion is facilitated by the instant flooding of information across national, class, ethnic, and economic boundaries via the mass media. As we noted in Chapter 8, the mass media consist of those organizations—newspapers, magazines, television, radio, and motion pictures—that undertake to convey information to the public. According to one view, the media functions as a kind of giant hypodermic needle. In the hands of a few skilled operators—crafty politicians, "Madison Avenue people," and other sell artists—the needle discharges into the passive body of the population endless propaganda that renders it susceptible to the manipulators' wares—whether products, ideas, values, or candidates. Another view depicts the media as affording a "marketplace of ideas" in which an enlightened public carefully and rationally sifts and winnows a variety of attitudes and behaviors. Both views are

yet we have never actually "observed" the "technical events." This insight leads McGrane to inquire of his students as to what other social practices and institutions escape our conscious notice as we go about our day-to-day lives.

McGrane also asks his students to watch a television program and a news program each for 10 minutes without turning on the sound. Some students reported that when they watched a program of their choice without sound, they were lulled into "a stupor of passivity." Nor had they previously appreciated how "boring" television can be. News programs also tended to dull their senses with an overloading of the mind with images of death, despair, murder, and sensationalism. Moreover, students often had difficulty recognizing when the news stopped and the commercials began because there were no "borders" between the different types of programming. McGrane observes that from a "functionalist" perspective such a practice is quite "functional" because "the first imperative of any institution is its own survival"—in brief, "the medium is the message."

Significantly, many students verbalize considerable anger and resentment over having to undertake the experiments (they also are instructed to "write up" their observations). They frequently voice the objection: "I wasted 30 minutes of my time." McGrane relates their experience to Weber's "Protestant ethic" in which time is associated with "being productive," "getting ahead," and "accruing value" (or in the words of Benjamin Franklin, "Remember that time is money!"). So in the process of studying others (namely, television), the students also come to study themselves. Our society places a considerable premium upon "keeping busy" and "not wasting time" (the notion that "Idle hands are the Devil's workshop"). In "watching" television in the manner prescribed by their instructor, they were violating societal expectations—indeed, they were not even being "entertained."

alike in assigning considerable weight and importance to mass communications in the shaping and changing of contemporary life. Yet the matter is not nearly as simple as the proponents of either view would have us believe.

Mass communication ordinarily does not serve as a necessary and sufficient cause of attitudinal and behavioral change. *Most* efforts at mass communication merely confirm the beliefs that people already hold. For one thing, people typically expose themselves to mass communications that are congenial or favorable to their existing opinions and interests. For another, selective perception operates so that people tend to misperceive and misinterpret persuasive communications in accordance with their existing opinions.

Although the mass media may not be the powerfully overwhelming force that they are sometimes credited with being, they nonetheless have not-so-minimal effects. Take the matter of the "news." We typically think of news coverage as the media bringing to public attention the "important" happenings of the day by reporting on an objective reality "out there." But as symbolic interactionists point out, "news" is "constructed"—some selected occurrences come to be translated into "public events" for a mass constituency while others are ignored. Because individuals and groups have differing and competing uses for events, they have differing conceptions of what constitutes a newsworthy occurrence. So social power takes on critical importance—the capacity to create and sustain the perceived reality of others. For instance, "news" about women is on the increase in American news media, but men continue to receive more attention from the nation's news organizations (a February 1994 survey found that men received some 75 percent of front page references, as against 25 percent for women) (Glaberson, 1994). See the box describing an "un-TV experiment."

The media perform other functions as well. They "agenda-set" by providing cues that people then use in deciding the importance of an issue. And they "prime" people to the criteria of judgment that they should use in evaluating such matters as presidential or congressional performance. Additionally, fictional media presentations have a "cultivation effect" in which images are provided that influence public attitudes and behavior about such social policies as crime, violence, and welfare. Moreover, programs like *The Oprah Winfrey Show* afford self-help remedies. Finally, although intellectuals often disdain television as a vast wasteland that corrupts its viewers and turns them into mindless, sedentary couch potatoes, the viewing of situation comedies and action-adventure programming may be a way of providing the public with a vehicle for getting rid of many stresses and tensions.

PERSPECTIVES ON SOCIAL CHANGE

Many of sociology's roots lie in the effort to unravel the "meaning" of history and to establish laws of social change and development. The founders of sociology, particularly Auguste Comte and Herbert Spencer, looked to the grand sweep of history, searching for an understanding of how and why societies change. Many contemporary sociologists continue to be intrigued by these "big questions." The major sociological perspectives on social change fall within four broad categories: evolutionary perspectives, cyclical perspectives, functionalist perspectives, and conflict perspectives.

Evolutionary Perspectives. Much sociological thinking during the nineteenth century was dominated by the doctrine of social progress and a search for underlying evolutionary laws. According to Social Darwinists like Spencer, social evolution resembles biological evolution and results in

the world's growing progressively better. In his theory of *unilinear evolution,* Spencer contended that change has persistently moved society from homogeneous and simple units toward progressively heterogeneous and interdependent units. He viewed the "struggle for existence" and "the survival of the fittest" as basic natural laws. Spencer equated this struggle with "free competition," insisting that "men ignore it to their sorrow." If unimpeded by outside intervention, particularly government, those individuals and social institutions that are "fit" will survive and proliferate while those that are "unfit" will in time die out.

As we pointed out in Chapter 1, Spencer's Social Darwinism mirrored the orientation of laissez-faire capitalism. Governmental regulation and welfare legislation were depicted as fostering social degeneration by "artificially preserving" the unfit and restricting the fit in their inheritance of the earth. Social Darwinism was a doctrine well suited to expansionist imperialism and provided a justification for Western colonialism. The white race and its cultures were extolled as the highest forms of "humanity" and "civilization." Other peoples and cultures were "lower" in evolutionary development, and so it was only proper that Europeans, being "fitter," should triumph in the "struggle for existence." However, such blatant ethnocentrism did not stand the test of scientific research. Simultaneously, the notion of unilinear evolution came under scientific scrutiny and was found wanting. Anthropologists demonstrated that non-Western societies—and many European nations as well—did not pass through the same sequence of stages. In brief, there is no one scenario, but many scenarios of social change. The course of change is not merely preprogrammed by natural law in some rigidly fashioned mold.

Although evolutionary theory fell into disrepute for some 50 years, it has undergone a revival in recent decades (Steward, 1955; White, 1959; Lenski, 1966; Service, 1971). Contemporary approaches take a *multilinear* view of evolution. Their proponents recognize that "change" does not necessarily imply "progress," that change occurs in quite different ways, and that change proceeds in many different directions. Indeed, interest in evolutionary theory has moved so centrally into mainstream sociology that even such a leading structure-function sociologist as the late Talcott Parsons (1966, 1977) came to fashion a theory of "evolutionary change." While disclaiming that societal evolution is either a continuous or a simple linear process, Parsons suggests that societies tend to become increasingly *differentiated* in their structures and functions. But differentiation is not sufficient since the new structural arrangements must be more functionally adaptive than previous arrangements, leading to *adaptive upgrading*.

Sociologist Gerhard Lenski (1966; Lenski and Lenski, 1987) likewise takes an evolutionary perspective that does not regard changes in social organization as necessarily leading to greater human happiness or satisfaction. He holds that evolution depends largely on changes in a society's level of technology and its mode of economic production. These changes in turn have consequences for other aspects of social life, including stratification systems, the organization of power, and family structures. According to Lenski, there is an underlying continuum in terms of which all societies can be ranked: hunting and gathering societies, simple horticultural societies, advanced horticultural societies, agrarian societies, and industrial societies. More specialized evolutionary bypaths include herding societies and "hybrid societies" such as fishing and maritime societies.

Cyclical Perspectives. Evolutionary theories, particularly those with a unilinear focus, depict history as divided into steplike levels that constitute sequential stages and that are characterized by an underlying trend. Cyclical theorists take a different approach and look to the rise and fall of civilizations. Their objective is not to predict the long-term direction of human history but rather to predict the course of a civilization or society. Nor do cyclical theorists seek to place societies on

some sort of linear or historical scale. Instead, they compare societies in a search for generalizations regarding their stages of growth and decline. In sum, evolutionalists tend to be relatively jolly people who see humankind as ever striving to reach new heights in a challenging future, whereas cyclical theorists tend to be relatively pessimistic individuals who forecast the demise of every civilization.

The nineteenth century was a time of faith in evolution and human progress. But the catastrophe of World War I and the periodic economic crises that have plagued industrial nations led some scholars to express doubt regarding the course of human history. One of these was the German scholar Oswald Spengler (1880–1936), whose *The Decline of the West* (1918/1926) became a best-seller. He contended that culture passes through the same stages of growth and decline as individuals: a period of development, followed by maturity, eventual decline, and death. Based on his examination of eight cultures, Spengler says that each culture possesses a life span of approximately 1,000 years. Western culture, he held, emerged about A.D. 900, and therefore its end is close at hand (hence the title of his book and the interest it provoked).

English historian Arnold J. Toynbee (1934/1954) also sought to depict uniformities in the growth and decline of civilization and to identify the principles that underlie this development. Like Spengler, he believes that the course of most civilizations is uniform, although he does not ascribe a time interval to their rise and decline. Toynbee says that civilizations arise in response to some challenge. A challenge may derive from natural forces, such as severe climate, or from human factors, such a warlike neighbors. A civilization grows and flourishes when the challenge is not too severe and when a creative minority (an intelligent elite) finds an adequate response to the challenge. When the creative minority fails to find a response adequate to a challenge, the civilization breaks down and disintegrates. In the course of disintegrating, the minority transforms itself into a ruling elite and imposes its will by force. This development hastens the decline because it intensifies internal strife. However, careful examination of Toynbee's work shows it to rely primarily upon Hellenic and Western experiences and to neglect Arabic, Egyptian, and Chinese histories that reveal somewhat different patterns. Thus his theory tends to be arbitrarily imposed on the history of other civilizations rather than being inductively derived from a study of them.

Functionalist Perspectives. As we saw in Chapter 2, the concept of system is central to the structure-function model of society. A system is a set of elements or components related in a more-or-less stable fashion over a period of time. One of the features of a system stressed by structure-function theorists is its tendency toward *equilibrium.* Even though contending forces are never equal, final, or permanent, there is a tendency for a system to achieve some sort of balance among them. Although time can be introduced as a factor within the model, American structure-function sociologists have stressed static over dynamic processes. Of course things are not static in the sense of being dead; things happen all the time. Children are born, people die, and institutional structures functionally contribute to the regular performance of essential tasks across time (Dahrendorf, 1968).

As we pointed out earlier in the chapter, structure-function sociologists like Parsons (1966, 1977) have introduced the notion of evolution to the perspective. In so doing, they have attempted to broaden the concept of equilibrium to include *developing* properties in addition to those that are *self-maintaining.* Following the organic analogy, the social group is portrayed as living in a state of dynamic or moving equilibrium. Upsetting forces introject themselves into the equilibrated system, functioning as innovative stimuli. The equilibrated social system responds adjustively to these disturbances, accommodating them within the functioning structure and establishing a new level of equilibrium. Hence, even though society

changes, it remains stable through new forms of social integration.

Sociologist William F. Ogburn (1922) drew upon evolutionary models to fashion a functionalist approach to social change. He distinguishes between *material* and *nonmaterial culture* and locates the source of change in material invention—tools, weapons, and technical processes. Nonmaterial culture refers to social values, norms, beliefs, and social arrangements, including law, religion, and the family. Ogburn saw the impetus for social change coming from material culture. Nonmaterial cultural must adapt or respond to changes in material culture. Since nonmaterial culture must constantly "catch up" with material culture, an adjustment gap develops between the two forms of culture. Ogburn called this gap **cultural lag.** Although the notion of cultural lag contains a valuable insight, it vastly oversimplifies matters. No one factor is capable of explaining social change since in real-life situations a vast array of forces converge in complex interaction with one another to give society its dynamic properties.

Social life abounds with examples where the rate of change in various segments of society is uneven and results in social dislocation. For instance, the automobile has fostered a whole host of changes. It spawned such secondary industries as oil refineries, tire and glass conglomerates, and the giant accident insurance industry. It induced massive investments in single-family homes and in extensive road systems that move traffic from the central city to outer suburban rings. But in doing so, the automobile has contributed to the despoiling of the natural environment and to an exodus of the central city's affluent population. Thus, as depicted by Ogburn, social problems ensue from the "social disorganization" that occurs when social institutions lag behind changing technology.

Conflict Perspectives. Conflict theorists hold that tensions between competing groups are the basic source of social change. Nowhere does one find a clearer exposition of the conflict perspective than that provided by Karl Marx, particularly as it finds expression in his notion of the *dialectic*. As we saw in Chapter 1, the dialectic depicts the world in dynamic terms as a world of *becoming* rather than *being*. According to Marxian dialectical materialism, every economic order grows to a state of maximum efficiency, at the same time developing internal contradictions or weaknesses that contribute to its decay. Class conflict is a particularly powerful source of change, and Marx saw it as the key to understanding human history. As noted in Chapter 6, class conflict derives from the struggle between those who own the means of producing wealth and those who do not.

Marx said that all change is the product of a constant conflict between opposites. It arises from the contradiction inherent in all things and all processes. All development—social, economic, or human—proceeds through the resolution of existing contradictions and the eventual emergence of new contradictions. The outcome of the clash between opposing forces is not a compromise (an averaging out of the differences among them). It is an entirely new product, one born of struggle. In this manner, both individuals and societies change. It is a dynamic process of complex interchanges between all facets of social life. As Marx (1867/1906) observed, "By acting on the external world and changing it, he [the individual] at the same time changes his own nature."

We have dealt with conflict theorists at some length in several chapters. We have noted that many conflict theorists regard Marx's view that "all history is the history of class conflict" as a vast oversimplification (Coser, 1956, 1957; Dahrendorf, 1958). They contend that other types of conflict are equally or, in some instances, more important, including conflict between nations, ethnic groups, religions, and economic interest groups. Sociologist Ralf Dahrendorf (1958: 174–175), an advocate of conflict theory, asserts:

1. *Every society is subjected at every moment to change: social change is ubiquitous.*

2. *Every society experiences at every moment social conflict: social conflict is ubiquitous.*
3. *Every element in a society contributes to its change.*
4. *Every society rests on constraint of some of its members by others.*

Dahrendorf sees these points as complementing the functionalist model, which highlights the integrated and configurational aspects of social life.

SOCIAL CHANGE IN THE UNITED STATES

To live in the United States is to gain an appreciation for Dahrendorf's assertions that social change is ubiquitous. It highlights the maxim that "To live is to change." Let us examine one aspect of change, that associated with the rapid introduction of technology into American life, particularly within the workplace. Most popular models draw upon a familiar but narrow understanding of society that is rooted in "black box" economics. New technologies are portrayed as entering the "box" at one end of the economy, where they are mixed with other components like the education of the work force and incentives for business investment, and in due course come out the other end of the "box" as economic growth and jobs. Viewed in this manner, technologies are simply components of a gigantic device—a national wealth-generating pump—whose sole purpose is to produce ever-greater quantities of wealth.

Sociological models, in contrast, depict technological innovations as a reweaving of the social fabric—a reshaping of the norms, roles, relationships, groups, and institutions that make up society. As political scientist Langdon Winner (1993) notes, a better analogy for technological change would be the "loom" rather than the "pump." Today we hear a good deal about the construction of "information highways" and "information infrastructures." The building of "highways" and "infrastructures" breeds new patterns of interaction and association. Consequently, technology is not the sole cause of the resulting social change. However, it frequently serves as the occasion and catalyst for redefinitions of the operating structures of society and of the family, work, and community experiences of people. In considering these matters it would be well to remind ourselves of the vast impact that another "highway system" had on American life—the building of the interstate system following World War II. The system was inspired by a wish to improve commerce, foster physical and social mobility, and bolster national defense. But the interstate system also had many unanticipated consequences that permanently changed the nation's social landscape. For instance, it fostered the rapid growth of strip and edge cities (see Chapter 11) and magnified the split between outlying communities and inner cities.

The Information Revolution.   Many of us are fascinated by the Industrial Revolution. But when we ask why the Industrial Revolution was a revolution, we find that it was not the machines that made it so. Certainly the steam engine, the cotton gin, the locomotive and rails, and the power loom were extraordinary inventions. But the primary reason that they were revolutionary is because they were agents for great social change. They took people out of the fields and brought them into factories. They gave rise to mass production and, through mass production, to a society in which wealth was not confined to the few. In somewhat like fashion, computers promise to revolutionize the structure of American life, particularly as they free the human mind, open new vistas in knowledge and communication, and allow technologies to increasingly take on human qualities—what some have termed the *Information Revolution.* See Figure 12.1. In fact, by the year 2000, it is predicted that school children will be playing with videogame and computer equipment as powerful as supercomputers were in 1990 (Markoff, 1991). It is the capacity of the computer for solving problems and making decisions that represents its greatest potential and poses the greatest difficulties in predicting its impact on society. Even so, a number of issues have been

repeatedly raised about the social impact of computers.

First, the computer promises to automate some workplace activities that are now performed by people. The Industrial Revolution centered on the supplementation and ultimate replacement of the *muscles* of humans and animals by introducing mechanical methods. The Information Revolution goes beyond this development to supplement and replace some aspects of the *mind* of human beings by electronic methods. Both changes have vast implications for the world of work. However, much of the computer's potential remains more promise than actuality. As yet, predictions of a computerized society have not been realized. In many cases, computers have simply been used as faster calculators and better typewriters without radically altering the way we live or work.

Second, information is a source of power, and computers mean information. The centralized accumulation of data permits the concentration of considerable power in those who have access to computers. A power gap tends to develop between those who are trained to use and understand computers and those who are not. Some authorities believe that widespread access to computers will produce a society more democratic, egalitarian, and richly diverse than any previously known. But the expectations of computer enthusiasts may be nothing more than wishful thinking. It may be that computer technology intelligently structured and wisely applied might help a society raise its standard of literacy, education, and general knowledgeability. But there is no automatic, positive link between knowledge and its enlightened use.

Third, computers alter the way people relate to one another. On a telephone, we hear the other person's voice. In fact-to-face contact, we see people smile, frown, and nod. But there is no such feedback in computer exchanges. When people use a computer to send electronic mail, they lack access to nonverbal cues. Thus computers may have consequences for our sense of individuality. It also makes computer exchanges less pre-

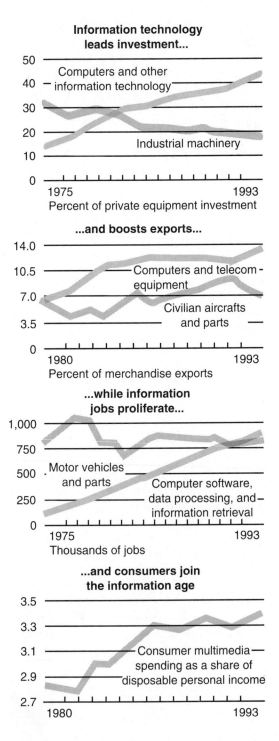

Figure 12.1 THE INFORMATION REVOLUTION
The Information Revolution is driving the economy in the 1990s, translating into mammoth social change.
(SOURCE: Commerce Department, Bureau of Labor Statistics and Morgan Stanley & Co. Adapted from May 18, 1994, issue of *Business Week* by special permission. Copyright © 1994 by McGraw-Hill, Inc.

"On the Internet, nobody knows you're a dog."

Drawing by P. Steiner; © 1993 The New Yorker Magazine, Inc.

as people handle more and more of their activities through electronic instruments—mail, banking, shopping, entertainment, and travel plans—it becomes technically feasible to monitor these activities with unprecedented ease. Such opportunities for matching and correlating data have a menacing, Orwellian potential to them.

Technology and Jobs. Visionaries look to technology to make human lives richer and freer. Today, ascendant corporations and nations are masters not so much of land and material resources but of ideas and technologies. Significantly, Japan, South Korea, Taiwan, Singapore, and Hong Kong are among the world's fastest growing economies. The advocates of modern technology say that the new electronics allows people to have access to vast stores of information, expanded human resources, and opportunities for working and relating with one another on a cheaper, more flexible, and convenient basis. More specifically, they see a variety of benefits deriving from technological advances. For one thing, tasks that are boring, repetitive, and narrowly defined can be performed by machines. As automation removes low-level work, opportunities grow for greater free time in which people can be more creative and productive. For another, new technologies dictate that workers understand how the entire production process fits together rather than seeing themselves as working with only a small piece of it. And as routine tasks are taken over by computers and robots, the ability and willingness of workers to solve unexpected problems and to reprogram production in response to shifting requirements assumes greater significance. Further, some experts see computer systems as offering opportunities to disadvantaged groups to acquire the skills and social ties they require to become fully functioning members of society.

dictable. For one thing, people are less likely to hold back strong feelings when communicating by computers; they show a greater tendency to swear, insult others, and communicate abruptly. For another, in face-to-face meetings, one person is likely to talk considerably more than another. But on a computer, people tend to talk about the same amount because they are less self-conscious and are protected by a feeling of anonymity. Moreover, computer technology changes people's awareness of themselves, of one another, and of their relationship with the world. A machine that appears to "think" challenges our notions not only of time and distance but also of mind.

Finally, computers have implications for individual privacy and the confidentiality of our communications and personal data. The growing use of computers to collect data and store information provides the technical capability for integrating several information files into networks of computerized data banks. With such networks, personal data that we provide for one purpose can potentially be accessed for other purposes. Thus

But not all experts are so optimistic. Some express fear that computers and robots will take over many office and factory duties so that jobs as janitors, cashiers, truck drivers, hospital orderlies, sales personnel, and fast-food helpers will primarily remain. Technology often has the double impact of job creation and job displacement, increasing the demand for technical workers while eliminating many semiskilled and unskilled jobs. According to the Office of Technology Assessment (1988), about 45 percent of the job growth in the United States between 1980 and 1986 was in professional and managerial occupations, and almost 50 percent of the new jobs created between 1983 and 1986 went to people with at least 3 years of college education.

Yet it is easy to overestimate the rapidness with which new technology is introduced within industry. Not too long ago some experts were predicting that millions of dangerous and repetitive jobs would be taken over by an army of robots. It was thought that by 1990 some 250,000 robots would be operating in American factories. Yet by 1990 only 37,000 robots had been put in place, and by 1994 there were not a great many more. Moreover, many people mistakenly assume that the number of employees an industry loses is proportional to the decline of its output. Yet between 1970 and 1994, the number of manufacturing jobs in the United States decreased from 19.4 to 17.7 million. But manufacturing output doubled during that period. Fewer workers are simply producing more (Rosenbaum, 1993).

Increasingly, critics are also questioning whether the new technology is improving the lot of office workers. Indeed, some labor leaders contend that office automation has created the electronic equivalent of the moving assembly line, with the computer system programmed to monitor workers' performance. A study by the U.S. Public Health Service offers some support for the criticism. The study looked at three categories of workers: clerical workers who did data processing with video-display terminals, professionals who occasionally used video-display terminals, and clerical workers who processed data by manual methods. The clerical workers using the video-display terminals reported substantially greater physical and mental stress than did workers in other categories. The terminal users had to follow rigid work procedures that did not allow them any control over their work. Instead, the machine controlled them. Contemporary "electronic factories" are mostly a creation of banks, insurance companies, credit-card concerns, and firms with large data-processing requirements. In appearance the work settings are quite similar: a large, quiet room with video-display terminals grouped in clusters or rows with data processors serving as electronic-age stevedores, loading and retrieving information.

Although considerable controversy surrounds the impact technology has on the workplace, it is clear that some individuals come out the losers. Frequently, the human consequences are so massive and pervasive that a single company, industry, or state cannot cope with them. Under these circumstances, a national response is essential if programs are to be set in place for shifting workers to industries and regions with jobs and for retraining workers for new jobs. A modern society ignores at its peril a situation where a growing number of its population cannot find gainful employment.

SOCIAL CHANGE IN THIRD WORLD NATIONS

It is difficult today to read a newspaper or view a television newscast without gaining a feeling for the powerful currents of change that continually encompass the world. Iran, the Middle East, Central America, South Africa, and countless other global centers conjure up images of boiling cauldrons of social transition and transformation. Sociologists have approached social change in Third World nations from two somewhat different perspectives: modernization and world systems.

Modernization. **Modernization** describes the process by which a society moves from traditional or preindustrial social and economic arrangements to those characteristic of industrial societies. Implicit in the notion of modernization is the assumption that there is basically one predominant course of development—namely, that followed by advanced Western nations and Japan. Viewed in this manner, modernization entails patterns of *convergence* in which societies become increasingly urban, industry comes to overshadow agriculture, the size and density of the population increase, the division of labor becomes more specialized, and the knowledge base grows larger and more complex. East Asia (Taiwan, South Korea, Hong Kong, and Singapore) is the showcase of modernization theories.

The momentum for change derives from *internal* forces and processes. The chances that a Third World country will evolve in the direction of liberal Western democracies are thought to be enhanced when a nation's economy provides for literacy, education, and communication, creates a pluralistic rather than a centrally dominated social order, and prevents extreme inequalities among the various social strata. Efficient systems of communication and a diversity of social groups and organizations are believed to distribute political resources and skills among multiple segments of the community and provide the foundation of effective opposition parties.

World System or Dependency. World-system (and dependency) approaches view the social structures of Third World nations as shaped by the historical experience of colonialism, the timing and manner of their incorporation into the global capitalist economy, and the perpetuation of their dependency through political domination, multinational corporations, and unfavorable exchange arrangements. For instance, sociologist Immanuel Wallerstein (1974a, b, 1989; 1991) considers development within the context of an international, geographical division of labor: the core, the periphery, and the semiperiphery (see Chapter 8). In general, the *core* geographical area dominates the world economy and exploits other social and economic units. The *periphery* consists of those regions that supply raw materials to the core and are severely exploited by it. The *semiperiphery* consists of those areas that fall somewhere between the exploiting and exploited segments of the world economy.

According to world-system and dependency analysis, Third World nations cannot recapitulate the developmental trajectory of Western nations and Japan. An unequal exchange takes place between core and periphery nations, with development at the former end of the chain coming at the cost of underdevelopment at the other end (London and Williams, 1990; Walton and Ragin, 1990; Chase-Dunn and Hall, 1993). More particularly, specialization in the production and export of raw materials is said to be detrimental to the long-term growth prospects of developing nations. Such specialization distorts these nations' economies because they become responsive to the demands of the world market rather than to internal developmental needs. Thus the momentum and course of development are shaped primarily by *external* forces and processes. Further, investments in the production or mining of raw materials monopolize capital to the detriment of other types of investment. And class formation in the dependent nations results in a small elite whose economic interests are linked to foreign investors in the core countries (Berberoglu, 1987; Bradshaw, 1988). Dependency theorists see Latin America and Africa as affording stark evidence of the limits that dependency imposes on nations. World-system theorists view current events in Eastern Europe and the former Soviet Union as offering testimony to the difficulty nations have in exiting the world system.

In sum, whereas modernization approaches look to convergences in political and economic development, world-system and dependency analysis looks to divergences. And whereas modernization theories view direct, private foreign investment as an asset in the development of Third World nations, world-system and dependency approaches consider foreign investment as the prime culprit in many Third World social ills. Overall, those in advantaged international positions tend to favor explanations that emphasize the internal features of development (modernization approaches), and those in disadvantaged positions to prefer explanations that look to external factors (world-system or dependency approaches). Fast-moving world events have also impacted the sociological study of change in Third World nations (Firebaugh, 1992; Bollen and Appold, 1993; Moaddel, 1994). The field has been in flux in recent years as it has confronted a host of new issues including: How will the demise of communism and Cold War tensions impact these countries? Will an information age enable Third World nations to leapfrog stages in economic development? How will new population policies and women's issues affect development policies?

☐ Collective Behavior

As we experience social life, it tends to be settled, patterned, and recurrent. We go about our daily activities, carrying out our roles and guiding our behavior by norms that define what we are supposed to do in given situations. Yet as we have seen in this chapter, it is easy to overemphasize the structured nature of social life. Some forms of group behavior are not organized in terms of established norms and institutionalized lines of action. This is particularly true of **collective behaviors**—ways of thinking, feeling, and acting that develop among a large number of people and that are relatively spontaneous and unstructured. Human history is replete with episodes variously labeled by contemporaries as "psychic epidemics," "collective seizures," "group outbursts," "mass delusions," "crazes," and "group pathologies." Indeed, from earliest recorded times people have

thrown themselves into a great many types of mass behavior, including social unrest, riots, manias, fads, panics, mass flights, lynchings, crowd excitement, religious revivals, and rebellions. All these forms of behavior are more likely to occur during times of rapid social change. Moreover, they often provide an impetus to social change. Accordingly, no discussion of social change can neglect collective behavior.

VARIETIES OF COLLECTIVE BEHAVIOR

Collective behavior comes in a great many forms. In order to gain a better appreciation for the impact such behavior has on our lives, let us consider a number of varieties of collective behavior at greater length.

Rumors. A **rumor** is a difficult-to-verify piece of information transmitted from person to person in relatively rapid fashion. We often think of rumors as providing false information, and in many cases this is true. But they also may be accurate, or, at the very least, contain a kernel of truth. Rumors typically arise in situations in which people lack information or distrust the official sources of information. They are a substitute for hard news, a collective attempt by people to achieve information and understanding about matters that are important to them but about which they are ignorant (Shibutani, 1966; Rosnow, 1991). As such, rumors are both a form of collective behavior and an important element in most other forms of collective behavior.

Periods of anxiety, tension, and sagging economic conditions provide an environment that leads to a proliferation of rumors (Rosnow and Kimmel, 1979; Koenig, 1982, 1985). Under these circumstances, rumors give people a way to make sense out of their social world and to structure reality. Indeed, the more frightened people are by a rumor, the more likely they are to repeat it. They often repeat a rumor that frightens them in hopes of finding that it is wrong. But since other people may not afford contrary information, the process serves to escalate popular fears (Goleman, 1991b).

One type of rumor that is particularly common involves alleged contamination (Turner, 1994). Indeed, in recent years a variety of unfounded rumors have hurt the sales of some of the nation's largest corporations. For instance, McDonald's has had to fight rumors that it puts earthworms in hamburgers (perhaps suggested by the fact that raw hamburger resembles red worms). Some people have seen a communist connection in the clenched-fist symbol of Arm & Hammer, the baking soda company. And Procter & Gamble has been plagued with persistent rumors that its 140-year-old moon-and-stars trademark is a satanic symbol.

Rumors tend to evolve and take on new details as people interact and talk. Some research suggests that highly anxious people spread rumors much more frequently than do less anxious ones. Likewise, rumor participants—people who are eager to listen to or pass on a rumor—are often individuals who wish to attract attention. Typically they are people who are on the edge of the group or relatively low in status. For a brief instant—at the time when they are circulating a sensational story—they become somebody (Koenig, 1982, 1985).

Fashion and Fads.   We typically think of folkways and mores as having considerable durability—as being relatively fixed and slow to change. But human beings often yearn for something new, for variety and novelty. At first it may seem impossible that this desire could be satisfied through norms since norms emphasize conformity (see Chapter 2). Yet curiously, human beings manage to be conformists even when they seek change. They achieve this strange anomaly by a set of norms that demand some measure of conformity while they endure but that last only a short time (Davis, 1949). Such norms are termed *fashions* and *fads*.

A **fashion** is a folkway that lasts for a short time and enjoys widespread acceptance within society. Fashion finds expression in such things as styles of clothing, automobile design, and home architecture. By virtue of fashion, the suit that was in vogue 5 years ago seems out of place today. The automobile of 3 years past that appeared so exquisitely beautiful and appropriate looks outdated and even somewhat odd now. And "gingerbread" and brownstone houses no longer suit the tastes of many home buyers.

A **fad** is a folkway that lasts for a short time and enjoys acceptance among only a segment of the population. Indeed, the behavior is often scorned by most people. Fads often appear in amusements, new games, popular tunes, dance steps, health practices, movie idols, and slang. Adolescents are particularly prone toward fads. It seems that the identities of adolescents are as yet rather diffuse, uncrystallized, and fluctuating, and that teenagers are frequently at sea with themselves and others. This ambiguity and absence of stable social anchorage lead many youths to overcommit themselves to fads. The fads become a vehicle whereby young people can gain a sense of identity and belonging, with aspects of dress and gesture arbitrarily serving as signs of an in-group or out-group status (Erikson, 1968). Adherence to a fad, then, is one way youths define themselves in relation to their peers. For the most part, fads typically play only an incidental part in the lives of the individuals who adopt them. Some fads, however, come to preoccupy individuals, becoming all-consuming passions. Such fads are called **crazes.** Financial speculation at times assumes craze proportions (Chatzky, 1992). In the famous Holland tulip mania in the seventeenth century, the value of tulip bulbs came to exceed their weight in gold; the bulbs were not planted, but bought and sold among speculators. In the Florida land boom of the 1920s, lands were sold and resold at skyrocketing prices without the purchasers even seeing their purchases.

Mass Hysteria.   **Mass hysteria** refers to the rapid dissemination of behaviors involving contagious anxiety, usually associated with some mysterious force. For instance, medieval witchhunts rested on the belief that many social ills were caused by witches. Likewise, some "epidemics" of assembly-line illness—*mass psychogenic illness*—derive from hysterical contagion. In recent years episodes of mass psychogenic illness have occurred in American plants packing frozen fish, punching computer cards, assembling electrical switches, sewing shoes, making dresses, and manufacturing lawn furniture. In most cases, the workers complain of headache, nausea, dizziness, weakness, and breathing difficulty. However, health authorities, including physicians, industrial hygienists, and toxicologists, find no bacteria, virus, toxic material, or other pathogenic agent to explain the symptoms. The episodes are most prevalent among poorly paid, female assembly-line workers who perform the same repetitive task over and over. Mass psychogenic illness is usually a collective response to severe stress caused by job dissatisfaction, monotony, overwork, noise, crowding, or poor management. An event such as speedup or required overtime commonly triggers the outbreak (Colligan, Pennebaker, and Murphy, 1982).

We should not conclude that illnesses associated with contagious hysteria are simply in the workers' "heads." The individuals suffer real physical symptoms. For example, something—perhaps unusual stress—causes them to breathe rapidly (hyperventilate). The more rapidly a person breathes, the more carbon dioxide is blown off, and the higher becomes the pH level (acid-alkaline content) of the blood. The human body performs poorly at high pH levels, and such symptoms as headache, nausea, numbness in the feet and hands, and weakness can ensue.

Panic. **Panic** involves irrational and uncoordinated but collective actions among people induced by the presence of an immediate, severe threat. For instance, people commonly flee from a catastrophe such as a fire or flood. The behavior is collective, since social interaction intensifies people's fright. Consider what happened on Halloween evening in 1938 when a radio drama (by Howard Koch) of H. G. Well's novel *War of the Worlds* stirred up incidents of panic behavior in the United States (Cantril, 1940). The broadcast, carried by CBS stations, purported to describe an invasion of Martians. The story, narrated by Orson Welles and a number of other actors, was related in the form of special news bulletins and on-the-spot reports interspersed with interviews with "eyewitnesses," "scientists," "public officials," and "commentators." The program began with dance music, purportedly coming from a hotel orchestra. Suddenly the music was interrupted with a special news bulletin (Cantril, 1940:22–23):

Ladies and gentlemen, I have a grave announcement to make. Incredible as it may seem, both the observations of science and the evidence of our eyes lead to the inescapable assumption that those strange beings who landed in the Jersey farmlands tonight are the vanguard of an invading army from the planet Mars. The battle which took place tonight at Grovers Mill has ended in one of the most startling defeats ever suffered by an army in modern times; seven thousand men armed with rifles and machine guns pitted against a single fighting machine of the invaders from Mars. One hundred and twenty known survivors. The rest strewn over the battle area from Grovers Mill to Plainsboro crushed and trampled to death under the metal feet of the monster, or burned to cinders by its heat-ray.

Dramatic announcements came in quick succession. As the broadcast proceeded, people ran to tell others by word of mouth and by phone. Some ran to the streets in panic. Others took to their cars to drive as far as possible from the place of invasion. Still others fell to the floor in prayer, or sat immobilized, waiting for the inevitable end. Estimates suggest that at least a million Americans were disturbed by the story. The following morning, when newspapers and radio broadcasts reported that the affair was a hoax, the excitement ended.

Crowds. The **crowd** is one of the most familiar and at times spectacular forms of collective behavior. It is a temporary, relatively unorganized gathering of people who are in close physical proximity. Since a wide range of behavior is encompassed by the concept, sociologist Herbert Blumer (1946; also see McPhail, 1989) distinguishes among four basic types of crowd behavior. The first, a **casual crowd,** is a collection of people who have little in common except that they may be viewing a common event, such as looking through a department store window. The second, a **conventional crowd,** entails a number of people who have assembled for some specific purpose and who typically act in accordance with established norms, such as people attending a baseball game or a concert. The third, an **expressive crowd,** is an aggregation of people who have gotten together for self-stimulation and personal gratification, such as occurs at a religious revival or a rock festival. And fourth, an **acting crowd** is an excited, volatile collection of people who are engaged in rioting, looting, or other forms of aggressive behavior in which established norms carry little weight.

Although crowds differ from one another in many ways, they also share a number of characteristics:

1. *Suggestibility.* Crowd members tend to be more suggestible than they are in established social settings. Their behavior is not guided in a straightforward manner by conventional norms. Accordingly, individuals are usually more susceptible to images, directions, and propositions emanating from others.

2. *Deindividualization.* **Deindividualization** is a psychological state of diminished identity and self-awareness (Zimbardo, 1969). Anonymity—a sense that one is among strangers and "lost in the crowd"—contributes to deindividualization. Under such circumstances people no longer feel as inhibited in committing disapproved acts as they would among close associates. Reduced self-consciousness and a lowered concern for social evaluation also contribute to the deindividualization process (Mann, Newton, and Innes, 1982). Thus feel-

ings of individual distinctiveness and uniqueness diminish as individuals increasingly make the group their focus of attention and activity.

3. *Invulnerability.* In crowd settings individuals often acquire a sense that they are more powerful and invincible than they are in routine, everyday settings. Moreover, they feel that social control mechanisms are less likely to be applied to them as individuals. Under these conditions, there may be an increase in behavior not normally approved by society, such as aggression, risk taking, self-enhancement, stealing, vandalism, and the uttering of obscenities (Dipboye, 1977; Mann, Newton, and Innes, 1982).

We will return to a consideration of crowds shortly, considering several theories of crowd behavior. But first, let us examine a number of preconditions for collective behavior.

PRECONDITIONS FOR COLLECTIVE BEHAVIOR

Sociologist Neil J. Smelser (1963) provides a framework for examining collective behavior based on the value-added model popular among economists. **Value-added** is the idea that each step in the production process—from raw materials to the finished product—increases the economic value of manufactured goods. Consider, for instance, the stages by which iron ore is converted into finished automobiles. As raw ore, the iron can be fashioned into an auto fender, a kitchen range, a steel girder, or the muzzle of a cannon. Once it is converted into thin sheets of steel, however, its possible uses are narrowed. Although it can still be fashioned into an auto fender or a kitchen range, it can no longer be employed for making a steel girder or the muzzle of a cannon. After the steel sheet is cut and molded in the shape of a fender, its use is further limited; it is no longer suitable for making a kitchen range. Each step in the process adds a specific "value" to the iron ore while simultaneously subtracting from previous possibilities.

As viewed by Smelser, episodes of collective behavior are like automobiles in that they are produced in a sequence of steps that constitute six determinants of collective behavior. In order of occurrence, they are (1) structural conduciveness, (2) structural strain, (3) growth and spread of a generalized belief, (4) precipitating factors, (5) mobilization of participants for action, and (6) the operation of social control. Each determinant is shaped by those that precede it and in turn shapes the ones that follow. Moreover, as in the case of automobiles, as each successive determinant is introduced in the value-added sequence, the range of potential final outcomes becomes progressively narrowed. Smelser contends that each of the six factors in the scheme is a *necessary* condition for the production of collective behavior, while all six are believed to make collective behavior virtually inevitable. Let us take a closer look at each of the determinants in Smelser's model.

Structural Conduciveness. **Structural conduciveness** refers to social conditions that *permit* a particular variety of collective behavior to occur. For instance, before a financial panic is possible, such as the stock-market crash of 1929, there must be a financial market where assets can be exchanged freely and rapidly. This basis does not exist in societies where property can be transferred only to the first-born son on the father's death because the holders of property lack sufficient maneuverability to dispose of their assets on short notice. In like manner a race riot—a battle between two racial groups—dictates that two racial populations be in close physical proximity to one another.

Structural Strain. **Structural strain** is said to occur when important aspects of a social system are "out of joint." Wars, economic crises, natural disasters, and technological change disrupt the traditional rhythm of life and interfere with the way people normally carry out their activities. As stress accumulates across time, individuals become increasingly susceptible to courses of action not defined by existing institutional arrangements. They experience *social malaise*—a feeling of underlying and pervasive discontent. Thus, as we noted earlier in the chapter, mass psychogenic illness typically is a response to job strain where workers are under pressure to increase production. What the workers seem to be saying when they become ill is, "This place makes me sick."

The Growth of a Generalized Belief. Structural strain and a sense of social malaise by themselves are not sufficient to produce collective behavior. People must define a situation as a problem in need of a solution. In the course of social interaction, they evolve a shared view of reality and common ideas as to how they should respond to it. A generalized belief is required that provides people with "answers" to their stressful circumstances. For instance, in panic behavior, a belief evolves that empowers an ambiguous element in the environment with a generalized capacity to threaten or destroy. It was this type of belief regarding Martian invaders that precipitated the panic associated with the 1938 Halloween broadcast.

Precipitating Factors. Still another ingredient is required. Some sort of event is needed to "touch off" or "trigger" mass action. A precipitating event creates, sharpens, or exaggerates conditions of conduciveness and strain. Additionally, it provides adherents of a belief with explicit evidence of the workings of evil forces or greater promise of success. Revolutions, for example, are often precipitated in this manner: General Gage's 1775 march from Boston to Concord and Lexington; the seizure of the royal prison fortress by an angry French crowd in 1789; and the March 11, 1917, Tsarist decrees against Petrograd strikers. Likewise, in panic behavior it is usually a specific event that sets the flight in motion. A dramatic event—a broadcast of a Martian "invasion," an explosion, a government collapse, or a bank failure—provides the structuring essential to such behavior.

The Mobilization of Participants for Action. Once the determinants have been put in place, the only necessary condition that remains is to bring the participants into action. Collective behavior requires a *critical mass*. Physicists view "critical mass" as the amount of radioactive material that is needed for a nuclear fission explosion to occur. Sociologists use the concept to refer to the threshold or number of participants that must be reached before collective behavior "erupts" or "explodes" (Oliver and Marwell, 1988; Macy, 1991).

In the Martian panic, the broadcast itself contained mobilizing communications (Cantril, 1940:29):

> *This is Newark, New Jersey . . .*
> *This is Newark, New Jersey . . .*
> *Warning! Poisonous black smoke pouring in from Jersey marshes. Reaches South Street. Gas masks useless. Urge population to move into open spaces . . . automobiles use routes 7, 23, 24. . . . Avoid congested area. Smoke is now spreading over Raymond Boulevard. . . .*

In turn, listeners sounded the alarm to others. Social ties are critical for collective behavior. For instance, they allow panic to feed on itself through the contagion of fear. Similarly, recruitment to religious sects and to social movements typically occurs through lines of preexisting social relationships, for example, among relatives, neighbors, friends, and work associates (Tilly, 1978a; Gould, 1991; Opp and Gern, 1993). In turn, intense and sustained social action is mediated through integration into organizational and personal networks of individuals (McAdam and Paulsen, 1993).

Operation of Social Control. The sixth factor in Smelser's scheme is the operation of social control. It is not like the other determinants of collective behavior. Social control is basically a counterdeterminant that prevents, interrupts, deflects, or inhibits the accumulation of the others. Social control typically takes two forms. First, there are controls designed to *prevent* the occurrence of an episode of collective behavior by lessening conduciveness and strain (for example, welfare programs that seek to pacify the underclasses). Second, there are controls that attempt to *repress* an episode of collective behavior *after* it has begun (for example, police measures and curfews). In the case of the Martian broadcast, 60 percent of the stations carrying the program periodically interrupted it to make local explanatory announcements when it became evident that a misunderstanding was abroad. Such announcements helped curb panic behavior in the localities that received them.

In some instances, however, the activities of the agents of social control precipitate collective behavior and even violence (Waddington, Jones, and Critcher, 1989). A good illustration of this occurred in the spring of 1963 when the Reverend Martin Luther King, Jr., took the civil rights fight to Birmingham, Alabama, alleged to be the most segregated large city in the South. He and his followers organized a "siege of demonstrations" against Birmingham's segregation ordinances. More than 3,000 Birmingham African Americans were arrested, while newspapers, magazines, and television stations beamed to the nation pictures of African Americans facing snarling police dogs and being bowled over by water from high-pressure fire hoses. Although the demonstrations did not immediately succeed in overturning Birmingham's racist laws, the civil rights issue quickly became the number-one topic not only in the South but throughout the United States. The brutality against Birmingham African Americans gave impetus to some 1,122 civil rights demonstrations in the following 4 months in cities throughout the nation. These demonstrations culminated on August 28, 1963, in the March on Washington in which some 200,000 civil rights marchers demonstrated "for jobs and freedom." The wave of demonstrations spurred the Kennedy administration to sponsor new civil rights legislation, which was passed by Congress the following year.

Assessing the Value-Added Model. Smelser's value-added model provides a useful tool for grasping the complexity of collective behavior. We see that collective behavior requires more than discontent and effective leaders (Marx and Woods, 1975). But the approach does have serious limitations. In some cases of collective action, all six stages do not necessarily occur, or they do not take place in the sequence Smelser specifies (Milgram, 1977). Additionally, some forms of crowd behavior are better explained by other perspectives. Let us consider a number of these approaches.

EXPLANATIONS OF CROWD BEHAVIOR

One of the characteristics of crowd behavior is the substitution of new forms and patterns of behavior for those that normally prevail in everyday life. Although crowd members differ in a great many ways, their behavior seems to derive from a common impulse and to be dominated by a single spirit. But is this indeed the case? What happens in the course of crowd behavior? And what processes fashion people's behavior under crowd conditions? Three somewhat different answers have been supplied by sociologists to these questions.

Contagion Theory. **Contagion theory** emphasizes the part that rapidly communicated and uncritically accepted feelings, attitudes, and actions play in crowd settings. Its proponents assume that unanimity prevails within a crowd since crowd members often seem to act in identical ways and to be dominated by a similar impulse. Thus a crowd is often spoken of in the singular, as if it were a real thing—"the crowd roars" and "the angry mob surges forward." This view of the crowd is embodied in the influential work of the nineteenth-century French writer Gustave Le Bon (1896:23–24), who set forth the "law of the mental unity of crowds":

Under certain given circumstances . . . an agglomeration of men [people] presents new characteristics very different from those of the individuals composing it. The sentiments and ideas of all the persons in the gathering take one and the same direction, and their conscious personality vanishes.

Hence, Le Bon believed that people undergo a radical transformation in a crowd. They can become cruel, savage, and irrational—Jekylls turned into Hydes. In the crowd people become capable of violent, destructive, and terrible actions that would horrify them if they engaged in the actions when alone.

Le Bon's contagion theory depicts the crowd as characterized by a "mob mind" that overpowers and submerges the individual. A uniform mood and imagery evolve contagiously through three mechanisms: *imitation*—the tendency for one person to do the same thing that others are doing; *suggestibility*—a state in which individuals become susceptible to images, directions, and propositions emanating from others; and *circular reaction*—a process whereby the emotions of others elicit the same emotions in oneself, in turn intensifying the emotions of others in a reciprocal manner (for instance, A sees B becoming excited and in response also becomes excited, intensifying the excitement of B, leading A to become all the more excited, and so on). However, Le Bon's concept of the crowd mind as some sort of supraindividual entity—one that is endowed with thinking processes and a capacity for feeling and believing-is rejected by most social scientists (Milgram and Toch, 1969). Only as individual entities with individual brains and nervous systems are human beings capable of thought and emotion.

Convergence Theory. The spread of an infectious disease is a good analogy for the contagion theory. In contrast, the heart surgery ward of a hospital provides the best analogy for **convergence theory**. The patients on the ward share a common problem, but not because they have transmitted the infection to one another. Rather, they select themselves out from the public because they share a common complaint and assemble on the ward with a common purpose. Likewise, some social scientists say that crowds select out a special class or category of people who are "crowd-prone." Whereas contagion theorists see normal, decent people being *transformed* under crowd influence, convergence theorists propose that a crowd consists of a highly unrepresentative body of people who assemble *because* they share the same predispositions. For instance, social psychologist Hadley Cantril (1941), in his study of the Leeville, Texas, lynching, contends that the active members came chiefly from the lowest economic bracket and several had previous police records. As a class, poor whites were most likely to compete for jobs with African Americans and were most likely to find their own status threatened by the presence of successful African Americans. These individuals provided a reservoir of people who were ready for a lynching with a minimum of provocation.

Emergent-Norm Theory.   The **emergent-norm theory** challenges the image of the crowd contained in both contagion and convergence theory. It stresses the *lack* of unanimity in many crowd situations and the *differences* in motives, attitudes, and actions that characterize crowd members: the presence of impulsives, suggestibles, opportunistic yielders, passive supporters, cautious activists, passers-by, and so on. The approach denies that people find themselves spontaneously infected with the emotions of others to the extent that they want to behave as others do (Turner, 1964; Turner and Killian, 1972; Shibutani, 1986).

Emergent-norm theory draws upon the work of Muzafer Sherif (1936) and Solomon Asch (1952) that deals with social conformity in ambiguous situations (see Chapter 4). According to sociologists like Ralph H. Turner and Lewis M. Killian (1972), collective behavior entails an attempt by people to find meaning in an uncertain social setting. Individuals search for cues to appropriate and acceptable behavior. And like the subjects in Sherif's experiments, who developed group norms that were different from the stan-

dards they developed when they were alone, crowd members collectively evolve new standards for behavior. For example, they may develop a norm that one should loot, burn, or harass police. Crowd members then proceed to enforce the norm: They reward behavior consistent with it, inhibit behavior contrary to it, justify proselytizing, and institute actions that restrain dissenters. Since the new behavior differs from that in non-crowd situations, the norm must be specific to the situation—hence, an *emergent* norm.

Assessing the Perspectives.   The three perspectives provide differing views of crowd behavior. Even so, they are not mutually exclusive. Consider what happens at a homecoming football game. Contagion contributes to the excitement through a process of circular reaction. Convergence operates since loyal alumni and football enthusiasts are selected out from the larger population and come together in the stadium. Finally, an emergent norm defines what constitutes an appropriate response to a particular event and suppresses incongruous behavior. In sum, each perspective affords a useful tool for understanding crowd behavior.

□ Social Movements

Like collective behavior, social movements often appear in times of rapid social change. Both frequently provide an impetus to social change. Indeed, both occur outside the institutional framework that forms everyday life and break through the familiar web of ordered expectations. But even though social movements and collective behavior resemble one another, they differ in an important way (Traugott, 1978). Whereas collective behavior is characterized by spontaneity and a lack of internal structure, social movements possess a considerable measure of internal order and purposeful orientation. It is this organizational potential that allows social movements to challenge established institutions. Thus sociologists view a **social movement** as a more-or-less persistent and organized effort on the part of a relatively large number of people to bring about or resist change.

Central to the concept of social movement is the idea that people intervene in the process of social change. Rather than responding passively to the flow of life or to its troubling aspects, people seek to alter the course of history. Of equal significance, they undertake joint activity. Individuals consciously act together with a sense of engaging in a common enterprise. In sum, social movements are vehicles whereby people collectively seek to influence the course of human events through formal organization (see Chapter 4). It is little wonder, then, that social movements are the stuff of which history books are written: accounts of great leaders, the rise and fall of political movements, and the social dislocations and changes brought about by revolutions. Christianity, the Crusades, the Reformation, the American Revolution, the antislavery movement, the labor movement, Zionism, and fascism—like other social movements—have profoundly affected the societies they have touched.

TYPES OF SOCIAL MOVEMENTS

Historian Crane Brinton (1938) in his classic study *The Anatomy of Revolution,* writes, "No ideas, no revolution." He might equally well have noted, "No ideas, no social movement." In brief, a set of ideas—an **ideology**—is critical to a social movement. An ideology provides individuals with conceptions of the movement's purposes, its rationale for existence, its indictment of existing conditions or arrangements, and its design for action (Moaddel, 1992). Thus an ideology functions as a kind of glue that joins people together in a fellowship of belief, thereby cementing solidarity. But an ideology does even more. It not only binds together otherwise isolated and separated individuals, but also unites them with a *cause.* In doing so, it prepares them for self-sacrifice on behalf of the movement—at times

even to lay down their lives for the "True God," "the New Nation," or "the Revolution."

Social movements can be distinguished on the basis of their ideologies or, more particularly, by the goals their ideologies set forth. Some movements pursue objectives that aim to change society through challenging fundamental values or by seeking modifications within the framework of the existing value scheme. In the former case, **revolutionary movements** advocate *replacement* of the existing value scheme; in the latter, **reform movements** pursue changes that will *implement* the existing value scheme more adequately. The civil rights movement identified with the leadership of the Reverend Martin Luther King, Jr., had a reform emphasis. It sought to extend values that were already acknowledged to inhere in political democracy to the African-American population of the United States. In contrast, a number of African-American nationalist groups that arose in the late 1960s had a revolutionary emphasis. They sought to institute basic changes in the American republican form of government, to rearrange the American class structure, and to inaugurate a system of greater African-American autonomy.

Movements arise not only for the purpose of instituting change but also to block change or to eliminate a previously instituted change—**resistance movements.** Indeed, movement begets countermovement. Thus the southern movement for civil rights unleashed a white counterattack beginning in the 1950s that found expression in the organization of white citizens' councils and Ku Klux Klan groups (Vander Zanden, 1965, 1983). Historian Arthur M. Schlesinger, Jr. (1986) has argued that from its earliest days the United States has been dominated by alternating political currents: the conservative (Tory or Hamiltonian) philosophy and the liberal (Whig or Jeffersonian) philosophy. Liberal periods witness an emphasis on popular rights, programs of reform, and efforts to share power with the unrepresented. In contrast, the emphasis during conservative periods falls on property rights, safety of the propertied classes, and efforts to perpetuate the power of the status quo. Schlesinger points out that liberal gains typically remain on the statute books even after the conservatives recover power. The conservatives acquiesce in the new social arrangements. However, they attempt to sabotage the reform measures by halfhearted enforcement and reduced appropriations.

Still other types of movements—**expressive movements**—are less concerned with institutional change than with a renovating or renewing of people from *within* (frequently with the promise of some future redemption). Pentecostal and holiness religious sects illustrate this kind of movement. Although they arise primarily among the underprivileged, these sects do not seek comprehensive social change; they do not aim to save the world but to save individuals from a world that is becoming progressively degenerate. They commonly believe that the second coming of the Messiah is near at hand and that there is no hope for the unsaved except through conversion and regeneration.

SOCIAL REVOLUTION

A **social revolution** involves the overthrow of a society's state and class structures and the fashioning of new social arrangements. Revolutions are most likely to occur under certain conditions (also see the discussion in Chapter 1 dealing with the work of Theda Skocpol and Jack Goldstone that focuses on state-centered revolutions). First, a good deal of political power is concentrated in the state, so that there is a centralized governing apparatus. Accordingly, the state can become the focus for collective anger and attack. Second, the military's allegiance to the established regime is weakened so that the army is no longer a reliable tool for suppressing domestic disorders. Where army officers are drawn from elites in conflict with the central government, or when troops sympathize with their civilian counterparts, the unreliability of the army increases the vulnerability of the state. Third, political crises—often associated with long-term international conflicts that

result in military defeat—weaken the existing regime and contribute to the collapse of the state apparatus. And fourth, a substantial segment of the population must mobilize in uprisings that bring a new elite to power. Peasant revolts usually stem from landlords' taking over peasant lands, substantial increases in taxation or rents, or famines. Urban uprisings commonly derive from sharp jumps in food prices and unusually high levels of unemployment (Skocpol, 1979; Goldstone, 1982, 1986, 1991).

A number of historians and sociologists have surveyed important revolutions of the West in search of common stages and patterns in their development (Edwards, 1927; Brinton, 1938; Goldstone, 1982, 1986, 1991). Among the revolutions that they have examined are the English Revolution of 1640, the American Revolution of 1776, the French Revolution of 1789, and the Russian Revolution of 1917. From this work have stemmed a number of observations regarding the sequence of events that typically unfold in the course of major social revolutions, an approach called the **natural history of revolutions.**

Prior to the revolution, intellectuals—journalists, poets, playwrights, essayists, lawyers, and others—withdraw support from the existing regime and demand major reforms. Under increasing attack, the state attempts to meet the criticisms by instituting a number of reforms (for example, the reforms of Louis XVI in France, the Stolypin reforms in Russia, and the Boxer reforms in China). The onset of the revolution is heralded by a weakening or paralysis of the state, usually brought on by the government's inability to deal with a major military, economic, or political problem. The collapse of the old regime brings to the forefront divisions among conservatives who attempt to minimize change, radicals who seek fundamental change, and moderates who try to steer a middle course. Coups or civil war often ensue. The first to gain the reins of power are usually moderate reformers (for instance, in Iran, Bazargan, the moderate critic, first took power after the shah's government was forced out).

The moderates seek to reconstruct governmental authority on the basis of limited reform, often employing organizational structures left over from the old regime. Simultaneously, radical centers of mass mobilization spring up with new organizations (in France, the moderate Girondin assembly confronted the radical Jacobin clubs; in America, the moderate Continental Congress was outpaced by the radical Patriots Societies; and in contemporary Iran the moderates led by Bazargan, Bani-Sadr, and Gotbzadeh were supplanted by the radical Islamic clerics). The moderates find themselves heirs to the same problems and liabilities that felled the old regime, and in turn they are replaced by the radicals. The disorder that follows the revolution and the seizure of power by the radicals results in coercive rule. This is the stage of "terror" that characterized the guillotine days of the French Revolution, Stalin's Gulag, and Mao's Cultural Revolution. Turmoil persists and allows military leaders to move into ascendancy (for instance, Washington, Cromwell, Napoleon, Ataturk, Mao, Tito, Boumedienne, and Mugabe). Finally, radicalism gives way to a phase of pragmatism and the consolidation of a new status quo. The "excesses" of the revolution are condemned, and the emphasis falls on the fashioning of stable institutions. In France, this phase was marked by the fall of Robespierre; in the Soviet Union, by Khrushchev's repudiation of Stalin; and in China, by the fall of Mao's allies (the "gang of four"). Although not all revolutions pass through the identical sequence of stages, this approach does draw our attention to recurrent patterns in the unfolding of revolutionary activity.

TERRORISM

Terrorism may be viewed as the use of force or violence against persons or property to intimidate or coerce a government, a formal organization, or a civilian population in furtherance of political, religious, or social objectives. In practice, as with a great many other behaviors, what constitutes terrorism is a matter of social definition. Thus it is often difficult to distinguish "your terrorist" from "our freedom fighter" or to differentiate "aid to terrorists" from "covert support of friendly forces," as with the Reagan administration's controversial support of the Nicaraguan Contras, or counterrevolutionary fighters, in the mid-1980s.

For many years social scientists and historians treated terrorism primarily as a nuisance. But more recently they have increasingly come to see it as a new mode of warfare with far-reaching implications. What distinguishes much contemporary terrorism is not so much its motivation or purpose but rather the extent of state involvement in carrying out well-planned and highly destructive acts against adversary nations (Perdue, 1989). In recent years, trials of terrorists in a number of nations have established that Syria, Iran, and Libya have actively sponsored terrorist activities. Moreover, disclosures from secret files of the former communist regimes in Eastern Europe reveal that well into the 1980s the governments gave sanctuary to Middle Eastern and Western European terrorist groups that were attacking Western targets (Whitney, 1990). Recent revelations also have implicated Western nations in terrorist activities (for instance, in 1985, French agents used two bombs to sink Greenpeace's flagship, the *Rainbow Warrior*, causing the loss of one life, because Greenpeace was challenging the French government's testing of nuclear devices in the South Pacific).

Another feature of contemporary terrorism has been the extent to which it has become a media event. Very often terrorism is aimed at a media audience, not the actual victims. Although the terrorists write the script and perform the drama, the "theater of terror" becomes possible only when the media afford the stage and access to a worldwide audience. Measured in terms of the worldwide attention terrorism garners, and not in terms of the number of lives lost, media coverage can be quite effective in the amount of terror it creates at relatively low cost to the perpetrators.

"I'm sorry, but this is the home base for the moderate rebel faction. You want the fundamentalist guerrilla organization, which is over on Elm Street."

Drawing by Ziegler; © 1992 The New Yorker Magazine, Inc.

The act of media coverage also often enhances the importance of the issue that allegedly led to the terrorist activities. Newspaper readers and television viewers see the issue as of substantially greater importance and as justifying resolution by national or international action. For instance, the 1983 bombing of the Marine barracks led many Americans, including members of Congress, to oppose American involvement in Lebanon. The media portrayed grotesque scenes of the bodies of young Marines being pulled out of the rubble, chilling a good many people and making the American public desirous of avoiding further entanglement in Lebanon's affairs.

When terrorists engage in brutality in the service of a cause, they can see themselves as acting to save the world and destroy evil. They are frequently teenagers and young adults who experience a strong sense of political powerlessness and helplessness that boils into burning rage. The more the individuals are impatient, desperate, and alienated from the power structures they wish to command and from the masses they seek to lead, the more likely they are to resort to violence (Reich, 1990). Somewhat similar patterns find expression in issue-oriented terrorism such as that associated in the United States with bombings of Planned Parenthood offices and women's health clinics that offer abortion services. In contrast to the close-knit, disciplined groups of the 1980s, more acts of terrorism are now being perpetrated by loose groupings of people of similar backgrounds and beliefs. People may engage in political violence when they view themselves as victims of repression and deem peaceful protest to be ineffective, a perspective that holds among many members of the Provisional Irish Republican Army (IRA) (White, 1989; Boswell and Dixon, 1990). Many of the same factors that underlie social movements also feed terrorism, a matter to which we now turn our attention.

CAUSES OF SOCIAL MOVEMENTS

Clearly the concept of social movement covers a good many different kinds of behavior. But why should a social movement form? What factors lead people to undertake joint action on behalf of some cause? Sociologists have been of two minds on these matters. There are those who seek the roots of social movements in social misery and, more particularly, in social and economic deprivation. Other sociologists do not find this argument particularly convincing. They note that most societies contain a considerable reservoir of social discontent and that oppression and misery have been widespread throughout history. Yet social movements are quite rare. These sociologists look to the resources and organizations that aggrieved persons can muster as providing the key to an understanding of social movements. Let us examine each of these approaches at greater length.

Deprivation Approaches. As noted in earlier chapters, Karl Marx held that capitalist exploitation leads to progressive impoverishment of the working class. He expected that over time conditions would become so abominable that workers would be compelled to recognize the social nature of their misery and overthrow their oppressors. Yet Marx also recognized that abject misery and exploitation do not necessarily result in revolutionary fervor. He pointed out that the suffering of the underclasses (which he labeled the *Lumpenproletariat*) can be so intense and their resulting alienation so massive that all social and revolutionary consciousness is deadened. Although the "progressive misery," or *absolute deprivation,* argument is found in Marx's more political writings, he also gave recognition to a type of *relative deprivation.* He foresaw that the working class could become better off as capitalism advanced but that the gap between owners and workers would widen and produce among the latter deepening feelings of comparative disadvantage (Giddens, 1973; Harrington, 1976).

A number of sociologists have suggested that a major factor in the evolution of the African-American protest in the 1960s was the emergence among African Americans of a growing sense of **relative deprivation**—a gap between what people actually have and what they have come to expect and feel to be their just due (Geschwender, 1964; Gurr, 1970). The prosperity of the 1950s and 1960s gave many African Americans a taste of the affluent society. They gained enough to arouse realistic hopes for more. Hence, grievances revolving about squalid housing, limited job opportunities, persistent unemployment, low pay, and police brutality were felt as severely frustrating. The civil rights movement arose not so much as a protest fed by despair as one fed by *rising* expectations.

Sociologist James Davies (1962, 1969, 1974) finds that relative deprivation may also be fostered under another condition—that characterized by his "rise-and-drop," or "J-curve," hypothesis (see Figure 12.2). He contends that revolutions are most likely to take place when a prolonged period of social and economic betterment is followed by a period of sharp reversal. People fear that the gains they achieved with great effort will be lost, and their mood becomes revolutionary. Davies illustrates the rise-and-drop hypothesis by events as varied as Dorr's rebellion in Rhode Island in 1842, the Pullman strike of 1894, the Russian Revolution of 1917, and the Egyptian Revolution of 1953.

Resource Mobilization Approaches. Deprivation approaches seek to find out why people are attracted to social movements. Resource mobilization approaches take a different tack. According to the resource mobilization school, social discontent is more or less constant and thus endemic within all modern societies (Tilly, 1978a; Taylor, 1989; Walton and Ragin, 1990). Accordingly, its proponents deem it unnecessary to explain the forces that energize and activate a social movement. Instead, they emphasize the importance of structural factors, such as the availability of

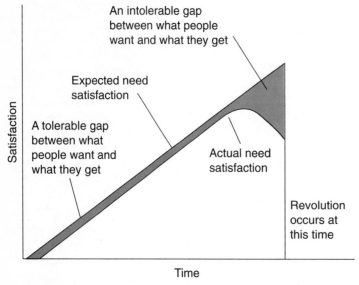

Figure 12.2 DAVIES' *J*-CURVE THEORY OF REVOLUTION
The figure illustrates Davies' theory that revolutions are often fostered when a period of social and economic betterment is succeeded by sharp reversals, fueling concern that the gains will be lost. (SOURCE: Adapted from James C. Davies, "Toward a Theory of Revolution," *American Sociological Review,* Vol. 27, February 1962, fig. 1, p. 6.)

resources for pursuing particular goals and the network of interpersonal relationships that serve as the focus for membership recruitment. People are seen as participating in a social movement not as the result of deprivation but as a response to a rational decision-making process whereby they weigh the costs and benefits of participation. Consequently, conditions of political opportunity—for instance, support from established elites, contemporary models of successful political activism, and preexisting organizational networks and organizations—play a critical part in the development of social movements.

In many cases, resources and organizations outside the protest group are crucial in determining the scope and outcomes of collective action. External support is especially critical for movements of the poor. Sociologist J. Craig Jenkins (1985) illustrates the point with historical materials dealing with farm worker insurgencies within the United States. He contrasts the unsuccessful

attempt to organize farm workers by the National Farm Labor Union from 1946 to 1952 with the successful organization of Mexican farm workers by the United Farm Workers from 1965 to 1972. Both groups pursued similar ends (union contracts), employed similar tactics (mass agricultural strikes and boycotts supported by organized labor), and encountered comparable obstacles. Yet the United Farm Workers prevailed where the National Farm Labor Union failed. Jenkins contends that the United Farm Workers succeeded because internal divisions in government neutralized oppositional elites, while the support of the liberal-labor coalition during the reform years of the 1960s and early 1970s turned the tide in favor of the farm workers.

The grievances of the farm workers did not change in the post–World War II period, nor did the basic conflicts of interest that were embedded in the nation's institutional life. What changed were the resources and opportunities for collective action that were available to the farm workers—most particularly, the availability of powerful allies. Hence, the success or failure of a social movement derives from strategic factors and the political processes in which it becomes enmeshed (Button, 1989; Burstein, 1991b; Morris, 1993).

Assessing the Approaches. Proponents of both the deprivation and resource mobilization approaches at times overstate their respective cases. Relative deprivation theorists neglect the part that resources and organization play in social movements and instead focus on people's grievances and psychological frustrations (Downey, 1986; Snow et al., 1986). On the other hand, it may be true, as resource mobilization theorists say, that social unrest is always present within society. But there are instances where suddenly imposed grievances do generate organized protest. The rapid emergence of organized action groups in the communities surrounding the Three Mile Island area following the 1979 nuclear accident provides a good illustration of this process (Walsh, 1981, 1988). Much the same holds for countermovements—resistance or "anti" movements—that arise in response to the social change pursued by other movements (Mottl, 1980; Buechler, 1990). The antisegregation movement in the South (Vander Zanden, 1965) and the Boston antibusing movement provide examples of movements that gain support among people who believe themselves threatened by impending change (Useem, 1980). These observations suggest that each approach contributes valuable insight to our understanding of social movements. Both factors are operative (Opp, 1988; Amenta and Zylan, 1991).

□ Looking to the Future

We look to the past for the roots of the present and to both the past and the present for what the future may hold. In fact, we undertake many of our daily activities in anticipation of the future. We carry out our job responsibilities in the expectation that we will be paid at the end of the week or the month. We make arrangements for future events, including football games, parties, spring break, final examinations, and graduation exercises. We invest our money, energy, and time in an education based on the assumption that there will be a job payoff down the road. We may involve ourselves in environmental and antinuclear movements in order to have a voice in the fashioning of tomorrow's world. Because the future is so important to us, we look to experts from a wide range of disciplines to give us some idea of what we can expect in the weeks, years, and decades ahead. Some individuals, known as **futurists,** specialize in the study of the future, seeking to understand, predict, and plan the future of society.

With the twenty-first century rapidly approaching, we can only speculate on the vast changes that await us. Most likely we will have little more success specifically anticipating the century ahead than did our compatriots 100 years ago at the time of the future-oriented World's Columbian Exposition that opened in Chicago in 1893. For the most part, the forecasts provided by seventy-four prominent Americans not only turned out to be wrong but hilariously wrong. Treasury Secretary Charles Foster expressed the prevailing view that in 1993 the railroad would still be the fastest means of travel. None of the 1893 forecasters apparently anticipated the automobile. Indeed, Postmaster General John Wanamaker was convinced that mail in 1993 would still travel by stagecoach and horseback rider. A few forecasters enthused about air travel—or, more precisely, "balloon travel." Senator John J. Ingalls speculated that by 1993, "it will be as common for the citizen to call for his dirigible balloon as it now is for his buggy or his boots." Then, as now, forecasters fell victim to two fundamental problems in attempting to predict the future. First, change is so much a part of our lives that we take it for granted, oblivious to or unimpressed by much of it (during the 1880s a number of Europeans had already produced experimental gasoline-powered cars but the 1893 forecasters either did not know about the primitive "horseless carriages" or else did not deem them to be important). Second, a "rearview-mirror effect" operates in which recent events color and dominate our thinking about the future (the railroads were developing feverishly in the 1880s and 1890s, and so it took little imagination to predict that they would become faster and more widespread in the future) (Cornish, 1993).

Clearly the complexity of society makes it exceedingly difficult to predict the distant future with accuracy, and even the not too distant future is often hard to anticipate. Even so, one thing seems certain: We shall not live all our lives in the world into which we were born, nor shall we die in the world in which we worked in our maturity. Futurists have identified two changes that seem to be central to contemporary social life (Coates and Jarratt, 1990; Halal and Nikitin, 1990). First, the United States is being restructured from an industrial to an information society. Second, modern societies are increasingly shifting from a national to a global economy. Futurists have applied a good many metaphors to these changes, including Daniel Bell's "postindustrial society" (1973), Alvin Toffler's "third wave" (1980, 1990), and John Naisbitt's "megatrends" (1982; Naisbitt and Aburdene, 1989). Common to these metaphors is the notion that American society is shifting from the production of goods to the production of services, and from a society based on the coordination of people and machines to a society organized around knowledge. These changes, it is contended, will afford a myriad of choices. The world will increasingly be one of many flavors, not just vanilla or chocolate.

Many observers of contemporary American life believe that we are witnessing a historical change and the first major impact of the shift from an energy economy to an information economy (Drucker, 1985). For 300 years technology has been cast in a mechanical model, one based on the combustion processes that go on inside a

star like the sun. The steam engine opened the mechanical age, and the mechanical age reached its apex with the discovery of nuclear fission and nuclear fusion, which replicated the energy-producing processes of a star. But we now seem to be moving toward a biological model based on information and involving the intensive use of materials. Although biological processes need physical energy and materials, they tend to substitute information for both. Biological processes "miniaturize" size, energy, and materials by "exploding" information. The human brain is some ten times the size and weight of the brain of a lemur (a lower primate). But it handles a billion times more information. The miniaturization is on the order of 10 to the ninth power, and it is far ahead of what the microchip has achieved with miniaturization. Increasingly, high-tech industries are becoming information-intensive rather than energy- or materials-intensive.

At the same time, a new international era is being shaped that bears only a slight resemblance to the Cold War universe in which East and West jockeyed for military and ideological dominance. The collapse of the communist bloc, the worldwide explosion of ethnic and nationalist sentiments and hatreds, the groping of Eastern European and Asian nations toward market economies, and the surge of Islamic fundamentalism have introduced profound social change. Simultaneously, in the absence of the Soviet military threat, the Americans, Japanese, and West Europeans have lost many of their incentives to set aside their economic differences. Much about this new world and this new agenda is in the process of unfolding. Even so, it is already amply clear that the new era will afford unbounded opportunities for sociologists to gain exciting new insights into social life and for applying these insights to the evolution of informed social policy.

As we have noted throughout this textbook, sociology invites us to scrutinize our prosaic world and notice what we otherwise often ignore, neglect, or take for granted. It looks behind the outer reaches of the social experience and discerns its inner structure and processes—suspending the belief that things are simply as they seem. As such, sociology is uniquely suited to fostering the skills necessary for living in an ever-changing world filled with countless choices and seemingly endless uncertainty. So you may well wish to consider a major in sociology, which, besides providing specific knowledge, affords you the opportunity for developing many of the interpersonal, analytical, problem-solving, and communication skills so essential for success in today's competitive job market. Indeed, sociology is a matter of curiosity, discovering things, and asking, Why? Why is it so? So, even more broadly, the challenges we confront as we move into the twenty-first century may well inspire you to pursue a sociological career.

Summary

1. Human life is never static but always in flux. However, the dynamic quality of life often eludes us because of our perceptual and conceptual limitations. Sociologists refer to fundamental alterations in the patterns of culture, structure, and social behavior over time as social change. It is a process by which society becomes something different while remaining in some respects the same.

2. Social change confronts people with new situations and compels them to fashion new forms of action. A great many factors interact to generate changes in people's behavior and in the culture and structure of their society. Sociologists identify a number of particularly critical factors, including the physical environment, population, clashes over resources and values, supporting values and norms, innovation, diffusion, and the mass media.

3. Many of sociology's roots lie in the effort to unravel the "meaning" of history and to establish laws of social change and development. The major sociological perspectives on social change fall within four broad categories: evolutionary perspectives, cyclical perspectives, functionalist perspectives, and conflict perspectives. Evolutionary theorists, particularly those with a unilinear focus, depict history as divided into steplike levels that constitute sequential stages and that are characterized by an underlying trend. Cyclical theorists look to the course of a civilization or society, searching for generalizations regarding their stages of growth and decline. Functionalist theorists see society as a system that tends toward equilibrium. And conflict theorists hold that tensions between competing groups are the basic source of social change.

4. The computer revolution is having a broad impact on people's lives. Computers promise to automate some workplace activities now performed by people. They have consequences for the use and manipulation of social power. Computers alter the manner in which people relate to one another. And they have implications for individual privacy and the confidentiality of communications and personal data. Visionaries look to technology to make human lives richer and freer. Pessimists see technology as creating a two-tier work force with a small group of creative people performing spirit-enriching and mind-challenging tasks at the top and a large work force of people with low job skills who are paid correspondingly low wages at the bottom.

5. Sociologists have approached social change in Third World nations from two somewhat dif-

ferent perspectives. The modernization approach sees development as entailing a pattern of convergence as societies become increasingly urban, industry comes to overshadow agriculture, the size and density of the population increase, the division of labor becomes more specialized, and the knowledge base grows larger and more complex. The world-system and dependency approaches view development within the context of an international, geographical division of labor. According to world-system and dependency analysis, an unequal exchange takes place between core and periphery nations, with development at the former end of the chain coming at the cost of underdevelopment at the other end.

6. Some forms of group behavior are not organized in terms of established norms and institutionalized lines of action. This is particularly true of collective behavior. Collective behavior comes in a good many forms, including rumors, fashions and fads, mass hysteria, panic, and crowds.

7. Sociologist Neil J. Smelser provides a framework for examining collective behavior based on the value-added model popular among economists. As viewed by Smelser, episodes of collective behavior are produced in a sequence of steps that constitute six determinants of collective behavior. In order of occurrence, they are (1) structural conduciveness, (2) structural strain, (3) growth and spread of a generalized belief, (4) precipitating factors, (5) mobilization of participants for action, and (6) the operation of social control. Each determinant is shaped by those that precede it and in turn shapes the ones that follow.

8. Sociologists offer three somewhat different approaches to crowd behavior. According to contagion theory, rapidly communicated and uncritically accepted feelings, attitudes, and actions play a critical part in crowd settings through processes of imitation, suggestibility, and circular reaction. Convergence theory suggests that a crowd consists of a highly unrepresentative body of people who assemble because they share the same predispositions. The emergent-norm theory challenges the image of the crowd contained in both contagion and convergence theory. According to this view, crowd members evolve new standards for behavior that they then enforce in normative ways.

9. Central to the concept of social movements is the idea that people intervene in the process of social change. Of equal significance, they undertake joint activity. Social movements are vehicles whereby people collectively seek to influence the course of human events through formal organizations. Common forms of social movements include revolutionary, reform, resistance, and expressive movements.

10. Social revolutions are most likely to occur under certain conditions. First, a good deal of political power is concentrated in the state, so that there is a centralized governing apparatus. Second, the military's allegiance to the established regime is weakened, so that the army is no longer a reliable tool for suppressing domestic disorders. Third, political crises weaken the existing regime and contribute to the collapse of the state apparatus. And fourth, a substantial segment of the population must mobilize in uprisings that bring a new elite to power. A number of historians and sociologists have surveyed important revolutions of the West in search of common stages and patterns in their development, giving rise to the natural history of revolutions approach.

11. Sociologists are of two minds regarding the causes of social movements. There are those who seek the roots of social movements in

social misery and, more particularly, in social and economic deprivation. Other sociologists do not find this argument particularly convincing. They note that most societies contain a considerable reservoir of social discontent and that oppression and misery have been widespread throughout history. These sociologists look to the resources and organizations aggrieved persons can muster as providing the key to an understanding of social movements.

Glossary

acting crowd An excited, volatile collection of people who are engaged in rioting, looting, or other forms of aggressive behavior in which established norms carry little weight.

casual crowd A collection of people who have little in common with one another except that they may be viewing a common event, such as looking through a department store window.

collective behavior Ways of thinking, feeling, and acting that develop among a large number of people and that are relatively spontaneous and unstructured.

contagion theory An approach to crowd behavior that emphasizes the part that rapidly communicated and uncritically accepted feelings, attitudes, and actions play in crowd settings.

conventional crowd A number of people who have assembled for some specific purpose and who typically act in accordance with established norms, such as people attending a baseball game or concert.

convergence theory An approach to crowd behavior that says a crowd consists of a highly unrepresentative body of people who assemble because they share the same predispositions.

crazes Fads that become all-consuming passions.

crowd A temporary, relatively unorganized gathering of people who are in close physical proximity.

cultural lag The view that immaterial culture must constantly "catch up" with material culture, resulting in an adjustment gap between the two forms of culture.

deindividualization A psychological state of diminished identity and self-awareness.

diffusion The process by which culture traits spread from one social unit to another.

discovery An addition to knowledge.

emergent-norm theory An approach to crowd behavior that says crowd members evolve new standards for behavior in a crowd setting and then enforce the expectations in the manner of norms.

expressive crowd An aggregation of people who have gotten together for self-stimulation and personal gratification, such as occurs at a religious revival or a rock festival.

expressive movement A movement that is less concerned with institutional change than with a renovating or renewing of people from within.

fad A folkway that lasts for a short time and enjoys acceptance among only a segment of the population.

fashion A folkway that lasts for a short time and enjoys widespread acceptance within society.

futurists Individuals specializing in the study of the future; they seek to understand, predict, and plan the future of society.

ideology A set of ideas that provides individuals with conceptions of the purposes of a social movement, a rationale for the movement's existence, an indictment of existing conditions, and a design for action.

invention The use of existing knowledge in a new form.

mass hysteria The rapid dissemination of behaviors involving contagious anxiety, usually associated with some mysterious force.

modernization The process by which a society moves from traditional or preindustrial social and economic arrangements to those characteristic of industrial societies.

natural history of revolutions   The view that social revolutions pass through a set of common stages and patterns in the course of their development.

panic   Irrational and uncoordinated but collective action among people that is induced by the presence of an immediate, severe threat.

reform movement   A social movement that pursues changes that will implement the existing value scheme of a society more adequately.

relative deprivation   A gap between what people actually have and what they have come to expect and feel to be their just due.

resistance movement   A social movement that arises to block change or eliminate a previously instituted change.

revolutionary movement   A social movement that advocates the replacement of a society's existing value scheme.

rumor   A difficult-to-verify piece of information that is transmitted from person to person in relatively rapid fashion.

social change   Fundamental alterations in the patterns of culture, structure, and social behavior over time.

social movement   A more-or-less persistent and organized effort on the part of a relatively large number of people to bring about or resist change.

social revolution   The overthrow of a society's state and class structures and the fashioning of new social arrangements.

structural conduciveness   Social conditions that permit a particular variety of collective behavior to occur.

structural strain   A condition in which important aspects of a social system are "out of joint."

terrorism   The use of force or violence against persons or property to intimidate or coerce a government, a formal organization, or a civilian population in furtherance of political, religious, or social objectives.

value-added   The idea that each step in the production process—from raw materials to the finished product—increases the economic value of manufactured goods.

world system   An approach that views development as involving an unequal exchange between core and periphery nations, with development at the former end of the chain coming at the cost of underdevelopment at the other end.

References

ABRAHAMIAN, ERVAND. 1989. *The Iranian mojahedin*. New Haven, Conn.: Yale University Press.

ABRAHAMSON, MARK. 1994. Stratification, mobility, and playing cards metaphor. *Teaching Sociology*, 22:183–188.

ACKER, JOAN. 1992. Gendered institutions. *Contemporary Sociology*, 21:565–569.

ACKERMAN, NATHAN W., and MARIE JAHODA. 1950. *Anti-Semitism and emotional disorder*. New York: Harper & Row.

ADAMS, DAVID S. 1993. "Who are your second cousins?" A lecture/discussion technique for introducing "status," "norm," and "role" in the first year sociology course. *Teaching Sociology*, 21:105–108.

ADLER, PATRICIA A., and PETER ADLER. 1989. The gloried self: The aggrandizement and the constriction of self. *Social Psychological Quarterly*, 52:299–310.

ADLER, STEPHEN J. 1991. Suits over sexual harassment prove difficult due to issue of definition. *Wall Street Journal* (October 9):B1.

ADORNO, T. W., ELSE FRENKEL-BRUNSWIK, DANIEL J. LEVINSON, and R. NEVITT SANFORD. 1950. *The authoritarian personality*. New York: Harper & Row.

AGGER, BEN. 1991. Critical theory, poststructuralism, postmodernism: Their sociological relevance. *Annual Review of Sociology*, 17:105–131.

AHLBURG, DENNIS, and CAROL J. DE VITA. 1992. New realities of the American family. *Population Bulletin*, 47, No. 2.

AKARD, PATRICK J. 1992. Corporate mobilization and political power: The transformation of U.S. economic policy in the 1970s. *American Sociological Review*, 57:597–615.

ALDRICH, HOWARD, CATHERINE ZIMMER, and DAVID MCEVOY. 1989. Continuities in the study of ecological succession: Asian businesses in three English cities. *Social Forces*, 67:920–944.

ALEXANDER, JEFFREY C. 1988. The new theoretical movement. In Neil J. Smelser, ed., *Handbook of sociology*. Newbury Park, Calif.: Sage.

ALEXANDER, PAMELA C., SHARON MOORE, and ELMORE R. ALEXANDER III. 1991. What is transmitted in the intergenerational transmission of violence? *Journal of Marriage and the Family*, 53:657–668.

ALLEN, WALTER R., and REYNOLDS FARLEY. 1986. The shifting social and economic tides of black America, 1950–1980. *Annual Review of Sociology*, 12:277–306.

ALLMENDINGER, JUTTA. 1989. *Career mobility dynamics: A comparative analysis of the United States, Norway, and West Germany*. Berlin: Max-Planck-Institut fur Bildungsforschung.

ALLPORT, GORDON W. 1954. *The nature of prejudice*. Boston: Beacon Press.

ALTMAN, LAWRENCE K. 1991. Many Hispanic Americans reported in ill health and lacking insurance. *New York Times* (January 9): A10.

ALTSCHILLER, DAVID. 1988. Selling the presidency: More dollars equal less message. *New York Times* (March 20): F3.

ALWIN, DUANE F., and JON A. KROSNICK. 1991. Aging, cohorts, and the stability of sociopolitical orientations over the life span. *American Journal of Sociology*, 97:169–195.

AMATO, PAUL R. 1993. Children's adjustment to divorce: Theories, hypotheses, and empirical support. *Journal of Marriage and the Family*, 55:23–38.

AMATO, PAUL R., and BRUCE KEITH. 1991. Parental divorce and the well-being of children: A meta-analysis. *Psychological Bulletin*, 110:26–46.

AMENTA, EDWIN. 1993. The state of the art in welfare state research on social spending efforts in capitalist democracies since 1960. *American Journal of Sociology*, 99:750–763.

AMENTA, EDWIN, and YVONNE ZYLAN. 1991. It happened here: Political opportunity, the new institutionalism, and the Townsend movement. *American Sociological Review*, 56:250–265.

AMERICAN ASSOCIATION OF UNIVERSITY WOMEN. 1992. *How schools shortchange girls*. Washington, D.C.: American Association of University Women Educational Foundation.

AMERICAN SOCIOLOGICAL ASSOCIATION. 1989. *Code of ethics*. Washington, D.C.: American Sociological Association.

ANDERSEN, SUSAN M., and STEVE W. COLE. 1990. "Do I know you?" The role of significant others in general social perception. *Journal of Personality and Social Psychology*, 59:384–399.

ANDERSON, ELIJAH. 1978. *A place on the corner*. Chicago: University of Chicago Press.

ANDERSON, ELIJAH. 1990. *Streetwise: Race, class, and change in an urban community*. Chicago: University of Chicago Press.

ANDERSON, ELIJAH. 1994. The code of the streets. *Atlantic Monthly* (May):81–94.

ANDERSON, L. S., THEODORE G. CHIRICOS, and GORDON P. WALDO. 1977. Formal and informal sanctions: A comparison of deterrent effects. *Social Problems*, 25:103–114.

ANDERSON, NELS. 1923. *The hobo*. Chicago: University of Chicago Press.

APPLE, MICHAEL W. 1982. *Education and power*. London: Routledge & Kegan Paul.

APPLE, MICHAEL W., and LOIS WEIS. 1983. *Ideology and practice in schooling*. Philadelphia: Temple University.

APPY, CHRISTIAN G. 1993. *Working-class war: American combat soldiers and Vietnam*. Chapel Hill: University of North Carolina Press.

ARENS, W. 1986. *The original sin: Incest and its meaning.* New York: Oxford University Press.

ARIÈS, PHILIPPE. 1962. *Centuries of childhood.* Trans. R. Baldick. New York: Random House.

ARIÈS, PHILIPPE. 1981. *The hour of our death.* New York: Knopf.

ASCH, SOLOMON. 1952. *Social psychology.* Englewood Cliffs, N.J.: Prentice-Hall.

ASENDORPF, JENS B. 1987. Videotape reconstruction of emotions and cognitions related to shyness. *Journal of Personality and Social Psychology,* 53:542–549.

ASENDORPF, JENS B. 1989. Shyness as a final common pathway for two different kinds of inhibition. *Journal of Personality and Social Psychology,* 57:481–492.

AXELROD, ROBERT. 1984. *The evolution of cooperation.* New York: Basic Books.

BACHU, AMARA. 1993. *Fertility of American women: June 1992.* Washington, D.C.: Government Printing Office.

BAER, ELLEN D. 1991. The feminist disdain for nursing. *New York Times* (February 23):17.

BAILEY, WILLIAM C., and RUTH D. PETERSON. 1989. Murder and capital punishment: A monthly time-series analysis of execution publicity. *American Sociological Review,* 54: 722–743.

BAKER, DAVID P., and DEBORAH PERKINS JONES. 1993. Creating gender equality: Cross-national gender stratification and mathematical performance. *Sociology of Education,* 66: 91–103.

BAKER, STEPHEN. 1993. The owners vs. the boss at Weirton Steel. *Business Week* (November 15):38.

BAKER, WAYNE E. 1990. Market networks and corporate behavior. *American Journal of Sociology,* 96:589–625.

BALES, ROBERT F. 1970. *Personality and interpersonal behavior.* New York: Holt, Rinehart and Winston.

BALES, ROBERT F., and EDGAR F. BORGATTA. 1955. Size of group as a factor in the interaction profile. In A. P. Hare, E. F. Borgatta, and R. F. Bales, eds., *Small groups: Studies in social interaction.* New York: Knopf.

BALKWELL, CAROLYN. 1981. Transition to widowhood: A review of the literature. *Family Relations,* 30:117–127.

BANDURA, ALBERT. 1971. *Psychological modeling: Conflicting theories.* Chicago: Aldine-Atherton.

BANDURA, ALBERT. 1973. *Aggression: A social learning analysis.* Englewood Cliffs, N.J.: Prentice-Hall.

BANK, LEW, MARION S. FORGATCH, GERALD R. PATTERSON, and REBECCA A. FETROW. 1993. Parenting practices of single mothers: Mediators of negative contextual factors. *Journal of Marriage and the Family,* 55:371–384.

BARAK, GREGG, ED. 1991. *Crimes by the capitalist state: An introduction to state criminality.* Albany: State University of New York Press.

BARAN, PAUL, and PAUL M. SWEEZY. 1966. *Monopoly capital: An essay on the American economic and social order.* New York: Monthly Review Press.

BARBER, BERNARD. 1988. *Effective social science: Eight cases in economics, political science, and sociology.* New York: Russell Sage Foundation.

BARCLAY, A. M., and R. N. HABER. 1965. The relation of aggression to sexual motivation. *Journal of Personality,* 33: 462–475.

BARENBOIM, CARL. 1981. The development of person perception in childhood and adolescence. *Child Development,* 52:129–144.

BARKEY, KAREN, and SUNITA PARIKH. 1991. Comparative perspectives on the state. *Annual Review of Sociology,* 11:523–549.

BARKOW, J. H. 1978. Culture and sociobiology. *American Anthropologist,* 80:5–20.

BARNET, RICHARD J., and JOHN CAVANAGH. 1994. *Global dreams: Imperial corporations and the new world order.* New York: Simon and Schuster.

BARNICOTT, N. A. 1964. Taxonomy and variation in modern man. In A. Montagu, ed., *The concept of race.* Westport, Conn.: Greenwood Press.

BARON, JAMES N., FRANK R. DOBBIN, and P. DEVEREAUX JENNINGS. 1986. War and peace: The evolution of modern personnel administration in U.S. industry. *American Journal of Sociology,* 92:350–383.

BARRINGER, FELICITY. 1991. Immigration brings new diversity to Asian population in the U.S. *New York Times* (June 12):A1, A9.

BARRINGER, FELICITY. 1992. A census disparity for Asians in U.S. *New York Times* (September 20):20.

BARRINGER, FELICITY. 1993. Sex survey of American men finds 1% are gay. *New York Times* (April 15):A1, A9.

BARRINGER, HERBERT, ROBERT W. GARDNER, and MICHAEL J. LEVIN. 1993. *Asian and Pacific Islanders in the United States.* New York: Russell Sage Foundation.

BARROW, CLYDE W. 1990. *Universities and the capitalist state: Corporate liberalism and the reconstruction of American higher education, 1894–1928.* Madison: University of Wisconsin Press.

BASS, BERNARD M. 1960. *Leadership, psychology, and organizational behavior.* New York: Harper & Row.

BATUTIS, MICHAEL. 1987. Lancaster's Amish. *American Demographics,* 9 (February):53–54.

BAUM, ANDREW, and GLENN E. DAVIS. 1980. Reducing the stress of high-density living: An architectural intervention. *Journal of Personality and Social Psychology,* 38:471–481.

BAUMANN, MARTY. 1991. Caring for parents. *USA Today* (January 8):D1.

BAUMEISTER, ROY F. 1984. Choking under pressure: Self-consciousness and paradoxical effects of incentives on skillful performance. *Journal of Personality and Social Psychology,* 46:610–620.

BAUMEISTER, ROY F., and ANDREW STEINHILBER. 1984. Paradoxical effects of supportive audiences on performance under pressure: The home field disadvantage in sports championships. *Journal of Personality and Social Psychology*, 47:85–93.

BAXTER, JANEEN. 1994. Is husband's class enough? Class location and class identity in the United States, Sweden, Norway, and Australia. *American Sociological Review*, 59:220–235.

BAYDAR, NAZLI, and JEANNE BROOKS-GUNN. 1991. Effects of maternal employment and child-care arrangements on preschoolers' cognitive and behavioral outcomes: Evidence from the children of the National Longitudinal Survey of Youth. *Developmental Psychology*, 27:932–945.

BEAN, FRANK D., and MARTA TIENDA. 1987. *The Hispanic population of the United States*. New York: Russell Sage Foundation.

BECK, E. M., PATRICK HORAN, and CHARLES TOLBERT. 1978. Stratification in a dual economy: A structural model of earnings determination. *American Sociological Review*, 43:704–720.

BECK, E. M., PATRICK HORAN, and CHARLES TOLBERT. 1980. Social stratification in industrial society: Further evidence for a structural alternative. *American Sociological Review*, 45:712–719.

BECK, E. M., and STEWART E. TOLNAY. 1990. The killing fields of the Deep South: The market for cotton and the lynching of blacks, 1882–1930. *American Sociological Review*, 55: 526–539.

BECK, SCOTT H. 1982. Adjustment to and satisfaction with retirement. *Journal of Gerontology*, 37:616–624.

BECKER, HOWARD S. 1963. *Outsiders: Studies in the sociology of deviance*. New York: Free Press.

BEER, WILLIAM. 1988. New family ties: How well are we coping? *Public Opinion*, 10 (March/April):14–15, 57.

BEGLEY, SHARON. 1991. Milking the laboratories for dollars. *Newsweek* (May 6):58.

BEHAR, RICHARD. 1990. The underworld is their oyster. *Time* (September 3):54–57.

BEIRNE, PIERS. 1979. Empiricism and the critique of Marxism on law and crime. *Social Problems*, 26:373–385.

BELANGER, SARAH, and MAURICE PINARD. 1991. Ethnic movements and the competition model: Some missing links. *American Sociological Review*, 56:446–457.

BELL, ALAN P., and MARTIN S. WEINBERG. 1978. *Homosexualities: A study of diversity among men and women*. New York: Simon and Schuster.

BELL, ALAN P., and MARTIN S. WEINBERG, and SUE K. HAMMERSMITH. 1981. *Sexual preference: Its development in men and women*. Bloomington: Indiana University Press.

BELL, ALEXA. 1991. Is the U.S. a two-tier society? *Investor's Business Daily* (October 9):1, 2.

BELL, DANIEL. 1973. *The coming of the post-industrial society*. New York: Basic Books.

BELLAH, ROBERT N. 1970. *Beyond belief*. New York: Harper & Row.

BELLAH, ROBERT N., and PHILLIP E. HAMMOND. 1980. *Varieties of civil religions*. New York: Harper & Row.

BELLAH, ROBERT N., RICHARD MADSEN, ANNE SWIDLER, WILLIAM M. SULLIVAN, and STEVEN M. TIPTON. 1985. *Habits of the heart: Individualism and commitment in American life*. Berkeley: University of California Press.

BELSKY, JAY. 1990. Parental and nonparental child care and children's socioemotional development: A decade in review. *Journal of Marriage and the Family*, 52:885–903.

BELSKY, JAY, and MICHAEL ROVINE. 1990. Patterns of marital change across the transition to parenthood: Pregnancy to three years postpartum. *Journal of Marriage and the Family*, 52:5–19.

BEM, SANDRA. 1981. Gender schema theory: A cognitive account of sex typing. *Psychological Bulletin*, 88:354–364.

BEM, SANDRA LIPSITZ. 1993. *The lenses of gender: Transforming the debate on sexual inequality*. New Haven, Conn.: Yale University Press.

BENAVOT, AARON, YUN-KYUNG CHA, DAVID KAMENS, JOHN W. MEYER, and SUK-YING WONG. 1991. Knowledge for the masses: World models and national curricula, 1920–1986. *American Sociological Review*, 56:85–100.

BENDIX, REINHARD. 1977. Bureaucracy. *International encyclopedia of the social sciences*. New York: Free Press.

BENNETT, AMANDA. 1990. Quality programs may be shoddy stuff. *Wall Street Journal* (October 4):B1.

BENOIT-SMULLYAN, EMILE. 1948. The sociologism of Emile Durkheim and his school. In Harry Elmer Barnes, ed., *An introduction to the history of sociology*. Chicago: University of Chicago Press.

BENSON, J. KENNETH. 1977. Organizations: A dialectical view. *Administrative Science Quarterly*, 22:1–21.

BEN-YEHUDA, NACHMAN. 1980. The European witch craze of the 14th and 17th centuries. *American Journal of Sociology*, 86:1–31.

BERBEROGLU, BERCH. 1987. *The internationalization of capital: Imperialism and capitalist development on a world scale*. New York: Praeger.

BERGER, BRIGITTE, and PETER L. BERGER. 1983. *The war over the family: Capturing the middle ground*. Garden City, N.Y.: Anchor Books.

BERGER, JOSEPH. 1989. All in the game. *New York Times* (August 6): EDUC 23–24.

BERGER, PETER L. 1963. *Invitation to sociology*. Garden City, N.Y.: Anchor Books.

BERGER, PETER L. 1967. *The sacred canopy: Elements of a sociological theory of religion*. Garden City, N.Y.: Doubleday.

BERGER, PETER L. 1979. *The heretical imperative: Contemporary possibilities of religious affirmation*. Garden City, N.Y.: Doubleday.

BERGER, PETER L. 1986. *The capitalist revolution*. New York: Basic Books.

BERGMANN, BARBARA R. 1987. *The economic emergence of women*. New York: Basic Books.

BERK, RICHARD A., and PHYLLIS J. NEWTON. 1985. Does arrest really deter wife battery? An effort to replicate the findings of the Minneapolis spouse abuse experiment. *American Sociological Review*, 50:253–262.

BERK, SARAH FENSTERMAKER. 1985. *The gender factory: The apportionment of work in American households.* New York: Plenum.

BERKE, RICHARD L. 1990a. An edge for incumbents: Loopholes that pay off. *New York Times* (March 20):A1, A10.

BERKE, RICHARD L. 1990b. Most of senators go out of state for contributions. *New York Times* (April 16):A1, A10.

BERKE, RICHARD L. 1990c. Bulk of $94 million in special interest gifts goes to incumbents. *New York Times* (August 31):A10.

BERKE, RICHARD L. 1990d. Study confirms interest groups' pattern of giving. *New York Times* (September 16):18.

BERKOWITZ, LEONARD. 1989. Frustration-aggression hypothesis: Examination and reformulation. *Psychological Bulletin*, 106:59–73.

BERLE, ADOLPH, JR., and GARDNER C. MEANS. 1932. *The modern corporation and private property.* New York: Harcourt, Brace & World.

BERNARD, JESSIE. 1987. *The female world from a global perspective.* Bloomington: Indiana University Press.

BERNSTEIN, AARON. 1991a. What happened to the American dream? *Business Week* (August 19):80–85.

BERNSTEIN, AARON. 1991b. Is Uncle Sam shortchanging young Americans? *Business Week* (August 19):85.

BERNSTEIN, AARON. 1993. The young and the jobless. *Business Week* (August 16):107.

BERNSTEIN, ILENE N., WILLIAM R. KELLY, and PATRICIA A. DOYLE. 1977. Social reactions to deviants: The case of criminal defendants. *American Sociological Review*, 42:743–755.

BERREMAN, GERALD. 1960. Caste in India and the United States. *American Journal of Sociology*, 66:120–127.

BETTELHEIM, BRUNO, and MORRIS JANOWITZ. 1950. *Dynamics of prejudice.* New York: Harper & Row.

BIANCHI, SUZANNE M. 1984. Children's progress through school: A research note. *Sociology of Education*, 57:184–192.

BIDERMAN, ALBERT D., and JAMES P. LYNCH. 1991. *Understanding crime incidence statistics: Why the UCR diverges from the NCS.* New York: Springer-Verlag.

BIELBY, DENISE D., and WILLIAM T. BIELBY. 1988. She works hard for the money: Household responsibilities and the allocation of work effort. *American Journal of Sociology*, 93:1031–1059.

BIELBY, WILLIAM T., and DENISE D. BIELBY. 1992. I will follow him: Family ties, gender-role beliefs, and reluctance to relocate for a better job. *American Journal of Sociology*, 97:1241–1247.

BIERSTEDT, ROBERT. 1950. An analysis of social power. *American Sociological Review*, 15:730–738.

BIERSTEKER, THOMAS J. 1987. *Multinationals, the state and control of the Nigerian economy.* Princeton, N.J.: Princeton University Press.

BILLINGS, DWIGHT B. 1990. Religion as opposition: A Gramscian analysis. *American Journal of Sociology*, 96:1–31.

BIRDWHISTELL, RAYMOND L. 1970. *Kinesics and context.* Philadelphia: University of Pennsylvania Press.

BIRKETT, DEA. 1991. Fletcher Christian's children. *New York Times Magazine* (December 8):66–78.

BITTLES, ALAN H., WILLIAM M. MASON, JENNIFER GREENE, and N. APPAJI RAO. 1991. Reproductive behavior and health in consanguineous marriages. *Science*, 252:789–794.

BLACKMAN, ANN, PRISCILLA PAINTON, and ELIZABETH TAYLOR. 1992. The war against feminism. *Time* (March 9):50–55.

BLAKE, JUDITH. 1989. *Family size and achievement.* Berkeley: University of California Press.

BLASI, JOSEPH R. 1988. *Employee ownership: Revolution or ripoff?* Cambridge, Mass.: Ballinger.

BLAU, PETER M. 1964. *Exchange and power in social life.* New York: Wiley.

BLAU, PETER M., and OTIS DUDLEY DUNCAN. 1972. *The American occupational structure*, 2nd ed. New York: Wiley.

BLAU, PETER M., and RICHARD A. SCHOENHERR. 1971. *The structure of organizations.* New York: Basic Books.

BLAU, PETER, and RICHARD SCOTT. 1962. *Formal organizations.* San Francisco: Chandler.

BLINDER, ALAN S. 1990. There are capitalists, then there are the Japanese. *Business Week* (October 8):21.

BLOCK, FRED. 1987. *Revising state theory: Essays in politics and postindustrialism.* Philadelphia: Temple University Press.

BLOCK, FRED. 1990. *Postindustrial possibilities: A critique of economic discourse.* Berkeley: University of California Press.

BLOSSFELD, HANS-PETER, and JOHANNES HUININK. 1991. Human capital investments or norms of role transition? How women's schooling and career affect the process of family formation. *American Journal of Sociology*, 97:143–168.

BLUESTONE, BARRY, and BENNETT HARRISON. 1982. *The deindustrialization of America.* New York: Basic Books.

BLUESTONE, BARRY, and BENNETT HARRISON. 1987. The grim truth about the job "miracle." *New York Times* (February 1):F3.

BLUHM, CAREY, THOMAS A. WIDIGER, and GLORIA M. MIELE. 1990. Interpersonal complementarity and individual differences. *Journal of Personality and Social Psychology*, 58:464–471.

BLUMBERG, PAUL. 1980. *Inequality in the age of decline.* New York: Oxford University Press.

BLUMENTHAL, RALPH. 1987. F.B.I. says public officials accepted 105 of 106 bribes offered in 2-year operation. *New York Times* (August 12):1.

BLUMER, HERBERT. 1946. Collective behavior. In A. M. Lee, ed., *New outline of the principles of sociology.* New York: Barnes & Noble.

BLUMER, HERBERT. 1961. Race prejudice as a sense of group position. In J. Masuoka and P. Valien, eds., *Race relations.* Chapel Hill: University of North Carolina Press.

BLUMER, HERBERT. 1969. *Symbolic interaction: Perspective and method.* Englewood Cliffs, N.J.: Prentice-Hall.

BLUMSTEIN, ALFRED, and JACQUELINE COHEN. 1987. Characterizing criminal careers. *Science,* 237:985–991.

BLUMSTEIN, PHILIP, and PEPPER SCHWARTZ. 1983. *American couples.* New York: Morrow.

BOBO, LAWRENCE, and JAMES R. KLUEGEL. 1993. Opposition to race-targeting: Self-interest, stratification ideology, or racial attitudes? *American Sociological Review,* 58:443–464.

BOGUE, DONALD J., and DAVID J. HARTMANN, EDS. 1990. *Essays in human ecology 3.* Chicago: Garcia-Bogue Research and Development.

BOHANNON, PAUL, and ROSEMARY ERICKSON. 1978. Stepping in. *Psychology Today,* 11 (January):53–59.

BOK, DEREK. 1993. *The cost of talent: How executive and professionals are paid and how it affects America.* New York: Free Press.

BOLLEN, KENNETH A., and STEPHEN J. APPOLD. 1993. National industrial structure and the global system. *American Sociological Review,* 58:283–301.

BOLLEN, KENNETH A., and ROBERT W. JACKMAN. 1989. Democracy, stability, and dichotomies. *American Sociological Review,* 54:612–621.

BONACICH, EDNA. 1972. A theory of ethnic antagonism: A split-labor market. *American Sociological Review,* 37:547–559.

BONACICH, EDNA. 1975. Abolition, the extension of slavery, and the position of free blacks: A study of split-labor markets in the United States, 1830–1863. *American Journal of Sociology,* 81:601–628.

BONACICH, EDNA, and JOHN MODELL. 1980. *The economic basis of ethnic solidarity.* Berkeley: University of California Press.

BONGER, WILLIAM A. 1936. *An introduction to criminology.* London: Methuen.

BOONE, LOUIS E., DAVID L. KURTZ, and C. PATRICK FLEENOR. 1988. The road to the top. *American Demographics,* 10 (March):34–37.

BORNSCHIER, VOLKER, and CHRISTOPHER CHASE-DUNN. 1985. *Transnational corporations and underdevelopment.* New York: Praeger.

BOROUGHS, DON L. 1992. *U.S. News & World Report* (May 4):50–52.

BOSERUP, ESTER. 1965. *The conditions of agricultural growth: The economics of agrarian change under population pressures.* Chicago: Aldine.

BOSSE, RAYMOND, CAROLYN M. ALDWIN, MICHAEL R. LEVENSON, and KATHRYN WORKMAN-DANIELS. 1991. How stressful is retirement? Findings from the normative aging study. *Journal of Gerontology,* 46:P9–14.

BOSWELL, TERRY. 1989. Colonial empires and the capitalist world-economy: A time series analysis of colonization, 1640–1960. *American Sociological Review,* 54:180–196.

BOSWELL, TERRY, and WILLIAM J. DIXON. 1990. Dependency and rebellion: A cross-national analysis. *American Sociological Review,* 55:540–559.

BOSWELL, TERRY, and WILLIAM J. DIXON. 1993. Marx's theory of rebellion: A cross-national analysis of class exploitation, economic development, and violent revolt. *American Sociological Review,* 58:681–702.

BOTTOMORE, THOMAS B. 1981. A Marxist consideration of Durkheim. *Social Forces,* 59:902–917.

BOUND, JOHN, GREG J. DUNCAN, DEBORAH S. LAREN, and LEWIS OLEINICK. 1991. Poverty dynamics in widowhood. *Journal of Gerontology,* 46:S115–124.

BOURDIEU, PIERRE. 1994. Rethinking the state: Genesis and structure of the bureaucratic field. *Sociological Theory,* 12:1–18.

BOVARD, JAMES. 1989. Lester, the sky hasn't fallen. *Wall Street Journal* (June 26):10.

BOWLES, SAMUEL, and HERBERT GINTIS. 1976. *Schooling and capitalist America.* New York: Basic Books.

BRADBURN, NORMAN M., and SEYMOUR SUDMAN. 1988. *Polls and surveys: Understanding what they tell us.* San Francisco: Jossey-Bass.

BRADBURY, KATHARINE L., ANTHONY DOWNS, and KENNETH A. SMALL. 1982. *Urban decline and the future of American cities.* Washington, D.C.: Brookings Institution.

BRADDOCK, JOMILLS HENRY, III, and JAMES M. MCPARTLAND. 1987. How minorities continue to be excluded from equal employment opportunities: Research on labor market and institutional barriers. *Journal of Social Issues,* 43:5–39.

BRADLEY, HARRIET. 1989. *Men's work, women's work: A sociological history of the sexual division of labour in employment.* Minneapolis: University of Minnesota Press.

BRADSHAW, YORK W. 1988. Reassessing economic dependency and uneven development: The Kenyan experience. *American Sociological Review,* 53:693–708.

BREINES, WINI. 1980. Community and organization: The New Left and Michels' "iron law." *Social Problems,* 27:419–429.

BREWER, MARILYN B., and RODERICK M. KRAMER. 1986. Choice behavior in social dilemmas: Effects of social identity, group size, and decision framing. *Journal of Personality and Social Psychology,* 50:543–549.

BRIDGES, GEORGE S., ROBERT D. CRUTCHFIELD, and EDITH E. SIMPSON. 1987. Crime, social structure and criminal punishment: White and nonwhite rates of imprisonment. *Social Problems,* 34:345–361.

BRIDGWATER, CAROL AUSTIN. 1982. Consumer psychology. *Psychology Today,* 16(May):16–20.

BRINTON, CRANE. 1938. *The anatomy of revolution.* New York: Vintage Books.

BRODY, ELAINE M. 1990. *Women in the middle: Their parent-care years.* New York: Springer.

BRODY, JANE E. 1981. Effects of beauty found to run surprisingly deep. *New York Times* (September 1):15–16.

BRODY, ELAINE M., SANDRA J. LITVIN, STEVEN M. ALBERT, and CHRISTINE J. HOFFMAN. 1994. Marital status of daughters and patterns of parent care. *Journal of Gerontology,* 49:S95–S103.

BROOKS, ANDREE. 1984. Birth rank: Effects on personality. *New York Times* (March 26):17.

BROUILLETTE, JOHN R., and RONNY E. TURNER. 1992. Creating the sociological imagination on the first day of class: The social construction of deviance. *Teaching Sociology,* 20:276–279.

BROWN, DON W. 1978. Arrest rates and crime rates: When does a tipping effect occur? *Social Forces,* 57:671–682.

BROWN, LESTER R., CHRISTOPHER FLAVIN, and SANDRA POSTEL. 1990. *State of the world 1990.* New York: Norton.

BROWN, LESTER R., CHRISTOPHER FLAVIN, and SANDRA POSTEL. 1991. *Saving the planet: How to shape an environmentally sustainable global economy.* New York: Norton.

BROWNE, ANGELA. 1993. Violence against women by male partners. *American Psychologist,* 48:1077–1087.

BRUCH, MONROE A., JANET M. GORSKY, TOM M. COLLINS, and PAT A. BERGER. 1989. Shyness and sociability reexamined: A multicomponent analysis. *Journal of Personality and Social Psychology,* 57:904–915.

BRZEZINSKI, ZBIGNIEW. 1993. *Out of control: Global turmoil on the eve of the 21st century.* New York: Scribner's.

BUCHMANN, MARLIS. 1989. *The script of life in modern society: Entry into adulthood in a changing world.* Chicago: University of Chicago Press.

BUECHLER, STEVEN M. 1990. *Women's movements in the United States: Woman suffrage, equal rights, and beyond.* New Brunswick, N.J.: Rutgers University Press.

BUMPASS, LARRY L., JAMES A. SWEET, and ANDREW CHERLIN. 1991. The role of cohabitation in declining rates of marriage. *Journal of Marriage and the Family,* 53: 913–927.

BUNZEL, JOHN H. 1988. Choosing freshmen: Who deserves an edge? *Wall Street Journal* (February 1):22.

BURAWOY, MICHAEL. 1979. *Manufacturing consent.* Chicago: University of Chicago Press.

BURAWOY, MICHAEL. 1983. Factory regimes under advanced capitalism. *American Sociological Review,* 48:587–605.

BURAWOY, MICHAEL, and PAVEL KROTOV. 1992. The Soviet transition from socialism to capitalism: Worker control and economic bargaining in the wood industry. *American Sociological Review,* 57:16–38.

BURBANK, VICTORIA KATHERINE. 1988. *Aboriginal adolescence: Maidenhood in an aboriginal community.* New Brunswick, N.J.: Rutgers University Press.

BURNHAM, JAMES. 1941. *The managerial revolution.* New York: John Day.

BURNS, GENE. 1990. The politics of ideology: The papal struggle with liberalism. *American Journal of Sociology,* 95: 1123–1152.

BURRIS, VAL. 1988. The political partisanship of American business. *American Sociological Review,* 52:732–744.

BURSTEIN, PAUL. 1991a. Policy domains: Organization, culture, and policy outcomes. *Annual Review of Sociology,* 17:327–350.

BURSTEIN, PAUL. 1991b. Legal mobilization as a social movement tactic: The struggle for equal employment opportunity. *American Journal of Sociology,* 96:1201–1225.

BUSS, TERRY F., and F. STEVENS REDBURN. 1983. *Shutdown at Youngstown: Public policy for mass unemployment.* Albany: State University of New York Press.

BUTTERFIELD, FOX. 1986. Why Asians are going to the head of the class. *New York Times* (August 3):EDUC 18–23.

BUTTERFIELD, FOX. 1992. Studies find a family link to criminality. *New York Times* (January 31):A1, A8.

BUTTON, JAMES W. 1989. *Blacks and social change: Impact of the civil rights movement in southern communities.* Princeton, N.J.: Princeton University Press.

BUZAWA, E. S., and C. G. BUZAWA. 1990. *Domestic violence.* Newbury Park, Calif.: Sage.

BYRNE, JOHN A. 1984. Worth his weight. *Forbes* (June 4):96–146.

BYRNE, JOHN A. 1990. Pay stubs of the rich and corporate. *Business Week* (May 7):56–64.

BYRNE, JOHN A. 1994a. That eye-popping executive pay. *Business Week* (April 25):52–58.

BYRNE, JOHN A. 1994b. The pain of downsizing. *Business Week* (May 9):60–61.

CALDERA, YVONNE M., ALETHA C. HUSTON, and MARION O'BRIEN. 1989. Social interactions and play patterns of parents and toddlers with feminine, masculine, and neutral toys. *Child Development,* 60:70–76.

CALHOUN, JOHN. 1962. Population density and social pathology. *Scientific American,* 206:139–146.

CAMPBELL, ANNE. 1993. *Men, women, and aggression.* New York: Basic Books.

CAMPBELL, JOHN L. 1987. The state and the nuclear waste crisis: Institutional analysis of policy constraints. *Social Problems,* 34:18–33.

CANTRIL, HADLEY. 1940. *The invasion from Mars: A study in the psychology of panic.* Princeton, N.J.: Princeton University Press.

CANTRIL, HADLEY. 1941. *The psychology of social movements.* New York: Wiley.

CAPLOW, THEODORE, HOWARD M. BAHR, BRUCE A. CHADWICK, REUBEN HILL, and MARGARET H. WILLIAMSON. 1982. *Middletown families: Fifty years of change and continuity.* Minneapolis: University of Minnesota Press.

CARLEY, KATHLEEN. 1991. A theory of group stability. *American Sociological Review,* 56:331–354.

CARMICHAEL, STOKELY, and CHARLES HAMILTON. 1967. *Black power.* New York: Random House.

CARROLL, PAUL B. 1991. IBM announces details of plan to break its business into more autonomous pieces. *Wall Street Journal* (December 6):B4.

CARRUTHERS, BRUCE G. 1994. When is the state autonomous? Culture, organization theory, and the political sociology of the state. *Sociological Theory,* 12:19–44.

CARTWRIGHT, SUSAN, and CARY L. COOPER. 1993. If cultures don't fit, mergers may fail. *New York Times* (August 29):9F.

CARVER, CHARLES S., and CHARLENE HUMPHRIES. 1981. Havana day-dreaming: A study of self-consciousness and the negative reference group among Cuban Americans. *Journal of Personality and Social Psychology,* 40:545–552.

CASTANEDA, CARLOS. 1972. *Journey to Ixtlan.* New York: Pocket Books.

CASTRO, JANICE. 1991. Watching a generation waste away. *Time* (August 26):10,12.

CATTON, WILLIAM R., JR. 1980. *Overshoot: The ecological basis of revolutionary change.* Urbana: University of Illinois Press.

CATTON, WILLIAM R., JR., GERHARD LENSKI, and FREDERICK H. BUTTEL. 1986. To what degree is a social system dependent on its resource base? In J. E. Short, Jr., ed., *The social fabric: Dimensions and issues.* Beverly Hills, Calif.: Sage.

CENTER FOR EDUCATION STATISTICS. 1990. *America's challenge: Accelerating academic achievement.* Washington, D.C.: Department of Education.

CHAFETZ, JANET SALTZMAN. 1990. *Gender equity: An integrated theory of stability and change.* Newbury Park, Calif.: Sage.

CHAFETZ, JANET SALTZMAN, and ANTHONY GARY DWORKIN. 1986. *Female revolt: Women's movements in world and historical perspective.* New York: Rowman & Allanheld.

CHAIKEN, JAN M., and MARCIA R. CHAIKEN. 1982. *Varieties of criminal behavior.* Santa Monica, Calif.: Rand Corporation.

CHAMBLISS, WILLIAM J. 1973. The Saints and the Roughnecks. *Society,* 2 (November):24–31.

CHAMBLISS, WILLIAM J., and ROBERT B. SEIDMAN. 1971. *Law, order and power.* Reading, Mass: Addison-Wesley.

CHASE, SUSAN E., and COLLEEN S. BELL. 1990. Ideology, discourse, and gender: How gatekeepers talk about women school superintendents. *Social Problems,* 37:163–186.

CHASE-DUNN, CHRISTOPHER. 1989. *Global formation: Structure of the world-economy.* Cambridge, Mass.: Blackwell.

CHASE-DUNN, CHRISTOPHER, and THOMAS D. HALL. 1993. Comparing world-systems: Concepts and working hypotheses. *Social Forces,* 71:851–886.

CHATZKY, JEAN SHERMAN. 1992. A brief history of stock fads. *Forbes* (September 14):253–268.

CHAVES, MARK. 1994. Secularization as declining religious authority. *Social Forces,* 72:749–774.

CHEEK, JONATHAN. 1983. Shyness: How it hurts careers and social life. *U.S. News & World Report* (October 31):71–72.

CHENG, LUCIE, and EDNA BONACICH. 1984. *Labor immigration under capitalism.* Berkeley: University of California Press.

CHERLIN, ANDREW. 1983. Changing family and household: Contemporary lessons from historical research. *Annual Review of Sociology,* 9:51–66.

CHERLIN, ANDREW J. 1992. *Marriage, divorce, remarriage,* rev. ed. Cambridge, Mass.: Harvard University Press.

CHERLIN, ANDREW J., FRANK F. FURSTENBERG, JR., P. LINDSAY CHASE-LANSDALE, KATHLEEN E. KIERNAN, PHILIP K. ROBINS, DONNA RUANE MORRISON, and JULIEN O. TEITLER. 1991. Longitudinal studies of effects of divorce on children in Great Britain and the United States. *Science,* 252:1386–1389.

CHESNAIS, JEAN-CLAUDE. 1992. *The demographic transition: Stages, patterns and economic implications—A longitudinal study of sixty-seven countries.* Trans. Elizabeth and Philip Kreager. New York: Clarendon.

CHILDE, V. GORDON. 1941. *Man makes himself.* London: Watts.

CHILDE, V. GORDON. 1942. *What happened in history.* Harmondsworth, Eng.: Penguin Books.

CHIRA, SUSAN. 1994a. Study confirms worst fears on U.S. children. *New York Times* (April 12):A1, A11.

CHIRA, SUSAN. 1994b. Women campaign for new plan to curb the world's population. *New York Times* (April 13): A1, A8.

CHIRICOS, THEODORE, and GORDON WALDO. 1975. Socioeconomic status and criminal sentencing: An empirical assessment of a conflict proposition. *American Sociological Review,* 40:753–772.

CHOLDIN, HARVEY M. 1978. Urban density and pathology. In R. H. Turner, J. Coleman, and R. C. Fox, eds., *Annual Review of Sociology.* Palo Alto, Calif.: Annual Reviews.

CHOMSKY, NOAM. 1957. *Syntactic structures.* The Hague: Mouton.

CHOMSKY, NOAM. 1975. *Reflections on language.* New York: Pantheon.

CHOMSKY, NOAM. 1980. *Rule and representations.* New York: Columbia University Press.

CHRISTIAN, J. J. 1963. The pathology of overpopulation. *Military Medicine,* 128:571–603.

CHURCH, GEORGE J. 1993. Gorzilla zaps the system. *Time* (September 13):25–28.

CICIRELLI, VICTOR G. 1978. The relationship of sibling structure to intellectual abilities and achievement. *Review of Educational Research,* 48:365–379.

CLARK, CANDACE. 1983. Sickness and social control. In H. Robboy and C. Clark, eds., *Social interaction: Readings in sociology.* New York: St. Martin's Press.

CLARK, KENNETH B. 1965. *Dark ghetto.* New York: Harper & Row.

CLARK, LINDLEY H., JR. 1993. The pay gap narrows—slowly. *Wall Street Journal* (July 2):A6.

CLARK, R. A. 1952. The projective measurement of experimentally induced levels of sexual motivation. *Journal of Experimental Psychology,* 44:391–399.

CLARK, REGINALD M. 1983. *Family life and school achievement: Why poor black children succeed or fail.* Chicago: University of Chicago Press.

CLAUSEN, JOHN A. 1993. *American lives.* New York: Free Press.

CLAUSEN, JOHN S. 1991. Adolescent competence and the shaping of the life course. *American Journal of Sociology,* 96:805–842.

CLAWSON, DAN, and ALAN NEUSTADTL. 1989. Interlocks, PACs, and corporate conservatism. *American Journal of Sociology,* 94:749–773.

CLAWSON, DAN, ALAN NEUSTADTL, and DENISE SCOTT. 1992. *Money talks: Corporate PACs and political influence.* New York: Basic Books.

CLINARD, MARSHALL B. 1990. *Corporate corruption: The abuse of power.* New York: Praeger.

CLINES, FRANCIS X. 1992. With casino profits, Indian tribes thrive. *New York Times* (January 31):1, 18.

CLINGEMPEEL, W. GLEN. 1981. Quasi-kin relationships and marital quality in stepfather families. *Journal of Personality and Social Psychology,* 41:890–901.

COALE, ANSLEY J., and SUSAN COTTS WATKINS, EDS. 1986. *The decline of fertility in Europe.* Princeton, N.J.: Princeton University Press.

COATES, JOSEPH F., and JENNIFER JARRATT. 1990. What futurists believe: Agreements and disagreements. *The Futurist* (November/December):22–28.

COCKBURN, ALEXANDER. 1987. Social Darwinism on the big and small screens. *Wall Street Journal* (June 11):23.

COHEN, ALBERT K. 1955. *Delinquent boys.* New York: Free Press.

COHEN, ALBERT K. 1965. The sociology of the deviant act: Anomie theory and beyond. *American Sociological Review* 30:5–14.

COHEN, ALBERT K. 1966. *Deviance and control.* Englewood Cliffs, N.J.: Prentice-Hall.

COHEN, JEAN L., and ANDREW ARATO. 1992. *Civil society and political theory.* Cambridge, Mass.: MIT Press.

COHEN, JERE. 1980. Rational capitalism in Renaissance Italy. *American Journal of Sociology,* 85:1340–1355.

COHEN, JERE. 1983. Peer influences on college aspirations. *American Sociological Review,* 48:728–734.

COHEN, MARK N. 1977. *The food crisis in prehistory: Overpopulation and the origins of agriculture.* New Haven, Conn.: Yale University Press.

COLASANTO, DIANE, and LINDA WILLIAMS. 1987. The changing dynamics of race and class. *Public Opinion,* 9 (January/February):50–53.

COLE, STEPHEN. 1972. *The sociological method.* Chicago: Markham.

COLE, STEPHEN. 1992. *Making science: Between nature and society.* Cambridge, Mass.: Harvard University Press.

COLEMAN, JAMES S. 1988. Social capital in the creation of human capital. *American Journal of Sociology:* 94: S95–S120.

COLEMAN, JAMES S. 1990. *Foundations of Social Theory.* Cambridge, Mass.: Bellknap Press.

COLEMAN, JAMES S. 1993. The rational reconstruction of society. *American Sociological Review,* 58:1–15.

COLEMAN, JAMES S., and THOMAS HOFFER. 1987. *Public and private high schools: The impact of communities.* New York: Basic Books.

COLEMAN, JAMES S., THOMAS HOFFER, and SALLY KILGORE. 1982a. *High school achievement: Public, Catholic, and other private schools compared.* New York: Basic Books.

COLEMAN, JAMES S., THOMAS HOFFER, and SALLY KILGORE. 1982b. Cognitive outcomes in public and private schools. *Sociology of Education,* 55:65–76.

COLEMAN, JAMES S., and LEE RAINWATER. 1978. *Social standing in America.* New York: Basic Books.

COLEMAN, JAMES W. 1985. *The criminal elite: The sociology of white-collar crime.* New York: St. Martin's Press.

COLEMAN, JAMES W. 1987. Toward an integrated theory of white-collar crime. *American Journal of Sociology,* 93:406–439.

COLEMAN, JAMES W. 1989. *The criminal elite: The sociology of white collar crime.* New York: St. Martin's Press.

COLEMAN, MARILYN, and LAWRENCE H. GANONG. 1990. Remarriage and stepfamily research in the 1980s: Increased interest in an old family form. *Journal of Marriage and the Family,* 52:925–940.

COLGAN, PATRICK. 1983. *Comparative social recognition.* New York: Wiley.

COLLIER, JANE FISBURNE. 1988. *Marriage and inequality in classless societies.* Stanford, Calif.: Stanford University Press.

COLLIGAN, MICHAEL J., JAMES W. PENNEBAKER, and LAWRENCE R. MURPHY, EDS. 1982. *Mass psychogenic illness: A social psychological analysis.* Hillsdale, N.J.: Erlbaum.

COLLINS, NANCY L. and STEPHEN J. READ. 1990. Adult attachment, working models, and relationship quality in dating couples. *Journal of Personality and Social Psychology,* 58:644–663.

COLLINS, RANDALL. 1975. *Conflict sociology.* New York: Academic Press.

COLLINS, RANDALL. 1976. Review of "Schooling in capitalist America." *Harvard Educational Review,* 46:246–251.

COLLINS, RANDALL. 1977. Some comparative principles of educational stratification. *Harvard Educational Review,* 47:1–27.

COLLINS, RANDALL. 1979. *Credential society.* New York: Academic Press.

COLLINS, RANDALL. 1980. Weber's last theory of capitalism: A systematization. *American Sociological Review,* 45:925–942.

COLLINS, RANDALL. 1981. *Sociology since midcentury: Essays in theory cumulation.* New York: Academic Press.

COLLINS, RANDALL. 1988a. *Sociology of marriage and the family,* 2nd ed. Chicago: Nelson Hall.

COLLINS, RANDALL. 1988b. *Theoretical sociology.* San Diego: Harcourt Brace Jovanovich.

COLLINS, RANDALL. 1993. Maturation of the state-centered theory of revolution and ideology. *Sociological Theory,* 11:116–128.

COLLINS, RANDALL, and MICHAEL MAKOWSKY. 1984. *The discovery of society,* 3rd ed. New York: Random House.

COLLINS, SHARON. 1983. The making of the black middle class. *Social Problems,* 30:340–377.

COLOMY, PAUL. 1991. To begin anew. *Contemporary Sociology,* 20:797–800.

COLVIN, MARK, and JOHN PAULY. 1983. A critique of criminology: Toward an integrated structural-Marxist theory of delinquency production. *American Journal of Sociology,* 89:513–551.

CONGER, RAND D., FREDERICK O. LORENZ, GLEN H. ELDER, JR., RONALD L. SIMONS, and XIAOJIA GE. 1993. Husband and wife differences in response to undesirable life events. *Journal of Health and Social Behavior,* 34:71–88.

CONNOR, WALTER D. 1979. *Socialism, politics, and equality.* New York: Columbia University Press.

CONRAD, PETER, and JOSEPH SCHNEIDER. 1980. *Deviance and medicalization: From badness to sickness.* St. Louis: Mosby.

COOLEY, CHARLES HORTON. 1902/1964. *Human nature and the social order.* New York: Scribner's.

COOLEY, CHARLES HORTON. 1909. *Social organization.* New York: Scribner's.

COONTZ, STEPHANIE. 1992. *The way we never were: American families and the nostalgia trap.* New York: Basic Books.

COPELAND, ANNE P., and KATHLEEN M. WHITE. 1991. *Studying families.* Newbury Park, Calif.: Sage.

COPP, TERRY, and BILL MCANDREW. 1990. *Battle exhaustion: Soldiers and psychiatrists in the Canadian army, 1939–1945.* Montreal & Kingston: McGill-Queen's University Press.

CORDES, COLLEEN. 1984. Behavior therapists examine how emotion, cognition relate. *APA Monitor* (February):18.

CORNISH, EDWARD. 1993. 1993 as predicted in 1893: If they could see us now! *The Futurist* (May–June):41–42.

CORNWALL, MARIE. 1989. The determinants of religious behavior. A theoretical model and empirical test. *Social Forces,* 68:572–592.

COSE, ELLIS. 1990. Do we ask too much of polls? *Time* (February 19):78.

COSER, LEWIS A. 1956. *The functions of social conflict.* New York: Free Press.

COSER, LEWIS A. 1957. Social conflict and the theory of social change. *British Journal of Sociology,* 8:170–183.

COSER, LEWIS A. 1962. Some functions of deviant behavior and normative flexibility. *American Journal of Sociology,* 68:172–181.

COSER, LEWIS A. 1975. Presidential address: Two methods in search of a substance. *Am Sociol Rev,* 40:691–700.

COUGHLIN, ELLEN K. 1988. Worsening plight of the "underclass" catches attention of researchers. *Chronicle of Higher Education* (Mar 30):A1.

COUGHLIN, ELLEN K. 1992. Sociologists confront questions about field's vitality and direction. *Chronicle of Higher Education* (August 12):A6–A8.

COWELL, ALAN. 1984a. African famine battle: Aid has been a villain. *New York Times* (November 29):1, 6.

COWELL, ALAN. 1984b. South of Sahara, the intrusive politics of hunger. *New York Times* (December 3):1, 4.

COWLEY, GEOFFREY. 1989. The plunder of the past. *Newsweek* (June 26):58–60.

COX, OLIVER C. 1948. *Caste, class, and race.* Garden City, N.Y.: Doubleday.

CRANE, JONATHAN. 1991. The epidemic theory of ghettos and neighborhood effects on dropping out and teenage childbearing. *American Journal of Sociology,* 96:1226–1259.

CREIGHTON, LINDA L. 1993. Kids taking care of kids. *U.S. News & World Report* (December 20):26–33.

CRESSEY, DONALD R. 1969. *Theft of the nation: The structure and operations of organized crime in America.* New York: Harper & Row.

CRISPELL, DIANE. 1993a. Interracial children pose challenge for classifiers. *Wall Street Journal* (January 27):B1.

CRISPELL, DIANE. 1993b. Sex surveys: Does anyone tell the truth? *American Demographics,* 15 (July):9–10.

CROCKER, JENNIFER, and RILA LUHTANEN. 1990. Collective self-esteem and ingroup bias. *Journal of Personality and Social Personality and Social Psychology,* 58:60–67.

CROSSETTE, BARBARA. 1991. India's poorest find an economic place. *New York Times* (January 29):A8.

CURTISS, SUSAN. 1977. *Genie: A psycholinguistic study of a modern-day "wild child."* New York: Academic Press.

CVETKOVICH, GEORGE, and TIMOTHY C. EARLE. 1992. Environmental hazards and the public. *Journal of Social Issues,* 48:1–20.

DAHL, ROBERT. 1961. *Who governs? Democracy and power in an American city.* New Haven, Conn.: Yale University Press.

DAHRENDORF, RALF. 1958. Toward a theory of social conflict. *Journal of Conflict Resolution,* 2:170–183.

DAHRENDORF, RALF. 1959. *Class and class conflict in industrial society.* Stanford, Calif.: Stanford University Press.

DAHRENDORF, RALF. 1965. *Gesellshaft und Demokratie in Deutschland.* Munich: Piper Verlag.

DAHRENDORF, RALF. 1968. *Essays in the theory of society.* Stanford, Calif.: Stanford University Press.

DAKE, KARL. 1992. Myths of nature: Culture and the social construction of risk. *Journal of Social Issues,* 48:21–37.

DAMON, WILLIAM, and DANIEL HART. 1982. The development of self-understanding from infancy through adolescence. *Child Development,* 53:841–864.

DANDEKER, CHRISTOPHER. 1990. *Surveillance, power and modernity: Bureaucracy and discipline from 1700 to the present day.* New York: St. Martin's Press.

DANIELS, ARLENE KAPLAN. 1987. Invisible work. *Social Problems,* 34:403–415.

DARNTON, NINA. 1991. The pain of the last taboo. *Newsweek* (October 7):70–72.

DATAN, NANCY. 1977. After the apple: Post-Newtonian metatheory for jaded psychologists. In N. Datan and H. W. Reese, eds., *Life-span developmental psychology: Dialectical perspectives on experimental research,* New York: Academic Press.

DAVIE, MAURICE R. 1937. The patterns of urban growth. In George P. Murdock, ed., *Studies in the science of society.* New Haven, Conn.: Yale University Press.

DAVIES, JAMES. 1962. Toward a theory of revolution. *American Sociological Review,* 27:5–19.

DAVIES, JAMES. 1969. The J-curve of rising and declining satisfactions as a cause of some great revolutions and a contained revolution. In H. D. Graham and T. R. Gurr, eds., *The history of violence in America.* New York: Bantam.

DAVIES, JAMES. 1974. The J-curve and power struggle theories of collective violence. *American Sociological Review,* 39:607–610.

DAVIS, F. JAMES. 1991. *Who is black? One nation's definition.* University Park: Pennsylvania State University Press.

DAVIS, JAMES. 1982. Up and down opportunity's ladder. *Public Opinion,* 5 (June/July):11–15+.

DAVIS, KINGSLEY. 1945. The world demographic transition. *Annals of the American Academy of Political and Social Science,* 237:1–11.

DAVIS, KINGSLEY. 1949. *Human society.* New York: Macmillan.

DAVIS, KINGSLEY. 1951. Introduction. In William J. Goode, *Religion among the primitives.* New York: Free Press.

DAVIS, KINGSLEY. 1955. The origin and growth of urbanization in the world. *American Journal of Sociology,* 60:429–437.

DAVIS, KINGSLEY. 1959. The myth of functional analysis as a special method in sociology and anthropology. *American Sociological Review,* 24:757–772.

DAVIS, KINGSLEY. 1960. Legitimacy and the incest taboo. In Norman W. Bell and Ezra F. Vogel, eds., *A modern introduction to the family.* New York: Free Press.

DAVIS, KINGSLEY. 1967. The urbanization of the human population. In *Cities.* New York: Knopf.

DAVIS, KINGSLEY. 1971. The world's population crisis. In Robert K. Merton and Robert A. Nisbet, eds., *Contemporary social problems,* 3rd ed. New York: Harcourt Brace Jovanovich.

DAVIS, KINGSLEY, and WILBERT MOORE. 1945. Some principles of stratification. *American Sociological Review,* 10:242–249.

DAVIS, NANCY J., and ROBERT V. ROBINSON. 1988. Class identification of men and women in the 1970s and 1980s. *American Sociological Review,* 53:103–112.

DAVIS, NANCY J., and ROBERT V. ROBINSON. 1991. Men's and women's consciousness of gender inequality: Austria, West Germany, Great Britain, and the United States. *American Sociological Review,* 56:72–84.

DEAUX, KAY, and LAWRENCE S. WRIGHTSMAN. 1984. *Social psychology in the 80s,* 4th ed. Monterey, Calif.: Brooks/Cole.

DEBOLD, ELIZABETH, MARIE WILSON, and IDELISSE MALAVE. 1993. *Mother daughter revolution: From betrayal to power.* Reading, Mass.: Addison-Wesley.

DECHICK, JOE. 1988. Childbirth deaths higher for minorities. *USA Today* (July 11):D1.

DEEGAN, MARY JO. 1988. *Jane Addams and the men of the Chicago school, 1892–1918.* New Brunswick, N.J.: Transaction.

DEEGAN, MARY JO. 1989. *American ritual dramas: Social rules and cultural meanings.* Westport, Conn.: Greenwood Press.

DEGLER, CARL. 1980. *At odds: Women and the family in America from the Revolution to the present.* New York: Oxford University Press.

DELONG, JAMES V. 1994. The criminalization of just about everything. *American Enterprise,* 5 (March/April):26–35.

DE LUCE, JUDITH, and HUGH T. WILDER. 1983. *Language in primates.* New York: Springer-Verlag.

DEMARIS, ALFRED, and K. VANINADHA RAO. 1992. Premarital cohabitation and subsequent marital stability in the United States: A reassessment. *Journal of Marriage and the Family,* 54:178–190.

DEMOS, VASILIKIE. 1990. Black family studies in the *Journal of Marriage and the Family,* and the issue of distortion. A trend analysis. *Journal of Marriage and the Family,* 52: 603–612.

DENEVAN, WILLIAM M., ED. 1992. *The native population of the Americas in 1492,* 2nd ed. Madison: University of Wisconsin Press.

DENTON, NANCY A., and DOUGLAS S. MASSEY. 1989. Racial identity among Caribbean Hispanics: The effect of double minority status on residential segregation. *American Sociological Review,* 54:790–808.

DENTZER, SUSAN. 1993. The dangers of economic insecurity. *U.S. News & World Report* (October 25):50.

DEPALMA, ANTHONY. 1991. How undergraduates can succeed: Study together, and in small classes. *New York Times* (November 6):B8.

DEPARLE, JASON. 1992. Report, delayed months, says lowest income group grew sharply. *New York Times* (May 12):A7.

DEPARTMENT OF EDUCATION. 1989. News release (December 27). Washington, D.C.

DESAI, SONALDE, and LINDA J. WAITE. 1991. Women's employment during pregnancy and after the first birth: Occupational characteristics and work commitment. *American Sociological Review,* 56:551–566.

DEVINE, JOEL A., MARK PLUNKETT, and JAMES D. WRIGHT. 1992. The chronicity of poverty: Evidence from the PSID, 1968–1987. *Social Forces,* 70:787–812.

DEVINE, PATRICIA G. 1989. Stereotypes and prejudice: Their automatic and controlled components. *Journal of Personality and Social Psychology,* 56:5–18.

DE VRIES, RAYMOND G. 1981. Birth and death: Social construction of the poles of existence. *Social Forces,* 59:1074–1093.

DE WITT, KAREN. 1991. Stanford, criticized by U.S., changes billing on research. *New York Times* (March 14):A12.

DILLMAN, DON A. 1991. The design and administration of mail surveys. *Annual Review of Sociology,* 17:225–249.

DIMAGGIO, PAUL. 1982. Cultural capital and school success: The impact of status culture participation on the grades of U.S. high school students. *American Sociological Review,* 47:189–201.

DIONNE, E. J., JR. 1980. Abortion poll: Not clear-cut. *New York Times* (August 10):A15.

DIONNE, E. J., JR. 1987. The 60's meet the 80's. *New York Times* (November 9):1, 19.

DIPBOYE, ROBERT L. 1977. Alternative approaches to deindividualization. *Psychological Bulletin,* 84:1057–1075.

DIPRETE, THOMAS A., and DAVID B. GRUSKY. 1990. Structure and trend in the process of stratification for American men and women. *American Journal of Sociology,* 96:107–143.

DIXIT, AVINASH K., and BARRY J. NALEBUFF. 1991. *Thinking strategically.* New York: Norton.

DJILAS, MILOVAN. 1957. *The new class.* New York: Praeger.

DJILAS, MILOVAN. 1988. What Gorbachev can learn from Yugoslavia's strikes. *Wall Street Journal* (March 16):31.

DOBRZYNSKI, JUDITH H. 1993. The "glass ceiling": A barrier to the boardroom, too. *Business Week* (November 22):50.

DODGE, KENNETH A., JOHN E. BATES, and GREGORY S. PETTIT. 1990. Mechanisms in the cycle of violence. *Science,* 250:1678–1683.

DOMHOFF, G. WILLIAM. 1970. *The higher circles.* New York: Random House.

DOMHOFF, G. WILLIAM. 1983. *Who rules America now? A view for the '80s.* Englewood Cliffs, N.J.: Prentice-Hall.

DOMHOFF, G. WILLIAM. 1990. *The power elite and the state: How policy is made in America.* New York: Aldine de Gruyter.

DOWNEY, GARY L. 1986. Ideology and the clamshell identity: Organizational dilemmas in the anti-nuclear power movement. *Social Problems,* 33:357–373.

DOYLE, SIR ARTHUR CONAN. 1927. *The complete Sherlock Holmes.* Garden City, N.Y.: Doubleday.

DRESSEL, PAULA L., and ANN CLARK. 1990. A critical look at family care. *Journal of Marriage and the Family,* 52:769–782.

DREW, PAUL, and ANTHONY WOOTTON, EDS. 1988. *Erving Goffman: Exploring the interaction order.* Boston: Northeastern University Press.

DRUCKER, PETER F. 1985. Depression cycle. *Wall Street Journal* (January 9):24.

DRUCKER, PETER F. 1993. *The post-capitalist society.* New York: Harper Collins.

DUBIN, ROBERT. 1976. Work in modern society. In Robert Dubin, ed., *Handbook of work, organization, and society.* Chicago: Rand McNally.

DUGGER, CELIA W. 1992. U.S. study says Asian-Americans face widespread discrimination. *New York Times* (February 29):1, 5.

DUMAINE, BRIAN. 1991. New weapons in the crime war. *Fortune* (June 3):180–188.

DUMONT, L. 1970. *Homo hierarchicus. The caste system and its implications.* London: Weidenfeld and Nicolson.

DUNCAN, GREG. 1984. *Years of poverty, years of plenty.* Ann Arbor: Institute for Social Research, University of Michigan.

DUNCAN, GREG J. 1987. On the slippery slope. *American Demographics,* 9 (May):30–35.

DUNCAN, GREG J., MARTHA S. HILL, and SAUL D. HOFFMAN. 1988. Welfare dependence within and across generations. *Science,* 239:467–471.

DUNCAN, GREG J., and WILLARD RODGERS. 1991. Has children's poverty become more persistent? *American Sociological Review,* 56:538–550.

DUNCAN, GREG J., TIMOTHY M. SMEEDING, and WILLARD RODGERS. 1992. The incredible shrinking middle class. *American Demographics,* 14 (May):34–38.

DUNCAN, OTIS DUDLEY. 1959. Human ecology and population studies. In Philip Hauser and Otis D. Duncan, eds., *The study of population.* Chicago: University of Chicago Press.

DUNCAN, OTIS DUDLEY. 1961. From social system to ecosystem. *Sociological Inquiry,* 31:140–149.

DUNN, ASHLEY. 1994. Southeast Asians highly dependent on welfare in U.S. *New York Times* (May 19):A1, A13.

DUNN, WILLIAM. 1993. Educating diversity. *American Demographics,* 15 (April):38–43.

DUNNING, DAVID, DALE W. GRIFFIN, JAMES D. MILOJKOVIC, and LEE ROSS. 1990. The overconfidence effect in social prediction. *Journal of Personality and Social Psychology,* 58:568–581.

DUPAQUIER, J., A. FAUVE-CHAMOUX, and E. GREBENIK, EDS. 1983. *Malthus past and present.* Orlando, Fla.: Academic Press.

DURKHEIM, EMILE. 1893/1964. *The division of labor in society.* New York: Free Press.

DURKHEIM, EMILE. 1895/1938. *The rules of sociological method.* Glencoe, Ill.: Free Press.

DURKHEIM, EMILE. 1897/1951. *Suicide.* New York: Free Press.

DURKHEIM, EMILE. 1912/1965. *The elementary forms of religious life.* New York: Free Press.

DUTTON, DONALD G., and ARTHUR P. ARON. 1974. Some evidence for heightened sexual attraction under conditions of high anxiety. *Journal of Personality and Social Psychology,* 30:510–517.

DWYER, JEFFREY W., and RAYMOND T. COWARD. 1991. Multivariate comparison of the involvement of adult sons versus adult daughters in the care of impaired parents. *Journal of Gerontology,* 46:S259–269.

EASTERLIN, RICHARD A. 1961. The American baby-boom in historical perspective. *American Economic Review,* 51:869–911.

EASTERLIN, RICHARD A. 1987. *Birth and fortune: The impact of numbers on personal welfare.* Chicago: University of Chicago Press.

EATON, WILLIAM W. 1986. *The sociology of mental disorders,* 2nd ed. New York: Praeger.

EBERSTADT, NICK, ED. 1981. *Fertility decline in the less developed countries.* New York: Praeger.

EBERSTADT, NICHOLAS. 1993. Mortality rates and nations in crisis. *American Enterprise,* 4 (September/October):46–53.

EBERSTADT, NICHOLAS. 1994. Marx and mortality: A mystery. *New York Times* (April 6):A13.

ECKHOLM, ERIK. 1994. The Apaches. *New York Times Magazine* (February 27):45–52.

EDWARDS, L. P. 1927. *The natural history of revolution.* Chicago: University of Chicago Press.

EDWARDS, RICHARD. 1978. The social relations of production at the point of production. *Insurgent Sociologist,* 8: 109–125.

EDWARDS, RICHARD. 1979. *Contested terrain.* New York: Basic Books.

EGAN, TIMOTHY. 1988. Despairing Indians looking to tradition to combat suicides. *New York Times* (March 19):1, 8.

EHRHARDT, ANKE A., and H. F. L. MEYER-BAHLBURG. 1981. Effects of prenatal sex hormones on gender-related behavior. *Science,* 176:123–128.

EHRLICH, PAUL R., and ANNE H. EHRLICH. 1970. *Population, resources, environment: Issues in human ecology.* San Francisco: Freeman.

EHRLICH, PAUL R., and ANNE H. EHRLICH. 1990. *The population explosion.* New York: Simon and Schuster.

EHRLICH, PAUL R., and ANNE H. EHRLICH. 1991. *Healing the planet: Strategies for resolving the environmental crisis.* New York: Addison-Wesley.

EICHAR, DOUGLAS M. 1989. *Occupation and class consciousness in America.* New York: Greenwood Press.

EISENBERG, DAVID M., RONALD C. KESSLER, CINDY FOSTER, FRANCES E. NORLOCK, DAVID R. CALKINS, and THOMAS L. DELBANCO. 1993. Unconventional medicine in the United States: Prevalence, costs, and patterns of use. *New England Journal of Medicine* (January 28):246–253.

EKMAN, PAUL. 1980. *The face of man: Expressions of universal emotions in a New Guinea village.* New York: Garland STPM Press.

EKMAN, PAUL, and WALLACE V. FRIESEN. 1987. Universals and cultural differences in the judgments of facial expressions of emotion. *Journal of Personality and Social Psychology,* 53:712–717.

EKMAN, PAUL, WALLACE V. FRIESEN, and JOHN BEAR. 1984. The international language of gesture. *Psychology Today,* 18 (May):64–67.

EKMAN, PAUL, WALLACE V. FRIESEN, and MAUREEN O'SULLIVAN. 1988. Smiles when lying. *Journal of Personality and Social Psychology,* 54:414–420.

ELDER, GLENN H., JR. 1974. *Children of the Great Depression.* Chicago: University of Chicago Press.

ELDER, GLENN H., JR. 1983. Families, kin, and the life course. In R. Parke, ed., *The family.* Chicago: University of Chicago Press.

ELDER, GLENN H., JR. 1985. Perspectives on the life course. In Glenn H. Elder, Jr., ed., *Life Course Dynamics.* Ithaca, N.Y.: Cornell University Press.

ELDER, GLENN H., JR. 1986. Military timing and turning points in men's lives. *Developmental Psychology,* 22:233–245.

ELDER, GLEN H., JR. 1994. Time, human agency, and social change: Perspectives on the life course. *Social Psychology Quarterly,* 57:4–15.

ELDER, GLENN H., JR., and ELIZABETH C. CLIPP. 1988. Wartime losses and social bonding: Influences across 40 years in men's lives. *Psychiatry,* 51:177–197.

ELIAS, MARILYN. 1994. Poverty impacts children's IQ. *USA Today* (May 9):D1.

ELLIOTT, DELBERT S. 1966. Delinquency, school attendance and dropout. *Social Problems,* 13:307–314.

ELLWOOD, DAVID T. 1988. *Poor support: Poverty in the American family.* New York: Basic Books.

ELLYSON, STEVE L., JOHN F. DOVIDIO, RANDI L. CORSON, and DEBBIE L. VINICUR. 1980. Visual dominance behavior in female dyads. *Social Psychology Quarterly,* 43:328–336.

ENGELS, FRIEDRICH. 1884/1902. *The origin of the family, private property, and the state.* Chicago: Kerr.

EPSTEIN, SUE HOOVER. 1983. Why do women live longer than men? *Science* 83, 4 (October):30–31.

ERICKSON, MAYNARD L., and JACK P. GIBBS. 1978. Objective and perceptual properties of legal punishment and the deterrence doctrine. *Social Problems,* 25:253–264.

ERIKSON, ERIK. 1963. *Childhood and society.* New York: Norton.

ERIKSON, ERIK. 1968. *Identity: Youth and crisis.* New York: Norton.

ERIKSON, KAI T. 1962. Notes on the sociology of deviance. *Social Problems,* 9:307–314.

ERIKSON, KAI T. 1966. *Wayward Puritans: A study in the sociology of deviance.* New York: Wiley.

ERIKSON, ROBERT, and JOHN H. GOLDTHORPE. 1992. *The constant flux: A study of class mobility in industrial societies.* Oxford: Clarendon Press.

ESPIRITU, YEN LE. 1992. *Asian American panethnicity: Bridging institutions and identities.* Philadelphia: Temple University Press.

ESPOSITO, JOHN L. 1992. *The Islamic threat: Myth or reality.* New York: Oxford University Press.

ETZIONI, AMITAI. 1964. *Modern organizations.* Englewood Cliffs, N.J.: Prentice-Hall.

ETZIONI, AMITAI. 1975. *A comparative analysis of complex organizations.* New York: Free Press.

ETZIONI, AMITAI. 1985. Shady corporate practices. *New York Times* (November 15):27.

EVANS, PETER B. 1981. Recent research on multinational corporations. *Annual Review of Sociology,* 7:199–223.

FAGOT, BEVERLY I., MARY D. LEINBACH, and CHERIE O'BOYLE. 1992. Gender labeling, gender stereotyping, and parenting behaviors. *Developmental Psychology,* 28:225–230.

FAIA, MICHAEL A. 1986. *Dynamic functionalism: Strategy and tactics.* New York: Cambridge University Press.

FAIA, MICHAEL A. 1989. Cultural materialism in the functionalist mode. *American Sociological Review,* 54:658–660.

FALTERMAYER, EDMUND. 1991. The deal decade: Verdict on the '80s. *Fortune* (August 26):58–76.

FALTERMAYER, EDMUND. 1994. Competitiveness: How U.S. companies stack up now. *Fortune* (April 18):52–64.

FARKAS, GEORGE, ROBERT P. GROBE, DANIEL SHEEHAN, and YAN SHUAN. 1990. Cultural resources and school success. *Gender,* ethnicity, and poverty groups within an urban school district. *American Sociological Review,* 55:127–142.

FARLEY, REYNOLDS, and WALTER R. ALLEN. 1987. *The color line and the quality of life in America.* Washington, D.C.: Russell Sage Foundation.

FARNSWORTH, CLYDE H. 1990. Report by World Bank sees poverty lessening by 2000 except in Africa. *New York Times* (July 16):A3.

FARNSWORTH, CLYDE H. 1991. Economic woes force Canada to re-examine medical system. *New York Times* (November 24):7.

FARNSWORTH, MARGARET, and MICHAEL J. LEIBER. 1989. Strain theory revisited: Economic goals, educational means, and delinquency. *American Sociological Review,* 54:263–274.

FASSINGER, POLLY A. 1989. Becoming the breadwinner: Single mothers' reactions to changes in their paid work lives. *Family Relations,* 38:404–411.

FAUNCE, WILLIAM A. 1989. Occupational status-assignment systems: The effect of status on self esteem. *American Journal of Sociology,* 95:378–400.

FEAGIN, JOE R. 1991a. Blacks still face the malevolent reality of white racism. *Chronicle of Higher Education* (November 27):A44.

FEAGIN, JOE R. 1991b. The continuing significance of race: Antiblack discrimination in public places. *American Sociological Review,* 56:101–116.

FEATHERMAN, DAVID L., and ROBERT M. HAUSER. 1978. *Opportunity and change.* New York: Academic Press.

FEINGOLD, ALAN. 1988. Matching for attractiveness in romantic partners and same-sex friends: A meta-analysis and theoretical critique. *Psychological Bulletin,* 104:226–235.

FEINGOLD, ALAN. 1990. Gender differences in effects of physical attractiveness on romantic attraction: A comparison across five research paradigms. *Journal of Personality and Social Psychology,* 59:981–993.

FELSON, RICHARD B., and MARK D. REED. 1986. Reference groups and self-appraisals of academic ability and performance. *Social Psychology Quarterly,* 49:103–109.

FENIGSTEIN, ALAN. 1984. Self-consciousness and the overperception of self as a target. *Journal of Personality and Social Psychology,* 47:860–870.

FENNEMA, MEINHERT. 1982. *International networks of banks and industry.* Boston: Martinius Nijhoff.

FENYVESI, CHARLES. 1991. Spreading scandal. *U.S. News & World Report* (February 4):22.

FERREE, MYRA MARX. 1990. Beyond separate spheres: Feminism and family research. *Journal of Marriage and the Family,* 52:866–884.

FERRISS, ABBOTT L. 1988. The use of social indicators. *Social Forces,* 66:601–617.

FIALA, ROBERT, and GARY LaFREE. 1988. Cross-national determinants of child homicide. *American Sociological Review,* 53:432–445.

FIELD, TIFFANY. 1991. Quality infant day-care and grade school behavior and performance. *Child Development,* 62:863–870.

FIERMAN, JACLYN. 1990. Why women still don't hit the top. *Fortune* (July 30):40–62.

FINDLAY, STEVEN. 1986. Cancer risk higher for poor. *USA Today* (October 7):D1.

FINE, MARK A., and LAWRENCE A. KURDEK. 1992. The adjustment of adolescents in stepfather and stepmother families. *Journal of Marriage and the Family,* 54:725–736.

FINKE, ROGER, and RODNEY STARK. 1992. *The churching of America, 1776–1990: Winners and losers in our religious economy.* New Brunswick, N.J.: Rutgers University Press.

FINKELHOR, DAVID. 1979. *Sexually victimized children.* New York: Free Press.

FIREBAUGH, GLENN. 1992. Growth effects of foreign and domestic investment. *American Journal of Sociology,* 98:105–130.

FIREY, WALTER. 1947. *Land use in central Boston.* Cambridge, Mass.: Harvard University Press.

FISCHER, MICHAEL M. J. 1980. *Iran: From religious dispute to revolution.* Cambridge, Mass.: Harvard University Press.

FISHER, ANNE B. 1992. When will women get to the top? *Fortune* (September 21):44–56.

FITZGERALD, LOUISE F. 1993. Sexual harassment. *American Psychologist,* 48:1070–1076.

FITZPATRICK, ELLEN. 1990. *Endless crusade: Women social scientists and progressive reform.* New York: Oxford University Press.

FLANDRIN, J. F. 1979. *Families in former times: Kinship, household, and sexuality.* New York: Cambridge University Press.

FLANIGAN, PETER M. 1991. A school system that works. *Wall Street Journal* (February 12):A12.

FLIGSTEIN, NEIL. 1990. *The transformation of corporate control.* Cambridge, Mass.: Harvard University Press.

FLIGSTEIN, NEIL, and PETER BRANTLEY. 1992. Bank control, owner control, or organization dynamics: Who controls the large modern corporation? *American Journal of Sociology,* 98:280–307.

FORAN, JOHN. 1993a. *Fragile resistance: Social transformation in Iran from 1500 to the revolution.* Boulder, Colo.: Westview Press.

FORAN, JOHN. 1993b. Theories of revolution revisited: Toward a fourth generation? *Sociological Theory,* 11:1–20.

FORD, C. S., and F. A. BEACH. 1951. *Patterns of sexual behavior.* New York: Harper & Row.

FOST, DAN. 1992. Education to back up affirmative action. *American Demographics,* 14 (April):16–17.

FRANKEL, MARTIN, and HUMPHREY TAYLOR. 1992. Suicide highest in wide-open spaces. *American Demographics,* 14 (April):9.

FREADHOFF, CHUCK. 1992. America goes back to school. *Investor's Business Daily* (August 28):1, 2.

FREEDMAN, J. L. 1975. *Crowding and behavior: The psychology of high-density living.* New York: Viking.

FREUD, SIGMUND. 1930/1961. *Civilization and its discontents.* London: Hogarth.

FREUD, SIGMUND. 1938. *The basic writings of Sigmund Freud.* Trans. A. A. Brill. New York: Modern Library.

FREUDENBURG, WILLIAM R. 1986. Social impact assessment. *Annual Review of Sociology,* 12:451–478.

FREY, WILLIAM H., and WILLIAM P. O'HARE. 1993. Vivan los suburbios! *American Demographics,* 15 (April):30–36.

FRIEDMAN, ANDREW. 1977. *Industry and labor: Class struggle at work and monopoly capitalism.* New York: Macmillan.

FRIEND, TIM. 1990. High death rate among blacks hard to explain. *USA Today* (February 9):D1.

FULLER, C. J. 1976. *The Nayars today.* Cambridge, Mass.: Cambridge University Press.

FURSTENBERG, FRANK F., JR., and ANDREW J. CHERLIN. 1991. *Divided families.* Cambridge, Mass.: Harvard University Press.

GAITER, DOROTHY. 1991. Although cures exist, poverty fells many afflicted with cancer. *Wall Street Journal* (May 1):A1, A4.

GALLUP ORGANIZATION. 1990. *The Gallup Poll Monthly* (February). Princeton, N.J.: Gallup Organization.

GANS, HERBERT J. 1972. The positive functions of poverty. *American Journal of Sociology,* 78:275–289.

GANZEBOOM, HARRY B. G., DONALD J. TREIMAN, and WOUT C. ULTEE. 1991. Comparative intergenerational stratification research: Three generations and beyond. *Annual Review of Sociology,* 17:277–302.

GARBARINO, JAMES, and DEBORAH SHERMAN. 1980. High-risk neighborhoods and high-risk families: The human ecology of child maltreatment. *Child Development,* 51: 188–198.

GARFINKEL, HAROLD. 1974. The origins of the term "ethnomethodology." In R. Turner, ed., *Ethnomethodology.* Harmondsworth, Eng.: Penguin Books.

GARGAN, E. A. 1986. George tried; Now queen is in Peking. *New York Times* (October 13):5.

GARGAN, EDWARD A. 1992. India faces worst case: War between the castes. *New York Times* (July 24):A5.

GARREAU, JOEL. 1991. Edge cities. *American Demographics,* 13 (September):24–31+.

GECAS, VIKTOR, and MONICA A. SEFF. 1990. Families and adolescents: A review of the 1980s. *Journal of Marriage and the Family,* 52:941–958.

GEERTZ, CLIFFORD. 1963. *Old societies and new states.* New York: Free Press.

GELLES, RICHARD J., and CLAIRE P. CORNELL. 1985. *Intimate violence in families.* Beverly Hills, Calif.: Sage.

GELLES, RICHARD J., MURRAY A. STRAUS, and JOHN W. HARROP. 1988. Has family violence decreased? *Journal of Marriage and the Family,* 50:286–291.

GELMAN, DAVID. 1991. Clean and sober—and agnostic. *Newsweek* (July 8):62–63.

GENERAL MILLS. 1981. *The General Mills American family report, 1980–1981: Families, strengths and strains at work.* Minneapolis: General Mills.

GESCHWENDER, JAMES A. 1964. Social structure and the Negro revolt: An examination of some hypotheses. *Social Forces,* 43:248–256.

GESCHWENDER, JAMES A. 1978. *Racial stratification in America.* Dubuque, Iowa: William C. Brown.

GEST, TED. 1989. Victims of crime. *U.S. News & World Report* (July 31):16–19.

GIBBONS, ANN. 1991. Does war on cancer equal war on poverty? *Science,* 253:260.

GIBBS, JACK P. 1975. *Crime, punishment, and deterrence.* New York: Elsevier.

GIDDENS, ANTHONY. 1973. *The class structure of the advanced societies.* New York: Harper & Row.

GIDDENS, ANTHONY. 1984. *The constitution of society.* Berkeley: University of California Press.

GIDDENS, ANTHONY. 1985. *A contemporary critique of historical materialism.* Vol. 2: *The nation-state and violence.* Berkeley: University of California Press.

GIDDENS, ANTHONY. 1990. *The consequences of modernity.* Stanford, Calif.: Stanford University Press.

GILBERT, C. 1967. When did a man in the Renaissance grow old? *Studies in the Renaissance,* 14:7–32.

GILBERT, JESS, and CAROLYN HOWE. 1991. Beyond "state vs. society": Theories of the state and New Deal agricultural policies. *American Sociological Review,* 56:204–220.

GILBERT, NEIL, and BARBARA GILBERT. 1989. *The enabling state: Modern welfare capitalism in America.* New York: Oxford University Press.

GILLIGAN, CAROL. 1982. *In a different voice: Psychological theory and women's development.* Cambridge, Mass.: Harvard University Press.

GILLIGAN, CAROL, ANNIE G. ROGERS, and DEBORAH L. TOLMAN, EDS. 1991. *Women, girls & psychotherapy: Reframing resistance.* New York: Haworth.

GILLIGAN, CAROL, J. V. WARD, and J. M. TAYLOR, EDS. 1989. *Mapping the moral domain.* Cambridge, Mass.: Harvard University Press.

GILMORE, D. D. 1990. *Manhood in the making: Cultural concepts of masculinity.* New Haven, Conn.: Yale University Press.

GINSBERG, BENJAMIN, and MARTIN SHEFTER. 1990. *Politics by other means: The declining importance of elections in America.* New York: Basic Books.

GLABERSON, WILLIAM. 1994. Study finds more news of, and by, women. *New York Times* (April 13):A10.

GLASS, DAVID, PEVERILL SQUIRE, and RAYMOND WOLFINGER. 1984. Voter turnout: An international comparison. *Public Opinion,* 6 (January):49–55.

GLASS, JENNIFER, and VALERIE CAMARIGG. 1992. Gender, parenthood, and job–family compatibility. *American Journal of Sociology,* 98:131–151.

GLASSMAN, RONALD M., WILLIAM H. SWATOS, JR., and PAUL L.

ROSEN, EDS. 1987. *Bureaucracy against democracy and socialism.* Westport, Conn.: Greenwood Press.

GLASTRIS, PAUL. 1992. A tale of two suburbias. *U.S. News & World Report* (November 9):32–36.

GLENN, NORVAL D. 1990. Quantitative research on marital quality in the 1980s: A critical review. *Journal of Marriage and the Family,* 52:818–831.

GLENN, NORVAL D. 1992. What does family mean? *American Demographics,* 14 (June):30–37.

GLENN, NORVAL, and C. N. WEAVER. 1981. The contribution of marital happiness to global happiness. *Journal of Marriage and the Family,* 43:161–168.

GLICK, CLARENCE. 1980. *Sojourners and settlers: Chinese immigrants in Hawaii.* Honolulu: University of Hawaii Press.

GLICK, PAUL C. 1984. How American families are changing. *American Demographics,* 6 (January):21–25.

GLOCK, CHARLES Y., BENJAMIN B. RINGER, and EARL R. BABBIE. 1967. *To comfort and challenge: A dilemma of the contemporary church.* Berkeley: University of California Press.

GLUCKMAN, MAX. 1955. *Custom and conflict in Africa.* Oxford: Blackwell.

GOFFMAN, ERVING. 1959. *The presentation of self in everyday life.* Garden City, N.Y.: Doubleday.

GOFFMAN, ERVING. 1961a. *Encounters.* Indianapolis: Bobbs-Merrill.

GOFFMAN, ERVING. 1961b. *Asylums: Essays on the social situation of mental patients and other inmates.* Garden City, N.Y.: Anchor Books.

GOFFMAN, ERVING. 1974. *Frame analysis: An essay on the organization of experience.* Cambridge, Mass.: Harvard University Press.

GOLDFARB, JEFFREY C. 1992. *After the fall: The pursuit of democracy in Central Europe.* New York: Basic Books.

GOLDIN-MEADOW, SUSAN. 1983. Gestural communication in deaf children: Noneffect of parental input on language development. *Science,* 221:372–373.

GOLDIN-MEADOW, SUSAN, and CAROLYN MYLANDER. 1984. Gestural communication in deaf children. *Monographs of the Society for Research in Child Development,* 49, No. 207.

GOLDSCHEIDER, FRANCES K., and CALVIN GOLDSCHEIDER. 1991. The intergenerational flow of income: Family structure and the status of black Americans. *Journal of Marriage and the Family,* 53:499–508.

GOLDSTONE, JACK A. 1982. The comparative and historical study of revolutions. *Annual Review of Sociology,* 8:187–207.

GOLDSTONE, JACK A. 1986. The comparative and historical study of revolutions. In J. A. Goldstone, ed., *Revolutions.* San Diego: Harcourt Brace Jovanovich.

GOLDSTONE, JACK A. 1991. *Revolution and rebellion in the early modern world.* Berkeley: University of California Press.

GOLDTHORPE, J. E. 1984. *The sociology of the Third World,* 2nd ed. New York: Cambridge University Press.

GOLEMAN, DANIEL. 1984. A bias puts self at center of events. *New York Times* (June 12):19, 23.

GOLEMAN, DANIEL. 1989. For many, turmoil of aging erupts in the 50's, studies find. *New York Times* (February 7):17, 21.

GOLEMAN, DANIEL. 1991a. Doctors find comfort is a potent medicine. *New York Times* (November 26):B5.

GOLEMAN, DANIEL. 1991b. Anatomy of a rumor: Fear feeds it. *New York Times* (June 4):B1, B7.

GOLEMAN, DANIEL. 1992. Family rituals may promote better emotional adjustment. *New York Times* (March 11):B6.

GOLEMAN, DANIEL. 1994. Mental decline in aging need not be inevitable. *New York Times* (April 26):B5, B7.

GONOS, GEORGE. 1977. "Situation" versus "frame": The "interactionist" and the "structuralist" analyses of everyday life. *American Sociological Review,* 42:854–867.

GOODE, ERICA E. 1993. The culture of illness. *U.S. News & World Report* (February 15):74–76.

GOODE, WILLIAM J. 1959. The theoretical importance of love. *American Sociological Review,* 24:38–47.

GOODE, WILLIAM J. 1960. Illegitimacy in Caribbean social structure. *American Sociological Review,* 25:21–31.

GOODE, WILLIAM J. 1963. *World revolution and family patterns.* New York: Basic Books.

GOODE, WILLIAM J. 1972. The place of force in human society. *American Sociological Review,* 37:507–519.

GORNICK, VIVIAN, and B. K. MORAN. 1971. *Women in sexist society.* New York: New American Library.

GOTTFREDSON, MICHAEL R., and TRAVIS HIRSCHI. 1990. *A general theory of crime.* Stanford, Calif.: Stanford University Press.

GOUGH, E. KATHLEEN. 1959. The Nayars and the definition of marriage. *Journal of the Royal Anthropological Institute,* 89:23–24.

GOULD, CAROL GRANT. 1983. Out of the mouths of beasts. *Science* 83, 4 (April):69–72.

GOULD, ROGER V. 1991. Multiple networks and mobilization in the Paris Commune, 1871. *American Sociological Review,* 56:716–729.

GOVE, WALTER R. 1970. Societal reaction as an explanation of mental illness: An evaluation. *American Sociological Review,* 35:873–884.

GOYDER, JOHN. 1987. *The silent minority: Nonrespondents on sample surveys.* Boulder, Colo.: Westview.

GRASMICK, HAROLD G., and GEORGE J. BRYJAK. 1980. The deterrent effect of perceived severity of punishment. *Social Forces,* 59:471–491.

GRASSIAN, STUART. 1983. Psychopathological effects of solitary confinement. *American Journal of Psychiatry,* 140:1450–1454.

GRAY, BRADFORD H. 1991. *The profit motive and patient care: The changing accountability of doctors and hospitals.* Cambridge, Mass.: Harvard University Press.

GREELEY, ANDREW M. 1989. *Religious change in America.* Cambridge, Mass.: Harvard University Press.

GREENHOUSE, STEVEN. 1994. State Dept. finds widespread abuse of world's women. *New York Times* (February 3):A1, A6.

GREENWALD, A. G., and A. R. PRATKANIS. 1984. The self. In R. S. Wyer and T. K. Srull, eds., *Handbook of social cognition.* Hillsdale, N.J.: Erlbaum.

GREENWOOD, PETER W. 1982. *Selective incapacitation.* Santa Monica, Calif.: Rand Corporation.

GREIDER, WILLIAM. 1992. *Who will tell the people: The betrayal of American democracy.* New York: Simon and Schuster.

GREIF, GEOFFREY L. 1985. *Single fathers.* Lexington, Mass.: Lexington Books.

GRENIER, GUILLERMO J. 1988. *Inhuman relations: Quality circles and anti-unionism in American industry.* Philadelphia: Temple University Press.

GRIGSBY, JILL S. 1992. Women change places. *American Demographics,* 14 (November):46–50.

GRIMES, MICHAEL D. 1991. *Class in twentieth-century American sociology: An analysis of theories and measurement strategies.* New York: Praeger.

GROB, GERALD N. 1983. *Mental illness and American society, 1875–1940.* Princeton, N.J.: Princeton University Press.

GROSS, A. 1977. Marriage counseling for unwed couples. *New York Times Magazine* (April 24):52+.

GRUSKY, DAVID, and ROBERT M. HAUSER. 1984. Comparative social mobility revisited: Models of convergence and divergence in 16 countries. *American Sociological Review,* 49:19–38.

GUBRIUM, JABER F., and JAMES A. HOLSTEIN. 1990. *What is family?* Mountain View, Calif.: Mayfield.

GUELZOW, MAUREEN, GLORIA W. BIRD, and ELIZABETH H. KOBALL. 1991. An exploratory path analysis of the stress process for dual-career men and women. *Journal of Marriage and the Family,* 53:151–164.

GURNEY, PATRICK J. 1981. Historical origins of ideological denial: The case of Marx in American sociology. *American Sociologist,* 16:196–201.

GURR, TED R. 1970. *Why men rebel.* Princeton, N.J.: Princeton University Press.

GUTFELD, ROSE. 1991. Eight of 10 Americans are environmentalists, at least so they say. *Wall Street Journal* (August 2):A1, A8.

GUTH, JAMES L. 1993. Secular scholars and the religious right. *Chronicle of Higher Education* (April 7):B3, B5.

HAAS, AIN. 1993. Social inequality in aboriginal North America: A test of Lenski's theory. *Social Forces,* 72:295–313.

HACKER, HELEN MAYER. 1951. Women as a minority group. *Social Forces,* 30, 60–69.

HACKER, HELEN MAYER. 1974. Women as a minority group: Twenty years late. In Florence Denmark, ed., *Who discriminates against women.* Beverly Hills, Calif.: Sage.

HADAWAY, C. KIRK, PENNY LONG MARLER, and MARK CHAVES. 1993. What the polls don't show: A closer look at U.S. church attendance. *American Sociological Review,* 58:741–752.

HADDEN, JEFFREY K. 1987a. Religious broadcasting and the mobilization of the New Christian Right. *Journal for the Scientific Study of Religion,* 26:1–24.

HADDEN, JEFFREY K. 1987b. Toward desacralizing secularization theory. *Social Forces,* 65:587–611.

HADLEY, ARTHUR T. 1978. *The empty polling booth.* Englewood Cliffs, N.J.: Prentice-Hall.

HAGAN, JOHN. 1980. The legislation of crime and delinquency: A review of theory, method, and research. *Law and Society Review,* 14:603–628.

HAGAN, JOHN. 1989. *Structural criminology.* New Brunswick, N.J.: Rutgers University Press.

HAGAN, JOHN, ILENE N. BERNSTEIN, and CELESTA ALBONETTI. 1980. The differential sentencing of white-collar offenders. *American Sociological Review,* 42:587–598.

HAGAN, JOHN, and JEFFREY LEON. 1977. Rediscovering delinquency: Social history, political ideology, and the sociology of law. *American Sociological Review,* 42:587–598.

HAGE, JERALD, and CHARLES H. POWERS. 1992. *Post-industrial lives: Roles and relationships in the 21st century.* Newbury Park, Calif.: Sage.

HAGEDORN, JOHN M. 1988. *People and folks: Gangs, crime and the underclass in a rustbelt city.* Chicago: Lakeview Press.

HALAL, WILLIAM E., and ALEXANDER I. NIKITIN. 1990. One world. *The Futurist* (November/December): 8–14.

HALL, EDWARD T. 1966. *The hidden dimension.* Garden City, N.Y.: Doubleday.

HALPERN, DIANE F. 1992. *Sex differences in cognitive abilities,* 2nd ed. Hillsdale, N.J.: Erlbaum.

HAMBURG, DAVID A., and RUBY TAKANISHI. 1989. Preparing for life: The critical transition of adolescence. *American Psychologist,* 44:825–827.

HAMPER, BEN RIVETHEAD 1991. *Tales from the assembly line.* New York: Warner.

HANLEY, RUTH. 1988. Students hesitant about teaching other races. Columbus (Ohio) *Dispatch* (February 4):2.

HANNIGAN, JOHN A. 1991. Social movement theory and the sociology of religion: Toward a new synthesis. *Sociological Analysis,* 52:311–331.

HARDEE-CLEAVELAND, KAREN. 1989. Is eight enough? *American Demographics,* 11 (June):60.

HARDIN, GARRETT J. 1968. The tragedy of the commons. *Science,* 162:1243–1248.

HARE, A. PAUL. 1976. *Handbook of small group research,* 2nd ed. New York: Free Press.

HARE, A. PAUL, and HERBERT H. BLUMBERG. 1988. *Dramaturgical analysis of social interaction.* New York: Praeger.

HAREVEN, TAMARA K. 1982. *Family time and industrial time.* New York: Cambridge University Press.

HAREVEN, TAMARA K. 1987. Historical analysis of the family. In Marvin B. Sussman and Suzanne K. Steinmetz, eds., *Handbook of marriage and the family.* New York: Plenum.

HARKINS, STEPHEN G., and KATE SZYMANSKI. 1989. Social loafing and group evaluation. *Journal of Personality and Social Psychology,* 56:934–941.

HARRINGTON, MICHAEL. 1976. *The twilight of capitalism.* New York: Simon and Schuster.

HARRIS, CHAUNCEY D., and EDWARD L. ULLMAN 1945. The nature of cities. *Annals of the American Academy of Political and Social Science,* 242:7–17.

HARRIS, LOUIS. 1989. Examine these myths of the 80's. *New York Times* (May 19):23.

HARSANYI, ZSOLT, and RICHARD HUTTON. 1979. Those genes that tell the future. *New York Times Magazine* (November 18):194–205.

HARTMAN, CURTIS, and STEVEN PEARLSTEIN. 1987. The job of working. *INC.* (November):61–71.

HARWOOD, JOHN, and GERALDINE BROOKS. 1993. Other nations elect women to lead them, so why doesn't U.S.? *Wall Street Journal* (December 14):A1, A9.

HAUSER, ROBERT, and DAVID FEATHERMAN. 1977. *The process of stratification.* New York: Academic Press.

HAWKINS, DARNELL F. 1987. Beyond anomalies: Rethinking the conflict perspective on race and criminal punishment. *Social Forces,* 65:719–745.

HAWLEY, AMOS H. 1963. Community power and urban-renewal success. *American Journal of Sociology,* 68:422–431.

HAYS, CHARLOTTE. 1984. The evolution of Ann Landers: From prim to progressive. *Public Opinion,* 6 (January):11–13.

HAYS, LAURIE. 1987. Pay problems: How couples react when wives out-earn husbands. *Wall Street Journal* (June 19):19.

HEARST, PATRICIA CAMPBELL. 1981. *Every secret thing.* Garden City, N.Y.: Doubleday.

HEATH, DWIGHT B. 1958. Sexual division of labor and cross-cultural research. *Social Forces,* 37:77–79.

HECKATHORN, DOUGLAS D. 1988. Collective sanctions and the emergence of prisoner's dilemma. *American Journal of Sociology,* 94:535–562.

HECKATHORN, DOUGLAS D. 1990. Collective sanctions and compliance norms: A formal theory of group-mediated social control. *American Sociological Review,* 55:366–384.

HECKHAUSEN, JUTTA, ROGER A. DIXON, and PAUL B. BALTES. 1989. Gains and losses in development throughout adulthood as perceived by different adult age groups. *Developmental Psychology,* 25:109–121.

HEILBRONER, ROBERT. 1993. *21st century capitalism.* New York: Norton.

HENDRICK, SUSAN S., and CLYDE HENDRICK. 1992. *Romantic love.* Newbury Park, Calif.: Sage.

HENRY, LAWRENCE. 1990. Companies combat rising employee theft. *Investor's Daily* (January 11):1.

HENRY, TAMARA. 1994. Violence in schools grows more severe. *USA Today* (January 6):D1.

HEPWORTH, JOSEPH T., and STEPHEN G. WEST. 1988. Lynchings and the economy: A time-series reanalysis of Hovland and Sears (1940). *Journal of Personality and Social Psychology,* 55:239–247.

HERBERG, WILL. 1955. *Protestant-Catholic-Jew.* Garden City, N.Y.: Doubleday.

HERBERT, BOB. 1993. Nurses on the advance. *New York Times* (December 15):A15.

HERDT, GILBERT. 1982. *Rituals of manhood: Male initiation in Papua New Guinea.* Berkeley: University of California Press.

HERMAN, EDWARD S. 1981. *Corporate control, corporate power.* Cambridge: Cambridge University Press.

HERMAN, JUDITH, and LISA HIRSCHMAN. 1981. Families at risk for father-daughter incest. *American Journal of Psychiatry,* 138:967–970.

HERRING, CEDRIC, and KAREN ROSE WILSON-SADBERRY. 1993. Preference or necessity? Changing work roles of black and white women, 1973–1990. *Journal of Marriage and the Family,* 55:314–325.

HERSKOVITS, MELVILLE J. 1945. The processes of cultural change. In Ralph Linton, ed., *The science of man in the world crisis.* New York: Columbia University Press.

HERTZLER, J. O. 1961. *American social institutions.* Boston: Allyn and Bacon.

HERZOG, A. RAGULA, JAMES S. HOUSE, and JAMES N. MORGAN. 1991. Relation of work and retirement to health and well-being in old age. *Psychology and Aging,* 6:202–211.

HETHERINGTON, E. MAVIS. 1989. Coping with family transitions: Winners, losers, and survivors. *Child Development,* 60:1–14.

HEWITT, JOHN P. 1979. *Self and society,* 2nd ed. Boston: Allyn and Bacon.

HICKSON, DAVID J. 1987. Decision making at the top of organizations. *Annual Review of Sociology,* 13:165–192.

HILBERT, RICHARD A. 1992. *The classical roots of ethnomethodology: Durkheim, Weber, and Garfinkel.* Chapel Hill: University of North Carolina Press.

HILL, REUBEN. 1964. Methodological issues in family development research. *Family Process,* 33:186–206.

HILLER, E. T. 1933. *Principles of sociology.* New York: Harper & Row.

HILLKIRK, JOHN. 1991a. High salaries draw fire in austere times. *USA Today* (April 26):B1, B2.

HILLKIRK, JOHN. 1991b. The pay gap. *USA Today* (April 26):B1.

HILTS, PHILIP J. 1994. 6% of pregnant women say they were battered. *New York Times* (March 4):A8.

HIMES, JOSEPH. 1973. *Racial conflict in American society.* Columbus, Ohio: Charles E. Merrill.

HIMMELFARB, GERTRUDE. 1984. *The idea of poverty: England in the early industrial age.* New York: Knopf.

HINKLE, ROSCOE. 1980. *Founding theory of American sociology: 1881–1915.* London: Routledge & Kegan Paul.

HOCK, ELLEN, and DEBRA K. DEMEIS. 1990. Depression in mothers of infants: The role of maternal employment. *Developmental Psychology,* 26:285–291.

HODGE, ROBERT, and DONALD TREIMAN. 1968. Class identification in the United States. *American Journal of Sociology,* 73:535–547.

HOEBEL, E. A. 1958. *Man in the primitive world,* 2nd ed. New York: McGraw-Hill.

HOFFERTH, SANDRA L., and DEBORAH A. PHILLIPS. 1991. Child care policy research. *Journal of Social Issues,* 47:1–13.

HOFFMAN, CURT, and NANCY HURST. 1990. Gender stereotypes: Perception or rationalization? *Journal of Personality and Social Psychology,* 58:197–208.

HOFFMAN, LOIS. 1989. Effects of maternal employment in the two-parent family. *American Psychologist,* 44:283–292.

HOLDEN, CONSTANCE. 1987. Why do women live longer than men? *Science,* 238:158–160.

HOLDEN, CONSTANCE. 1989. Street-wise crack research. *Science,* 246:1376–1381.

HOLDEN, KAREN C., and PAMELA J. SMOCK. 1991. The economic costs of marital dissolution: Why do women bear a disproportionate cost? *Annual Review of Sociology,* 17:51–78.

HOLLAND, EARLE. 1983. Science. Columbus (Ohio) *Dispatch* (November 13):E6.

HONAN, WILLIAM H. 1994. Cost of 4-year degree passes $100,000 mark. *New York Times* (May 4):A13.

HOOKS, GREGORY. 1990a. The rise of the Pentagon and U.S. state building: The defense program as industrial policy. *American Journal of Sociology,* 96:358–404.

HOOKS, GREGORY. 1990b. From an autonomous to a captured state agency: The decline of the New Deal in agriculture. *American Sociological Review,* 55:29–43.

HORAN, PATRICK. 1978. Is status attainment research atheoretical? *American Sociological Review,* 43:534–541.

HORN, JACK C., and JEFF MEER. 1987. The vintage years. *Psychology Today,* 21 (May):76–84+.

HORNING, DONALD. 1970. Blue-collar theft: Conceptions of property, attitudes toward pilfering, and work-group norms in a modern industrial plant. In Erwin O. Smigel and H. Laurence Ross, eds., *Crimes against bureaucracy.* New York: Van Nostrand/Reinhold.

HOROWITZ, CARL. 1994. What's environmental racism? *Investor's Business Daily* (March 2):1, 2.

HOSTETLER, JOHN A. 1980. *Amish society.* Baltimore: Johns Hopkins University Press.

HOUT, MICHAEL. 1988. More universalism, less structural mobility: The American occupational structure in the 1980s. *American Journal of Sociology,* 93:1358–1400.

HOUT, MICHAEL, and JOSHUA R. GOLDSTEIN. 1994. How 4.5 million Irish immigrants became 40 million Irish Americans: Demographic and subjective aspects of the ethnic composition of white Americans. *American Sociological Review,* 59:64–82.

HOWLETT, DEBBIE. 1992. Chicago flood was tip of the iceberg. *USA Today* (April 29):1A, 2A.

HOYT, HOMER. 1939. *The structure and growth of residential neighborhoods in American cities.* Washington, D.C.: Federal Housing Administration.

HSU, FRANCES L. K. 1943. Incentives to work in primitive communities. *American Sociological Review,* 8:638–642.

HUEY, JOHN. 1994. The new post-heroic leadership. *Fortune* (February 21):42–50.

HUFF-CORZINE, LIN, JAY CORZINE, and DAVID C. MOORE. 1991. Deadly connections: Culture, poverty, and the direction of lethal violence. *Social Forces,* 69:715–732.

HUGHES, CHARLES C. 1968. Medical care: Ethnomedicine. In D. Sills, ed., *International Encyclopedia of Social Sciences,* Vol. 10. New York: Macmillan.

HUMPHREY, JOHN A., and TIMOTHY J. FOGARTY. 1987. Race and plea-bargained outcomes: A research note. *Social Forces,* 66:176–182.

HUNTLEY, STEVE. 1983. America's Indians: "Beggars in our own land." *U.S. News & World Report* (May 23):70–72.

HURLEY, DAN. 1988. Getting help from helping. *Psychology Today,* 22 (January):63–67.

HUSTON, ALETHA C., VONNIE C. McLOYD, and CYNTHIA GARCIA COLL. 1994. Children and poverty: Issues in contemporary research. *Child Development,* 65:275–282.

HYDE, JANET SHIBLEY. 1984. How large are gender differences in aggression? A developmental meta-analysis. *Developmental Psychology,* 20:722–736.

HYDE, JANET SHIBLEY. 1991. *Half the human experience: The psychology of women.* Lexington, Mass.: Heath.

HYDE, JANET S., ELIZABETH FENNEMA, and SUSAN J. LAMON. 1990. Gender differences in mathematics performance: A meta-analysis. *Psychological Bulletin,* 107:139–155.

HYMAN, HERBERT H., and ELEANOR SINGER. 1968. Introduction. In H. H. Hyman and E. Singer, eds., *Readings in reference group theory and research.* New York: Free Press.

IANNACCONE, LAURENCE R. 1988. A formal model of church and sect. *Supplement to the American Journal of Sociology,* 94:S241–268.

IMPERATO-McGINLEY, J., R. E. PETERSON, E. GAUTIER, and N. STURLA. 1979. Androgens and the evolution of male-gender identity among male pseudohermaphrodites with a 5a-reductase deficiency. *New England Journal of Medicine,* 300:1233–1237.

IM THURN, E. F. 1883. *Among the Indians of Guiana.* London: Kegan Paul, Trench & Trubner.

INGHAM, ALAN G. 1974. The Ringelmann effect: Studies of group size and group performance. *Journal of Experimental Social Psychology,* 10:371–384.

INGRASSIA, LAWRENCE. 1993. Gay, lesbian groups seek to expunge bias they see in language. *Wall Street Journal* (May 3):A1, A8.

INTONS-PETERSON, MARGARET JEAN. 1988. *Gender concepts of Swedish and American Youth,* Hillsdale, N.J.: Erlbaum.

ISAAC, LARRY, and WILLIAM R. KELLY. 1981. Racial insurgency, the state, and welfare expansion: Local and national level evidence from the postwar United States. *American Journal of Sociology,* 86:1348–1386.

ISHIDA, HIROSHI, JOHN H. GOLDTHORPE, and ROBERT ERIKSON. 1991. Intergenerational class mobility in postwar Japan. *American Journal of Sociology,* 96:954–992.

IYENGAR, SHANTO. 1991. *Is anyone responsible? How television frames political issues.* Chicago: University of Chicago Press.

JACKMAN, MARY R., and ROBERT W. JACKMAN. 1983. *Class awareness in the United States.* Berkeley: University of California Press.

JACKSON, PHILIP W. 1969. *Life in classrooms.* New York: Holt, Rinehart and Winston.

JACKSON, WALTER A. 1990. *Gunnar Myrdal and America's conscience: Social engineering and racial liberalism, 1938–1987.* Chapel Hill: University of North Carolina Press.

JACOBS, JERRY A. 1989. Long-term trends in occupational segregation by sex. *American Journal of Sociology,* 95:160–173.

JACOBSON, ROBERT L. 1992. Professors who teach more are paid less, study finds. *Chronicle of Higher Education* (April 15):A17.

JAFFEE, DAVID. 1993. The unique nature of the human factor: A theme for courses in organization. *Teaching Sociology,* 21:60–67.

JAIN, UDAY. 1989. *The psychological consequences of crowding.* Newbury Park, Calif.: Sage.

JAMES, DAVID R., and MICHAEL SOREF. 1981. Profit constraints on managerial autonomy: Managerial theory and the unmaking of the corporation president. *American Sociological Review,* 46:1–18.

JAMES, JOHN. 1951. A preliminary study of the size determinant in small group interaction. *American Sociological Review,* 16:474–477.

JANIS, IRVING. 1972. *Victims of groupthink.* Boston: Houghton Mifflin.

JANIS, IRVING L. 1982. *Groupthink,* 2nd ed. Boston: Houghton Mifflin.

JANIS, IRVING L. 1989. *Crucial decisions: Leadership in policy-making and crisis management.* New York: Free Press.

JAYNES, GERALD D., and ROBIN M. WILLIAMS, EDS. 1989. *A common destiny: Blacks and American society.* Washington, D.C.: National Academy Press.

JENCKS, CHRISTOPHER. 1992. *Rethinking social policy: Race, poverty, and the underclass.* Cambridge, Mass.: Harvard University Press.

JENKINS, J. CRAIG. 1985. *The politics of insurgency: The farm worker movement in the 1960s.* New York: Columbia University Press.

JENKINS, J. CRAIG, and BARBARA G. BRENTS. 1989. Social protest, hegemonic competition, and social reform: A political struggle interpretation of the origins of the American welfare state. *American Sociological Review,* 54:891–909.

JENKINS, J. CRAIG, and BARBARA G. BRENTS. 1991. Capitalists and social security: What did they really want? *American Sociological Review,* 56:129–132.

JENNESS, DIAMOND. 1922. The life of the Copper Eskimo. *Report of the Canadian Arctic Expedition, 1913–1918,* Vol. 12.

JENSEN, ARTHUR R., and L. B. ROSENFELD. 1974. Influence of mode presentation, ethnicity, and social class on teachers' evaluations of students. *Journal of Educational Psychology,* 66:540–547.

JENSEN, MICHAEL C. 1994. A revolution only markets could love. *Wall Street Journal* (January 3):A6.

JESSOP, BOB. 1985. *Nicos Poulantzas: Marxist theory and political strategy.* New York: St. Martin's Press.

JESSOP, BOB. 1990. *State theory: Putting the capitalist state in its place.* University Park: Pennsylvania State University Press.

JOHNSON, HAYES. 1988. Hispanics, blacks are dropping out. *USA Today* (March 23):D3.

JOHNSON, ROBERT. 1990. Heavenly gifts: Preaching a gospel of acquisitiveness, a showy sect prospers. *Wall Street Journal* (December 11):A1, A6.

JONES, JACQUELINE. 1992. *The dispossessed: America's underclasses from the Civil War to the present.* New York: Basic Books.

JOSEPHY, ALVIN M., JR. 1991. *The Civil War in the American West.* New York: Knopf.

KAGAN, JEROME, RICHARD B. KEARSLEY, and PHILIP R. ZELAZO. 1978. *Infancy: Its place in human development.* Cambridge, Mass.: Harvard University Press.

KAIN, EDWARD L. 1984. Surprising singles. *American Demographics,* 6 (August):16–19+.

KAIN, EDWARD L. 1990. *The myth of family decline: Understanding families in a world of rapid social change.* Lexington, Mass.: Lexington Books.

KALISH, SUSAN. 1994. International migration: New findings on magnitude, importance. *Population Today,* 22:1–3.

KAMEDA, TATSUYA, MARK F. STASSON, JAMES H. DAVIS, CRAIG D. PARKS, and SUZI K. ZIMMERMAN. 1992. Social dilemmas, subgroups, and motivation loss in task-oriented groups: In search of an "optimal" team size in division of work. *Social Psychology Quarterly,* 55:47–56.

KAMERMAN, JACK B. 1988. *Death in the midst of life: Social and cultural influences on death, grief, and mourning.* Englewood Cliffs, N.J.: Prentice-Hall.

KAMOLNICK, PAUL. 1988 *Classes: A Marxist critique.* Dix Hills, N.Y.: General Hall.

KANE, EMILY W. 1992. Race, gender, and attitudes toward gender stratification. *Social Psychology Quarterly,* 55:311–320.

KAPLAN, DAVID A. 1993. Is it torture or tradition? *Newsweek* (December 20):124.

KAPLAN, HOWARD B., ROBERT J. JOHNSON, and CAROL A. BAILEY. 1987. Deviant peers and deviant behavior: Further elaborations of a model. *Social Psychology Quarterly,* 50:277–284.

KARAU, STEVEN J., and KIPLING D. WILLIAMS. 1993. Social loafing: A meta-analytic review and theoretical integration. *Journal of Personality and Social Psychology,* 65:681–706.

KAREN, DAVID. 1990. Toward a political-organizational model of gatekeeping. The case of elite colleges. *Sociology of Education,* 63:227–240.

KATZ, IRWIN, and R. GLEN HASS. 1988. Racial ambivalence and American value conflict: Correlational and priming studies of dual cognitive structures. *Journal of Personality and Social Psychology,* 55:893–905.

KATZ, SIDNEY. 1983. Active life expectancy. *New England Journal of Medicine,* 309:1218–1224.

KAUFMAN, MICHAEL T. 1979. Abandoned effort after the Gandhi era. *New York Times* (November 11):E7.

KEATLEY, ROBERT. 1994. Cure for Sweden's current economic ills may lie in dismantling model system. *Wall Street Journal* (April 1):A4.

KEITA, GWENDOLYN PURYEAR, and STEVEN L. SAUTER, EDS. 1992. *Work and well-being: An agenda for the 1990s.* Washington, D.C.: American Psychological Association.

KELLER, HELEN. 1904. *The story of my life.* Garden City, N.Y.: Doubleday.

KELLER, JOHN J. 1992. Some AT&T clients gripe that cost cuts are hurting service. *Wall Street Journal* (January 24):A1, A4.

KELLER, SUZANNE. 1963. *Beyond the ruling class.* New York: Random House.

KEMPER, THEODORE D., and RANDALL COLLINS. 1990. Dimensions of microinteraction. *American Journal of Sociology,* 96:32–68.

KENDALL-TACKETT, KATHLEEN A., LINDA MEYER WILLIAMS, and DAVID FINKELHOR. 1993. Impact of sexual abuse on children: A review and synthesis of recent empirical studies. *Psychological Bulletin,* 113:164–180.

KENISTON, KENNETH. 1970. Youth: A "new" stage in life. *American Scholar* (Autumn):586–595.

KERBO, HAROLD R. 1983. *Social stratification and inequality.* New York: McGraw-Hill.

KERR, NORMAN L. 1983. Motivation losses in small groups: A social dilemma analysis. *Journal of Personality and Social Psychology,* 45:819–828.

KERR, PETER. 1988a. Crime study finds high use of drugs at time of arrest. *New York Times* (January 22):1, 9.

KERR, PETER. 1988b. Measuring how drugs, crime mix. *New York Times* (January 24):E26.

KERTZER, DAVID I. 1991. Household history and sociological theory. *Annual Review of Sociology,* 17:155–179.

KESSLER, RONALD C., and JAMES A. McRAE, JR. 1981. Trends in sex and psychological distress. *American Sociological Review,* 46:443–452.

KESSLER-HARRIS, ALICE. 1990. *A women's wage: Historical meanings and social consequences.* Lexington: University Press of Kentucky.

KETT, J. F. 1977. *Rites of passage: Adolescence in America, 1870 to the present.* New York: Basic Books.

KIDD, ROBERT F., and ELLEN F. CHAYET. 1984. Why do victims fail to report? The psychology of criminal victimization. *Journal of Social Issues,* 40:39–50.

KILBORN, PETER T. 1992. Sad distinction for the Sioux: Homeland is no. 1 in poverty. *New York Times* (September 20):1, 14.

KILLIAN, LEWIS M. 1990. Race relations and the nineties: Where are the dreams of the sixties? *Social Forces,* 69:1–13.

KILPATRICK, JAMES J. 1990. U.S. poverty study poorly misleading. Columbus (Ohio) *Dispatch* (September 29):A6.

KIM, JAE-ON. 1987. Social mobility, status inheritance, and structural constraints: Conceptual and methodological considerations. *Social Forces,* 65:783–805.

KIMMEL, D. C. 1980. *Adulthood and aging.* New York: Wiley.

KINGSTON, PAUL WILLIAM, and STEVEN L. NOCK. 1987. Time together among dual-earner couples. *American Sociological Review,* 52:391–400.

KISER, EDGAR, and MICHAEL HECHTER. 1991. The role of general theory in comparative-historical sociology. *American Journal of Sociology,* 97:1–30.

KITSON, GAY C., and WILLIAM M. HOLMES. 1992. *Portrait of divorce: Adjustment to marital breakdown.* New York: Guilford.

KITSON, GAY C., and LESLIE A. MORGAN. 1990. The multiple consequences of divorce: A decade review. *Journal of Marriage and the Family,* 52:913–924.

KLASS, PERRI. 1987. When the doctor-patient relationship breaks down. *Discover,* 8(March):16.

KLEIN, KATHERINE J. 1987. Employee stock ownership and employee attitudes: A test of three models. *Journal of Applied Psychology,* 72:319–332.

KLINEBERG, OTTO. 1986. SPSSI and race relations, in the 1950s and after. *Journal of Social Issues,* 42:53–59.

KLUCKHOHN, CLYDE. 1960. *Mirror for man.* Greenwich, Conn.: Fawcett.

KLUEGEL, JAMES R. 1990. Trends in whites' explanations of the black-white gap in socioeconomic status, 1977–1989. *American Sociological Review,* 55:512–525.

KLUEGEL, JAMES R., and ELIOT R. SMITH. 1982. Whites' beliefs about blacks' opportunity. *American Sociological Review,* 47:518–532.

KNEALE, DENNIS. 1987. Cutting output, IBM tells some workers: Move, retire or quit. *Wall Street Journal* (April 8): 1,18.

KNODEL, JOHN E. 1988. *Demographic behavior in the past: A study of fourteen German village populations in the eighteenth and nineteenth centuries.* Cambridge, Mass.: Cambridge University Press.

KNOTTNERUS, J. DAVID. 1987. Status attainment research and its image of society. *American Sociological Review,* 52:113–121.

KNOTTNERUS, J. DAVID. 1991. Status attainment's image of society: Individual factors, structural effect, and the transformation of the class structure. *Sociological Spectrum,* 11:147–176.

KOENIG, FREDERICK. 1982. Today's conditions make U.S. "ripe for the rumor mill." *U.S. News & World Report* (December 6):40.

KOENIG, FREDERICK. 1985. *Rumor in the marketplace: The social psychology of commercial hearsay.* Dover, Mass.: Auburn House.

KOHLBERG, LAWRENCE. 1966. A cognitive-developmental analysis of children's sex-role concepts and attitudes. In Eleanor

E. Maccoby, ed., *The development of sex differences.* Stanford, Calif.: Stanford University Press.

KOHLBERG, LAWRENCE. 1969. Stage and sequence: The cognitive-developmental approach to socialization. In D. A. Goslin, ed., *Handbook of socialization theory and research.* Chicago: Rand McNally.

KOHLBERG, LAWRENCE, and D. Z. ULLIAN. 1974. Stages in the development of psychosexual concepts and attitudes. In R. C. Friedman, R. N. Richart, and R. L. Van de Wiele, eds., *Sex differences in behavior.* New York: Wiley.

KOHN, MELVIN L., and CARMI SCHOOLER. 1973. Occupational experience and psychological functioning: An assessment of reciprocal effects. *American Sociological Review,* 38:97–118.

KOHN, MELVIN L., and CARMI SCHOOLER. 1982. Job conditions and personality: A longitudinal assessment of their reciprocal effects. *American Journal of Sociology,* 87:1257–1286.

KOHN, MELVIN L., and CARMI SCHOOLER. 1983. *Work and personality: An inquiry into the impact of social stratification.* Norwood, N.J.: Ablex.

KOHN, MELVIN L., ATSUSHI NAOI, CARRIE SCHOENBACH, CARMI SCHOOLER, and KAZIMIERZ M. SLOMCZYNSKI. 1990. Position in the class structure and psychological functioning in the United States, Japan, and Poland. *American Journal of Sociology,* 95:964–1008.

KOLATA, GINA. 1993. Strong family aid to elderly is found. *New York Times* (May 3):A7.

KOLBERT, ELIZABETH. 1991. Sexual harassment at work is pervasive survey suggests. *New York Times* (October 11):A1, A11.

KOLKO, GABRIEL. 1962. *Wealth and power in America.* New York: Praeger.

KOLLOCK, PETER. 1993. "An eye for an eye leaves everyone blind": Cooperation and accounting systems. *American Sociological Review,* 58:768–786.

KOMAROVSKY, MIRRA. 1991. Reflections on feminist scholarship. *Annual Review of Sociology,* 17:1–25.

KOMORITA, SAMUEL S., and JOAN M. BARTH. 1985. Components of reward in social dilemmas. *Journal of Personality and Social Psychology,* 48:364–373.

KONNER, MELVIN. 1993. *Medicine at the crossroads: The crisis in health care.* New York: Pantheon.

KORETZ, GENE. 1992. Just how welcome is the job market to college grads? *Business Week* (November 9):22.

KORNHAUSER, WILLIAM. 1959. *The politics of mass society.* New York: Free Press.

KORPI, WALTER. 1989. Power, politics, and state autonomy in the development of social citizenship: Social rights during sickness in eighteen OECD countries since 1930. *American Sociological Review,* 54:309–328.

KOSELKA, RITA. 1993. Businessman's dilemma. *Forbes* (October 11):107–109.

KRAAR, LOUIS. 1990. The U.S. mood: Ever optimistic. *Fortune* (March 26):19–26.

KRAFFT, SUSAN. 1994. Why wives earn less than husbands. *American Demographics,* 15 (January):16–17.

KRAMER, RODERICK M., and MARILYNN B. BREWER. 1984. Effects of group identity on resource use in a simulated commons dilemma. *Journal of Personality and Social Psychology,* 46:1044–1057.

KRAUTHAMMER, CHARLES. 1993. The indictment of Ozzie and Harriet. *The Globe and Mail* (November 27):D5.

KRIESI, HANSPETER. 1989. New social movements and the new class in the Netherlands. *American Journal of Sociology,* 94:1078–1116.

KRYMKOWSKI, DANIEL H. 1991. The process of status attainment among men in Poland, the U.S., and West Germany. *American Sociological Review,* 56:46–59.

KRYMKOWSKI, DANIEL H., and TADEUSZ K. KRAUZE. 1992. Occupational mobility in the year 2000: Projections for American men and women. *Social Forces,* 71:145–157.

KÜBLER-ROSS, ELISABETH. 1969. *On death and dying.* New York: Macmillan.

KÜBLER-ROSS, ELISABETH. 1981. *Living with death and dying.* New York: Macmillan.

KUHN, MANFORD. 1964. Major trends in symbolic interaction theory in the past twenty-five years. *Sociological Quarterly,* 5:61–84.

KUHN, THOMAS, 1962. *The structure of scientific revolutions.* Chicago: University of Chicago Press.

KULIK, JAMES A., PAUL SLEDGE, and HEIKE I. M. MAHLER. 1986. Self-confirmatory attribution, egocentrism, and the perpetuation of self-beliefs. *Journal of Personality and Social Psychology,* 50:587–594.

KURDEK, LAWRENCE A. 1993. The allocation of household labor in gay, lesbian, and heterosexual married couples. *Journal of Social Issues,* 49:127–139.

KURZ, KARIN, and WALTER MULLER. 1987. Class mobility in the industrial world. *Annual Review of Sociology,* 13:417–442.

KUTTNER, ROBERT. 1994. Pat Moynihan's blarney on health care. *Business Week* (February 14):18.

LABICH, KENNETH. 1994. Class in America. *Fortune* (February 7):114–126.

LADD, EVERETT C. 1987. Polls help map political terrain but hold pitfalls. *Christian Science Monitor* (November 6):3–4.

LANG, O. 1946. *Chinese family and society.* New Haven, Conn.: Yale University Press.

LANGAN, PATRICK A. 1991. America's soaring prison population. *Science,* 251:1568–1573.

LANGLEY, MONICA. 1984. AT&T has call for a new corporate culture. *Wall Street Journal* (February 28):32.

LARSON, JAN. 1991. Cohabitation is a premarital step. *American Demographics,* 13 (November):20–21.

LARSON, JAN. 1992. Understanding stepfamilies. *American Demographics,* 14 (July):36–40.

LASLETT, PETER. 1974. *Household and family in past time.* New York: Cambridge University Press.

LASLETT, PETER. 1976. Societal development and aging. In R. Binstock and E. Shanas, eds., *Handbook of aging and the social sciences.* New York: Van Nostrand/Reinhold.

LASSWELL, HAROLD. 1936. *Politics: Who gets what, when and how.* New York: McGraw-Hill.

LATANE, BIBB, KIPLING WILLIAMS, and STEPHEN HARKINS. 1979. Many hands make light the work: The causes and consequences of social loafing. *Journal of Personality and Social Psychology,* 37:822–832.

LAUB, JOHN H., and ROBERT J. SAMPSON. 1991. The Sutherland-Glueck debate: On the sociology of criminological knowledge. *American Journal of Sociology,* 96:1402–1440.

LAUER, ROBERT H., and WARREN H. HANDEL. 1983. *Social psychology,* 2nd ed. Englewood Cliffs, N.J.: Prentice-Hall.

LAWLER, EDWARD J. 1992. Affective attachments to nested groups: A choice-process theory. *American Sociological Review,* 57:327–339.

LAWLER, EDWARD J., CECILIA RIDGEWAY, and BARRY MARKOVSKY. 1993. Structural social psychology and the micro-macro problem. *Sociological Theory,* 11:269–290.

LAWLER, EDWARD J., and JEONGKOO YOON. 1993. Power and the emergence of commitment behavior in negotiated exchange. *American Sociological Review,* 58:465–481.

LAWSON, CAROL. 1989. Girls still apply makeup, boys fight wars. *New York Times* (June 15):15, 19.

LEARY, MARK R., and ROBIN M. KOWALSKI. 1990. Impression management: A literature review and two-component model. *Psychological Bulletin,* 107:34–47.

LEARY, WARREN E. 1991. Hypertension among blacks tied to bias, poverty and diet. *New York Times* (February 6):A12.

LE BON, GUSTAV. 1896. *The crowd: A study of the popular mind.* London: Ernest Benn.

LECHNER, FRANK J. 1991. The case against secularization: A rebuttal. *Social Forces,* 69:1103–1119.

LEE, FELICIA R. 1989. Poor self-image hurts blacks' health, doctors say. *New York Times* (July 17):9.

LEE, FELICIA R. 1990. "Model minority" label adds to the burdens of Asian students. *New York Times* (March 20):A14.

LEE, GARY R. 1977. *Family structure and interaction: A comparative analysis.* Philadelphia: Lippincott.

LEE, VALERIE E., and ANTHONY S. BRYK. 1989. A multi-level model of the social distribution of high school achievement. *Sociology of Education,* 62:172–192.

LEHMAN, EDWARD W. 1988. The theory of the state versus the state of theory. *American Sociological Review,* 53:807–823.

LEISINGER, KLAUS M. 1988. Multinationals and the Third World. *New York Times* (February 21):F3.

LEMERT, EDWIN M. 1951. *Social pathology: A systematic approach to the theory of sociopathic behavior.* New York: McGraw-Hill.

LEMERT, EDWIN M. 1972. *Human deviance, social problems and social control,* 2nd ed. Englewood Cliffs, N.J.: Prentice-Hall.

LENSKI, GERHARD E. 1966. *Power and privilege.* New York: McGraw-Hill.

LENSKI, GERHARD, and JEAN LENSKI. 1982. *Human societies: An introduction to macrosociology,* 4th ed. New York: McGraw-Hill.

LENSKI, GERHARD E., and JEAN LENSKI. 1987. *Human societies: An introduction to macrosociology,* 5th ed. New York: McGraw-Hill.

LEPENIES, W. 1988. *Between literature and science: The rise of sociology.* Cambridge, Mass.: Cambridge University Press.

LESLIE, STUART W. 1993. *The Cold War and American science: The military-industrial-academic complex at M.I.T. and Stanford.* New York: Columbia University Press.

LEUNG, ELEANOR H. L., and HARRIET L. RHEINGOLD. 1981. Development of pointing as a social gesture. *Developmental Psychology,* 17:215–220.

LEVINSON, DANIEL J. 1986. A conception of adult development. *American Psychologist,* 41:3–13.

LEVINSON, DANIEL J., ET AL. 1978. *The seasons of a man's life.* New York: Knopf.

LEVINSON, HARRY. 1964. Money aside, why spend life working? *National Observer* (March 9):20.

LEVI-STRAUSS, CLAUDE. 1956. The family. In Harry L. Shapiro, ed., *Man, culture and society.* New York: Oxford University Press.

LEVY, FRANK. 1987. *Dollars and dreams: The changing American income distribution.* New York: Russell Sage Foundation.

LEVY, FRANK. 1989. What's really squeezing the middle class? *Wall Street Journal* (July 26):A14.

LEVY, FRANK, and RICHARD C. MICHEL. 1991. *The economic future of American families.* Washington, D.C.: Urban Institute.

LEWIN, KURT, RONALD LIPPITT, and RALPH K. WHITE. 1939. Patterns of aggressive behavior in experimentally created "social climates." *Journal of Social Psychology,* 10:271–299.

LEWIN, TAMAR. 1990. Too much retirement time? A move is afoot to change it. *New York Times* (April 22):1, 36.

LEWIS, MICHAEL, MARGARET WOLAN SULLIVAN, CATHERINE STANGER, and MAYA WEISS. 1989. Self development and self-conscious emotions. *Child Development,* 60:146–156.

LEWIS, OSCAR. 1959. *Five families: Mexican case studies in the culture of poverty.* New York: Basic Books.

LEWIS, OSCAR. 1961. *The children of Sanchez.* New York: Random House.

LEWIS, OSCAR. 1966. *La vida: A Puerto Rican family in the culture of poverty, San Juan and New York.* New York: Random House.

LEWIS, SUZAN, DAFNA N. IZRAELI, and HELEN HOOTSMANS, EDS. 1992. *Dual-earner families: International perspectives.* Newbury Park, Calif.: Sage.

LEWONTIN, R. C., STEVEN ROSE, and LEON J. KAMIN. 1984. *Not in our genes.* New York: Pantheon.

LIBBY, ROGER W. 1977. Creative singlehood as a sexual lifestyle: Beyond marriage as a rite of passage. In R. W. Libby and R. N. Whitehurst, eds., *Marriage and alternatives.* Glenview, Ill.: Scott, Foresman.

LIEBERSON, STANLEY. 1970. Stratification and ethnic groups. *Sociological Inquiry,* 40:172–181.

LIEBERSON, STANLEY, and MARY C. WATERS. 1993. The ethnic responses of whites: What causes their instability, simplification, and inconsistency? *Social Forces,* 72:421–450.

LIEBOW, ELLIOT. 1967. *Tally's corner.* Boston: Little, Brown.

LIMBER, JOHN. 1977. Language in child and chimp? *American Psychologist,* 32:280–295.

LINDBLOM, CHARLES E. 1990. *Inquiry and change: The troubled attempt to understand and shape society.* New Haven, Conn.: Yale University Press.

LINDEN, DANA WECHSLER, and NANCY ROTENIER. 1994. Goodbye to Berle & Means. *Forbes* (January 3):100–103.

LINDEN, EUGENE. 1990. Is the planet on the back burner? *Time* (December 24):48–50.

LINDEN, FABIAN. 1984. Myth of the disappearing middle class. *Wall Street Journal* (January 23):18.

LINDEN, FABIAN. 1986. The dream is alive. *American Demographics,* 8 (June):4–6.

LINDEN, FABIAN. 1989. What's really squeezing the middle class? *Wall Street Journal* (July 26):A14.

LINDORFF, DAVE. 1992. *Marketplace medicine: The rise of the for-profit hospital chains.* New York: Bantam Books.

LINDSEY, ROBERT. 1987. Colleges accused of bias to stem Asians' gain. *New York Times* (January 19):8.

LINK, BRUCE G., FRANCIS T. CULLEN, ELMER STRUENING, PATRICK E. SHROUT, and BRUCE P. DOHRENWEND. 1989. A modified labeling theory approach to mental disorders: An empirical assessment. *American Sociological Review,* 54:400–423.

LINK, BRUCE G., MARY CLARE LENNON, and BRUCE P. DOHRENWEND. 1993. Socioeconomic status and depression: The role of occupations involving direction, control, and planning. *American Journal of Sociology,* 98:1351–1387.

LINK, BRUCE G., JERROLD MIROTZNIK, and FRANCIS T. CULLEN. 1991. The effectiveness of stigma coping orientations: Can negative consequences of mental labeling be avoided? *Journal of Health and Social Behavior,* 32:302–320.

LINTON, RALPH. 1936. *The study of man.* New York: Appleton-Century-Crofts.

LINTON, RALPH. 1937. One hundred per cent American. *American Mercury,* 40 (April):427–429.

LINTON, RALPH. 1945. *The cultural background of personality.* New York: Appleton-Century-Crofts.

LIPSET, SEYMOUR MARTIN. 1982. Social mobility in industrial societies. *Public Opinion,* 5 (June/July):41–44.

LIPSET, SEYMOUR MARTIN. 1993. Reflections on capitalism, socialism and democracy. *Journal of Democracy,* 4:43–53.

LIPSET, SEYMOUR MARTIN. 1994. The social requisites of democracy revisited. *American Sociological Review,* 59:1–22.

LIPSET, SEYMOUR M., and REINHARD BENDIX. 1951. Social status and social structure. *British Journal of Sociology,* 2:150–160.

LIPSET, SEYMOUR MARTIN, MARTIN A. TROW, and JAMES S. COLEMAN. 1956. *Union democracy.* New York: Free Press.

LIPTON, DOUGLAS, ROBERT MARTINSON, and JUDITH WILKS.

1975. *The effectiveness of correctional treatment: A survey of treatment evaluation studies.* New York: Praeger.

LISKA, ALLEN E. 1987. A critical examination of macro perspectives on crime control. *Annual Review of Sociology,* 13: 67–88.

LIVESLEY, W. J., and D. B. BROMLEY. 1973. *Person perception in childhood and adolescence.* New York: Wiley.

LIZOTTE, ALAN J. 1978. Extra-legal factors in Chicago's criminal courts: Testing the conflict model of criminal justice. *Social Problems,* 25:564–580.

LOBEL, THALMA E., and JUDITH MENASHRI. 1993. Relations of conceptions of gender-role transgressions and gender constancy to gender-typed toy preferences. *Developmental Psychology,* 29:150–155.

LOCKE, JOHN L. 1993. *The child's path to spoken language.* Cambridge, Mass.: Harvard University Press.

LOGAN, WILLIAM BRYANT. 1993. The futurists. *Worth* (December/January):62–67.

LONDON, BRUCE, and BRUCE A. WILLIAMS. 1988. Multinational corporate penetration, protest, and basic needs provision in non-core nations: A cross-national analysis. *Social Forces,* 66:747–773.

LONDON, BRUCE, and BRUCE A. WILLIAMS. 1990. National political, international dependency, and basic needs provision: A cross-national analysis. *Social Forces,* 69:565–584.

LOO, CHALSA M. 1991. *Chinatown: Most time, hard time.* New York: Praeger.

LOOMIS, CAROL J. 1988. The new J.P. Morgans. *Fortune* (February 29):44–52.

LOPATA, HELENA ZNANIECKI. 1973. *Widowhood in an American city.* Cambridge, Mass.: Schenkman.

LOPATA, HELEN Z. 1981. Widowhood and husband satisfaction. *Journal of Marriage and the Family,* 43:439–450.

LOPEZ, JULIE AMPARANO. 1992. Study says women face glass walls as well as ceilings. *Wall Street Journal* (March 3):B1.

LOWENTHAL, MARJORIE F. 1964. Social isolation and mental illness in old age. *American Sociological Review,* 29:20–30.

LOWIE, ROBERT H. 1935. *The Crow Indians.* New York: Farrar & Rinehart.

LUBLIN, JOANN S. 1993. As more men become "trailing spouses," firms help them cope. *Wall Street Journal* (April 13):A1, A4.

LUCAL, BETSY. 1994. Class stratification in introductory textbooks: Relational or distributional models? *Teaching Sociology,* 22:139–150.

LUKACS, GEORG. 1922/1968. *History and class consciousness.* Cambridge, Mass.: MIT Press.

LUKES, STEVEN. 1977. Alienation and anomie. In *Essays in social theory.* New York: Columbia University Press.

LUMSDEN, CHARLES J., and EDWARD O. WILSON. 1981. *Genes, mind, and culture.* Cambridge, Mass.: Harvard University Press.

LYND, ROBERT S., and HELEN MERRILL LYND. 1929. *Middletown: A study in American culture.* New York: Harcourt, Brace & World.

LYND, ROBERT S., and HELEN MERRILL LYND. 1937. *Middletown in transition: A study in cultural conflicts.* New York: Harcourt, Brace & World.

LYNN, MICHAEL, and ANDREW OLDENQUIST. 1986. Egoistic and nonegoistic motives in social dilemmas. *American Psychologist,* 41:529–534.

LYON, DEBORAH, and JEFF GREENBERG. 1991. Evidence of codependency in women with alcoholic parent: Helping out Mr. Wrong. *Journal of Personality and Social Psychology,* 61:435–439.

MCADAM, DOUG, and RONNELLE PAULSEN. 1993. Specifying the relationship between social ties and activism. *American Journal of Sociology,* 99:640–667.

MCCAULEY, CLARK. 1989. The nature of social influence in groupthink: Compliance and internalization. *Journal of Personality and Social Psychology,* 57:250–260.

MACCOBY, ELEANOR E. 1990. Gender and relationships. *American Psychologist,* 45:513–520.

MACCOBY, ELEANOR E., and CAROL N. JACKLIN. 1974. *The psychology of sex differences.* Stanford, Calif.: Stanford University Press.

MACCOBY, ELEANOR E., and CAROL N. JACKLIN. 1980. Sex differences in aggression: A rejoinder and reprise. *Child Development,* 51:964–980.

MACCOUN, ROBERT J. 1993. Drugs and the law: A psychological analysis of drug prohibition. *Psychological Bulletin,* 113: 497–512.

MACEWEN, KARYL, and JULIAN BARLING. 1991. Effects of maternal employment experiences on children's behavior via mood, cognitive difficulties, and parenting behavior. *Journal of Marriage and the Family,* 53:635–644.

MCFADDEN, ROBERT D. 1987. The Mafia of the 1980's: Divided and under siege. *New York Times* (March 11):1, 19.

MACFARQUHAR, EMILY. 1994. The war against women. *U.S. News & World Report* (March 28):42–48.

MCGEE, REECE. 1975. *Points of departure.* Hinsdale, Ill.: Dryden Press.

MCGRANE, BERNARD. 1993a. Zen sociology: Don't just do something, stand there! *Teaching Sociology,* 21:79–84.

MCGRANE, BERNARD. 1993b. Zen sociology: The un-TV experiment. *Teaching Sociology,* 21:85–89.

MCGUIRE, MEREDITH B. 1981. *Religion: The social context.* Belmont, Calif: Wadsworth.

MACKINNON, CAROL E., and DONNA KING. 1988. Day care: A review of literature, implications for policy, and critique of resources. *Family Relations,* 37:229–236.

MACKLIN, ELEANOR D. 1974. Going very steady. *Psychology Today,* 8 (November):53–59.

MACKLIN, ELEANOR D. 1978. Nonmarital heterosexual cohabitation. *Marriage and the Family Review,* 1:2–10.

MCLAUGHLIN, STEVEN D., BARBARA D. MELBER, JOHN O. G. BILLY, DENISE M. ZIMMERIE, LINDA D. WINGES, and TERRY R. JOHN-SON. 1988. *The changing lives of American women.* Chapel Hill: University of North Carolina Press.

MCLAUGHLIN, STEVEN D., and MICHAEL MICKLIN. 1983. The timing of the first birth and changes in personal efficacy. *Journal of Marriage and the Family,* 45:47–55.

MCMICHAEL, PHILIP. 1990. Incorporating comparison within a world-historical perspective: An alternative comparative method. *American Sociological Review,* 55:385–397.

MCNALL, SCOTT G., RHONDA F. LEVINE, and RICK FANTASIA, EDS. 1991. *Bringing class back in: Contemporary and historical perspectives.* Boulder, Colo.: Westview Press.

MCNAMEE, STEPHEN J. 1987. Du Pont-state relations. *Social Problems,* 34:1–17.

MCPHAIL, CLARK. 1989. Blumer's theory of collective behavior: The development of a non-symbolic interaction explanation. *Sociological Quarterly,* 30:401–423.

MCQUILLAN, KEVIN. 1984. Modes of production and demographic patterns in nineteenth-century France. *American Journal of Sociology,* 89:1324–1346.

MACY, MICHAEL W. 1990. Learning theory and the logic of critical mass. *American Sociological Review,* 55:809–826.

MACY, MICHAEL W. 1991. Chains of cooperation: Threshold effects in collective action. *American Sociological Review,* 56: 730–747.

MACY, MICHAEL W. 1993. Backward-looking social control. *American Sociological Review,* 58:819–836.

MADDOX, GEORGE L., and JAMES WILEY. 1976. Scope, concepts and methods in the study of aging. In R. H. Binstock and E. Shanas, eds., *Handbook of aging and the social sciences.* New York: Van Nostrand.

MAHAR, MAGGIE. 1994. A change of place. *Barron's* (March 21):33–38.

MALABRE, ALFRED L., JR. 1991. U.S. living standards are slipping and were even before recession. *Wall Street Journal* (June 17):A1, A4.

MALINOSKY-RUMMELL, ROBIN, and DAVID J. HANSEN. 1993. Long-term consequences of childhood physical abuse. *Psychological Bulletin,* 114:68–79.

MALINOWSKI, BRONISLAW. 1929. *The sexual life of savages in northwestern Melanesia.* New York: Eugenics Press.

MALINOWSKI, BRONISLAW. 1964. Parenthood—the basics of social structure. In Rose Coser, ed., *The family: Its structure and functions.* New York: St. Martin's Press.

MANCHESTER, WILLIAM. 1993. A world lit only by change. *U.S. News & World Report* (October 25):6–9.

MANIS, JEROME G., and BERNARD N. MELTZER. 1994. Chance in human affairs. *Sociological Theory,* 12:45–56.

MANN, JAMES. 1983. One-parent family: The troubles and the joys. *Newsweek* (November 28):57–62.

MANN, LEON, JAMES W. NEWTON, and J. M. INNES. 1982. A test between deindividuation and emergent norm theories of crowd aggression. *Journal of Personality and Social Psychology,* 42:260–272.

MARE, ROBERT D., and MEEI-SHENN TZENG. 1989. Father's ages

and the social stratification of sons. *American Journal of Sociology,* 95:108–131.

MARGLIN, STEPHEN. 1974. What the bosses do: The origins and functions of hierarchy in capitalist production. *Review of Radical Political Economics,* 6:60–112.

MARKOFF, JOHN. 1991. Denser, faster, cheaper: The microchip in the 21st century. *New York Times* (December 29):F5.

MARKS, CAROLE. 1991. The urban underclass. *Annual Review of Sociology,* 17:445–466.

MARMOR, THEODORE R., JERRY L. MARSHAW, and PHILIP L. HARVEY. 1990. *America's misunderstood welfare state: Persistent myths, enduring realities.* New York: Basic Books.

MARS, GERALD. 1974. Dock pilferage: A case study in occupational theft. In *Deviance and social control.* London: Tavistock.

MARSH, HERBERT W. 1986. Global self-esteem: Its relation to specific facets of self-concept and their importance. *Journal of Personality and Social Psychology,* 51:1224–1236.

MARTIN, CAROL LYNN, and JANE K. LITTLE. 1990. The relation of gender understanding to children's sex-typed preferences and gender stereotypes. *Child Development,* 61:1427–1439.

MARTINSON, ROBERT. 1974. What works?—Questions and answers about prison reform. *The Public Interest,* 35:22–54.

MARTY, MARTIN E., and R. SCOTT APPLEBY. 1992. *The glory and the power: The fundamentalist challenge to the modern world.* Boston: Beacon Press.

MARX, GARY T., and JAMES L. WOODS. 1975. Strands of theory and research in collective behavior. *Annual Review of Sociology,* 1:363–428.

MARX, KARL. 1844/1960. Estranged labour—Economic and philosophic manuscripts of 1844. In C. W. Mills, ed., *Images of man.* New York: Braziller.

MARX, KARL. 1867/1906. *Capital* Vol. 1. New York: Modern Library.

MARX, KARL. 1970. *Critique of Hegel's "philosophy of right."* Trans. A. O'Malley and J. O'Malley. London: Cambridge University Press.

MARX, KARL, and FRIEDRICH ENGELS. 1848/1955. *The communist manifesto.* S. H. Beer, ed. New York: Appleton-Century Crofts.

MASSEY, DOUGLAS S. 1990. American apartheid: Segregation and the making of the underclass. *American Journal of Sociology,* 96:329–357.

MATSUEDA, ROSS L., and KAREN HEIMER. 1987. Race, family structure, and delinquency: A test of differential association and social control theories. *American Sociological Review,* 52:826–840.

MAUGH, THOMAS H., II 1990. Chimp uses grammar, Georgia researcher says. Columbus (Ohio) *Dispatch* (November 4):D7.

MAUKSCH, HANS O. 1972. Ideology, interaction, and patient care in hospitals. *Social Science and Medicine,* 7:817–830.

MAYER, MARTIN. 1990. *The greatest-ever bank robbery: The collapse of the savings and loan industry.* New York: Scribner's.

MAYNARD, DOUGLAS W., and STEVEN E. CLAYMAN. 1991. The diversity of ethnomethodology. *Annual Review of Sociology,* 17:385–418.

MAZUR, ALLAN. 1985. A biosocial model of status in face-to-face primate groups. Social groups. *Social Forces,* 64:377–402.

MAZUR, ALLAN, EUGENE ROSA, MARK FAUPEL, JOSHUA HELLER, RUSSELL LEEN, and BLAKE THURMAN. 1980. Physiological aspects of communication via mutual gaze. *American Journal of Sociology,* 86:50–74.

MEAD, GEORGE HERBERT. 1934/1962. *Mind, self, and other.* Chicago: University of Chicago Press.

MEAD, LAWRENCE M. 1992. *The new politics of poverty: The nonworking poor in America.* New York: Basic Books.

MEHAN, HUGH. 1992. Understanding inequality in schools: The contribution of interpretive studies. *Sociology of Education,* 65:1–20.

MEHRABIAN, ALBERT. 1968. Communication without words. *Psychology Today,* 2 (September):53–55.

MEIER, ROBERT F., and WELDON J. JOHNSON. 1977. Deterrence as social control: The legal and extralegal production of conformity. *American Sociological Review,* 42:292–304.

MELLOAN, GEORGE. 1993. Why America tops Europe in job creation. *Wall Street Journal* (December 13):A15.

MELTZER, BERNARD, JAMES PETRAS, and LARRY REYNOLDS. 1975. *Symbolic interactionism: Genesis, varieties, and criticisms.* London: Routledge & Kegan Paul.

MENAGHAN, ELIZABETH G. 1991. Work experiences and family interaction processes: The long reach of the job? *Annual Review of Sociology,* 17:419–444.

MENDES, H. A. 1976. Single fathers. *Family Coordinator,* 25:439–444.

MERTON, ROBERT. 1968. *Social theory and social structure,* rev. ed. New York: Free Press.

MESSICK, DAVID M., HANK WILKE, MARILYNN B. BREWER, RODERICK M. KRAMER, PATRICIA E. ZEMKE, and LAYTON LUI. 1983. Individual adaptations and structural change as solutions to social dilemmas. *Journal of Personality and Social Psychology,* 44:294–309.

MESSNER, STEVEN F. 1989. Economic discrimination and societal homicide rates: Further evidence on the cost of inequality. *American Sociological Review,* 54:587–611.

MESSNER, STEVEN F., and MARVIN D. KROHN. 1990. Class, compliance structures, and delinquency: Assessing integrated structural-Marxist theory. *American Journal of Sociology,* 96:300–328.

MEŠTROÍC, STJEPAN G. 1991. Point of view. *Chronicle of Higher Education* (September 25):A56.

MEYER, JOHN W., FRANCISCO O. RAMIREZ, and YASEMIN NUHOGLU SOYSAL. 1992. World expansion of mass education, 1870–1980. *Sociology of Education,* 65:128–149.

MICHELS, ROBERT. 1911/1966. *Political parties.* New York: Free Press.

MICKELSON, ROSLYN ARLIN. 1990. The attitude-achievement

paradox among black adolescents. *Sociology of Education,* 63:44–61.

MIDDLETON, RUSSELL. 1962. A deviant case: Brother-sister and father-daughter marriage in ancient Egypt. *American Sociological Review,* 27:603–611.

MILGRAM, STANLEY. 1977. *The individual in a social world.* Reading, Mass.: Addison-Wesley.

MILGRAM, STANLEY, and HANS TOCH. 1969. Collective behavior. Crowds and social movements. In G. Lindzey and E. Aronson, eds., *The handbook of social psychology,* 2nd ed., Vol. 2. Reading, Mass.: Addison-Wesley.

MILIBAND, RALPH. 1969. *The state in capitalist society.* New York: Basic Books.

MILLER, JOANNE, KAZIMIERZ M. SLOMCZYNSKI, and MELVIN L. KOHN. 1985. Continuity of learning-generalization: The effect of job on men's intellective process in the United States and Poland. *American Journal of Sociology,* 91:593–615.

MILLER, JUDITH. 1992. The Islamic wave. *New York Times Magazine* (May 31):23–42.

MILLER, WALTER B. 1958. Lower-class culture as a generating milieu of gang delinquency. *Journal of Social Issues,* 14:5–19.

MILLER, WALTER B. 1975. *Violence by youth gangs and youth groups as a crime problem in major American cities.* Washington, D.C.: U.S. Government Printing Office.

MILLS, C. WRIGHT. 1956. *The power elite.* New York: Oxford University Press.

MILLS, C. WRIGHT. 1959. *The sociological imagination.* New York: Oxford University Press.

MILNE, L. 1924. *The home of an eastern clan.* Oxford: Clarendon Press.

MILNER, MURRAY, JR. 1987. Theories of inequality: An overview and a strategy for synthesis. *Social Forces,* 65:1053–1089.

MINER, ANNE S. 1991. Organizational evolution and the social ecology of jobs. *American Sociological Review,* 56:772–785.

MINER, HORACE. 1956. Body ritual among the Nacirema. *American Anthropologist,* 58:503–507.

MINTZ, BETH, and MICHAEL SCHWARTZ. 1985. *The power of American business.* Chicago: University of Chicago Press.

MINTZ, STEVEN, and SUSAN KELLOGG. 1988. *Domestic revolutions: A social history of American family life.* New York: Free Press.

MIROWSKY, JOHN, and CATHERINE E. ROSS. 1990. The consolation-prize theory of alienation. *American Journal of Sociology,* 95:1505–1535.

MISCHEL, WALTER. 1970. Sex-typing and socialization. In P. H. Mussen, ed., *Carmichael's manual of child psychology,* 3rd ed., Vol. 2. New York: Wiley.

MITCHELL, JANE E., LAURA A. BAKER, and CAROL NAGY JACKLIN. 1989. Masculinity and femininity in twin children: Genetic and environmental factors. *Child Development,* 60:1475–1485.

MOADDEL, MANSOOR. 1992. Ideology as episodic discourse: The case of the Iranian revolution. *American Sociological Review,* 57:353–379.

MOADDEL, MANSOOR. 1994. Political conflict in the world economy: A cross-national analysis of modernization and world-system theories. *American Sociological Review,* 59:276–303.

MOLM, LINDA D. 1989. Punishment power: A balancing process in power-dependence relations. *American Journal of Sociology,* 94:1392–1418.

MOLM, LINDA D. 1991. Affect and social exchange: Satisfaction in power-dependence relations. *American Sociological Review,* 56:475–493.

MONEY, JOHN. 1987. Sin, sickness, or status? Homosexual gender identity and psychoneuroendocrinology. *American Psychologist,* 42:384–399.

MONK, RICHARD C., and JOEL HENDERSON. 1986. Teaching concepts: Culture and ethnocentrism. In Norman R. Layne and Patrick E. Fontane, *Innovative techniques for teaching sociology: Essays from the teaching newsletter.* Washington, D.C.: ASA Teaching Resources Center.

MONEY, JOHN, and P. TUCKER. 1975. *Sexual signatures: On being a man or a woman.* Boston: Little, Brown.

MOORE, DIDI. 1984. It's either me or your job! *Working Woman* (April):108–111.

MOORE, JOAN W. 1991. *Going down to the barrio: Homeboys and homegirls in change.* Philadelphia: Temple University Press.

MORELL, VIRGINIA. 1994. An anthropological culture shift. *Science,* 264:20–22.

MORRIS, ALDON D. 1993. Birmingham confrontation reconsidered: An analysis of the dynamics and tactics of mobilization. *American Sociology Review,* 58:621–636.

MORRIS, MARTINA, ANNETTE D. BERNHARDT, and MARK S. HANDCOCK. 1994. Economic inequality: New methods for new trends. *American Sociological Review,* 59:205–219.

MORROW, LANCE. 1991. Rough justice. *Time* (April 1):16–17.

MORTENSON, THOMAS G., and ZHIJUN WU. 1991. *High school graduation and college participation of young adults by family income backgrounds 1970 to 1989.* Iowa City, Iowa: American College Testing, Educational and Social Research.

MORTIMER, JEYLAN T., and ROBERTA G. SIMMONS. 1978. Adult socialization. *Annual Review of Sociology,* 4:421–454.

MOSKOWITZ, BREYNE ARLENE. 1978. The acquisition of language. *Scientific American,* 239 (November):92–108.

MOUZELIS, NICOS. 1992. The interaction order and the micro-macro distinction. *Sociological Theory,* 10:122–128.

MOTTL, TAHI L. 1980. The analysis of countermovements. *Social Problems,* 27:620–635.

MOYNIHAN, DANIEL PATRICK. 1985. *Family and nation.* Cambridge, Mass.: Harvard University Press.

MOYNIHAN, DANIEL PATRICK. 1993. *Pandaemonium: Ethnicity and International Politics.* New York: Oxford University Press.

MOYNIHAN, MARY MINARD. 1989. Writing in sociology classes: Informal assignments. *Teaching Sociology,* 17:346–350.

MULKEY, LYNN M., ROBERT L. CRAIN, and ALEXANDER J. C. HARRINGTON. 1992. One-parent households and achievement:

Economic and behavioral explanations of a small effect. *Sociology of Education,* 65:48–65.

MULLER, EDWARD N. 1988. Democracy, economic development, and income inequality. *American Sociological Review,* 53:50–68.

MURA, DAVID. 1992. Bashed in the U.S.A. *New York Times* (April 2):A15.

MURDOCK, GEORGE P. 1934. *Our primitive contemporaries.* New York: Macmillan.

MURDOCK, GEORGE P. 1935. Comparative data on the division of labor by sex. *Social Forces,* 15:551–553.

MURDOCK, GEORGE PETER. 1949. *Social structure.* New York: Macmillan.

MURDOCK, GEORGE P. 1950a. Feasibility and implementation of comparative community research. *American Sociological Review,* 15:713–720.

MURDOCK, GEORGE P. 1950b. *Outline of cultural materials,* 3rd ed. New Haven, Conn.: Yale University Press.

MURDOCK, GEORGE PETER. 1967. *Ethnographic atlas.* Pittsburgh: University of Pittsburgh Press.

MURRAY, CHARLES. 1986. What does the government owe the poor? *Harpers* (April):35–47.

MURRAY, CHARLES. 1994. Does welfare bring more babies? *American Enterprise,* 5 (January/February):52–59.

MURSTEIN, BERNARD I. 1972. Physical attractiveness and marital choice. *Journal of Personality and Social Psychology,* 22:8–12.

MURSTEIN, BERNARD I. 1976. *Who will marry whom?* New York: Springer.

MUSTO, DAVID F. 1987. *The American disease: Origins of narcotic control.* New York: Oxford University Press.

MUTCHLER, JAN E., and JEFFREY A. BURR. 1991. Racial differences in health and health care service utilization in later life: The effect of socioeconomic status. *Journal of Health and Social Behavior,* 32:342–356.

MYDANS, SETH. 1990. Study of Indians' remains: Science or sacrilege? *New York Times* (October 19):A9.

MYDANS, SETH. 1991. Videotape of beating by officers puts full glare on brutality issue. *New York Times* (March 18):A1, A8.

MYRDAL, GUNNAR. 1944. *An American dilemma.* New York: Harper.

NAGEL, JOANE. 1994. *American Indian ethnic renewal: Red power and the transformation of identity and culture.* New York: Oxford University Press.

NAISBITT, JOHN. 1982. *Megatrends.* New York: Warner Books.

NAISBITT, JOHN, and PATRICIA ABURDENE. 1989. *Megatrends 2000.* New York: Morrow.

NASAR, SYLVIA. 1987. Do we live as well as we used to? *Fortune* (September 14):32–44.

NASAR, SYLVIA. 1992. Fed report gives new data on gains by richest in 80's. *New York Times* (April 21):A1, A6.

NATIONAL CENTER FOR HEALTH STATISTICS. 1993. *Annual summary of births, marriages, divorces, and deaths: United States, 1992. Monthly Vital Statistics Report,* 41 (September 28).

NATIONAL COMMISSION ON EXCELLENCE IN EDUCATION. 1983. *A nation at risk: The imperative for educational reform.* Washington, D.C.: U.S. Department of Education.

NAVARRO, MIREYA. 1992. Agencies slowed in effort to widen definitions of AIDS. *New York Times* (February 10):A1, A12.

NAZARIO, SONIA L. 1992. Medical science seeks a cure for doctors suffering from boorish bedside manner. *Wall Street Journal* (March 17):B1.

NEFF, ROBERT. 1994. The many faces of free enterprise. *Business Week* (January 24):17–18.

NEUGARTEN, BERNICE L. 1979. Time, age, and the life cycle. *American Journal of Psychiatry,* 136:887–894.

NEUGARTEN, BERNICE L., and DAIL A. NEUGARTEN. 1987a. *Forum,* 62:25–27.

NEUGARTEN, BERNICE L., and DAIL A. NEUGARTEN. 1987b. The changing meanings of age. *Psychology Today,* 21 (May):29–33.

NEUHOUSER, KEVIN. 1992. Democratic stability in Venezuela: Elite consensus or class compromise? *American Sociological Review,* 57:117–135.

NEW YORK TIMES. 1991. New York bridges found failing. (April 2):A12.

NEW YORK TIMES. 1993. Rise in health-care costs is linked to social behavior. *New York Times.* (February 23):B-7.

NEWCOMB, THEODORE M. 1950. *Social psychology.* New York: Holt, Rinehart and Winston.

NEWMAN, BARRY. 1979. Do multinationals really create jobs in the Third World? *Wall Street Journal* (September 25):1, 16.

NEWMAN, KATHERINE S. 1993. *Declining fortunes: The withering of the American dream.* New York: Basic Books.

NIEBUHR, H. RICHARD. 1929. *The social sources of denominationalism.* New York: Holt, Rinehart and Winston.

NOBLE, BARBARA PRESLEY. 1992. And now the "sticky floor." *New York Times* (November 22):F23.

NOBLE, KENNETH B. 1989. Low commodity prices vex life in Ivory Coast. *New York Times* (November 19):6.

NOEL, DONALD M. 1972. *The origins of American slavery and racism.* Columbus, Ohio: Charles E. Merrill.

NOTESTEIN, FRANK W. 1945. Population—The long view. In Theodore W. Schultz, ed., *Food for the world.* Chicago: University of Chicago Press.

NOTTELMANN, EDITHA D. 1987. Competence and self-esteem during transition from childhood to adolescence. *Development Psychology,* 23:441–450.

NULAND, SHERWIN B. 1994. *Reflections on life's final chapter.* New York: Knopf.

NUSSBAUM, BRUCE. 1988. Help wanted from the multinationals. *Business Week* (February 29):68–70.

O'CONNOR, JAMES. 1973. *The fiscal crisis of the state.* New York: St. Martin's Press.

O'DELL, JERRY W. 1968. Group size and emotional interaction. *Journal of Personality and Social Psychology,* 8:75–78.

OFFICE OF TECHNOLOGY ASSESSMENT. 1988. *Technology and the American economic transition.* Washington, D.C.: U.S. Government Printing Office.

OGBURN, WILLIAM F. 1922. *Social change.* New York: Huebsch.

O'HARE, WILLIAM. 1987. Separating welfare fact from fiction. *Wall Street Journal* (December 14):22.

O'HARE, WILLIAM P. 1992. America's minorities—the demographics of diversity. *Population Bulletin,* 47, No. 4.

OLIVER, CHARLES. 1994. Freedom and economic growth. *Investor's Business Daily* (May 27):1, 2.

OLIVER, PAMELA E., and GERALD MARWELL. 1988. The paradox of group size in collective action: A theory of the critical mass. II. *American Sociological Review,* 53:1–8.

OLSEN, MARVIN E. 1970. *Power in societies.* New York: Macmillan.

OLSON, DANIEL V. A., and JACKSON W. CARROLL. 1992. Religiously based politics: Religious elites and the public. *Social Forces,* 70:765–786.

OLSON, DAVID J., and PHILIP MEYER. 1975. *To keep the republic.* New York: McGraw-Hill.

OLZAK, SUSAN. 1990. The political context of competition: Lynching and urban racial violence, 1882–1914. *Social Forces,* 69:395–421.

OLZAK, SUSAN. 1992. *The dynamics of ethnic competition and conflict.* Stanford, Calif.: Stanford University Press.

OMI, MICHAEL, and HOWARD WINANT. 1987. *Racial formation in the United States: From the 1960s to the 1980s.* New York: Routledge & Kegan Paul.

OPINION ROUNDUP. 1987. Class differences. *Public Opinion,* 10 (May/June):21–29.

OPP, KARL-DIETER. 1988. Grievances and participation in social movements. *American Sociological Review,* 53:853–864.

OPP, KARL-DIETER, and CHRISTIANE GERN. 1993. Dissident groups, personal networks, and spontaneous cooperation: The East German revolution of 1989. *American Sociological Review,* 58:659–680.

ORESKES, MICHAEL. 1990a. America's politics loses way as its vision changes world. *New York Times* (March 18):1, 16.

ORESKES, MICHAEL. 1990b. Alienation from government grows. *New York Times* (September 19):A15.

ORLOFF, ANN SHOLA. 1993. Gender and the social rights of citizenship: The comparative analysis of gender relations and welfare states. *American Sociological Review,* 58:303–328.

OTTEN, ALAN L. 1989. Wives may not benefit when men do chores. *Wall Street Journal* (October 30):B1.

OTTEN, ALAN L. 1990. Healthy aging hinges on income, education. *Wall Street Journal* (December 24):B1.

OTTEN, ALAN L. 1991. Asian-Americans become more heterogeneous. *Wall Street Journal* (March 13):B1.

OTTEN, ALAN L. 1992. Poor health is linked to lack of education. *Wall Street Journal* (January 3):B1.

OTTEN, ALAN L. 1994. Gender pay gap eased over last decade. *Wall Street Journal* (April 15):B1.

PADILLA, FELIX M. 1992. *The gang as an American enterprise.* New Brunswick, N.J.: Rutgers University Press.

PALMORE, ERDMAN B., BRUCE M. BURCHETT, GERDA G. FILLENBAUM, LINDA K. GEORGE, and LAWRENCE M. WALLMAN. 1985. *Retirement: Causes and consequences.* New York: Springer.

PAMPEL, FRED C. 1993. Relative cohort size and fertility: The socio-political context of the Easterlin effect. *American Sociological Review,* 58:496–514.

PARCEL, TOBY L., and ELIZABETH G. MENAGHAN. 1994. Early parental work, family social capital, and early childhood outcomes. *American Journal of Sociology,* 99:972–1009.

PARK, ROBERT E., ERNEST W. BURGESS, and RODERICK D. MCKENZIE. 1925. *The city.* Chicago: University of Chicago Press.

PARKER, STEPHEN. 1990. *Informal marriage, cohabitation and the law, 1750–1989.* New York: St. Martin's Press.

PARKINSON, C. NORTHCOTE. 1962. *Parkinson's Law.* Boston: Houghton Mifflin.

PARNES, H. S. 1981. *Work and retirement—A longitudinal study of men.* Cambridge, Mass.: MIT Press.

PARNES, H. S., J. E. CROWLEY, R. J. HAURIN, L. J. LESS, W. R. MORGAN, F. L. MOTT, and G. NESTEL. 1985. *Retirement among American men.* Lexington, Mass.: Lexington Books.

PARSONS, TALCOTT. 1949. *The structure of social action,* 2nd ed. New York: McGraw-Hill.

PARSONS, TALCOTT. 1951. *The social system.* New York: Free Press.

PARSONS, TALCOTT. 1966. *Societies: Evolutionary and comparative perspectives.* Englewood Cliffs, N.J.: Prentice-Hall.

PARSONS, TALCOTT. 1977. On building social system theory: A personal history. In Talcott Parsons, ed., *Social systems and evolution of action theory.* New York: Free Press.

PARSONS, TALCOTT, and ROBERT F. BALES. 1955. *Family socialization and interaction process.* New York: Free Press.

PASSELL, PETER. 1992. Twins study shows school is sound investment. *New York Times* (August 19):A14.

PASSELL, PETER. 1994. Controlling world population growth: Where to put the money. *New York Times* (April 21):C2.

PATERNOSTER, RAYMOND. 1989. Absolute and restrictive deterrence in a panel of youth: Explaining the onset, persistence/desistance, and frequency of delinquent offending. *Social Problems,* 36:289–309.

PATERNOSTER, RAYMOND, and LEANN IOVANNI. 1986. The deterrent effect of perceived severity. A reexamination. *Social Forces,* 64:751–777.

PATTERSON, ORLANDO. 1991. *Freedom.* Vol. 1: *Freedom in the making of western culture.* New York: Basic Books.

PEAR, ROBERT. 1987. Women reduce lag in earnings but disparities with men remain. *New York Times* (September 4):1, 7.

PEAR, ROBERT. 1991. Rich got richer in 80's; others held even. *New York Times* (January 11):A1, A13.

PEAR, ROBERT. 1992. New look at the U.S. in 2050: Bigger, older and less white. *New York Times* (December 4):A1, A10.

PEARLIN, LEONARD I. 1992. Structure and meaning in medical sociology. *Journal of Health and Social Behavior,* 33:1–9.

PEBLEY, ANNE R., and DAVID E. BLOOM. 1982. Childless Americans. *American Demography,* 4 (January):18–21.

PERDUE, WILLIAM D. 1989. *Terrorism and the state: A critique of domination through fear.* New York: Praeger.

PERLEZ, JANE. 1993. Why Poland swung to left. *New York Times* (September 21):A4.

PERROW, CHARLES. 1979. *Complex organizations,* rev. ed. Glenview, Ill.: Scott, Foresman.

PERROW, CHARLES. 1982. Disintegrating social sciences. *Phi Delta Kappan,* 63:684–688.

PERRY, DAVID G., LOUISE C. PERRY, and PAUL RASMUSSEN. 1986. Cognitive social learning mediators of aggression. *Child Development,* 57:700–711.

PERRY, JAMES M. 1991. A remembrance of things past—the Nixon Tapes II. *Wall Street Journal* (June 5):A1, A4.

PERSELL, CAROLINE HODGES, SOPHIA CATSAMBIS, and PETER W. COOKSON, JR. 1992. Differential asset conversion: Class and gendered pathways to selective colleges. *Sociology of Education,* 65:208–225.

PETERSEN, TROND. 1992. Individual, collective, and systems rationality in work groups: Dilemmas and market-type solutions. *American Journal of Sociology,* 98:469–510.

PETERSEN, WILLIAM. 1960. The demographic transition in the Netherlands. *American Sociological Review,* 25:334–347.

PETERSON, KAREN S. 1984. Child-care benefits in infancy. *USA Today* (September 25):B1.

PETERSON, KAREN S. 1988. Working moms like family life. *USA Today* (February 9):D1.

PETTIGREW, THOMAS F., and JOANNE MARTIN. 1987. Shaping the organizational context for black American inclusion. *Journal of Social Issues,* 43:41–78.

PILIAVIN, IRVING, ROSEMARY GARTNER, CRAIG THORTON, and ROSS MATSUEDA. 1986. Crime, deterrence and rational choice. *American Sociological Review,* 51:101–119.

PILL, CYNTHIA J. 1990. Stepfamilies: Redefining the family. *Family Relations,* 39:186–193.

PIÑA, DARLENE L., and VERN L. BENGTSON. 1993. The division of household labor and wives' happiness: Ideology, employment, and perceptions of support. *Journal of Marriage and the Family,* 55:901–912.

PINES, AYALA, and ELLIOT ARONSON. 1988. *Career burnout: Causes and cures.* New York: Free Press.

PINKER, STEVEN. 1994. *The language instinct: How the mind creates language.* New York: Morrow.

PLUMB, J. H. 1972. *Children.* London: Penguin Books.

POLAKOW, VALERIE. 1993. *Lives on the edge: Single mothers and their children in the other America.* Chicago: University of Chicago Press.

POMER, MARSHALL I. 1986. Labor market structure, intragenerational mobility, and discrimination: Black male advance-ment out of low-paying occupations, 1962–1973. *American Sociological Review,* 51:650–659.

POPKIN, SUSAN J. 1990. Welfare: Views from the bottom. *Social Problems,* 37:64–79.

POPULATION REFERENCE BUREAU. 1991. *African Americans in the 1990s.* Washington, D.C.: Population Reference Bureau.

POPULATION REFERENCE BUREAU. 1994. *1994 world population data sheet.* Washington, D.C.: Population Reference Bureau.

PORTES, ALEJANDRO, and CYNTHIA TRUELOVE. 1987. Making sense of diversity: Recent research on Hispanic minorities in the United States. *Annual Review of Sociology,* 13:359–385.

POULANTZAS, NICOS. 1973. *Political power and social classes.* London: New Left Review.

POUNDSTONE, WILLIAM. 1992. *Prisoner's dilemma.* Garden City, N.Y.: Anchor Books.

PRESS, ROBERT M. 1988. Africa struggles to hold back desert. *Christian Science Monitor* (May 19):7, 10.

PRESTHUS, ROBERT. 1978. *The organizational society,* rev. ed. New York: St. Martin's Press.

PREWITT, KENNETH, and ALAN STONE. 1973. *The ruling elite.* New York: Harper & Row.

PRINCETON RELIGION RESEARCH CENTER. 1994. Religion index hits all-time low mark. *PRRC Emerging Trends,* 16 (March):1, 2.

PUTKA, GARY. 1991. Education reformers have new respect for Catholic schools. *Wall Street Journal* (March 28):A1, A8.

QUADAGNO, JILL S. 1982. *Aging in early industrial society.* New York: Academic Press.

QUADAGNO, JILL S. 1984. Welfare capitalism and the Social Security Act of 1935. *American Sociological Review,* 49:632–647.

QUINNEY, RICHARD. 1974. *Criminal justice in America.* Boston: Little, Brown.

QUINNEY, RICHARD. 1980. *Class, state, and crime.* New York: Longman.

RAAB, SELWYN. 1990. A battered and ailing Mafia is losing its grip on America. *New York Times* (October 22):A1, A12.

RAGIN, CHARLES C. 1987. *The comparative method: Moving beyond qualitative and quantitative strategies.* Berkeley and Los Angeles: University of California Press.

RAPHAEL, RAY. 1988. *The men from the boys: Rites of passage in male America.* Lincoln: University of Nebraska Press.

RAPOPORT, AMNON. 1988. Provision of step-level public goods: Effects of inequality in resources. *Journal of Personality and Social Psychology,* 54:432–440.

RAYMOND, CHRIS. 1990a. Bush and advisers are viewed as sympathetic to a bigger role for social-science research. *Chronicle of Higher Education* (March 21):A25, A28.

RAYMOND, CHRIS. 1990b. New studies by anthropologists indicate Amish communities are much more dynamic and diverse than many believed. *Chronicle of Higher Education* (December 19):A7, A9.

RAYMOND, CHRIS. 1991. Racial stereotypes. *Chronicle of Higher Education* (January 16):A8.

RECTOR, ROBERT. 1990. Poverty in U.S. is exaggerated by census. *Wall Street Journal* (September 25):A18.

REICH, WALTER, ED. 1990. *Origins of terrorism: Psychologies, ideologies, theologies, states of mind.* New York: Cambridge University Press and Woodrow Wilson International Center for Scholars.

REINHOLD, ROBERT. 1991. Study of Los Angeles police finds violence and racism are routine. *New York Times* (July 10):A1, A11.

RENO, RAYMOND R., ROBERT B. CIALDINI, and CARL A. KALLGREN. 1993. The transsituational influence of social norms. *Journal of Personality and Social Psychology,* 64:104–112.

RESKIN, BARBARA F., and PATRICIA A. ROOS. 1990. *Job queues, gender queues: Explaining women's inroads into male occupations.* Philadelphia: Temple University Press.

REYNOLDS, ALAN. 1992. The middle class boom of the 1980s. *Wall Street Journal* (March 12):A12.

RHEINGOLD, HARRIET L., and K. V. COOK. 1975. The contents of boys' and girls' rooms as an index of parents' behavior. *Child Development,* 46:459–463.

RHEINGOLD, HARRIET L., DALE F. HAY, and MEREDITH J. WEST. 1976. Sharing in the second year of life. *Child Development,* 47:1148–1158.

RICHARDS, LESLIE N. 1989. The precarious survival and hardwon satisfactions of white single-parent families. *Family Relations,* 38:396–403.

RICHARDS, ROBERT J. 1988. *Darwin and the emergence of evolutionary theories of mind and behavior.* Chicago: University of Chicago Press.

RIESMAN, DAVID. 1953. *The lonely crowd.* Garden City, N.Y.: Doubleday.

RIGDON, JOAN E. 1991. Asian-American youth suffer a rising toll from heavy pressures. *Wall Street Journal* (July 10):A1, A4.

RILEY, GLENDA. 1991. *Divorce: An American tradition.* New York: Oxford University Press.

RILEY, MATILDA WHITE. 1987. On the significance of age in sociology. *American Sociological Review,* 52:1–14.

RILEY, MATILDA WHITE, ED. 1988a. *Social change and the life course.* Vol. 1: *Social structures and human lives.* Newbury Park, Calif.: Sage.

RILEY, MATILDA WHITE, ED. 1988b. *Social change and the life course.* Vol 2: *Sociological lives.* Newbury Park, Calif.: Sage.

RISMAN, BARBARA J., CHARLES T. HILL, ZICK RUBIN, and LETITIA ANNE PEPLAU. 1981. Living together in college: Implications for courtship. *Journal of Marriage and the Family,* 43:77–83.

RITZER, GEORGE. 1983. *Sociological theory.* New York: Knopf.

RITZER, GEORGE. 1990. The current status of sociological theory: The new syntheses. In George Ritzer, ed., *Frontiers of social theory.* New York: Columbia University Press.

RIVERS, W. H. R. 1906. *The Toda.* New York: Macmillan.

ROBERTS, PRISCILLA, and PETER M. NEWTON. 1987. Levinsonian studies of women's adult development. *Psychology and Aging,* 2:154–163.

ROBERTS, SAM. 1984. A profile of the American Mafia. *New York Times* (October 4):1, 18.

ROBERTSON, HECTOR M. 1933. *Aspects of the rise of economic individualism.* London: Cambridge University Press.

ROBINSON, JOHN P. 1989. Time for work. *American Demographics,* 11 (April):68.

RODWIN, MARC A. 1993. *Medicine, money, and morals: Physicians' conflicts of interest.* New York: Oxford.

ROETHLISBERGER, FRITZ J., and WILLIAM J. DICKSON. 1939. *Management and the worker.* Cambridge, Mass.: Harvard University Press.

ROKEACH, MILTON, and SANDRA J. BALL-ROKEACH. 1989. Stability and change in American value priorities, 1968–1981. *American Psychologist,* 44:775–784.

ROMANELLI, ELAINE. 1991. The evolution of new organizational forms. *Annual Review of Sociology,* 17:79–103.

ROOF, WADE CLARK. 1992. The baby boom's search for God. *American Demographics,* 14 (December):50–56.

ROONEY, JAMES F. 1980. Organizational success through program failure: Skid Row rescue missions. *Social Forces,* 58:904–924.

ROSECRANCE, RICHARD. 1990. Too many bosses, too few workers. *New York Times* (July 15):F11.

ROSEN, GEORGE. 1963. The hospital: Historical sociology of a community institution. In E. Freidson, ed., *The hospital in modern society.* New York: Free Press.

ROSENBAUM, DAVID E. 1993. Beyond a trade pact. *New York Times* (November 11):A10.

ROSENBERG, MORRIS. 1986. Self-concept from middle childhood through adolescence. In J. Suls and A. Greenwald, eds., *Psychological perspectives on the self,* Vol. 3. Hillsdale, N.J.: Erlbaum.

ROSENBERG, MORRIS. 1989. *Society and the adolescent self-image,* rev. ed. Middletown, Conn.: Wesleyan University Press.

ROSENFELD, ANNE, and ELIZABETH STARK. 1987. The prime of our lives. *Psychology Today,* 21 (May):62–72.

ROSENHAN, DAVID L. 1973. On being sane in insane places. *Science,* 179:250–258.

ROSENTHAL, ELISABETH. 1993. Medicine suffers as fewer doctors join front lines. *New York Times* (May 24):A1, A11.

ROSNOW, RALPH L. 1991. Inside rumor. *American Psychologist,* 46:484–496.

ROSNOW, RALPH, and ALLAN J. KIMMEL. 1979. Lives of a rumor. *Psychology Today,* 13 (June):88–92.

ROSOW, IRVING. 1974. *Socialization to old age.* Berkeley: University of California Press.

ROSSI, ALICE S. 1973. *The feminist papers.* New York: Columbia University Press.

ROSSI, ALICE S. 1984. Gender and parenthood. *American Sociological Review,* 49:1–19.

Rossi, Alice S., and Peter H. Rossi. 1990. *Of human bonding: Parent-child relations across the life course.* New York: Aldine de Gruyter.

Rothchild, John. 1993. Sacred cows. *Worth* (December/January):55–58.

Rothenberg, Randall. 1990. Surveys proliferate, but answers dwindle. *New York Times* (October 5):A1, A6.

Rubenstein, Carin. 1982. Real men don't earn less than their wives. *Psychology Today,* 16 (November):36–41.

Rubinson, Richard. 1976. The world-economy and the distribution of income within states: A cross-national study. *American Sociological Review,* 41:638–659.

Ruble, Diane N., Alison S. Fleming, Lisa S. Hackel, and Charles Stangor. 1988. Changes in the marital relationship during the transition to first time motherhood: Effects of violated expectations concerning division of household labor. *Journal of Personality and Social Psychology,* 55: 78–87.

Ruggie, Mary. 1992. The paradox of liberal intervention: Health policy and the American welfare state. *American Journal of Sociology,* 97:919–944.

Ruggles, Patricia. 1990. The poverty line—Too low for the 90's. *New York Times* (April 26):A14.

Ruggles, Steven. 1987. *Prolonged connections: The rise of the extended family in nineteenth-century England and America.* Madison: University of Wisconsin Press.

Ruth, Robert, and Sylvia Brooks. 1993. Convicts set up rigid system. Columbus (Ohio) *Dispatch* (April 26):1A, 2A.

Rutter, Michael. 1979. *Fifteen thousand hours: Secondary schools and their effects on children.* Cambridge, Mass.: Harvard University Press.

Ryder, Robert G. 1973. Longitudinal data relating marriage satisfaction and having a child. *Journal of Marriage and the Family,* 35:604–606.

Rymer, Russ. 1993. *Genie: An abused child's flight from silence.* New York: Harper Collins.

Sadker, Myra, and David Sadker. 1994. *Failing at fairness: How America's schools cheat girls.* New York: Scribner's.

Sagarin, Edward. 1975. *Deviants and deviance.* New York: Praeger.

Sakamoto, Arthur, and Meichu D. Chen. 1991. Inequality and attainment in a dual labor market. *American Sociological Review,* 56:295–308.

Sampson, Robert J., and W. Byron Groves. 1989. Community structure and crime: Testing social-disorganization theory. *American Journal of Sociology,* 94:774–802.

Sampson, Robert J., and John H. Laub. 1990. Crime and deviance over the life course: The salience of adult social bonds. *American Sociological Review,* 55:609–627.

Samuelson, Robert J. 1987. Bureaucracy as life. *Newsweek* (January 12):43.

Samuelson, Robert J. 1994. The more and less deserving rich. *Newsweek* (April 25):43.

Samuelsson, Kurt. 1961. *Religion and economic action: A critique of Max Weber.* Trans. E. G. French. New York: Harper Torchbooks.

Sanchez, Sandra. 1992. Most women in jail held for drug crimes. *USA Today* (March 23):3A.

Sanchez, Sandra. 1993. Equality of sexes? Give it 1,000 years. *USA Today* (February 5):A1.

Sanders, William B. 1974. *The sociologist as detective.* New York: Praeger.

Sapir, Edward. 1949. *Selected writings in language, culture, and personality.* Berkeley: University of California Press.

Saporito, Bill. 1986. The revolt against "working smarter." *Fortune* (July 21):58–65.

Sassen, Saskia. 1991. *The global city: New York, London, Tokyo.* Princeton, N.J.: Princeton University Press.

Sassen, Saskia, and Alejandro Portes. 1993. Miami: A new global city? *Contemporary Sociology,* 22:471–477.

Satchell, Michael. 1993. Trashing the reservations? *U.S. News & World Report* (January 11):24–25.

Savin-Williams, Ritch C., and David H. Demo. 1984. Developmental change and stability in adolescent self-concept. *Developmental Psychology,* 20:1100–1110.

Scanzoni, John, Karen Polonko, Jay Teachman, and Linda Thompson. 1989. *The sexual bond: Rethinking families and close relationships.* Newbury Park, Calif.: Sage.

Scarf, Maggie. 1976. *Body, mind, behavior.* Washington, D.C.: New Republic.

Scarr, Sandra, Deborah Phillips, and Kathleen McCartney. 1989. Working mothers and their families. *American Psychologist,* 44:1402–1409.

Schlenker, Barry R., Michael F. Weigold, and John R. Hallam. 1990. Self-serving attributions in social context: Effects of self-esteem and social pressure. *Journal of Personality and Social Psychology,* 58:855–863.

Schlesinger, Arthur M., Jr. 1986. *The cycles of American history.* Boston: Houghton Mifflin.

Schmemann, Serge. 1993. A once-proud force finds itself impoverished and demoralized. *New York Times* (November 28):1, 6.

Schmidt, Peter, and Ann Dryden Witte. 1988. *Predicting recidivism using survival models.* New York: Springer-Verlag.

Schoen, Robert, and Robin M. Weinick. 1993. Partner choice in marriages and cohabitations. *Journal of Marriage and the Family,* 55:408–414.

Schopmayer, Kim D., and Bradley J. Fisher. 1993. Insiders and outsiders: Exploring ethnocentrism and cultural relativity in sociology courses. *Teaching Sociology,* 21:148–153.

Schor, Juliet B. 1992. *The overworked American: The unexpected decline of leisure.* New York: Basic Books.

Schor, Juliet B. 1993. All work and no play: It doesn't pay. *New York Times* (August 29):F9.

Schorr, Alvin L. 1984. Redefining poverty levels. *New York Times* (May 9):27.

SCHULZ, RICHARD, PAUL VISINTAINER, and GAIL M. WILLIAMSON. 1990. Psychiatric and physical morbidity effects of caregiving. *Journal of Gerontology,* 45:P181–191.

SCHUMAN, HOWARD, and JACQUELINE SCOTT. 1987. Problems in the use of survey questions to measure public opinion. *Science,* 236:957–959.

SCHUR, EDWIN. 1965. *Crimes without victims.* Englewood Cliffs, N.J.: Prentice-Hall.

SCHUTZ, ALFRED. 1971. *Collected papers.* The Hague: Martinius Nijhoff.

SCHWARTZ, JOE. 1989. Future lock. *American Demographics,* 11 (November):16.

SCHWARTZ, JOE. 1990. Million markets. *American Demographics,* 12 (September):9–11.

SCHWARTZ, MICHAEL, NAOMI ROSENTHAL, and LAURA SCHWARTZ. 1981. Leader-member conflict in protest organizations: The case of the Southern Farmers' Alliance. *Social Problems,* 29:22–36.

SCHWARTZ, SHALOM H., and WOLFGANG BILSKY. 1987. Toward a universal psychological structure of human values. *Journal of Personality and Social Psychology,* 53:550–562.

SCHWENDINGER, HERMAN, and JULIA SIEGEL SCHWENDINGER. 1985. *Adolescent subcultures and delinquency.* New York: Praeger.

SCOTT, JOHN. 1991. Networks of corporate power: A comparative assessment. *Annual Review of Sociology,* 17:181–203.

SECRETARY'S COMMISSION ON ACHIEVING NECESSARY SKILLS. 1992. *Learning a living.* Washington, D.C.: Government Printing Office.

SEEMAN, MELVIN. 1959. On the meaning of alienation. *American Sociological Review,* 24:783–791.

SEIDLER, JOHN, and KATHERINE MEYER. 1989. *Conflict and change in the Catholic Church.* New Brunswick, N.J.: Rutgers University Press.

SEKULIC, DUSKO, GARTH MASSEY, and RANDY HODSON. 1994. Who were the Yugoslavs? Failed sources of a common identity in the former Yugoslavia. *American Sociological Review,* 59:83–97.

SELIGMANN, JEAN. 1990. Variations on a theme. *Newsweek* (Winter/Spring Special Issue):38–46.

SELLTIZ, CLAIRE, LAWRENCE S. WRIGHTSMAN, and STUART W. COOK. 1976. *Research methods in social relations,* 3rd ed. New York: Holt, Rinehart and Winston.

SELMAN, R. L. 1980. *The growth of interpersonal understanding: Developmental and clinical analyses.* New York: Academic Press.

SELZ, MICHAEL. 1994. Testing self-managed teams, entrepreneur hopes to lose job. *Wall Street Journal* (January 11):B1, B2.

SERBIN, LISA A., and CAROL SPRAFKIN. 1986. The salience of gender and the process of sex typing in three- to seven-year-old children. *Child Development,* 57:1188–1199.

SERVICE, ELMAN. 1971. *Primitive social organization: An evolutionary perspective.* New York: Random House.

SERVICE, ELMAN. 1973. The ghosts of our ancestors. In *Primitive Worlds.* Washington, D.C.: National Geographic Society.

SEWELL, WILLIAM H., JR. 1992. A theory of structure: Duality, agency, and transformation. *American Journal of Sociology,* 98:1–29.

SHANNON, THOMAS RICHARD. 1989. *An introduction to the world-system perspective.* Boulder, Colo.: Westview Press.

SHAPIRO, JOSEPH P. 1993. Straight talk about gays. *U.S. News & World Report* (July 5):42–48.

SHAPIRO, SUSAN P. 1990. Collaring the crime, not the criminal: Reconsidering the concept of white-collar crime. *American Sociological Review,* 55:346–365.

SHARPE, ROCHELLE. 1994. Women make strides, but men stay firmly in top company jobs. *Wall Street Journal* (March 29):A1, A8.

SHAW, CLIFFORD R. 1930. *Natural history of a juvenile career.* Chicago: University of Chicago Press.

SHAW, CLIFFORD R., and HENRY MCKAY. 1942. *Juvenile delinquency in urban areas.* Chicago: University of Chicago Press.

SHEA, JOHN C. 1984. *American government: The great game of politics.* New York: St. Martin's Press.

SHEEHY, GAIL. 1976. *Passages.* New York: Dutton.

SHELDON, WILMON HENRY. 1954. *God and polarity.* New Haven, Conn.: Yale University Press.

SHELLENBARGER, SUE. 1992. Flexible policies may slow women's careers. *Wall Street Journal* (April 22):B1.

SHELLENBARGER, SUE. 1994. More day-care centers help the aging attend to the aged. *Wall Street Journal* (March 8):B1, B9.

SHERBOURNE, CATHY DONALD, and RON D. HAYS. 1990. Marital status, social support, and health transitions in chronic disease patients. *Journal of Health and Social Behavior.* 31:328–343.

SHERIF, MUZAFER. 1936. *The psychology of social norms.* New York: Harper & Row.

SHERIF, MUZAFER, O. J. HARVEY, B. JACK WHITE, WILLIAM R. HOOD, and CAROLYN W. SHERIF. 1961. *Intergroup conflict and cooperation: The Robbers' Cave experiment.* Norman: University of Oklahoma Book Exchange.

SHERMAN, LAWRENCE W., DOUGLAS A. SMITH, JANELL D. SCHMIDT, and DENNIS P. ROGAN. 1992. Crime, punishment, and stake in conformity: Legal and informal control of domestic violence. *American Sociological Review,* 57:680–690.

SHIBUTANI, TAMOTSU. 1966. *Improvised news: A sociological study of rumor.* Indianapolis: Bobbs-Merrill.

SHIBUTANI, TAMOTSU. 1986. *Social processes: An introduction to sociology.* Berkeley: University of California Press.

SHILLS, DAVID. 1957. *The volunteers.* New York: Free Press.

SHILS, EDWARD A., and MORRIS JANOWITZ. 1948. Cohesion and disintegration in the Wehrmacht in World War II. *Public Opinion Quarterly,* 12:280–315.

SHILTS, RANDY. 1993. *Conduct unbecoming: Gays & lesbians in the U.S. military, Vietnam to the Persian Gulf.* New York: St. Martin's Press.

SHORTER, EDWARD. 1975. *The making of the modern family.* New York: Basic Books.

SHORTER, EDWARD. 1991. *From paralysis to fatigue: A history of psychosomatic illness in the modern era.* New York: Free Press.

SILBERSTEIN, LISA R. 1992. *Dual-career marriage: A system in transition.* Hillsdale, N.J.: Erlbaum.

SIMMEL, GEORG. 1908/1955. *Conflict and the web of group affiliations.* New York: Free Press.

SIMMEL, GEORG. 1908/1959. How is society possible? In Kurt Wolff, ed., *Essays in sociology, philosophy, and aesthetics.* New York: Harper & Row.

SIMMEL, GEORG. 1950. *The sociology of George Simmel.* Ed. and trans. Kurt Wolff. New York: Free Press.

SIMMONS, ROBERTA G., and DALE A. BLYTH. 1987. *Moving into adolescence: The impact of pubertal change and school context.* New York: Aldine de Gruyter.

SIMON, JULIAN L. 1981. *The ultimate resource.* Princeton, N.J.: Princeton University Press.

SIMON, JULIAN L. 1989. *The economic consequences of migration.* Cambridge, Mass.: Blackwell.

SIMON, JULIAN L. 1990. Bring on the wretched refuse. *Wall Street Journal* (January 26):A12.

SIMON, JULIAN L., and HERMAN KAHN. 1984. *The resourceful earth: A response to Global 2000.* New York: Blackwell.

SIMON, RITA J., and GLORIA DANZIGER. 1991. *Women's movements in America: Their successes, disappointments, and aspirations.* New York: Praeger.

SIMONS, RONALD L., JAY BEAMAN, RAND D. CONGER, and WEI CHAO. 1993. Stress, support, and antisocial behavior trait as determinants of emotional well-being and parenting practices among single mothers. *Journal of Marriage and the Family,* 55:385–398.

SIMONS, RONALD L., CHRISTINE JOHNSON, JAY BEAMAN, and RAND D. CONGER. 1993. Explaining women's double jeopardy: Factors that mediate the association between harsh treatment as a child and violence by a husband. *Journal of Marriage and the Family,* 55:713–723.

SIMONS, RONALD L., LES B. WHITBECK, RAND D. CONGER, and WU CHYI-IN. 1991. Intergenerational transmission of harsh parenting. *Developmental Psychology,* 27:159–171.

SIMPSON, GEORGE EATON, and J. MILTON YINGER. 1972. *Racial and cultural minorities.* 4th ed. New York: Harper & Row.

SJOBERG, GIDEON. 1960. *The preindustrial city.* New York: Free Press.

SKLAIR, LESLIE. 1991. *Sociology of the global system.* Baltimore: Johns Hopkins University Press.

SKOCPOL, THEDA. 1979. *States and social revolution.* Cambridge, Mass.: Cambridge University Press.

SKOCPOL, THEDA. 1980. Political response to capitalist crisis: Neo-Marxist theories of the state and the case of the New Deal. *Politics and Society,* 10:155–201.

SKOCPOL, THEDA. 1992. *Protecting soldiers and mothers: The political origins of social policy in the United States.* Cambridge, Mass.: Harvard University Press.

SKOCPOL, THEDA, and EDWIN AMENTA. 1986. States and social politics. *Annual Review of Sociology,* 12:131–157.

SKOLNICK, ARLENE. 1981. The family and its discontents. *Society,* 18 (January):42–47.

SKOLNICK, ARLENE. 1991. *Embattled paradise: The American family in an age of uncertainty.* New York: Basic Books.

SLOTKIN, JAMES S. 1955. Culture and psychopathology. *Journal of Abnormal and Social Psychology,* 51:269–275.

SMALL, STEPHEN A., and DAVE RILEY. 1990. Toward a multidimensional assessment of work spillover into family life. *Journal of Marriage and the Family,* 52:51–61.

SMELSER, NEIL J. 1959. *Social change in the Industrial Revolution.* Chicago: University of Chicago Press.

SMELSER, NEIL J. 1963. *Theory of collective behavior.* New York: Free Press.

SMITH, ALTHEA, and ABIGAIL J. STEWARD. 1983. Approaches to studying racism and sexism in black women's lives. *Journal of Social Issues,* 39:1–15.

SMITH, BRUCE D. 1989. Origins of agriculture in eastern North America. *Science,* 246:1566–1571.

SMITH, DOUGLAS A., and PATRICK R. GARTIN. 1989. Specifying specific deterrence: The influence of arrest on future criminal activity. *American Sociological Review,* 54:94–105.

SMITH, ERIC R. 1989. *The unchanging American voter.* Berkeley: University of California Press.

SMITH, KEVIN B. 1981. Class structure and intergenerational mobility from a Marxian perspective. *Sociological Quarterly,* 22:385–401.

SMITH, RICHARD M., and CRAIG W. SMITH. 1981. Child rearing and single-parent fathers. *Family Relations,* 30:411–417.

SNAREY, JOHN. 1987. A question of morality. *Psychology Today,* 21 (June):6–8.

SNIPP, C. MATTHEW. 1989. *American Indians: The first of this land.* New York: Russell Sage Foundation.

SNOW, DAVID A., E. BURKE ROCHFORD, JR., STEVEN K. WORDEN, and ROBERT D. BENFORD. 1986. Frame alignment processes, micromobilization, and movement participation. *American Sociological Review,* 51:464–481.

SNOWDEN, FRANK M., JR. 1983. *Before color prejudice: The ancient view of blacks.* Cambridge, Mass.: Harvard University Press.

SOBEL, RICHARD. 1989. *The white-collar working class: From structure to politics.* New York: Praeger.

SOLOMON, PATRICK. 1992. *Black resistance in high school: Forging a separatist culture.* Albany: State University of New York Press.

SOLOMON, ZAHAVA, MARION MIKULINCER, and STEVEN E. HOBFOLL. 1986. Effects of social support and battle intensity on loneliness and breakdown during combat. *Journal of Personality and Social Psychology,* 51:1269–1276.

SOMMER, ROBERT. 1969. *Personal space.* Englewood Cliffs, N.J.: Prentice-Hall.

SORENSEN, AAGE B. 1975. The structure of intragenerational mobility. *American Sociological Review,* 40:456–471.

SOROKIN, PITIRIM. 1959. *Social and cultural mobility.* New York: Free Press.

SOUTH, SCOTT J., and GLENNA SPITZE. 1994. Housework in marital and nonmarital households. *American Sociological Review,* 59:327–347.

SOUTH, SCOTT J., and KATHERINE TRENT. 1988. Sex ratios and women's roles: Cross-national analysis. *American Journal of Sociology,* 93:1096–1115.

SOUTHERN SCHOOL NEWS. 1954. Segregation. *Southern School News,* 1 (November):3.

SPENGLER, OSWALD. 1918/1926. *The decline of the West.* New York: Knopf.

SPIEGEL, DAVID. 1994. Compassion is the best medicine. *New York Times* (January 10):A11.

SPITZE, GLENNA, and JOHN LOGAN. 1990. Sons, daughters, and intergenerational social support. *Journal of Marriage and the Family,* 52:420–430.

SPREY, JETSE. 1979. Conflict theory and the study of marriage and the family. In Wesley R. Burr, Reuben Hill, F. Ivan Nye, and Ira L. Reiss, eds., *Contemporary theories about the family,* Vol. 2. New York: Free Press.

STACK, JOHN F., JR., ED. 1986. *The primordial challenge: Ethnicity in the contemporary world.* Westport, Conn.: Greenwood Press.

STAGNER, R. 1975. Boredom on the assembly line: Age and personality variables. *Industrial Gerontology,* 2:23–44.

STARK, DAVID. 1992. The great transformation? Social change in Eastern Europe. *Contemporary Sociology,* 21:299–304.

STARK, RODNEY, and WILLIAM S. BAINBRIDGE. 1979. Of churches, sects, and cults: Preliminary concepts for a theory of religious movements. *Journal for the Scientific Study of Religion,* 18:117–133.

STARK, RODNEY, and WILLIAM S. BAINBRIDGE. 1981. American-born sects: Initial findings. *Journal for the Scientific Study of Religion,* 20:130–149.

STARR, PAUL. 1982. *The social transformation of American medicine.* New York: Basic Books.

STEARNS, PETER N. 1977. *Old age in European society.* London: Croom Helm.

STEEH, CHARLOTTE, and HOWARD SCHUMAN. 1992. Young white adults: Did racial attitudes change in the 1980s? *American Journal of Sociology,* 98:340–367.

STEFFENSMEIER, DARRELL, and CATHY STREIFEL. 1991. Age, gender, and crime across three historical periods: 1935, 1960, and 1985. *Social Forces,* 69:869–894.

STEIN, HERBERT. 1993. Who's subsidizing whom? *Wall Street Journal* (September 15):A22.

STEIN, JUDITH A., SARAH A. FOX, and PAUL J. MURATA. 1991. The influence of ethnicity, socioeconomic status, and psychological barriers on use of mammography. *Journal of Health and Social Behavior,* 32:101–113.

STEIN, ROBERT S. 1993. Who are the rich and the poor? *Investor's Business Daily* (October 28):1, 2.

STEINBERG, LAURENCE D., RALPH CATALANO, and DAVID DOOLEY. 1981. Economic antecedents of child abuse and neglect. *Child Development,* 52:975–985.

STEINBERG, LAURENCE, JULIE D. ELMEN, and NINA S. MOUNTS. 1989. Authoritative parenting, psychosocial maturity, and academic success among adolescents. *Child Development,* 60:1424–1436.

STEINMETZ, GEORGE. 1990. The local welfare state: Two strategies for social domination in urban Imperial Germany. *American Sociological Review,* 55:891–911.

STEINMETZ, GEORGE, and ERIK OLIN WRIGHT. 1989. The fall and rise of the petty bourgeoisie: Changing patterns of self-employment in the postwar United States. *American Journal of Sociology,* 94:973–1018.

STEPHENS, GENE. 1990. Future justice. *The Futurist* (September/October):21–24.

STEPHENS, JOHN D. 1989. Democratic transition and breakdown in western Europe, 1870–1939: A test of the Moore thesis. *American Journal of Sociology,* 94:1019–1077.

STEPHENS, WILLIAM N. 1963. *The family in cross-cultural perspective.* New York: Holt, Rinehart and Winston.

STERBA, JAMES P. 1982. New study defends the social sciences. *New York Times* (June 22):20.

STEVENS, WILLIAM K. 1991. What really threatens the environment? *New York Times* (January 29):B7.

STEVENS, WILLIAM K. 1993. Scientists confront renewed backlash on global warming. *New York Times* (September 14):B5, B6.

STEVENS, WILLIAM K. 1994. Third-world gains in birth control: Development isn't only answer. *New York Times* (January 2):1, 4.

STEVENSON, DAVID LEE. 1991. Deviant students as a collective resource in classroom control. *Sociology of Education,* 64:127–133.

STEVENSON, HAROLD W., CHUANSHENG CHEN, and SHI-YING LEE. 1993. Mathematics achievement of Chinese, Japanese, and American children: Ten Years later. *Science,* 259:53–58.

STEVENSON, HAROLD W., and JAMES W. STIGLER. 1992. *The learning gap: Why our schools are failing and what we can learn from Japanese and Chinese education.* New York: Summit.

STEVENSON, RICHARD W. 1992. Huge fund turns up proxy heat. *New York Times* (March 21):17, 23.

STEWARD, JULIAN H. 1955. *Theory of culture change.* Urbana: University of Illinois Press.

STINCHCOMBE, ARTHUR L. 1983. *Economic sociology.* New York: Academic Press.

STINCHCOMBE, ARTHUR L. 1990. *Information and organizations.* Berkeley: University of California Press.

STITH, SANDRA M., and ALBERT J. DAVIS. 1984. Employed mothers and family day-care substitute caregivers: A comparative analysis of infant care. *Child Development,* 55:1340–1348.

STOKES, RANDALL G. 1975. Afrikaner Calvinism and economic action: The Weberian thesis in South Africa. *American Journal of Sociology*, 81:62–81.

STOKES, RANDALL G., and ANDY B. ANDERSON. 1990. Disarticulation and human welfare in less developed countries. *American Sociological Review*, 55:63–74.

STOKES, RANDALL G., and JOHN P. HEWITT. 1976. Aligning actions. *American Sociological Review*, 41:838–849.

STOLLER, ELEANOR PALO. 1983. Parental caregiving by adult children. *Journal of Marriage and the Family*, 45:851–858.

STOLLER, ELEANOR PALO, and KAREN L. PUGLIESI. 1990. Other roles of caregivers: Competing responsibilities or supportive resources. *Journal of Gerontology*, 44:S231–238.

STONE, KATHERINE. 1974. The origins of job structures in the steel industry. *Review of Radical Economics*, 6:61–97.

STRANG, DAVID, and NANCY BRANDON TUMA. 1993. Spatial and temporal heterogeneity in diffusion. *American Journal of Sociology*, 99:614–639.

STRAUS, MURRAY A., and RICHARD J. GELLES. 1986. Societal change and change in family violence from 1975 to 1985 as revealed by two national surveys. *Journal of Marriage and the Family*, 48:465–479.

STRAUS, MURRAY A., and RICHARD J. GELLES, EDS. 1989. *Physical violence in American families: Risk factors and adaptations to violence in 8,145 families.* New Brunswick, N.J.: Transaction.

STRAUS, MURRAY A., and RICHARD J. GELLES. 1990. *Physical violence in American families: Risk factors and adaptions to violence in 8,145 Families.* New Brunswick, N.J.: Transaction.

STRAUSS, ANSELM, and BARNEY GLASER. 1970. *Anguish.* San Francisco: Sociology Press.

STRAUSS, ANSELM, LEONARD SCHATZMAN, RUE BUCHER, DANUTA EHRLICH, and MELVIN SABSHIN. 1964. *Psychiatric ideologies and institutions.* New York: Free Press.

STROUD, MICHAEL. 1990. More job control can lessen harmful work strains. *Investor's Daily* (April 17):8.

STRUBE, MICHAEL J. 1988. The decision to leave an abusive relationship: Empirical evidence and theoretical issues. *Psychological Bulletin*, 104:236–250.

STRUBE, MICHAEL J., and LINDA S. BARBOUR. 1983. The decision to leave an abusive relationship: Economic dependence and psychological commitment. *Journal of Marriage and the Family*, 45:785–793.

STRYKER, ROBIN. 1994. Rules, resources, and legitimacy processes: Some implications for social conflict, order, and change. *American Journal of Sociology*, 99:847–910.

STRYKER, SHELDON. 1980. *Symbolic interactionism: A social structural version.* Menlo Park, Calif.: Benjamin/Cummings.

STRYKER, SHELDON. 1987. The vitalization of symbolic interactionism. *Social Psychology Quarterly*, 50:83–94.

STRYKER, SHELDON, and ANNE STATHAM. 1985. Symbolic interaction and role theory. In G. Lindzey and E. Aronson, eds., *Handbook of social psychology*, 3rd ed. Vol. 1. New York: Random House.

SUDNOW, DAVID. 1967. *Passing on: The social organization of dying.* Englewood Cliffs, N.J.: Prentice-Hall.

SUITOR, J. JILL. 1991. Marital quality and satisfaction with the division of household labor across the family life cycle. *Journal of Marriage and the Family*, 53:221–230.

SUMNER, WILLIAM GRAHAM. 1906. *Folkways.* Boston: Ginn.

SUNDSTROM, ERIC. 1978. Crowding as a sequential process: Review of research on the effects of population density on humans. In A. Baum and Y. M. Epstein, eds., *Human responses to crowding.* Hillsdale, N.J.: Erlbaum.

SURO, ROBERTO. 1990. Where America is growing: The suburban cities. *New York Times* (February 23):1, 10.

SURO, ROBERTO. 1991. Your tired, your poor, your masses yearning to be with relatives. *New York Times* (January 6):4E.

SUTHERLAND, EDWIN H. 1939. *Principles of criminology.* Philadelphia: Lippincott.

SUTHERLAND, EDWIN H. 1949. *White-collar crime.* New York: Dryden Press.

SUTTON, JOHN R. 1991. The political economy of madness: The expansion of the asylum in progressive America. *American Sociological Review*, 56:665–678.

SWANN, WILLIAM B., JR., and CRAIG A. HILL. 1982. When our identities are mistaken: Reaffirming self-conceptions through social interaction. *Journal of Personality and Social Psychology*, 43:59–66.

SWANSON, GUY E. 1992. Doing things together: Some basic forms of agency and structure in collective action and some explanations. *Social Psychological Quarterly*, 55:94–117.

SWEDBERG, RICHARD. 1991. *Joseph A. Schumpeter: His life and work.* Princeton, N.J.: Princeton University Press.

SYMONDS, WILLIAM C. 1994. Whither a health-care solution? Oh, Canada. *Business Week* (March 21):82–85.

SYMPOSIUM. 1992. *The American Occupational Structure.* Reflections after twenty-five years. *Contemporary Sociology*, 21:596–668.

SZYMANSKI, ALBERT. 1976. Racial discrimination and white gain. *American Sociological Review*, 41:403–414.

SZYMANSKI, ALBERT. 1981. *The logic of imperialism.* New York: Praeger.

TAMÁS, GÁSPAR M. 1992. Socialism, capitalism, and modernity. *Journal of Democracy*, 3:60–74.

TAWNEY, R. H. 1926. *Religion and the rise of capitalism.* New York: Harcourt.

TAYLOR, VERTA. 1989. Social movement continuity: The women's movement in abeyance. *American Sociological Review*, 54:761–775.

TERRACE, HERBERT S. 1979. How Nim Chimpsky changed my mind. *Psychology Today*, 13 (November):65–76.

't HART, PAUL. 1990. *Groupthink in government: A study of small groups and policy failure.* Lisse, The Netherlands: Swets & Zeitlinger.

THOMAS, GEORGE M., and JOHN W. MEYER. 1984. The expansion of the state. *Annual Review of Sociology,* 10:461–482.

THOMAS, MELVIN E., and MICHAEL HUGHES. 1986. The continuing significance of race: A study of race, class, and quality of life in America, 1972–1985. *American Sociological Review,* 830–841.

THOMAS, W. I. 1923. *The unadjusted girl.* Boston: Little, Brown.

THOMAS, WILLIAM I., and DOROTHY S. THOMAS. 1928. *The child in America: Behavior problems and programs.* New York: Knopf.

THORNBERRY, TERENCE P., and MARGARET FARNWORTH. 1982. Social correlates of criminal involvement. *American Sociological Review,* 47:505–518.

THRASHER, FREDERIC M. 1927. *The gang.* Chicago: University of Chicago Press.

THUROW, LESTER C. 1987. A surge in inequality. *Scientific American,* 256 (May):30–37.

TICE, DIANNE M. 1992. Self-concept change and self-presentation: The looking glass self is also a magnifying glass. *Journal of Personality and Social Psychology,* 63:435–451.

TIEGER, TODD. 1980. On the biological basis of sex differences in aggression. *Child Development,* 51:943–963.

TIEN, H. YUAN. 1992. China's demographic dilemmas. *Population Bulletin,* 47 (June), No. 1.

TIENDA, MARTA, and DING-TZANN LII. 1987. Minority concentration and earnings inequality: Blacks, Hispanics, and Asians compared. *American Journal of Sociology,* 93:141–165.

TIENDA, MARTA, SHELLEY A. SMITH, and VILMA ORTIZ. 1987. Industrial restructuring, gender segregation, and sex differences in earnings. *American Sociological Review,* 52:195–210.

TIERNEY, JOHN. 1990. Betting the planet. *New York Times Magazine* (December 2):52–53+.

TIGER, LIONEL. 1990. When "corporate" and "culture" clash. *Wall Street Journal* (April 9):A10.

TILGHMAN, SHIRLEY M. 1993. Science vs. women—A radical solution. *New York Times* (January 26):A19.

TILLY, CHARLES. 1978a. *From mobilization to revolution.* Reading, Mass.: Addison-Wesley.

TILLY, CHARLES, ED. 1978b. *Historical studies of changing fertility.* Princeton, N.J.: Princeton University Press.

TILLY, CHARLES. 1984. *Big structures, large processes, huge comparisons.* New York: Russell Sage Foundation.

TILLY, CHARLES. 1990. *Coercion, capital, and European states, AD 990–1990.* Cambridge, Mass.: Blackwell.

TIMES MIRROR CENTER FOR THE PEOPLE AND THE PRESS. 1990. Press release (June 12). Los Angeles.

TINBERGEN, NIKO. 1954. The origin and evolution of courtship and threat display. In J. S. Huxley, A. C. Hardy, and E. B. Ford, eds., *Evolution as a process.* London: Allen & Unwin.

TITTLE, CHARLES R., and C. H. LOGAN. 1973. Sanction and deviance: Evidence and reexamining questions. *Law and Society Review,* 7:372–392.

TITTLE, CHARLES R., and ALAN R. ROWE. 1974. Certainty of arrest and crime rates: A further test of the deterrence hypothesis. *Social Forces,* 52:455–462.

TOFFLER, ALVIN. 1980. *The third wave.* New York: Morrow.

TOFFLER, ALVIN. 1990. *Powershift: Knowledge, wealth, and violence at the edge of the 21st century.* New York: Bantam.

TOWNSEND, BICKLEY, and KATHLEEN O'NEIL. 1990. Women get mad. *American Demographics,* 12 (August):26–32.

TOYNBEE, ARNOLD J. 1934/1954. *A study of history.* 10 vols. New York: Oxford University Press.

TRACY, PAUL E., MARVIN E. WOLFGANG, and ROBERT M. FIGLIO. 1990. *Delinquency careers in two birth cohorts.* New York: Plenum.

TRAUGOTT, MARK. 1978. Reconceiving social movements. *Social Problems,* 26:38–49.

TREASTER, JOSEPH B. 1990. Study finds many drug dealers hold other jobs. *New York Times* (July 11):A12.

TRICKETT, PENELOP K., and ELIZABETH J. SUSMAN. 1988. Parental perceptions of child-rearing practices in physically abusive and nonabusive families. *Developmental Psychology,* 24:270–276.

TROELTSCH, ERNST. 1931. *The social teachings of the Christian churches.* 2 vols. Trans. Olive Wyon. New York: Macmillan.

TROEN, SELWYN K. 1985. Technological development and adolescence: The early twentieth century. *Journal of Early Adolescence,* 5:429–440.

TROST, CATHY. 1990. Census survey on child care increases concern about how much poor can pay. *Wall Street Journal* (August 15):A10.

TUCKER, COMPTON J., HAROLD E. DREGNE, and WILBUR W. NEWCOMB. 1991. Expansion and contraction of the Sahara Desert from 1980 to 1990. *Science,* 253:299–301.

TURNER, BRYAN S. 1987. *Medical power and social knowledge.* Beverly Hills, Calif.: Sage.

TURNER, JONATHAN H. 1982. *The structure of sociological theory.* Homewood, Ill.: Dorsey Press.

TURNER, JONATHAN H. 1990. Emile Durkheim's theory of social organization. *Social Forces,* 68:1089–1103.

TURNER, PATRICIA A. 1994. *I heard it through the grapevine: Rumor in African-American culture.* Berkeley: University of California Press.

TURNER, RALPH H. 1964. Collective behavior. In R. E. L. Faris, ed., *Handbook of modern sociology.* Chicago: Rand McNally.

TURNER, RALPH H. 1968. The self-conception in social interaction. In C. Gordon and K. J. Gergen, eds., *The self in social interaction.* New York: Wiley.

TURNER, RALPH H., and LEWIS M. KILLIAN. 1972. *Collective behavior,* 2nd ed. Englewood Cliffs, N.J.: Prentice-Hall.

TYLER, TOM R. 1990. *Why people obey the law.* New Haven, Conn.: Yale University Press.

UCHITELLE, LOUIS 1989. U.S. businesses loosen link to mother country. *New York Times* (May 21):1, 12.

UCHITELLE, LOUIS. 1990. Not getting ahead? Better get used to it. *New York Times* (December 16):E1, E6.

UCHITELLE, LOUIS. 1991a. But just who is that fairy godmother? *New York Times* (September 29):E1, E4.

UCHITELLE, LOUIS. 1991b. Trapped in the impoverished middle class. *New York Times* (November 17):F1, F10.

UDRY, J. RICHARD. 1965. Structural correlates of feminine beauty in Britain and the United States. *Sociology and Social Research,* 49:330–342.

U.S. NEWS & WORLD REPORT. 1979. In hot pursuit of business criminals. (July 23):59–60.

U.S. NEWS & WORLD REPORT. 1994. Cost of crime: $674 billion. (January 17):40–41.

USA TODAY/CNN/GALLUP POLL. 1994. Poll: Discipline OK, abuse isn't. *USA Today* (April 8):8A.

USDANSKY, MARGARET L. 1992. Poor whites get more help than others. *USA Today* (October 9):3A.

USEEM, BERT. 1980. Solidarity model, breakdown model, and the Boston anti-busing movement. *American Sociological Review,* 45:357–369.

USEEM, MICHAEL. 1983. *The inner circle.* New York: Oxford University Press.

VALENTE, JUDITH. 1991. A century later, Sioux still struggle, and still are losing. *Wall Street Journal* (March 25):A1, A12.

VALENTINE, CHARLES. 1968. *Culture and poverty.* Chicago: University of Chicago Press.

VAN CREVELD, MARTIN. 1982. *Fighting power: German and U.S. Army performance, 1939–1945.* Westport, Conn.: Greenwood Press.

VAN DEN BERGHE, PIERRE. 1963. Dialectic and functionalism: Toward a theoretical synthesis. *American Sociological Review,* 28:695–705.

VANDER ZANDEN, JAMES W. 1965. *Race relations in transition.* New York: Random House.

VANDER ZANDEN, JAMES W. 1983. *American minority relations,* 4th ed. New York: Knopf.

VANDER ZANDEN, JAMES W. 1993. *Human development,* 5th ed. New York: McGraw-Hill.

VANNEMAN, REEVE, and LYNN WEBER CANNON. 1987. *The American perception of class.* Philadelphia: Temple University Press.

VANNOY, DANA, and WILLIAM W. PHILLIBER. 1992. Wife's employment and quality of marriage. *Journal of Marriage and the Family,* 54:387–398.

VEBLEN, THORSTEIN. 1899. *The theory of the leisure class.* New York: Viking.

VEBLEN, THORSTEIN. 1921. *Engineers and the price system.* New York: Viking.

VEGA, WILLIAM A. 1990. Hispanic families in the 1980s: A decade of research. *Journal of Marriage and the Family,* 52:1015–1024.

VERANO, JOHN W., and DOUGLAS H. UBELAKER, EDS. 1992. *Disease and demography in the Americas.* Washington, D.C.: Smithsonian Institution Press.

VERBA, SIDNEY, NORMAN H. NIE, and JAE-ON KIM. 1978. *Participation and political equality: A seven-nation comparison.* New York: Cambridge University Press.

VERBRUGGE, LOIS M. 1988. A life-and-death paradox. *American Demographics,* 10 (July):34–37.

VERBRUGGE, LOIS M. 1989. The twain meet: Empirical explanations of sex differences in health and mortality. *Journal of Health and Social Behavior,* 30:282–304.

VERNEZ, GEORGES, and DAVID RONFELDT. 1991. The current situation in Mexican immigration. *Science,* 251:1189–1193.

VISGAITIS, GARY. 1994. A look at Native Americans across the USA. *USA Today* (April 28):7A.

VOGEL, LISE. 1983. *Marxism and the oppression of women.* New Brunswick, N.J.: Rutgers University Press.

WADDINGTON, DAVID, KAREN JONES, and CHAS CRITCHER. 1989. *Flashpoints: Studies in disorder.* New York: Routledge.

WADMAN, MEREDITH K. 1992. Mothers who take extended time off find their careers pay a heavy price. *Wall Street Journal* (July 16):B1, B2.

WAGLEY, CHARLES, and MARVIN HARRIS. 1964. *Minorities in the New World.* New York: Columbia University Press.

WAITZKIN, HOWARD. 1983. *The second sickness: Contradictions of capitalist health care.* New York: Free Press.

WALDO, GORDON P., and THEODORE G. CHIRICOS. 1972. Perceived penal sanction and self-reported criminality: A neglected approach to deterrence research. *Social Problems,* 19:522–540.

WALDROP, JUDITH. 1989. Feeling good. *American Demographics,* 11 (May):6.

WALKER, LENORE E. A. 1989. Psychology and violence against women. *American Psychologist,* 44:695–702.

WALLACE, STEVEN P. 1990. Race versus class in the health care of African-American elderly. *Social Problems,* 37:517–533.

WALLERSTEIN, IMMANUEL. 1974a. *The modern world-system: Capitalist agriculture and the origins of the European world economy in the 16th century.* New York: Academic Press.

WALLERSTEIN, IMMANUEL. 1974b. The rise and future demise of the world capitalist system: Concepts for comparative analysis. *Comparative Studies in Society and History,* 16:387–415.

WALLERSTEIN, IMMANUEL. 1980. *The modern world-system II: Mercantilism and the consolidation of the European world-economy, 1600–1775.* New York: Academic Press.

WALLERSTEIN, IMMANUEL. 1989. *The modern world-system III: The second era of great expansion of the capitalist world-economy, 1730–1840.* New York: Academic Press.

WALLERSTEIN, IMMANUEL. 1991. *Geopolitics and geoculture: Essays on the changing world-system.* Cambridge: Cambridge University Press.

WALLERSTEIN, JUDITH S., and SANDRA BLAKESLEE. 1989. *Second chances: Men, women, and children a decade after divorce.* New York: Ticknor and Fields.

WALLIS, ROY. 1975. *Sectarianism: Analyses of religious and non-religious sects.* New York: Wiley.

WALMER, TRACY. 1990. For USA's "Third World," illness a way of life. *USA Today* (November 14):A9.

WALMER, TRACY. 1991. Costs, lack of health care hurt rural poor most. *USA Today* (March 13):A8.

WALSH, EDWARD J. 1981. Resource mobilization and citizen protest in communities around Three Mile Island. *Social Problems,* 29:1–21.

WALSH, EDWARD J. 1988. *Democracy in the shadows: Citizen mobilization in the wake of the accident at Three Mile Island.* Westport, Conn.: Greenwood Press.

WALTON, JOHN, and CHARLES RAGIN. 1990. Global and national sources of political protest: Third World responses to the debt crisis. *American Sociological Review,* 55:876–890.

WANDERSMAN, ABRAHAM H., and WILLIAM K. HALLMAN. 1993. Are people acting irrationally? *American Psychologist,* 48:681–686.

WANDYCZ, KATARZYNA. 1993. Divorce kills. *Forbes* (October 25):240.

WARNER, R. STEPHEN. 1993. Work in progress toward a new paradigm for the sociological study of religion in the United States. *American Journal of Sociology,* 98:1044–1093.

WARNER, W. LLOYD. 1949. *Democracy in Jonesville.* New York: Harper & Row.

WARNER, W. LLOYD, and PAUL S. LUNT. 1941. *The social life of the modern community.* New Haven, Conn.: Yale University Press.

WEBER, MAX. 1904/1958. *The Protestant ethic and the spirit of capitalism.* New York: Scribner's.

WEBER, MAX. 1916/1964. *The religion of China: Confucianism and Taoism.* New York: Macmillan.

WEBER, MAX. 1917/1958. *The religion of India: The sociology of Hinduism and Buddhism.* New York: Free Press.

WEBER, MAX. 1921/1968. *Economy and society.* 3 vols. Totowa, N.J.: Bedminster Press.

WEBER, MAX. 1946. *The theory of social and economic organization.* Ed. and trans. A. M. Henderson and Talcott Parsons. New York: Macmillan.

WEBER, MAX. 1947. *From Max Weber: Essays in sociology.* Ed. and trans. Hans H. Gerth and C. Wright Mills. New York: Oxford University Press.

WEINBERG, MARTIN S., and COLIN J. WILLIAMS. 1980. Sexual embourgeoisment? Social class and sexual activity: 1938–1970. *American Sociological Review,* 45:33–48.

WEINSTEIN, EUGENE, and JUDITH M. TANUR. 1976. Meanings, purposes and structural resources in social interaction. *Cornell Journal of Social Relations,* 11:105–110.

WEISMAN, STEVEN R. 1988. Broken marriage and family brawl pose hard test for a cohesive caste. *New York Times* (February 21):12.

WEISS, ROBERT S. 1984. The impact of marital dissolution on income and consumption in single-parent households. *Journal of Marriage and the Family,* 46:115–127.

WESSEL, DAVID. 1991. Racial bias against black job seekers remains pervasive, broad study finds. *Wall Street Journal* (May 15):A9.

WESSEL, DAVID. 1992. Low-income mobility was high in 1980s. *Wall Street Journal* (June 2):A2.

WHELLER, STANTON. 1976. Trends and problems in the sociological study of crime. *Social Problems,* 23:525–534.

WHEELER, STANTON, KENNETH MANN, and AUSTIN SARAT. 1988. *Sitting in judgment: The sentencing of white-collar criminals.* New Haven, Conn.: Yale University Press.

WHITBECK, LES, DANNY R. HOYT, and SHIRLEY M. HUCK. 1994. Early family relationships, intergenerational solidarity, and support provided to parents by their adult children. *Journal of Gerontology,* 49:S85–S94.

WHITE, GREGORY L. 1980. Physical attractiveness and courtship progress. *Journal of Personality and Social Psychology,* 39:660–668.

WHITE, JAMES M. 1991. *Dynamics of family development: A theoretical perspective.* New York: Guilford.

WHITE, LESLIE. 1959. *The evolution of culture.* New York: McGraw-Hill.

WHITE, LYNN, and JOHN N. EDWARDS. 1990. Emptying the nest and parental well-being: An analysis of national panel data. *American Sociological Review,* 55:235–242.

WHITE, RALPH K., and RONALD O. LIPPITT. 1960. *Autocracy and democracy.* New York: Harper & Row.

WHITE, ROBERT W. 1989. From peaceful protest to guerrilla war: Micromobilization of the Provisional Irish Republican Army. *American Journal of Sociology,* 94:1277–1302.

WHITE, THEODORE H. 1961. *The making of the president, 1960.* New York: Atheneum.

WHITEHEAD, ALFRED NORTH. 1929. *Process and reality.* New York: Macmillan.

WHITESIDE, MARY F. 1989. Family rituals as a key to kinship connections in remarried families. *Family Relations,* 38:34–39.

WHITNEY, CRAIG R. 1990. East's archives reveal ties to terrorists. *New York Times* (July 15):5.

WHITT, J. ALLEN. 1979. Toward a class-dialectical model of power: An empirical assessment of three competing models of political power. *American Sociological Review,* 44:81–100.

WHITT, J. ALLEN. 1982. *Urban elites and mass transportation: The dialectics of power.* Princeton, N.J.: Princeton University Press.

WHORF, BENJAMIN L. 1956. *Language, thought, and reality.* Cambridge, Mass.: MIT Press.

WHYTE, MARTIN KING. 1990. *Dating, mating, and marriage.* New York: Aldine de Gruyter.

WICKS, JERRY W., and EDWARD G. STOCKWELL. 1984. A comment on the neonatal mortality–socioeconomic status relationship. *Social Forces,* 62:1035–1039.

WIDOM, CATHY SPATZ. 1989a. Does violence beget violence? A critical examination of the literature. *Psychological Bulletin,* 106:3–28.

WIDOM, CATHY SPATZ. 1989b. The cycle of violence. *Science,* 244:160–166.

WILCOX, CLYDE. 1992. *God's warriors: The Christian right in twentieth-century America.* Baltimore: Johns Hopkins University Press.

WILKE, JOHN R. 1993. Computer links erode hierarchical nature of workplace culture. *Wall Street Journal* (December 9):A1, A7.

WILKIE, JANE RIBLETT. 1991. The decline in men's labor force participation and income and the changing structure of family economic support. *Journal of Marriage and the Family,* 53:111–122.

WILLIAMS, DAVID R., DAVID T. TAKEUCHI, and RUSSELL K. ADAIR. 1992. Socioeconomic status and psychiatric disorder among blacks and whites. *Social Forces,* 71:179–194.

WILLIAMS, KIPLING, STEPHEN HARKINS, and BIBB LATANE. 1981. Identifiability as a deterrent to social loafing: Two cheering experiments. *Journal of Personality and Social Psychology,* 40:303–311.

WILLIAMS, RHYS H., and N. J. DEMERATH III. 1991. Religion and political process in an American city. *American Sociological Review,* 56:417–431.

WILLIAMS, ROBIN M., JR. 1964. *Strangers next door.* Englewood Cliffs, N.J.: Prentice-Hall.

WILLIAMS, ROBIN M., JR. 1970. *American society,* 3rd ed. New York: Knopf.

WILLIE, CHARLES V. 1979. *Caste and class controversy.* New York: General Hall.

WILLIE, CHARLES V. 1991. Universal programs are unfair to minority groups. *Chronicle of Higher Education* (December 4):B1, B3.

WILLS, GARRY. 1990. *Under God: Religion and American politics.* New York: Simon and Schuster.

WILSON, BRYAN R. 1990. *The social dimensions of sectarianism: Sects and new religious movements in contemporary society.* New York: Oxford University Press.

WILSON, JAMES Q. 1967. The bureaucracy problem. *The Public Interest,* 6:3–9.

WILSON, JAMES Q. 1975. *Thinking about crime.* New York: Basic Books.

WILSON, JAMES Q. 1990. *What government agencies do and why they do it.* New York: Basic Books.

WILSON, JAMES Q. 1993. Mr. Clinton, meet Mr. Gore. *Wall Street Journal* (October 28):A18.

WILSON, PETER J. 1988. *The domestication of the human species.* New Haven, Conn.: Yale University Press.

WILSON, WILLIAM JULIUS. 1978. *The declining significance of race.* Chicago: University of Chicago Press.

WILSON, WILLIAM JULIUS. 1987. *The truly disadvantaged: The inner city, the underclass, and public policy.* Chicago: University of Chicago Press.

WILSON, WILLIAM JULIUS. 1991. Studying inner-city social dislocations: The challenge of public agenda research. *American Sociological Review,* 56:1–14.

WILSON, WILLIAM JULIUS, and ROBERT APONTE. 1985. Urban poverty. *Annual Review of Sociology,* 11:231–258.

WINCH, ROBERT F. 1958. *Mate selection: A study of complementary needs.* New York: Harper & Row.

WINKLER, KAREN J. 1990. Scholar whose ideas of female psychology stir debate modifies theories, extends studies to young girls. *Chronicle of Higher Education* (May 23): A6, A7.

WINN, EDWARD A. 1981. Looking at good schools. *Phi Delta Kappan,* 62:377–381.

WINNER, LANGDON. 1993. How technology reweaves the fabric of society. *Chronicle of Higher Education* (August 4):B1–B3.

WINNICK, LOUIS. 1991. *New people in old neighborhoods.* New York: Russell Sage Foundation.

WINSHIP, CHRISTOPHER. 1992. Race, poverty, and *The American Occupational Structure. Contemporary Sociology,* 21:639–643.

WISE, PAUL H., MILTON KOTELCHUCK, MARK L. WILSON, and MARK MILLS. 1985. Racial and socioeconomic disparities in childhood mortality in Boston. *New England Journal of Medicine,* 313:360–366.

WITT, LINDA, KAREN M. PAGET, and GLENNA MATTHEWS. 1993. *Running as a woman: Gender and power in American politics.* New York: Free Press.

WOLFGANG, MARVIN E., ROBERT M. FIGLIO, and THORSTEN SELLIN. 1972. *Delinquency in a birth cohort.* Chicago: University of Chicago Press.

WOODARD, MICHAEL D. 1987. Voluntary association membership among black Americans: The post-civil-rights era. *Sociological Quarterly,* 28:285–301.

WOODIWISS, MICHAEL. 1988. *Crime crusades and corruption: Prohibition in the United States, 1900–1987.* Totowa, N.J.: Barnes & Noble.

WOODS, JAMES D. 1993. *The corporate closet: The professional lives of gay men in America.* New York: Free Press.

WOODWARD, C. VANN. 1966. *The strange career of Jim Crow,* 2nd rev. ed. New York: Oxford University Press.

WRIGHT, ERIK OLIN. 1978a. *Class, crisis, and the state.* New York: Schocken.

WRIGHT, ERIK OLIN. 1978b. Race, class, and income inequality. *American Journal of Sociology,* 83:1368–1388.

WRIGHT, ERIK OLIN. 1979. *Class structure and income determination.* New York: Academic Press.

WRIGHT, ERIK OLIN. 1985. *Classes.* New York: Schocken.

WRIGHT, ERIK OLIN. 1993. Typologies, scales, and class analysis: A comment on Halaby and Weakliem's "Ownership and authority in the earnings function." *American Sociological Review,* 58:31–34.

WRIGHT, ERIK OLIN, and DONMOON CHO. 1992. The relative permeability of class boundaries to cross-class friendships: A comparative study of the United States, Canada, Sweden, and Norway. *American Sociological Review,* 57:85–102.

WRIGHT, ERIK OLIN, ANDREW LEVINE, and ELLIOTT SOBER. 1992. *Reconstructing Marxism.* London: Verso.

WuDunn, Sheryl. 1991. China, with ever more to feed, pushes anew for small families. *New York Times* (June 16):1, 4.

Wysocki, Bernard , Jr. 1991. Influx of Asians brings prosperity to Flushing, a place for newcomers. *Wall Street Journal* (January 15):A1, A10.

Xiaohe, Su, and Martin King Whyte. 1990. Love matches and arranged marriages: A Chinese replication. *Journal of Marriage and the Family,* 52:709–722.

Yamagishi, Toshio, and Karen S. Cook. 1993. Generalized exchange and social dilemmas. *Social Psychology Quarterly,* 56:235–248.

Yamaguchi, Kazuo, and Denise Kandel. 1993. Marital homophily on illicit drug use among young adults: Assortative mating or marital influence? *Social Forces,* 72: 505–528.

Yates, Alayne. 1987. Current status and future directions of research on the American Indian child. *American Journal of Psychiatry,* 144:1135–1142.

Yinger, J. Milton. 1965. *Toward a field theory of behavior.* New York: Macmillan.

Yinger, John. 1991. *The housing discrimination study.* Washington, D.C.: Department of Housing and Urban Development.

Yllo, Kersti, and Murray A. Straus. 1981. Interpersonal violence among married and cohabiting couples. *Family Relations,* 30:339–347.

Zeitlin, Maurice. 1989. *The large corporation and contemporary classes.* New Brunswick, N.J.: Rutgers University Press.

Zey-Ferrell, Mary. 1981. Criticisms of the dominant perspective on organizations. *Sociological Quarterly,* 22:181–205.

Zick, Cathleen, and Ken R. Smith. 1991. Marital transitions, poverty, and gender differences in mortality. *Journal of Marriage and the Family,* 53:327–336.

Zigler, Edward, and Sally J. Styfco. 1993. Using research and theory to justify and inform Head Start expansion. *Social Policy Report, Society for Research in Child Development,* Vol. VII, No. 2.

Zigli, Barbara. 1984. Asian-Americans beat others in academic drive. *USA Today* (April 25):D1.

Zimbardo, Philip G. 1969. The human choice: Individuation, reason, and order versus deindividualization, impulse, and chaos. In W. Arnold and D. Levine, eds., *Nebraska Symposium on Motivation,* 17:237–307.

Zimbardo, Philip G. 1978. Misunderstanding shyness: The counterattack. *Psychology Today,* 12 (June):17–18+.

Zimmer, Lynn. 1988. Tokenism and women in the workplace: The limits of gender-neutral theory. *Social Problems,* 35:64–77.

Zimmerman, Don H. 1971. The practicalities of rule use. In Jack Douglas, ed., *Understanding everyday life.* Chicago: Aldine.

Zipp, John F., Richard Landerman, and Paul Luebke. 1982. Political parties and political participation. *Social Forces,* 60:1140–1153.

Zuckerman, Marvin. 1990. Some dubious premises in research and theory on racial differences. *American Psychologist,* 45:1297–1303.

Zuckerman, Miron, M. H. Kernis, S. M. Guarnera, J. F. Murphy, and L. Rappoport. 1983. The egocentric bias: Seeing oneself as cause and target of others' behavior. *Journal of Personality,* 51:621–630.

Credits and Acknowledgments

PHOTO CREDITS FOR CHAPTER OPENERS

Chapter 1: Eli Reed/Magnum.
Chapter 2: Rene Burri/Magnum.
Chapter 3: Lawrence Migdale/Stock, Boston.
Chapter 4: Lisa Quinones/Black Star.
Chapter 5: Dr. Jürgen Gebhardt/Stern/Black Star.
Chapter 6: Edward Keating/NYT.
Chapter 7: Lionel Delevingne/Stock, Boston.
Chapter 8: Dennis Brack/Black Star.
Chapter 9: Joel Gordon.
Chapter 10: Stephen Ferry/Gamma Liaison.
Chapter 11: Kathleen Campbell/Gamma Liaison.
Chapter 12: Ansell Horn/Impact Visuals.

FIGURES, TABLES, AND TEXT

Acknowledgments are listed by page number in order of appearance.

28, Extract: "Code of Ethics," American Sociological Association, 1989. Reprinted by permission.

33–34, Extract: From "Fletcher Christian's Children" by Dea Birkett in *The New York Times Magazine,* December 8, 1991. Copyright © 1991 by The New York Times Company. Reprinted by permission.

42–43, Box Extract: From "Insiders and Outsiders" by Kim Schopmeyer and Bradley Fisher in *Teaching Sociology,* 21:1993. Copyright © 1993 American Sociological Association. Reprinted by permission.

72–73, Box: Reprinted with the permission of The Free Press, a Division of Simon & Schuster, Inc. from *Rules of Sociological Method* by Emile Durkheim, translated by S. A. Solovay and J. H. Mueller. Edited by George E. G. Catlin. Copyright © 1938 by George E. G. Catlin; copyright renewed 1966 by S. A. Solovay, J. H. Mueller, and G. E. G. Catlin.

132–133, Box: From "Creating the Sociological Imagination on the First Day of Class: The Social Construction of Deviance" by John R. Brouilette and Ronny E. Turner in *Teaching Sociology,* 20:276–279. Copyright © 1992 American Sociological Association. Reprinted by permission.

148, Figure 5.2: From *The Wall Street Journal,* February 18, 1994. Reprinted by permission of *The Wall Street Journal,* © 1994 Dow Jones & Company, Inc. All rights reserved worldwide.

180, Figure 6.3: From *Fortune,* December 28, 1992, © 1992 Time Inc. All rights reserved.

185, Figure 6.5: Copyright, March 2, 1992, U.S. News & World Report. Reprinted by permission.

263, Figure 8.1: From *The New York Times,* August 29, 1993. Copyright © 1993 by The New York Times Company. Reprinted by permission.

281, Extract: From "New Realities of the American Family" by Dennis Ahlburg and Carol De Vita from *Population Bulletin,* Vol. 47, No. 2, 1992. Reprinted by permission of Population Reference Bureau.

296, Table 9.2: Adapted from *American Demographics* magazine, June 1994, ©. Reprinted with permission.

320, Figure 10.1: Adapted from Roy Wallis, *Sectarianism: Analyses of Religious and Non-Religious Sects.* New York: Wiley, 1975, p. 41. Reprinted by permission of Peter Owen Ltd.

376, Figure 11.5: Adapted from "The Baby Boom—Entering Midlife," by Leon F. Bouvier and Carol J. De Vita from *Population Bulletin,* Vol. 46, No. 3, 1991. Reprinted by permission of Population Reference Bureau, Inc.

375, Figure 11.4: Adapted from *American Demographics* magazine, September 1992, ©. Reprinted with permission.

NAME INDEX

SUBJECT INDEX